TOCQUEVILLE *on* AMERICA *after* 1840

Letters and Other Writings

Edited and translated, with an interpretative essay and notes, by

Aurelian Craiutu

Indiana University, Bloomington

Jeremy Jennings

Queen Mary University of London

CAMBRIDGE
UNIVERSITY PRESS

CAMBRIDGE UNIVERSITY PRESS
Cambridge, New York, Melbourne, Madrid, Cape Town, Singapore, São Paulo, Delhi

Cambridge University Press
32 Avenue of the Americas, New York, NY 10013-2473, USA

www.cambridge.org
Information on this title: www.cambridge.org/9780521676830

First published 2009

Printed in the United States of America

A catalog record for this publication is available from the British Library

Library of Congress Cataloging in Publication data

Tocqueville, Alexis de, 1805–1859.
[Selections. English. 2009]
Tocqueville on America after 1840 : letters and other writings / edited by
Aurelian Craiutu, Jeremy Jennings.
   p. cm.
Includes bibliographical references and index.
ISBN 978-0-521-85955-4 (hardback) – ISBN 978-0-521-67683-0 (pbk.)
1. United States – Politics and government – 1841–1845. 2. United States – Politics and
government – 1845–1861. 3. Tocqueville, Alexis de, 1805–1859 – Correspondence.
I. Craiutu, Aurelian, 1966– II. Jennings, Jeremy, 1952– III. Title.
JK216.T71915   2009
320.973 – dc22   2008031330

ISBN 978-0-521-85955-4 hardback
ISBN 978-0-521-67683-0 paperback

Contents

PART II: SPEECHES, ARTICLES, AND DIPLOMATIC PAPERS

Editors' Note and Acknowledgments

This book has been a long time in the making. While working on it, most often on two continents, we have had the good fortune to accumulate many debts to a great number of persons and institutions, and it is a pleasure to acknowledge them here.

The inspiration for this project came from two essays by Françoise Mélonio and Hugh Brogan, who convinced us of the importance of studying the evolution of Tocqueville's views on America after 1840. We initially set out to write a paper on this topic which we presented at the Annual Meeting of the American Political Science Association, Philadelphia, August 31–September 3, 2003. A substantially revised version of our essay was published as "The Third Democracy: Tocqueville's View of America after 1840" in *American Political Science Review*, 98: 3 (2004): 391–404. Subsequently, Ed Parsons of Cambridge University Press encouraged us to develop our article into a larger project and patiently worked with us over the past years to improve the contents of this volume.

The book project that evolved out of our original article underwent significant transformations over time and greatly benefited from the advice we received from many distinguished Tocqueville scholars in the United States and Europe. We began working on our project with the idea of including only translations of Tocqueville's letters to his American correspondents after 1840 (originally published in *OC*, VII) along with translations of other documents written after 1840 in which he made substantial references to America. Since the texts included in *OC*, VII represent only half of the story, we attempted to retrieve the letters that Tocqueville received from his American friends after 1840. This evolved into a full-fledged subsection of our volume whose completion required substantial archival research in various libraries in the United States and Europe. Some of these letters are available only as copies, the originals having been lost. Matthew Holbreich and David Belanich played an important role in transcribing most of the Bonnel copies from the Beinecke Rare Book and Manuscript Library at Yale University and we would like to thank them again for their research assistance.

The editing of the letters received by Tocqueville from America posed significant challenges. Apart from minor exceptions, we decided to leave intact the grammar, punctuation, and the spelling of the original letters (written in English). Where appropriate, for the sake of clarity, we silently corrected a few obvious errors and standardized the use of quotations. Occasionally, we added square brackets indicating the editors' best guess for the missing words or illegible passages in the original texts.

We would like to thank the Beinecke Rare Book and Manuscript Library at Yale University for the opportunity to work in the Tocqueville archives and the Quai d'Orsay, Paris for the permission to consult Tocqueville's diplomatic correspondence during his short tenure as Minister of Foreign Affairs in 1849. Françoise Mélonio encouraged us to examine this neglected part of Tocqueville's archives, and we would like to express again our gratitude for her suggestions.

The completion of this project would not have been possible without the generous financial help provided by many institutions, to which we would like to express our special thanks here. In particular, our gratitude goes to Indiana University's Institute for Advanced Study; the College of Arts and Sciences Arts and Humanities Institute, the Vice-President Office for Research, the Office of International Scholars, the West European Studies, the Department of Political Science at Indiana University, Bloomington; and the Social Philosophy and Policy Center at Bowling Green State University. In 2006, Aurelian Craiutu received a Rose and John Jackson research fellowship from the Beinecke Rare Book and Manuscript Library at Yale University. Jeremy Jennings received research grants from the Indiana University's Institute for Advanced Study (2005, 2006) and the British Academy (2006, 2007) to finance research in Bloomington, New Haven, Boston, and Cambridge, Massachusetts. Several colloquia organized by Liberty Fund gave us the opportunity to work together in Bloomington and Indianapolis at key stages of this project.

We would also like to thank the libraries and the librarians who provided invaluable assistance during various stages of our project in locating original sources and documents: the University of South Carolina Library; the Beinecke Rare Book and Manuscript Library, Yale University; the Huntington Library, San Marino, California; the Massachusetts Historical Society Library (Boston); the Virginia Historical Society Library, Richmond; the Houghton Library, Harvard University; the Wells Library and the Lilly Library at Indiana University; the Bibliothèque Nationale in Paris; and the Quai' d'Orsay, Paris.

Numerous colleagues and friends have read and made valuable suggestions on various parts of this manuscript. Special thanks are due to Barbara Allen, Richard Boyd, Seymour Drescher, Sheldon Gellar, Christine D. Henderson, James Farr, Robert T. Gannett, Russell L. Hanson, Ivona Hedin, Jeffrey C. Isaac, Lucien Jaume, Daniel J. Mahoney, Matthew Mancini, Françoise Mélonio, Joshua Mitchell, Eduardo Nolla, Elinor and Vincent Ostrom, Jennifer Pitts, Jean-Bertrand Ribat, Filippo Sabetti, James T. Schleifer, Barry Shain, Richard Shannon, Lee Siegelman, and Cheryl Welch.

We also thank Joohyung Kim, who provided the index of this volume. Our current and previous home institutions – Indiana University, Queen Mary University of London, and the University of Birmingham – have provided congenial places for completing this book. We would like to thank our colleagues for their intellectual companionship which has supported us over the past years. Portions of this book have been presented at various colloquia and conferences, and we would like to thank all those who commented on them.

Finally, we would like to express our deepest gratitude to Ed Parsons of Cambridge University Press who endorsed our project from the very beginning and deftly stewarded it through a long editorial process. Thanks are also due to four anonymous referees who provided extremely useful suggestions for revising the manuscript, as well as to Peter Katsirubas and his colleagues at Aptara who turned the manuscript into a book.

Finally, we would like to dedicate this volume to Sophia Alexandra Craiutu, whose first steps into the world were accompanied by the completion of this project.

A.C. & J. J.

The Third *Democracy*: Tocqueville's Views of America after 1840[1]

"What happens now in America must be of interest to all civilized people and is of particular interest to me, who am half Yankee" (Tocqueville, 1856).[2]

I. How Many Democracies?

The famous French literary critic Sainte-Beuve once predicted that Tocqueville would become an inexhaustible subject of reflection for future generations of scholars.[3] A century and a half after his death, the writings of Alexis de Tocqueville remain a source of inspiration for political theorists, sociologists, philosophers, legal scholars, and historians. Today, Tocqueville is celebrated as the most prominent theorist of the modern democratic revolution. It is no mere coincidence that in the past decade alone, four new English translations of *Democracy in America* have been published.[4] A fifth new translation by James T. Schleifer and edited by Eduardo Nolla (forthcoming with Liberty Fund) will give English-speaking readers the opportunity to familiarize themselves with Tocqueville's fascinating notes for *Democracy in America*. Two new translations of Tocqueville's *The Old Regime and the Revolution* have also been published in the last decade.[5]

Moreover, a significant number of new and provocative interpretations of Tocqueville's works have appeared in both French and English, shedding fresh light on lesser-known facets of Tocqueville's persona: the philosopher, the moralist, the writer, the politician and the defender of French colonization of Algeria.[6] The publication of *The Tocqueville Reader, The Cambridge Companion to Tocqueville*, along with the third volume of his works in the prestigious Bibliothèque de la Pléiade, have added new dimensions to our appreciation of Tocqueville. In 2005, the bicentenary of his birth was widely cele-brated, with conferences in France, the United States, Italy, Belgium, Spain, Germany, Poland, Canada, Argentina, and Japan, and else-where across the world, thus showing that Tocqueville's works have an appeal transcending national boundaries.

Our own interest in Tocqueville can be explained by the fact that his work, to quote Cheryl Welch, "seems to retain a greater measure of normative and exploratory power – and intellectual provocation – than that of many other nineteenth-century thinkers."[7] Tocqueville's universal appeal, Sheldon Wolin argued, can be accounted for by the acuity with which he grasped and described the key features and dilemmas of modern democracy, the complexity of democratic political culture, the importance of civil society, and the far-reaching consequences of high social mobility.[8] In Wolin's words, "to reflect on present day American politics invites reflection on *Democracy in America* and vice versa."[9]

At the time of its first publication in France, the two volumes of *Democracy in America* (1835, 1840) offered the image of an accom-plished and successful democracy based on the equality of conditions and the sovereignty of the people. The political system of the New World, Tocqueville argued, combined administrative decentralization and political centralization, allowed for self-government, and provided for a judicious separation of powers and a genuine system of checks and balances. Tocqueville contrasted the regular, stable, and effective institutions and mores of America with those existing in Europe where the relics of an aristocratic past proved to be a barrier against politi-cal democracy. In America he saw more than America. He perceived the image of democracy itself, with all its inclinations, prejudices and passions.

The extraordinary success of Tocqueville's masterpiece provided the lenses through which generations viewed and interpreted the virtues and limitations of American democracy. It also explains the often idealized image of America that admirers of Tocqueville derived from reading his book. Yet, an interesting debate arose among Toc-queville scholars as to whether Volume One of *Democracy in America* (1835) was part of the same intellectually coherent project as Volume Two published five years later in 1840[10] or whether it reflects radically different concerns and preoccupations.

But was Volume Two of *Democracy in America* itself Tocqueville's definitive statement on America? After all, Tocqueville lived for nineteen more years (he died in 1859, two years before the start of the Civil War). During this period, when he became more and more involved in French politics, Tocqueville often despaired that his native country would ever be able to achieve a political regime comparable to that of America. He continued to be interested in American political events and exchanged many letters with his American friends, old and new, some of whom – such as Theodore Sedgwick and Jared Sparks – had been instrumental in providing him with essential information about the United States while Tocqueville was completing the two volumes of *Democracy in America*.

Tocqueville's letters to his American friends were published in Volume VII of his *Œuvres Complètes* (1986) and have not previously been translated into English.[11] The letters that he received from his American correspondents after 1840 have remained, for the most part, in the archives and have not been published to this day. In addition, Tocqueville referred to America in his published articles in the 1840s and he made frequent references to America in his parliamentary speeches and interventions in the Constituent and Legislative Assemblies of the Second Republic (1848–1851). He also spoke of America in the letters that he sent to many of his French friends. Even less known perhaps is the fact that, as Minister of Foreign Affairs for a brief period in 1849, Tocqueville was faced with an embarrassing diplomatic incident with America. Tocqueville's correspondence regarding this event has remained in the archives of the French Foreign Ministry at Quai d'Orsay in Paris and it is published here for the first time.

The existence of this important body of post-1840 writings about America prompted us to ask the following questions. Did Tocqueville change his views on America outlined in the two volumes of *Democracy* published in 1835 and 1840? If so, which of his views did change and why? What were the continuities and discontinuities in his perceptions of America? How did Tocqueville come to view the American republic as it edged ever closer to civil war? And more importantly, did the evolution of his views of America affect his theory of democracy and what were the implications of any failure of American democracy? Would it be possible to contemplate what a hypothetical "third" volume of *Democracy in America* might have looked like, had it ever been written? The materials collected in this volume answer these questions by examining Tocqueville's diverse writings on America in the period between 1840 and 1859. As obvious an inquiry as this might be, these very questions have been largely ignored by the majority of Tocqueville's interpreters.[12] Even classic books such as André Jardin's and Hugh Brogan's biographies of Tocqueville, George Wilson Pierson's and James T. Schleifer's studies of the writing of *Democracy in America*, have virtually nothing to say about Tocqueville's *later* impressions of America.[13]

✖

A few words about the present introductory study are in order here. It begins by exploring the image of America in France *before* the publication of Volume One of Tocqueville's masterpiece. This preliminary discussion provides the necessary background for interpreting Tocqueville's engagement with America. It also gives us a better understanding of the nature and originality of Tocqueville's analysis of American democracy placed in its original historical context. As we shall see, Tocqueville came to share some – though not all – of the opinions held by his predecessors who had espoused a critical view of America. The discussion of the image of America in France will also address, if only obliquely, the rhetoric of American exceptionalism.[14]

The second part of our essay examines the main points and concerns about America raised by Tocqueville in his letters to his American friends written after 1840. As we shall see, his warnings against the effects of the instability of the market on the functioning of political institutions and the damaging effects of unbridled materialism sound surprisingly fresh today when economics dominates politics to an unprecedented degree and the relationship between democracy and the market has become a key topic in our public debates. More generally, Tocqueville's remarks invite us to reflect upon the problems and dilemmas faced by an America where, according to many social critics, the vitality (as well as viability) of political and civil life seem to be on the decline.[15]

Tocqueville's letters represent an invaluable source of information for any student of his work. Their seminal importance is documented not only by the wide array of topics they addressed but also by his request to some of his friends to keep his correspondence. Indeed, one might go as far as to argue that, in some respects, Tocqueville's letters are as important as his published writings. Tocqueville writes so beautifully that his readers enjoy his letters both for their style and substance. As much as in his published books, Tocqueville's correspondence demonstrates his strong passion for liberty as well as the seriousness with which he sought to apply his political and philosophical ideas to the public realm. And unlike his published writings, Tocqueville's letters allow us to trace his hopes, fears, and disillusionment with politics, such that, to quote Roger Boesche, "when we know the man better, we find him no less political."[16]

There is a further consideration to be borne in mind. Since Tocqueville's correspondents remained substantially the same during the entire period, covering the twenty-eight years from 1831 to 1859, we can assume that he felt no need to adopt new epistolary strategies or to tailor his comments to suit the views of his correspondents. Moreover, if the recipients of his letters remained unchanged, the views expressed by Tocqueville certainly did change over time, the most significant shift occurring in the 1850s. The early letters were usually designed to solicit information, advice, or guidance. It is only in the later exchanges beginning around 1852 that his deep misgivings and criticisms became evident and when they did so they became matters of central importance to his correspondence.

Nor should we underestimate the significance that Tocqueville attached to his career and aspirations as a politician. From his youth, he aspired to political glory and longed for recognition in the political world. Tocqueville's correspondence with Gustave de Beaumont is revealing in this regard. "It goes without saying, it is the political man that we must foster in us," Tocqueville wrote to his friend on October 25, 1829.[17] Eleven years later, in August 1840, Tocqueville confessed to Beaumont: "You know what a taste I have for great events and how tired I am of our little democratic and bourgeois pot of soup."[18] In 1848, upon his election to the Constituent Assembly, Tocqueville experienced an overwhelming sensation as he took his seat along his new colleagues. "I felt at once," he wrote, "that the atmosphere of this Assembly suited me and in spite of the seriousness of the situation, *I had a sense of happiness I had never known before.*"[19] Thus, his parliamentary speeches, public interventions and political journalism are integral to our understanding of Tocqueville the *political* man.

Finally, Tocqueville's reappraisal of American democracy (in his correspondence) did not draw upon a rereading of his earlier evidence of American life and institutions but upon a close observation of contemporary political and social developments in America that postdated the publication of his earlier account. It was these developments, and

not the reassessment of earlier evidence, that led him in the late 1850s
to the stark conclusion that America no longer held out hope for the
friends of liberty around the world.

II. America in France before Tocqueville

A thorough analysis of Tocqueville's assessment of American democracy before and after 1840 requires that we first survey French attitudes toward America during the Bourbon Restoration (1814–1830)
and the early years of the July Monarchy (1830–1835). This account
will allow us to place Tocqueville's views on American democracy
into the larger historical and cultural context to which they belonged.
This is all the more significant since his analysis of America has too
often been detached from this background.

Tocqueville was by no means the first person in France to write
on the nature of American democracy.[20] Before it came to be seen
as a political model for nineteenth-century Europe, America had previously acquired the almost mythic image of a country unspoiled
by luxury, a land where the main occupation was agriculture and
where people lived peacefully in austerity and virtuous simplicity.
Crèvecour's letters describing the modes of farming, the manners and
peculiar customs of the Americans contributed greatly to the dissem-
ination of this pastoral and idyllic image of an American Arcadia.[21]
As such, America appeared as a boundless and bountiful continent,
a virgin environment and a territory of adventure and discovery that
inspired the travelers' imagination.

Eventually, this ideal came to be replaced by the image of an economic life in constant transformation, a society bent on indefinite
progress and innovation. Individuals were no longer seen as deriving their happiness from living a frugal life. On the contrary, their
happiness was directly related to rising living standards, comfort, and
material prosperity, resulting from an ever-expanding commerce and
navigation. Over time, America came to be regarded as the hallmark
of utilitarianism, a country in which everything and everyone was on
the move, and in constant search for ways of improving the conditions
of daily life. It is worth noting that this dynamic face of America was
seen as an outcome of its democratic institutions.

What is less known, however, is that in France the idea that the
study of the political organization and institutions of the United States

might profit those interested in the future of democracy had appeared *before* the publication of the first volume of Tocqueville's *Democracy in America*. In fact, some ideas about America that Tocqueville used in his work were commonplace at that time. Tocqueville's analysis gained wide recognition not so much because of the originality of his ideas on America as because of the way in which he developed the commonplace into the extraordinary. As René Rémond pointed out in his magisterial study of the image of the United States during the first half of the nineteenth century in France, from 1815 to 1830 French public opinion looked favorably at America and was relatively optimistic with regard to the stability and future of its political institutions.[22] In his important history of the United States published in 1825, Charles-Arnold Scheffer (1796–1853), the secretary of La Fayette and, later, editor of *Le Commerce*, claimed that the American federation showed the entire world "true popular government and liberty."[23] The suggestion made by Scheffer was that the successful republican political experiment in America would pave the way for similar political developments in Europe. The same theme appeared in *La Revue Américaine*, edited by Armand Carrel from July 1826 to June 1827.[24] For example, Armand Carrel described the American constitution as "a model constitution," adding that this was not due to the fact that the Americans possessed an instinctive political genius. "The American constitution," he commented, "is not foreign to us; it is the daughter of eighteenth-century French political doctrines, fortunately combined with the most reasonable and tested elements of English institutions."[25] Admirers of America such as Madame de Staël, Birbeck, Barboux, Vinet, Scheffer, and Barbé-Marbois invoked the wisdom of its laws, principles, and institutions.[26] Vinet argued that "this state seems to have solved the problem which consists in reconciling the highest degree of individual liberty and the supreme conditions of security and order."[27] Other French writers claimed that, in America, power was limited, no one was above the law, and everyone obeyed the laws that were clearly formulated to serve the common good.[28] The American government, it was argued, imposed low taxes and treated its citizens with respect. "As the hand of Providence, it governs without being felt and almost without being perceived," wrote the author of an article published in *La Revue Encyclopédique* in August 1819.[29] Other virtues of the American system highlighted by French writers included a strong educational system,[30] the abolition of hereditary power, the presence of exceptional political leaders, civic–minded citizens and a solid work ethic. As importantly, French commentators emphasized the connection between liberty and religion in the United States and pointed to the important role played by religious toleration, liberty of conscience, and freedom of the press in securing civil liberties. Also worth noting in these accounts is the identification of America with liberty and the awareness of the relation that existed between freedom, reason, and civic virtue, themes that were to re-appear in Tocqueville's work a few years later.

Nonetheless, doubts about the proper functioning of American institutions began to appear gradually in France, as the United States entered a new stage of its political development with the coming of age of a new generation of politicians who brought a new political style. Thus, America appeared as a country with an uncertain future, facing a complex set of problems and challenges, and therefore unlikely to serve as a political model for Europe. What was the substance of French disquiet? The question is particularly important in light of our attempt to reevaluate Tocqueville's criticism of American democracy against the background of earlier analyses of America.

The concerns expressed in the French press in the early 1830s ranged from doubts regarding the maintenance of the unity of the country confronted with the problem of slavery to the calling into question of the existence of a genuine national character of the American people.[31] The expanding territory of the Union now appeared as a serious challenge to national unity. Critics wondered if the American republic would be able to survive and surmised that it might be replaced by either monarchy or a new form of military dictatorship.[32] More importantly, the French began questioning not only the possibility of importing the American institutions, but also their very *raison d'être*. Two of the principles that had previously been considered as pillars of American democracy – bicameralism and federalism – came to be regarded with increasing skepticism by the French. Some of them denounced American individualism as a form of "narrow rationalism" and "Protestant egoism"[33] that fueled "the materialization of human destiny."[34]

A further common theme in this period was the image of America as a young and immature society. "The government of the United States," claimed François Guizot in a famous discourse from 1834, "is a good and wonderful government for the United States, in the circumstances in which this society found itself at the moment of its birth, because it is a society that has just been born, une *société enfant*."[35]

Progressive republicans on the left of the political spectrum also expressed their discontent with a number of aspects of American democracy and made a fundamental distinction between the *moral* aspects of the American democracy and its *political* institutions and principles, questioning the former but approving of the latter. This dichotomy appeared, for example, in the following fragment of André Marchais and J. F. Dupont published in *La Revue Républicaine* in 1834. "From the moral point of view," they wrote, "we do not belong to the American school. From the practical point of view, we belong to the American school . . . in this sense that we invoke the example of America as a practical proof that demonstrates the application of the republican doctrine of universal suffrage and its consequences."[36]

Finally, the early 1830s saw the emergence of a new topic – slavery – that had been previously underplayed by the French. The idea that slavery tended to undermine the status and future of American democracy began gaining wide currency in France at that time. In an article published in *La Revue Britannique* in 1831, its director J.-L. Saulnier denounced the hypocrisy of American democracy, which, he wrote, combined "this liberty without any limits on one side, and this abject servitude on the other."[37] Alphonse de Lamartine was struck by the contrast between "this Congress where the nice words independence, human dignity, imprescriptible rights, and the inviolability of natural rights could constantly be heard" and the miserable condition of the black population that cried out against "so much philanthropic hypocrisy."[38]

If some critics pointed out that equality remained a mere ideal in a country with extreme forms of racial inequality, others began to see the dangers of extreme forms of equality. Théodore Jouffroy, for example, feared that the general leveling of conditions would lead to "a form of mediocre civilization."[39] Many French travelers such as Édouard de Montulé, author of *Travels in America, 1816-1817*, focused on the interplay between nature, culture, and politics, raising questions about the possibility of a good life in the New World.[40] Others, like Achille Murat, chose to settle permanently in America. In *A Moral and Political Sketch of the United States of North America* (1833), Murat noted that the America of the late 1820s was an agricultural rather than a trading country, a land marked by great divisions between the slave

states and the free states, between New England and the central-
Atlantic states, and between the South and the West. Murat, who
settled in Florida and supported the emancipation of slaves, regarded
not without bewilderment the proliferation of Protestant sects and
espoused a critical view of religion in America. He praised the gracious society of the South[41] and was taken aback by the absence
of the art of conversation in the North, where people talked only
about business and politics. In the territories west of the Mississippi,
Murat remarked, social life was characterized by "a rude instinct of
robust liberty, degenerating often into licentiousness, a simplicity of
morals, and an uncouthness of manners, approaching occasionally
to coarseness and cynical independence."[42] Murat also commented
on the attitudes of the Americans toward government, competition –
"the secret of the American system" – and federalism. He had words
of praise for the Supreme Court and judicial review and criticized the
electoral college system, which, in his view, thwarted the will of the
majority.

    Asked to clarify his own position on America, Murat concluded
on a Tocquevillian note *avant la lettre*: "You will immediately ask
me if I think the constitution of the United States the best possible,
and if I think it applicable to France? This question has been asked
me a thousand times: I do not answer it, at least at present, for it
is not that which is of immediate concern. It is not so much the
constitution and laws of the United States that I admire and love, as
the reason why the United States have this constitution, and these
laws. . . . This principle, from which so much good has emanated, and
which is destined to govern the world, is what is called in America
'Self-government,' Government by the people themselves."[43]

    Murat's political assessment differed from the emphasis that other
French visitors of the New World put on the uncivilized, mercan-
tile, and materialistic character of American society. During his
trip to America in 1833, Benjamin Saint-Victor wryly noted: "The
main question here (and it's the *alpha* and *omega* of life), is to gain
money, and then to use this money to gain ever more. . . . The entire
world does not seem to suffice to their cupidity."[44] In the eyes of
the sophisticated French, American life was monotonous and coarse
because it lacked poetry and *savoir-vivre*. "America," claimed La Mennais, "is struck by the plague of commerce. The outcome is a spirit
of calculation that stifles or weakens all generous sentiments."[45]
In turn, Saint-Victor deplored the restless competition and frantic

commercial life that created "this perpetual and boundless movement of all cupid passions, the endpoint of all the worried thoughts of this multitude of people, who constantly turned to earth, exhaust themselves under the sun in order to build a treasure or to increase without measure the one that they have already amassed."[46] One exception was Chateaubriand, who visited America in the 1820s. Fascinated by the "primitive" America, he drew an exotic portrait of the New World that, for the most part, had little to say about politics and economy.[47]

An interesting critique of America was advanced by Victor Jacquemont who visited the New World in 1826–1827, five years before Tocqueville. Educated in the pro-American milieu of the Idéologues, a group with whom Jefferson was closely connected, Jacquemont came to America with an open mind. He was enthusiastic about learning English and refrained from passing superficial judgments about the country. Yet, toward the end of his journey, he could not conceal his dissatisfaction with the American way of life. "I dislike the American mores," he wrote in a forty-page letter to Victor de Tracy in September 1827; "their aspect, sometimes severe, is most often cold, flat, and vulgar."[48] Jacquemont referred to the great American leaders as republicans by principle and aristocrats in their mores and concluded that, for all its virtues, the American way of life did not provide a civilized type of liberty. What is particularly interesting in Jacquemont's case is that his conclusion that individual happiness was more or less independent from forms of government coexisted with a sincere appreciation of many political aspects of American democracy. In this regard, he echoed the fundamental distinction made by French republicans between the *moral* aspects of American democracy and its *political* institutions and principles.

A similar argument appeared in Stendhal's *On Love* (originally written in 1821) in which the well-known novelist drew an ultimately unflattering portrait of daily life in the United States (although he never visited America). "All their attention," wrote Stendhal, referring to Americans, "seems to be concentrated on a sensible arrangement of the business of living, and on foreseeing all mishaps." But these efforts came at a high price: "When at last," he continued, "they reach the point of harvesting the fruit of so much care and orderly planning, they find no life left . . . to enjoy."[49] Yet, unlike other critics, Stendhal did not see American mores as rude. On the contrary, it was their politeness and rationality that he found problematic and unsatisfying.

He acknowledged that America had a free government which "does its citizens no harm, but rather gives them security and tranquility."[50] But, in Stendhal's opinion, this was not enough to create true happiness; political happiness, and true happiness are different and they do not always coincide. Happiness meant much more than being free from the interference of a bad, harmful, and incompetent government. The spirit of American liberty, Stendhal concluded, is "a coarse spirit" that gives the people the illusion of being happy simply because they enjoy security and tranquility.[51]

More importantly, the unflattering picture of American mores led to a questioning of some of the political principles underlying American democracy. Thus, one commentator claimed that American government was not as cheap as had previously been argued.[52] Other French observers of American political life deplored an extreme form of partisan politics that triggered violent attacks on political opponents and overheated electoral campaigns. President Jackson's unsophisticated political style was also criticized. The country no longer had the brilliant statesmen who had fought for its independence from England and who had been instrumental in drafting its Constitution. By reflecting on the recurrent episodes of popular agitation such as the mob violence and riots of 1834, French observers of American politics feared that law-abidingness in America was waning and concluded that the American people was impulsive and bellicose. Last but not least, the weakness of the federal government – previously seen as an advantage – now came to be interpreted as a major weakness. This perception fueled the image of a democracy prone to degenerate into mobocracy, a regime that engendered violence and risked descending into popular autocracy.[53] Moreover, the French increasingly came to suspect that the presence of slavery was going to cause the break-up of the Union. These themes were to loom large in Tocqueville's letters of the 1840s and 1850s, in which he referred to inadequate trials and summary executions, lynching, and the flagrant violation of individual rights.

III. Tocqueville's Views of America before 1840

The various accounts of America presented in the previous section demonstrate that, by the time that Tocqueville had finished writing Volume One of *Democracy in America*, the viability of the American political model was questioned in France. Serious doubts had emerged concerning the possibility of transplanting it onto French soil as well as with regard to its own effectiveness. America, its critics argued, could not serve as a political model for France.[54]

Tocqueville participated in this French debate,[55] although he was probably not familiar with important first-hand accounts of America such as those given by Jacquemont and Murat. In his published writings, as well as in his private correspondence, Tocqueville advanced a series of arguments that were meant to respond to the ideas of his contemporaries. In 1835, Tocqueville presented a relatively optimistic image of American institutions and constitution. He described how Americans practiced the art of self-government, how they felt attached to their townships and participated in their local administration. More importantly, Tocqueville demonstrated that, contrary to what its critics argued, the sovereignty of the people could be channeled into effective and regular institutions that promoted the common interest and the common good. While the unusually long chapter that concluded Volume One of *Democracy in America* ("Some Considerations Concerning the Present State and Probable Future of the Three Races that Inhabit the Territory of the United States") voiced a series of concerns about the probable future of the country, Tocqueville stopped short of suggesting that the stability of the country itself was at risk. He foresaw the gradual and inevitable disappearance of the native races and predicted that the destiny of the blacks would be intermingled with that of the white population. "The most dreadful of all the evils that threaten the future of the United States," Tocqueville surmised, "arise from the presence of blacks on its soil."[56] Although Tocqueville saw that, in a certain part of the country, the legal barrier that separated the two races was falling, he was convinced that slavery remained a formidable challenge because the three prejudices – of the master, of race and of the white – to which slavery had given birth still remained untouched.[57]

The twin issues of race relations and slavery were not the only major topics discussed by this chapter. Tocqueville also analyzed the relations between the federal government and the states and noted that federal power was decreasing at the time he visited the country. He claimed that "Americans have much more to expect and to fear from the state than from the Union.... The federal government...is...by its very nature a weak government."[58] Furthermore, Tocqueville expressed optimism regarding the survival of the republic in America, by which he meant that form of government based on "the slow and tranquil action of society on itself."[59] Because the institutions of the country were essentially republican and enjoyed "a sort of *consensus universalis*,"[60] Tocqueville believed that it would be extremely difficult to found a monarchy or an aristocracy in the United States. In spite of his reflections about the dangers of the tyranny of the majority, Tocqueville's words spoke with reassuring confidence of the future of the country. He perceived his America as an accomplished and mature democracy, capable of overcoming its challenges (slavery, territorial expansion, the growth of population), destined to rise to the status of one of the world's premier powers, and expected to serve as a political model for the rest of the world. The idea of an immature and unstable American democracy that figured prominently in his later letters did *not* appear in Volume One.

Published in 1840, Volume Two of *Democracy in America* qualified this optimistic view by introducing a series of new themes and concerns about the democratic individual. Yet, in the end, Tocqueville's thoughts on the shortcomings of democracy did not call into question the viability and maturity of American democracy. He seemed less interested in making predictions about its future than in drawing the portrait of the democratic individual living in the age of equality. In spite of his distrust of the bourgeoisie and of his anxieties about the pernicious effects of rampant individualism in modern democratic society, Tocqueville did not question what he took to be the foundational virtue of the American middle class, "self-interest rightly understood." The vices of individualism, he argued, can be successfully mitigated and combated by religion, free institutions, and local freedoms. Tocqueville also noted that *l'intérêt bien entendu* "forms a multitude of citizens who are regulated, temperate, moderate, farsighted, master of themselves"[61] and concluded that self-interest rightly understood, while preventing some individuals from mounting far above the ordinary level of humanity, prevented many more from falling below it.

Three things are worth noting in Tocqueville's analysis in Volume Two of *Democracy in America*. First, he suggested that the Americans were moderate and responsible individuals, who knew well their interests and rights, were capable of controlling their passions, and were not easily swayed by mob flatterers or demagogues. The idea that democracy might engender violence and turmoil or that the market might become uncontrollable because of the growing multiplicity of interests seemed implausible. On Tocqueville's account, Americans displayed common sense, temperance, and moderation. Although Volume Two of *Democracy in America* addressed to some extent the perils of prosperity and the limits of abundance, one finds many more details about these issues in Tocqueville's correspondence.[62]

Second, Tocqueville had little to say here about the possibility of the economic sphere invading the political realm and corrupting its institutions. Yet, in Volume Two of *Democracy in America*, he discussed the possibility of the rise of an "industrial aristocracy" in democratic America. This new type of manufacturing aristocracy, he argued, would be different from the old one, since its goal would be only to make use of the population rather than to govern the country. "It is one of the hardest [aristocracies] that has appeared on earth," Tocqueville surmised, "but it is at the same time one of the most restrained and least dangerous."[63] The possible emergence of an industrial aristocracy was therefore not enough to call into question the image of an accomplished American democracy. For the author of *Democracy in America*, this was to change after 1850, as he became more and more concerned about the consequences of the unbridled spirit of enterprise at the core of the American way of life.[64]

Finally, in spite of his dislike of the French rising bourgeoisie of his time, Tocqueville praised the outstanding spirit of enterprise of the American middle class and showed how democracy favors new developments in industry and multiplies the opportunity for various lucrative enterprises. He wrote *sine ira et studio* about the independent spirit of the American middle class, its restlessness, and the multiplicity of its economic enterprises that opened up new vistas and careers to all individuals, regardless of their station in life. To be sure, one finds in Tocqueville's balanced account neither the vitriolic attacks on the boundless cupidity of the Americans that underlay conservative critiques of America such as Saint-Victor's *Letters from the United States of America* (1835), nor the profound dislike for the vulgar mores and the prosaic American way of life expressed by Victor Jacquemont and Stendhal in the 1820s.[65]

IV. Tocqueville's American Critics

The publication of Tocqueville's *Democracy in America* was hailed as a major intellectual event on both sides of the Atlantic. When Volume

One came out in France in January 1835, Tocqueville's work was immediately compared with Aristotle's *Politics* and Montesquieu's *The Spirit of the Laws*. "I have read it five times," the venerable Royer-Collard confessed, "it is for me an inexhaustible source of instruction and pleasure."[66] Tocqueville also gained the recognition and admiration of American readers, who enthusiastically applauded his sociological acumen, the finesse of his observation on mores, and his love of truth.[67] Tocqueville was described as "an original thinker, an acute observer, and an eloquent writer."[68] At the same time, Tocqueville's American admirers did not shy away from pointing out some shortcomings in his arguments. As Edward Everett, one of Tocqueville's correspondents, argued, "there are several mistakes, as to matters of fact, some of considerable importance; there is occasionally a disposition shown, almost universal among intelligent original thinkers, to construct a theory, and then find the facts to support it." Nonetheless, Everett added, these were only "slight defects in an excellent work."[69]

That Tocqueville might have committed a few factual errors was not surprising in a book of such scope and depth as *Democracy in America*. In an important letter written in June 1837, President John Quincy Adams called Tocqueville's attention to a passage relating to himself in Volume One, containing an erroneous statement of facts. The passage in question mistakenly alleged that President Adams had dismissed many individuals named by his predecessor. He politely expressed his hope that in future editions of the work it would be corrected or omitted.[70]

In a letter of May 9, 1840, Joseph Story, a member of the Supreme Court of the United States, wrote to Francis Lieber complaining about the ignorance of constitutional law among Europeans, especially when applied to forms of government such as the American one. "Europeans know little on the subject," Story wrote, adding that "it is surprising how little they read of what has been written here." He then extended this criticism to include Tocqueville, in effect questioning his intellectual honesty. "The work of de Tocqueville," he wrote, "has had a great reputation abroad, partly founded on their ignorance that he has borrowed the greater part of his reflections from American works, and little from his own observation. The main body of his materials will be found in the *Federalist*, and in Story's *Commentaries on the Constitution*; *sic vos non vobis*. You know ten times as much as he does of the actual workings of our system and of its true story."[71] Another acquaintance and correspondent of Tocqueville's, George

Ticknor, expressed a nuanced criticism of Tocqueville's treatment of slavery: "Tocqueville's acute book, which contains so much truth as well as error about us – and which Talleyrand says is the ablest book of this kind published since Montesquieu's *Spirit of the Laws* – has explained the matter [slavery] with a good degree of truth, but with great harshness."[72]

Other critics went so far as to challenge even some of the key concepts of Tocqueville's account of American democracy. In a letter of February 1, 1841 to Guillaume-Tell Poussin (author of an important book on the government and institutions of the United States in which he sought to amend some of Tocqueville's observations),[73] Jared Sparks, a close friend of Tocqueville, pointed out his disagreement with the latter's theory of the tyranny of the majority in America. "Your criticisms of Mr. de Tocqueville's work," Sparks wrote, "also accord for the most part with my own sentiments. Notwithstanding the great ability with which his book is written, the extent of his intelligence, and his profound discussions of many important topics, I am persuaded that when applied to the United States, sometimes lead him astray. For instance, in what he says of the tyranny of the majority, I think, he is entirely mistaken. His ideas are not verified by experience. The tyranny of the majority, if exercised at all, must be in the making of laws; and any evil arising from this source operates in precisely the same manner on the majority itself as on the minority. Besides, if the majority passes an oppressive law, or a law which the people generally disapprove, this majority will certainly be changed at the next election, and be composed of different elements. Mr. de Tocqueville's theory can only be true where the majority is an unchangeable body and where it acts exclusively on the minority, as distinct from itself – a state of things which can never occur where the elections are frequent and every man has a voice in choosing the legislators."[74]

Similar points were raised by Sparks at about the same time in another letter, this time addressed to Professor William Smyth, of Cambridge, England. Sparks criticized Smyth's lectures on America because, in his view, the Cambridge professor placed too much confidence in Tocqueville's ideas of the tyranny of the majority. "On this subject," Sparks wrote on October 13, 1841, "his imagination leads him far astray. In practice we perceive no such consequences as he supposes. If the majority were large and always consisted of the same individuals, such a thing might be possible; but with us, as in all free governments, parties are nearly equal, and the elections are so frequent that a man who is in the majority at one time is likely to find himself in the minority a few months afterwards. What inducement has a majority thus constituted to be oppressive? Moreover, Mr. de Tocqueville often confounds the majority with public opinion, which has the same tendency, or nearly so, in all civilized countries, whatever may be the form of government. Yet his work has great merit, and on most points is remarkably accurate where facts only are concerned. He is apt to theorize."[75] John C. Spencer was to make exactly the same point to Jean-Jacques Ampère a decade later when Tocqueville's close friend visited him in America.[76]

The catalogue of Tocqueville's alleged errors and omissions did not stop there. Jacksonian democrats such as Senator Thomas Hart Benton complained about his unflattering treatment of Andrew Jackson in *Democracy in America* and claimed that Tocqueville's dislike of the Jackson presidency was a residue of the influence exercised by his (allegedly biased) Whig sources.[77] Other commentators emphasized that Tocqueville ought not to be regarded first and foremost as an empirical observer of the American society, since his analysis of American democracy was informed by his more general views of democracy in modern society. As Sean Wilentz remarked two decades ago, "where Tocqueville saw many things in Jacksonian America and called them one thing, there were in fact many democracies. Behind what he called the Americans' universal consensus, there were fundamental differences about the first principles of democracy itself."[78] To his credit, Tocqueville himself was not unaware of these problems. As he was finalizing Volume One of *Democracy in America*, he pointed out in one of his notes "the great difficulty in untangling what there is democratic, commercial, English, and puritan" in America.[79] In this respect, he could have hardly been more prescient.

V. Tocqueville's Views on America after 1840

In spite of Tocqueville's cautionary words about the possibility of the emergence of a new type of soft democratic despotism, Volume Two of *Democracy in America* offered the image of a relatively solid and stable democratic regime that, for all its inherent shortcomings, managed to reconcile successfully the demands for equality, liberty, and justice. A major participant in the French parliamentary politics of the 1840s, Tocqueville never published a sequel to *Democracy in*

America or any major statement on American democracy between 1840 and his death in 1859. After 1850, Tocqueville's research interests eventually shifted to studying the Old Regime and the origins of the French Revolution.[80] But what happened with Tocqueville's interest in America? Did he change his views on American democracy? What did he make of America as it moved towards Civil War?

To answer these questions we shall turn primarily to the correspondence between Tocqueville and his American friends. At the same time, we shall also examine a number of lesser-known texts of Tocqueville (speeches, parliamentary reports, and diplomatic correspondence) in which he referred to – and drew upon – the values, principles, and institutions of American democracy. From October 1840 until his death, Tocqueville sent more than one hundred letters to his American friends and received an almost equal number of letters from them. Some of these letters have been lost, while others exist only in transcribed form in the Beinecke Library at Yale University. Tocqueville's addressees were mostly individuals whom he and Beaumont had met during their voyage to America. The group included, among others, Jared Sparks (1789–1866), the president of Harvard University and editor of the papers of Washington and Franklin; Francis Lieber (1798–1872), editor of the *Encyclopaedia Americana* and professor at South Caroliniana College;[81] Edward Everett (1794–1865), ambassador to London, Secretary of State and senator; Theodore Sedgwick (1811–1859), who provided Tocqueville with essential information while he was writing Volume One of *Democracy in America*; Charles Sumner (1811–1874), a Harvard law professor and Republican senator; N. W. Beckwith, a wealthy American businessman who lived in Geneva and traveled to the Far East; and last but not least, Edward Vernon and Edward Lee Childe, members of an American family living temporarily in France and with whom Tocqueville had close relations in the 1850s (Mildred Childe was Robert E. Lee's sister). Two other important correspondents were the American diplomats Richard Rush and George Bancroft.[82]

As Benedict G. Songy pointed out three decades ago, "these letters are important not only as commentaries on the social and political situation in America, but as reflections of Tocqueville's own thought. They reveal his predominant concern for the future of the Union and the fate of the democratic experiment. For Tocqueville, Democracy was on trial, or rather, the American form of Democracy was tested."[83] Some of Tocqueville's letters, as well as those received from his correspondents, are short and limit themselves to brief comments on political events in both America and Europe. Many deal with the mundane matters of everyday life (planned visits, illnesses and deaths within the family, and other such matters which figure prominently in the correspondence between friends as they get old). Some letters focus on professional matters such as the publication of the newspaper *Le Commerce*, the sessions of the French Academy, and the Chamber of Deputies whose member Tocqueville was. A regular topic of inquiry, especially in the exchanges with Theodore Sedgwick, was the economic stability of America. Tocqueville owned shares in a few American railway companies and was frequently worried about them.

Tocqueville's letters from the 1850s also reaffirmed his interest in American politics as the political developments in the United States led to an intensification of the struggle between the defenders and opponents of slavery. The correspondence with N. W. Beckwith and the Childes includes some of the best letters that Tocqueville ever wrote or received and gives us an invaluable opportunity to gaze into his mind and soul.[84] The letters that Tocqueville exchanged with his American friends from 1852 onward raised a series of new concerns and perspectives on America. References were made to an emerging American imperialism, the excesses of American democracy, the decline of mores and the rise of lawlessness, the revolutionary fervor of American politics, as well as to poor political leadership and the reckless spirit of American capitalism. Lurking behind all of these issues was Tocqueville's growing concern about the issue of slavery and the possible break up of the Union as the country entered a new turbulent era paving the way for the Civil War.

As already mentioned, we shall also turn elsewhere in search of answers to our questions. To this effect, we shall examine Tocqueville's journalism, his speeches and academic presentations, his participation in French constitutional debates as well as his career as a diplomat and his occasional writings.[85] Taken together, these sources represent a substantial body of work and allow us to identify four distinct timeframes. We have arranged the material in two main parts, each divided in turn in five separate sections in keeping with the four aforementioned timeframes. The editors' introductions lay out the main themes of each section and highlight the relevant intellectual and political background of Tocqueville's writings.

The first period is 1840–1847, when Tocqueville was primarily concerned with geo-political questions concerning the United States and its foreign policy. The second period covers the Second Republic (1848–1852), when Tocqueville renewed his interest in the American Constitution and American political institutions. The third and the fourth periods (1852–1856, 1857–1859) comprise the last seven and a half years of Tocqueville's life, when Tocqueville continued to follow closely political developments in the United States, especially the debates on slavery and immigration as well as the growing corruption of democratic institutions. The inauguration of the Buchanan Administration in early 1857 marked a turning point in American politics, in the aftermath of the Kansas–Nebraska Act that led to an increasing number of cases of mob violence and lawlessness.

It is no coincidence that Tocqueville's correspondence reached a peak in 1857, when he exchanged no less than forty-two letters with his American friends in which he openly expressed his growing concerns about the vitality of American democracy triggered by the controversies surrounding the extension of slavery into the Western territories. All these developments led Tocqueville to utter harsh criticisms about the excesses and corruption of American democracy, harsher in any case than those which can be found in either of the two volumes of *Democracy in America*. Finally, in the 1850s, amidst growing skepticism about America's political future, Tocqueville came to regard the corruption of American institutions and mores, along with slavery, as a major threat to American democracy. It was in this context that Tocqueville began reflecting on the invasion of the political by the economic sphere as well as on the inevitable shortcomings of a market society, two topics that had *not* loomed large in his previous writings.

VI. Tocqueville and America in the 1840s

During the first half of the 1840s, Tocqueville remained confident that American political institutions offered the best combination of liberty and security and continued to believe that the future of liberty in the world depended to a significant extent on the preservation of a democratic republic in the United States. Describing himself as "half Yankee,"[86] Tocqueville argued that, in spite of temporary misunderstandings and rivalries between the two countries, France and the United States shared so many interests that they were two natural allies united by profound ties that needed to be strengthened. "Nothing interests me more than anything concerning this great and strong nation [America]," he wrote to Nathaniel Niles in 1843, "I have lately broken somewhat the chain of my relations with the United States. I regret this and would like to renew them. I take a particular interest in this issue both from my heart and my patriotism, since one of the guiding principles of my politics is that in spite of the preconceptions and disagreements on small details, France and the United States are allies so natural and necessary to each other that they should never lose sight of each other for a single moment."[87] In the American system of government, Tocqueville admired those safety valves that had preserved it from major convulsions and allowed it to make gradual changes in the constitution, by parliamentary means. The implicit suggestion was that America could serve as a political model *sui generis* for France, a point that he reiterated in an important speech given at a popular banquet in Cherbourg in March 1848.

In the 1840s, Tocqueville also made frequent references to America in his parliamentary speeches and reports on prison reform in France.[88] It will be recalled that, in 1833, Tocqueville had co-authored with Gustave de Beaumont a prize-winning report entitled *On the Penitentiary System in the United States and Its Application in France* (it was reedited in 1836 and 1845).[89] Tocqueville and Beaumont commented at length on the virtues and limitations of the Philadelphia system (based on solitary confinement by day and night) and the Auburn System (cellular isolation at night, work during the day under a strict rule of silence). Hesitating between the two systems, Tocqueville initially pointed out the beneficial effects of the Auburn system.[90] A decade later, however, he changed his mind and affirmed the superiority of the Philadelphia system. Serving as *rapporteur* of a committee entrusted with the task of presenting a project of prison reform to the Chamber of Deputies, Tocqueville argued that the Philadelphia system was, all things considered, less damaging than any other prison system and could be used in France as well.[91] Regrettably, his hopes for prison reform in France failed to materialize during his lifetime.

Tocqueville also made favorable remarks about American democracy in two texts on democracy in Switzerland written in mid-1840s. In an untitled article from 1845 that contained a number of critical remarks about the perplexing weakness of the Swiss government of the time, Tocqueville praised the virtues of American democracy in unambiguous terms: "When the American government decides to raise money it has its own tax collectors who tell every American citizen the share that he must pay. When it recruits its army, it has its own agents to muster the troops. When it sets up customs posts, it has its own customs officers. When, finally, the taxpayer refuses to pay, the soldier to march, and the customs officer to obey, it has its courts which represent only itself and which oblige the citizens to obey its laws."[92] Tocqueville took up the same comparison between Switzerland and America a few years later in his important review of Cherbuliez's *Democracy in Switzerland*, which Tocqueville decided to include as an appendix to the twelfth edition of *Democracy in America* published in 1848.

That Tocqueville remained convinced that the American model had something to offer to France is also illustrated not only by the flattering remarks on American democracy in the preface to the twelfth edition of *Democracy in America* (1848), but also by his remarks in the intense constitutional debates that accompanied the birth of the Second Republic in 1848.[93] The preface he wrote in 1848 is particularly instructive here. Tocqueville remarked that, unlike European nations that had always been devastated by war or torn by civil discord, the American republic was not a disruptive force but the preserver of civil rights and of individual property. He concluded his short preface as follows: "Let us not turn our eyes to America in order to copy in a servile manner the institutions that she has established for herself, but in order to understand better those institutions that suit us, less in order to find there examples than to draw lessons, in order to borrow her principles rather than the details of her laws. The laws of the French Republic can and must be in many cases different from those that govern in the United States, but the principles on which the American constitutions rest, the principles of order, balance of powers, true liberty, sincere and deep respect for law, all these principles are indispensable to all republics and must be common to all of them."[94]

The constitutional debates of 1848 faced Tocqueville with the challenge of moderating the (French) revolutionary obsession with unity and equality. As a fervent advocate of both bicameralism and federalism, he found himself at odds with those republicans who remained hostile toward these principles because they were seen as unsuitable to France. The genius of France, it was frequently stated, was "unitary" and there could be no grounds for dividing up the sovereign will of people by reference to artificial institutional mechanisms designed to thwart its wishes. More specifically, both bicameralism and federalism were associated with aristocratic influence and power and, in the eyes of their French opponents, could be easily discredited by reference to the allegedly aristocratic English constitution.

Tocqueville strongly opposed these views. Recognizing that his ideas would never secure majority support, he nonetheless persisted in arguing that France had much to learn from the American experience.[95] This was from within a perspective which, at this early stage, saw Tocqueville expressing the view that one of the consequences of the 1848 revolution would be to give more liberty to individuals. In particular, Tocqueville opposed the preferred republican model of a single chamber by reference to the American system. There was, he confidently pointed out, only one democratic republic in the world, the United States, and the Americans had chosen bicameralism which they regarded as a bulwark of liberty.[96]

Tocqueville doubted that France could borrow indiscriminately from the American model, but made the curious point that in America each state was "in a position similar to ours" and all of them possessed two chambers. Not a single American, he remarked, wished the system to operate differently. Tocqueville was, in fact, echoing the views of his American friends who also considered bicameralism as one of the main causes of the survival of a democratic republic in the United States. The presence of two chambers, it was argued, offered the best protection not only against mob flatterers and demagogues, but also against the encroachment of the executive power. In a letter sent to Tocqueville in June 1848, John C. Spencer emphasized all these points and added that the two Chambers must also have different modes of election that would allow them to withstand the whims of public opinion. The senators, elected for a longer time, could resist the various demands of the masses and learn to form a healthy and sober second thought. "It is this second thought," Spencer argued, "that has saved us from many disasters."[97] Tocqueville agreed with this view. In a letter to Everett from March 12, 1849, he defended bicameralism as a pillar of constitutionalism. In turn, Everett reiterated this point by arguing that "the utility of a twofold chamber is one of those empirical mysteries of representative government, which are learned by practice; by the positive experience of England and the United States of America in its favor; by the negative experience of your Convention in 1793 against it."[98] Furthermore, in a draft of a speech in 1848, Tocqueville insisted that two chambers ought not to be considered as an aristocratic institution. He also warned that a single Assembly would inevitably amount to poor government with significant long-term consequences for the entire country. "You will not re-establish the Terror," Tocqueville remarked, "even with the aid of a single Assembly, but you will produce an execrable government."[99]

Moreover, in the 1848 debates Tocqueville denied that the two-chamber model used in America was an English invention, as some of its critics argued. States such as Pennsylvania and Massachusetts had begun life with one chamber: "public reason" had demonstrated the necessity of two chambers. This example, Tocqueville remarked, is revealing. Likewise, he disputed the claim that a two-chamber system automatically institutionalized aristocratic power, arguing that "in America, the two chambers represent in a similar manner and through similar means, the same interests and the same classes of people." He then outlined the three advantages of such a system – it prevented executive power from abuse; it strengthened the executive in its relations to parliament; and it prevented "legislative intemperance" – commenting that "two chambers do not prevent revolutions but they prevent the bad government which leads to revolutions."[100]

Tocqueville's next reference to the American model was in the context of the heated debate that surrounded the election and powers of the president. First, Tocqueville opposed the principle of re-election at the end of a president's mandate. This, he acknowledged, was what existed in America, and even there it posed an increasing problem, but fortunately the American president possessed "little power." In France, by contrast, a president would undoubtedly abuse his power in order to secure election.[101] Next, Tocqueville recommended the American system of electoral colleges as the best means of securing the election of the French president.[102]

With the exception of the mandate of the president, Tocqueville was roundly defeated by the majority republican party, intent on reliving the days of the Convention of 1793. For Tocqueville, it was a deeply troubling experience, and one that left him convinced that France would again fall prey to political instability. He did not believe that the American model could be copied without due consideration to France's own particularities, but he did believe that politicians in France should have the wisdom to learn from the experience and rules of a constitution which he did not hesitate to refer to as "a work of art." This, as we shall see, was all the more remarkable given that he himself was having growing doubts about the direction in which America itself was moving.

Tocqueville's confidence in the ability and wisdom of the American political class was affected by his dealings with the administration of President Zachary Taylor. In 1849, during his brief tenure as Minister of Foreign Affairs, Tocqueville tried in vain to find a solution to the "Poussin Affair" that created significant tensions in the diplomatic relations between the two countries.[103]

VII. Tocqueville and America in the 1850s

In the 1850s, Tocqueville's faith in the vitality of American institutions was challenged by political developments in the New World that brought into prominence, arguably more than ever before, the growing corruption of America's democratic institutions. True, his own political experience in France made him prone to pessimism, as his own country demonstrated once more that the French nation lacked a political tradition of moderation and practical wisdom. Tocqueville's own tendency to discouragement and his declining health due to the onset of tuberculosis also undoubtedly played an important role in deepening a sense of isolation that constantly frightened him. "I would have liked to shake off for good my tendency to discouragement," Tocqueville confessed in a letter to Madame de Swetchine from January 1856. "I have had this ailment, however, for most of my life.... You cannot imagine, Madame, how painful and often cruel it is for me to live in this kind of moral isolation, to feel excluded from the intellectual community of my times and my country. To be alone in the desert often strikes me as being less painful than being alone among men."[104] While Tocqueville's pessimism and tendency to political spleen can be explained to a degree by his own physical and spiritual constitution (he was a truly restless mind in constant search for certainty and intellectual companionship), political developments in America and France unquestionably contributed to his disillusionment and to his acute sense of distance from his contemporaries.[105]

In short, Tocqueville's views of American democracy did not change independently of other events in the last decade of his life. Consumed by a permanent revolutionary fervor, the French proved to be incapable of changing the constitution through peaceful parliamentary reform. They were also unable to conceive long-term political plans that would reconcile the immediate goals of all political actors with the interests of the country at large. Democracy again faltered and the year 1852 saw the birth of the Second Empire, this time under the leadership of the man Victor Hugo referred to contemptuously as *Napoléon le Petit*.[106] In the late 1840s and early 1850s, Tocqueville continued to believe in the practical sense of Americans as displayed by the country's strong tradition of self-government, and expressed again and again his hope that, in spite of its problems, American democracy would survive and prosper.[107] Yet, the tone of Tocqueville's letters[108] became more severe and pessimistic as he approached the end of his life and saw the future of liberty threatened and compromised in both France and the United States. America was entering a time of fierce party conflict that led to the blurring of previous ideological boundaries and the realignment of the political scene, with the disappearance of the Whig party in the early 1850s.[109]

In his correspondence, Tocqueville expressed serious concerns regarding the emergent American imperialism which he described as a sign of the bad health of American democracy. For Tocqueville, the idea of conquering new territories to be annexed to the already existing ones was absurd because, in his view, the country had already acquired a vast territory. Stressing again his American credentials as "half an American citizen," Tocqueville wrote to Theodore Sedgwick on December 4, 1852: "As your compatriot, I have not seen without apprehension this spirit of conquest, and even plunder, which has manifested itself among you for several years now. It is not a sign of good health for a people that already have more territories than it can fill."[110] In one of his letters from this period, Jared Sparks confirmed Tocqueville's worries, while also stressing the unprecedented material prosperity in the country: "Your apprehensions of the tendencies of the popular mind are not without foundation," Sparks wrote. "The history of the last few years, the acquisitions of Texas and California, prove that the spirit of adventure and conquest excites the aspirations and moves the will of the people. Perhaps it is inherent in the democratic element. The clamor for acquiring Cuba springs from the same spirit; and a slight cause could carry the arms of the United States again into Mexico. Where will this end, and how are such vast accessions and discordant materials to be held together in a confederated republic?"[111]

A related problem in Tocqueville's eyes was the growing immigration to America that brought into the country a considerable number of individuals who did not belong to the English race and had a different political culture.[112] Referring to the issue of the physical composition of America, Tocqueville expressed his concern about the fact that America was annually receiving around 140,000 German immigrants. How could they possibly be assimilated into American life, he wondered, given the lack of public life in Germany and the historic absence of free institutions in that country? The Germans, Tocqueville wrote in a letter to Sedgwick (August 15, 1854), "are what two centuries of absolute government, sixty years of centralization, and a very long habit of administrative dependence, as bureaucrats or administered individuals, have made them; that is to say, they lend themselves very well only to servitude or revolution. What can you do with these people when they arrive among you in America?"[113] Tocqueville also took up the immigration issue in other letters in which he expressed his concern for a possible break-up of the Union. Moreover, the large number of immigrants now present in American society made it impossible any longer to refer to the original nature of America. Unfortunately, Tocqueville commented in another letter to Sedgwick (August 29, 1856), "each new day brings to you so many foreign elements that soon you will no longer be yourselves."[114]

In December 1852, Tocqueville wrote to Sparks that American democracy had nothing more to fear than its own excesses. He also argued that an immoderate spirit of adventure, risk, and conquest would endanger the stability of democratic institutions. American democracy, Tocqueville wrote, "has nothing more to fear than from itself, from the abuse of democracy, the spirit of adventure and conquest, from the sense and exaggerated pride in its strength, and from the impetuosity of youth."[115] The solution proposed by Tocqueville was moderation: "I could not recommend moderation enough among such good fortune. Nations need it no less than individuals."[116] What is remarkable in these passages is Tocqueville's emphasis on the *excesses of democracy*, a theme that was in stark contrast with the earlier image of an accomplished and stable American democracy, more or less immune to chronic turmoil and violence. In 1852, Tocqueville realized much better than he had in 1835 or 1840 that it was in the very nature of democracy, even in the most advanced democratic regime in the world, to transgress its limits and to subvert its own foundations.

To be sure, the cacophonic spectacle of American political life in the 1850s only fueled Tocqueville's increasing skepticism and provided numerous examples of the decay of its democratic institutions. The image of a law-abiding and tranquil citizenry that Tocqueville presented in Volume One of *Democracy in America* seemed a relic of the past or, at best, a mere theoretical ideal. In a letter to Sedgwick from September 19, 1855, Tocqueville denounced "the violent, intolerant, and lawless spirit"[117] manifested in some parts of the country. He reiterated the same concern two years later, in an important letter to Lieber (October 9, 1857), in which he deplored the acts of personal revenge and violence that tended to subvert the authority of the law and the judicial system in America. As the country was preparing for the inauguration of President James Buchanan in early 1857, America was "a nation on the brink."[118] Tocqueville perceptively grasped this point, and became concerned with the rapid degradation of mores which he had previously described as the pillar of American democracy. He suggested that if political parties offered the spectacle of a ruthless competition for power, punctuated by uncivilized electoral campaigns and unacceptable attacks on their political opponents, it was because political mores and habits had become violent and rude in America.[119]

This conclusion allowed Tocqueville to make a surprising claim that cannot be found in *Democracy in America*. The deterioration of mores, he argued, fostered a kind of revolutionary fervor and the country seemed to be heading toward revolution. "What is certain," Tocqueville wrote in 1856, "is that in Europe the idea that you are approaching rapidly the time of revolution is more and more accepted and is spreading very quickly."[120] If Tocqueville stopped short of endorsing this prevailing opinion, doubts had already entered his mind, and they seemed strong enough to call into question some of his previously held opinions about the stability of American democracy.

Furthermore, confronted with the spectacle of a democracy that tended to transgress its limits and to engender chronic violence, Tocqueville came to rethink what made America original. In 1835, Tocqueville had stressed self-government and the successful alliance between the spirit of liberty and the spirit of religion. In 1840, he had emphasized the Cartesianism, individualism, and religious beliefs of Americans and had shown how self-interest rightly understood underlay their actions. In the later letters, the story was somewhat different. Religion no longer played a major role in his account of

American democracy and was conspicuously absent from his correspondence with his American friends.[121] While Tocqueville earlier believed that religion properly practiced could provide the foundation for sound mores and a virtuous form of materialism in an age of individualism and skepticism, by the 1850s this belief appeared to have waned. Tocqueville no longer made mention of America's originality in combining liberty and religion.[122]

Rather, Tocqueville now claimed that America's particularity lay in combining a degree of primitivism with the most advanced elements of civilization. This primitivism was manifested by the extreme forms of the spirit of adventure and risk which had been fostered by the growing abundance and the limitless opportunities for gain, the very same elements that Tocqueville had previously considered as the causes of the restlessness amongst Americans. In a letter to Sedgwick from October 14, 1856, Tocqueville expressed his concern regarding "this race of desperate gamblers that your prosperity, in a land that is half empty, has brought forth, a race which combines the passions and instincts of the savage with the tastes, needs, vigour, and vices of civilized men. The world, I think, has never seen anything like it before. Who can say where this might lead if ever they gain the upper hand in your affairs?"[123] What is particularly striking in this passage is the suggestion that the endless quest for increased comfort and material prosperity was the most important cause of these excesses. Far from softening human nature, as Tocqueville argued in Volume Two of *Democracy in America*, abundance now stood accused of encouraging an excessive spirit of enterprise, adventure, and risk by arousing boundless desires and fueling an unbridled materialism. Also implicit in this passage is the idea that the market was difficult to control once free reign was given to individual ambitions and interests.

Nonetheless, Tocqueville did not draw the conclusion that this was the stage of an advanced democracy. On the contrary, he came to believe that he was witnessing the symptoms of a young and immature democracy that, like a child unable to control its emotions and passions, takes the liberty of indulging its own whims and desires without considering their pernicious long-term effects. In taking up the issue of the alleged immaturity of American democracy – a new theme in his writings – Tocqueville conjured up a powerful image to capture the sense of America as a young and inexperienced society. In a letter to Sedgwick from August 29, 1856, Tocqueville referred to America, in a phrase borrowed from Thomas Hobbes, as a *puer robustus*,[124] as a robust child who responded only to being either spoilt or punished."What is certain," Tocqueville wrote, "is that, for some years now, you have strangely abused the advantages given to you by God, advantages which have allowed you to commit great errors with impunity.... Viewed from this side of the ocean, you have become the *puer robustus* of Hobbes. Being so, you upset all the friends of democratic liberty and delight all of its opponents."[125] He used the same image in letters to Lieber and to Nassau Senior from 1856. America, Tocqueville argued, risked disappointing the hopes of millions of people for a better future, because it offered in reality the disquieting spectacle of an unstable regime led by incompetent and dishonest leaders, relying on corrupt institutions, and incapable of controlling the excesses of the spirit of enterprise and adventure.[126] Echoing some of the points made by his American correspondents in the mid-1850s, Tocqueville remarked that the greatest plague of America, after slavery, was the government of the country by the least honest, if not the least capable, part of the nation.

Similar claims also appeared in the American press of that time. In early 1857, *Harper's Weekly* published an editorial which decried "the pecuniary corruption omnipresent in our Legislative Halls, which control land grants and steamer contracts, and is incarnated in that gigantic corruption-fund, the public printing."[127] In turn, Emerson did not conceal his profound dislike of the politicians of his time who formed a class of "privileged thieves who infest our politics . . . and get into government and rob without stint and without disgrace."[128]

Tocqueville's concerns for America's future, however, paled into insignificance by the side of those he voiced concerning slavery. Here we must remember that upon his election as a member of the Chamber of Deputies in 1839, one of the principal responsibilities allotted to Tocqueville had been that of drafting a law abolishing slavery in the French colonies. The report that he prepared was subsequently translated and published in America, leading him to hope that it might have some useful impact, especially in the South. In the context of this report, Tocqueville wrote to Sparks (October 13, 1840) that "slavery has deeper and stronger roots on your soil than anywhere else."[129] It was a source of great sadness to him that America had incorporated slavery in itself in the way that it had. In his view, it was because these roots were so deep that slavery would survive for longer in America than elsewhere. Indeed, Tocqueville predicted that neither he nor Sparks would see its end.

Tocqueville's profound concern about the impact of slavery continued long after his retirement from active politics in 1851. Like some of his American correspondents, Tocqueville was worried about the "terrible antagonism between freedom and slavery"[130] that seemed only to increase in force over time. This concern was made abundantly clear when, in 1856, Tocqueville published an open letter in *The Liberty Bell*. Describing himself as "the persevering enemy of despotism everywhere," Tocqueville indicated in the strongest terms that he was "pained and astonished" by the fact that "the freest people in the world is, at the present time, almost the only one among civilized and Christian nations which yet maintains personal servitude."[131] Slavery, he went on, retarded America's progress, gave support to her detractors, and threatened the future of the Union. As a man, and not just as "an old and sincere friend of America," he was moved by "the spectacle of man's degradation by man" and hoped to see the day when the law would grant equal civil liberty to all citizens.[132] As Benedict Songy put it, "even though [Tocqueville] loved America, he could not love its faults, especially when it failed in the area of liberty."[133] Toward the end of 1857, Tocqueville's letters struck a more pessimistic tone, as he received new information from his American correspondents such as N. W. Beckwith and E. V. Childe. The election of Buchanan as president significantly increased his fears that slavery would be extended.

It was this theme that came to dominate the remaining letters Tocqueville wrote to his American friends prior to his untimely death in April 1859. For example, while he appeared to agree with Sedgwick that the greatest danger facing the northern states was political corruption, the prospect of the extension of slavery filled him with horror and despair. While distancing himself from the abolitionist position[134] (because he was fearful of the consequences of a policy which he described as premature and dangerous), Tocqueville vehemently opposed the extension of slavery into the western territories. Such a possibility, he indicated in a letter to Theodore Sedgwick from January 10, 1857, could only be viewed as "one of the greatest crimes that men could commit against the general cause of humanity."[135] Tocqueville could not accept that a great people had no right to express an opinion about the extension of what he did not hesitate to describe as "the most horrible of all social evils."[136] Fortunately, Tocqueville added, as a Frenchman he did not have to face the terrible dilemmas that such action would entail for the Union.

Increasingly, however, Tocqueville felt that the Union was in danger. An equivalent level of political agitation and passion would have been such, he recognized, as to lead to civil war in Europe. In July 1857 he identified the cause of the Union with "that of liberty across the world."[137] To the end, he continued to hope that slavery would be vanquished. Nevertheless, it is hard not to conclude that the debate about the possible extension of slavery added to the mounting political pessimism that characterised the final decade of Tocqueville's life.

VIII. *"L'Amérique en sucre"?*

If Tocqueville's ideas have become extremely influential today among academics and elected politicians (in the United States), it is also true that the richness of his writings has sometimes generated a tendency to over praise his work, turning the Frenchman into an intellectual guru. Reacting against this trend, a number of perceptive critics of Tocqueville have raised important questions regarding the accuracy of his analysis of American democracy and expressed doubts regarding the validity of his method of inquiry and theoretical conclusions. It has even been suggested that Tocqueville "got America wrong,"[138] that he failed to see the reality of America, and this because he worked with a flawed method that made him perceive only what suited his ideological biases and intellectual inclinations. For these interpreters, Tocqueville's conclusions are a strange concoction of mostly unwarranted generalizations and impressionistic observations based on *a priori* ideas that he had brought with him from France. According to Gary Wills, "what Tocqueville did not see is often more interesting than what he did.... Most of his opinions were formed at his first encounters with an idea and they were rarely altered afterwards."[139]

In "Beyond Tocqueville, Myrdal and Hartz," Rogers Smith argued a similar case, contending that "the Tocquevillian story is deceptive because it is too narrow."[140] In Smith's opinion, the relevance of Tocqueville's interpretation is limited by the fact that he used "categories derived from the hierarchy of political and social statuses men have held in Europe."[141] As such, concluded Smith (echoing a point previously made by Sean Wilentz), Tocqueville's analysis, at the heart of which lies the concept of the equality of conditions, fails to give due consideration "to the inegalitarian ideologies and conditions that have shaped the participants and the substance of American politics just as deeply."[142] The charge, both in Tocqueville's day and now, has been that Tocqueville presented an idealized and saccharine version of America.

More recently, the scientific nature of Tocqueville's method has been emphasized again by Raymond Boudon. He has argued that Tocqueville had "an explicative and not interpretative conception of social-historical phenomena," because he aimed at providing a scientific explanation rather than a literary interpretation of facts.[143] Tocqueville's own method combined in an original way explanation and interpretation, descriptive and normative analysis by using a mixture of quasi-formal methods and a very effective research strategy that should be evident to anyone who has carefully studied the writing process of *Democracy in America* (as well as *The Old Regime and the Revolution*). Far from "imagining" America, as some critics claimed, Tocqueville carefully and painstakingly studied its mores and social conditions before drawing his own set of political conclusions or recommendations.

The examination of Tocqueville's often-neglected correspondence with his American friends after 1840 confirms Boudon's argument. The Frenchman did not overlook the issue of slavery and he was not oblivious to the fact that the equality of conditions extended only to a part of the population. He saw that industrialization was changing the face and mores of America. He grasped the significance of American expansionism. The perceptive letters sent to his American friends in the 1850s clearly show that Tocqueville's image of American life was neither deceptive nor too narrow. Indeed, in some ways they offer a more poignant account than the one to be found in the two volumes of *Democracy in America*. Twenty years earlier, Tocqueville had seen in America "more than America,"[144] the image of democracy itself, and wanted to find lessons there from which everyone in his native country could profit. Tocqueville was fully convinced that the future of democracy and freedom in the world depended on the success of the democratic experiment in the United States. He also believed that the development and progress of American democracy responded to a secret design of Providence. Tocqueville's subtle and elegant analysis of American mores and institutions sought to convince his compatriots that American democracy was stable and orderly and represented a great step forward for the cause of justice in the entire world.

For all his nuanced and sometimes critical portrait of the democratic individual, it can be argued that Tocqueville did not radically change his views when he came to write Volume Two of *Democracy in America*, although it was undoubtedly the case that his focus eventually shifted from what was distinctively American to what was democratic in general. This is not meant to understate the originality of Volume Two of *Democracy in America*. He there expressed an uneasiness about the mediocrity of democratic life, bent on commerce and imbued with utilitarian values, and wanted rather to see more individuals capable of conceiving loftier plans than that of gaining money and of making their lives more comfortable. As illustrated by the last book of Volume Two of *Democracy in America*, in the late 1830s Tocqueville believed that the greatest dangers to democracy were not anarchy and the ensuing collapse of political and social order but a new form of "democratic" despotism, one that strikes the mind rather than the body, and transforms all citizens into a mass of docile individuals in perpetual need of an enlightened tutor who relieves them "entirely of the trouble of thinking and the pain of living."[145] The main idea of Tocqueville's analysis in the last book of Volume Two of *Democracy in America* was that democratic despotism was the inevitable companion of centralization and the outcome of the multiplication of the functions and agencies of government demanded by the growing equality of conditions. In addressing such a despotism, he confided in a letter to Royer-Collard, "I feel that I am treating here the most important idea of our time."[146]

Nonetheless, the final image of American mores and institutions presented in Volume Two, in stark contrast to the more negative assessments of American democracy offered in his post-1840 correspondence, gave significant reasons for optimism. In his book, Tocqueville drew four important conclusions that are worth restating. First, the instincts and passions of democracy ought to be constantly moderated and held in check because democracy goes hand in hand with materialism, the tyranny of the majority, rampant individualism, and centralization. Second, this task of moderating and purifying democracy can be *successfully* accomplished by a regime such as that of America.[147] Third, Tocqueville believed that "political liberty is the greatest remedy for nearly all the evils with which equality menaces man."[148] Fourth, he argued that since "there is only Democracy (by this word I understand self-government) which can lessen and make bearable the inevitable evils of a democratic social state, . . . it is necessary with all one's might to hasten to give enlightenment and liberty to people who have already such a social state."[149] All these points show that Tocqueville arrived at the conclusion that soft (bureaucratic) despotism and centralization of power posed much greater threats to democracy than unruly legislative assemblies, power-driven individuals, or the process of industrialization. Yet, as his letters demonstrate, a decade and a half later, Tocqueville came to doubt *some* of these conclusions and claimed that the hopes pinned on American democracy and freedom had been severely compromised. The hypothetical "Volume Three" of *Democracy in America*, if it had ever been written, would have probably mirrored his disenchantment and skepticism and would have called into question *some* of the most significant ideas of his widely acclaimed book.

In some respects, Tocqueville did not alter his previous assessment. He continued to believe in democracy's capacity to overcome internal crises, in spite of its own tendency to decline. If there was a crisis in America, the real cause lay not so much in its democratic institutions and instincts as in the presence of slavery; but even under those circumstances, universal suffrage and free institutions remained the sole hope for curing these problems. This point was made repeatedly by one of Tocqueville's most astute and thorough American correspondents, N. W. Beckwith. "If America as compared with herself is worse than she was," Beckwith wrote in a letter from 1857 (or 1858), "I must confess that she is worse, much worse; that she degenerates in morals and manners, manifestly and clearly – I have not a doubt of it. You have also heard it said that the principal causes are: 1st the predominant influence of "the people" in public affairs; 2nd the increase of adventurers from all parts; and 3rd the ultra democratic constitution of the courts of justice, the judges being elected by universal suffrage, for short tenures of offices, dependant on party or popularity, whereby justice is rendered uncertain and people will not resort to the tribunals, but prefer to redress their own grievances in their own way. I admit the degeneracy in its full length and breadth, but I reject the cause to which it is assigned. [. . .] Slavery is the cause, I do not say the sole cause, but cause enough obvious and certain, to produce the progressive demoralization you have indicated."[150]

The high stakes and implications of a possible failure of the American model for Tocqueville were unambiguously illustrated by a letter sent to Francis Lieber on September 1, 1856, in which he expressed his disenchantment with American political life. "I have passionately wished to see a free Europe," Tocqueville wrote, "and I realize that the cause of liberty is more compromised now than it was at the moment of my birth. I see around me nations whose souls seem to weaken as their prosperity and physical force grow, nations that remain, to borrow Hobbes's phrase, robust children who deserve only to be treated by means of the stick and the carrot. Your America itself, to which once turned the dream of all those who lacked the reality of liberty, has, in my view, given little satisfaction to the friends of liberty for some time."[151]

The implicit assumption was that America should remain exceptional and must continue to offer a hopeful example to all those who lacked liberty. Moreover, the reference to the cause of true liberty being discredited by political developments in Europe shows the magnitude of Tocqueville's disappointment and disillusionment in the last years of his life. It is well known that he wrote *Democracy in America* for French readers in the hope that they would profit from the lessons taught by American democracy. The unflattering remark in the passage above about America's alleged failure to fulfill the dream of the friends of liberty suggests the extent to which Tocqueville was still seeing in America more than America. What is so striking in the letters written in the decade following his retirement from political life is a growing and generalized pessimism which fed off his disenchantment with the Second Empire of Napoléon III.[152] Tocqueville commented: "All those who have received a liberal education and have been involved directly or indirectly in public affairs feel and see clearly that we have destroyed all the public liberties in the name of the sovereignty of the nation, and that we have employed the outward forms of popular election only to establish a more absolute despotism than any other that has ever appeared in France"[153] As he neared the end of his time, there appeared little reason to believe that the cause of liberty would triumph and now not even the inspiration derived from America remained.[154]

There are a few references to America in Volume One of *The Old Regime and the Revolution* (1856), the most significant intellectual undertaking of the last decade of Tocqueville's life. Most of these are passing remarks to New England townships, a comparison between the United States and Canada, the role of cities, religion, and the rule of law in America. The main point of comparison is England and where America appears it is, as Seymour Drescher pointed out, "as England's partner in a seamless Anglo-American heritage."[155] All things considered, America disappeared as a major reference in Tocqueville's last book and, in the incomplete Volume Two that Tocqueville began writing in 1857–1858, he went so far as to warn his readers that the most dangerous imitators of America were those who had not been there.[156] One might conclude, as Seymour Drescher has done, that this curious silence on Tocqueville's part was due to the fact that America was increasingly ill suited to be the success story of liberty.

The degree of Tocqueville's disenchantment can only be explained by the magnitude of his hopes. When writing Volume One of *Democracy in America*, he swam against the current of the French public opinion as America lost its previous Arcadian image and was regarded in France as a decaying society. Tocqueville revealed to his compatriots a different image, that of a healthy and prosperous society, which according to one of his critics, Victorien Sardou, was an idealized or "sweetened" version of America, *"l'Amérique en sucre."*[157] By drawing upon America, Tocqueville suggested that democracy should and could be moderated and channeled into regular institutions that promote the common good and successfully reconcile the demands for equality and liberty. The American model, he argued, showed that this aim could be achieved thorough a combination of healthy and stable mores, federalism, self-interest rightly understood (that softens the negative effects of extreme individualism), religion, and the art of association. Twenty years later, he feared, however, that he might have been mistaken and that his critics might have been right after all. In Tocqueville's opinion, American public and political life was dominated by individuals "who lacked moderation, sometimes probity, above all education"[158] and who resembled mere political adventurers, violent, gross, and devoid of principles. The institutions in place were able to do relatively little to stave off this growing corruption. As such, American politics appeared to Tocqueville more and more as an arena for brute instincts and appetites.

What a disappointment must have felt the man who once claimed to have perceived in America more than America and who, in the last years of his life, saw the cause of freedom compromised not only in Europe but also in the United States! We should be grateful then to the vagaries of French political life (which absorbed his energies and occupied his attention in the last two decades of his life) for the fact that Tocqueville never came to write what would have been "Volume Three" of *Democracy in America*. Reading the correspondence with his American friends after 1840 gives us a bitter taste of what the message of that hypothetical volume might have been, had it ever been written.

PART I

LETTERS

Introduction

Part I, sections A–D, contains Tocqueville's correspondence with his American friends after the publication of Volume Two of *Democracy in America*. Although some of the letters that Tocqueville wrote to and received from his American colleagues and friends during this period were either lost or destroyed, the letters that have been preserved offer a comprehensive view of Tocqueville's sustained intellectual dialogue with his American correspondents after 1840.

Most of Tocqueville's letters collected in this volume were originally published in French,[1] whereas several letters are new to our edition.[2] However, with one exception, none of Tocqueville's letters to his American friends after 1840 have previously been translated into English.[3] As for the letters that Tocqueville received from his American correspondents, they have not been published before in their entirety (either in France or elsewhere) and appear in print here for the first time. These letters have been collected from libraries in the United States (more information about the sources of the texts included here can be found in Appendix 3).[4]

The majority of the letters received by Tocqueville from America after 1840 were written in English; a small number of them were originally written in French and have been translated for this edition. Some letters are available only as copies, the originals having been lost, and are to be found at Yale University's Beinecke Rare Book and Manuscript Library. In the late 1920s, a local schoolteacher from Normandy by the name of Bonnel was asked by Yale University to transcribe documents from the archives preserved at the Tocqueville chateau. Bonnel dutifully completed this complex task, but his transcriptions occasionally contain obvious errors. We have pointed them out in footnotes and, where appropriate, have indicated possible corrections.

Tocqueville's American correspondents were distinguished "notables" – lawyers, professors, diplomats, historians belonging to the upper bourgeoisie. Most were from New England, many from the city of Boston, and nearly all, like Tocqueville himself, were born around the turn of the nineteenth century. Tocqueville had met some of them during his voyage in 1831–1832 and remained in close contact with them ever after. Others, such as Richard Rush, Robert Walsh, George Sumner, and George Bancroft, became acquaintances of Tocqueville in Paris in the 1840s and 1850s.[5]

Despite his perception that he was "the worst, the most irregular, and the most intermittent of correspondents,"[6] Tocqueville had a particular gift for letter writing. His letters were often beautifully written and were used both to explore ideas and to deepen friendships. They also provide an insight into his unique and passionate personality. As Hugh Brogan pointed out in his recent biography, Tocqueville "required the stimulus of other men's ideas, other men's criticism, to set his creative impulses free, and they had to be men whom he loved and trusted without reserve, men whose sympathy he could retain."[7] Not surprisingly, Tocqueville's correspondence with his French friends (Gustave de Beaumont, Jean-Jacques Ampère, and Louis de Kergorlay),[8] as well as with his American correspondents presented in this volume (such as Theodore Sedgwick, Edward Everett, N. W. Beckwith, and Edward Vernon Childe) is a rich source for any student of Tocqueville's political thought.

These letters (along with the other writings included in Part II) show that Tocqueville kept himself well informed about events in America until the very end of his life. The importance of the letters included in Part I, sections A–E, derives in part from the fact that they shed new light on the kind of information about America made available to Tocqueville after 1840. He exchanged letters with no fewer than twenty-six American correspondents. These documents touch on a wide variety of personal, professional, and political issues, ranging from the relations between France and America and American domestic policy to the topic of slavery and the despotic regime of Napoléon III.

These letters clearly show that Tocqueville continued to follow political and economic events in America with great interest after

1840. Although at times, as Tocqueville himself acknowledged in a letter to Nathaniel Niles from 1843, he had allowed his contacts with America to weaken a little, he never lost interest in American politics and society and always considered himself "a half American citizen." As Tocqueville wrote to Edward Vernon Childe in December 1856, "What happens now in America must be of interest to all civilized people and is of particular interest to me, who am half Yankee."[9] Another convincing testimony of Tocqueville's abiding interest in America can be found in a letter of Charles Sumner from 1858, in which the famous U. S. senator gratefully acknowledged that Tocqueville's interest in America did not abate after the publication of *Democracy in America* and thanked him for often having "a kind word" for the Americans.

As already mentioned in the general introduction to this volume, we have divided Tocqueville's correspondence into four major timeframes: 1840–1847, 1848–1852, 1853–1856, and 1857–1859. In general, the image that Tocqueville retained of American democracy during the period 1840–1847 was a positive and optimistic one. His American correspondents insisted on the vitality of American mores and institutions. America, they claimed, was blessed with many things, among them (as Lieber wrote on September 25, 1846) "cheap, fertile, undisputed and similar land, readiness and impulse to move on, . . . strongly social adhesion in political matters; consciousness of rights and authority to act, and instead of a feeling of debasement rather pride."[10]

U. S. foreign policy also occupied Tocqueville's attention during this period. "The beginning of the new administration," Tocqueville wrote to Lieber in 1844, "its domestic and foreign policy, the state of the country, its attitude toward England, its likely decisions on the great issues of Texas, Oregon, and the Tariff . . . they all greatly excite our curiosity."[11] He advised Americans to stay away from the political intrigues of the "old" Europe.

In particular, Tocqueville took a strong interest in the territorial issues of Texas and Oregon and, more generally, the expansion of the United States toward the Pacific Ocean. Given the intense diplomatic and political rivalry between France and England, he was concerned with finding a countervailing power to the maritime supremacy of England. The United States, Tocqueville hoped, could serve as such a power. Oregon had previously been under the joint occupation of England and the United States, but disagreements about the future of Oregon were quick to appear. Rejecting the official position of the Guizot-Soult government in Paris, Tocqueville believed that France could not remain neutral in this dispute and was entitled to side with the Americans in order to free the Pacific Ocean from English domination. On numerous occasions, Tocqueville reiterated his belief that the United States and France, although separated by the ocean, had a common interest, the liberty of the seas, a liberty threatened at that time by the British. Accordingly, in Tocqueville's opinion, the two great states had only to follow the natural tendency that encouraged them to form an intimate political union.[12]

As the letters from 1840 to 1847 also show, Tocqueville continued to invoke the American example in his reports and interventions on prison reform from the 1840s. His interest in this issue was far from being new, since both Tocqueville and Beaumont initially came to America to study its penitentiaries. The report they completed upon their return to France was published in 1833 as *On the Penitentiary System in America and Its Application to France* and received wide acclaim, being quickly translated into English, German, and Portuguese. Between 1833 and 1845, three editions of this work were published.[13] In the 1840s, Tocqueville remained involved in the debates on prison reform in France. He followed closely the discussions between the advocates of the Philadelphia system, based on solitary confinement, and those of the Auburn system, in which persons worked during the day and were kept in solitary confinement at night, with enforced silence at all times. It is telling that Tocqueville asked his correspondents, in particular Francis Lieber, to send him information about similar attempts at reform abroad.

The letters exchanged during 1848–1852 focused on a different set of issues and conveyed essential information about various aspects of political life and the political system in mid-nineteenth-century America. As a member of the parliamentary committee entrusted with the task of writing a new constitution for France, Tocqueville did not hesitate to draw again on the example of America. Correspondents, such as John C. Spencer (June 10, 1848) and Edward Everett (May 12, 1849), warned Tocqueville against the dangers of unicameralism and described bicameralism as one of the pillars of American liberty that successfully moderated the less desirable tendencies of popular sovereignty and political democracy. Referring to the division of the legislative branch into two chambers, Spencer wrote: "In fact, we believe it to be the great secret discovered by modern democracy and the ignorance of which was the ultimate cause of the downfall of ancient republics." He added a few words on the need to differentiate between the two chambers: "If one of the chambers is more permanent than the other," Spencer wrote, "it will afford the advantage of a matured public opinion, rather than of a hasty and evanescent outburst."[14] Everett's letters echoed these points. He remarked that it was the division of the legislative power in two houses that afforded the Americans the invaluable benefit of a "second thought" that had saved the country from many disasters. Furthermore, Everett remarked, the ability to make gradual changes in due course was essential to the establishment and consolidation of a free government. All these points were found in Tocqueville's interventions as a member of the committee for drafting and revising the French constitution in 1848 and 1851.

The tone and content of the letters written and received by Tocqueville from 1852 to the end of his life are strikingly *different* from those of his previous correspondence with the Americans. New themes appeared, such as immigration and economic crises, whereas older themes such as slavery gained new prominence during this period. Tocqueville was not only an avid reader of news about political events in America, but he followed with equal interest and anxiety the economic trends in the New World. In particular, Tocqueville was troubled about the fate of his financial investments in U. S. railroad companies. Some of Tocqueville's letters during this period bring to light his anxiety caused by the volatility of the U. S. stock market in which he had invested his money.

Predictably, the tone of these letters is far from uniform, and we see in particular that the letters received by Tocqueville provided him with two very different diagnoses of the state of the Union. On the one hand, the Frenchman continued to receive many testimonies brimming with optimism with regard to the unprecedented material prosperity of the United States. For example, in June 1853, Jared Sparks wrote: "The material prosperity of the country goes onward with an amazing acceleration. The rapid growth of cities, towns, and villages, the expansion of commerce, the increasing products of agriculture, the multiplication of railroads forming a network from the eastern extremity of Maine to the Mississippi, and steamboats floating on all navigable rivers and lakes, the vast increase of manufactures of every description – all these present a scene of rapid change, activity, enterprise, and progress, which certainly has no parallel in the history of civilization. Nor is mental culture neglected."[15] Similarly, in December 1853, Theodore Sedgwick informed Tocqueville that "the country has never been happier and has never enjoyed greater material progress than today... There is very little interest among us now in political questions with the exception of the distribution of positions. The entire country is busy doing business."[16] A few years later, the same optimistic tone could be detected in a letter of Charles Sumner, in which the U. S. senator, predicting a revival in trade, reiterated that the country had never before been as rich and as abundant in resources.

On the other hand, the information that Tocqueville received from his American correspondents after 1852 led him to nuance some of his previous views about the vitality of American democratic institutions and mores. During this period, his concerns about the effects of slavery and the degradation of democratic mores significantly increased and Tocqueville began to wonder about the future of American democracy as a valuable and enduring form of government. For example, the letter from Sparks cited earlier spoke not only of American prosperity but also, in the wake of the acquisition of Texas and California, of the clamor to acquire Cuba and to invade Mexico, and concluded that "Your apprehensions of the tendencies of the popular mind are not without foundation."[17] As Tocqueville's correspondence with Sedgwick, Everett, Lieber, Sumner, Childe, and Beckwith clearly shows, the Frenchman was careful to distinguish between fundamental symptoms of political and moral decline and accidental ones. And, as Benedict Songy pointed out, Tocqueville "did really understand the distinction that some anti-slavery men (like E. Everett, N. W. Beckwith, and even Abraham Lincoln) were making between the preservation of slavery and the extension of slavery."[18]

At times, Tocqueville came to express serious doubts about the long-term effects of the westward territorial expansion on the stability of American democracy. He was also concerned about the massive influx of new immigrants (mostly of German extraction) and the unorthodox traditions of the Mormons in the West. Many letters during this period demonstrate that Tocqueville was preoccupied by the extreme forms of the spirit of adventure, risk, and enterprise that, he felt, were coming increasingly to characterize American individualism. In his letters to Sedgwick from 1856, Tocqueville referred to the violent and intolerant spirit that was spreading quickly throughout a good part of the Union and voiced his concern about the excessive forms of individualism that coexisted with the unprecedented prosperity in the country. It was this unusual combination of extreme forms of civilization, prosperity, and primitivism characteristic of the New World that explains why, in spite of his sincere admiration for its institutions, Tocqueville displayed a certain ambivalence toward American mores.

Many letters from 1853 onward also show that Tocqueville followed with greatest interest the issue of slavery as the country expanded west of the Mississippi and south into Texas. The short piece that Tocqueville wrote for *Liberty Bell* at the invitation of Maria W. Chapman in 1855 was an unambiguous testimony of his antislavery views. As Seymour Drescher pointed out four decades ago, "Tocqueville's slavery articles strike one as the most assured of his reformist work.... They were less indecisive than his works on poverty and less defensive than those on prison reform."[19] In a letter to Edward Vernon Childe from April 2, 1857, after denouncing the folly of those who sought to expand slavery in the Western territories following the Kansas–Nebraska Act, Tocqueville warned that "spreading that horrible plague onto a large portion of the earth which had been free from it until now, imposing all the crimes and miseries accompanying slavery on millions of future people (masters or slaves) who could otherwise be spared it, all this is an unpardonable crime against mankind."[20] Other letters reflect on the expansionist policies of the United States in the West and comment on the formidable challenges posed by slavery to the future of the Union.

The letters received by Tocqueville during the last four years of his life gave him a pessimistic assessment of the future of the Union and led him to wonder, to quote Songy again, "whether democracy were not its own worst enemy."[21] On September 19, 1856, Sedgwick confessed to Tocqueville: "We have lost our simplicity and modesty, not to mention our virtue. I believe that we shall be punished by this great hand which holds the reigns of the universe. And in fact we have already been punished. The administration of the current president has only been a repetition of the most disgusting errors and we shall not be spared very serious blows in the future."[22] Worried by the prospect of slavery spreading into the territories west of Mississippi, Edward Vernon Childe denounced the increasing disregard for law and the stronger disposition to substitute might for right that manifested itself in many portions of the land. In turn, Edward Everett had this to say about the excesses of democracy in America: "How unfortunate that everywhere people abuse so much their privileges! In our country, where people fully enjoy freedoms so dearly obtained, so painfully acquired elsewhere, they push them so far beyond their legitimate exercise that the abuse threatens to become a more unbearable evil than their total absence."[23]

A more sober note can be found in the letters of Sparks in which he acknowledged that there was an intense conflict between parties, but, he added, this was a constant feature of all free governments. And, in a letter of December 1857, without minimizing the corrupting effects of slavery, Sedgwick ascribed the domestic turmoil of the Americans to their lack of discipline and mania for decentralization, their recklessness in speculation, and unbridled love of gain and money. All this, he concluded, threatened America much more than slavery. This account was challenged by Charles Sumner who, in his letter of May 5, 1858, acknowledged that "Many of those things by which we are degraded are caused by slavery, even in States where slavery does not exist. This has demoralized our government, and introduced everywhere the vulgar principles of force, which, as you know, underlies slavery."[24]

Therefore, it is not a mere coincidence that Tocqueville's correspondence with his American friends and acquaintances reached a peak during 1857 and again shifted in tone. In 1857 America arrived at a dangerous point in its political development with the unfolding of the Kansas crisis that came to monopolize the business of the U. S. Congress. The vigorous controversy triggered by the Lecompton pro-slavery constitution[25] in Kansas marked, as Kenneth M. Stampp wrote, "the point where discussion and negotiation gave way to accusations and inflexible demands, and where concession was equated with humiliating defeat."[26] The year 1857 also witnessed the Supreme Court's famous Dred Scott decision, endorsing the right of slaveholders to carry their slaves into all the states of the country. Several letters received by Tocqueville during this period stand out and shed fresh light on what Tocqueville knew of the intense political atmosphere at that time. Four of these letters came from the pen of N. W. Beckwith and offered Tocqueville invaluable information about the debates on slavery in America prior to the Civil War. Beckwith was an implacable opponent of slavery, regarding it as the main cause of the deterioration of the political and moral climate in the United States in the 1850s. A democrat at heart, Beckwith was persuaded that "the people is really and truly pretty well behaved, and though you may meet with croakers who, seeing these evils and not perceiving the cause of them, ascribe them to universal suffrage, elective judges and the influence of the people, be assured, my friend, they are totally mistaken. It is not the people who are corrupting the manners and morals, it [is] the leaders who corrupt the people."[27]

In particular, Beckwith's long letter of February 20, 1857 (written from Geneva, Switzerland), is full of interesting concrete details meant to demonstrate the irrationality of slavery. As Benedict Songy commented, Beckwith's surprisingly long letter was a remarkable "descriptive and analytic essay" and it is a pity that Tocqueville's answer has been lost. Beckwith gave not only an exhaustive account of happenings up to that time but also a fairly comprehensive commentary on the American political scene as it appeared in early 1857. Beckwith's account only confirmed Tocqueville's premonition about the approaching crisis that would ultimately lead to the Civil War a few years later. Moreover, Beckwith's letter ended with an unambiguous profession of faith in the supremacy of freedom that must have appealed to Tocqueville: "Nothing but freedom, absolute freedom and equal justice for all can give that scope for individual volition and action which are the essential conditions. It is, I trust, the 'mission' of America, not from foresight and design, but from necessity, driven along by higher laws, to work out some problems, social problems, which have never yet received the development they are capable of – and that thus driven to right principles, driven to be just, we may have reason to unite with the blacks in recognition of the good fortune which brought us together for mutual benefit, instead of regarding it as a mutual calamity."[28]

Beckwith also shared with Tocqueville his belief that the evils that he lamented sprang neither from democratic elective institutions and universal suffrage nor from the exercise of civil and political liberties, but were to be ascribed mostly to the corrupting and nefarious effects of the presence of slavery on U. S. soil. He also pointed out that the crisis was not to be reduced to a mere struggle between slavery and freedom but was, in its essence, a struggle for political power. This, Beckwith insisted, was not primarily democracy's fault. Attempting to calm Tocqueville's fears about the results of a rapid emancipation, he concluded on a confident note: "I rely on 'the people' to do, what nothing else could do, which is to exterminate slavery."[29]

Yet, in spite of all these troubling signs, Tocqueville continued to believe that the Americans had a core of good practical wisdom, which would prevent the country from rushing into a thoughtless and damaging adventure. Ultimately, perhaps under the influence of Sedgwick's opinion, Tocqueville came to believe that the greatest domestic danger threatening the northern states was less slavery than the corruption of democratic institutions. He attributed this phenomenon to the movement of an unlimited democracy that had failed to elevate the best individuals to the government of society.

A few words about Tocqueville's qualified ambivalence concerning the stability of American democracy in the late 1850s are in order here. The evolution of Tocqueville's views must be interpreted in light of his belief that America was destined to be a beacon of hope for all friends of freedom struggling for survival across the world. Consequently, he was extremely sensitive to any signs suggesting a possible deterioration of democratic mores in the New World. As Tocqueville told Sedgwick as early as December 1852, the Europeans had begun looking unfavorably at America. "They view the United States," Tocqueville warned, "as the pit of the abyss from where nothing but a putrid stench comes out; and people reproach you for having made them believe in the Democratic Republic."[30] After describing America as a robust child in another letter to Sedgwick from August 14, 1854, Tocqueville voiced his fear that the country was growing too quickly and predicted that it was "carried away by an inevitable destiny toward greatness and dangers."[31] The stakes, Tocqueville pointed out to Lieber on September 1, 1856, could not be any higher: "Your America itself, to which once turned the dream of all who lacked the reality of liberty, has, in my view, given little satisfaction to the friends of liberty for some time. One would say that the despots of the old world have entrusted you with performing the same role that the Spartans bid the helots play in front of their children, and that through the follies and vulgarities that liberty gives rise to, they want to cure them of the desire ever to be free."[32] Tocqueville made a similar point in a letter to Sparks in July 1857: "Everything that you might tell me about your country will also be of great interest to me. The crisis into which it is thrown by the issue of slavery is the subject of my worries and I would very much wish that you could reassure me about the future of the Union, to which that of liberty in the world perhaps is attached."[33]

Finally, some of the letters included here allow us to understand better Tocqueville the man. We see him trying to arrange for the visits of his American friends in France or recommending to his American correspondents some of his French acquaintances traveling across the Ocean. We can also trace Tocqueville's ultimately unsuccessful attempts to edit the newspaper *Le Commerce* and, in Francis Lieber, to find an American correspondent. The correspondence with Edward Lee Childe is particularly illuminating, as it shows the lesser-known paternal side of Tocqueville's character. He did not shy away from giving intimate advice to his younger friend whose mother, Mildred Childe, had been close to Tocqueville's heart.

Moreover, by reading Tocqueville's correspondence during the last four years of his life, we see the famous writer seeking and cherishing the close friendship of Beaumont, Ampère, and Sedgwick at a critical stage in his life, when he was fighting the illness that ultimately claimed his life at the age of fifty-four. We also feel in these pages the restless mind of a man who described himself, in a melancholic voice, as being "over the top of the mountain" and who confessed to being ready to descend toward his inevitable demise.

Letters: 1840–1847

1. Jared Sparks to Alexis de Tocqueville

London, September 5, 1840

Dear Sir,

Some months ago, I received a copy of your able and excellent *Report on the Emancipation of the Slaves in the French Colonies.*[34] It seemed to me to contain many things highly interesting and important to the American public. I procured a translation to be made by a lady who was much pleased with the task and executed it well. When I left the United States on the 1st of July it was in the press and I presume that it is published before this time.

I am busily engaged here examining the papers in the public offices relating to the American Revolution. I find the material abundant and valuable. In November I expect to go to Paris, for the purpose of making similar researches in the French offices.

I have not had the opportunity to read the second part of your great work; but I hear it spoken of by good judges in terms of high approbation & praise.

> With great regard, I am, dear Sir,
> Most truly yours,
> Jared Sparks

Houghton Library, Harvard University, Ms Sparks, 132, Vol. IX (G. 29).

2. Alexis de Tocqueville to Jared Sparks

Chateau de Tocqueville, October 13, 1840

My dear Mr. Sparks,

I apologize for not having replied sooner to the letter that you sent me at the beginning of last month. That letter was first mailed to Paris where I was no longer residing. It was forwarded here, from where I was also temporarily away. It is only now that I am able to answer you.

I am very happy that you approve of my report on the abolition of slavery and that the latter has been translated in the United States.[35] However, I have little hope that it will make a useful impression in that country (I am speaking of the South). Slavery has deeper and stronger roots on your soil than anywhere else. Neither you nor I will see its end. It is sad for me to realize that, as your nation grows, slavery expands with it to such an extent that it makes humanity wail, even though you are making progress is which all civilized peoples should rejoice. There is almost no example in which servitude has ever been abolished at the initiative of the master. It has always been abolished only by the endeavor of a power that had control at one and the same time over the master and the slave. Because you are entirely independent, slavery will last longer among you than anywhere else.

You give me good news by announcing that you intend to come to Paris in November. I shall be there at that time in order to attend the debates in the Chamber of Deputies of which I am a member. I hope, my dear Mr. Sparks, that you will come to see me. My wife will be pleased to make your acquaintance. I live at 11 rue Castellane. You can be reassured that I shall do my best to assist you in your historical research[36] whose worth I know so well.

Please believe in my esteem and my sincere affection.

Alexis de Tocqueville

3. John C. Spencer to Alexis de Tocqueville

Albany, November 21, 1840

My dear Sir,

I avail myself of the opportunity afforded by my friend Mr. I. Townsend going to Europe, to send you a copy of the American edition of the second part of your work on *Democracy in America*. It has been well received in this country, and has added to the fame you had so justly acquired.[37]

I regretted that my public duties did not allow me time to have written a more extended notice of the work, by way of Preface. But in truth there was little occasion for any.

I informed you in a former letter that the bookseller, with whom I was negotiating on your behalf, Mr. Adlard, had become bankrupt and was unable to complete the arrangement. And before an opportunity occurred to open a new negotiation with another, the English copy of Mr. Reeve's translation arrived in this country, and of course prevented my offering any inducement to an American publisher.

We take great interest here in the question of War or Peace between your country and the four Powers.[38] To us it appears very mysterious how any cause of hostility can be found in the event and circumstances connected with the Eastern question, and we cannot believe that such nations as France and England would plunge all Christendom in war, without the direst necessity. As neutrals we should profit by your conflicts, but as men and Christians, we deplore a return to the barbarism of brute force. There is something so *animal* in War, that refinement condemns it as much as it would any other grossness.

I am obliged to you for the report and speech you sent me, and if I was aware of any thing that would be acceptable to you on this side of the Atlantic, it should be forwarded.

> Believe me,
> My dear Sir,
> Truly and sincerely your friend,
> John C. Spencer

Beinecke Rare Book and Manuscript Library, Yale University, Uncat MSS 324; also available as Bonnel copy, MS Vault Tocqueville, D II a, Paquet 12, pp. 56–58.

4. Alexis de Tocqueville to Jared Sparks

Paris, December 9 (or 16), 1840

My dear Mr. Sparks,

It has been several days since I came to look for you at your hotel without being able to find you. I hope that they have not forgotten to give you my card. My intention was – and still is – to return there tomorrow between 1 and 2 p.m. I hope to have the opportunity to meet you. I wanted to have the pleasure of seeing you and to tell you that we spend every *Wednesday* evening with friends at our home and that we would be extremely delighted if you were to come here on one of these occasions. This evening, for example, Madame de Tocqueville and I would be happy to receive you.

Please accept the expression of my consideration and my affection.

Alexis de Tocqueville

5. Samuel Griswold Goodrich to Alexis de Tocqueville

Paris (27 Boulevard des Italiens)
June 16, 1841

Sir,

The homage from every American to the author of *Democracy in America*, induces me to send you the accompanying book.[39] It will, I trust, be an excuse for presenting you with so very humble a performance.

I have the honor to be, Sir, with great respect, your respectful,

S. G. Goodrich

Beinecke Rare Book and Manuscript Library, Yale University, Uncat MSS 324; also available as Bonnel copy, MS Vault Tocqueville, D II a, Paquet 12, p. 69.

6. A. W. Paull to Alexis de Tocqueville[40]

Princeton, State of New Jersey, U.S.A.,
September 30, 1841

M. de Tocqueville,

Sir, I have the honor of addressing you at this time to inform you of your election as an honorary member of the American Whig Society of the College of New Jersey.[41] In so doing we feel conscious that we are honoring ourselves rather than you: yet acknowledging as we do the debt of admiration and gratitude which our country owes you, we will willingly throw in our mite to conceal that debt. To you, Sir, is awarded the high honor of being the first of foreigners who had the genius to comprehend and the candor to commend the true principles of our government. And while we trust that by the publication of your volumes on the United States of America, Europe, enthralled and oppressed, may be regenerated and exalted to the true standards of equality and independence, we are free to confess that from them we have learned more of ourselves and do, if possible, more dearly prize our own excellent institutions. We are proud therefore to insert your name among the honored ones who dignify and adorn our association.

The American Whig Society was formed previous to the Revolution of '76. The country was then divided into two great political parties, the Whigs and the Tories: the latter advocating the high classes of England and anxious to keep us under her tyranny and misrule, the former maintaining those glorious principles of liberty which we owe to revolution and the establishment of our freedom and independence. These latter principles our Society was established to support, but when they were obtained and hence dispensed [its][42] blessings over the land, the society was ranged into one lively literary[43] and has ever retained this distinctive character. It has not now, nor since 1782 has had any thing to do with politics. James Madison, late President of the United States, was one of our earliest members. Since that time, we had had in our roll of members Attorney General Bradford,[44] Gov. Lee of Virginia,[45] Brockholst and Edward Livingston,[46] James A. Bayard,[47] Rob[ert] Goodloc Harper,[48] Dr. David Hosack[49] of New York, Judge Johnson of the Supreme Court of the U. S.,[50] John Sergeant,[51] John Forsyth,[52] Richard Rush,[53] Hugh L. White,[54] John C. Calhoun,[55] Lewis Cass,[56] President Tyler,[57] Daniel Webster,[58] and very many more living and dead who held high places in the government. Should you dignify us [with] your acceptance of a membership, we would be happy to enroll you among the illustrious men who have been of our members. Be pleased to accept, Sir, the assurance of my highest admiration.

By the order of my society,
A.W. Paull, Secretary, etc.

Beinecke Rare Book and Manuscript Library, Yale University, Bonnel copy, MS Vault Tocqueville, D II a, Paquet 10, pp. 63–64.

7. Isaiah Townsend[59] to Alexis de Tocqueville

Paris, Nov[ember] 2, 1841,
Hotel Maurice

Dear Sir,

On applying at your lodgings, I find you are in the country and likely to remain beyond the period I have fixed for my stay in Paris. Last winter my passage through this capital was so hurried as not to allow me an opportunity of testing whether I might not be in a second call more fortunate than in my first when you were not at home. Being thus neither then nor now so happy as to see you, I cannot think of being again so near you without informing you of my presence and at the same time of the pleasure it will give me to take charge of any commissions you may wish executed in the United States whither I purpose returning after perhaps a month's sojourn in Paris and a like period in England.

You will have been gratified to hear of the closing at least for a season of the wound which had been opened anew by the arrest of MacLeod[60] and had been since festering more and more between England and my country. I think I may say that with the exception of certain persons on the Atlantic coast whose fortunes are embarked in our trade with Great Britain, of certain politicians raised by accident or of placemen whose merits and salaries might be much reduced by a right-earnest ordeal – and of certain old women of both sexes – the people of the U. States without courting the battle would have cheerfully accepted it. Yet they are not the less disposed to think that war ought to be the *ultima ratio* of Republics as well as of Kings, and they will hail the prospect of peace with a pleasure nearly universal. For my own part, I trust I would not have been among the last to uphold the honor – the rights of our noble commonwealth, as far as we may, nor will I be among the last to rise superior to an excitement that has not been without motive and to check peradventure a selfish inkling for military fame, and frankly confess that I am glad for the sake of all of the decision of the Utica Jury.[61] So you who of all strangers – whether English, French or German – know best my country, who know that newspaper rumours and political declamations as little indicate general confusion and uproar as the sullen and constant break of the daily surge on your Breton or Normand coast does the casual tempests of the ocean. I need not say that no American apprehends – now that the law has spoken – a rupture of the present quasi-harmony by extra-legal violence. We may have trouble on our frontiers because they teem with refugees and the refuse of ourselves at certain points – but nothing more than whatever the state government may easily quell.

You will be glad to hear that your friend and my relative, Mr. John C. Spencer from the secretaryship of state of New York, has been promoted to the head of the War Department at Washington. No step more conclusively showed the disposition of the Government to be prepared against the emergency half-expected – for they could scarcely have found among our public men one who to keen and comprehensive intelligence, unites such untiring activity, such a spirit of order, such promptness of decision, and such inflexibility of purpose – all these qualities which constitute talents for administration – as Mr. Spencer. I differ with him too widely in many of his views to be his political friend – yet am I persuaded much benefit will accrue to the country from the appointment though peace should continue undisturbed.

I believe this is the first occasion I have had to offer you my felicitations on your marriage.[62] Believe me they are not the less sincere for coming late. If my memory be not treacherous, you almost promised us something on England which, but for being a sister, should make us jealous for our "Democracie" [sic]. And yet more lately, I have seen your visit to Africa and Algeria chronicled.[63] But here, I presume, you intend your first public to be that of the Chamber. Do what you will, the public of America will be long in forgetting, how most nobly you have achieved the right of citizenship.

Permit me in conclusion to repeat the unreserved offer of my services, and to assure you of the continuous esteem with which I remain,

Very sincerely yours,
Isaiah Townsend

Beinecke Rare Book and Manuscript Library, Yale University, Uncat MSS 324; also available as Bonnel copy, MS Vault Tocqueville, D II a, Paquet 12, pp. 61–64.

8. Alexis de Tocqueville to John C. Spencer[64]

Tocqueville, November 10, 1841

Sir,

I have been waiting a long time for an appropriate opportunity to recall myself to you. It has presented itself today. I have received a letter from our common friend, Mr. Townsend,[65] who wrote to me to let me know that he had just arrived in Paris and will leave soon to return to America. He asked me if I have any commissions for you. I cannot let him leave without entrusting him with a few friendly words for you. Moreover, I deeply regret not being able to place my letter directly into Mr. Townsend's hands. Unfortunately, my obligations keep me in the country. I shall return to Paris only for the reopening of the Chambers, that is, towards the end of this year.

I have learned with great satisfaction of your entry into the government.[66] I am happy not for you – I follow public affairs closely enough to know that one can derive little happiness from them – but for your country and even for the general affairs of the world; because the United States already enjoy a sufficiently large role among nations for everyone to be interested in the choice of those who will govern them. This interest is especially strong in France among all those who are educated and thoughtful. Everyone justifiably considers the Union as our natural and necessary ally. Although separated by the ocean, we have in fact an identical interest, which is the liberty of the seas. We all suffer and are destined to suffer even more from England's maritime superiority if we do not know how to act in concert. For all the peoples who have not abandoned the sea, Great Britain is today what Louis XIV was for Europe in the 17th century. It has destroyed the majority of these peoples and threatens all others more or less with the same fate. I foresee that sooner or later this state of affairs will become so intolerable that it will bring into existence a new League of Augsburg[67] and that, in the end, all the navies will unite to combat such a dangerous and distressing dominance.[68] This would have already occurred in Europe if the French Revolution had not turned the attention of princes and peoples elsewhere, and if it had not divided, through questions of government and domestic policy, nations whose interests would otherwise have made them act in concert. Fortunately, no such issue could appear between the American Union and France. The two great states are therefore free to follow their natural tendency and this tendency encourages them to form an intimate union. Accidental circumstances and the whims of the people will try to separate them in vain, because a permanent and irresistible force will always bring them closer together.

Among the accidents capable of separating for a time the two nations which have such a great need to support each other, I shall cite with profound regret the last bill which takes away from French commerce the advantages that it has enjoyed until now.[69] I dare to say that, regardless of how strong the reasons were which prompted American statesmen to take these measures, in so doing they moved away from a fundamental law of politics of their country as well as ours, and that experience will demonstrate this to them one day. And I doubly congratulate myself when I see a man like you, who is such a friend of his country and at the same time such an enlightened person, entering the world of political affairs at such an important moment.

Farewell, dear Mr. Spencer. Please believe in all the sentiments of esteem and affection that I have toward you.

Alexis de Tocqueville

9. Francis Lieber to Alexis de Tocqueville

Columbia, S.C., June 30, 1842

My dear de Tocqueville,

Will you pardon me if I take the liberty of troubling you? The Committee of the Library of South Carolina College is desirous of subscribing for a *weekly* Paris paper, which contains the most important news, political, social etc., reports of interesting debates, similar to the London Spectator. Or have you no such papers? If there is one and you think it worthy of being subscribed for, would you have the kindness to hand this letter to the manager of the paper? I shall beg Messrs. Wiley & Putnam, one of our first publishing houses in New York, to inform you at the end of this letter how the payment for that paper may best be effected. The paper ought to be sent by Havre packets via New York to:

Francis Lieber
Columbia, S.C.
United States

The S. C. after Columbia must not be forgotten; there are several Columbias in the U. S. as you may remember.

If there is a semi-weekly paper which you think much better than any weekly, you might take that. But in the latter case I would beg you to subscribe for half a year only; in the first for a whole year.

Have you received my *Essays on Property and Labour*?[70] I sent you two copies long ago.

You have seen that they are in good earnest in Prussia about reforming prisons. Dr. Julius wrote me that he is building a model prison in Berlin. He praises the London model prison as far the most superior in existence in any country. I see from the papers that you too have decided to adopt the principle of perpetual seclusion in the new Paris prison. Did the late N. York act relating to prison labour ever reach you? It is the most retrograde step that has been made for many years in any branch.[71]

Why are you so silent like a grave? To be sure, a man may hear of you frequently without hearing from you – I mean through reviews and reports of debates, still I should be very glad to have once more a few lines from you. Excuse the liberty I have taken. Remember me kindly to de Beaumont.

Ever yours most faithfully,
Francis Lieber

[Note written by Wiley & Putnam] Mon[sieur] Hector Bossange will please pay the amount of subscription for such paper as may be selected by Mon[sieur] A. de Tocqueville for South Carolina College and change the same to the account of

Very truly yours,
Wiley & Putnam,
New York, July 9, 1842.

The University of South Carolina Library, Columbia, S.C.

10. Alexis de Tocqueville to Francis Lieber[72]

Paris, August 14, 1842

My dear Lieber,

Please forgive me for not having written sooner. Legislative activities, public affairs, the academies, and finally the numerous concerns that occupy the life of a man who has both a political and a literary career, all these have prevented me from writing to you until now. Nonetheless, I am full of remorse and beg you to believe me that forgetfulness and indifference are not to be found among the reasons that I had for not writing to you.

In response to your letter of June 30, I answer that I do not know any French weekly newspaper which has the least value and hence which would be worth crossing the Atlantic. We have papers that appear every two weeks and give a summary of the events or the publications of that fortnight. Would a paper of this kind be of interest to you? If so, please write to me. As far as the choice is concerned, I would recommend to you, all things considered, the *Revue des Deux Mondes*.[73] It is our best publication, without being an excellent one. Contrary to the English custom, all the articles are signed and, as a consequence, those who write them are always concerned more with themselves than with the author whose work they pretend to analyze. Most often, even this paper contains many articles whose sole aim is to make known the ideas of those who write them. But most of these people are well-known individuals and several of them enjoy considerable fame. I will take out for you a subscription to this journal as soon as I know that this is what you want.

In spite of our sincere desire to secure your election as a foreign correspondent of our Academy, it was impossible for Beaumont and me to do so on the occasion of the last election. At that moment, Mr. Wheaton was in Paris and had just published a remarkable work on the right of visitation.[74] This work brought him to the attention of the public and highlighted his credentials for being elected. But I am very hopeful that the next time the opportunity arises to select a new correspondent from America, which might happen soon, you will be the choice of the Academy.[75] The members of this learned body are familiar with your name and we shall not let them forget you. I have passed on the books that you sent me.

I am writing to you from Paris where I am attending a short session of the Chambers. We have just had, as you know, a general election in which I have been reelected with a large majority. I do not know if you have learned that I was elected a member of the French Academy a year ago.[76] If this might be of interest to you, I shall send you the speech that I gave on that occasion as well as the speech given in response by Count Molé.[77] This oratorical contest of a more political nature than an academic one might perhaps excite your curiosity. If you wish, I shall also send you the report that I gave in the Chamber of Deputies on the penitentiary system.[78] I am not familiar with the Statutes of New York to which you refer, and if you can send them to me, I would be obliged to you.

Farewell, my dear Lieber. Please think of me sometimes and believe in all my sentiments of esteem and affection.

Alexis de Tocqueville

11. Alexis de Tocqueville to N. Niles[79]

June 15, 1843

My dear Mr. Niles,

Thank you very much for the document that you have sent me[80] and which I regard as important. I thank you even more for your kind offer concerning the period when you will be in the United States. As you know, nothing interests me more than whatever concerns this great and strong nation. Documents which could shed light on its internal condition and which, above all, might inform me about its relations with England and ourselves would be extremely valuable in my eyes and I would be especially obliged to you for bringing them to my attention.

I would also have a more special request to address to you. As you know, I am responsible for writing a report on prison law, a very important law for the drafting of which we draw constant inspiration from the knowledge and experience of America. The discussion of this law will not take place this year but it will most likely open the next session.[81] You can understand how important it would be for me to obtain between now and then all the American documents capable of shedding light on this important question. In particular I do not have the last two *reports of the state prison of Philadelphia* (Cherry Hill prison). Neither do I have the two last *reports of the Prison Discipline Society of Boston*. These documents are essential and I would be extremely obliged to you if you could obtain them for me. *Any other* important document on this issue would be of great interest to me.

I have lately broken somewhat the chain of my relations with the United States. I regret this and would like to renew them. I take a particular interest in this issue both from my heart and my patriotism, since one of the guiding principles of my politics is that in spite of the preconceptions and disagreements on small details, France and the United States are allies so natural and necessary to each other that they should never lose sight of each other for a single moment.

If, in turn, I could be of use to you in France in order to obtain any documents that you want, I am entirely at your disposal.

Please present my respectful compliments to Mrs. Niles and believe in all my sentiments of esteem and affection.

Alexis de Tocqueville

12. Robert Walsh to Alexis de Tocqueville

Paris, Dec[embe]r 9, 1843

Dear Sir,

I have just rec[eive]d your note of the 7[th].[82] You know how M. Léon Faucher[83] generally writes – with great confidence in himself, but very little accurate knowledge of his subject. I would place no reliance on his statistics. He is now writing, in *La Revue des Deux Mondes*, crude notions and unilateral statements of British affairs. I will address myself at once to proper sources of information in Rhode Island and New Jersey. But, unluckily, no steamer will go from England to the United States before the 4th of next month. There will be a packet from Havre on the 16th; the passages are long at this season of the year. Some time must, therefore, elapse before an answer can be received. I shall endeavor, meanwhile, to find here what may refute M. Faucher. Two recent and important publications in my hands (American) contain materials concerning the mortality in the Eastern Penitentiary of Pennsylvania, and in regard to the question of Slavery in the United States, which will deserve your attention on your return to Paris. My letter to the Mayor of Philadelphia was duly transmitted by our Chargé d'affaires. I have removed to my apartment n° 2, rue Neuve des Mathurins.

Be pleased to accept, dear Sir, the high respect of your faithful serv[an]t.
Robert Walsh

Beinecke Rare Book and Manuscript Library, Yale University, Uncat MSS 324, Folder "Robert Walsh, Four letters, 1843–59"; also available as Bonnel copy, MS Vault Tocqueville, D II a, folder "Bonnel's copies of letters from Americans to Tocqueville."

13. Robert Walsh to Alexis de Tocqueville

Paris, Dec[embe]r 13, 1843

Dear Sir,

The enclosed article is from a Philadelphia paper of the 10[th], inst. I send it to you at once in order that you may see how much M. Faucher has erred. If I can find a series of a Rhode Island journal, I shall probably succeed in getting similar testimony concerning the penitentiary of that State. I have written to Mr. Charles King, of New-York, for the entire official documents.

There is conclusive testimony that the mentality of the *whites* in the two Penitentiaries of Pennsylvania is less, on the average, than that of the people of Philadelphia and Pittsburg [sic], out of the prisons. The negroes do not bear confinement as well. The same ratios are noted in regard to insanity and idiocy.

I have the honor to be,
very respectfully,
your ob[edien]t serv[an]t,
Robert Walsh

n° 2
Rue Neuve des Mathurins

Beinecke Rare Book and Manuscript Library, Yale University, Uncat MSS 324, Folder "Robert Walsh, Four letters, 1843–59"; also available as Bonnel copy, MS Vault Tocqueville, DII a, "Bonnel's copies of letters from Americans to Tocqueville."

14. Alexis de Tocqueville to Francis Lieber

Paris, April 22, 1844

My dear Lieber,

I only have time to send you a few words, being overwhelmed by various things at the present time; but I do not need long sentences to express how delighted Beaumont and I will be to see you again. You do not imagine, I hope, that the thirteen years which have elapsed since we said farewell to you have in any way diminished the sentiments of esteem and friendship that we then professed for you.

I answer your questions without delay:

The exhibition[84] will begin next May 1 and will last, I believe, for six weeks or two months.

Regarding the Chamber of Deputies, I think that it will be in session, as usual, until the end of June.

My address in Paris is 11 rue Castellane. I shall remain here until the end of the session. After that, I shall go home to the country. My address is *Tocqueville par St. Pierre Église* (Manche).

Since I expect to see you soon, I shall not tell you more today. Please be assured of my sentiments of true friendship.

Alexis de Tocqueville

15. Alexis de Tocqueville to Robert Walsh[85]

Versailles, July 27, 1844

Sir,

I ask you to forgive me for not having responded earlier to the letter with which you have honored me and for not having thanked you for the documents that it contained.

The chief reason for my silence was that I had great difficulty in obtaining the legislative documents that you wanted. I have finally received them and shall send them to the address that you indicated to me. They consist of the Report of the Budgetary Committee[86] and that of M. Thiers.[87] If other documents should be useful to you, please let me know; I shall do my best to send them to you.

The newspaper *Le Commerce*[88] has lately partly come under the political influence of some of my friends and under my own influence. Hence we would very much like the newspaper to have a distinguished editorial team. A reliable contribution from America would be useful to us. But it should come from a distinguished person who would be able to explain well to a French audience the events that are taking place in your country and the ethos that prevails there. I thought that you could perhaps suggest such a correspondent and tell me what terms it would be appropriate to offer to him. You would afford me great pleasure and would render me a great service if you could shed light for me on this issue.

Please accept the expression of my most distinguished consideration.

Alexis de Tocqueville

16. Alexis de Tocqueville to Henry Wheaton

Tuesday evening (1844–45)

Sir,

Thank you very much for having sent me your work on the history of the peoples of the North. I had already heard a lot about it but have never read it. I shall remedy this omission.

I would like to be able to write a review of the book for *Le Commerce*. But apart from the fact that I rarely happen to write for newspapers, I fear that I do not have the time to write the article that your book deserves. I therefore might perhaps be obliged not to fulfil my wish in this regard. If so, at all events I will ask one of the principal editors of the newspaper to take this matter in hand.

Please accept, Sir, with my thanks, the expression of my most distinguished consideration.

Alexis de Tocqueville

17. Alexis de Tocqueville to Francis Lieber

Tocqueville, par St. Pierre Église (Manche)
September 18, 1844

My dear Lieber,

A few days ago, I received the letter that you had sent me from Paris.[89] I would have preferred to meet you in person and to be able to greet you before your return to America. But your affairs and mine have not allowed that to happen. At all events, please receive the expression of the most sincere wishes on the part of Madame de Tocqueville and myself, for your happiness and for your pending and appointed return. You are not made to live in America. Europe is the true homeland of your spirit and you should come and live on this continent even if you were not born here. From what I know of you, you will breathe with difficulty in the midst of the atmosphere of American society. As you say, a free country in Europe is your stage. I would very much wish that that country were our own. Politically speaking, this nation may not be the freest in the world, but it is certainly the one in which the individual is least hindered by the obligations imposed by society on daily actions. I shall insist, I promise you, that in the near future the Institute establishes a new link between you and France. Beaumont is full of zeal for the same project and I think Mignet[90] is also well disposed toward it.

I have a proposal to make to you and I would be happy if you accepted it. I exercise considerable influence over an important Parisian newspaper called *Le Commerce*, and I am extremely interested that this newspaper, which is the principal political organ of my friends and myself, should acquire real worth in the eyes of serious people. The best means of achieving this goal is to obtain for the paper that which gives English newspapers their greatest value and which is completely missing from ours, namely interesting contributions from abroad. I have already managed to obtain for the next issue a contribution of this kind from England, from where a distinguished member of the House of Commons is willing to write for us twice a month.[91] You understand how much I would like to obtain something similar from the United States. You would be in a better position than anyone else to render this service to us, if that were to your liking. You would have to write a letter once a month or more often, if you think fit, amounting to two or three columns of a French newspaper, and whose aim would be to inform us about what is going on in the Union, whether in politics, commerce, industry, or the arts. Several people have already offered to render this service to us.[92] But in order to write such contributions well one would need sufficient tact and knowledge of Europe to grasp not only what is interesting in itself, but also what could be of interest to us, the Europeans and the French. You alone would be capable of doing this very well. Would you like to do it? If you want to do it anonymously, you can be reassured that your confidentiality will be fully preserved. I shall be the only one to know. It goes without saying that these kinds of contributions are not free of charge. We could talk about this issue later if you find the proposal appealing.

In the meantime, you could be useful to us in another manner. Thus far we have tried unsuccessfully to find good contributors in Germany, mainly in northern Germany and in particular, in Prussia and the Hanseatic towns. Nonetheless, we are extremely interested in every detail concerning what is going on in Prussia, the German Customs Union, the commerce in the Baltic Sea, the general movement of public opinion in northern Germany. Any information of a commercial nature would be particularly valuable for a newspaper that adds the specialty of commerce to politics. If you could find for us good contributors either in Prussia with regard to general politics, or in Hamburg to cover the industrial and commercial affairs of northern Germany, you would render us an extremely great service. I would repeat what I have said above, that you can *be sure of confidentiality* if confidentiality is what you desire. I would be the only intermediary and as far as the other conditions are concerned, we could easily come to an agreement. I think that for the coverage of politics, a university professor would perhaps be preferable to anyone else. But could we find such a person?

I end this long letter by wishing you a safe voyage and ask that you do not forget the true and good friends whom you are leaving behind in France. My wife wishes to be especially remembered to you.

Alexis de Tocqueville

18. Francis Lieber to Alexis de Tocqueville

Hamburg, November 7, 1844

My dear de Tocqueville,

I have received your warm and friendly letter in Berlin, but have not been able to find time to answer it until now. If I lived at the North of the

U. S., in Boston, New York, or Philadelphia, I would easily accept your offer,[93] but living as I do, out of the way, in the South, the matter becomes more difficult for me and less acceptable for you. Still, the trial might be made, provided you find it agreeable to concede to the following points.

1. I make my communications in English. French would take me too much time, at least at the beginning, and indeed, would save you none. For the correction and smoothing over of my French would require quite as much time as translating from the English into French.

2. You must consider that it will happen at times that my communication does not touch upon something which has just transpired at the North shortly before the sailing of a packet, and too short a time to reach me.

3. It must be kept strictly and absolutely secret that I rend these communications, not that I shall have to fear to avow what I write, but a man cannot afford to fight battles in all directions. Besides, the thing would be misunderstood. Indeed, I do not well know how shall I be able to send you every month a pretty thick letter without drawing attention to it in so small a place as the one I live in; for I must pay each time for the letter as far as N. York, and therefore make it known that it comes from me.

4. You will consider that my communications may at times not arrive at the precise day when they ought to arrive to leave the U. States by steam. Still I will try to make the best possible arrangement with some friend or other at the North.

Weigh these difficulties well and if you think them not insuperable let me know what remuneration the paper can afford to give and how it will be paid. It would be best to let me have an answer as soon as possible so that I might write to you yet once before I leave Europe.

I wish I could see you; I could then tell you many interesting things which it will not do to confide to paper. I have been several times with the King of Prussia.[94]

You know my view that the highest interests of the cause of civilization require France and England to be united. My journey has strengthened this opinion a thousand times. All the governments, except those of France and England, and, perhaps, some petty one[s], not worth mentioning, are at heart for absolutism – in many cases, maybe, with a general and not very definite wish, to do good to the people, but absolutism is their creed, their love, and their hope. England was once the only spot on earth where brilliant and absolute centralization found no footing; shall the world never go on, and shall not mankind have at least two nations toward which they may look with some confidence, that they will form a breakwater? I own, the older I grow the more fervent I love liberty, true and substantial freedom, and the more I hate absolutism, be it monarchical or democratic. But I forgot the small size of this paper when I entered upon the subject of so vast a size.

I shall do all to find you here a German correspondent. In Berlin the thing was impossible. Give my best regards to Madame de Tocqueville, who, I trust, will not absolutely forget me when in America. Remember me kindly to the Beaumonts. I should have liked so much to see you all four once more. A propos, I wish to make one additional condition if I write for your paper, viz. that you send me your paper and that sometimes, even though it be rarely, you write me, mentioning in your letter a list[95] of the most prominent works which interest me. If you have not time, why may not Madame de Tocqueville do me the favour ? My wife begs to offer, although unknown to you, her best regards. Write soon, my dear friend, and whether I become your *correspondent politique* or not, consider me always your affectionate friend,

Francis Lieber

The University of South Carolina Library, Columbia, S.C. Fragments from this letter were published in *The Life and Letters of Francis Lieber*, edited by Thomas Sergeant Perry (Boston: Osgood & Co, 1882), pp. 191–92.

19. Alexis de Tocqueville to Francis Lieber

Paris, November 13, 1844

My dear Lieber,

The letter that I received from you yesterday[96] pleased me all the more as I was beginning to be concerned or rather I was blaming the mail and was thinking that you had left Europe without having received what I had sent you from Tocqueville. I had written you a second letter to America. Your last one arrived on the same day as I was about to mail it and hence I threw it into the fire. Now, I answer your questions by considering them in the order that you ask them:

I have always understood that your contributions would be written in English. Hence, there are no problems on this point.

I understand that it would be more useful if you were in New York than South Carolina. But this is an inconvenience that I was aware of and which has always seemed to me to be inferior to the advantage of having a correspondent like you.

As to confidentiality, I give you my word that it will be absolute. *No one* working on the newspaper will know your name. Beaumont, who has the same political interest as I do in the success of *Le Commerce*, and my wife, will be the only persons who will know that you are a correspondent and I am certain of their discretion as of mine.

As to the regularity of dispatches, one hopes, of course, that they will be as regular as possible, and that no more than a month would pass without the reader being able to follow what is happening in America; nonetheless, in these matters, punctuality is impossible. Moreover, events must have some influence on the timing of dispatches. If, in the interval between two letters, an important event were to occur, you should not wait for the moment of the regular dispatch to make it known and to indicate its significance to us. This is a matter of which you are the sole judge.

What we demand from you is the equivalent of a two- or three-column article. I shall send you a copy of the newspaper to Hamburg so that you can ascertain what this entails in terms of its actual length. It would be more difficult to tell you in advance what ought to be included in these two or three columns. But, on this point, I readily rely on you. Please do not forget that you speak to France and choose among American affairs those which could interest us the most. Do not forget, moreover, that you speak to readers who have little knowledge of the people, history, institutions, and the social state of the United States, and with whom one must therefore be clear and more explicit than if one were to write for Americans or even for the English.

Everything regarding the behavior of Americans considered as a people in relation to other nations, especially in relation to the English and Mexico, will naturally excite our curiosity. But we are also very much interested in the internal affairs, the intellectual life, the development of the social prosperity of the country, its industrial and commercial greatness.... As an inhabitant of the Union, you will know better than me those of its affairs which should be selected for this type of monthly review of events and I imagine that you will undertake this task without any problems whatsoever.

You ask me to send you a copy of the newspaper. This is reasonable; but how can I send it without letting the administration of the paper know your name? Would it not be possible to have it sent to one of your friends or under a different name than yours? Please give me instructions on this point.

As to remuneration, this is the policy of the journal. In England, we have a very distinguished man, a Member of Parliament, who, like you, wants confidentiality and agrees to do for us what we are asking you to do with regard to America. He wished that we should give him two guineas or approximately fifty francs per article. Please tell me frankly if you find this payment suitable; in the contrary case, please tell me your figure and I think that I shall have the owners of the paper agree to it. As for the manner of sending the money, it seems to me that it will be very easy to give it to a banker who will forward it to you.

I would like you to become our correspondent for many reasons, among others because this would establish more frequent and intimate relations between you and us. I do not need to tell you that I shall have to write to you often in order to indicate what we want to know. For your part, do not forget that Beaumont and I are at your disposal in order to give you all the information that you might need.

Have you learned in Germany and particularly in Prussia anything that might be useful for us to know regarding the penitentiary system? If so, we would be obliged to you if you could bring it to our attention, because during the forthcoming parliamentary session the debate on this great question will necessarily be reopened.

Farewell, my dear friend. It is with sadness that I see you leaving again this Europe in which you were made to live. Please be reassured that our wishes and our friendship will follow you beyond the ocean. Madame de Tocqueville remembers you fondly. She would tell you herself if she were here. But three days ago she left me in order to see one of her aunts who lives in the country. She had added a word for you to the letter which I mentioned at the beginning of this one and which I threw into the fire because it was redundant. The opportunity to correspond again will appear soon, I hope. In the meantime, please receive the expression of our sincere affection.

Alexis de Tocqueville

P.S. I would very much appreciate it if you could find for us in Hamburg the German correspondent we are looking for. At all events, it seems to me that it should be easy to find a merchant there who could send us business news.

20. Francis Lieber to Alexis de Tocqueville

Hamburg, Nov[ember] 26, 1844

It is always unpleasant, my dear de Tocqueville, between friends to talk of small money business. I feel it strongly now; do me then at least the favour to remember that I write to you *en ami*,[97] with perfect candour in answer to your last of Paris, Nov. 13th.

I do not know by any means yet whether I shall be able to do myself justice as a correspondent of a European paper, in that hole down there, nor whether, after some time you and de Beaumont would like my epistles from Negretia.[98] It will be a trial. That I could be a fair correspondent from the North, I hope; but that is not the question. I also acknowledge that the *Commerce* cannot pay as much, when the names of the correspondents are not to be divulged, as it might do, if known names could be frankly given. I see that very well. I also see that a pound a column is a fair remuneration, if a man can write much and is not far from you. But as the case will be with me, writing but once a month – and I could not well engage to write more frequently – being obliged to take some more American journals and paying a good deal of postage, which you know, is far from being low in the U. States, two pounds for my monthly article would not be sufficient for me, while three pounds may be too much for the *Commerce*, considering what I said just now, that I write from an out of the way place and that my name cannot be given. You and de Beaumont must reflect upon the subject, and if you think three pounds too much, let me know it, and I will do my best to find you some person at the North, willing to write for the conditions that you have proposed. Whether I should be able to find a proper subject is another question; in Germany I have not succeeded; I would do however my best. Even if you accept my proposition, I should still consider the matter a trial, for I may find that I cannot do myself satisfaction, or you may find that that it will not do. Absolute candour ought always to be the rule between us.

If I become your correspondent you will be particularly careful not to let Americans in Paris come on the scent.

If you write to me in America, do not use any envelopes, for we pay there yet by sheets.

I should not know how to arrange the directing of the paper to me; for if, as you propose, I have the paper sent to some friend in America, it would be inconvenient and dangerous. He would ask at once "why not have it sent direct to you"?

You ask me about penitentiary matters in Prussia. Let me tell you, *under the seal of the strictest secrecy*, that the King is unconditionally for the Pennsylvania system,[99] but most of his ministers are not. So is Humboldt[100] (who is every evening until 11 o'clock with the King) against it. He repeated to me all the old stories against solitary confinement, not forgetting Lafayette's saying that he never brooded so many revolutions in his mind as when at Olmütz. The King asked me to go to his ministers, in his name, "and to convert them." Tellkamp, a German now residing in the U. S. and lately here – a fool, *entre nous soit dit*[101] – has done a great deal of mischief. He has written a book, in which he proposes the silliest things – solitary confinement, among other things, until the convict is corrected, say for a year or a year and a half – and then [the] Auburn system[102] !!! Yet this book has taken in Berlin, especially with General de Thile,[103] the Prime Minister, in some such [sic] – a man of good intentions but very limited views and narrow mind. Tellkamp wants to be called to Prussia and wrote his book – suddenly changing his previous opinion, when he found how the wind blew here. Yet I feel convinced that that book will be served up in your Chamber next winter. Prepare yourself therefore by reading the article on this book by Dr. Varntrapp, in the last number of his *Annals on Prison Matters*, publ[ished] in September or October last. Varntrapp is one of the best penologic statistical writers. He wrote to the U. S. and found among other things that, while Tellkamp says, Germans easily get deranged in the American Penitentiaries on the Pennsylv[ania] plan,[104] and cites instances, *not one German* ever became crazy. The King said to me that he must have me in Prussia and that he occupies himself constantly with the thought [of] how to get me there. I repeat, that I trust all this to your honour as a *perfect* secret. *La Prusse ne me plaît pas.*[105]

As to Dickens' lachrymose story of the mulatto girl in Philadelphia, I sent de Beaumont my letter, containing my personal observation of the case. It will be worth at least Dickens' statement. Besides, have you not Eugène Sue's opinion? One novel writer against another. And Sue's remarks in the *Mystères de Paris* are worth a hundred of Dickens' remarks in the *Notes*, at least.[106]

My best regards to your and Beaumont's circle.

Pray write me in your next with a few words how many *inspecteurs généraux des prisons*[107] you have, and whether the prisons stand partly under the minister of justice.

I have strongly recommended to the King of Prussia to appoint inspectors general of prisons, with the duty to lecture in the Universities on Penology, as I have called the whole branch of criminal sciences[108] which occupies itself (or ought to do so) with the *punishment* and the *criminal*, not with the definition of crime, the subject of accountability and the proving of the crime, which belongs to criminal law and the penal process. Thus I would call you and Beaumont *deux penologistes distingués*.[109] Add that word to the *Dictionnaire de l'Académie!*[110]

I have an article on Intramural and Extramural executions (you see I coin words pretty fast) in Mittermaier's last number of the *Annals of Foreign Legislation*. I wish you could draw attention to the essay. The subject is important. I call intramural executions those which are performed before proper witnesses within walls of the prison yard, as is done in N.Y., Massachusetts, New Jersey, Rhode Island, Ohio etc. etc. etc. Extramural executions are a scandal and fearfully immoral.[111] Pity you do not read German, else I could wish you to [read] that article which Foeling could lend you.

Let me hear soon from you. Remember me kindly to Mesd[ames] de Tocqueville and de Beaumont.

> Ever yours most faithfully,
> Francis Lieber
> [Illegible word] Esplanade

Do not send the *Commerce* any more here. I see it at the Club. Thank you for the copies you sent me.

The University of South Carolina Library, Columbia, SC; this letter was partially reproduced in *The Life and Letters of Francis Lieber*, edited by Thomas Sergeant Perry (Boston: Osgood & Co, 1882), pp. 192–93.

21. Marie and Alexis de Tocqueville to Francis Lieber[112]

Paris, December 2, 1844

My dear Mr. Lieber,

I wrote to you about three weeks ago, in a letter of M. de Tocqueville's, which from some circumstance that I have forgotten he threw into the fire instead of putting it into the post. As I desire most particularly the kindly feelings you have hitherto expressed towards me should not change from any negligence on my part, I will not longer delay assuring you that the rapid moments I passed in your society in Paris were most pleasing. How much I regret that the wide Atlantic is so soon to divide you from your very good friends in Paris. Unfortunately, during your residence here we were some time absent which prevented our meeting as often as we desired. Be assured we shall not forget you. Monsieur de Tocqueville is very anxious to see you elected a corresponding member of the Institute, and I am quite as zealous in the affair as he is, but you know very well that the rarest merit does not obtain its reward in this intriguing age without much manoeuvering; nevertheless, I hope a nomination which would do so much honour to the Institute will not be delayed beyond measure. Several of its members are well known to us, and one of our most intimate and valuable friends has much chance of adding soon to the number; how happy should I be to see him contribute to an election in every way so desirable as yours.[113] Is there no chance of your ever coming to settle in Europe? If you were in Prussia we should see you occasionally, but in America the hope of meeting again more than once during our life seems faint. M. and Mme de Beaumont are still at Lagrange and will remain there until the opening of the Session which is fixed for the 26th. The change of Ministry so much desired by the opposition is not very likely to be brought about, I understand, tho' the King's ardent desire to obtain a donation for the Duke de Nemours may be a stumbling block, his Majesty is so infatuated with himself, and considers himself so completely master of his position that it is said he insists on the presentation of that very unpopular *projet de loi*.[114] You see of course the French newspapers at Hamburg, what do you think of the *Juif errant*[115]? I hope you don't admire it, for in that case we should differ essentially. In the first place I don't think it amusing, which is a fault without redemption for a novel, and in the second, I think its moral tendencies are scandalous. M. Eugène Sue would never have my good opinion were he to walk to Rome barefooted in sign of repentance of having propagated such detestable doctrines. I see in the French newspapers several indirect attacks on the Penitentiary System and I have no doubt but that they will be renewed more openly ere long. M. Thiers[116] and his corrupted party are enemies to all measures that do not please the multitude. You do not say if Mrs. Lieber leaves Europe without too much sorrow. We greatly regretted she did not accompany you to Paris, we should have been most happy to make her acquaintance. I must now say adieu, for M. de Tocqueville wishes to write to you in the same letter, believe me then, my dear Mr. Lieber, with every sentiment of regard most truly yours,

Marie de Tocqueville

My dear Lieber,[117]

I have let Madame de Tocqueville write to you in my place, first of all because she wanted to send you a word of friendship, and also because I would not have had time to write you a long letter, being overwhelmed today by various matters, but not wanting to delay in giving you news about us. Immediately after receiving your letter, I saw the owners of the paper and I assured myself that the arrangement that you desire is feasible. Therefore, we are set for *3 pounds* as you reasonably requested. As to confidentiality, I repeat that it will be *as complete as possible*. I know your adoptive country. I know that the smallest criticism of America coming from an American might create irreparable harm. Therefore, be reassured that I would not want at any price to put you in a difficult situation. Hence, you are entirely free to write whatever you wish. Now, I very much want to see you out of Europe and arrived safely in America. The current situation is extremely interesting. The nomination of a new President and the beginning of a new policy,[118] the importance for us of the relations between the English and you, all these things make me wish that your correspondence will not be long waited for. You will no doubt disembark in New York. I would ask you to write for us your first letter from there.

I deeply regret that you have not been able to find a correspondent for us in Germany. Nonetheless, I was expecting this. Germany is still the country of silence, and I fear that it will never be different, at least during our lifetime. Have you tried at all events to put us in touch with someone in Hamburg, even if it were only regarding business issues? Such a correspondent would be very valuable to us.

If, on your arrival in the United States, there are newly published official reports on prisons or any other important documents of any kind on this issue, please be so kind to send them to me, since we shall have another battle on the penitentiary system this year. Farewell, my dear friend. Be assured that our strong and sincere affection will follow you everywhere.

[Alexis de Tocqueville]

22. Alexis de Tocqueville to Francis Lieber

December 14, 1844

My dear Lieber,

I have just received your letter[119] and respond briefly in haste. You ask me 1° if you should write via England and steamship. I answer in the affirmative if, as I believe, this way is the shortest. You should not send your letter to me, but to M. Scheffer,[120] Editor-in-Chief of the newspaper, 6 rue St. Joseph. You should not sign it, since he does not know your name. If you have something special to ask from me, you should put everything in an enclosed sealed envelope. M. Scheffer will be informed of this and will give me this package; the administration will pay for the postage. If you think that it might be dangerous to let M. Scheffer see the stamps on the letter, you should address it directly to me. 2° You ask how you should send me, either from Hamburg or from America, documents with officially paid postage. As long as Parliament is in session, that is, until the end of July, you can send them to me care of the President of the Chamber of Deputies. An enclosed sealed envelope with my name on it would cover the letters or the documents; upon reflection, this is also the best way to send your monthly letters during the parliamentary session. Therefore, please use it instead of addressing your letters to M. Scheffer.

As to the pamphlets, after the end of the session, you should send them to me care of the Minister of the Interior, making sure to indicate on the package sent to me *"penitentiary documents."*

You will be well advised to speak to Mr. Humboldt about the Institute. We shall talk about you in Paris and his word can be of great help to us.

Write to us as soon as you can after your arrival in America. You know that current events there are of great interest to us. The beginning of the new administration, its domestic and foreign policy, the state of the country, its attitude toward England, its likely decisions on the great issues of Texas, Oregon, and the Tariff . . . they all greatly excite our curiosity.

Farewell, my dear friend. I am leaving you now, but not before wishing you all good fortune. My wife wishes you the same, and both of us ask you to believe in our sincere friendship.

Alexis de Tocqueville

P.S. Please tell me how we can send you the small sum that you were so kind as to accept. If you can find a German correspondent for us, it will be greatly appreciated.

23. Marie de Tocqueville to Francis Lieber[121]

Paris, January 8, 1845

My dear Mr. Lieber,

I cannot let you depart from Europe without writing you a word of advice, without telling you once more that our best wishes will accompany you everywhere. M. de Tocqueville is more than ever occupied or he would have joined a few lines to my letter. He asked me to say to you that he will open a credit for you in New York and when the definitive arrangements are made he will duly inform you. He begs you will let him know the amount of the sum you wish him to transmit at a time, as he supposes it would not be worthwhile to send the amount of each single letter. Perhaps you will be able to get some subscribers to *Le Commerce* in America, in New York it might be possible to place a few or in any part of the Union it would be very desirable to introduce that newspaper; if the American newspapers could give extracts from it, I think it would produce an excellent effect. What M. de Tocqueville desires is that *Le Commerce* should obtain as much publicity as possible out of France as well as within. Should you have an opportunity of attracting the attention thereto during your sort stay in England you would do a good deed, for I consider the propagation of sound and elevated ideas a good deed. I am happy to say that the success of the journal exceeds our expectations in this country,[122] tho' its opinions on the question which agitates the public mind in this moment are very unpopular.[123] I need not say, I believe, that that question is the Secondary Instruction Bill; it is far from sure that it will be discussed in the Chamber of Deputies, owing to the unfortunate malady of the unfortunate M. Villemain,[124] however there is nothing yet decided on that hand. For my part, I hope that the law will be withdrawn. The Ministry was much in danger a week ago, but the King seems to have taken them again into favour and I suppose they will struggle through the session. M. de Tocqueville is quite delighted with the perspective of having a correspondent at Heidelberg,[125] he offers you his best thanks for your friendly efforts in his favour. He has received the pamphlets you were good enough to forward to him through the President of the Chamber; unfortunately for him they are in German and I am but a poor translator. However I will do my best to give him the pith of the work. The *Constitutionnel* (M. Thiers' newspaper) attacks repeatedly and violently the cellular system,[126] our friends seems to go to sleep, and I fear the law passed last year is in great danger. M. de Tocqueville is *infatigable* but really he cannot do everything at once. M. de Beaumont seems *apathique*.[127] Pray be good enough when you write to tell my husband everything you can collect favorable to that system. How much good there is to be done and, *hèlas*! how inadequate are the powers of any single man to find remedies to the evils he perceives. However we must not be too ambitious and we must try to content ourselves with doing the little good that is in our power. I indulge myself with the hope that my husband will ever find an active cooperation in you, and I rejoice that your relations will be more close and frequent than formerly. I hope you won't forget me when you are on the other side of the Atlantic. Write to me, I take an interest in everything. With kindest and best regards to Mrs. Lieber and yourself, believe me yours most truly,

Marie de Tocqueville

24. Alexis and Marie de Tocqueville to Francis Lieber

Paris, May 18, 1845

My dear Lieber,

We have already received three of your letters which have been published in the newspaper and have been read with great interest by the public. I would have informed you earlier and would have asked you to continue to write for us in the same manner if I had not been preoccupied by the likely occurrence of a fact that is taking place at the present moment and which should bring about the end of this correspondence. My intention is to withdraw from the direction of the newspaper. Various problems that have arisen among the owners prompt me to take this decision. As you have been in correspondence with *Le Commerce* only through me and because of me, I hasten to pass onto you this news so that you do not continue writing letters that I could not publish without revealing your name and address. Until now, the secret has been kept *completely and absolutely*. Only Madame de Tocqueville and I know your name. The originals of your letters are in my hands; hence there is nothing to fear from this point of view. I also have your money. Please let me know how you would like to receive it. What I can send you now is the expression of my profound gratitude.

At the present moment, there is no vacancy for foreign correspondents at the Academy. I hope that you have no doubt that as soon as a vacancy appears in the sections for which you can compete, I shall deploy all my zeal to initiate and support your candidacy. I have no doubt that Beaumont will be of great help in this regard.

Although I can no longer ask you to write new letters for the newspaper, I do not need to tell you that, as a politician, I would place high value in knowing from you, every now and then, what is going on in America in times of great crisis, something that you are so good at explaining. Nor do I need to tell you that, as your friend, it would be very pleasant and precious to me to receive news from you and your family from time to time. I hope that you count on our friendship as we do on yours.

Alexis de Tocqueville

My dear Mr. Lieber,[128]

I open M. de Tocqueville's letter in order to add one little word of remembrance. We think your letters most interesting, but unfortunately the newspaper has not succeeded as we expected and the *ennuis* & difficulties of the *entreprise* have determined my husband to retire from direction. We often talk of you and ever bear in mind the affair you have at heart. M. de Tocqueville is watching for a favorable occasion to bring forward your claims which he considers to be of the first order. In a long conversation with M. de Beaumont yesterday I drew his attention towards the same object and I have no doubt he will join his efforts to my husband's, who is ever on the *qui-vive*, whenever an opportunity presents itself. I have a friend waiting for me, therefore must terminate hastily my post-scriptum, and with kindest regards believe me, my dear Mr. Lieber,

Your most attached,
Marie de Tocqueville

25. Alexis de Tocqueville to Francis Lieber

Paris, July 1, 1845

My dear Lieber,

I have just deposited at the bank of M. de Rothschild the sum of 300 francs that the newspaper owes you for the four letters. I could not send you more because, since yesterday, I have completely ended any relations with *Le Commerce* which is passing into other hands.[129] I have waited until the last moment to ask for the money owed to you because I was hoping for the arrival of a fifth letter. Only yesterday morning did I receive from the administration the amount that was owed to you up to that point. M. Rothschild was not able to send the money to the person that you indicated to me. But you can get it in New York from Mr. A. Belmont[130] whom everyone knows, I am told. I add to this letter a small note that was given to me for you at the office of M. Rothschild.

Nobody has suspected your name which I have not revealed to anyone whatsoever; hence you do not have to fear any unpleasant consequence for your contribution to the newspaper. I only regret that it could not have been longer. But there was a disagreement between the owners of *Le Commerce* and myself and I had to withdraw along with my political friends.

I would be very pleased if you could send via the Embassy or even via the Ministry of Interior a few interesting American documents of a political or other nature. If you do so via the Ministry of the Interior, you should indicate on the address *"penitentiary papers."* The truth is that these kinds of documents continue to interest me profoundly, since this issue has not been fully resolved among us.

We are in the middle of the tumult accompanying the last days of the session.[131] I can only spare you these few words.

Many friendly and sincere regards,
Alexis de Tocqueville

P.S. I was mistaken when saying that I was going to add a note to my letter. This note, which is an acknowledgment from Rothschild, must remain in my hands.

26. Robert Walsh to Alexis de Tocqueville

Paris, Febr[uary] 6, 1846

Dear Sir,

When you happen to have no further use for the volumes which I had the pleasure of sending to you, you will oblige me by returning them to my bureau. I am exceedingly sorry that you did not find any opportunity to speak on the question of Texas.[132] Much remains to be said.

I have the honor to be,
Dear Sir,
Your very resp[ectfu]l serv[an]t,
Robert Walsh
Rue de Rivoli,
n° 32.

P. S. Be so kind as to give me the address of M. de Corcelle.

Beinecke Rare Book and Manuscript Library, Yale University, Uncat MSS 324; also available as Bonnel copy, MSS Vault Tocqueville, Paquet 12, p. 66.

27. Alexis de Tocqueville to Benjamin P. Poore[133]

April 6, 1846 Monday

Sir,

I have the honor of sending you a note for tomorrow, Tuesday. It would be enough to be at the Chamber by 11.30. Unfortunately, the session will be, I think, of little interest.

I have the honor of being your most humble servant,
Alexis de Tocqueville

28. Isaiah Townsend to Alexis de Tocqueville[134]

June 13, 1846

I imagine, Sir, that the author of *Democracy in America*, the Montesquieu of the Romans of the New World,[135] could not lose any interest in the affairs of a country whose institutions he so wonderfully managed to understand and explain. He would like, I think, to obtain more accurate ideas about the current situation of the United States than those he finds in the newspapers which the political passions on this side of the ocean and the biases and prejudices on the other side render very little trustworthy. I count myself happy to be able to provide him with this occasion, by referring him to one of my most esteemed friends, Mr. J. V. L. Pruyn, who is leaving soon for England and France. Mr. Pruyn is one of my most respectable fellow citizens from Albany. Admitted to the Bar, he occupies a distinguished place in the Chancery Court and is already Regent of the State University [of New York], although he is quite young for that honorable position. He is a man very capable of completing the imperfect ideas and correcting the wrong impressions that you might have received from reading our journals or from your correspondence, either with regard to the Oregon question, or the war against Mexico, or our domestic affairs. In turn, since you know the monarchy in France as well as democracy in America, I shall take the liberty of asking that you give to my friend information about the people and events from your own country that nobody would be in a better position to share than you. Both he and I will be grateful to you for that.

A Convention has just assembled in this town in order to reform the State Constitution.[136] Mr. Pruyn will explain to you the abuses that people decry and the remedies that are being proposed. I shall limit myself solely to informing you, based on the information received from some of the most profound and clear-sighted of this Assembly, that it is very likely that the Chancery Court will be abolished and a commission will be appointed in order to codify, once and for ever, either the customary laws or the statutory laws that govern the state.

Mrs. Pruyn will accompany her husband. She is a young woman equally pleasant and full of wit whom I cordially recommend to Madame de Tocqueville.

I take this opportunity, Sir, to renew the expression of all my sentiments as well as of those that my compatriots have toward you,

Your devoted servant,
Isaiah Townsend,
Albany, June 13, 1846

Beinecke Rare Book and Manuscript Library, Yale University, Uncat MSS 324; also available Bonnel copy, in MS Vault Tocqueville, D II a, folder "Bonnel's copies of letters from Americans to Tocqueville."

29. Alexis and Marie de Tocqueville to Francis Lieber

Tocqueville, July 22, 1846

My dear Lieber,

Your letter dated February 14 reached me only at the end of June at the very moment when I was leaving Paris.[137] I did not answer immediately because, on my return here, I was extremely busy. Our general elections will take place on the first of next month. You know as well as I do that the time before the election is not a period of tranquillity for the candidates. As for me, however, I cannot complain of having been very troubled. No competitor has presented himself until now and my election is therefore certain.[138]

I have read with great pleasure the small brochure and the manuscript that you have sent me.[139] I find both of them worth submitting to the attention of the Institute. As for their inclusion into the transactions of our Academy, this does not seem possible to me. The Academy prints in its transactions only the texts that have been read by their authors. Here is how you could accomplish your goal in part. I could present to the Academy as a gift the two works that you have sent me, and on this occasion I would present a short analysis of both of them, making known who you are. The report that I shall make will be printed *de iure* in the transactions. I do not think that it would be possible to do more that that, but this would suffice to accomplish two goals: to signal your name to the public and especially to recall your name to the Academy.

You asked me to which weekly newspaper I would advise you to subscribe in Paris. I do not know what to tell you. Until now, we have not paid too much attention to these types of newspapers and the existing ones are little known in the political world. The publication that would best serve your goal would be the *Revue des Deux Mondes*. It appears every two weeks and contains, apart from regular articles, a chronicle of the events of the last fortnight that, although clearly written in a partisan spirit, gives foreigners the opportunity to familiarize themselves with the facts and evolution of ideas. In France, it costs 50 francs per year. I do not know what the price is for foreign subscribers.

As I was telling you above, we are on the eve of a general election. I think that the opposition will lose more than it will win in this great contest.[140] Nonetheless, I do not know if our government will survive for long. The arrival of the Whigs in power is certainly a great problem for M. Guizot.[141] Moreover, although his politics, or rather the politics of the King, are prevailing, the person of M. Guizot continues to be very unpopular,[142] and if the conservative party were to regain its majority in the Chamber, it is likely that it will split, which might bring a change of personnel, but not a great change in the conduct of affairs. As for a change of this kind, you can be certain that it will never occur as long as the King lives and perhaps even for a certain period after him. For he has created a school that will survive him: reason without genius, skill without greatness, and order without morality.[143]

At this moment, I am very busy with our affairs in Africa which are becoming more and more important every day. For us, the war has become the secondary aspect of our enterprise and will remain so for as long as we shall have no quarrels in Europe. The most important issue today is colonization. How to attract and, above all, to retain a great number of European farmers in Algeria? We already have 100,000 Christians in Africa without counting the army, but almost all of them are settled in towns which become great and beautiful cities, while the countryside remains depopulated. It is impossible to deal with the colonization of Africa without thinking of the great examples given by the United States on this issue. But how to study them? Have any books been published in the United States, or any documents of any kind, which could shed light on this point and might reveal how things are in reality? Could this information be found in official reports or elsewhere? I would be extremely grateful to receive from you anything that you might find on this subject.[144] If you cannot give me any information but do know someone who might help me in this regard, please let me know the person to whom I might write. At all events, please afford me the pleasure of answering as soon as possible.

Many sincere and friendly regards,
Alexis de Tocqueville

P.S. I have written again to *Le Commerce*.

Tocqueville, July 22, 1846[145]

My dear Mr. Lieber,

I must add the expression of my thanks for your so amiable remembrance, to M. de Tocqueville's letter. We read your highly interesting observations on Laura Bridgman together, he intends to communicate them to the Academy, and I hope it will not be long before you will become a corresponding member. It is our greatest desire that your election should not be much longer delayed and we hope this last work will, by drawing the attention to you, facilitate your election. We are expecting our dear friends, Mr. and Mrs. Grote[146] to spend a fortnight with us in the beginning of August. I know you are an admirer of theirs and we shall often speak of you together. The two first volumes of Mr. G[rote]'s *History of Greece* has [*sic*] appeared, it is a work of great merit and shows the profound erudition of the author. I shall give them your work to read and am sure it will have great success. Why are you so far away across the Ocean? When I think that perhaps we shall never meet again it quite damps my courage. Are you really fixed in America for ever? Pray tell me when next you write your plans for the future, for I should be too sad if I thought you would never take up your permanent abode in Europe. It would give me so much pleasure to make Mrs. Lieber's acquaintance. I hope your children satisfy your *amour propre* and your heart. But I must say adieu and with most sincere regards believe me most truly yours,

Marie de Tocqueville

30. Alexis de Tocqueville to Robert Walsh

Thursday morning
August 20, 1846[147]

Sir,

An important question on the verification of powers is being discussed today in the Chamber.[148] Could you tell me what is going on in this regard in the deliberative assemblies of America and, in particular, in Congress? Do these assemblies have the right to annul or to postpone elections? And if so, how do they proceed? I would be very obliged to you if you could give me some information on these issues.

The library of the Chamber will subscribe to the *National Intelligencer*[149] and a few of the publications that you have suggested.

Believe in my sentiments of most distinguished consideration.
Alexis de Tocqueville

31. Francis Lieber to Alexis de Tocqueville

Columbia, S. C.,
Sept[ember] 25, 1846

My dear Tocqueville,

Your kind letter of July and Madame de Tocqueville's charming lines came into my hands a few days ago only, when I returned from a journey to the West – that great West where a mighty future is unfolding itself. I thank you for your offer to give to the Institute an account of my communication on the Sounds of Laura Bridgman and venture to beg you to do so as soon as you may find it convenient. I was mistaken. I thought communications on subjects of peculiar interest might be read to your Institute though coming from non-members. Is there no way of publishing my paper in French – all expenses of course to be borne by me? Or is there some good widely read periodical which would think it worthwhile to translate and publish it, giving me a fair number of copies? But first I would really feel much obliged to you to give the account you speak of to the Institute. And now to that part of your letter which is naturally the most important to you, the colonization of Algeria and the question whether the U. St[ates] may serve as example as well as your desire to have books and reports on the subject. As to books, there are none I feel sure, and as to reports, I have written the very day I received your letter to the Vice President and several Senators and Representatives, to direct every document to be sent to me in which a description of new settlements especially of Oregon, or an incidental account of the process of peopling and *politiking* of uninhabited parts of our territory, may be contained. They are my personal friends and will do what they can, but I feel sure that they will not be able to find anything because that whole process with us is a natural and not a planned one. There is in the Anglican race an instinctive impulse of establishing governments with the principle of vitality and self-action *within*, not depending upon a *vis matrix* from without – there is a *nisus*, if I can call it so, of forming polities in this race, that people no more speak about it than about the fact that the settlers eat, sleep, and walk. The cases of America and Algeria are essentially different. To see this and discover where they may possibly not differ, it will be best if I state the elements which constitute and characterize our process of peopling. You may then compare and apply. But before I proceed I must warn you that in all probability you will find not a word which you – the philosophical and faithful painter of the U. S. – do not know, and very possibly better than myself. But the distance is too far; I cannot lose time by inquiry whether I shall give you my views or not, so here they are.

1. The Teutonic race and the Irish have a readiness of emigration which the French have not; this readiness becomes in America, where it can so easily be satisfied, a desire of moving onward. The Far, the Distant has a charm, and many people move merely because they can do so. They, therefore, do not cling to cities.

2. The American is not half as social as the Frenchman who loves his coffee house with all the buzz of talk and clicking of the domino. Mathews calls the Americans a moping race. They therefore have not only no objection to settling separately, but they prefer it, because economically speaking it is preferable and they have perfect independence. They *dot* a country and consequently subdue it easier.

3. Although the land belongs to the U. S., the pre-emption law makes it for all purposes of first settling as though it absolutely belonged to no one. You settle down and clear land where you list.

4. The land is wild, none but hunters have lived there; it is fine and fertile, yet characterized by the same features and fit for the same branches of agriculture with that from which they emigrate.

5. They have to do with no enemies except Indians, who recede with the buffalo. Besides what are they, compared to your Arabs?

6. The same power of opinion which you observe in operation when on an emergency something – say thanks on board a steamboat, are to be voted[150] – is in operation with the new settlers – the same instinctive skill, the same submission. A chairman is everywhere elected at once, where any social action is requisite and this chairman is the nucleus of all Anglican political crystallisation. The process is astonishing yet natural. One collection of men, one assembly leads to another, courts are even held and at last *Legislatures* established, without sanction except that of the spontaneous action and social consciousness in all. You may have read of the Legislature of Willamette for Oregon, of acts and actions and some very stringent too. Well, this whole Legislature was a self-constituted one – yet very active and well obeyed. Read, if

you please, an article "Moderator" which I gave in the *Encycl[opedia] Am[ericana]* of which you remember I sent a copy to the Institute. By and bye, the regular government, i.e. Congress establishes a *"Territory;"* the self-constituted government passes over into or furnishes the rudiments of a legalized one, and sanctioned action begins. People have been tried and executed in the farthest West by self-conglomerated or rather self-organized courts, where every thing was most regular – judge, jury, prosecutor, counsel, clerk – everything except the origin, and this origin, too, appears not irregular because every individual in America stands so near the first source of sovereignty that he feels it almost as natural to act on own self-sufficient power in cases of emergency, as Christina[151] thought it natural that, though having resigned the crown, she tried and killed her enemy at Paris, and *others* did *not* try and hang *her* for it.

7. Every American who emigrates knows he does not sink into a colonist; he *is* and *remains* full citizen, which aids much in inducing people to emigrate. And by the bye, this is one of the points by which the English have shown their wisdom and fairness, compared to Spain. A colonist was always at least in England, a full Englishman.

We have then these elements: cheap, fertile, undisputed and similar land, readiness and impulse to move on, dissocial settlements and strongly social adhesion in political matters; consciousness of rights and authority to act, and instead of a feeling of debasement rather pride, for the Western settler considers himself more of a man than the Philadelphian. He has no Paris, no "belle France" to long for, for he is in America and means to remain for ever in the West. The wisdom of Congress is chiefly shown, in my opinion, in these two points: 1. in making the acquisition of land as easy as it is possible; 2. in showing no jealousy on the part of the old states, but on the contrary a regular process of organisation, assimilation, and equalisation, in which the U. St[ates] have given the first example in history. Everywhere else we see Athens sovereign, but all Attica subject; or Napoleon Empereur *des Français* but *Roi d'Italie*.

I wish, dear Tocqueville, I could give you more accurate information. If you will put detailed questions, I will endeavour to answer them. In the meantime you shall get what I receive [. . .][152]

Huntington Library, San Marino, California. A copy of the original letter is available at Beinecke Rare Book and Manuscript Library, Yale University, MSS Vault Tocqueville, C I d.

32. Alexis de Tocqueville to Charles Sumner[153]

Tocqueville, August 6, 1847

My dear Sir,

I read in the June 1 issue of the *Daily Advertiser* the summary of the session in which you proposed to the Boston Prison Discipline Society[154] a resolution whose effect was to declare that this Society did not have to be considered *the pledged advocate* of the Auburn system or any other system; the resolution proposed that all of these systems should be assessed in an unbiased and unprejudiced manner. I have learned since from the same newspaper that the Society refused to adopt the resolution. This vote surprised and saddened me. I follow with great interest the question of prison reform and have always professed a respectful attachment to the Society that granted me the honor of generously admitting me as a member[155] and which is deservedly renowned in the world of philanthropists. It is under the impression of these two sentiments that I felt the desire to write to you.

The vote that I have just mentioned will cause, I am not afraid to say, a distressing surprise to almost all of those who concern themselves with the issue of prisons in Europe. They will interpret it as a solemn pledge by the Society to champion the Auburn system and to become the systematic opponent of solitary confinement. From being judge, it seems to have become the jury.

I do not need to tell you that in Europe today, both discussion and experience have, on the contrary, convinced everyone to adopt the system of solitary confinement and to reject the Auburn system.[156] Most of the governments of the old world have pronounced themselves more or less in this direction, not suddenly, but after serious inquiry and long debates. I shall speak here only of the two great nations of Europe, those I know best, and which are most entitled to be followed as an example in this regard, France and England. They reached their conclusions only after extensive discussions conducted openly and in accordance with public opinion. I can assure you that in these two countries, the Auburn system is almost universally rejected. The majority of those who were once favourably disposed toward this system have completely abandoned it and adopted, fully or partly, the system of solitary confinement. The two governments have followed the same trend. You know that a few years ago, the French government presented a law based on the system of solitary confinement. After a five-week debate, the longest and most profound one that has ever taken place on any question in our Parliament, this law was passed by an *immense majority*. If this same law has not yet been discussed in the Chamber of Peers, this is because of circumstances wholly unrelated to the question of penitentiary reform. The Chamber of Peers will address it at the beginning of the next session and the majority of the most prominent members of this Chamber have already strongly pronounced themselves in favor of its principles.[157] In the press, almost all the newspapers endorse the system of solitary confinement. The journal that has attacked most strongly and adroitly this system has recently declared itself convinced of its virtues.[158] This change was partly triggered by the experiments made in a large number of our prisons over the last few years. Moreover, it is beyond doubt that, when the law is submitted to the Chamber of Deputies, no one will challenge its *principle*.

Given this situation and these opinions, the vote just passed by a Society as enlightened and famous as the Boston Society will not be understood among us, and I avow that I cannot prevent myself from fearing that it will damage the high esteem that it enjoys on this side of the ocean, or, at least, that it will diminish its authority. I would very much regret this, not only in the interest of an association to which I have the honor of being a member, but also in the interest of humanity whose cause it could serve so effectively.

Please accept, Sir, the expression of my most distinguished consideration.

> Alexis de Tocqueville
> Member of the Institute
> and of the Chamber of Deputies

33. Charles Sumner to Alexis de Tocqueville

> Boston, U. S. of America,
> September 15, 1847

My dear Sir,

I have received your important and interesting letter of August 6th. Let me thank you much for this prompt and authoritative expression of opinion in a way that cannot fail to exert great influence. Feeling unwilling that it should be confined to those only who could peruse your manuscript, I have ventured to regard it as for the public. I have accordingly translated it & caused it to be printed in one of our newspapers. It has already been extensively copied by the newspapers of the country. Your name is so familiar to the enlightened minds among us, that nothing from you can fail to attract attention or inspire confidence.

The discussions which have recently taken place in Boston on the subject of Prison Discipline have been the means of diffusing much information, awakening an interest which will be productive of good. Everything relating to it is now read with avidity.

The Government of our own Society is in the hands of a few persons who are strongly prejudiced against all change. I think, however, that its course will now be altered. Mr. Dwight, the Secretary, has become insane – whether incurably so, I do not know.

The New York Society promises great usefulness. Its last Report is a document of great research & candour, & contains some remarkable admissions, particularly when we consider that it belongs to a State which is the cradle of the Auburn System.

I cherish a lively recollection of my brief intercourse with you in Paris. It will always be a source of gratification to me to hear from you, & to be of service to you in any way in my country.

> Believe me, my dear Sir,
> Very faithfully yours,
> Charles Sumner

Houghton Library, Harvard University, Ms Am1, Reel 063/191.

SECTION B

Letters: 1848–1852

34. Richard Rush to Alexis de Tocqueville[1]

Paris, May 27, 1848

Mr. Rush presents his compliments to M. de Tocqueville and referring to the conversation on the subject of the provincial parliaments of France when last it was his good fortune to see M. de Tocqueville, ventures to send him on the sheets enclosed an extract of a letter from the Secretary of State of the United States, dated the 31st of March last, which perhaps M. de Tocqueville might take an interest in looking over (and possibly some of his associates of the Committee also might) whilst engaged in the important work of reporting a draft of the new constitution of France.

In thus enclosing it, Mr. Rush has to request that it may be considered as a communication wholly informal and unofficial; and he is happy in this opportunity of tending to M. de Tocqueville the assurances of his high consideration.

Firestone Library, Princeton University. Rush Family Papers (C0079), IV. Papers, Documents, and Correspondence (1846–1849) Relating to the French Mission, Correspondence, in Letterbook, Box 11, No. 129.

35. John C. Spencer to Alexis de Tocqueville

Albany, State of New York,
June 10, 1848

My dear Sir,
I cannot refrain from addressing you a few lines to congratulate you

93

upon the late wonderful revolution in your country. Wonderful, we regard it here, not as much on account of the event being unexpected, as for the sublime forbearance exhibited by the people. Of course, you had the warmest sympathies of our citizens but you have more – their most profound respect and admiration.

We have watched your progress from step to step, with an anxiety not less intense than your own; and we have rejoiced that at the first and most critical stages of your progress, you have avoided the dangers of ultra-radicalism, as it is called, but which should be called anarchy.

It gives your friends here special pleasure to observe that you are one of the Committee of the Assembly to frame a Constitution.[2] You have so thoroughly studied the principle of Democracy, have so carefully observed its operations and witnessed its results, that you are peculiarly qualified to embody its safeguards in written elements of government.

I presume you are overwhelmed with advice, and you are justly sensitive to the impertinent interference of strangers. But claiming as I do, that our relations are of a different character, I wish to avail myself of time to communicate with you on a single point, respecting which there is great apprehension so entertained here that there may be a fatal error committed. And at the hazard of giving offence I will state frankly to you the views of the most intelligent and zealous friends of France, in this country, upon that point.

The point to which I refer, is, the organization of a single legislative body.[3] It is the firm belief of our wisest men, that under Providence we owe the continuance of our fine institutions, more than to any other one cause, to the institution of two legislative chambers. The object, as you of course know, is to secure deliberation, by interposing the delay of forms, to hasty action. The same result is not accomplished by committees or bureaux; nor by rules of order, requiring delays, because it is always in the power of the body to dispense with these rules and committees by a majority. And all our experience teaches us that when an assembly is under great excitement, and has a particular object to accomplish, rules and orders of proceeding are mere chaff before the wind, and are driven before the tempest of passion. I have myself repeatedly seen instances in legislative bodies of which I have been a member, of the most violent and dangerous measures being adopted, in defiance of all rules, but which were arrested by the necessity of being sanctioned by another body; and which on the very next day were deeply regretted by the very persons who urged them. Popular tyrants, for such are demagogues, know well how to play on the passions of multitudes, and they dread no check to their schemes so much as time – deliberation. In fact we believe it to be the great secret discovered by modern democracy and the ignorance of which was the ultimate cause of the downfall of ancient republics. Our own Franklin, in the Constitution which he prepared for the State of Pennsylvania, made provisions for only one legislative chamber, with the veto of the Executive. It was adopted; but so ruinous was its operation, so disastrous to sound legislation, that it was abrogated in a very short time, and two chambers created.[4]

The value of the Executive veto in restraining hasty legislation depends so entirely on the character of the individual who is to exercise it, that you cannot rely upon it. If the proposed measure is a favored object of the Executive, he will avail himself of the means always in his hands, of procuring its rapid passage. In truth two chambers afford the best guard and protection against Executive encroachments.

If one of the chambers is more permanent than the other, it will afford the advantage of a matured public opinion, rather than of a hasty and evanescent outburst. For persons elected two or three years since express the opinions of their time; and members who have two or three years to serve, can and will brave a temporary sentiment, until time is afforded to entertain what we call the sound and sober "second thought." This second thought has saved us from many disasters. But this could have been no opportunity for its indulgence, had not constitutional provisions (that could not be altered at the moment) interposed delays and sent the propositions to a different body of men, acting under different impulses, and who had time to reflect.

Many of these ideas I presume have occurred to you; but perhaps not precisely in the light, or in the same angle of view in which I present them.

It seems to me there is no difficulty in your forming a Senate in France. Your departments furnish territorial divisions sufficiently convenient. If they are unequal in population, I suppose they could be equalised. It will be found very advantageous to collect what may be called the provincial sentiments of a department, particularly in reference to its own local affairs. And the contrariety and diversity of their sentiments on general subjects will produce the *juste milieu*.[5] In this Senate, the land owners should be collected as the most conservative class in [the] community, and if not always the most intelligent, yet always the most honest. And if for this branch the qualification of ownership of land should be exacted, you would possess a real aristocracy, without its name or its odious privileges. Agriculture is the basis of all your wealth, and has not been sufficiently encouraged by making the occupation honorable.

I could say much more on this topic, as it is one on which I have long and often reflected, and in which I feel a deep interest. But I must not fatigue you with my prolixity. I wish it were in my power to render you and your country any service. And if these hints should awaken reflections in your active mind, and lead you to pursue them to such results as to satisfy you that our American views on this point, are correct, I should indulge the most confident belief that your liberty would be as permanent as it has been glorious.

I know well that your avocations must leave you little time, yet I should be happy to receive a single line of acknowledgment of this communication, and of my not being forgotten by one whom I so highly esteem. If M. de Beaumont, your colleague in this country, has not forgotten me, please present him my cordial regards.

> With profound respect
> and the highest esteem,
> Your friend,
> John. C. Spencer

Beinecke Rare Book and Manuscript Library, Yale University, Uncat MSS 324; also available as Bonnel copy, Paquet 12, pp. 51–56.

36. William Alexander Duer[6] to Alexis de Tocqueville

> Inglewood, near Morristown, N. J.
> July 1, 1848

My dear Sir,

Presuming upon the acquaintance I had the pleasure of forming with you upon your visit to this country, I take the liberty of introducing to you my friend and family connection, General Theodore Lyman of Massachusetts, who is about visiting France, and hopes to have the opportunity of delivering this into your hands.

It is not improbable that General Lyman is already known to you as the author of a work on the "Diplomacy of the United States";[7] but be this as it may, you will find him well entitled to your consideration and esteem for his worth as a man, as well as for his merits as an author.

I avail myself of this opportunity to transmit to you the lectures, at large, on the Constitutional Jurisprudence of the United States, of which I had the honour some years ago, of sending you the "Outlines," and receiving your flattering acknowledgement in return. I also transmit a copy of a Discourse delivered by my brother[8] on the life and character of the late Chancellor Kent,[9] with whom you probably became acquainted in New York, and whose reputation, at all events, as one of our most distinguished jurists, must be known to you.

The late events in France have, as you may well suppose, excited the greatest attention in this country, especially among those who, like myself, feel an interest in her political regeneration and national honor, and prosperity, and who await with corresponding anxiety, their results. I was therefore the more glad to learn that you were not only elected a member of the National Assembly, but appointed upon the Committee to frame a new constitution. Your name in conjunction with those of the majority appointed with you, afforded assurance to all friends of rational freedom, that the form of Government you will devise and recommend will be founded on the solid bases of law, order, and public morality. From the experience of our own Constitution, I am led to suggest the adoption of a single Executive, as most likely to secure the advantages of vigour, promptness and responsibility so essential in that Department; and a division of the Legislature into two coordinate branches, in order to insure the caution and deliberation requisite to the enactments of wise and wholesome laws.

The establishment of the judicial power as a coordinate Department of the Government seems also to be necessary where the Executive and Legislative branches are limited in their powers in order to interpret finally these powers as well as to restrain their exercise within the constitutional bounds. The independence therefore of the judges should be secured by their tenure of office, and permanent provision for their support. With every apology for venturing upon these suggestions,

> I have the honor to be,
> Dear Sir,
> With great respect and esteem,
> Faithfully yours,
> W. A. Duer

Beinecke Rare Book and Manuscript Library, Yale University, Uncat MSS 324; also available as Bonnel copy, Paquet 12, pp. 70–72.

37. Alexis de Tocqueville to George Sumner[10]

Paris, October 14, 1848
Sunday morning

My dear Sir,

I am greatly obliged to you for the communication you have been so kind as to send to me. I shall take care to return the volume which you have lent me as soon as I have finished with it.

I can easily obtain the report of M. [. . .][11] and, I believe, also that of M. Bauchart.[12] As for the documents which will be published in support of the latter, the difficulty will be perhaps much greater. This publication will form, I think, several volumes, and I do not know whether each representative will be able to obtain more than one copy. I hope, however, to fulfil your wishes in this matter.

Mme de Tocqueville asks me to tell you that hereafter we shall be at home on Monday and no longer on Thursday as formerly; Thursday being the day of the President's reception,[13] I am often obliged to be absent on that day.

Please believe, in all my feelings of esteem and friendship.
Alexis de Tocqueville

38. Alexis de Tocqueville to George Sumner

Paris, January 16, 1849

My dear Mr. Sumner,

Please forgive me a thousand times for my silence. I have been almost continuously ill for the past two weeks. I had a fever even yesterday and I cannot leave my residence today. I shall gladly obtain two tickets for your compatriots as soon as I can get to the Assembly. I shall send you these tickets.

As to the *Conseil d'État*,[14] you will find plenty of materials in all the writings on administrative law, Macarel, Boulatignier, and Cormenin.[15] In particular, the latter, in his book *Questions de Droit* (this is the title, I think) will familiarize you with the examples that you seem to be looking for.

Please believe in all my sentiments of esteem and friendship.
Alexis de Tocqueville

39. Alexis de Tocqueville to Edward Everett[16]

Paris, March 6, 1849

Sir,

Please allow me to recommend to you one of my compatriots, a very talented painter and a most honorable character, who is traveling to America to practice his art. His name is M. *Henri Delattre*.[17] M. Delattre has already visited the United States and the happy memory that he has preserved of it has encouraged him to return there in order to free himself from the all too frequently sterile preoccupations of our old societies. I believe that no one is better placed than you to assist him in his pursuit and to extend to him an honorable patronage.

I shall not speak at all about our internal affairs. There would be too much to report. I only want you to know that, although I have been one of the members of the constitutional committee in the National Assembly of France, I do not take any responsibility for the outcome of that committee. I have criticized vigorously some of the most important parts of our new constitution both before the committee and the Assembly. In particular, I spoke and voted against the establishment of a single chamber[18] and on several occasions I expressed the opinion that if the current constitution is not to be modified soon, the republic will not last.

Please accept, Sir, the expression of my most distinguished consideration.

Alexis de Tocqueville

40. Alexis de Tocqueville to Francis Lieber

Paris, March 7, 1849

My dear Lieber,

Please allow me to recommend warmly to you one of my compatriots, *M. Henri Delattre*, a very talented painter and a most honorable character, who is going to America to practice his art. I would be extremely delighted if you could be of assistance to him. I do not write more on this occasion, not being sure if this letter will ever reach you. We have not received any news from you for a long time. Both Madame de Tocqueville and I are concerned about this.

Many friendly and sincere regards,
Alexis de Tocqueville

41. Alexis de Tocqueville to George Sumner

Friday morning (March 9, 1849)

Dear Sir,

I forgot the other day, when you promised to come on Sunday evening, that I have a family reunion at my father's home that very evening. Could you, please, change the day and come tomorrow, Saturday?

Many friendly and sincere regards,
Alexis de Tocqueville

If Saturday is not convenient, please come on Tuesday.

42. Alexis de Tocqueville to George Sumner

Paris,
Monday evening, March 12, 1849

My dear Sir,

I am truly unlucky. I had arranged to stay at home tomorrow for the whole of Tuesday evening. I had even refused several invitations. But a letter from the President of the Republic has just arrived inviting me to dinner on that day. I cannot refuse. Therefore, I am obliged again to ask you to postpone our meeting. Could we rearrange it for Friday evening, if you are willing to do so?

Many friendly and sincere regards,
Alexis de Tocqueville

43. Edward Everett to Alexis de Tocqueville

Cambridge, U. S. [of] America
May 12, 1849

My dear M. de Tocqueville,

Your letter of the 6th of March recommending M. Henri Delattre to my good offices was forwarded to me by that gentleman from Philadelphia, a few days ago. I assure you it afforded me sincere pleasure to hear from you. I immediately wrote to M. Delattre, enclosing to him a letter for a friend in Philadelphia, who I thought would be both able and willing to be useful. Should M. Delattre come to Boston, I shall do everything in my power to promote his interest.

I was much gratified to learn by your letter that you had protested, in the formation of a new Constitution, against a *single* chamber. Shortly after the breaking out of the Revolution of February, I wrote to Mr. Walsh[19] on this subject, and begged him to endeavour to impress upon members of your assembly the importance of considering the American precedents on this point, which I think one of the vital points of a representative government. All our assemblies, as you know so well – not only the national Congress, but the State Legislatures – consist of two chambers. It is an organization which has descended to us from the colonial period, and there is no doubt that our forefathers borrowed it from the British Constitution. The principle of the composition of the British Parliament – of an hereditary house of Lords and an elective house of Commons – of course, had no application to the state of things existing in the American Colonies; neither is there, at the present day, any analogy between the United States Senate, in which each State, large and small, is represented by two senators, and the Senate of our different States, which differs only from the House of Representatives, in being a small body and consequently chosen from larger districts. It would accordingly be impossible to establish this *duplication* of the legislative body, upon any *philosophical principle*, drawn from the different character of the Constituencies represented by the two bodies. Even in England, at the present day, the House of Peers is a very different body, in its relations to the State, from what it was in the origin of the parliamentary organization. But the utility of a twofold chamber is one of those empirical mysteries of representative government, which are learned by practice; by the positive experience of England and the United States of America in its favor; by the negative experience of your Convention in 1793 against it. I am so sure of the necessity of two Chambers, that I most fully concur with you in the opinion *"que si la Constitution actuelle n'est pas bientôt modifiée, la république n'aura aucune durée."*[20] Not only will the *Republic* be short lived; but no constitutional monarchy can stand with a single chamber. I am aware that the house of Peers, under your Restoration, was a feeble body, unable to cope with the *Deputés*. That arose from the facts, that the hereditary principle had been so undermined in France, and the Royal Prerogative had not regained its hold on the public mind. But if you cannot have an hereditary house of Lords like England; and if a chamber of Peers nominated for life by the King does not command respect; establish an elective Senate to be chosen in large districts, perhaps by the Departments.[21]

But I feel the absurdity of attempting to discuss these topics, with a person who is so thoroughly versed as yourself in the theory of constitutional government, and who has studied with so much care its practical operation. I much wish you would write to me, and give me some information as to the present state and the probable future of your new Republic. I need not attempt to tell you how completely electrified we were last year with the events of February; how much we sympathized with you in those terrible days of June. That you are not yet *au bout*[22] seems certain; your destiny will no doubt be affected by events in foreign countries, which France cannot control. I look forward to a succession of action and reaction, between the different powerful members of the European family, of a most critical character.

We are at present quite prosperous in the U. States. The Mexican war was a fearful experiment.[23] Our President plunged into it haphazard and for mere party motives. It resulted in bringing forward as a candidate for the Presidency, a general whose politics were opposed to the President, and his election has been a defeat of the party which made the war.[24] The territorial acquisition of California – with its almost fabulous, though well authenticated abundance of gold – will be productive no doubt of serious consequences both economical and political of a grave character. But their nature can as yet be only conjectured. I fear our success in Mexico will teach a lesson of territorial ambition and military adventure to my countrymen of a most pernicious character.

Though our correspondence has been interrupted for many years, you may have learned that after the close of my mission to London (from which I was recalled by Mr. Polk), I was chosen President of the University[25] in this place. My health suffered so much by the labors and confinement incident to the office, that, after holding it for three years, I was compelled to resign it. My movements for the future are undecided. I should take great pleasure in visiting Europe, renewing my intercourse with numerous friends both in England and on the Continent, especially in France, and in contemplating from a near point of view the mighty changes in progress. But whether I am able to effect this purpose is quite doubtful. In the mean time I should be extremely grateful to hear from you, and I beg to say (what is hardly necessary, but what in these critical times may not be wholly superfluous) that you may rely on the entire discretion, which I shall practice, in reference to any facts you may communicate or opinions you may express to me.

Should you have the opportunity, I pray you to remember me kindly to those friends in Paris who may recollect me, and especially to your ancient colleague M. de Beaumont, and to the members of the Lafayette family.

I remain, my dear M. de Tocqueville, sincerely yours,

Edward Everett

P. S. A letter would reach me by the English steamers dropped into your Post office *sans façon*.[26]

Beinecke Rare Book and Manuscript Library, Yale University, Uncat MSS 324; also available as Bonnel copy, Paquet 12, pp. 15–20.

44. Richard Rush to Alexis de Tocqueville

H. E. M. de Tocqueville   Legation of the U. States
Min. For. Aff.   Paris, June 7, 1849

Sir, I had the honor to receive Your Excellency's note informing me that the President of the Republic has confided to you the Portfolio of Foreign Affairs.

I receive, Sir, this information with peculiar satisfaction and shall lose no time in imparting it to my government, regarding it as a new pledge that the exercise of the important functions of the office in your hands will tend to promote and strengthen the harmony and friendship so happily existing between the Am[erica]n and French Republics. In these feelings I pray Y[our] E[xcellency] to accept assurances etc.

Rich[ar]d Rush

Firestone Library, Princeton University. Rush Family Papers (C0079), IV. Papers, Documents, and Correspondence (1846–1849) Relating to the French Mission, Correspondence, in Letterbook, Box 11, No. 317.

45. Alexis de Tocqueville to George Bancroft[27]

Paris, June 15, 1849

My dear Mr. Bancroft,

Many thanks for your letter of June 5; I was very grateful to receive it. I saw in it not only the expression of your sentiments to which I attach great value, but also a token of sympathy which was granted to me in the name of your great and happy nation, for which I have retained so much affection and gratitude.

I accepted a position in government against my inclinations;[28] I was ill in my bed when I was offered the ministry. I accepted it only in the hope of contributing to the restoration of order and, as you say, to the strengthening of the moderate and constitutional Republic. My friends and I are devoted to this great cause. I want to serve it with my feeble means by trying to maintain peace in the world. I do not know if we shall succeed, nor do I know if success is at all possible. But I hope, at all events, that all sensible people of good faith will be grateful to us for having tried to do so.

Believe in all my sentiments of high consideration and friendship.

Alexis de Tocqueville

46. Alexis de Tocqueville to Richard Rush[29]

Paris, June 27, 1849

Sir,

Please allow me to express the profound regret that your letter has caused me.[30] It is with great sadness that I see you leaving the position you have occupied here and which you have filled so well in the interest of your country and ours, since I like to merge these interests in my thoughts. I am sure that the President of the Republic and the members of his government will share the same regret; but I shall feel these regrets more so than anyone else. The extremely pleasant personal relations that I have had with you led me to place great importance upon seeing you remain among us.

Please, Sir, remember me and Madame de Tocqueville to Misses Rush and believe in all my sentiments of high consideration.

Alexis de Tocqueville

47. Richard Rush to Alexis de Tocqueville

| H. E. M. de Tocqueville | Legation of the U. States |
| Min. For. Aff. | Paris, July 8, 1849 |

Mr. Rush, Minister of the U. States, has the honor to acknowledge with his thanks the new ticket of admission to the Diplomatic tribune of the National Legislative Assembly, which H[is] E[xcellency] M. de Tocqueville, Min. of For. Aff. has had the kindness to send him, with his note of yesterday. And he prays etc.

Firestone Library, Princeton University. Rush Family Papers (C0079), IV. Papers, Documents, and Correspondence (1846–1849) Relating to the French Mission, Correspondence, in Letterbook, Box 11, No. 332.

48. Richard Rush to Alexis de Tocqueville

Legation of the U. States
July 31, 1849

The Minister of the United States has the honor to present his best compliments to H[is] E[xcellency] the Minister of Foreign Affairs, and in answer to his note only just now received, begs to state that he has no information leading him to suppose that either Mr. James Hendebert or Mr. John L. Hodge, appointed Consul of the U. States for Marseilles and Lyons, are already domiciled at those places. The despatch conveying the commissions enclosed to H[is] E[xcellency] on the 27th inst., was received by the Minister of the U. States on the 25th, and did not mention the places of their actual residence at present. Mr. Rush is happy to avail himself of this new occasion to tender to M. [de] Tocqueville the assurance of his distinguished consideration.

Firestone Library, Princeton University. Rush Family Papers (C0079), IV. Papers, Documents, and Correspondence (1846–1849) Relating to the French Mission, Correspondence, in Letterbook, Box 11, No. 338.

49. Richard Rush to Alexis de Tocqueville

Legation of the U. States
Paris, August 4, 1849

Mr. Rush, Minister of the U. States, has the honor to present his compliments to M. de Tocqueville, Minister of Foreign Affairs, and to represent to H[is] E[xcellency] the following case.

That Mr. Erhard Richter, a native of Germany, a person of good repute, domiciled for several years in New York, proprietor of real estate there and having duly declared his intention according to law of becoming a citizen of the U. States, arrived lately in Europe on his private affairs with the intention of a speedy return to New York, was arrested in some part of Alsace and is now imprisoned at Strasbourg under a charge or suspicion of having been concerned in the disturbances at Baden; but that by the information communicated to Mr. Rush, he is fully innocent of the charge, the most that can be alleged against him being the use of some unguarded words, and that he has done nothing whatever in violation of the laws, the security or the tranquility of France.

If these be the facts, Mr. Rush prays that H[is] E[xcellency] will have the goodness to cause such directions to be given as may lead to the indulgent consideration of his case in reference to any demand for his surrender from the soil of France by any foreign power; as well as for his discharge from prison at Strasbourg that he may return to this home and family in the U. States.

And Mr. Rush gladly avails himself of this opp[ortunit]y to present to M. de Tocqueville the assurances etc.

Firestone Library, Princeton University. Rush Family Papers (C0079), IV. Papers, Documents, and Correspondence (1846–1849) Relating to the French Mission, Correspondence, in Letterbook, Box 11, No. 339.

50. Alexis de Tocqueville to Richard Rush

1849[31]

My dear Sir,

You had written to me that you would come to see me this morning at half past nine. I waited for you until a quarter past ten, after which I had to go to a cabinet meeting. I add that I shall be happy to see you at whatever hour you might return during the day. Should it be possible for you, I would prefer half past four.

Please accept the expression of my most distinguished consideration.

Alex. [de] Tocqueville

51. Alexis de Tocqueville to Richard Rush

Paris, Wednesday, August 8, 1849

My dear Sir,

I have learned with great regret that you have come twice to see me without finding me. You told my ushers that you would be willing to make a new attempt to meet me tomorrow morning at ten o'clock. I hope you would not mind if I ask you to move the time of your visit forward a little and to arrive at my home at half past nine. If so I shall have more time to talk to you.[32]

Please believe in all my sentiments of high consideration and friendship.

Alexis de Tocqueville

Mr. Rush, Plenipotentiary Minister of the United States of America

52. Alexis de Tocqueville to Richard Rush

Ministry of Foreign Affairs   Monday morning [August, 1849]
The Office [of the Minister]

My dear Sir,

Please forgive me if I have not thanked you as yet for the spontaneous visit that you were so kind as to pay me. Be reassured that I was very touched by it. Madame de Tocqueville was equally extremely moved by the visit that the Mlles Rush were so kind to pay her during her absence. She expects to seek them out as soon as she is able to do so. Moreover, Sir, you should not doubt at all my eagerness to come to see you, as soon as I have a *single* moment of freedom.

Please believe in all my sentiments of high consideration and friendship.

Alexis de Tocqueville

Mr. Rush, Special Envoy of the United States of America

53. Richard Rush to Alexis de Tocqueville

H. E. M. de Tocqueville   Legation of the U. States
Min. For. Affs   Paris, September 10, 1849

Mr. Rush, Minister of the U. States, has the honor to present his compliments to H[is] E[xcellency] M. de Tocqueville, Minister of Foreign Affairs, and in answer to the inquiries contained in his note of the 8th inst. Respecting Mr. Ruhl lately appointed Consul of the U. States at Bordeaux, begs leave to say that he is not a resident of France; nor is this Legation aware of his possessing a commercial establishment at Bordeaux. Mr. Rush prays the Minister of Foreign Affairs to accept etc.

Firestone Library, Princeton University. Rush Family Papers (C0079), IV. Papers, Documents, and Correspondence (1846–1849) Relating to the French Mission, Correspondence, in Letterbook, Box 11, No. 345.

54. Richard Rush to Alexis de Tocqueville

H. E. M. de Tocqueville   Legation of the U. States
Min. For. Affs   Paris, September 14, 1849

Sir,

I beg leave to state to Y[our] E[xcellency] that I have this day received a note from Mr. Barringer Esq. now in London, on his way to Madrid, to which court he is appointed Minister Plenipotentiary from the U. States. Intending to pass through France, and expecting to arrive in two or three days at Boulogne, I have the honor to request that Y[our] E[xcellency] will have the goodness to cause such directions to be given to the Custom House officers of that port as may be usual, to pass his baggage and effects with that of his family and suite without examination or detention.

I pray Y[our] E[xcellency] to receive assurances etc.

Richard Rush

Firestone Library, Princeton University. Rush Family Papers (C0079), IV. Papers, Documents, and Correspondence (1846–1849) Relating to the French Mission, Correspondence, in Letterbook, Box 11, No. 345.

55. Richard Rush to Alexis de Tocqueville

H. E. M. de Tocqueville   Legation of the United States
Minister of Foreign Affairs   Paris, October 3, 1849

Sir,

Having verbally informed your Excellency that Mr. Rives, a distinguished citizen of the United States formerly accredited to this government as Minister Plenipotentiary, and now appointed my successor, has arrived in Paris, I have to beg that Your Excellency will have the goodness to appoint a time when I may have the honor of presenting him to you in that capacity.[33]

It is with great pleasure that I avail myself of this occasion of tendering to Your Excellency the cordial assurances of high consideration with which I have the honor to be

Your most obedient
humble servant,
Richard Rush

Firestone Library, Princeton University. Rush Family Papers (C0079), IV. Papers, Documents, and Correspondence (1846–1849) Relating to the French Mission, Correspondence, in Letterbook, Box 11, No. 347.

56. Alexis de Tocqueville to Richard Rush

Paris, Friday, October 5, 1849

Sir,

I would very much like to converse with you. I would be very obliged if you could come to my home between 5 and 6, if that is possible.

Please accept the expression of my most distinguished consideration.

Alexis de Tocqueville

57. Richard Rush to Alexis de Tocqueville

H. E. M. de Tocqueville   Legation of the United States
Minister of Foreign Affairs   Paris, October 6, 1849

Sir,

It is known to Your Excellency by communications I have had the honor to make in person that the government of the United States has recalled me from this mission.

A letter has been addressed to [the] President of the Republic by the President of the United States announcing my recall, and I now beg leave to enclose an official copy of it requesting that Your Excellency will be pleased to take the directions of the President of the Republic as to the time which I may be honored with an audience to deliver the original, and have the goodness to afford me information of the same.

I seize this last occasion of renewing to Your Excellency constant assurances of the high consideration with which I have the honor to be

Your most faithful and
most obedient servant,
Richard Rush

Firestone Library, Princeton University. Rush Family Papers (C0079), IV. Papers, Documents, and Correspondence (1846–1849) Relating to the French Mission, Correspondence, in Letterbook, Box 11, No. 347.

58. Alexis de Tocqueville to Richard Rush

Ministry of Foreign Affairs
The Office [of the Minister]
Paris, October 10, 1849

My dear Sir,

I do not want to send you the document that you requested without expressing to you my regret for not having been at home to receive you and to say farewell. I wish sincerely that your return to your country takes place under the most favorable auspices. I hope, as I do myself, that you will find the United States as prosperous as you can possibly desire. I do not need to tell you that the unfortunate incident that has just occurred[34] does not change at all the sentiments I have for the American nation nor the opinions which I have formerly expressed about that great people. I believe that, in these circumstances, its government acted with great haste and without giving itself the time to get to know the real state of things. Above all, I believe that the publication of official documents was not in keeping with diplomatic usages and was, at all events, very premature. But, I repeat, the unpleasant impression caused by these circumstances does not change in any way whatsoever the sentiments of strong and sincere sympathy that I have for a country in which I was previously received so well and to which I shall always return with pleasure. In this respect, the impressions of the minister do not have any influence on those of the private individual.

I take this opportunity to express to you again how much we regret your departure and to ask you to accept the expression of my most distinguished consideration.

Al. de Tocqueville

59. W. W. Mann to Alexis de Tocqueville

Paris, November 23, 1849

My dear Sir,

Will you excuse the liberty I take in communicating to you the enclosed *letter* of the Paris correspondent of the New York *Courier and Enquirer?* You will remark in it a not unkind allusion to yourself.[35] I pray you to believe, Sir, that my sole motive in making the communication is the sincere desire to remove an unfavorable impression which the unexplained statements of "Cosmopolite" are likely to make in the *United States* where the name of *de Tocqueville* is known, respected, and admired by every intelligent well read man. I dare say the charges of *La Presse*,[36] to which reference is made, have been already answered through some public medium which has escaped my notice. If so, will you not have the kindness to direct my attention to such articles?

After you have read the letter of "Cosmopolite" please reinclose it to

Most respectfully,
Y[ou]r ob[edien]t ser[van]t
Wm. W. Mann

8 Place du Palais Bourbon

Beinecke Rare Book and Manuscript Library, Yale University, Uncat MSS 324; also available as Bonnel copy in MS Vault Tocqueville, D II a, Paquet 12, pp. 72–73.

The following explanatory note was written by W. W. Mann on November 27, 1849, drawing upon his letter of November 23, 1849. The note can be found at Beinecke Rare Book and Manuscript Library, Uncat MSS 324; it is also available as Bonnel copy in MS Vault Tocqueville, D II a, Paquet 12, pp. 73–74.

Nov. 27, 1849

Mr. Mann would have been happy to find in the little incident to which allusion was made in his late note, the occasion of making the acquaintance of M. de Tocqueville: but he regrets that an engagement for tomorrow morning will deprive him of the pleasure of accepting M. de T.'s invitation to breakfast.

Mr. Mann had no intention to provoke from M. de Tocqueville, for publication, a formal reply to the charge of *La Presse*. M. de T. pronounces the charge a calumny. *That* is quite sufficient to satisfy every one. *La Presse* has misinterpreted and perhaps mis-stated the facts. *Du reste,*[37] the American public will probably be of the opinion of Mr. Rush, with whom Mr. Mann conversed upon the subject – viz. that in order to entitle a charge derogatory to M. de Tocqueville, to the slightest consideration, it must rest upon something *more substantial* than the malicious insinuations and inferences, however ingenious, of *La Presse*.

M. de. Tocqueville is in error in supposing *Cosmopolite* to be the name of an American *journal*. It is but the borrowed name of a letter writer, the correspondent in Paris of an American journal. The printed letter, signed *"Cosmopolite"* to which the attention of M. de T. was called, was published in *The Courier and Enquirer* of New-York, a journal which M. de T. will probably recognize as at the head of the Whig press in the United States.

60. George Sumner to Alexis de Tocqueville

Sunday, 4 [December 1849][38]

Dear Sir,

Mr. Mann of whom I have talked to you is called *Dudley* Mann. I am not sure that he is in Paris at the present moment.

There is another Mr. Mann, who lives on *rue de Bourgogne*. He is the correspondent of a New York newspaper, and unlike Mr. Dudley Mann, he is not an agent of the United States government.

This fact will perhaps modify your plans regarding the answer that you should give him.

Yours devoted,
Geo[rge] Sumner

Beinecke Rare Book and Manuscript Library, Yale University, Uncat MSS 324.

61. Alexis de Tocqueville to Edward Everett

Paris, December 12, 1849

My dear Sir,

Please allow me to recommend particularly to your attention M. de Cessac, who is traveling to America. M. de Cessac is the son of the person with the same name who was successively an important member of the first

Constituent Assembly, Minister of War during the greater part of the reign of Napoléon, a Peer of France, and member of the French Academy.[39] I replaced him in that illustrious company. His son will have the honor of explaining to you the reason that has made him undertake the voyage to the United States.[40] I hope that you will receive him with kindness. For this I will be especially grateful to you.

Please accept the expression of my sentiments of high consideration and friendship.

Alexis de Tocqueville

62. Alexis de Tocqueville to George Bancroft

Paris, December 12, 1849

My dear Sir,

I have the special honor of recommending to your kind attention M. de Cessac, who is traveling to America. M. de Cessac is the son of the famous minister of the Emperor Napoléon. His goal in coming to the United States is to deal with the regrettable affair of MM. de Montesquiou, the eldest of whom, in a moment of insanity, according to the reports, committed several murders in Louisville. As you know, MM. de Montesquiou belong to one of the oldest and most honorable families in France. M. de Cessac is a close relative of the convicted and he has accepted the painful mission of going to meet them in order to inquire into what has occurred and to help his relatives, should this be possible. I would be very grateful for any expression of interest that you could give to M. de Cessac.

Please accept, Sir, the expression of all my sentiments of high consideration and friendship.

A. de Tocqueville

63. Edward Everett to Alexis de Tocqueville

Cambridge, U. States of America
Jan. 8, 1850

My dear Sir,

M. de Cessac, in hastening through Boston the other day, had not time to come to this place, nor did I have the pleasure of seeing him. I received the letter which you wrote to me by him; but not till after he had proceeded on his journey. I have written to him at St. Louis, and have sent him a letter to my old congressional friend and associate Mr. Edward Bates of that place. Mr. Bates is a lawyer of great eminence; a man of principle and honor; and should M. de Cessac consult him, he will be sure to receive the best advice.

I was quite sorry to hear of your retirement from the ministry, and I regretted while you were in office the occurrence of a momentary mis-understanding with the government of the United States, which happily seems to have left no unpleasant consequences.[41]

When I regret your retirement from the government, it is not on your own account; for public service, in the present state of the world, either in Europe or America, is not to be coveted by men of character. I was very sorry that the Department of Foreign Affairs in France, that department on which depends the peace of Europe, should lose the benefit of your intelligence and moderation.[42]

Your President will find it impossible to unite the two systems of responsible ministerial government and uncontrolled executive power. I presume he does not wish to unite them; but to pass, as rapidly as the public opinion of France will permit, from the former to the latter. He wants, I fear, the capacity to follow in his uncle's steps; – although thus far he has certainly exhibited greater *moyens*[43] than the world gave him *crédit*[44] for.

I should be extremely gratified to receive information from you as to the present condition and aspect of things in France; and I remain,

My dear M. de Tocqueville,
With the highest respect,
Very faithfully yours,
Edward Everett

P.S. A letter thrown into the Post Office in Paris will at all times be sure to find me.

Beinecke Rare Book and Manuscript Library, Yale University, Uncat MSS 324; also available as Bonnel copy, MS Vault Tocqueville, D II a, Paquet 12, pp. 20–21.

64. Alexis de Tocqueville to George Bancroft

Paris, February 15, 1850

Sir,

I am limiting myself to giving two letters of recommendation to M. de Bois-le-Comte[45] who will represent us in America. One of them is for you. I hope that M. de Bois-le-Comte will be able to hand it over to you in person and will find in you what I myself have found, that is, a lot of kindness. He fully deserves to be treated with kindness for he is a worthy man, as honorable in his private as in his public life, and one who will receive, I hope, a warm welcome in the United States. I take all the more interest in his success since, even before the regrettable behavior of Mr. Clayton became known in France, I was the one who nominated him for the post in Washington, as the replacement for M. Poussin.[46] Hence, I particularly wish that M. Bois-le-Comte be received and esteemed as he has the right to be and that he should meet people as distinguished as you who would be willing to assist him.

Please accept, Sir, the expression of my special consideration and friendship.

A. de Tocqueville

65. Alexis de Tocqueville to Edward Everett

Paris, February 15, 1850

Sir,

M. de Bois-le-Comte, our new minister to the United States, has asked me for two or three letters of recommendation for distinguished persons with whom, in my view, he could establish useful and friendly relations. I have naturally thought of you. This should not come as a surprise to you since my personal recollections have guided me in this choice. Hence I take the liberty of asking you to receive M. de Bois-le-Comte as he has the right to be received, that is, as a worthy man who has rendered us great service at his embassy in Sardinia and who, I am sure, will render us even more important services in the position which is now entrusted to him. I myself recommended him to the President when, even before the unfortunate quarrel between Mr. Clayton and myself took place, I had recalled M. Poussin. M. de Bois-le-Comte is a man as respectable in his private as in his public life, and I hope that he will gain the sympathy of all enlightened Americans. Here he belongs to the republican party, but he would like the republic of Washington and not that of Robespierre.

I would like to thank you, Sir, for what you so kindly did for my compatriot, M. de Cessac, and for his relatives, who seem to me more worthy of pity than anger. I hope that the American courts will think so too.

Our country is calm and more prosperous than one could believe after such violent crises. But confidence in the future continues to be lacking, and although sixty years of revolution have rendered this feeling of instability less detrimental to social progress and less unpleasant to us than to other peoples, it has produced a number of very disturbing results. This great nation in its entirety finds itself in the state of mind of a sailor at sea or a soldier in the field. It seeks to do the best every day, without thinking of tomorrow. But such a state is precarious and dangerous. Moreover, it is not limited to us. With the exception of Russia, in the whole of continental Europe one can see society undergoing a profound transformation and the old world that has crumbled into pieces. Please believe me when I say that all the restorations of former powers that are taking place around us are nothing but temporary incidents which do not prevent the great drama from following its course. This drama is the complete destruction of the old society and the building in its stead of I do not know what kind of human edifice whose contours the mind cannot clearly yet perceive.

Farewell, my dear Sir. You know the high esteem that I have for you and the great importance I always attach to your letters.

A. de Tocqueville

66. Edward Everett to Alexis de Tocqueville

Cambridge, U. S. A.
March 29, 1850

My dear M. de Tocqueville,

I received yesterday from Washington a note from M. Bois-le-Comte[47] with your letter of the 15th of January. I have written to him this morning to say, that if he comes to the Eastern States, during his mission – which I think he will hardly fail to do – I shall be most happy to make his personal acquaintance and to render him every service in my power. I have not heard from M. de Cessac since I wrote to him at St. Louis. I perceive by the papers that Mr. Edward Bates, the lawyer to whom I recommended him, has appeared as his counsel. The painful affair could not be in better hands.

M. Bois-le-Comte, as you will have perceived from the newspapers, has been officially received by the President. The addresses on both sides were of the most satisfactory description.

I regret to find you under the conviction that the continent of Europe is destined to still further and more critical changes. No one can be insensible – certainly no American – that there is much in the systems of government which existed before February 1848 that greatly required reformation. How deeply it is to be regretted, that the continental governments cannot enjoy the benefit of that *safety valve*, which for a century and a half has preserved England from convulsions; I mean the facility of making gradual changes in the constitution, by parliamentary means! This and the moral stability derived from religious education appear to me the main protection of England.

We are going through a crisis in the United States.[48] That terrible antagonism between freedom and slavery which you witnessed, and so well described in your book, has, since you were here, increased in force. The acquisition of territory from Mexico and the rapid settlement of California have forced the question on Congress in various forms. The Californians have formed a constitution of state government which excludes slavery. They have done this, although the emigrants from the free states were not a majority in the constituent assembly. The southern members of Congress are annoyed at this prohibition; but they cannot well resist the admission of California into the Union *on that ground*, because it is their favorite maxim, that this is a subject which the people of each state must settle for themselves. They accordingly object to the boundaries of California as unreasonably comprehensive, and purpose to couple with her admission to the Union the passage of more stringent laws for the extradition of fugitive slaves; an incident of slavery of all others most distasteful to the free states. I am however of opinion that California will come into the Union at this session of Congress. The territory included within her boundaries is about equal to the whole space between Charleston S. Carolina and Boston, east of the Mississippi! It will of course be hereafter subdivided.

It always affords me great pleasure to hear from you; and I pray you to believe me, my dear M. de Tocqueville, ever sincerely yours,

Edward Everett

P. S. I read the article of our friend Mr. Senior on Lamartine's book with the greatest pleasure, from knowing that it had been approved by you.[49]

Beinecke Rare Book and Manuscript Library, Yale University, Uncat MSS 324; also available as Bonnel copy, MS Vault Tocqueville, D II a, Paquet 12, pp. 26–28.

67. John C. Spencer to Alexis de Tocqueville

Albany, State of New York
July 3, 1850

Dear Sir,

One of my respected fellow citizens, Mr. George W. Newell,[50] is about to visit Europe, and expecting to be in Paris naturally desires an introduction to a gentleman who has done so much to illustrate the political and social condition of our country. Mr. Newell has had important public stations under our State government and is well informed on all public subjects. I beg to commend him to your consideration and ask for him such facilities for inquiry as your numerous avocations, and the many calls upon you by Americans, may enable you to dispense.

> Respectfully and truly,
> Your friend and servant,
> John G. Spencer

Beinecke Rare Book and Manuscript Library, Yale University, Uncat MSS 324; also available as Bonnel copy, MS Vault Tocqueville, D II a, Paquet 12, p. 51.

68. George Bancroft to Alexis de Tocqueville

New York, October 14, 1850

My dear M. de Tocqueville,

I beg leave to ask for my particular friend Mr. Sedgwick, the honor of being presented to you. He is highly esteemed among us as among those who take the lead in jurisprudence; and to general culture adds the merit of firm, liberal and statesmanlike opinions on public affairs. The care of his health takes him to Europe; and nothing, I am sure, can more conduce to his restoration, than the cultivated society of Paris.[51]

I read with great interest and hearty conscience your remarks on the reception of the President by your constituents. I hope all France will listen to the counsels you suggested.[52]

Let me ask to be presented most respectfully and most kindly to Madame de Tocqueville.

> I remain ever
> Very faithfully yours,
> George Bancroft

Beinecke Rare Book and Manuscript Library, Yale University, Uncat MSS 324; also available as Bonnel copy, MS Vault Tocqueville, D II a, Paquet 12, pp. 39–40.

69. George Bancroft to Alexis de Tocqueville

New York, June 13, 1851

Dear M. de Tocqueville,

My friend Mr. Tappan,[53] one of the very best metaphysicians in the United States, visits Paris. Pray spare for him some half hour, that in returning home, he may have the satisfaction of remembering you as one whom he has seen personally. I need not add how well he knows your writings: every American does that. You will find Mr. Tappan very sensible as well as very modest. He holds a very high rank among our men of letters, and will return after a short stay in Paris, to rise, I trust, still higher in that career.

> I beg my best regards to Madame de Tocqueville,
> and remain ever faithfully
> yours,
> George Bancroft

Beinecke Rare Book and Manuscript Library, Yale University, Uncat MSS 324; also available as Bonnel copy, MS Vault Tocqueville, D II a, Pacquet 12, pp. 40–41.

70. W. W. Mann to Alexis de Tocqueville

Paris, June 28, 1851

My dear Sir,

An American gentleman, a friend of mine, President of the Legislative Assembly of the State of New York, is at present in Paris on a visit of a few days.[54]

He desires before leaving to attend a sitting of the French Legislative Assembly: and I know not to whom I can apply with more confidence than yourself, who so well understands, and has[55] so profoundly commented [on] American institutions, for procuring this gratification to one of our most promising young public men.

I am sure there is no public man in France to whom he would more pleasantly remember the having been indebted for the favour.[56]

Will you oblige us by sending me a couple of tickets, one to be used by him, the other by myself, for the sitting of Tuesday next the first of July?

Accept, Sir, in advance our thanks with the assurance of our high consideration,

W. W. Mann
8 Place du Palais Bourbon

Beinecke Rare Book and Manuscript Library, Yale University, MS Vault Tocqueville, D II a, also available as a Bonnel copy, Paquet 12, pp. 106–107.

71. Alexis de Tocqueville to W. W. Mann[57]

Versailles, July 2, 1851

Sir,

I have been in the country for several days and your letter of the 28th reached me only yesterday. Hence, I have been unable to send you the tickets that you have requested. Moreover, I could not have obtained them from here. I hope to make up for this by sending you the attached letter addressed to the Chief Usher of the Assembly. The letter, I hope, will give you and your friend the opportunity to attend our debates. I do not need to add that it is with great pleasure that I render this small service to you. I consider the Americans as compatriots and it is always a pleasure for me to be useful to them.

Please accept, Sir, the expression of my most distinguished consideration.

A. de Tocqueville

72. W. W. Mann to Alexis de Tocqueville

Paris, July 12, 1851

My dear Sir,

The kind letter that you were good enough to address to me the 2nd inst.[58] from Versailles inclosing a note to the *chef des huissiers*[59] reached me so late that Mr. Raymond of the assembly of New York for whom I then especially desired entrance into the assembly of France, *was made unable to make use of it.*

This note is therefore to inform you that unless [I receive] from you an intimation that you would prefer I should not do so, I propose to make use of your note to the *chef des huissiers* to obtain admission into the National Assembly on *Monday* or *Tuesday* next, in order that with an American friend I may have[60] the pleasure of being present at the discussion of your very able and statesmanlike report upon the revision of the constitution: a report that is worthy of the author of *Democracy in America*, and which possesses a quality still rarer than ability and statesmanship – viz. a patriotism that forgetful of self and party, anxiously selects, and then resolutely marches upon what seems the least of many dangers. But, alas, it is not the enlightened patriotism of any one man that can resolve the present crisis and save Liberty in France. A Washington himself, if you had one, would have to retire in despair before the irreconcilable parties which rule the country, or be overwhelmed in the attempt to oppose them. But come what may, there will be consolation in the thought of having earnestly and intelligently striven to overcome them: and that consolation will ever belong to the reporter of the committee on revision.

Respectfully your obedient servant,
W. W. Mann
8 place du Palais Bourbon

Beinecke Rare Book and Manuscript Library, Yale University, Uncat MSS 324; also available as Bonnel copy, MS Vault Tocqueville, D II a, Paquet 12, pp. 105–106.

73. Alexis de Tocqueville to Edward Everett

Paris, August 5, 1851

Sir,

One of my best friends and most eminent colleagues, M. Ampère,[61] a member of the French Academy and the Academy of Inscriptions and Belles-Lettres, and a professor at the Collège de France, is going to America with the intention of spending a few months there. I did not think I could render him a greater service than by directing him to you. I recommend him to your attention. Both his merit and his works speak for him better than I can.

I eagerly avail myself of this opportunity to thank you for sending me your two volumes entitled *Orations and Speeches*.[62] I have received them with gratitude and am reading them with the greatest interest. I have placed them in the best location of my library and I carefully keep them there. Nothing that reaches me from America is indifferent to me; but I attach a particular value to anything that comes from you.

For my part, I hope that, from time to time, you think, if not of me, at least of France, whose situation is so singular and so critical. Nobody can predict what will happen to us a year from now. Nonetheless, I do not believe in the likelihood of long and violent crises. I have more confidence in the common sense of the people than in the wisdom of those who are at the helm. Everything that has happened since the revolution of 1848 has shown the progress that this kind of moderation and practical wisdom, born out of experience, has made among our people. I do not believe that any nation, taken so much by surprise by a great revolution, could have conducted itself with greater firmness and more tranquillity than the French during the last three years. Even today, in spite of the anxiety caused by the approach of the year 1852,[63] everyone pursues their business with energy and perseverance, as if they were certain of tomorrow and, contrary to predictions, the development of commerce does not slow down.

Farewell, Sir. Do you expect to return to Europe one day, where your worth is known and esteemed? For my part, I would very much wish that this were the case. Please accept, in the meantime, the expression of my sentiments of great consideration and friendship.

A. de Tocqueville

74. Alexis de Tocqueville to Richard Rush

Paris, August 6, 1851

Sir,

Please allow me to introduce to you one of my oldest and best friends, M. Ampère. He is the son of a famous scholar with the same name who helped the natural sciences make immense progress. He is himself a most eminent member of our Institute and one of our most brilliant writers. I would be particularly grateful if you would be willing to receive him with kindness.

I eagerly avail myself of this opportunity of bringing myself to your recollection and to tell you that I have not forgotten and shall never forget the excellent relations that we enjoyed together during your sojourn in Europe. I hope they left the same impression on you as they did on me.

Please remember me to your daughters and believe in all my sentiments of friendship.

A. de Tocqueville

75. Maurice Wakerman to Alexis de Tocqueville

Fairfield, Connecticut
U. States of America,
Nov[ember] 29, 1851

Sir,

You will doubtless feel surprised to receive a letter from an entire stranger. But when you are informed that the object of it is simply to obtain your autograph, I trust it will be deemed pardonable. If at your leisure, you do me the honour of acknowledging its receipt, I shall regard it as a favour. Your name, as well as political character, is generally well understood. On this side of the water, among others, I entertain a high regard for your talents, as well as private virtues. I recollect of your traveling through this country some years since, and of having published an account of the same, soon after your return in France, in which, (upon the whole) you have done in more justice, than British travelers have usually awarded us. I did not have the pleasure of seeing you while among us. But I am quite sure, that you made a very favorable impression wherever you went. As it does not become an American Citizen to address another otherwise than in a direct and candid manner, I trust you will receive what I have to say with a calm and unruffled temper. It is quite possible, Sir, that some of the suggestions I shall offer may be worthy of your attentive reflection. I write with a knowledge of the sentiments of my countrymen, both North and South. The American people feel that they owe a debt of gratitude to France, for nobly coming to their aid, in their struggle with Great Britain, to obtain our liberties. And there is a deep interest felt among us in the success of the movement, now in progress among your people, for the establishment of a Republican Government. We hope that you will be induced to accept our form of Government as a model, feeling quite sure, that if you do so, the people of France, cannot be otherwise than prosperous and happy.

With others of my countrymen, I very much regretted the movement, recently made by your Government in relation to Cuba. The recent attack upon Cuba was made by a lawless set of adventurers, who went there without the sanction or knowledge of this Government.[64] One unvarying principle of this Government, since its formation (as you are doubtless aware) has been the observance of a strict non-interference in the affairs of other Powers, and an equally firm resolve, that other Powers, shall not be permitted to meddle with our own. I scarcely need say to you, that this principle will be maintained to the letter, at all hazards. If therefore our Government should think proper to deal with Spain and Cuba, in any manner she may choose, it is no concern of France or England. And I beg to assure you, Sir, that it will be extremely unfortunate for either Great Britain or France, or both countries combined, to provoke a quarrel with this Government, by interfering in a matter that does not concern them. Knowing the temper of my countrymen, and their sentiments on this subject, I beg distinctly to assure you, that if the American people are pushed into a war with France and England, my countrymen will not accept of a peace, short of depriving both Great Britain and France, of their possession on this Continent, and the islands adjacent.

It is a matter of surprise to us, that France should allow itself to be made a stool-pigeon of, by Great Britain. The latter is quite willing that the former shall do the fighting (not having the stomach to encounter us alone), and in a division of the spoils (if any) come in for a share. We have supposed that France had by this time understood England well enough, not to permit herself to be made a tool of by the latter. The truth perhaps is, our brother of England dare not provoke us to an encounter. He therefore persuades his French neighbour to fight for him. But I fear I am trespassing upon your forbearance. As I am a stranger, I beg to refer to the Honorable John Griswold of New-York, who has commercial relations with the Messrs. Baring of London. With sentiments of high regard,

I have the honour to be, Sir,

Very faithfully y[ou]r ob[edien]t serv[an]t,

Maurice Wakerman

Beinecke Rare Book and Manuscript Library, Yale University, Uncat MSS 324; also available as Bonnel copy, MS Vault Tocqueville, D II a, "Bonnel's copies of letters from the Americans."

76. Edward Everett to Alexis de Tocqueville

(Confidential)   Boston, March 15, 1852

My dear M. de Tocqueville,

I have more than one very agreeable letter from you unanswered, especially those in which you did me the favor to recommend to me M. de Boislecomte[65] and M. Ampère. Of the former gentleman, during his short residence in this country, I saw but little; enough however to make me deeply regret that I did not see more of him and of his amiable family. They were much esteemed at Washington. I was rather more fortunate with regard to M. Ampère. It will always afford me sincere pleasure to be useful to any friends of yours coming to this country.

I forbear to write to you on the subject of politics, and the particular motive of this letter is altogether personal to myself. Some time ago, M. Alex. Vattemare proposed to me to present a copy of my *Orations and Speeches* to the Academy of Moral and Political Sciences of the Institute, which I was extremely happy to do. In due time I received the usual letter of thanks from M. Mignet. In transmitting this letter to me, M. Vattemare expressed the opinion that before long the Academy would do me the honor to elect me as a foreign member. This was wholly unexpected by me, nor had the subject directly or indirectly attended to in my correspondence with M. V. with whom I am not *intimement lié*.[66] I answered, of course, that I should be much flattered by such a mark of the favorable opinion of the Academy; and I added that, though I was not much known in France, I had some friends there, who, I thought, would take an interest in my election, and I ventured to name you as one of them.

In his reply of the 23rd of February, M. Vattemare makes the following remarks; a portion of which leads me to fear some *misunderstanding*. Pardon me for repeating the whole passage: "I wanted to confirm the hopes that it was very pleasant for me to give you on the part of the Academy of Moral and Political Sciences by my letter of the 19th of October, 1851. For this reason, I saw M. Guizot and M. Alexis de Tocqueville, both of whom have very favorable intentions. The former, who remembers with pleasure to have been your colleague in London, will support your candidature with all his power. He declared it to me with an ardor that marks his esteem for your character as well as for your talent. The latter requested me to ask you for the exact and complete list of works that you have published in order to determine the section of the Academy to which you will belong. I say *will belong* because the success is not doubtful. The next vacancy, I am sure will open the doors of our institution to you. Let me advise you, Sir, to send me without delay the list that M. [de] Tocqueville is waiting for."[67]

Now, I did not name M. Guizot as among my friends at Paris, nor were we colleagues at London. I did not go to London till November 1841, at which time M. Guizot was in office in France; I never saw him except at one of his receptions *aux Affaires étrangères*.[68] This makes me admit as a painful *possibility* (and I am unwilling to think it more than a bare possibility) that M. Vattemare is trifling with me, for some selfish purpose of his own, and that he has grossly colored what there may be of fact, in his statements to me. I am very loath to admit this even as a possibility: but how else explain what he says of M. Guizot?

But supposing him (M. V.) to be *de bonne foi*,[69] and that you have expressed a wish for an exact list of my publications, I would say that it is not quite easy to furnish it, on account of their number. My intellectual labors – such as they are – have not been condensed into one or two elaborate treatises, but are spread over a great many *pièces d'occasion*.[70] My two volumes of *Orations* you have and I am grateful for the kind manner in which you speak of them in your letter of the 5th of August 1851. Besides these, there are speeches and reports in Congress and political tracts which would fill two volumes more. I have also written more than one hundred articles in the *North American Review*,[71] on subjects of Literature, History, and Politics, the greater part of them prepared with labor and care. I will take the liberty, in a few days, to forward you the numbers of the Review containing my articles on your *Système Pénitentiaire* and *Démocratie en Amérique*.[72] My life has been an active one; and so much occupied with official duties as a member of Congress ten years, governor of Massachusetts four years, Minister in London four years, and President of the University at Cambridge,[73] three years, that I have not found leisure for my work *de longue haleine*.[74] I have, however, been making collections and preparations for an elementary treatise on the Modern Law of Nations, which I have ventured to announce as the object of my studies in the preface to the Collection of my *Orations*, Vol. I. p. XI.

If the Academy consists of two classes, I conceive that my writings would point to the political class, unless the law of Nations is regarded in a very large sense as a branch of morals. In writing to M. Vattemare, I observed that I could hardly promise myself the honor of an election, if, as

I understood, personal canvassing was a necessary condition; for, besides the difficulty of conducting this by letter, it is entirely repugnant to my tastes and habits. I have never solicited an office or an honor in my life. But I have thought that I might with propriety write what I have written to you, my dear M. de Tocqueville, an old friend and correspondent, and in compliance (as M. Vattemare informs me) with your expressed wish.

If the subject is really one that has been considered, I think – if you thought fit to name it to them – you would find my colleague at London M. de Ste. Aulaire would take some interest in it; as also M. Cousin whom I knew in Germany in my youth. I think also your friend Ampère will remember me with some kindness.

I will only add one more remark, that if my friends in Paris have ever thought of doing me the honor of proposing my election, I hope it will not be done unless there is a very fair prospect of success. I had much rather not be nominated than fail *au scrutin*.[75]

Pardon this long letter and believe me, my dear M. de Tocqueville, with sincere attachment faithfully yours,

Edward Everett

Beinecke Rare Book and Manuscript Library, Yale University, Uncat MSS 324; also available as Bonnel copy, MS Vault Tocqueville, D II a, Paquet 12, pp. 10–15.

77. Alexis de Tocqueville to Edward Everett

Paris, April 16, 1852

My dear Mr. Everett,

M. Vattemare,[76] with whom I also am not *intimately connected*, has given you a very accurate account in what he wrote to you about myself and M. Guizot. I have indeed expressed to M. Vattemare the idea that a man like you must be a corresponding member of the Academy of Moral and Political Sciences for America and that, for my part, I would like to take the first opportunity to propose your nomination to this learned body. I have added, as M. V. has reported to you, that before taking this step, I would like to know the complete list of your works, and would like you to afford me the pleasure of sending this list to me. Thus, as far as I am concerned, the account of M. V. was thoroughly accurate. I have checked with M. Guizot himself that the same can also be said of him regarding the desire he expressed to see you elected to the Academy. M. V. might have misunderstood what M. Guizot told him about the place where he had made your acquaintance, but what he said was generally accurate. It seemed to me that M. Guizot was as desirous as myself to see your nomination as a corresponding member of the Academy; he believes this choice to be suitable and useful. He assured me that he had already spoken of you to some of our colleagues and, finally, he told me formally that he intended to propose you as first choice when a vacancy appears in his section. This is the history section.

Perhaps you would do well to write to him in order to thank him for his good intentions. A very useful step would be to send to the Academy an unpublished work on a historical, political, or moral topic. This work or study, if it were translated into French, could be read in one of the meetings and would render the audience favorably disposed toward you. An almost equally effective step, which would give you less trouble, would be to send the Academy, as a gift, two volumes similar to the ones that you were so kind as to send me. If you agree to forward them to me, I would present them in your name to the Academy as a token of respect, making known the nature and worth of the work.

The Academy of Moral Sciences, which, as you know, is part of the Institute, consists of five sections, namely: 1. Philosophy; 2. Ethics; 3. Legislation, Public Law; 4. Political Economy; 5. General and Philosophical History.

This is, my dear Sir, all I can tell you about this subject. I have no doubt that we shall have you among our colleagues soon and, for my part, I shall be extremely delighted. Moreover, I understand very well the desire that you have expressed not to be presented as a candidate, if you were not certain of being elected. Please be reassured that we shall undertake this only if we have great chances of success. In this matter, as in all those that are decided by election, no success can be guaranteed in advance. But I am asking you to bear in mind that there are few eminent people in our Institute who have been successful in their first attempt, and that the possibility of failure has not stopped anyone. In your case, the setback would be even less vexing, since you do not present yourself, but are proposed, without having asked to be so, by the members of the body itself

Please accept, my dear M. Everett, the expression of my highest consideration.

A. de Tocqueville

78. Edward Everett to Alexis de Tocqueville

Boston, May 11, 1852

My dear M. de Tocqueville,

I received by the last steamer your letter of the 16 April. I am very sensible to your kindness in writing to me so promptly, and I am a good deal relieved by the reasons which you give me for thinking that M. V[attemare] is *de bonne foi*.[77]

You propose that I should send you a copy of my volumes to be presented to the Academy. This I shall have much pleasure in doing, and whatever be the result of my nomination, I shall deem it a very gratifying circumstance to have the attention of the Academy called to my humble efforts by you. The parcel containing the volumes shall be sent by the next steamer.

I feel some hesitation as to the preparation of "a memoir" to be addressed to the Academy. Such a step, on my part, would look, under the present circumstances, like a tacit application for the honor of admission, which I am desirous of avoiding.

I am much obliged to you for the suggestion about writing to M. Guizot, to thank him for the interests which he has expressed in reference to my nomination. I will, if possible, obey your intimation by this steamer.

You will probably see something in the public journals of the reception of Kossuth in this country.[78] It is a history which does not reflect much credit upon our discernment. The homage paid to him is somewhat exaggerated in the journals favorable to him. It is partly founded upon an honest enthusiasm in favor of a People believed to be struggling for Constitutional liberty. But the greater part of the demonstration is the work of our domestic demagogues, who, for their own party purposes *exploitent*[79] the feeling of the people in favor of Kossuth. The amount of "material aid" which he will obtain, by the sale of his ridiculous Hungarian bonds, will not exceed fifty-thousand dollars. This sum he is expending as absurdly as it is raised *viz.* in the purchase of old muskets, at two dollars each, and on the manufacture of saddles for imaginary squadrons of Hungarian cavalry. Measures like these go near to indicate a disordered mind.

I remain, my dear M. de Tocqueville,

>   With sincere attachment,
>   faithfully yours,
>   Edward Everett

Beinecke Rare Book and Manuscript Library, Yale University, Uncat MSS 324; also available as Bonnel copy, MS Vault Tocqueville, D II a, Paquet 12, pp. 8–9.

79. Theodore Sedgwick to Alexis de Tocqueville[80]

New York, May 20, 1852,
53 Broadway

My dear M. de Tocqueville,

I am sending through M. Ampère the last volume of the history of our friend, Mr. Bancroft.[81] Please receive it as a token of remembrance for your kindness in Sorrento and Versailles.[82] But your most real act of friendship, for which I am most grateful, was the *temporary loan* of M. Ampère. He made a great number of friends here and we lost him with the deepest regret.[83] I do not dare speak to you about your politics and our politics are of little interest. The presidential battle can never be entirely devoid of interest in our country, given the immense number of *positions* which, according to our system of *rotation in office*, depend on the outcome. But there is so little to choose among the two parties, and all the big questions of our politics are either already decided or dormant, that for the moment the struggle cannot greatly interest those who have nothing to win or lose.

A question has come up lately which you might be able to answer without any difficulty. To whom do the *Churches* of France belong? I mean their material part. Who is the *owner*? Is it the state or the bishop? Or someone else? I [. . .][84] that they belong to *corporations* organised under a general law. I hope that your Italian winter has completely restored your health and that one of these fine days we shall see you again at the helm.

Please remember me to Madame de Tocqueville and accept, Sir, the expression of my most distinguished consideration and my most sincere devotion.

Theodore Sedgwick

P. S. Mr. Bancroft, to whom I made known my intention to send you his book wanted to precede me, but I have not allowed him to do so. He lives very quietly and appears to have said farewell to a political career.[85] *Ma, chi lo sa?*[86]

Beinecke Rare Book and Manuscript Library, Yale University, MS Vault Tocqueville, D II a, available only as Bonnel copy, Paquet 12, pp. 95–96.

80. Edward Vernon Childe to Alexis de Tocqueville

Paris, July 9, 1852

My dear Mon[sieu]r de Tocqueville,

According to the expectation expressed in my last note,[87] my friend Mr. Cotting arrived here the next day. Of course, I immediately questioned him as to the value of the property about which we had been speaking, and as he is the best businessman I ever knew, his options are, in my esteem, of no small value.

He does *not*, like the correspondent of the *Times*, believe in an approaching crisis in the commercial affairs of the U. S., but yet, he adds, that he would have nothing whatever to do with railway shares or bonds. He, however, did not say this till he had answered me as to the value and safety of Michigan Central railway bonds, *which he regards as good, and to be held without danger.*

The Indiana state stocks, he says, he knows nothing about, but the city of St. Louis bonds, he looks upon as unexceptionable and he is in a way to be well acquainted with property in that region, as he has two sons who are engaged in business there. He tells me of an investment which is the surest in the world, and which is now just on the point of being presented to the commercial public. It is an issue of 5 per. cent bonds, created by the city of Boston for the purpose of paying off its 6 per. cent securities, which are soon falling due. I regard this as the *best* investment, if one be content to receive but 5 per cent, because every house and stone in the place is pledged for payment of principal and interest, a security which I believe exists in no other case.

I am very sorry that I cannot give you more full and satisfactory information, but as I shall possibly go to America for a few weeks in the autumn, it will there perhaps be in my power to be of some real service to you.

Believe me, I pray you, most respectfully and faithfully your friend and servant.

E. V. Childe

I shall be most happy to hear from you *"aux Eaux de Hamburg, près de Francfort sur le Mein."*[88]

Beinecke Rare Book and Manuscript Library, Yale University, MS Vault Tocqueville, D II a, available only as Bonnel copy, Paquet 12, pp. 107–109.

81. Alexis de Tocqueville to Francis Lieber

Tocqueville, August 4, 1852

My dear Lieber,

A few days ago I received the letter that you wrote to me on June 28.[89] I shall share its content with Beaumont and I thank you for my part. You desire to have news of both of us. Here it is. On December 2, we were arrested at the same time as all the independent and law-abiding members of the Assembly.[90] Soon afterwards, we were released. Each of us retired to our homes in the country, Beaumont in Touraine, where he owns a small property bearing his name, and myself, in the heart of Normandy, close to Cherbourg. It is from there that I am writing to you now. Although it would have been quite easy for us to return, we have entirely left public life, and have decided to remain withdrawn from it for as long as we will not be able to defend the ideas and sentiments that have guided us until now. You will understand that while leaving politics, we have not succumbed to inaction. We have resumed the studies interrupted thirteen years ago; for my part, I am working hard in my solitude where a few friends often come to visit me. A long time ago I conceived the idea of a work[91] that current circumstances have allowed me to undertake. For more than a year I have been working on its outline; for I easily foresaw that the mistakes of 1848 were going to bring, as a reaction, a government so illiberal that I would not want to serve it. The events at the end of last year[92] did not surprise me, and soon after they took place, I was already at work. I would be perfectly happy with the life I am living now if I could entirely forget what is happening in my country and did not see the ridiculous, but very well-known, role that we play in the world, having overturned a monarchy because we did not find it to be sufficiently a friend of liberty in order to satisfy ourselves with a power that not only obstructs liberty but also eliminates it. Moreover, do not deceive yourself; this is not the end of the French Revolution, it is only a manifestation of it. While in fact placing the people in servitude, this government legally proclaims the dogma of the sovereignty of the people and conspicuously uses this dogma more so than any other government has ever done. Those who think that they can play with such a dogma and, after having established it in the government, can prevent it for long from spreading and bearing fruit, are truly stupid. The new constitution, at the same time as taking all kinds of tyrannical precautions to prevent people from becoming enlightened and from listening to a voice other than that of government, as well as to ensure that its representatives have no power whatsoever, has allowed the people not only to elect the silent assembly which votes the taxes, but all the local powers which direct the affairs of the departments and communes.[93] The government flatters itself that by isolating the masses from the enlightened classes and by making the former, so to speak, *impervious* to the knowledge and influence of the latter, it will always succeed in making the masses choose those individuals whom it will select for them and in making the latter act according to its will. By this skilful combination, the government thinks that it will be able to unite the advantages possessed by an absolute government to the strength of a popular government. I repeat that this is a mistake and a moment will arrive when this government will be obliged to deny entirely the dogma of popular sovereignty on which it pretends to rest and to abolish the right to vote which it has allowed it to survive, lest it will be destroyed by the consequences of this dogma and by the exercise of this right. It seems to me as clear as daylight that one or the other of these two hypotheses must come to pass in the shorter or longer term.

Furthermore, do not believe that the majority of our nation gives way before violence. No! The French, believe me, are always impossible to restrain. The enlightened classes see well what is going on. The people properly speaking, with their incomplete education, do not see it. The property owners, the bourgeois, the educated, in a word all those who have received a liberal education and have been involved directly or indirectly in public affairs, feel and see clearly that we have destroyed all public liberties in the name of the sovereignty of the nation, and that we have employed the outward forms of popular election only to establish a more absolute despotism than any other that has ever appeared in France. The people of the countryside, the peasants, do not see this at all. They hold on to appearances and are attached to the act in which they have played a part; they chose the President, the legislature, the members of general and municipal councils, and that is enough for them. They imagine that they are the true sovereigns, without seeing that, with the exception of the President, all the individuals whom they were allowed to choose have no real power and no effective influence on affairs. They do not see that all the guarantees of public liberties, and even of individual security, have been suppressed and that, deprived of all the means of enlightening themselves, of speaking with each other, of acting in common and understanding each other, they are nothing but mere voting machines. They still see nothing of this as yet. But such tangible truths cannot fail to appear to them sooner or later, in spite of the jealous care with which those in power oppose any attempt to reveal these truths to the people or even to let the people hear of them.

But this is more than enough about politics. I do not need to tell you that this letter, at least as far as my name is concerned, is *absolutely* only for you. Why do you not speak to me in your letter about affairs in America? Do you think that this subject has ceased to be of interest to me? Please make good this neglect the first time you write to me again.

Farewell, my dear Lieber. My wife wishes that I remember her to you and I ask you to believe in all my sentiments of sincere friendship.

A. de Tocqueville

We shall return to spend the next winter in Paris.

82. George Sumner to Alexis de Tocqueville[94]

Boston, August 10, 1852

My dear M. de Tocqueville,

I am writing to you to remind you about your promise to respond to me. Please tell me what is the situation in France? Are you right in the middle of Empire, are you going to remain a republic? Or will you have a restoration of the constitutional monarchy? The latter seems to me the least favorable of all the possible solutions. Due to your Léon de Mallevilles,[95] your Thiers, and *tutti quanti*, you have lost the Constitution of '48, and I very much fear that the nation is not grateful toward the party which, more so than any other one, has brought forth the current situation. But you will tell me yourself what is going on.[96]

One word for Madame de Tocqueville, to whom I beg the [...][97] and [...][98] respectful remembrance. Tell her to keep her *Michigan Central Bonds*. They pay 8 per cent interest, *and are perfectly safe*. At the same time, they can be converted into Stock of the Road, which will pay about 12 percent interest. The stock is now selling at 115. The bonds are payable to bearer and if lost, there is no recourse; but the Stock is inscribed *nominativement*. Madame de T. asked me about other American Stocks, but there are none [...][99] at prices low enough to price large dividends. In fact, every thing has risen in value here in presence of the immense prosperity which every where prevails. The bonds of some of the Western Counties may be [...][100] at little over 5 will yield 8 and 10 percent interest. These if discreet [...][101] may[102] will form a safe investment.

I am delighted with the appearance of all things in America. The material progress is immense, and what pleases me, as much, is to see how greatly the aesthetic sentiment is developed. Music, sculpture and architecture seem here to find their chosen home. It is well, that the example of high development of art, [. . .][103] in Republican Greece, Republican Rome, and in the Republic of Florence, Genoa and Venice, should be repeated here. *Vive la République*!![104]

The next Presidential elections promise to be animated. The probabilities are that [Winfield][105] Scott the Whig Candidate will be chosen. He was born in Virginia, a slave-holding State, but he in early life emancipated his slaves, and is in everything an anti-slavery man. The other candidate, i.e. of the Democratic [Party] is obliged in order to [. . .][106] the [. . .][107] of the [. . .][108] to accept the programme which they propose.

In a few days the Free-Soil Party will nominate a 3rd Candidate, whose election will be impossible, but who will probably draw [. . .][109] the so-called democratic ticket enough really democratic to destroy Pierce's chance for election, and thus open the doors for Scott.[110]

My brother,[111] as you [are] aware, represents in the Senate the Free-Soil sentiment. Acting [. . .][112] the *Abolitionists* who are aggressive, the *Free-Soilers* seek to drive slavery from every point where it has the protection of the National [. . .][113] or to use my brother's phrase in debate to make freedom not slavery national and slavery not freedom *sectional*. Both the old parties have been disposed to do exactly the reverse.

It cannot be derived that the Free-Soil sentiment [. . .][114] every day. Even at the approaching elections of '52 (November) they will *possibly* indirectly decide the contest between the old parties – in '56 the possibilities are that they will hold in their hands the balance of power.

Let me beg pardon for this long [letter].[115] I honestly avow that my great aim in writing is to provoke a reply. I am anxious to hear of France – *ma seconde patrie*[116] – anxious also to hear of Madame de Tocqueville [. . .].[117] Pray do not disappoint me. Every body here from President [. . .][118] down enquires after you – where you are? What you are doing? What you think of things in France? *Mettez moi à même de leur répondre.*[119] Address your letter simply to me care of Messrs. Baring Brothers & Co., London, *jettez-la à la poste sans affranchir- et elle me parviendra en 15 jours. Adieu! au plaisir d'avoir de vos nouvelles.*[120]

Your devoted,

G. Sumner

Beinecke Rare Book and Manuscript Library, Yale University, MS Vault Tocqueville, available only as Bonnel copy, Paquet 12, pp. 28–31.

83. Alexis de Tocqueville to Theodore Sedgwick

Paris, December 4, 1852
30 rue de Courcelles

My dear Mr. Sedgwick,

I found your letter of May 20 only upon my arrival here; this explains why I am so late in answering. But, although belated, my thanks will not be the less sincere. I was very touched by your token of remembrance and am very grateful to you for having sent me the fourth volume of Mr. Bancroft. I know the entire work; it is a model of accurate history, in which the truth of the details does not make one lose interest in the whole. Why did you not bring the book yourself? This is the only thing with which I can reproach you. You will be nowhere better received than in Paris, where people think that you are the most pleasant and most brilliant American conversationalist that has ever been seen in France. You know that our Frenchmen, who continue to attribute to themselves a merit that they no longer have, admit with difficulty that intelligence exists anywhere else than in France.

You are right to thank me for having lent Ampère to you. He is one of the best and most agreeable men I know, and one of those whose charm is universally recognized, because taking an interest in all things, he always has a subject of conversation ready for everyone. Moreover, he returns enraptured about your country, and says this openly and loudly, although this is not the most favorable moment for saying so. The great taste he has developed for America is a new link between him and me, for you know that I am half an American citizen. Moreover, this is a way of being a citizen somewhere. As your compatriot, I have not viewed without apprehension this spirit of conquest, and even plunder, which has manifested itself among you for several years now. It is not a sign of good health for a people that already has more territories than it can fill. I confess that I would be very saddened if the nation embarked on an enterprise against Cuba, or, what might be worse perhaps, if it allowed it to be carried out by its forlorn children. Believe me, if not conducted with great prudence, this entire affair would end by putting you at odds with the great nations of Europe.

I do not need to tell you that, on our continent, you are not in good odor. Governments loathe you. They view the United States as the pit of the abyss from where nothing but a putrid stench comes out; and people reproach you for having made them believe in the Democratic Republic. Never would people be so ready to come together to create difficult problems for you and to show you that you are not as entirely sheltered from the blows of the old world as you seem to think.

I have been constantly ill since my arrival in Paris, which accounts for the fact that I have not been able to leave the house to make the acquaintance of Mr. Beckwith and to thank him.[121] I shall go to see him as soon as I am able to pay visits. Moreover, it is not my health that will prevent me from *being seen again at the helm*, as you say. How could you believe that a man who has written, spoken, and acted as I have done for the past twenty years would like, I would not say to return to the helm – that does not depend on anyone's will – but to enter at this moment into public affairs? The impossibility in which I find myself of expressing in writing the reasons which keep me in private life is sufficient to explain to you that I do not want to leave it.[122] No, my dear Mr. Sedgwick, I am nothing and I do not want to be anything, apart from always being a member of the Academy, a title that Piron scorned,[123] but only after it was refused to him. Farewell. Return soon to France and count on the fact that nobody will receive you with greater pleasure and eagerness than me. I should say we, since my wife has retained a very pleasant recollection of your visits.

A. de Tocqueville

Do not forget to remember me to Mr. Bancroft and to tell him that I shall never be indifferent to anything that might happen to him, either in private or public life.

84. George Sumner to Alexis de Tocqueville

Boston, December 8, 1852

My dear Sir,

In one of Swift's letters addressed to Bolingbroke,[124] when the English statesman was at the *Source du Loiret*,[125] is the following passage: "I thank you, my Lord, the more, for your having condescended to write to me when you had the *honor* to be an exile."

This "condescension" you have not shown me, during these your days of dignified retreat, although I have twice written, and often expected to hear from you.

In the first place I sent messages of remembrance and of financial wisdom to Madame de Tocqueville, and then I asked a thousand questions of you. Of some of these time has kindly undertaken the answer, but he has told me nothing personal to yourself. Let me therefore ask for news of you, of your health, and of your mode of employing your time during these days of moral stagnation. I am here asked by many persons and I am unable to answer. I have told all of your noble conduct on the 2nd December,[126] and moreover of your conduct so worthy of all praise, before that day when you honestly toiled, during days of doubt and peril, to make the Republic possible. Will it ever return? Will this actual despotism run into Constitutional Monarchy or into the Republic again? These are questions which I am most anxious to have light upon. If you knew how much pleasure your letter would give, you would surely not refuse to write me. Where is Beaumont? Where Rémusat?[127] Beaumont stood honorably for the Republic, but I have always thought that M. de Rémusat *might* have done *more* than he did, though I am far from classing him with Léon de Malleville and others of that stamp. What is Dufaure[128] about now and what view does he take of things? How long will it all last?

Shall we have war in the Spring, and with what power? *Voilà bien des questions.*[129]

As to America, everything is going on well. An extraordinary degree of prosperity tends to stimulate material developments, and, at the same time, it permits the gratification of those refined and elegant tastes which are native to the soil of Republics. A few days since, in this *metropolis*, we had, on the same evening, Sontag and Alboni![130] Pray tell this to Madame de Tocqueville. The knowledge of the musical banquet we can offer here may induce her to migrate to these shores, quitting your village of Paris, where the two luminaries in question have never shone upon the same night.

The new President Pierce is a man who, so far, keeps his own counsel. Many Whigs, angry that Webster was not nominated,[131] voted for him. I believe that he will show as much moderation as any of his predecessors. Mr. King, the Vice President, whom you know some years since in Paris, is although called a Democrat, very Conservative in his feelings.[132] As to Cuba, I do not believe that any movement upon it will here be made. If the Southern States reclaim its annexation, the North will cry out for Canada, which, like ripe fruit, is ready to fall into the open lap of the Union.

Pray give my best remembrances to Madame de Tocqueville, and receive for yourself the assurances of high regard with which I remain, always,

Your faithful servant and friend,
Geo[rge] Sumner

P.S. A letter for me sent to care of Messrs. Baring Brothers & Co. London, will be at once forwarded to me. They will send by steamer. If you are in France, you can send to Greene & Co.[133]

Beinecke Rare Book and Manuscript Library, Yale University, Uncat MSS 324; also available as Bonnel copy in MS Vault Tocqueville, D II a, Paquet 12, pp. 32–34.

85. Alexis de Tocqueville to Jared Sparks

Paris, December 11, 1852

My dear Mr. Sparks,

I would like to add to the official letter that I am writing to you in your capacity as President of the University a word of friendship that recalls me to your memory. Moreover, I wish especially to tell you that I could not have been more moved by the testimony of esteem that I received on this occasion from your colleagues and yourself.[134] As I said openly in my official letter, I have a high appreciation for Harvard College and nothing could appear to me more agreeable and honorable than to belong to this great and fine institution. Moreover, at no other time have literary honors been more dear to me. Since December 2, 1851, I have left public life completely and am entirely determined not to return to it as long as there exists in my country an order of things contrary to anything that I have wanted and hoped for. Hence, I am now living a purely literary life, surrounded by a small number of friends and many books. From the depths of my withdrawal from public life, I often turn my eyes with great pleasure, mixed sometimes with a certain anxiety, toward your America, whose citizen I almost consider myself to be, so much do I desire its prosperity and greatness. It has nothing to fear but from itself, from the excesses of democracy, the spirit of adventure and conquest, the sentiment of and the excessive pride in its strength, and the passions of youth. I could not recommend moderation enough among such great good fortune. Nations need it no less than individuals. Do not let yourselves be drawn lightly into disputes with Europe. At the present moment, people here are very badly disposed toward you, and they would happily seize an occasion to give you proofs of this ill will. Regardless of how great and powerful you are, a conflict with Europe could bring you, if not serious dangers, at least grave inconveniences and might have many repercussions on your internal affairs that would be difficult to foresee.

Please excuse me for speaking to you at such length about the country that I left a long time ago, and please see in my language only a testimony of the interest that I continue to have in it.[135]

I have received the little booklet in which you respond to the critical comments made in England on your great edition of Washington's letters.[136] These criticisms are unknown in France and your work translated by M. Guizot continues to enjoy a most deserved reputation here.[137]

Beaumont, who is in Paris at the present moment, asks particularly to be remembered to you. Please kindly remember both of us to M. E. Everett if he is still close by and tell him that in Paris he has friends who do not forget him.

Believe, my dear Mr. Sparks, in all my sentiments of esteem and friendship.

Alexis de Tocqueville

86. Alexis de Tocqueville to Jared Sparks[138]

Paris, December 11, 1852

Mr. President,

About a month ago, the Minister of the United States in Paris delivered to me the diploma that the University of Cambridge[139] had granted me and the letter that you enclosed with it. A quite serious illness has not allowed me to respond to you sooner.[140] I am using my newly regained energies to acquit myself of this duty.

Nothing could touch or honor me more than the testimony of esteem that the university generously wishes to grant me. I am so sincerely and profoundly a friend of America that everything which tends to bind me to her is extremely valuable in my eyes. I am particularly pleased to adhere to her by the new bond that you have just established. For more than twenty years, I have known and admired the great scientific and literary institution over which you preside. I know that Harvard's College, almost as old as the colony of Massachusetts, has not ceased to be the principal source of enlightenment, not only in New England but on your whole continent. I recall that it was within its walls that the first and greatest doctrines of civil and political liberty were defended almost a century ago, during an era when even in England similar doctrines were not professed so boldly. Finally, I know that many of your great statesmen were its students and that it still contains an assembly of able and wise professors such as one would encounter only with difficulty in any of the universities of Europe. Thus, I say again, I feel greatly honored for being the recipient of the favor of which you have informed me. Please, Mr. President, repeat this to your colleagues on my behalf and, with them, accept the expression of my true gratitude.

I am, Mr. President, your very humble and very obedient servant.
Alexis de Tocqueville

SECTION C

Letters: 1853–1856

87. Theodore Sedgwick to Alexis de Tocqueville[1]

New York, January 31, 1853

My dear Sir,

Before thanking you for your good and kind letter, please allow me to introduce to you Colonel Hughes, the carrier of this letter. As Captain of the *Topographical Engineers* in the service of the United States, Colonel in the war against Mexico, first Chief Engineer of the Panama Rail Road and finally, as a kind-hearted and talented man, Mr. Hughes is worthy of the fullest consideration.

But the main issue is not the Colonel's personal worth. You know perhaps that we are building here a *Crystal Palace* and I am entrusted with chairing this task.[2] Mr. Hughes is going to Europe as our agent in order to represent us to European governments and ask for their cooperation. In fulfilling his functions, Mr. Hughes will perhaps need that advice which can come only from highly placed persons who have great experience and perfect loyalty, advice whose worth is truly invaluable.

That is why, my dear M. de Tocqueville, I have taken the liberty of giving him this letter for you. I believe that your interest in our country and perhaps the personal kindness that you have showed me will permit you to offer to Colonel Hughes the information and advice that he will need.

Mr. Bancroft was very delighted by your letter. I have dined with him recently. Please remember me to Madame de Tocqueville whose distinction and charm have strongly impressed me. Accept my sincere

142

wishes for the restoration of your health and believe in my respect and devotedness,

Theodore Sedgwick

Beinecke Rare Book and Manuscript Library, Yale University, MS Vault Tocqueville, D II a, Bonnel copy, Paquet 12, pp. 88–89.

88. Alexis de Tocqueville to Theodore Sedgwick[3]

[May 8?] 1853

My dear Mr. Sedgwick,

I am writing to you today on behalf of a very distinguished family, a member of which is in a very critical situation at this moment in New York. I am speaking of a certain Frenchman named M. de Corn who killed another Frenchmen after having – so they say – seduced his wife.[4] This M. de Corn has among his close relatives here one of my closest friends, M. Rivet, who I arranged to dine with you in Versailles two years ago.[5] As for M. Corn, he denies having had relations with the wife of the man whom he killed (I know nothing about this), but he asserts (and I believe it to be so) that he killed only in self-defense. It was perhaps an exaggerated gesture of self-defense, but one in which, at all events, there was no question of premeditation or desire to murder. A series of circumstances and highly convincing occurrences led him to believe that he was being sought to be struck down and that he was on the point of being attacked, and in this belief, he himself struck first. If this is the way things really happened, the murder – while no less blameworthy – no longer merits the full severity of the law, at least according to our ideas and jurisprudence. If you share this view and could do something to mitigate the punishment threatening M. de Corn, I would be particularly grateful to you. Ampère, who is also very close to M. Rivet, wanted to write to you about the same matter, but I kept him from doing so by telling him that I would speak to you in his name as well as in my own. Thus, I ask you to consider this letter as coming from both M. Ampère and myself.

Mr. Hughes gave me the letter that you wrote on January 31st. I met Mr. Hughes at the Institute and later I went to his home to talk more with him. I have not seen him again, nor have I heard anything about him since. I presume that he spent only a very short time in Paris. I regret that I was not able to let him know more clearly how much I value your letters of recommendation and how eager I am to be of service to those of your countrymen who come recommended by you. They should count on being very well received.

My wife wants me to remember her to you, and as for myself, I assure you of all my esteem and friendship.

A. de Tocqueville

P. S. I hope that next year you will come to France where you have many friends.

89. Jared Sparks to Alexis de Tocqueville

Cambridge, June 13, 1853

My dear Sir,

I have delayed too long to answer the kind letter, which accompanied your official communication, acknowledging the receipt of your Diploma from our University. The sentiments expressed by you on the occasion were gratifying to the Corporation, as showing an interest in the institution, and good wishes for its continued prosperity.[6]

Through the usual channels of intelligence, you are so well informed of the general state of affairs in this country, that any remarks from me with the view of enlarging your knowledge, or enlightening your opinions, might seem superfluous. Your own observations and experience have made you familiar with the principles upon which our political system is founded, and with many of the details of its operations. Yet there have been changes in twenty years; and indeed it would not be wise to predict with any degree of precision what developments time may bring to pass.

The material prosperity of the country goes onward with an amazing acceleration. The rapid growth of cities, towns, and villages, the expansion of commerce, the increasing products of agriculture, the multiplication of railroads forming a network from the eastern extremity of Maine to the Mississippi, and steamboats floating on all navigable rivers and lakes, the vast increase of manufactures of every description – all these present a scene of rapid change, activity, enterprise, and progress, which certainly has no parallel in the history of civilization. Nor is mental culture neglected. The New England school system, modified as local circumstances may require, is established in nearly all the free states, patronized by the governments, and sustained by the people. Higher seminaries and colleges are well supported. But it must doubtless be a long time, in the midst of so many temptations to active and political life, before there will be a large class who will seek eminence by triumphs in literature or purely intellectual achievements.

Your apprehensions of the tendencies of the popular mind are not without foundation. The history of the last few years, the acquisitions of Texas and California, prove that the spirit of adventure and conquest excites the aspirations and moves the will of the people. Perhaps it is inherent in the democratic element. The clamor for acquiring Cuba springs from the same spirit; and a slight cause could carry the arms of the Untied States again into Mexico. Where will this end, and how are such vast accessions and discordant materials to be held together in a confederated republic? But the slave question presents the most formidable problem. How is this to be solved? No political geometer has yet devised a method. You know the extreme difficulties attending this question, as connected both with the form and extent of slavery as it exists in this country. Its political aspects are dark and ominous.

There is not the least reason to fear that the United States will meddle with the agitations of Europe. The experiment tried by Kossuth proved a total failure.[7] The people were ready enough to *sympathize*, but not a voice was raised for action, unless from a few German emigrants and restless agitators.

Mr. Everett is now a member of the United States Senate, from Massachusetts, and one of the prominent leaders of what we call the Whig party.[8] Indeed, since the death of Mr. Clay and Mr. Webster, he may be regarded as the head of that party.

When you again see M. Beaumont, pray present to him my kind remembrances.

Accept, my dear Sir, the assurance of the sincere regards of your most truly,

Jared Sparks

Beinecke Rare Book and Manuscript Library, Yale University, MS Vault Tocqueville, D II a, Bonnel copy, "Bonnel's copies of letters of Americans to Tocqueville." Originally published in Herbert B. Adams, *Jared Sparks and Alexis de Tocqueville* (Baltimore: The Johns Hopkins University Press, 1898), pp. 45–46.

90. Francis Lieber to Alexis de Tocqueville

Columbia S. C., September 29, 1853

My dear de Tocqueville,

You will receive through M. Bossange a copy of the work on which

I was engaged when I last wrote to you. Its title is *On Civil Liberty and Self Government*. Accept it in kindness. I do not know that there is a man living, whose opinion that there is some substance in the work, I should value more than yours. You will see that I have several times quoted you with that esteem which I sincerely feel for you. If you peruse the book, you will see the reason why I have abstained from sending a copy to the Institute, which otherwise I should have been proud to do. I do not know in what precise relation the Institute may stand to a power of which I have repeatedly spoken in the work in no favourable terms. If, however, you think that it would nevertheless not be inappropriate to lay a copy of it before the academy, I wish you would write me so, and a copy shall be sent immediately. I suppose in such a case, I ought to direct it to the Secretary. I shall be most happy to hear from you after you have glanced at my book. Do not omit writing me how you are, how Madame de Tocqueville is, and how you personally are "getting on," as the phrase is.

I have sent a copy to de Beaumont. I trust these letters, which I send to Paris, for want of a more particular direction, will safely reach you.

I cannot help writing with a certain emotion, whenever I write nowadays to a French friend.

May God protect you all. Give my very best regards to Madame de Tocqueville, and believe me always your sincerely attached friend.

Ever yours,
Francis Lieber

Beinecke Rare Book and Manuscript Library, Yale University, MS Vault Tocqueville, D II a, Bonnel copy, Paquet 12, pp. 49–51.

91. Francis Kidder[9] to Alexis de Tocqueville

Boston, Oct[ober], 1853

Sir,

At the suggestion of a friend I take the liberty of sending you this volume[10] not for any inherent value in the work but that it may leave to show the rise and progress of a New England town in the last century.

Truly yours,
Frederic Kidder

Beinecke Rare Book and Manuscript Library, Yale University, Bonnel copy, D II a, folder "Bonnel's copies of letters from Americans to Tocqueville."

92. Alexis de Tocqueville to Theodore Sedgwick

St.-Cyr-près-Tours (Indre-et-Loire)
November 7, 1853

My dear Mr. Sedgwick,

I would like to have your opinion on a subject that it is very important for me to clarify. This is the true state of industrial affairs in America and what those Europeans who have placed a part of their fortune in the United States might in reality have to fear from it. Here is my situation. In 1848, being worried by the financial state of France, I bought a certain number of American bonds that I have kept ever since. These are: 1. New York and Harlem Railroad bonds; 2. Galena-Chicago Union Railroad bonds; 3. Michigan Central Railroad bonds. These funds, thus invested, have since paid me good interest and I have had no reason to believe that the capital might be under the smallest danger. But the newspapers are full of more or less alarming news on the state of business affairs in America. Many people are beginning to fear that a new industrial crisis, similar to those crises that we have already seen, might again occur in your country.[11] These rumors have alarmed me a little; for, although having wealth enough to meet my wants, and am therefore, of means, I am not rich and the loss of a portion of what I own in America would have the most unfortunate consequences for me. I have thought that under these circumstances, I could address myself to no one in the United States who inspired me with more confidence than you. Hence, I ask that you be so kind as to tell me: 1. If you believe that the fear of a crisis is well founded; 2. If, even in the event of a crisis, the funds that I have just mentioned appear to you to be under any danger; 3. What do you advise me to do under the present circumstances? I do not need to tell you how grateful I would be to you if you were so kind as to give me this advice. When responding, please do not mention anything about political affairs in France, which might prevent your letter from reaching me, since the confidentiality of letters does not exist at all among us. But, please, do tell me something about your country in which, it seems to me, I become more and more interested as my interest distances itself from other places.

I am not writing from my home where, unfortunately, my health has prevented me from spending the last winter, but from near Tours where I have rented a small house for a year.[12] I have been living here for five months and expect to stay until next summer. The air that one can breathe on the banks of the Loire and, especially, the tranquility of spirit and the profound calmness in which I live, seem to have restored my health. I very much enjoy this return to life and I profit from it to pursue again studies and projects that are more suitable to my inclinations than public affairs and from which the latter have kept me separated. Hence, it is with calm that I look forward to what the future has yet in store both for this country and myself.

Our common friend, Ampère, has come to spend two summer months with me here. Winter drove him to Italy. You know that he is like a swallow.

While in Paris last winter, I saw much of Mr. Beckwith and his charming wife whose acquaintance I owe to you. They should have returned to America by now. Please remember me to them and tell them that I shall regret not finding them in Paris upon my return. Please do not forget to remember me to Mr. Bancroft as well.

Do you know Mr. George Sumner, the Senator's brother, in person? And do you have any opportunity to see him? If so, please tell him that I wrote him a letter a year ago to which he has not yet responded. This makes me fear that he has not received it, although I sent it via England, in keeping with the instructions he had given me.

I do not know where to send this letter. I have your address from last year but I am too familiar with American mores not to know that you probably no longer live in the same house. Nonetheless, I shall send this letter there, in the hope that people will know your current address. Moreover, your name alone will be enough for the letter not to get lost.

Have you received the observations that I sent to you via Ampère as a response to the questions that you had asked me regarding the property of the Church? I do not need to tell you that if you need books or information on this country, I am entirely at your disposal as well as to your friends whom you might introduce to me.

Please believe in all my sentiments of esteem and friendship.

Alexis de Tocqueville

93. Alex Vance to Alexis de Tocqueville[13]

Beaumont le Roger (Eure),
November 10, 1853

Sir,

Having just brought to a close a little work commenced by me some two years ago in the back-woods of America, upon a subject I should hardly suppose any man living were so competent as the author of "*La Démocratie en Amérique*" to estimate the nature and the value; am I, Sir, in finally committing it to the press, taking too great a liberty in soliciting the permission to submit it to your perusal. It is entitled "*An apology for Hebrew prophecy; or Christianity identified with Democracy.*" I may briefly state that it is an attempt to establish thro[ugh] the medium of the mosaic and prophetic writings that *prophecy* was prophetic of *Democracy*, and *not* of Christianity; and you will perhaps catch my meaning when I state that the rolling *stone* in the fable of the *mighty image* in the Book of Daniel is assumed to be prophetic of the final conquests of Democracy.

It is not conceived in a spirit hostile to Christianity; had it been, I trust I had been too well aware what was due to M. de Tocqueville to make the request I am this moment doing.

I have no other apology, Sir, to offer for the very great liberty I am taking with an utter and so distinguished a stranger, further than assuring you that I am a very young man, and far too conscientious a one not to be most painfully alive to all the responsibilities [that] may possibly be attached to such a publication.

As it is not my intention to prefix my name to the work, should by any chance it ever be thrown upon your notice; you will much oblige me by ignoring the name of the author.

I remain, Sir, your most obed[ient] ser[van]t,

Alex Vance

94. Theodore Sedgwick to Alexis de Tocqueville[14]

New York, December 1, 1853

My dear M. de Tocqueville,

I have just received your letter of November 7. It is always a genuine pleasure for me to be able to be useful to you. Your first question is "*if I believe* the *fear* of a crisis to be justified?" And the two others derive from it. The crisis, such as it has been, is now over. We have passed through one of those *crises*, as they are called, which occur here almost every year. There is a *dearness of money* or a lack of sufficient stocks affecting all financial operations that forces the banks to cut down their discounts and sometimes brings down great speculators who owe a lot of money. But these crises do not affect in any way the great industrial development of the country, neither the cotton planters nor the northern farmers nor (to arrive at your subject) the railroads. During my lifetime, we have had only one crisis of this *last type* – that of 1837 – which had the most disastrous consequences. But at this moment we are not at all threatened by such a financial revolution. The country has never been happier and has never enjoyed greater material progress than today. I am not giving you only my personal opinion, for I am neither a banker nor a speculator. After receiving your letter, wanting to compare my opinions to those of the persons best placed to read the barometer of affairs, I have spent a part of the morning on *Wall Street* (our *Thread Needle Street*). What I give you is the outcome of my conversations. The publicity here is so great and the *intellectual* movement of affairs so quick and powerful that it is quite easy to obtain all the possible information on a public question such as the one you asked, unless, of course, everyone has lost their mind, as in fact, one must admit, did occur in 1834 and 1835. But unfortunately you cannot rely on our *newspapers* and above all on those that are mostly read in Europe. These are very cheap newspapers that thrive on all kinds of excitement and [. . .].[15] Today there is a general war in Europe, tomorrow a war in Mexico. The future of the Union is in danger and there is *uproar* about a poor runaway slave, and then the next day there is a financial crisis. We pay for our *freedom of the press*, and sometimes even a high price, although, of course, I would not want to diminish it. Please do not rely on the *newspapers* of this country.

In short, I am giving you my firm opinion that there will be no crisis and all the bonds of railroad companies are excellent investments. There is one other question that you have not asked me: it concerns the special nature of your bonds. All three of them are excellent and you can do nothing better than to keep them for now. Regarding the [Galena] and Chicago bonds, I am sending you a brochure which perhaps will be of interest to you. It will give you interesting details on all railroads and on this part of the Union. There is a map that will show you the current position of the railroads in this *district*. I believe that what I have just said should allay your fears about what to do; or, if you want further information, the only thing you have to do is to ask.

I very much regret to learn that you are still not well; I was thinking that your winter in Italy had completely restored your health. Every now and then, I receive a few words from our friend Ampère. I like him greatly and would be delighted to see him here again. Why would it not be a good idea for you to come here for a second visit? If you can persuade Madame de Tocqueville to undertake the voyage, you will revive your recollections from twenty years ago. You will see the progress of the sciences [...][16] that you revealed to Europe and you will be able to judge for yourself and with your own eyes about your *bonds*. Please try to come; you will receive a cordial reception everywhere.

I have recently sent you engravings and publications regarding our Crystal Palace. The delay of the opening has caused us great problems, but the final process has been completed. We will convert it into a permanent museum or rather a permanent exhibition. I have taken a great interest in it, but am now returning to my law studies and my profession that I love more than anything else. Bancroft is doing well and is fully occupied with his history. I know Mr. George Sumner very little [...][17] But I shall try to send him your message for his brother, the senator, who is a good man, although he is very taken by the issue of slavery and his extreme views make it impossible for him to act with any political party of our country. There is very little interest among us now in political questions with the exception of the distribution of positions. The entire country is busy doing business.

Now I am going to ask you a question. I take a strong interest in the religious wars of your country during the sixteenth century, from 1550 to 1600. (1°) What is the best bookseller or agent in Paris whom I could ask to discover for me what can be found on this period in writings, brochures, engravings etc.? You realize that this is not an ordinary request and I would need an intelligent person who is also a great *rummager* (if that is good French). (2°) Do you know or do you believe that there is in government offices any correspondence from that time which is original and might be important, and do you believe that a foreigner might obtain permission to examine those old papers? If you could shed light for me on these issues, I would be much obliged to you. I received what you kindly wrote to me regarding the property of the Church and I thank you greatly for it. You made the subject clear to me and it was very interesting.

You also wrote to me regarding one of your compatriots accused of *murder, M. de Corn.* I have inquired about his fate. He had good lawyers and, fortunately, I was able to assist him a little with his defense, but the *fact* was established and the excuse was not so convincing. He was found guilty of fourth degree murder and was condemned to state prison for 2 years and 10 months. But he has been placed on the *medical staff*, that is, he is attached to the Health Department in virtue of which he is neither obliged to wear a *uniform* nor is he condemned to forced labor – and *Kent* and I will take care of his release by asking for the clemency of the state government after he has served a part of his sentence.

Farewell, my dear M. de Tocqueville. I hope that your health is fully restored soon and that you might be able in person to examine our railroads and your *bonds*. I ask you to remember me to Madame de Tocqueville and to present to her my most sincere compliments and to accept the expression of my devotedness as well as my profound respect.

Theodore Sedgwick

Beinecke Rare Book and Manuscript Library, Yale University, MS Vault Tocqueville, D II a, Bonnel copy, Paquet 12, pp. 89–94.

95. Alexis de Tocqueville to Theodore Sedgwick

St.-Cyr-près-Tours, January 4, 1854

Dear Mr. Sedgwick,

I cannot thank you enough for your last letter.[18] It allayed all my fears. The newspapers have worried me and you have completely reassured me. Thank you a thousand times. I hope that your friendship does not limit itself to this, and if you perceive any reason to worry either about business affairs in general or regarding the three issues that I mentioned to you: 1. the Harlem and New York Railway, 2. the Chicago-Galena Railway, 3. the Michigan Central Railway (we own only bonds in these three companies), please write a few words to warn me. I have absolute confidence in you.

In your letter, you asked me a few questions which I could not answer in detail.[19] I am not sufficiently knowledgeable about these matters. It seems to me that the only person in France who could fully satisfy you is Mignet, an eminent historian, as you know; moreover, for the last twenty years, he has been pursuing research on the period that interests you. I have therefore written to him and am sending you the fragment from his letter that regards yourself. You will see that Mignet has done his job thoroughly, as someone who understands that the reason for contacting him is not an idle curiosity, but rather a serious desire to know more. The only point upon which, in my view, he does not shed enough light is that regarding the manuscripts that can be found in the National Archives or at the Ministry of Foreign Affairs. Since it concerned governmental papers, Mignet was more reserved about this (I have already told you that people avoid talking about the government, even in private letters). Nonetheless, I shall tell you that you should not expect much from this source. Even if you were to obtain authorization from ministers or from the master himself, you would still encounter fairly significant obstacles from the agents of the administration; the two persons who, at the present moment, are placed at the head of the state archives and those of Foreign Affairs are obsessed about the secrecy of old papers.[20] Moreover, secrecy is the general law of the day. A few years ago, you would have easily obtained everything that you could have wanted; and even today, if you *specify* a document, you will obtain, I believe, permission to examine it. But you will not be allowed, as was done previously for so many Americans, to browse at random, which is however the only means of discovering genuine treasures.

I have informed the family of M. de C[orn] of what you have already been so kind as to do and of what, in agreement with Mr. Kent, you still plan to do for him. Would both of you please accept the expression of the warmest gratitude of the family? For my part, I would be very grateful to you for your efforts to obtain the pardon of M. de C[orn], toward whom the jury seems to me to have been a little harsh. What a difficult job it is to be a husband in America! And how dangerous it is to risk your reputation with this pillar of the community, especially if one had had any relationship with the wife!

Madame de Tocqueville does not wish me to end this letter without telling you that she thanks you as much as I do for your advice and that she is equally grateful for it. Please accept, in the name of both of us, the expression of our sentiments of esteem and friendship.

A. de Tocqueville

P. S. I do not need to tell you that I am at your disposal with regard to what you have to do in France. You forgot to give me your current address again.

96. Alexis de Tocqueville to Edward Vernon Childe[21]

St.-Cyr-près-Tours, January 15, 1854

My dear Mr. Childe,

It is with great sadness that I have learned of the recent loss of your mother. I realize that, although she might have reached the farthest limits of human life, you had reasons to hope that she would still live a little longer, and therefore the unexpected nature of the event must have increased the pain that you have suffered. Please accept the expression of my deep sympathy.

Thank you for your kind offer regarding my business affairs in America. I would have benefited from it three months ago, when the reports in the newspapers made me extremely worried about the state of the economy in the United States. I feared a similar crisis to the one that, a few years ago, had ruined so many fortunes among you. But today I am completely reassured. What I was told about the general state of business and, in particular, about the three companies in which I have placed my money has convinced me that the best thing I should do at the present moment is to leave these funds where they are. Hence, I do not want, at least at the present time, to avail myself of your friendship. I ask only that you alert me if, contrary to my expectations, the state of the economy in America would seem a matter of concern to you either now or in the future.

Why do you tell me, dear Mr. Childe, that I helped you last year? These services were insignificant, infinitely less than I would have hoped them to be. I would have been happy to be able to do more; the solicitude that I showed toward you was so natural that it requires no gratitude. Who would not sympathize with such a great misfortune, so little deserved?[22] Moreover, what you tell me about Krakow indicates that this unfortunate matter is resolved and I am extremely happy about this, since I have a sincere affection for you and your family, and nothing that could happen to you would leave me indifferent. I thank you for having thought the same yourself when giving me news about your other children. I have always found little Mary to be a charming child and I am not surprised that she is popular at the boarding school where you have sent her.[23] I am as concerned as you are that a young man as pleasant as Edward has not taken steps as yet to take up a useful occupation.[24] If at least he were to learn to do something and, above all, if he were to take an interest in the things with which he might occupy himself, the evil would be much smaller. After all, one can do without a profession, but what one cannot dispense with is the taste for an occupation of some kind.

Farewell, dear Mr. Childe. Have a safe journey, and many thanks. Do not forget to remember me to Edward, and above all, please remember me especially and very fondly to Mrs. Childe.

A. de Tocqueville

97. Francis Lieber to Alexis de Tocqueville

Columbia, S. C., March 12, 1854

Your letter of the 30th of January, my dear friend, brought me the disagreeable news that my book had not yet arrived. Since then, I had one from Mittermaier, dated Heidelberg the 8th of February, and informing me that at length he had received the copies destined for that place. His letter gave me both the greatest delight on account of what he says of my work and the manner in which he expresses it, and much grief, because he speaks in almost desponding terms of the future of Germany. I make no doubt but that you have now your copies also. From a letter I had from my publisher, I see that instead of three copies there have been sent to Paris, only two, one for you, my dear de Tocqueville, and one for our common friend de Beaumont.

I would now beg you to use the copy destined for you, as a presentation copy for the Institute, if, after perusal, you find that without impropriety it can be presented. Nothing, indeed, can ever make me solemnly say what I do not believe, but I do not wish, on that account, to intrude and to force my views and theories into places where they may not be welcome, and where I myself am only a guest. If you think my *Civ[il] Liberty* can be presented you shall have another copy. I hope I can then send you the second edition, a good deal improved and a little enlarged. But remember, much as I desire that a report of my book be made to the Institute, and proud as I shall be to see such a report made by Alexis de Tocqueville, I am still more anxious to have a few private words on the subject from you. What a reward it would be to me, if my book were to suggest an idea or two to you for your book on the French Revolution, which will be, I know, a noble and a wise work. Only, I do not see how you will manage to navigate through the censorship; for, it strikes me that a man like you cannot well speak out on the first revolution without giving umbrage to some men having risen out of the second. How large will your work be? Will it suit for a translation? I mean, will a translation command a sufficient sale in the U.S.? No one in Europe can have an idea of the enormous sale of books in the U. States. Few thousand copies is now a common thing, but (with the exception of school books) this is true only of entertaining or semi-good and semi-trashy, or wholly bad books. There is now a book in vogue, which has the title of *Hot Corn*,[25] and has already sold to the tune of 50,000 copies. This part made me read it by way of philosophical study, and I found it a half sentimental and vicious, thoroughly bad book, with an ample sprinkling of bible, philanthropy and puritancy [sic].[26] But is it not so in all spheres? A dancer, a singer can beat at any day a philosopher, and an earnest and truthful statesman stands but little chance, on his own times,[27] against a demagogue.

This reminds me of our Nebraska Bill.[28] I suppose you know its import. It has passed the Senate and I fear there is no chance of preventing its being passed in the House of Representatives. It is a wicked and, even with reference to the South, a most unwise law. Whenever, in the unavoidable course of events there is an abstract question or principle irritating a nation, it is of the last importance to narrow down the debatable ground to distinct laws or positive pacts. This had been wisely done by our statesmen, now departed, in the Missouri Compromise.[29] It was of great importance to the South, but this mischievous Nebraska Bill sets everything afloat again, and will recoil, with tremendous force, upon the South. For the North is now set wholly free with reference to the sad slavery question. There are some men in the South that view things as I do; but we are very few. We shall see great agitation within the next ten years. And why is all this? Simply, because Senator Douglas, an able, bold, self-seeking, [. . .][30] man, looks for the presidency, and, I dare say, will obtain it. He gets by this unhallowed bill the whole South, which imprudently flies towards this bill as moths fly into the candle.

Let us talk of other things. How infinitely wiser the English are! No nation whatever, either in antiquity or modern times, seems so rarely to have failed against the wise precept to open the gates at the proper time, sufficiently wide and not too wide. No nation has so rarely abandoned the golden rule that in all spheres of human action, the highest and the lowest, in diplomacy, legislation, the family or the school, our acts are in the same degree efficient as our object is direct, our aim positive and our end distinctly adequate to the means at our disposal.

My first edition of *Civil Liberty* – now nearly sold – was of 2,000 copies.

You would do an essential service to your friend if you would now and then mention in your letters some truly important book on my theme[31] that may have lately appeared.

There is a work on the History of the Constitution in the U.S. by Mr. Custis[32] soon to appear in Boston. I believe it will be a very important book. I think it would be worth your while to get it through Bossange.

I was delighted to hear of your improved health. Give my very best regards to Madame de Tocqueville. How charmed I would be to have once more a letter from her.

Remember me very kindly to the Beaumonts.

I wish I was near you to teach you German, since you write that you are studying it. I pride myself upon being an efficient teacher of languages – if I take an interest in the student. With what ardor I would teach de Tocqueville that language which with all its leaden weight has wide pinions of its own.

If a report be made on my book, and a mention of it should appear in the papers, I should thank my friend, whom I shall never forget, for sending me the paper.

Francis Lieber

Beinecke Rare Book and Manuscript Library, Yale University, MS Vault Tocqueville, D II a, Bonnel copy, Paquet 12, pp. 42–47.

98. Henry D. Gilpin[33] to Alexis de Tocqueville

Hotel de Hollande (20 rue de la Paix)
May 30, 1854

Dear Sir,

I cannot deny myself the pleasure – in passing through Paris – in seeking to renew the acquaintance I had the pleasure to make with you – now many years since – in America; and though I learned from M. Ampère, in Rome, that your present residence is at Tours, yet as some accident may perhaps bring you to Paris, in the course of the next two weeks. I leave this note where I understand it may probably reach you, hoping that it may enable me to see you.

With the assurance of my great consideration,
I am very faithfully yours,
Henry D. Gilpin

Beinecke Rare Book and Manuscript Library, Yale University, Uncat MSS 324; also available as Bonnel copy in MS Vault Tocqueville, D II a, Paquet 12, pp. 74–75.

99. Alexis de Tocqueville to Theodore Sedgwick

Bonn, July 17, 1854

My dear Mr. Sedgwick,

Your two letters, after having followed me for a long time, have finally reached me.[34] The second arrived a long time before the first one. I cannot thank you enough for the friendly zeal that inspired you to write them. I shall follow your advice and change the old *bonds* into new ones. It is very kind of you to occupy yourself with our affairs and to send us your warnings and opinions from the other side of the Atlantic. We are very touched by this. For my part, I would like to be able to be of service to you one day in France. If this were the case, I hope that you would ask for my help without any hesitation; be reassured that I would be very pleased to do anything that could be useful or agreeable to you.

I am writing to you from Bonn where I have come to stay for a while. I left St.-Cyr at the end of last month, having almost fully achieved the goal that I had in mind when I initially went there (a thing so rare in this world as to be worth noting). There, the health of my wife has been completely restored and I have restored mine to the state in which it was two years ago. I am still not a very vigorous man, but, God be praised, nor am I any longer a sick man. We have benefited from this fruit of our solitude in order to travel a little in the world. We have come to Germany and are settled for a month or two on the banks of the Rhine.[35] Here, while war afflicts and agitates the whole of Europe,[36] I have quietly made myself a study. I am studying the history of Germany in order better to understand its current state. I am trying to immerse myself as much as possible in the atmosphere of Germanic mores and ideas. This is so different from our own. I live only with Germans and seek to speak to them only about their country. I find them pleasant and refined in their private life, although still poorly fit for public life.[37] But who could be fit for public life on the continent of Europe, where the free institutions of the Middle Ages have everywhere been extinct for the last two hundred years, and where civilization, instead of preparing men to live without any master other than themselves, seems to have served only to gild and legitimate their servitude?

But you probably are not interested in my *philosophy*. You would prefer to have some news. Unfortunately, I have none to give you. In France, only those who are in the office of the master know anything, and you are aware that I neither can be there nor, above all, do I want to enter therein. Hence, I am only familiar with what the newspapers tell us. The great question of the moment is that of knowing what the two central powers, Prussia and Austria, will do. People repeat every day that they are in agreement or will come soon to an agreement with France and England.[38] This is quite possible for the first act of the play, but not for the others. The Emperor of Austria and the King of Prussia might very well want to contain Russia and to oblige it to sue for peace, but they will never want to plunder and ruin it. For them, the question of principle still trumps that of territory, and they have far too little confidence in their own peoples to seek to destroy in advance the power that might be most capable of maintaining them in obedience, if need be. Now, it is no longer peace and the *status quo* that France and England want. It is war and the dismemberment of the colossus; they are perfectly right to do so. In spite of all this, it would not be *impossible* for the war to end as winter draws near. But that is quite unlikely and if no peace is made in the next six months, everything indicates that there will be no peace for a long time, and then everything will be uncertain on our continent. God willing that our examples might teach you how to remain tranquil on yours!

My wife wishes that I thank you in her name, as I have already done in mine, and that I remember her particularly to you. Believe, my dear Mr. Sedgwick, in all my sentiments of esteem and sincere friendship.

A. de Tocqueville

P. S. When you write, please address your letter to my father, the Count de Tocqueville, 19 place de la Madeleine, Paris.

100. Theodore Sedgwick to Alexis de Tocqueville[39]

New York, July 20, 1854

My dear M. de Tocqueville,

I have recently written to you about the new [. . .][40] *Haarlem R[ail] Road* bonds.

Since then, at the beginning of last month, it has been discovered that Mr. Robert Schuyler has committed an enormous fraud involving the shares of the *New York and New Haven Rail Road & Co.*, and that a similar fraud involving a smaller amount had been committed by Mr. Kayle, the treasurer of *Harlem R[ail] R[oad]* (your company). These frauds consist in the signature of these two agents on false *stock certificates*, in other words in the creation of *false shares*.

The discovery of these frauds along with the current uncertainty with regard to their magnitude has created a true *panic*, not only concerning the affairs of these companies, but also of almost *all* the *railroad companies*. I am writing to reassure you and to tell you that, based on the best information that I have been able to obtain thus far, in my opinion you have nothing to fear either for your *Harlem* bonds or for the *Michigan Central* and *Galena-Chicago* bonds. These are, I believe, all the bonds that you have.

First, the fraud is limited to *shares* and does not extent to bonds; and moreover there is at the present moment a *panic* that will gradually subside. You would not be able to sell your bonds for anywhere near their exact value, but I have no doubt that things will change. I do not say *when*, for public confidence is badly shaken by these frauds in all the *railroad* companies and it will take some time for them to settle down. I am writing to you because you asked me to keep you abreast of our financial world. There is no doubt that several of our railroad companies have great financial difficulties and will continue to have them for a long time to come. But the country is prospering and I think that those companies like yours, which regularly make money, will not fail to pay their interest promptly.

If you want more information, the only thing you have to do is to ask me. I send my compliments to Madame de Tocqueville and I ask you to accept the [expression][41] of my most sincere and distinguished [consideration].[42]

Theodore Sedgwick

Beinecke Rare Book and Manuscript Library, Yale University, MS Vault Tocqueville, D II a, Bonnel copy, Paquet 12, pp. 75–77.

101. Alexis de Tocqueville to Theodore Sedgwick[43]

Bonn, August 14, 1854

Dear Mr. Sedgwick,

I received your letter of last July 20 three days ago. It brought me great relief. I had been very concerned about the state of business affairs in America and, in particular, about the panic which seemed to reign in railroad transactions. Thanks to you, I now clearly see the causes and the extent of the problem. Based on what you tell me, I do not believe that I have anything to fear, since I do not need my capital at this moment and I can wait for the crisis to pass and for the prices to go up again. I could not properly express to you how grateful we are for the constant care that you are taking to provide us with information that you think might be useful or reassuring to us. This is to act like a true friend and one can only respond with genuine friendship to such behavior. This is, I assure you, what I am doing now and from all my heart. I hope that you would count on me if, for my part, I could ever do anything that would be agreeable to you in France.

I wrote to you from Bonn on the 17th of last month. It is still from Bonn that I am writing to you today, but I am about to leave this small town in which I have spent two very profitable and even pleasant months. I am fortunate to derive great pleasure from observing new mores and adjusting myself comfortably to them. Being introduced into a society of German professors and being admitted in the midst of their families, it has not taken me long to feel like one of them. I have found here a lot of education, often much intelligence, and almost always a genuine simplicity of habits and good-heartedness of character. What I have observed of the private mores of Germany has seemed to me very interesting and even engaging. But, as far as public mores are concerned, it is best not speak of them. They are what two centuries of absolute government, sixty years of centralization, and a very long habit of administrative dependence, both as bureaucrats and administered individuals, have made them; that is to say, they lend themselves very well only to servitude or revolution. What can you do with these people when they arrive among you in America? Nonetheless, they come to you in an ever growing number, already 140,000 per year, I am told.[44] Regardless of your power of assimilation, it is quite difficult to *digest* so many foreign bodies so quickly in such a way as to be able to incorporate them into your substance and such that they do not disturb the economy and the health of your social body. I wish that you were growing less quickly. But you are carried forward by an inevitable destiny toward greatness and dangers.

Farewell, dear Mr. Sedgwick, and thank you a thousand times again. Do not write to me any longer at St.-Cyr-près-Tours, which I have left, but at my father's home, the Count de Tocqueville, at *Clairoix, near Compiègne (Oise)*. I shall go there soon. With many heartfelt regards,

A. de Tocqueville

102. Francis Lieber to Alexis de Tocqueville

New York, September 4, 1854

Before I return to my everlasting South, my dear de Tocqueville, I wish to write a line to you, not that I have anything particular [to say], but the older I grow the more I see and feel[45] of two things – that in politics almost everything depends upon good *institutions* and people trained in them, and that, in private life, one of the greatest comforts and joys is a letter from a noble and high-minded friend. Therefore, let me hear from you. You must have received the copy of my *Civil Liberty* long ago, to judge from the fact that Mettermaier has had it these 4 months, and he has received his copy through Bossange through whom your copy went likewise. I am somewhat curious to hear whether you have thought it advisable to give an account of it to the Institute.

Of course you have heard of our infamous Grahamstown affair.[46] There is but one comfort, namely that there is not one American, not one newspaper (except of course the *Union*) that does not execrate it. The matter will be severely overhauled in next Congress. But the main business is the Nebraska Bill. You cannot conceive what a decided and absolute effect this has had on the *whole* North. Douglas, who hoped to become president by it, has, on the contrary, killed[47] by this bad measure. Another [. . .][48] attracting much attention is the "Know-Nothing," a secret society having arisen out of the old "Natives."[49] Their essential point is *anti-Irish Catholicism*. They will carry many, many votes next election, but must fall to the ground after that. I shall write a series of articles against them in the *N. Y. Daily Times*. I shall probably be in some permanent connexions with that paper – the most rising American paper. This is strictly [. . .][50] now. I have the offer to contribute to it.

You see, I write politics to you, indeed, but not of trans-Atlantic ones. I have not even mentioned the Russian war.[51]

Give my very best regards to Madame de Tocqueville and to the Beaumonts.

A propos, my agents in New York will be henceforth B. Westermann and C°, German Booksellers, New York, and anything for them given to Hector Bossange would be sure to reach me, so that for those cases the direction would be:

Francis Lieber

Care of B. Westermann and C°

German Booksellers

New York

For letters, my address is the same as formerly. Let me soon hear from you, in Columbia.

> Ever your sincere fr[ien]d,
> Lieber

Beinecke Rare Book and Manuscript Library, Yale University, MS Vault Tocqueville, D II a, Bonnel copy, Paquet 12, pp. 47–49.

103. Alexis de Tocqueville to Theodore Sedgwick

Tocqueville, September 4, 1855

Dear Mr. Sedgwick,

I have *just* received your letter, even though dated the first, no doubt by mistake. I am sending a messenger on horseback to the nearest post office so that this letter can reach you as quickly as possible. Nothing would please us more than your visit and you should not deny us this pleasure. Our common friend, Ampère, is with us, and like us, loudly expressed his joy upon learning that we might perhaps see you. Please come, the sooner the better! If you leave for Le Havre on Saturday, a steamship goes in eight hours from Le Havre to Cherbourg on Sunday. Once arrived there, you will have to be taken to the *Hotel de l'Europe*. The owner is one of our friends. She will find for you a barouche that will bring you here in two hours. If you prefer to travel over land, you must reserve your place in a stagecoach or in the mail coach from Paris to Valognes, a small neighbourhood town, or to Cherbourg. Seat reservations are made in Paris, although the coach can be taken only at the half-way point, at Lisieux. One can get to Lisieux by train. Since this route is a busy one, you should make a reservation in advance to be sure of having a place and a good seat. Perhaps the mail coach no longer runs, but the stagecoaches always do. Nonetheless, before going to the stagecoach, try the mail coach. The latter is always more comfortable and faster than the former. Once arrived in Valognes, go to the *Hotel du Louvre*; we also have friends there and you will be easily provided with a good coach to come here, also in two hours.

Goodbye for now, I hope; my wife, Ampère, and I will be very happy to see you again. A thousand friendly and sincere regards,

A. de Tocqueville

P. S. If this is not inconvenient to you, could you, please, stop by at the Lévy booksellers, 5 rue Vivienne, to obtain for me, on behalf of M. Ampère, a copy of *Promenade en Amérique*? This is the same work that you saw in the *Revue des Deux Mondes*. Since it was well received, Ampère turned it into a book, changing it a little in the process.[52]

The best person in charge of coaches in Valognes is called Alexandre. He is the one I use myself. He will provide you with a good coach that will bring you here quickly.

104. Alexis de Tocqueville to Theodore Sedgwick

Tocqueville, September 11, 1855

Dear Mr. Sedgwick,

We were greatly fearing that my letter might have arrived too late due to the delay of the post. It is with an even greater joy that we have received your announcement that your arrival here is certain and imminent. Even if you were to find in our home nothing of the sumptuous hospitality of the English castles, at least you will be received here by good friends, something that gives a certain charm and worth even to the simplest inn. Moreover, you will have the opportunity to see the old life of the French chateau, which is quite opposed to convention and ceremony, and does not carry into the countryside anything from the city, apart from the taste for conversation and books. Ampère will certainly remain here and greatly rejoices at the idea of spending a few days with you; I, too, think that the four of us will have a great time together. If you desire to see truly massive building works, I shall take you to Cherbourg and we shall visit the sea wall and dock basins which certainly are, if not among the most useful, at least among the most wonderful endeavours of the human spirit.

If you have time to give us one-day's advance notice, you will be certain to find us at home upon your arrival rather than paying a visit to a neighbour. But this is not really important since we are never far away. As a rule, it takes only two days for the post to arrive here and usually it takes no more than that, unless the letter is dropped into the box, either in Paris or here, after the mail is picked up. This is what happened with the letter that I had written to you. It left only on the next day after I wrote it.

But this is already writing too much to someone whom we shall soon see. Hence, I end here by greeting you and assuring you again of how delighted we are to be welcoming you.

A. de Tocqueville

105. Alexis de Tocqueville to Theodore Sedgwick

Tocqueville, September 19, 1855

Dear Mr. Sedgwick,

Your last letter caused us great disappointment and, I could even say, genuine sadness. My wife, Ampère, and I had been waiting continually for you for the last four days. You were the regular subject of our conversation and we were making all kinds of plans for spending our time together. You would have taught us many things about America that would have interested us to the highest degree and, perhaps, we too might have told you a few things about France that would have not been uninteresting to you. But destiny has been stronger than the will of all of us. I say *all* of us because I believe that you had the sincere desire to come here and that you were prevented from doing so only by circumstances independent of your will. I do not give up all hope of seeing this plan coming to fruition in another year. Nor do I need to tell you that your young son would be as well received here as yourself, especially if he were to accompany you. Two years from now, a railway will connect Cherbourg to Paris and then, undoubtedly, a regular steamship service will be established between Cherbourg and Southampton. Hence, I hope that you will begin your journey on the continent of Europe by passing through Tocqueville. Please remember this and take it as said.

You are very kind to offer your help with regard to our affairs in America. For the time being, we do not have cause to benefit from this friendly offer and we ask you only to act as you have already done of your own accord and to alert us whenever you think fit. Our funds continue to be invested in the same way; they are invested in bonds in the railway companies of Chicago-Galena, Michigan Central Railway, and New York Harlem. Mr. Green has lately encouraged us to buy the bonds of Marietta-Cincinnati. But this is of little importance.

Have a safe journey, dear Mr. Sedgwick; our wishes will accompany you across the Atlantic. Do write to us upon reaching your destination. After having spoken to us about yourself, please give us news of your country. Tell us if the Know-Nothing Party is as dangerous to the internal peace of the Union as it seems to us from afar. In the West, you have just provided examples of popular disorder that do not strengthen the cause of declining liberty in Europe.[53] The English do harm to liberty by the weakness and incapacity of their government and you do the same by the violent, intolerant, and lawless spirit that seems to be spreading throughout a good part of the Union. And yet, in my view, its cause remains the old good cause and it will nevertheless remain so for as long as I shall live.

You were instrumental in our making a very pleasant acquaintance by putting us in touch with the Beckwith family. When distinguished Americans and your friends come to Europe, do not hesitate to recommend them to us. We shall always honor your recommendation. Farewell. Everyone here joins me in expressing to you our regrets and in giving you the testimony of our friendship.

A. de Tocqueville

106. Theodore Sedgwick to Alexis de Tocqueville[54]

New York, February 15, 1856

My dear M. de Tocqueville,

It is useless to make excuses for myself when you think that I can be of help to you. I was traveling when your letter arrived; hence, in responding to you I have missed a steamer, but I think that this should reach you in time.

I addressed myself to the *Harpers* (it is the most important establishment here and the most likely to give a wide circulation to any writing). They have very willingly agreed to do it but hesitated about the translator.[55] They told me that it is almost impossible to find here a *translator* capable of translating *well* a serious work. All those who could do it are occupied either with newspapers or with other things, and those who are available are not capable of it. They told me that if you intend to publish the work in England, it would be better to use the English translation here. For the book might be translated better and more cheaply in London than here. Thus far, I have given you an account of a conversation I had with the Harpers. After finishing it, I made them a proposal in writing for the record and they have responded to me. I am sending you the correspondence and you will see that they believe they have found an adequate translator. I do not know the Dr. James to whom they refer, but they should be perfectly capable of [. . .][56] and I believe that you can trust them. Hence, if you send me the proof sheets as they become available, I shall pass them onto the Harpers and the book will appear in due course. I shall make a formal contract with them. And I shall be very pleased to serve you as a gentleman of the Chamber in order to present you to the "Sovereign people" to whom, moreover, you need no one to introduce you. If only you could give instructions in writing to the translator. I take the liberty of advising you, in your own interest, to write in a manner that is a little more in tune with the mores of our time. Your last letter is something between hieroglyphics and cuneiforms and I believe that only Ampère and I could decipher it. Also please make sure you conform to the post regulations if the proof sheets are sent by English steamers.

I owe you a sincere apology indeed for not having thanked you earlier for your kind and hospitable letter that I received in Brighton. I shall not forget your invitation to enter Europe by Cherbourg and Tocqueville on the occasion of my next visit. When I received it, I was about to leave and ever since my return, I have been very busy. My voyage has been of immense benefit to my health, but we are having a terrible winter here. For the last fifteen days, we have had only two or three days of thaw and mountains of ice and snow on our streets. Our political affairs are not very interesting. The members of the *Know-Nothing Party* have little power in the country, and the issue of slavery, in spite of *Kansas*, has lost a good deal of interest in the eyes of the people. The worst symptom of our affairs is that nobody cares any more about politics except the rabid fanatics and the [. . .].[57] Those who have any sense at all have withdrawn almost completely from politics. I would not dare to claim that we honor our time except in so far as material progress is concerned.[58] The growth of our power from this point of view is prodigious.

Please remember me to Madame de Tocqueville and believe me, my dear M. de Tocqueville, to be always your devoted,

Theodore Sedgwick

My friendly memories and greetings to Ampère.

107. Theodore Sedgwick to Alexis de Tocqueville[59]

New York, March 5, [1856]

My dear M. de Tocqueville,

The present letter will be rendered to you by *Mr. Alfred Pell* of our bar, who is leaving to visit Europe for the first time. I would very much like him to see you; and perhaps you will be so kind as to make him the acquaintance of one of your lawyer friends, who could initiate him into the mysteries of the Palace and the Public Prosecutor's Office. Mr. Pell is one of our young distinguished men and I very much desire that he should see those things that are most worth visiting in Paris.

I have recently written to you regarding your letter and am waiting for the proofs.

Please believe in my most sincere devotedness and in my most distinguished consideration.

Theodore Sedgwick

108. Theodore Sedgwick to Alexis de Tocqueville[60]

New York, March 23, [18]56

My dear M. de Tocqueville,

I have just received your letter of March 3, and I find the whole situation very annoying. I mean Fortune, not your letter.

When I received your *first* letter I contacted the Harpers who accepted to have your work translated and printed at their own risk and peril upon receiving the proof sheets from Paris, and to give you ten per cent of the revenues. I immediately wrote to you about all this by enclosing copies of my correspondence with the H[arpers]. I cannot conceive how my letter has not reached you, except for the fact that the address that you had given me in you first letter was *Place de la Madeleine*, whereas I see that this one has another address. At any rate, there was not the smallest delay on my part and I hope that this letter will reach you on time. The only thing you have to do is to send me the proof sheets. From a *financial* point of view, the contract you were offered is similar to what they agree with the best authors. I received your kind letter in England and perhaps I shall see you again this summer.

In great hurry (to catch the steamer), your devoted,

Theodore Sedgwick

Please remember me to Madame de Tocqueville.

Beinecke Rare Book and Manuscript Library, Yale University, MS Vault Tocqueville, D II a, Bonnel copy, Paquet 12, pp. 81–82.

109. Theodore Sedgwick to Alexis de Tocqueville[61]

N. Y., March 29, 1856

My dear M. de Tocqueville,

I am writing to you for the *third time*.

1° I answered your first letter concerning your work by enclosing copies of my correspondence with the Harpers.

2° Having received your second letter announcing that you had not received my news, I wrote again in order to inform you of what I had done.

3° I am enclosing again a copy of the Harpers' letter *ex majore*[62] in order to inform you that the agreement has been made here, and that you have nothing to do except to send me the proof sheets as they become available.

I would be very distressed if my countrymen were to be deprived of your work because you have not received my letters. In a hurry, please believe in my most sincere devotedness.

Theodore Sedgwick

Beinecke Rare Book and Manuscript Library, Yale University, MS Vault Tocqueville, D II a, Bonnel copy, Pacquet 12, p. 82.

110. Alexis de Tocqueville to *The Liberty Bell*[63]

Testimony against Slavery

I do not think it is for me, a foreigner, to indicate to the United States the time, the measures, or the men by whom Slavery shall be abolished.

Still, as the persevering enemy of despotism everywhere, and under all its forms, I am pained and astonished by the fact that the freest people in the world is, at the present time, almost the only one among civilized and Christian nations which yet maintains personal servitude; and this while serfdom itself is about disappearing, where it has not already disappeared, from the most degraded nations of Europe.

An old and sincere friend of America, I am uneasy at seeing Slavery retard her progress, tarnish her glory, furnish arms to her detractors, compromise the future career of the Union which is the guarantee of her safety and greatness, and point out beforehand to her, to all her enemies, the spot where they are to strike. As a man, too, I am moved at the spectacle of man's degradation by man, and I hope to see the day when the law will grant equal civil liberty to all the inhabitants of the same empire, as God accords the freedom of the will, without distinction, to the dwellers upon earth (France, 1855).

[Alexis de Tocqueville]

111. Alexis de Tocqueville to Theodore Sedgwick

Paris, May 18, 1856

Dear Mr. Sedgwick,

I wrote to you a month ago, sending you the first proof sheets of my book.[64] I have since sent you two other batches; the third one was sent yesterday and will perhaps arrive only at the same time as my letter. These three parcels should have placed into your hands the first sixteen proof sheets.[65] Ever since these parcels were sent out, a worrying thought occurred to me. I forgot to add to each parcel a thread that would make it more solid and I very much fear that an accident might have occurred and that everything that I have sent you might not have arrived intact at the final destination. Upon further reflection, I have found this fear so warranted that tomorrow I shall send you again, with all the necessary precautions, the sixteen sheets in one single batch. I would have already done so if I had not been annoyed at the idea of forcing you to pay an extra postage. I was reassured at the post office that the postage to America can be paid here, but that there is a local postage which the sender cannot pay in advance. Nevertheless, I have decided to impose upon you this small fee for which I am asking you, as a friend, to excuse me.

I am beginning to have a sense of the size of the book. It will have 330 to 340 pages of text and approximately 100 pages of notes. The printing is under way.

What is even more important to me, if that is possible, than the arrival of my proof sheets in your hands is your judgment of them once you receive them. God willing that this judgment should be favorable! I attach great importance to knowing your opinion. For, if a judge who is such a close friend of the one who is judged condemns it, what could one expect from the public at large?

Nothing interesting is occurring at the present moment in Europe that might help me render this letter less boring, at least nothing that I can bring to your attention. Moreover, an author who publishes is like a lover: the great interest he takes in his own affairs prevents him from seeing and hearing what is going on around him. Nevertheless, I believe I can affirm that nothing happens which the newspapers (which I do not read at all) could not directly tell you. We are enjoying peace here, without trusting too much in its duration.[66] Everyone understands that the entire political system followed in Europe for the past forty years has changed, that all the old alliances are being loosened or destroyed, that new interests and new forces are in place, and that the past no longer teaches us anything about the future. But of all the elements of this future, the most obscure part is inside the mind of the man who holds in his own hands the immense force that France has at her disposal.[67]

Farewell. Be well. Please give me news about yourself and retain a little friendship for us.

A. de Tocqueville

P.S. Henceforth you should reply to me at Tocqueville, St. Pierre-Église (Manche).

112. Theodore Sedgwick to Alexis de Tocqueville

New York, May 21, 1856

My dear M. de Tocqueville,

My eyes are troubling me a little, and as I am compelled to employ an amanuensis, I also am obliged to write in English.

I have received proof sheets one to seven of your work and have handed them over to Messrs. Harper and Brothers for translation.

I do not know what arrangements you have made about publishing a translation of your work in England but the Harpers wish me to call your attention to the fact, that if a translation of your work was published in England before that of the Harpers was published here, the English translation might reach this country and a cheap reprint of it be issued here much to their prejudice and that of the work.

I have told them that I would request you to obviate this difficulty by letting them have the proof sheets here in abundant time so as to be completely ahead of any translation that may be going on in England. Be good enough to let me have a word in reply on this subject in order to satisfy the Harpers.

I have been somewhat afraid of the difficulty of finding a good translator here but I believe a competent one has now been secured. I have read with great pleasure the seven sheets already received though I have not given them the careful perusal that I could have wished. On two points, viz: the extent of the division of landed property in France before the Revolution and the centralized administration of the Old Regime your views are very striking and interesting. It is very presumptuous in a foreigner to speak of style, but your sentences are as clear as crystal. I cannot but think that the critics of your own country will consider your work eminently happy in this respect. I am very glad to be instrumental in any way in bringing your book to the knowledge of my countrymen.

I shall be absent from the city for some time this summer, but I have given directions in my office which will prevent any delay in regard to your proof sheets. M. Desplaces is here on behalf of M. de Lamartine.[68] M. de L.'s name and works have great popularity here but if any thing was to have been done in a pecuniary way on a great scale, he should have come himself. Enthusiasm cannot be roused by a *fondé de pouvoir*.[69]

I beg my most particular remembrances to Madame de Tocqueville and pray you to be assured of my faithful regard,

Theodore Sedgwick

P.S. I have just received the proof sheets 8 to 12. The Harpers ask me how many pages the volume will have.[70]

T. S. Beinecke Rare Book and Manuscript Library, Yale University, MS Vault Tocqueville, D II a, Bonnel copy, Paquet 12, pp. 77–79.

113. Alexis de Tocqueville to Theodore Sedgwick

Paris, May 23, 1856

Dear Mr. Sedgwick,

The person bringing you this letter is a young Frenchman for whom I particularly request your kind attention. His name is the Viscount de Chambrun.[71] He belongs to a very good family and has an idea that must be encouraged, namely the idea of visiting the United States with his wife and to this effect to spend there, six or seven months. M. de Chambrun has already traveled a lot in Europe and has done so like a man who wants to learn and not only to see. All the information that you could give him about your country, all the useful contacts that you might help him make, will have great value in his eyes, and he is, I believe, very capable of fully appreciating the advantage of meeting a man like you.

I wrote to you some time ago and am waiting impatiently for a sign from you announcing that my proof sheets have begun to reach you.

Please believe in all my sentiments of most sincere friendship.

A. de Tocqueville

114. Theodore Sedgwick to Alexis de Tocqueville[72]

New York, May 28, 1856

My dear M. de Tocqueville,

I have just sent to you a letter by the last steamer (in English) and I realize that I addressed it by mistake to 19 Place de la Madeleine, your former residence. Please claim it, if it has not already reached you, since I did not keep a copy of it. I have just received your proofs up to page *no. 12*. I am enchanted by the work, but with regard to the *title*, how should it be translated, since we do not have any equivalent words for *Ancien Régime*? It is for this reason that we have naturalized them *in part*.

Would it be appropriate to say *The French Revolution and its relations to the old monarchical government of France*? How does this look to you? It is quite long – *On the Old French Monarchy and the Revolution*. Would that be better? I am so delighted by your book and have always been so interested in the great work of 1789 that I would not mind writing a small volume as an introduction to the translation, but I fear I might diminish the number of volumes sold. But, please, tell me something regarding the *title*.

"*Trade Price*" means retail price or *exchange price*.

Farewell, my dear M. de Tocqueville, and believe me to be always your devoted,

Theodore Sedgwick

Please excuse my letter; it is by mistake that I began on a half page and I do not have time to start again. As for "the good faith of the Francs" and the "current accounts," all our contracts without exception are made as [. . .][73]

Beinecke Rare Book and Manuscript Library, Yale University, MS Vault Tocqueville, D II a, Bonnel copy, Paquet 12, pp. 79–81.

115. Alexis de Tocqueville to Theodore Sedgwick

Paris, June 6, 1856

Dear Mr. Sedgwick,

I am beginning to be surprised and worried by your silence. Seven weeks ago, I started sending you the first proof sheets of my book. Since then, I have not heard a single word from you. In the meantime, I have been sending you the corrected proof sheets as they reached me and finally, on the 24th of last month, I sent you in one batch all the proof sheets that I had already sent to you separately, sixteen in total. I was fearful that some of the main parcels might have been lost. As I point out at the beginning of this letter, your silence not only surprises me but also worries me. I fear that you might have had an accident. Nevertheless, I feel reassured at the thought that those of your compatriots whom I already know would have informed me of anything that might have happened to you. Moreover, I know that, in spite of the ease of communications, the great abyss between us cannot be eliminated; nor can one be absolutely certain of journeying safely from one shore to the other. In spite of these reassuring thoughts, I very much desire to see your handwriting again.

People are very concerned here about the turn taken by events between England and yourselves.[74] They fear that a war might come out of all this. I cannot persuade myself that these fears are well-founded, nor can I imagine that two nations which have so many reasons to live in peace would resort to arms without being forced to do so, either out of interest or honor. Hence, until the very last moment I shall believe that a means of reaching an amicable agreement will be found. If you must finally settle this by arms, your government, in seeking to bring the question to a *successful* conclusion, will have committed an enormous mistake in waiting for peace to be re-established in Europe, if only temporarily.[75] For, on the one hand, this peace returns to England all its resources and, on the other hand, the treaty itself which has ended the war contains a clause which goes very much against your interests: it is the one which, while recognizing that the flag covers the merchandise, prohibits *letters of marque*.[76] This last arrangement appeared to England to be of such importance that, in order to obtain it, she abandoned the principle for which she had always fought. And I believe that in this regard she was right. This clause can only be very useful for her in a war against you. Because your principal means of action against her lies precisely in the recognition of the use of *letters of marque*.

But that is enough about this issue. The first rule that any Frenchmen must follow when writing to his friends, if he wants his letter to reach the person to whom it is addressed, is not to speak about politics. This is one of the consequences of our glorious institutions. Farewell then. A thousand friendly and affectionate regards.

A. de Tocqueville

P. S. I am mailing today the proof sheets numbered 17, 18, 19, 20, 21, 22, and 23.

116. Alexis de Tocqueville to Theodore Sedgwick

Paris, June 16, 1856

Dear Mr. Sedgwick,

I have finally received a letter from you. It is the first one. It is dated May 21 and arrived in Paris on June 10. I was absent at the time. I had just been summoned by telegraph to see my father who was very ill and who died in my arms a few hours later,[77] causing the most profound sorrow that has ever struck my family.

Having returned to Paris two days ago, I hastened to send you the last proof sheets of the book. They left yesterday. The baptism of our future emperor,[78] having closed the post office at an unusual hour, did not allow me to send this letter with the proof sheets as it had not yet been written.

I noted with deep regret the recommendations that you make in your letter regarding the dispatch of the proof sheets. You would have preferred them to have been sent first to America, rather than to England. Unfortunately, this recommendation arrives too late, since the book is finished.

In the letter that you wrote to Mr. Harper on February 11 of this year, a copy of which you sent me, you forewarned these gentlemen that you did not know if I was going to have my book translated in England. Messrs. Harper were therefore forewarned that this might be the case. Since, in their response to the letter of February 11, they made no observation whatsoever on this subject, I was led to believe that they had no particular wish in this respect. Therefore, as soon as each proof sheet reached me, I sent on the same day a copy to the English translator and one to the American translator. I thought that, given the silence of the contractees, justice obliged me to act in this way. You will easily understand that if I had wanted to favor one of the two editors, my private interest would have led me to favor the American editor, especially so when you learn that in England I sold the copyright for a one-time paid sum (according to the terms of international agreements which now regulate these matters) whereas in America, the material gain, if there is ever such a thing for me, will depend on how large or small the sale of the book is. From a monetary point of view, anything that can promote this sale in England is indifferent to me whereas this is of great importance to me as far as the American edition is concerned. Hence, I have acted as I did only because I was not aware of the wishes that the editors in the United States might have had. Moreover, I hope that by hurrying things along, the American edition will appear much earlier than the English one.

I would be very distressed, dear Sedgwick, if I had reason to believe that this small affair, independent of the annoyance and perhaps a few expenses that might have been incurred by you, could have caused you the least displeasure. Please reflect upon the circumstances that I am bringing to your attention and I hope that you will not think that I am at fault. What a pleasure it would be for me to see you and to be able to talk to you about all of this, instead of being reduced to correspondence. My wife wishes me to remember her to you. Please believe in my most sincere friendship.

A. de Tocqueville

117. Alexis de Tocqueville to Edward Vernon Childe

[end of] June 1856

Dear Mr. Childe,

Please excuse me if I do not come to see you and do not return to this funeral house. The catastrophe that has just occurred, so close in time to the death of my poor father, fills me with despair and horror.[79] I am sick in both body and spirit. I leave this cursed city to retire into solitude. But my brother has kindly agreed to give me news about you and your family in whom I shall have a profound interest for as long as I shall live.

A. de Tocqueville

118. Alexis de Tocqueville to Edward Lee Childe

[end of] June 1856

Dear Mr. Edward,

I do not know where this letter will reach you, or if it will ever reach you. I cannot send it to your father since I am told that he has left Paris. Therefore, I shall send it to a friend of your family who will perhaps know where to address it to you. Through a deep and profound sympathy, I felt the need to tell you how much I share your sorrow. You have lost a mother who was passionately attached to you; just a few days before the cruel event that took her away from you, I had heard her speaking about you with the greatest possible fondness. She venerated her son, that *dear Edward,* as she called you, with such a motherly tone that I can still hear it. Alas! How much she was rejoicing at the idea of seeing you again! Who could have believed that that joy would be refused to her in the prime of life and shining with such good health ? Your mother honored me with a special friendship; I shall never forget her and shall always recall her for the rest of my life with affection and respect; never shall I become indifferent to the fortunes of her children and particularly your own, dear Mr. Edward, whom she loved so deeply. The world only knew the sparkling and agreeable qualities of your mother, the brilliance of her mind, the vivacity of her imagination; but her friends appreciated even more things in her. They knew what there was of real worth under that attractive exterior. For my part, I often admired the vigor and clarity of her mind, the soundness of her judgment; nobody gave better advice than your mother. On several occasions, I asked for her opinion on the most serious and confidential matters and I always benefited from it. Moreover, she had a quality that is so rare even among superior women: she lacked all that petty envy, all those petty feelings, all those miserable petty passions that women often mix with their greatest qualities. Truly, I am writing to you with a genuine and profound sadness; the death of your mother, so close in time to the loss of my beloved father, has thrown me into a grief from which I am finding it difficult to recover. I hope that the terrible news did not arrive all of a sudden and that you were not alone in that cruel moment. I know from past experience what it means to learn suddenly of a great domestic tragedy, being far away from one's family, in the middle of foreigners from whom one can expect no sympathy. If this happened to you, you have my entire sympathy. You have a delicate health and I cannot refrain from fearing that such a great shock might have had a strong impact on it. I would be very happy to receive news from you. Furthermore, I do not know when I shall have the pleasure of seeing you again. I left Paris with the intention of not returning there, at least in a permanent manner, for a long time, perhaps for a few years; but, whether present or absent, I shall not cease to take a sincere and profound interest in anything that might concern you and your family.

A. de Tocqueville

119. Alexis de Tocqueville to Theodore Sedgwick

> Tocqueville, par St.-Pierre-Eglise (Manche)
> July 1856

Dearest Mr. Sedgwick,

I do not know by what turn of *untoward*[80] circumstances but your very kind letter of last May 28 has only now arrived here. Anything that I can say in response to your questions will unfortunately reach you too late. Nonetheless, I answer as if it would serve some useful purpose. *L'ancien régime* is untranslatable into English; it is an essentially French expression. You must resort therefore to a paraphrase. The two solutions that you propose seem to me equally good. I would incline, however, toward the second: *the old French monarchy and the Revolution.*

Your endorsement of the book brings me great joy. Nothing could flatter me more than such a favorable judgment coming from you. God willing that you should maintain this favorable opinion until you will have finished reading the entire book! I hope that without waiting for an answer from me, you will have followed the idea that you expressed in your letter and that you will have agreed to serve as the person *introducing* me to the American public. I assure you sincerely that this would make me very happy and I would be very saddened to learn that you have abandoned your intention.

The book appeared in France about two weeks ago. The death of my beloved father that coincided in such an unfortunate manner with an event which he had been so impatiently waiting for and which, alas, he was unable to enjoy, has entirely prevented me from taking the measures that, after having ceased to address the public as an author for twenty years, it is always wise to take at the moment of reappearing before it. Nonetheless, I have reasons to hope that my book, although left to itself, fares pretty well. My editor seems very happy about the sales;[81] almost all the newspapers have already written about it,[82] and every day I receive many letters informing me that the work and the author are well liked. These are good signs but nothing more than signs. Only time ranks the works of the mind and assigns them their definitive place.

How much trouble, how many worries have I given you with this book, my dear Mr. Sedgwick! I would be overwhelmed by the heavy obligation that I have toward you under these circumstances if I did not feel such a genuine sense of friendship and gratitude toward you. Will you not give us the pleasant opportunity to greet you soon? How happy would we be to see you arrive at the end of the long carriage drive flanked by oaks leading to my home! You would be received by hosts who would be truly delighted to have you under their roof and who would be determined not to let you leave easily. Please make sure that all this soon becomes something more than a dream!

I am waiting for the arrival of Ampère here in less than a month. I can assure you, without exaggeration, that he would be no less happy to see you than us.

Many friendly and sincere regards.

A. de Tocqueville

120. Alexis de Tocqueville to Edward Lee Childe

July 17, 1856

Dear Mr. Edward,

Your letter has profoundly moved me and, at the same time, has given me great pleasure.[83] I was worried about you. I feared that the announcement of the terrible tragedy that had struck you, having suddenly reached you in the middle of unknown people and on a cold foreign land where no sympathy can be found, might be too harsh for such a frail health as yours. When I saw that the condition of your mother seemed serious, I allowed myself to consult her doctors in order to know if it was not appropriate to ask you by telegraph to return quickly. They answered that, regardless of the final course of the illness, its ending was going to be too swift for you to be able to return in time. Moreover, your father, whom I had informed of my actions, told me that he did not know where you were to be found at that time. Your return, dear Edward, must have been very difficult. How much I, like you, regret that you were not there, at the approach of the terrible moment! Your presence would have sent a gesture of joy even into the horrors of death. Your mother was so passionately attached to you, so fully devoted to you! For her, you were the object of such a constant care! She loved all of her children, but you, she adored; and although she was not too forthcoming with regard to her own personal feelings, she could not prevent herself from constantly speaking to me about her son. I could not pay her memory the respectful and affectionate remembrance that I shall always have for her without taking the deepest and most genuine interest in you. It is impossible to think of her without your image being present.

You seem, dear Mr. Edward, to expect from me advice on the situation in which you find yourself. You have an inkling of what this advice will be, and you are right; there is, in fact, only one course of action. The first of all your duties is toward your father. You have in him a rare friend; I have never met a man who is more devoted to his children than him and who derives all the pleasure of his life from them. He must be very unhappy since, apart from the terrible suffering that such an event cannot fail to cause, his entire life is disturbed at a moment in life when such changes can no longer be repaired. For some time, at all events, you should think only of him and must think only of alleviating the transition from one way of life to another. Like you, I believe that, at least at first, a stay in Paris would be a great source of discomfort and sadness for both of you. Your father has friends here, even among the French; but in spite of this, everything would constantly remind him, as well as you, of how much your situation has changed and would cause you daily and in a painful manner to perceive the immensity of your loss. I imagine that, given these circumstances, Mr. Childe feels the need to return to his own country.[84] If this were the case, there is no doubt that you must accompany and help him as much as you can, regardless of how little you are attracted to that country, in order to make his stay there pleasant and not leave him before he finds a tranquil situation and habits to occupy his time. I am certain that this would be the advice of your mother if she could speak. Today America and Europe are at such a small distance from one another that this would not prevent you from coming to visit us soon and greeting the sincere friends that you are leaving behind in France. I would very much wish that you should choose a *profession*. But I have little hope of that. Dear Mr. Edward, you cannot imagine how useful that would be to you! A profession is like a roof under which a person designs the course of his life following his own preferences. It is the foundation to which one can add all kinds of accessories. Without a profession, one's actions lack the common point which makes them form a whole and by dint of which all the parts support each other. But, as I was saying, I very much fear that nothing has prepared you to make this step; try, at all events, to continue to occupy your mind and preserve the intellectual tastes that you have acquired in Europe. If I were to judge by what is being published in the United States at the moment, I have reason to believe that the number of those who have the same preferences as you is greater there than you might think; the only thing is that they are not gathered together as in France, and one must go to great lengths to look for them and discover them. From time to time, return to Europe to renew your contacts. From now on, please do not leave me without any news about you. I have a genuine affection for you and shall always be happy to give you all the proofs of it that may be in my power. Farewell, dear Mr. Edward. Remember me to your father and be reassured that you will have in me, for as long as I shall live, a true and sure friend.

A. de Tocqueville

121. Theodore Sedgwick to Alexis de Tocqueville[85]

New York, July 29, 1856

My dear M. de Tocqueville,

Thank you very much for your kind and friendly letters. Until last week, I had always thought it possible to see you in Europe this summer, for I have promised myself not to revisit France without seeing you at your home and without resting in the shade of the oaks at Tocqueville. But I must give up this pleasure this year. If I am alive, I hope to see you again next year and perhaps then I shall introduce one of my daughters to Madame de Tocqueville; I hope she will allow me to do so. Please believe in the sentiments of sympathy with which I received the news of the death of your father. These events, even when they arrive late, are always a turning point in life; if they do not break our heart as they do in our youth, they profoundly sadden us. The sounds of the bells are calling us.

As for your book, all is in order. The translation is finished and is now in the hands of the Harpers. The translator (a man full of wit) is very impressed by the talent of the book and tells me "that it will be *the* book on the subject." I believe him. As soon as the book is published, I shall send you a copy through a friend so that you can judge for yourself. If you find it well done, the translator would be very pleased if you sent him, through me, a flattering message which, coming from your mouth, would be very precious to him.

Our political affairs are in a total disorder and it is impossible to predict the name that will come out of the presidential ballot box. But I do not fear for the Union – we are not so stupid that we would slaughter each other.

When you see Ampère please "give him my love" as we say in English to those who are very dear to us. Please pass on my compliments to Madame de Tocqueville and believe always in my most sincere friendship,
Theodore Sedgwick

P. S. Thank you for your permission to serve as your godfather.[86] I would have attended your private baptism with great pleasure, but I have severely sprained my ankle lately. This has bothered me considerably and I now fear that it is too late to do it as it should be done – I could not appear in your company except properly attired.

Beinecke Rare Book and Manuscript Library, Yale University, MS Vault Tocqueville, D II a, Bonnel copy, Paquet 12, pp. 99–104.

122. Alexis de Tocqueville to Theodore Sedgwick

Tocqueville, par St.-Pierre-Église (Manche)
August 29, 1856

Dear Mr. Sedgwick,
    I received your letter of July 29 a few days ago. It would have arrived a day earlier had you addressed it to me at Tocqueville (as you should do

from now on) instead of sending it to a residence in Paris where I have not been living for some time. I probably forgot to inform you of this. Be that as it may, your letter has finally arrived and has given me immense pleasure, a feeling that was, however, mixed with the disappointment caused by learning that you will not be introducing me to your public. You know that I would have been particularly delighted by this manner of being presented in America and I abandon it only with great regret. You tell me that one of the reasons that has diverted you from this small undertaking has been the problems caused by a sprain. The cause upsets me as much as its effect. It seems to me that you have had some problems with your leg for a very long time. I fear that this new mishap might aggravate that old injury. Please respond to this point when writing to me again; because you must know that we take a sincere interest in all that concerns you and that we are not indifferent to anything good or bad that might befall you. Another sad piece of news contained in your letter is the postponement of the trip that you intended to make to Europe this year. We were excited by the idea of this trip and were already trying to guess the likely period of your visit. It is a real disappointment to give up this plan. Our only consolation is your renewed promise to come to see us upon disembarking on the continent upon the first occasion that you return to Europe. I assure you sincerely that you will be received here with genuine pleasure – not just you, but also those of your family who would be willing to accompany you – and that you will quickly feel *at home*[87] in my house. Is it your wish to postpone giving us this pleasure indefinitely?

In France, the success of the book in which you have shown interest surpasses all my expectations. The first edition was sold out in seven weeks. This edition came out, however, at the most unfavorable time of the year and was printed in as many copies as the three first editions of *Democracy* put together. If any important American newspapers or any major journal from the same country were to publish any articles about this work that might be of interest to me, I would be very obliged if you would send those issues to me. I hope also that someone will be kind enough to send me the American translation.

In Europe, people are beginning to believe that you are not far from the time when you will separate yourselves from one another. As far as I am concerned, I hope that this moment is even farther away than people usually think. I believe that you have a core of good practical sense, which will prevent you for a long time from rushing into such an adventure. Unfortunately, each new day brings you so many foreign elements that soon you will no longer be yourselves, and all the arguments about your *natural condition* will become more and more uncertain. For having so many races among you today, who can justly claim what your *natural condition* is nowadays? What is certain is that for some years, you have strangely abused the advantages given to you by God, advantages which have allowed you to commit great errors with impunity, and that you have come to inspire in the whole of Europe a sentiment combining little esteem for your wisdom with fear of your power. Viewed from this side of the ocean, you have become the *puer robustus* of Hobbes.[88] Being so, you upset all of the friends of democratic liberty and delight all of its opponents. People regard you as an unpredictable and dangerous force. But on the other hand, the public becomes more and more hostile toward you and the number of those who would happily see you fall into great shame and great disgrace grows every day.

Farewell, dear Sedgwick. Trust in our true friendship and our great desire to see you again.

A. de Tocqueville

123. Alexis de Tocqueville to Francis Lieber

Tocqueville, par St.-Pierre-Église (Manche)
September 1, 1856

My dear Lieber,

I have just received your letter of July 19 and noticed with sadness that you have left Columbia where, it seems to me, you had enjoyed a fairly happy time.[89] I would be very interested to know what consequences this event will have for you and what new changes you are going to make in your life. You live in a country where life is more erratic than in ours. Even in your private life, you are subject to more ups and downs than in Europe; but you also have many more means than the Europeans have of taking advantage of the new situations that the course of events create for you.

Thank you very much for the interest you have taken in advance in the book that I have just published. I am very eager to know what you will think of it once you have read it. I entreat you to read it in French. You know our language well enough for me to be interested in showing you my ideas in their national costume. The best translation is never more than a poor copy. In France, this book has had great success thus far. The first edition, which was quite large, was sold out in seven weeks, and I am presently occupied with the second. It is impossible for you not to be able to obtain a French copy in New York.

At the very moment when the book was released, I had the great misfortune of losing my father who, despite his advanced age, had remained the best support and the infallible guide for all of his children. Our sorrow was profound and every day new circumstances remind us how great is the irreparable loss that we have suffered. Soon after this sad event, towards the end of June, we left Paris and came to settle in the place from where I am writing to you now. We shall remain here until spring. It is to here that you should, in general, address your letters. Now that I no longer have any public functions, I do not spend more than a few months in Paris every year. The rest of the time is passed in the retreat where I am residing at the present moment. It is an old house belonging to my family, built near the sea, set in beautiful countryside. Here, I find many books that my predecessors or I have collected. I live a pleasant and healthy life, with no great luxuries, but in comfort and security, and I ask of God nothing more than to give health to my dear wife and I such that we may spend the rest of our life happily living here. Our life passes by. I have just turned fifty-one. Hence, I am over the top of the mountain and can only descend from here. I often gain comfort from this when seeing how little worldly affairs turn out as I would have liked them to. I have passionately wished to see a free Europe and I realize that the cause of liberty is more compromised now than it was at the moment of my birth. I see around me nations whose souls seem to weaken as their prosperity and physical force grow, nations that remain, to borrow Hobbes' phrase, robust children who deserve only to be treated by means of the stick and the carrot. Your America itself, to which once turned the dreams of all those who lacked the reality of liberty, has, in my view, given little satisfaction to the friends of liberty for some time. One would say that the despots of the old world have entrusted you with performing the same role that the Spartans bid the helots play in front of their children, and that through the follies and vulgarities that liberty gives rise to, they want to cure them of the desire ever to be free. After all, our time presents a curious and entirely new sight; and it is worth living through it, if only out of curiosity.

Farewell. Please believe in all my sentiments of sincere friendship. My wife wishes to be especially remembered to you.

A. de Tocqueville

124. Theodore Sedgwick to Alexis de Tocqueville[90]

New York, September 19, [18]56

My dear M. de Tocqueville,

I have just received your letter of August.[91] I have returned from the house of my mother where I spent a sad summer. But my sadness is not of recent date. I have never spoken to you about my personal life because I almost always avoid the subject, except when I am unable to do so, but the tone of your letters, so amicable (so friendly, as we say in English) makes me break the silence. My wife has been dying from a lung ailment – very slowly, very gradually, but also very painfully – for the last three years, with all the vicissitudes of improvement and decline which always mark this terrible malady. There were moments when we almost thought that she would recover, but for the last three months her condition has worsened considerably and now we only have to wait for her death which is approaching with slow but sure steps. So as to change the atmosphere, we left our home here, close to the city where Ampère found me, and for the last year and a half she has been staying with my mother in Massachusetts[92] where I first saw you twenty-five years ago. This has deprived me of my *home*[93] here and of my children, for I cannot deprive her of their society – the two oldest are nineteen and seventeen year-old girls, the two others are too young. My daughters are exactly at that age when they most need the guardian eye of a mother, so that this blow strikes me from all sides and in the most sensitive places. I spent the summer at my mother's home, close to the bed of my wife, and have just returned to town in order to occupy myself with the affairs of my profession which I like greatly. For, in the last resort, there is only enforced, obligatory work that can make us withstand life's evils. Please excuse this long and sad story; your letters, I repeat, are so kind and you exaggerate so much the little I have done for you that I could not desist.

I still do not know anything about the success of your work. It has just been published and in the solitude of the mountains of Massachusetts I saw almost nobody. Today I have asked for a copy that I will send (probably tomorrow) through Mr. Fulton to your address, care of *J. Monroe & Co*, 6 rue de la Paix, I believe, but the firm is well known. At any rate, the volume will arrive shortly. My friend in the firm is *Mr. G. J. Richards* and if you look for him, address yourself to him in my name. I shall write to him about this.

The book appears here at a very bad moment since we are in the middle of a very serious and acrimonious election and everything is now neglected for the sake of politics. [. . .][94] etc. etc. Your observations on the subject of our affairs do not surprise me, since there is enough room for even more severe reproach. Adversity is necessary to man, to nations as well as to individuals, and now, for almost three generations (at least two and a half) we have only had the most complete and striking prosperity. We have lost our simplicity and modesty, not to mention our virtue. I believe that we shall be punished by this great hand that holds the reigns of the universe. And in fact we have already been punished. The administration of the current president has only been a repetition of the most disgusting errors and we shall not be spared very serious blows in the future. Nonetheless, I do not believe in the separation. There is a little good sense that remains to us. I am delighted by what you tell me about the success of your work in France. That could not have been otherwise. Today I have been to see *Bonner* the translator, but I could not find him. I shall write more after seeing him. As for my sprain, it has made me suffer considerably, but it is better now. It was *the other foot*. I promise to see you again under the oaks of Tocqueville. Please let me know if this letter reaches you.

Your sincere friend,
Theodore Sedgwick

Beinecke Rare Book and Manuscript Library, Yale University, MS Vault Tocqueville, D II a, Bonnel copy, Paquet 12, pp. 96–99.

125. Alexis de Tocqueville to Edward Vernon Childe

September 24, 1856

Dear Mr. Childe,

I have received and read with the most profound emotion the letter that you wrote to me.[95] It brought bitter sweet recollections to my memory. I thank you for having left with M. D.[96] the package that you mentioned.[97] Upon arriving in Paris my first preoccupation will be to go to look for it, open it, and remove the letter to which you allude; I shall send it to you or shall copy it for you. But that will not occur immediately, since I cannot return to Paris before two or three months from now. I am held here by matters necessitated by the partition of the inheritance of my father. I would have been extremely delighted to greet you before your departure, as well as your children. But I must give up this idea for now. What I am not prepared to renounce is the idea of seeing you and them again. I hope that you all know, without any need for me to tell you again, that you have and will have in me, for as long as I shall live, a devoted friend, whose affection will not be diminished in any way by distance or years. I very much want to know, dear Mr. Childe, how you will arrange your life; how you will get on in America; if you can create for yourself a new life which might give you both the satisfactions of mind and heart that you need. I take the most profound interest in your children. I often think of Edward, who has so many pleasant and attractive qualities, but who until now has lacked the first condition of happiness on earth, namely, a prevailing liking for something and a regular occupation. How much I would love to learn that he has finally found his own path in life! I hope that Miss Mary will be a great source of consolation for you. The little that I have been able to see of this young woman confirmed in me this opinion of her. In general, dear Mr. Childe, I hope that you will find in the heart of your children the only consolation that could touch your own heart. They certainly have good reasons to love you, for I have never met a father who is more affectionate and has a more profound sensibility than you. These rare qualities, combined with the extreme refinement and the noble nature of your feelings, have gained you genuine friends in a country that was foreign to you. I do not speak only of myself but also about others; in fact, all those who knew you well have retained for you an esteem whose trace you will easily find if you ever return among us, as I hope you will do. As for me, I repeat, independent of the respectful and affectionate recollection that will always link me to the memory of Mrs. Childe, I shall never cease to have a genuine friendship for you and your family. Please write to me from time to time and give me news about yourself; you could not do this for anyone who takes a deeper and more sincere interest in you than I do. Farewell, I pray that Heaven protect and guide you and your children. Please embrace them affectionately on my behalf and do not forget me.

A. de Tocqueville

126. Alexis de Tocqueville to Theodore Sedgwick

Tocqueville, par St.-Pierre-Église (Manche)
October 14, [18]56

Dear Mr. Sedgwick,

Your letter of September 19, which arrived a few days ago, has profoundly touched me. It is only now that I believe that you really have a little friendship for me, since you spoke to me about your private affairs and about what is happening in the bosom of your family. I assure you that you could not communicate on this subject with anyone who might listen to you more sympathetically and would be more sincerely interested in what you tell him than me. Please be reassured that I deeply empathize with the family problems that you describe. Please do not delay in writing to us again (I say *us* because my wife very much shares the interest that I take in all that concerns you). Give us news about your dear ailing wife and your family. I hope that you stay healthy in the midst of these harsh trials and that the sight and interest of your children will give you to the end the courage that you will need.

Many thanks for letting me know that a copy of the translation of my book has been sent to me. I am writing today to Mr. Richards in order to let him know how the volume might reach me. I think I told you in my last letter that we have already been obliged to reprint the French text. If you read the English journals and major newspapers, you will observe that I have no complaints about the impact that the book seems to have in England. The German newspapers that I receive are also very favorable to me. With regard to America, I realize that the timing for publishing a book is not well chosen and that, regardless of the concern that an author might have for his own importance, I am obliged to acknowledge that at the present moment your fellow citizens have better things to do than to read what is being published in Europe.[98] Please God that they at least extricate themselves well from what preoccupies them! Moreover, a book on the French Revolution can never excite as much interest in America as in Europe. The French Revolution is a significant part of the special history of each of the peoples of this continent, and one cannot say anything about it that does not immediately prompt them to reflect on their own situation.

Like you, I was led to believe that, no matter how worrying the state of public affairs appears to be in your country, you would not let yourself be drawn toward separation and civil war. I desire this in the interest of the whole of mankind. I would hope for it even more if you were still the same people you were sixty years ago, or even the people that I saw twenty-five years ago, although even then I had already perceived a few distressing changes. But what scares me is, on the one hand, the prodigious number of foreigners that are turning you into a new people; and, on the other hand, this race of desperate gamblers that your prosperity, in a land that is still half-empty, has brought forth, a race that combines the passions and instincts of the savage with the tastes, needs, vigor, and vices of civilized men. The world, I think, has never seen anything like it before. Who can say where this might lead you if they ever gained the upper hand in your affairs? What is certain is that in Europe the idea that you are rapidly approaching the time of revolution is more and more accepted and is spreading very quickly. I do not share these fears as yet, or at least, I do not think that this event is so imminent. This is what determines me to leave the funds of which I have spoken to you invested in your railroad bonds. I count on you to tell me when you think it appropriate to withdraw them. To be honest, I still do not see any serious risk at the present time.

Our mutual friend, Ampère, is the one who has been charged with bringing from Paris the translation you mentioned to me. I expect him here at the end of the month and hope to keep him for two whole months before letting him go to Italy, where he absolutely wants to spend the end of winter. We shall go to Paris around February, as is our custom. Far from fearing winter in the countryside, once I am well settled here, I do marvellously well. There one is free from unwelcome visitors and can still hope to receive good friends. I am sure that we shall spend many lovely evenings with Ampère in December, around a large fireplace, facing a roaring wood fire, while the wind whistles around our age-old trees and the ocean rumbles two miles away from us. It is then that one remembers fondly by-gone times and absent friends. I assure you that we shall speak about you around this hearth and shall sincerely wish that your affairs may take a happier course. It is my hope to see both you and your family here one day, for you know that we are resolved to welcome you into our family. Dear Mr. Sedgwick, please give us news about yourself and write again, I pray, about the personal circumstances of your life. Be reassured that nowhere else will you find more sincere sympathy than within the old walls of Tocqueville. A thousand friendly regards.

A. de Tocqueville

127. Alexis de Tocqueville to Edward Vernon Childe

Tocqueville, December 12, 1856
par St. Pierre Église (Manche)

Dear Mr. Childe,

Two days ago I received your letter from Boston dated the 18th of last month. I had already been reassured about your situation by a letter that you had written to M. Mérimée;[99] but I was a little upset at not receiving news directly from you, since I like to think that there is no one in Europe who takes a more genuine interest in you and your children than me. I am extremely delighted by what you tell me about your children and yourself. I see that you were welcomed in Boston as you deserved to be, and that your sojourn there provides you with enjoyment. During my brief passage through the United States, more than twenty years ago, Boston seemed to me the most pleasant city to live in. There I found a great number of educated and pleasant people, and if I had had to settle somewhere in America, I believe that I would have chosen Boston.

The small token of remembrance that you mentioned to me has certainly arrived by now in the hands of my agent in Paris. But it will not reach me for some time, regardless of how much I desire to have it. I have ordered the person in question to keep anything that comes for me from you until my return to Paris so that he might hand everything over into my own hands. This will not happen, I think, before February. I am extending my stay here for as long as I can. For the return to Paris this year will seem to me quite sad. As you know, in the countryside I live an active and pleasant life that suits my health. Thank God, I have no reason to complain about the latter! . . . I very much fear that I shall have to wait for my return to Paris before I can send you the copy of my book that you want, as I do not have an available copy here. As you will easily understand, I shall send it to you with a very pleasant but also very sad emotion. How delighted I would have been to offer this book to her who has been taken away from among us in such a sudden and cruel manner! How much I would have wanted to have her opinion and to profit from the sound judgment that she had on all the works of the mind! How many conversations did we not have on the subject of this work, on its composition, its chances! Alas, who could have imagined that she was never going to read it? I am very touched, dear Mr. Childe, by the interest that you are taking in the fortunes of this book. It has already been translated twice into English[100] and once into German. The first edition of the French edition was sold out in less than two months. The second edition has almost sold out; in general, the reception of this work has surpassed all my hopes.

At the beginning of your letter, you told me, dear Mr. Childe, that you do not want to talk to me about your political issues. I very much object to this decision and hope that you will not persist in it the next time that you write to me again. What happens now in America must be of interest to all civilized people and is of particular interest to me, who am half Yankee. It would be very valuable for me to know what a man endowed with so much common sense like you and who, although being an American in his heart, has lived such a long time outside of the movement of parties, thinks about the current political situation of the Union and what he imagines the behavior of the new president will be. Hence, I do not release you from the obligation of speaking about politics when writing to me again.

Do you happen to have the opportunity sometimes to see M. Edward Everett? If so, please remember me to him. I also once had very good relations with Mr. J. Sparks. Please tell him that I have not in the least forgotten him.

Farewell, dear Mr. Childe. Remember me most affectionately to Edward and Mary, and believe in my deep and sincere friendship.

A. de Tocqueville

P. S. When writing to me, you should send the letter here, if it is intended to arrive before January 1, or send it later to M. Dosseur, 21 rue de Turenne, who will hand it to me. I do not know what my address in Paris will be.

Ampère, who is with me at this moment, asks me to remember him particularly to you and your son.

I re-open my letter to tell you that I have just received a letter from Edward that touches and interests me greatly. Please tell him that. I shall write to him soon.

Letters: 1857–1859

128. Alexis de Tocqueville to Edward Lee Childe

Tocqueville, January 4, 1857

Dear Mr. Edward,

I have received your letter of November 28 and I thank you for it.[1]
Everything in it that refers to your mother, Mrs. Childe, has particularly
touched me. I can imagine your profound emotion when placing that
coffin in your family vault. The account alone has profoundly moved me.
I still cannot accustom myself to the thought of her death, or to the idea
that I shall never see her again. Such thoughts had never come to my
mind before that terrible event occurred. In seeing her still so young,
so full of life, so outwardly healthy, so cheerful, so sparkling, who could
have imagined that she would abruptly plunge into death! This event –
so sudden and so unexpected – has filled me not only with sadness but
also with horror and made an impression on me that will never fade
away. Mrs. Childe had many sincere friends, but I doubt that she had
met anyone else who could penetrate into the depths of her soul more
than me. She took as much care to conceal from the world her most truly
attractive qualities as others do to display them. One needed, as it were,
to force her to remove this casual and easy-going appearance with which
she loved to cover herself in order to perceive what was serious, noble,
and right in her heart, what was sound and singularly powerful in her
mind. She allowed others only to see her more modest qualities. Anyone
could easily notice that she was witty and likeable. But, I believe, only
very few were given the opportunity to know that she had even better
qualities.

Before receiving your letter, I had received one from your father. I noted with great pleasure that in Boston he had met friends whose sympathetic welcome had done him a great deal of good. He seemed to me to be in a reasonably good state. I rejoiced with all my heart, since I have a genuine friendship for him. I hope that he is persuaded of this and that he will sometimes give me news about himself. In his last letter, he asked me to send him my new book. I was not able to do so immediately because I did not have a copy of the book here. At my request, my bookseller has just sent me a copy. I shall write a few words on its first page and M. Ampère, who is here with me but will return to Paris a day after tomorrow, will take it upon himself to give this volume to M. G.,[2] who will pass it onto Mr. Childe. The second edition of this book will soon be sold out.

You have told me, dear Edward, about how you spend your time in a very interesting way and have enabled me to understand in a manner that I enjoyed very much what is going on in your mind. I understand only too well that a man who has received your kind of education and spent the whole of his early youth in the midst of the society where I saw you, feels an almost insurmountable aversion toward embracing ordinary occupations and taking upon himself the annoyances brought about by a profession, and especially a profession in America. Between the world of affairs in your country and everything that has become necessary to you there is an incompatibility which, I fear, is absolute. I confess to you that I am distressed about this, for I persist in believing that the most solid foundation of happiness can be found in a regular life, where one is busily employed and has certain social connections. But I recognize that nothing has prepared you for this kind of life; you have acquired a second nature which it has become impossible for you to change. The main question now is to benefit as much as possible from this. To that end, it seems to me, you are doing the best that can be done. You compensate for this lack of imposed obligations by engaging in voluntary activities as much as you can. I could not approve of you more. Cultivate more and more this natural taste that you have for beautiful literature and the fine arts, and if, in fact, you are as receptive, as I think you are, to the refined pleasures that these things give, you will be able to fill your life and happily escape the general law which links happiness to having a permanent and fixed employment. With the inclinations that you describe and I know that you have, you will often return to see us in Europe, for here is the true native land of those who think like you. I am sure that you will always be well received here. You have knowledge, wit, and manners that will ensure that you will always be well regarded even by those who, unlike me, have not remained very faithful friends to you and your family. You amuse me with your fears of losing the habits that France has given you and of reappearing here as a stranger. Do not worry about this. Do not force yourself to acquire what you already have and do not force yourself to retain what is now part of your nature. Remain yourself as simply and naturally as you can. You will always easily discover yourself to be a European. It would be more difficult to turn you into a citizen of the United States. It is quite certain that, at the beginning, Paris will appear to you much changed when you return here. In your mother, Mrs. Childe, you had a great support: you will greatly miss her salon, which was unique even in France by the great number of distinguished people who used to attend it and by the variety of persons that the lady of the house was able to attract and gather together. It formed a center that was extremely conducive to the kind of life that you wanted to live. Nonetheless, if you no longer find these advantages here, you will still discover many traces of them. I imagine that you do have a few friends of your age. Your father has left among us a great deal of sincere affection, based on the incomparable esteem that he was able to inspire. His son will always be welcome among all those who knew him. I observe, as a good trait of our character, that a foreigner who sought to show himself in society as little as Mr. Childe did, was however widely known and appreciated by all those who had the opportunity to come close to him, and that he inspired a sentiment of friendship in so many people. Hence, do not worry and allow me to repeat to you: do not think of anything but of being yourself, without worrying in advance about what our world might think of you when seeing you again. Dear Mr. Edward, please forgive this advice from an old man. My age is more than twice yours and I take a profound interest in you. This is my excuse!

I shall end now in order to avoid sending you a whole volume. We are here until the end of the next month. After that, we shall spend a few months in Paris; I do not know where I shall reside there, but I imagine that a letter addressed to the Institute will always reach me.

Ampère who, as I have told you, is here, wants to be especially remembered to your father. He also wants me to mention him to you. He has not forgotten that he met you in Rome; nor has he forgotten the pleasure of being with you there.

A thousand friendly and sincere regards.

A. de Tocqueville

129. Alexis de Tocqueville to Theodore Sedgwick

Tocqueville, par St.-Pierre-Église (Manche)
January 10, 1857

Dear Mr. Sedgwick,

A letter that I have just received from our common friend Beckwith informs me that the great tragedy that you were fearing has finally occurred.[3] My wife and I are truly saddened and we ask you to accept the expression of our deep sympathy. We do not need to have known Mrs. Sedgwick in order to mourn her death. The sincere friendship that we have for you is enough for us to be very upset by this event. We know that in losing her, you are incurring an immense loss; for she was, we are told, a very rare person. Moreover, we ourselves fully understand how painful such a separation must be, since we also get on well together and each of us feels that losing the other would be the most terrible misfortune that could happen. Please therefore accept, I repeat, dear Mr. Sedgwick, the expression of our most deeply felt sympathy. Since you are no longer retained in America by such a strong obligation, I hope, moreover, that we can expect to see you in Europe next summer. I do not need to repeat what I have already told you so many times, namely, that it will be a great joy for us to welcome you and your children, and to keep you here for as long as possible. Hopefully, this time you will not make us regret that you visited our continent without meeting us. Your daughters, the Misses Sedgwick, if they accompany you, will find in my wife almost a compatriot and will be welcomed in the friendliest possible manner.

The affairs of your country continue greatly to worry the friends of America and of liberty. On this side of the ocean, the election of a new President[4] has been seen as the triumph of the cause of slavery, more so perhaps than is the case in reality. As for me, who has never been an abolitionist in the usual sense of the word, that is, who has never believed in the possibility of destroying slavery in the old states, I am, I shall confess to you, vehemently opposed to the extension of this horrible evil beyond the already too extensive limits within which it is confined today. That would seem to me to be one of the greatest crimes that human beings could commit against the general cause of humanity, and on this issue I feel in me powerful political passions, if it is allowed to a fifty-year-old Frenchman, who has seen four or five revolutions, to still have any passion whatsoever and to take human affairs very seriously. With what interest would I listen to you if, as I hope, I were able to speak with you next summer! I flatter myself that I could tell you a few things about France that you do not know, and I am sure that you would teach me many things about America of which I am unaware.

I have finally received, although after a great delay, the American translation of my book. I find this translation to be very good and would like to write to its author. How should I proceed? The second edition of the French text has just sold out. Four thousand copies in less than one year is a fact with which, I dare say, the booksellers in France today are not accustomed.

I am a little unhappy, dear Mr. Sedgwick, at having learned from a third party about an event that is so tragic and critical for you. I complain gently as one must always do between friends; but I complain nonetheless, since you know well enough how interested we are in you for you to be convinced that news of this kind could not fail to have great importance in my eyes.

Farewell. Please believe in all our sentiments of esteem and friendship.

A. de Tocqueville

P. S. Ampère has just left us, after having spent two months under our roof. I do not need to tell you what he thinks of you. He has announced that he will return next July or August. Hence, you have advance notice about the place where you will be able to find him.

We will leave Tocqueville next month in order to live in Paris until June. But we do not know as yet where we shall reside in that city. If you write to me, please address your letter to the *Palais de l'Institut*, care of *M. Pingard*, *Chief-Secretary*.

130. Edward Vernon Childe to Alexis de Tocqueville

Boston, January 13, 1857

My dear M. de Tocqueville,

Owing to the severity of the weather on the Atlantic this winter, letters arrive on this side of the water rather late. But, happily, your most kind epistle of Dec. 12th reached me a few days since, and I hasten to answer it. You say well (and as my children and their father can also say from long experience) that no one in Europe (perhaps I may add, in America) interests himself in our welfare more than you. Nor are we ungrateful. If we were, *she* to whom we are in so great a measure indebted for this interest, if she could witness our ingratitude, would not spare reproaches justly merited.

It is a source of happiness that your health is so good – you have so much to do before you that is worth doing, and impossible to others, while your affections are so much needed by those you love. Being here for the winter, we make the best that can be made of life at a hotel. Our friends and acquaintances, as I have already said, are kind and attentive, but there is such an air of soberness, not to say sadness, pervading both the physical and moral atmosphere that our hearts are at times the reverse of gay, dwelling, as they are too apt to do, on all which we have suffered – on all which was and alas! is not. I am sometimes asked respecting our future life and movements, and if anyone could answer for me, it would save me a world of embarrassment. What to do, and where to reside, I know not, there are so many contradictory elements to be considered. Two years are required for Mary (who, on learning this moment that I am writing to you, bids me say that she "hopes you are well, that she desires to be kindly remembered and that she wishes you a happy new year"). Two years, I was observing, are required for Mary's education. She must remain here, then, till the time arrive[s] for her entering society. In Europe how could she be presented, motherless as the poor child is, and without a single *female* friend? Her wants, therefore, and the peculiarities of her position, will of necessity regulate the movements of Edward and of me. Otherwise you might see us, and we might have the happiness of meeting our dear and excellent friends in France in the course of a few months. I do not know what may be the change which will come over us when we shall visit the South. Our friends there are waiting with outstretched arms to receive us, but I cannot quit my daughter even for a day. Edward, however, I have persuaded to precede us, the poor fellow finds life here so dull and unsympathetic. There is a possibility, though no great probability, of my son's finding some thing to do in Washington, which, while it diverts and occupies him, will serve as a sort of string whereon to attach the results of his studies and the products of his mind. Such is my ardent hope, but not my expectation. Not that I fear disappointment in being able to put him where my object could be accomplished, could I imbue him with my notions, but that Edward is not a man made for public life, such as public life is in America, not being ambitious in the common sense of the word, not being anxious of notoriety, nor as yet conscious of his powers, whatever they may be; free, too, from extravagance in every respect, he does not feel the necessity of exertion, nor till now, however he may admit it theoretically, does he appreciate the full value of a "career."

He wearies himself notwithstanding, no hour of his day is allowed to pass unoccupied. Having powerful means to employ, wherever we may be in Washington, and such services as Edward can render in the Foreign Office, for example, not being always at command in the capital, I have no fear of failure, should he feel disposed to avail himself of what can be had for the asking. But I have learned to be sanguine in nothing. Let me speak to you – you a sincere and faithful friend, who knew better than any one else concerning me from *her* who is lost to us – let me speak to you with open heart. That heart is not broken, though within the last 3 and 4 years it has sometimes seemed well nigh bursting; nor is hope crushed within it, though its hopes are indeed faint; but life, this small chapter in our interminable existence (although I feel and acknowledge the absurdity, perhaps too the iniquity, of the thing), appears now and then rather wearisome to me.

It is a source of real pleasure to Edward and me, the great success of your last work.[5] Although no judge in the premises, and although on reading it, and even before, there was no doubt in my mind as to its merits – its peculiar merit beyond, I presume, the exact or special talent of every other distinguished author – I should not have been surprised, however grieved, had the *[Old] Regime* not proved a popular book. That it has proved so I am truly delighted to learn. But, however content you may be, I figure to myself how much your satisfaction would have been enhanced, could you have been permitted to enjoy the congratulation of *one*, whose nice discrimination, clear judgment and virtuous habit of thought, could not but have been welcome even to you, independent as by necessity must be a mind like yours of others' opinion. But alas! in every cup of joy there is a dragon tooth.

A little before receiving your favor, I was dining with Mr. Everett, and I had been to see Mr. Sparks in Cambridge. Since then I have been on the look out for both these gentlemen, who will be both happy and proud to receive your friendly message, which I shall soon deliver to them.

You overrate the value of any communication that I am capable of making respecting American affairs. If I had been in Washington I might have had something authentic to tell, but *here* there seems to be little or no interest taken in the great questions of the nation, if one is to judge by the general conversation. Politicians are to be found without number, but without exception, so far as my observation reaches, northern *gentlemen* of education and position avoid mixing themselves up with persons of 2nd and 3rd rate rank. They are wrong. Hamilton, the greatest statesman, perhaps, of our country, remarked on a certain occasion to the leading men of Boston, "you err when, quitting the political arena in disgust, you deliver it over to the occupations of your inferiors in birth, talents, and acquirements."

I have no apprehension of a dismemberment of the Union. *Within* the slave states there is a populous, and numerically potent element which will ever keep down and neutralize the separationists' folly. The free states regard the frantic contortions of southern demagogues as grown men look on the freaks of a child.

The North can do without the South. The South without the North would not! Kansas, I believe, will be a free state. Public opinion in America is like "an army with banners." The question of the right of slave owners to carry their slaves into territories must be decided by the Supreme Court. However, contrary to every worthy feeling and to every true maxim of economy, that decision ought, in my poor opinion, legally to be in the affirmative.

Edward and Mary join me in all affection and respect.

E. V. Childe

Beinecke Rare Book and Manuscript Library, Yale University, Uncat MSS 324; also available as Bonnel copy in MS Vault Tocqueville, D II a, folder "Bonnel's copies of letters from Americans to Tocqueville."

131. Theodore Sedgwick to Alexis de Tocqueville[6]

New York, Febr[uary] 5, 1857

My dear M. de Tocqueville,

Thank you very much for your kind letter. I have thought several times of writing to you, but I have never been up to the task. My silence has not been caused by the fear of not finding sympathy, for you belong to the small number of people who participate in the great battles and pursue great careers without losing neither their heart, nor their humanity or their belief. But I have been sad and I shall continue to be so for a long time. As I believe I have told you, my wife was English, Puritan by birth, but she came here with her father at the age of ten and from that moment on, we have always been together; my sister was her friend from childhood — her brother, mine — so that we have lived in a close intimacy almost from the youngest age. I do not need to tell you what a death like this means to me. She takes with her in the tomb my youth and my courage. But I am not complaining. She was a noble heart and gave me four children who bear the imprint of her aristocratic nature in the best sense. She was of a rare beauty and that beauty never struck me more than the last time when I embraced her. She was so tranquil after so many anxieties of all kinds, so beautiful after three long years of illness.

I cannot speak about my wife – I never speak of her – but I love writing about her as she deserves. But to what avail? Thank you again for your sympathy. I shall speak about other things.

The election of Mr. Buchanan is in no way the triumph of the extreme party of the South. In the *Nominating Convention*, this party had two candidates, the current President[7] and Mr. Douglas, the author of the repeal of the *Missouri Compromise*.[8] Both have failed;[9] Mr. Buchanan was nominated candidate of our party broadly for three reasons: (1) He was absent from the country for three years and was not discredited in the recent affairs;[10] (2) He was in no way responsible for the Kansas-Nebraska Bill of Mr. Douglas; (3) He belonged to a free state[11] and the result seems to prove that we could not have elected any other person but him. He is completely free to pursue a[12] firm and independent policy. I am not ready to guarantee either the courage or the independence of party leaders, but I find good reasons to believe and hope that the administration of Mr. B.[13] will be wise and moderate. It is certain, and he sees it perfectly, that if this were not the case, we shall find ourselves in the most serious danger four years from now.

As for Mr. *Frémont*,[14] his nomination was, in my opinion, an insult to the good sense of the country, and even to the distinguished men of the party opposed to slavery. It offered no guarantee of wisdom or moderation. His election would have simply been a revolution – an abrupt and violent revolution. It is certain that the power of the Union will finally settle down in the free states. Their numerous representation in the lower Chamber cannot fail to achieve its goal. But in order to carry out this change of power in a furious onslaught to the country a much wiser and much more moderate approach is needed than the election of a dragoon colonel under the impression produced by civil war or the civil skirmishes in Kansas.

As for slavery, I detest it as you do, as any reasonable person does. But one must recognize that our Union is an alliance between *free* states and *slave* states; one must recognize that neither the climate nor the products of the southern or south-eastern states are appropriate to the work of the whites; one must finally recognize that the three million black slaves can never be admitted and incorporated into our political and social body; and one must admit and accept the logical consequences of these facts.

Slavery has spread with our dominion mainly to the states that produce cotton and sugar; I think that it will do the same in the future. Its growth will amount to nothing or little in the countries that cultivate wheat and the other products of the North. In other words, I believe that the solution of the difficulty will come from the laws of nature or, in other words, from *God* and not from man. Political parties will poison it – they will not solve it. I also think that for us, those from the North, we have other more serious dangers to fear than slavery. Our lack of discipline and mania for decentralization (at the antipodes of your French spirit), our recklessness in speculation, our unbridled love of gain and money, finally corruption of all kinds, all this threaten us much more than slavery.

All things considered, I believe that our national politics should seek to follow the fundamental idea of our system – that is to say, the complete independence of older and newer states in their local affairs, including slavery; and complete neutrality of the federal government toward the ideas of liberty and slavery. The current misfortune is that for their part, all the extreme parties of the North and South want to seize central power in order to augment their own power. If this antagonism prolongs itself for a long time, I consider it certain that we – you and me – shall see the dissolution of the Union; and thinking, as I do, that this event would infinitely be the greatest disaster that mankind can currently experience, I shall do my best to avoid it. The election of Mr. Buchanan is not the triumph of any of the extreme parties; it gives us, the friends *par excellence* or, above anything else, of the Union, a new and better lease which we shall use wisely. I am ashamed of the length of this letter – but the question is of an immense interest and has carried me away; please excuse me.[15]
[...]

Beinecke Rare Book and Manuscript Library, Yale University, Uncat MSS 324; also available as Bonnel copy in MS Vault Tocqueville, D II A, folder "Bonnel's copies of letters from Americans to Tocqueville." Massachusetts Historical Society Ms N-600.

132. N. W. Beckwith to Alexis de Tocqueville

Geneva, Feb[ruary] 20, 1857

My dear M. de Tocqueville,
    Your kind note of the 11th reached us on the 16th inst., and gave us a great deal of pleasure.

Anything from you is a pleasure at all times, but in this dull place, a letter full of living fresh thoughts, and on a subject so interesting to us, brings with it an electrical force which stirs the mind with agreeable emotions and makes us grateful.

The new administration[16] is not yet formed: the President will go into office in March; public curiosity has not been able to draw from him an intimation of his choice of assistants, and seems to have become tired of guessing; it is probable indeed that he has not yet made up his own mind, but is observing the progress of events and will keep himself free to act in accordance with circumstances, at the latest moment.

His own character is not so decided and positive as to enable us to judge of the specific character of his Cabinet till it is chosen, nor especially of its precise aspect with regard to slavery.

But it is safe to assume that it will somewhat resemble himself and will be moderately progressive or what we term conservative, with a hash-up policy, shirking responsibility and decision and throwing upon Congress the settlement of most questions.

This is as favorable as we can hope for, and is indeed of the best, because it leaves freer scope for the voice of the people, and we never go so nearly right as when that *vulgar* voice is listened to; the people has no object in going wrong, desires to go right and in general when it appears to go wrong – only *appears* so, because its wishes are willfully perverted and turned aside by a captious and arrogant government – like that of Pierce.

I do not know whether your confidence in the good dispositions and good intentions of the people increases or diminishes with experience and years, but I am more and more satisfied that it is the safest and best guide for the policy of the government: public feeling and public opinion are the most just and err the least, and in America surely there is never any difficulty for an honest man to know what the public opinion is, that is, the opinion of the great majority, for it is always abundantly expressed – and there are very few questions which arise with us, upon which the public is not competent to form good practical opinion.

The recent insurrectionary movement among the slaves was, to considerable extent, but did not amount to a rising in any instance and was easily stifled; it was the immediate result of the election agitations, produced not by abolitionists, but by the discussion of the planters and politicians themselves in presence of the blacks; they naturally sought for victims on whom to lay the blame, but found none, except among their own people, who (right or wrong) were condemned.

Some attempts have been made to throw the blame on the north but they gained no credit, not even in the south.

The north treats the matter coolly, as an occurrence incidental to slavery, and to be expected with increasing frequency and gravity, and the south has little to say in reply to this; indeed it seems by its moderation and silence to be of the same opinion.

Coming at the moment of the *great defeat which the slave holding interest has sustained* a deep impression has been made on the south and it cannot be otherwise than beneficial to the cause of freedom.

Some attempt at argument, it is true, has been made on this ground, to show the necessity of extension and dispersion of slaves for safety, but the argument has no force and has not, I believe, excited a serious reply.

The real condition of things, based upon statistical facts, is too well known to the public to have room for argument.

The following brief figures will suggest my meaning –

area of 15 slave states *1,029,396* square miles

Population – free 7,000,000

slave 4,000,000,

———————————

11,000,000

D[itt]o of 16 free states *542 847* d[itt]o d[itt]o: Population – 17,000,000.

———————————

28,000,000

Thus, the area of the slave states in proportion to the inhabitants as composed with the free states, is about 3/1 in favor the slave states. Yet there is abundance of room in the free states and a superabundance of unoccupied territory in the area already conceded to slavery.

They have no want of room to spread in; and every body knows that the late contest for new ground was a political contest, and nothing else.

The object was political power in the general government, and not room for slaves. You know that by our system, the balance of power in the senate is determined by the members of states; there are still 1, 744 millions of square miles of territory to be made into states, and the question is, shall they be slave or free? for that decides the question of power in the senate.

There are in fact but *350, 000 proprietors* of slaves in the Union and the question is, shall this minority, this clique govern?

One might imagine that such a question could not arise in a country where the majority principle is acknowledged, and lies at the foundation of all its institutions. But the world has always been governed by small numbers of men; a skillful and experienced politician like yourself does not need to be reminded of the power of small bodies, who are wealthy and intelligent, united by interest, unscrupulous, skillful and desperate – whose resolution is equal to all hazards and who are resolved to "rub or ruin."

The value of industrial products last year (1856) was 4,500,000,000 dollars; say 22,000,000,000 francs: of this $1/4$ (not quite) was the product of the slave states; thus, the ratio of population (as above) is 11 in the slave to 17 in the free states, but the ratio of the products of labor is as 22 to 11 in favor of freedom (very nearly).

It is not, then, want of room to spread in, nor the profits of slave labor as compared with free labor which excite the slave holders to such desperate efforts; the same capital employed by free labor would yield larger returns; it is not a question of pecuniary gains. Why then do the slave owners hold on so firmly to an institution so dangerous, so wicked, so degrading, and vicious?

You are accustomed to study human motives, and to fathom the impulses of men, and can answer this question better than I can.

To me it presents itself in this aspect: 1st. the Constitution of the U. S., in fixing the bases of representation in the federal Congress, counts 5 slaves as 3 freemen, which in effect makes the proprietor of 500 slaves not my political equal, not my peer, but my superior, he is equal to 300, such as I am, and he looks on me with contempt. This, in my judgment, was a vicious bargain; it is the most vicious feature in the whole American system; we have now some 28 members of Congress, what we may call extra members, against whom there is no northern counterpoise; and these extra men are sent to Congress by the slave owners, their seats resting on the bases of slave property – the only property representation we have.

A political bargain on such terms is a temptation to the slave owners to aim at still greater power, to increase their superiority, in fine to absorb all power, for it is of the nature of power to seek its own aggrandizement.

I cannot blame the slave owners for yielding to this temptation and I think we deserve to suffer for conceding it to them.

(I forget at this moment how you have treated this subject in your work on America, but of course it did not escape you).

2nd. There is no stronger passion than the love of power: it is common to all, and the same in a monarch or a merchant, a prince or a planter, all crave it, and the planter *is* a monarch, an absolute sovereign, in his small territory, and among his black subjects. His wish and his caprice are law, he loves to exercise and indulge them; he prefers labor which he can command, to that which he has to buy and bargain for on equal terms; he cannot come down to "will you?" – but he prefers "you shall" – and he loves this power with a desperate love, especially after being bred in the exercise of it. It is not a question of profit or of interest; put the money question to a sovereign or a slaveholder, and ask him to abdicate; he will turn from it with contempt, in both cases, for the feeling is identical in both – the meanest black sovereign is as ready to risk his life for his power as any monarch.

The attempted insurrection will not quicken nor diminish the efforts to extend slavery; these efforts being a political move, depend on the state of political elements and not on the condition of the blacks; if they come equally scattered over the territory conceded to them, you will observe, there would be less than 4 souls to each square mile – room for ages to come; undoubtedly insurrectional movements do open to the planters fearful glimpses of the future, but they will not on that account relax; their minds are made up and bred up to all the hazards; and from king Pharaon to this day, no sovereign willingly "lets this people go."

The people of the north are neither excited nor calmed by the movement of the blacks; they may feel a little stronger for it – as it shows slavery to be more odious and dangerous, but they neither exult nor relax in their zeal. The real question is not the condition of the blacks, but who is to rule? And any movement of the slaves, if it has any influence on the north, tends to strengthen their resolution not to take their places by the side of the slaves and submit like them to be governed by their masters.

It should not be lost sight of that although the south elected its President and gained in that respect an *apparent victory*, this is matter of little moment, and perhaps it is well that they were successful in this, because they have been totally defeated in the vital object of the contest. Events since the election every day render this fact more clear and more important.

They had deliberately matured their plans for years, gradually introduced them, removed step by step all the compromises, all the barriers, opened the door to free extension of slavery, and secured the influence of the govt to their views.

This slowly aroused the north, and Kansas became the battle ground, the first trial of strength in the open field, with slavery and the govt on one side and the people of the free states on the other.

That contest has been continued for more than a year – and in the midst of it, the election took place.

The result is that in Kansas the People is victorious: it has thoroughly beaten the south and the govt. Kansas must be a free state: the south has exploded its mines and fired its last gun, and is retiring from all points, without having gained a foot of new ground, but having hastened the peopling and forming a new state which will soon take place in the scale against them. This is the fact, in comparison with which the election of a President is a bagatelle; finding they had neither men nor money to contend with the north in peopling a new territory, they resolved to force – in this they appeared to be more successful, but it was a mere burst of passion and madness; it only increased the efforts of the north – and the stream of men (settlers) and money poured in the faster for it.

The result is, they are outnumbered and beaten, and are retiring, only a few, perhaps 200 blacks and a few masters remain against our thousands, some 30,000 – free people – who with the aid of our Eastern people have bought up nearly all the good lands in the territory. There will yet be some delay, and some squabbling in Congress etc., but *Kansas must be free*. (N. B. If you my friend wish to invest in wild lands, I am ready to supply you: I have got more than I want; we have all got more than we want, but were obliged to do this to shut out slavery – and we preferred it to war taxes and blood, and felt confident of victory *in time*: it is a new way of fighting – that I recommend as a substitute for bayonets).

It was not expected that success by peaceable means could be attained in so short a time and by the voluntary action of the people, in the manner which they resolved to adopt; but the election hastened the result.

The south gained, but barely gained; it was a narrow escape for them, and it exhibited a union and feeling growing to irresistible magnitude, in the free states, against the further spread of slavery. This fact, so manifest with this other fact, that they were already at their wits end for ways and means in Kansas, gave the *coup de grâce* to that contest, and they have been running away from it every since.

The dust of the election having blown away, the press in Europe remarks how quietly all has settled down, with the presidential victory in favor of the south, in which the north submits, but they do not look beyond that and see *why* the north is so quiet – they do not observe that the north is really the winning party – much less that the south is silent from despair more than from victory.

Notwithstanding the counting of blacks in the southern representation, the numerical majority in the House of Representatives has for a considerable period been on the side of the free states, but this superiority is neutralized by the composition of the senate.

There is a majority of one free state in the senate, but the southern influence retains a large working majority, in favor of the slave policy in the senate and will probably continue to do this, so long as this equality of states continues; the senate being so nearly equally divided, places it in the power of two or three politicians like Douglas, by forming a small party and uniting with the south, to control the action of the senate, and to a large extent, that of the government. It is so easy to do this and the temptation is so great, for those who love power, that the south always finds a "traitor" or two and that is enough.

Therefore, to bring back the government to the majority of the people and to limit the spread of slavery, it is indispensable to obtain a safe majority in the senate, and this can only be done by additional free states. Hence the contest and the importance of the contest in regard to Kansas; it is the turning point: because Nebraska and Oregon are already asking to come in as free states, and Deseret[17] and New Mexico are lying in wait, to see how it will go with Kansas.

I have said that I consider the question as to Kansas virtually settled in favor of freedom, and this decides the fate of the others – so that there is the strongest prospect of an accession of free states, probably during Buchanan's term, which will change the character of the senate, for ever. A reliable and permanent majority in the House and in the Senate, from the free states, is the only possible barrier to the further spread of slavery and this result is now fairly in view and I do not see how it can fail to be realized. I do not believe that any more territory will ever be given to slavery, nor that any more slave states will ever be made, unless at some future day the State of Texas which is very large should be divided, but mean time the free states will be quite out of reach in representation as compared with the slave states, and Texas can be delivered only by the consent of the free states which if given will be for special reasons and because they have nothing more to fear from the ascendancy of the slave power in the government.

This process of settlement, from the nature of the case is slow – but it must be permanent, because it does not rest on acts of legislation which may be repealed, but on a basis which cannot be repealed nor changed. It rests upon *free labor*, as against slave labor; a free laborer will not work beside a slave. Free labor feels itself dishonored and disgraced by slavery and shuns the contact; it is the first time that the question in this aspect has been brought home to the people, and it is they, the laboring people who are rising in self defense; their interest and their pride is touched. Thanks to a free and cheap Press, and the industrious pens of many men, *the people* has been brought to comprehend this, and as the government is in their hands, and must always be in their hands, with their rapidly increasing members – the future of this settlement looks to me secure.

Free labor, once awakened and enlightened, as to its own interests, may be relied on; it will never go backwards, against itself.

It was the stupid vote of the great body of foreigners, and the equally dull Dutchmen of Pennsylvania, who thought they must vote for a man from their own state, which lost us the Presidency.[18] But all this will soon get right and you see now, since the presidential election, Pennsylvania has rejected the nominee of Buchanan (and his personal and intimate friend) Forney[19] and elected to the Senate Cameron,[20] a thorough free soil man, which gives Pennsylvania to freedom in the Senate, in spite of Buchanan and *his great personal exertions*.

I do not represent that the contest is yet over; we shall have plenty of new schemes from the south and agitations and squabbles, but I do believe that the future is for us; we shall win all and hold all.

I have no doubt, as you suggest, that the south may for some years keep up the appearance of electing a president etc. because there will be party divisions on other questions at the north, and the south by uniting with one of these fractions *and accepting its candidate*, may thus appear to win. But this will be of no consequence as respects the extension of slavery, because the character of the Senate and House of Representatives, does not depend in the slightest degree on the Presidency – but the contrary; the govt to a great extent takes its character from Congress, and this body coming directly from the people, by local district elections, separate from the Presidential election, will retain its free soil, free labor character. There is no chance for intrigue and bargain here.

This review of the subject (which I am afraid you will find very tedious) relates only to the question of the extension of slavery, and to its political power in the federal government. It does not touch the question of emancipation, or of the future condition of the slaves.

This is not the question at issue and it never has been. The south, it is true, has raised the cry of abolition, and pretended to believe this to be the aim of the north, while the action, of a few individuals at the north, has been such as to give some color to pretended southern fears. But in point of fact, the south feels but *too safe* on this subject; they do not fear it and never have feared it, from the action of the north. Indeed they rely on the good faith of the north, and with entire safety, for the north will not disturb slavery where it exists, and in case of insurrections would go to the aid of the south to suppress them – not from a wish to preserve slavery, but it would be their interest and duty to suppress insurrection, because insurrection, which it would be of great injury to both parties, could not possibly better the condition of the slaves, but make it worse.

The south, it is true, pretends that limitation is equivalent to emancipation; that it is emancipation in disguise.

It is not absolutely impossible that this way may prove well founded, but if so, it must be very slow in its operation, extending over a long period of time, for they have still great room to spread in, and it is to be hoped that it will turn to that result. It is certainly no good objection to limitation that it tends to ultimate emancipation; good faith does not require us to adopt no measures necessary to our own safety, which may not be favorable to the enemy!

The north does not believe that slavery is to be the perpetual condition of the blacks; but it sees the great difficulties of the case, and does not wish to force the south in a matter so difficult to deal with. It prefers to leave to time and circumstances the solution of this problem, contenting itself with fixing boundaries to the spread of the evil, and securing the government against its encroachments.

Beyond this it has no hostility to the south, no conflicting interests and no ill will; but desires to be on good terms and to aid them.

There are few things in this world so bad but some good comes out of them! The indirect benefits resulting from slavery are worth regarding. It has kept freedom and free labor in a compact mass at the north, spreading west, but always in the cool and temperate latitudes, most favorable to the best moral and physical development of man, thus forming a favorable base for freedom and intelligence in the future – instead of permitting the current of free labor to spread over the south and warmer latitudes, and become enervated and demoralized in climates neither requiring nor permitting the same moral and physical exertions.

It has kept alive debates and secured the development of clear and definite ideas of state rights, practical notions of which are so peculiarly necessary to our system of government.

And it has led to ardent and *endless* discussions of personal rights and the relations of men in the social state, which brings home to the people well defined and practical notions on these subjects – a species of political knowledge so indispensable to government by the people.

I do not allude to these things as any apology for slavery, but as instances of good of no trifling character, coming out of evil.

He must be a bold man who will attempt to foretell the future of slavery or of the Union – if for no other reason, because the circumstances, take them all together, are so completely original, that there is no precedent, no analogies to help the judgment: there is great energy and incessant action. Events move fast; and every day presents a new aspect, and new problems to solve; for one I do not participate in the fears for the perpetuity of the Union. And as to slavery, I have great hopes for it; it is most evident that the south is driving on as if impelled by fate, to a solution of some sort.

By the force of natural ardor and the violent passions developed by slavery, they have driven themselves, and in the most logical manner, to the avowal of opinions and places, which completely *outlaws* them in the public opinion of the civilized world. They cannot retain that position; practically it is impossible, for the world would rise in arms against the reopening of the African slave trade – and morally they cannot retain it, for human nature cannot long stand the open scorn and contempt of all civilized men. They must break down, and the most ardent abolitionist can do nothing so good as leave them to themselves.

I have only one suggestion to make with regard to the future of the blacks. There is nothing more observable in the economy of nature, than the wise and beautiful provision, which diversifies and graduates the scale of human capacities, from the highest to the lowest, among all races, and all the individuals of a race, in a manner which renders each a necessity and a benefit to the other. The highest and the lowest, and intervening gradations, are equally fitted for their places, and equally dependent on each other. A blind or willful disregard of this arrangement is a fruitful source of oppression and wrong and the inferior are compelled to serve the superior, on unjust and unequal terms.

The full benefits of this natural provision can never be realized but on the terms of liberty and justice to all.

In America, the rapid accumulation of property and general diffusion of it and education presents society in a new aspect; all are lifted above inferior occupations; there is nobody left to discharge those necessary but lower functions; and a man must often act in the double capacity of gentleman and servant.

But for the considerable stream of emigration I don't know what we should do for many sorts of the most useful laborers and servants, and this resource is not permanent.

We must of necessity *do a wise thing*: we must avail of the provisions of nature, and since there are all sorts [of] capacities and colors, black and red and yellow and brown, we must get over ignorance and prejudice, and open the door of freedom to all these sorts of people.

They will serve us and we will serve them, each according to his capacity, but to make this acceptable and beneficial, there must be complete freedom and justice and protection for all. What excellent and intelligent servants the Chinese are, and how grateful for good pay and good treatment!

We have room now, not for 4, but for 10 millions of blacks – but they must be civilized and educated and free, and when fully developed under the influences which develop the white race, they will be of just the right *attitude*, just fit the place that is open for them, and will attain a higher civilization in this way than in any other, and we shall be mutually useful and necessary to each other. The black man has physical force, the white man skill. Let them agree on fair terms that skill shall guide force and the compact will be mutually beneficial.

If we can live with savage slaves, we can surely live with the same race when civilized and free.

This is my solution of slavery. I think it must come to this; it would be a happy solution for them and for us, and I do not see a single serious obstacle to it, but the will of the plantation sovereigns. If those who now oppress the blacks would do them justice and make amends for their past wrongs the black *citizens* would be as great a benefit and blessing to us, as the black slave is a stumbling block and a curse.

I do not expect so great a change from the voluntary action of slaveholders nor of non-slaveholders, but one must be blind who does not perceive how impotent are human plans and human wills, as compared with that mysterious and higher influence, that "destiny" which shapes all things and in regard to which the wisest thing to be done is, not to combat, but accept and shape our plans and actions to it. Destiny is working for us more reforms and doing more good, than we ever did or shall do for ourselves.

I do not believe in any natural hostility, aversion or enmity of nations, peoples or races – but that those feelings have been generated and perpetuated be erroneous policy and artificial systems, which ignore the provisions of nature and the true relations of men. It seems to me that the existing development of commerce between all peoples, which is without parallel in the past, displays not only the endless diversity and exhaustless fertility of human skill and capacity, but displays still more amply and clearly the wonderful adaptation and necessity of each to all and all to each. Every obstruction of this intercourse and to the exchange of labor and service, is an obstacle to human progress. It is in this direction we are to look for the greatest general prosperity, the highest development of civilization, the highest social development of man – for these last are based upon general prosperity and easiness of condition.

The amplification of this commercial idea approximates peoples and races, brings them into closer intercourse, even to social and domestic relations, from attic to basement (of the social and domestic edifice) and realizes the highest benefits and uses of all to all.

The policy of nations and the structure of society hitherto have never been very favorable to the development of this principle; they are often a bar to it and there is enmity and bitterness where there ought to be amity and harmony. Nothing but freedom, absolute freedom and equal justice for all can give that scope for individual volition and action which are the essential conditions.

It is, I trust, the "mission" of America, not from foresight and design, but from necessity, driven along by higher laws, to work out some problems, social problems, which have never yet received the development they are capable of, and that thus driven to right principles, driven to be just, we may have reason to unite with the blacks in recognition of the good fortune which brought us together for mutual benefit, instead of regarding it as a mutual calamity.

I do not talk of human perfectibility – I should be sorry to be thought a dreamer. I wish to be practical, and by observing that which is, and the course in which thing are drifting – to guess at that which may be, and probably will be – by and by.

Tell me, my friend, if these speculations are wild and dreamy, mere moon-shine? – or if they are possible and probable? If they are not founded I must dismiss them ; the only men fit for this world are practical men.

We are all in excellent health, and as far as the climate goes, and it goes for much with people who have nerves – the winter in Geneva astonishes me.

The temperature is cool and steady, very little wind, clear dry air, and bright sun; there is no snow nearer than the mountains; the valley is bare as summer and the roads are dry hard and dusty. Since about the 5th January, we have scarcely had a change, sometimes clouds, but no snow to remain beyond a few hours, not rain enough to moisten the surface, and very little fog. No weather could be finer for exercise and I live out of doors – walk the whole country over, which reminds me strongly of the sunny campagna of Rome, cooler and more bracing and without its humidity. I have not had a cold or a cough this winter, and have walked 4 times over the summit of the Salève 3,100 feet above the lake, for the mere pleasure of climbing in the snow and drinking the air.

Nothing restores and preserves the vitality in man, like changes of air and out of doors life. I only lack one thing, a friend who can walk and talk as long as I can and enjoy it as I do – because it is impossible to get up a laugh when one is alone, and laughing is next to a good digestion the essential thing for health.

This must be an exceptional winter, (as they say it is) or Geneva has been misrepresented as to climate in winter.

I do not ask for a finer winter climate. But I cannot understand why the Genevese are so monotonous, dry, bloodless, emotionless, (and as seems to me) unhappy.

After half an hour I can get nothing out of them to keep me from going to sleep; I try to agree and try to disagree with them, but it all comes to the same thing and is no use.

I am not a theologian and never could find time to play cards, consequently I am always *de trop*[21] everywhere, and no doubt a bore.

By way of diversion I have found a boy, an engraver of watches, of a peculiar nervous temperament, whom I am able to somnanbulise, magnetise, and I don't exactly know what, but by forming a circle with my wife and *children*, including the boy, he becomes the medium or channel of very curious physical and psychological phenomena.

I have no superstitions nor theories to explode nor to confirm, no old ideas to defend nor new ones to reject, or accept on this subject, but what I perceive is that this method does lay open a whole field of curious mental phenomena unexplored and unexplained, and let *savan[t]s*[22] laugh as they may, their philosophy is not yet up to any rational explication of this matter. If they don't look sharp the people will go ahead of them, as they have often done in recognizing and accepting facts, before they could be scientifically explained.

I see that an academic *confrère*[23] of yours, le comte Gasparin,[24] has written a book to explore these pretended phenomena. I have sent for it, but have not yet received it; but I have just read a book, a well written book on the same side, by a clergyman and professor of philosophy. But such unskillful handling of the facts and such logic! If this is a specimen of the per contra, I recommend every man who balances and hesitates in adopting an opinion, to read his enemy that he may see how feeble the other side is. I suppose all these things are according to law – but let them develop that law instead of obscuring the phenomena and ignoring the facts.

I have just received a few hasty lines from our friend Sedgwick; I am glad you wrote him, it will do him good. He has suffered much; he was at Washington and writes as he runs, so that I can hardly read him; but he is much more cheerful and in better spirits; is occupied with writing a law-book etc.

If you have not fallen asleep before reading thus far I beg you to express my best regards and those of Mrs. Beckwith to Madame de Tocqueville. I should be glad if I could have an hour at billiards with her; I should not have too much gallantry to beat her if [I] could.

Very truly yours,
N. W. B.

I am afraid the winds and damps of the sea coast in winter are not the most favorable for you; I don't see how it is possible for you to be enough out of doors – to lay in a good stock of strength for summer and for library work.

Beinecke Rare Book and Manuscript Library, Yale University, Uncat MSS 324; also available as Bonnel copy in MS Vault Tocqueville, D II A, folder "Bonnel's copies of letters from Americans to Tocqueville."

133. Edward Vernon Childe to Alexis de Tocqueville

Boston, Febr[uary] 22, 1857

My dear M. de Tocqueville,

I have already acknowledged your last and most kind letter. In it you said that no one feels a warmer interest than you in the welfare of my little family. This we know, and more than that, we feel; and we are not ungrateful for a sentiment, whose existence and origin we are far from attributing to ourselves alone. A week or two since a letter, very kind and acceptable, reached me from M. Ampère. It, as well as your letter, speaks of a copy of your last work, which I have taken the necessary steps to have sent to me from Paris. I thank you for it in advance. It will be dearly prized by me and by my children. And now I must tell you something of them. We intended to stay in Boston, for Mary's education, till perhaps the month of May; but after an experience of about four months, we have been forced to modify our scheme. Even at the best of seasons, and even when no obvious disturbing cause, either internally or externally, besets a man, it will happen, as you know, that his spirits fail, the whole economy of his being is deranged, and he ceases to be himself, that is, either for enjoyment or for usefulness. Such, or something like it, has befallen Edward and me. Mary, busy and interested in her studies, is content to go on as she is now doing; but her brother and papa are not so well off. In fact, Edward was so sad that I have advised him to visit Cuba, and he will quit this place on his journey the day after tomorrow. I, of course, shall not remain here long, but in three of four weeks Mary and I will be on our way to our friends in the south. We have had, indeed, quite enough here to render a change of place desirable, even if health of mind were alone concerned. But such is, and has been, the weather, that health of body must also be taken into consideration. Were you ever in Boston during the winter? Only think of cold so intense that one could not expose himself to it, however well clad, without danger, if not certainty, of ears and nose being frozen, and then, in two or three weeks, of heat so excessive as to be obliged to keep the windows open – open too during the evening in the months of January and February.

It affords me real pleasure to know that your health is so good. God grant you health and happiness! is my prayer. I am not, it must be admitted, wholly unselfish (who is?) in this my aspiration, for you are one of the very few of those whom I call in my "heart of heart" friends.

For my own condition, I have not known a well day during the last eight months. But I live on hoping for better things. One of the few real friends that I have, Mr. Cotting, is, it is feared, very near his end. His chance of life is minutely small, and his death will be to me an irreparable loss.

The more I examine affairs in America, the less do they please me – the political affairs, I mean. It is not merely that there is an angry feeling subsisting among the several States of Union – that might die out in the course of time if common wisdom and prudence prevailed –, but that offices, especially the most important, throughout the country are not filled by the most worthy. By some persons this menacing fact is imputed to those men who in their own persons are the first to suffer by exclusion from offices, and at one time I was myself of opinion that no small share of blame belonged to them; but on inquiry I am forced to believe that it is the people themselves, and themselves almost alone, who are accountable for the evil under which they sweat. I see no instant remedy, but I have great faith in time, in the self-correcting sense of man, and in an over-ruling Providence. I need not tell you, whose study has been man, and, too, man in the "States," how much beating and abuse our race will submit to (especially if they always feel conscious of an innate power and legal right to reform), before they turn in their might and make clean the stable. The aspect of things, I remarked, does not please me. Some persons, not wanting in intelligence, regard it as extremely threatening. I, too, think it threatening of much mischief, perhaps, but not of an overthrow of the Union. I look upon it as a most serious aspect, nevertheless, and quite sufficient to cause serious apprehension. And I do so because of the universal want of principle that pervades our public men, and the grounds in which they are elected. Let no one tell me that it was always, and will always be, the case in a popular form of government. Thirty years ago it was not so, nor do I believe that twenty years hence the same rule will prevail. The evil, I believe, is working its own remedy. In regard to the present Chief Magistrate, Mr. Pierce, friend and foe, both agree that the country was imposed upon. There is also, or I greatly mistake, a universal conviction that Mr. Buchanan, the incoming President, is a blunder. He will work his appointed mischief – he has, indeed, already begun, if well credited reports speak truth, by appointing for his chief secretary Mr. Cass, a man of little mind, narrow views, a loose tongue, and of unbounded prejudice. With these two men at the head of the nation a war with England is very possible – it is almost probable. Buchanan, when lately in England whence I got my information, withheld information he was bound to give to his government, thereby causing much dissension. He also was one of the three diplomatists who concocted the "Ostend manifesto," – got up for mere party-purposes, buccaneering in its nature and a disgrace to the 19th century. Why, Mr. Mason, who did me the honor frequently to talk (not to say consult) with me on many important subjects, never even opened his mouth upon the subject of the *manifesto*, for which I was ever grateful, because to have spoken of it as I thought (and in no other fashion should I have spoken), would have produced, perhaps, an estrangement from one who, with his family, was kindness itself to me and to mine in the hour of adversity. Then, as for Cass, he is a time-serving, sycophantic twaddler. His vanity too is of no harmless kind. Once upon a time having been appointed to represent his country in France, when visiting England, on his way to his post, it so happened, for what reason I know not, that he was, or fancied himself to be, neglected by the English aristocracy. Hence his bitter tears, and hence his biting words. If, in spite of this dumocrate,[25] we are able to tide over the next four years, as I believe we shall, without any signal misfortune, my impression is that the country will begin to see that we have been putting round men into square holes and square men into round holes.

Today is the birthday of Washington, and I know not whether to be more alarmed at the serious thoughts it suggests, or to be amused at the contemptible facts it recalls. It makes one serious to reflect on the high, the holy, the almost awful ends and means which crowded the brains of Washington and his companion patriots;[26] and then one can hardly help smiling to see the world go on glibly and jauntily, notwithstanding that constituencies seem to delight in rejecting men of education and character as their representatives, and notwithstanding that the greater bully and blackguard a man is, the better is his chance of being returned to Congress. I have very considerably examined the propriety of taking part in public life, for I hate idleness, home I have none, and it seems to me at times as though I could be of use to my country; but my best and wisest counselors dissuade me. Even in our state councils, the same pernicious rule holds good as in the assemblies of the nation. "Men of the people" – "self-made men" – vile panderers to the mob, are the successful candidates at elections. Our taxes are increased, unreasonable expenses having been saddled upon us by those who have nothing, or next to nothing, to be taxed. But the reverse of the picture is not discouraging. Material prosperity reigns throughout the land, but even this cannot for ever keep the eyes of the community closed to the fact that mis-representation is the worst sort of representation.

I observed above that I am *homeless*. I know that many others are so too – poor devils who are not only without a house but without a dinner, and therefore will not complain. Yet it may be permitted to speak of facts – to say, I cannot but remember that such things were and that they exist no longer. Edward wearies of this country, and I cannot well bear to see him pining, as it were, in this (to him) foreign atmosphere. Indeed, were it not for Mary's sake, I would accompany him to Paris in the course of a month or two. But my little motherless girl's interests must govern me, and control all my wishes and movements. And it is just to this subject that I beg you seriously to consider and to advise me. Boston is out of the question as a place of residence. The people are cold, unsocial, unsympathetic. They are good, it is true, as some folk count goodness; they are hospitable too in a way peculiar to themselves: that is, visit them when and how you may, one is always received as "company." The consequence in affecting Edward naturally is, that he loathes the place, and this very morning (the 24th) I have just returned from the railway, whither I went to see him off on his way to Cuba. There then remain to us only Baltimore and a place – a country residence, near Washington, called Arlington-house, belonging to Mr. Custis, which is the home of my children's maternal uncle, colonel Robert Lee, who married the only child of Mr. Custis. To think of furnishing a house when my son is yearning to quit the country, would be an absurdity: to pass another winter in Boston (at the hotel of necessity) is not to be thought of. I must therefore spend it in Baltimore, where Mary's education can be continued. As things look now, neither she nor I can go abroad for the space of 2 years, that is, till she is 18 years of age. Now, two years are a long time for a man at Edward's age to waste. *Is it not better, then, for him, to go to Europe alone?* This is question first. He dreads the idea of leaving his father, but had I not better (for his sake) to submit to the sacrifice, and to make him go – that is, a few months hence? Should I, for what seemed to me potent reasons, also leave this country, *with Mary, of course*, when the day came for her being "presented" in French society, *what practicable means will there be within my reach?* This is question second. There is not an American lady in Paris who takes any interest in her. There is not a French lady there on whom we have any claim. The only one who might have had the will, as she certainly has the means – the Duchess[27] – is an invalid, and from what I hear will never be in better health. My daughter will not be marriageable for at least two years to come. Should I be justified in removing her (unmarried) from a country where she will be sought for, and where her position is assured, to another where all is uncertain? I much fear that it will be my fate to be separated from one or the other of my dear children. In Baltimore, should we make that our temporary home, the only maternal aunt of my children is confined to her bed, and past all cure; her life is to me a miracle so that even this refuge promises no permanency. Her husband's life also is less certain than the lives of men of his age in general. And besides these two, there is no one in Baltimore to be reckoned on for an instant, although they have a daughter-in-law, living with them, who is highly spoken of, and who, I trust, will prove an acceptable companion to Mary. I repeat, then, my inquiry, even at the expense of boring you (but I am sure of your friendship and have unbounded confidence in your judgment): can I venture (and if so, at what period) to carry my daughter to Europe before her marriage? What chance of happiness do you think she stands on the other side of the Atlantic, compared to that she may fairly count on here in the course of 2, 3 or 4 years? I am in a decided embarrassment. Mr. Custis's home, I should have added, though very pleasant for some months in the year, is wholly unfitted, by its sadness and isolation, for a girl like Mary. It, as well as Mr. Marshall's house in Baltimore, has always been open to us, in their own words, "as a home." I am aware that you have not in this letter *all* the data required, but you can easily supply the missing ones. As you perceive, there is nothing in all this – the subject matter of my disquiet – which demands haste; but the result of your reflections will aid me, and, however inopportune it may be, you will see that "out the abundance of (my) heart the mouth speaketh."

I delivered your message to Mr. Everett, and he was as much pleased as is the nature of such a cold-blooded being to be. I expect to see

Mr. Sparks today, as I am going to Cambridge, where he dwells, and I will execute your behest.

Believe me your most faithfully, I pray you. E. and M.[28] join me in affection to you.

E. V. Childe

134. George Sumner to Alexis de Tocqueville

Boston, March 4, [18]57

My dear M. de Tocqueville,

I write only one line to be handed [to] you by my brother Mr. Charles Sumner, Senator of the Untied States.

I have asked him, in case you should not be in Paris, to hand this to M. Gustave de Beaumont.

I write that you or Beaumont could make it convenient to bring him *en rapport* with Cavaignac, Dufaure, Rivet[29] and some other of these honest and patriotic men, who, not having labored to bring in the Republic, yet stood honestly by that which represented a free and dignified people.

Pray present my best respects to Madame de Tocqueville and believe me always, with high regard,

Your faithful friend & servant,

Geo[rge] Sumner

135. Edward Lee Childe to Alexis de Tocqueville[30]

Havana, March 27, [18]57

My dear M. de Tocqueville,

I received your kind letter of January 4 some time before leaving Boston. My answer, instead of being sent from a country covered by snow and ice, will arrive to you heavy with the scent of orange trees and sugar cane. I have in me something that prevents me from remaining for a long time in the same place and makes any sojourn appear dull to me. I have been here since the beginning of the month; everything is new and extraordinary; the richness of the vegetation, the bright colors, the habits of the country, everything strikes me, everything amazes me, but that does not interest me. The origin of the inhabitants is betrayed by the blue, red, and yellow colors with which they paint their houses and churches. That matches quite well the blue of the sky and the contrasting colors of the fruits of the earth. The palm tree, the coconut palm, the banana tree, the cedar tree[31] are as familiar to me as the lime tree and the oak; the most bizarre fruits can be found in abundance but they do not have the taste of those that grow under more temperate climates. The fish market is one of the curiosities here; having all kinds of forms and colors, the inhabitants of the sea compete with those of the earth in order to amaze the foreigner, but they do not manage to enchant him. During the day, everything is calm, the houses are closed, and only the port is always busy. As the heat (80 degrees in the shade since my arrival three weeks ago) diminishes and the evening approaches, the window shutters open and behind the bars of immense windows appears the beautiful sex exchanging greetings and words with the passers-by. The streets are very narrow; the cabin of the coal merchant is located next to the palace of a great landowner, where one can see an interior court, a fountain, a palm tree or two, then endless corridors, everything reminding me of the stories from the East. The means of transportation in the country is specific to the island. Two horses or mules harnessed in the Spanish fashion, a negro postilion, three quarter riding boots, an embroidered morning jacket, topped off with a straw hat; some distance from the team of horses a cabriolet, where one has every facility to stretch oneself, finally two enormous wheels which hardly look to be part of the carriage. The public promenade is very lively; the military music and the cafés conclude the evenings.

I made several expeditions on the southern coast of the island up to Trinidad and in the interior. Everyone was very kind to me and the planters initiated me into the secrets of the production of sugar, coffee, and other products. I shall leave tomorrow for another trip on the northern coast. The nature of the tropics is quite beautiful, but it is tiresome. These contrasting colors, this variety in the forms of anything that catches the eye, end up by making you dizzy. There is also another feeling which it will be difficult for me to describe. It is a form of awe of the soul. The silence, the immobility of nature, has something terrifying for the man whose destiny is to always march forward. Little by little, the soul grows numb; the senses take more and more control over the intellectual and moral part. Here everything is beautiful for the eye, but there is no voice which touches the heart. The plumage of the birds is magnificent, but they have no voice. The same green covers the fields in the summer and winter, the trees do not lose any of their leaves; the delicious awakening of spring, the freshness of rejuvenated sensations are missing; the weakened soul loses its vigour, it no longer watches over itself and allows itself to be fascinated by the insidious attractions of the rich and fertile nature of the tropical zone. It feels that it is on a fatal and speedy slope; hence the malaise that one experiences after having lived here for some time. One loses sight of any order of more elevated ideas; torpor is followed by prostration and sadness, and nonetheless, nowhere else the beauties of physical nature show themselves more abundantly than here. I would like to see this feeling developed and explained psychologically by someone who understands it.

According to the latest news (March 16), my father and sister are doing well; they must be in Baltimore where I expect to join them. I follow a route which is somewhat of a detour; from here, I shall go to New Orleans, then I expect to go up the Mississippi to the lakes and return to the East in May. The pages in which you speak to me so nicely about my mother are and will always be for me very precious. Nobody was able to get to know her better than you, and your recollection will always be linked to her in my memory. This should tell you enough about the place that you occupy in it. You tell me, my dear Sir, in a very pleasant manner, and even more than necessary, everything that I [...].[32] You take care to add "you are or should be happy." In spite of all these advantages with which you gratify me, I often find myself envying the frank and sincere laughter of older people who have attached their happiness to permanent and fixed occupations. The Anglo-Saxon blood has a hard time dealing with inaction. On my return to Washington, I shall see what possibilities are there for me with regard to a political or diplomatic career. You speak to me about a possible return to Paris. To tell you the truth, I am fearful of returning there. It seems to me that if I were to visit Europe, I would be incapable of avoiding that city which in the past has meant so much to me that I would not be able to find there anything else besides cruel and overwhelming recollections. I lack courage when thinking about the life that I could live there and how different it would be from the *other one*. Let us not talk about it any longer; time, the doctor of the soul, will take care, under the will of Providence, to arrange things for the better.

I willingly enter into my inner self and adopt the habit of attaching myself as little as possible to anything that is exterior and constantly changing; it is possible that my true education only begins now. In any case, I shall be an obedient disciple, easy to persuade. I shall lack the impulse, the flexibility, and the liveliness of those who ignore the true goal of existence which is to suffer in order to become a better person. But at least I shall not lose my time dreaming. Happiness is rarely unpredictable, it is easy to guess when it might appear to you; misfortune can also be sometimes anticipated, but it has reserved for itself the privilege of striking in an unpredictable manner that changes the nature of the individual who is a victim.

When you write to M. Ampère, please thank him for his kind regards; if my father were sitting next to me, he would ask me to remember him to you. He is now in the city for which I have made a genuine passion – Rome; where each stone looks at you with a sympathetic eye; where one feels that Rome has nothing to learn in the way of suffering and it shares in the pain of all its children. Unlike Paris, Rome does not have personal recollections; everything becomes general, the individual loses himself there. Is that not precisely what one has to do, especially when one is called Edward Childe? Please believe in my genuine and deeply felt affection. I shall keep you informed about our movements. Goodbye for now, I hope.

Beinecke Rare Book and Manuscript Library, Yale University, Bonnel copy in MS Vault Tocqueville, D II A, folder "Bonnel's copies of letters from Americans to Tocqueville."

136. Alexis de Tocqueville to Edward Vernon Childe

April 2, 1857

Dear Mr. Childe,

I have just returned to Paris, and my first concern has been to go to M. D.[33] in order to retrieve what you left for me there. The package did indeed contain the papers that we were expecting. I found in it everything, including a letter that I had written after the death of my father, that is, a few days before the fatal operation took place and when undoubtedly the decision had been taken. I do not need to tell you how profoundly touched I was to see that, in such a moment, Mrs. Childe had thought of collecting the papers that she knew were so precious to me. In her care I saw a last proof of a friendship whose memory will always be dear and worthy of respect to me. I thank you from all my heart, dear Mr. Childe, for the small mementos that you enclosed in the first package. Your small ink pot will always be my travel companion. But I shall not need it in order to think often of you and your dear children. I have given much thought to what you told me about them and about yourself, as you can easily imagine. It is very difficult for me to give any advice on such matters! There are so many factors that are always poorly known! The first of them is the particular disposition of the friends to whom one speaks, of which they alone can judge and which must exercise a legitimate influence on their acts. For in the end, man cannot act only out of calculation and reasoning, but also out of inclination and inner impulse. As for Mr. Edward, it seems obvious to me that the best thing he can do is to come to Europe, at least for some time and often. Europe has become the homeland of his soul; I fear that he will never be able to live a normal life elsewhere. He likes to be busy in his own way and he will find the activities he loves only in the countries of the Old World. Hence, I think that, in his case, only a stay in Europe can countervail the influence of a temperament that is a little melancholic and whose effects are still augmented by idleness and boredom. As for Miss Mary, to tell you frankly what I think, I believe that, on the contrary, she has the best chance to find happiness in her own country. I confess that I would be more eager to see her find a husband in America than in France. It is rare that marriages turn out well when races are mixed and, above all, when different educations and religions are blended. Sometimes, they turn out well, but more often the outcome is a false situation and a painful inner torment. For my part, I would never advise a young woman to choose her husband from outside her nation, whatever that nation may be.[34] I think therefore that if Miss Mary could remain in America until her marriage, it would be best for her. But this does not only concern her. It also concerns you, and this is what your friends cannot forget, and what you yourself are not allowed to forget either. For, in the end, it is in the interest of your child that you should not make your life so sad and uncomfortable that your soul becomes depressed. Nothing good can arise from such a disposition, and one should not succumb to it at any price. From my point of view, the most desirable thing would be for you to marry off your daughter in America, to settle, if possible, close to her, in such a way as to find in her marriage an interior space and those intimate joys of the heart that your nature needs more than one might think when meeting you. You should undoubtedly come to Europe, but only as a recreation and in order to see, from time to time, the good friends that you have left behind here, while always preserving the foundation of your life and your position in your country. Dear Mr. Childe, this is, it seems to me, what might bring you the greatest possibility of happiness. But I return to what I was saying at the beginning: who can judge for another what is happiness? Each of us makes or imagines happiness in his own way, and in the end, one must direct one's actions according to the notion that one has of oneself, and not according to the image that others might have of you. Therefore, I would be very distressed if I exercised any influence upon your actions. You are a man of judgment and a good man, you love dearly your children; you know them, and you know yourself; anything that you do will seem wise to me, for you are better placed than me to ascertain what must be done.

You have given me very interesting details about your domestic affairs and I was extremely delighted to read them. I have great confidence in your judgment and everything that you might write to me concerning a country that has played such a great role in my private life and which should have such an influence on the general destiny of mankind, will always be extremely valuable to me. The greatest scourge of America after slavery is, as you put it well, the government of the country by the least honest, if not the least capable, part of the nation. I cannot believe that this evil has not been brought forth by a great good, namely domestic prosperity and exterior peace. I believe that more difficult circumstances would soon lead the people to choose more worthy representatives. Today they follow their tastes, because they believe that they can do so without any danger. As with all sovereigns, the people naturally love courtiers and flatterers; but I have enough confidence in their practical sense to believe that, in times of crisis, they would place their confidence in better hands. At least I hope so, for I passionately desire to see the success of the great experiment of *Self Government*[35] that is currently taking place in America. If it fails, that will be the end of political liberty on earth. What makes me despair is what is going on with the issue of slavery. I have always been very opposed to the abolitionist party, as far as that party wanted to bring forth the premature and dangerous abolition of slavery in those districts where this abominable institution has always existed. But introducing it into new states, spreading this horrible plague onto a large portion of the earth which has been free from it until now, imposing all the crimes and miseries accompanying slavery on millions of future people (masters or slaves) who could otherwise be spared it, all this is a crime against mankind and seems to me to be both dreadful and unpardonable.

I am familiar with your American winters, although I have not spent one in Boston. I remember that the day when I arrived in Washington, in January 1832; it was extremely hot; during the night, the Potomac froze. After this occurrence, which I witnessed personally, nothing surprises me. I am staying here for at least three months; but as I am living for the moment in a hotel which I may leave at any time, I ask you to write to me at the Institute, care of M. Pingard. Your letter will be sent to me wherever I might be. Farewell, dear Mr. Childe. Do not ever tire of speaking to me about your affairs and about anything that regards you. Be reassured that there is no other subject that interests me more and about which I would be more willing to talk to you than this one. I only regret having so few means of being of service to you. Please believe in all my sentiments of sincere and profound friendship. Remember me to Miss Mary. As for Mr. Edward, he is probably no longer with you.

A. de Tocqueville

137. Alexis de Tocqueville to Theodore Sedgwick

Paris, April 13, 1857

Dear Mr. Sedgwick,

Upon my arrival here I found your letter of February 5 waiting for me. I regret that it has taken me eight days to respond to it, but you will forgive me if you consider all the problems facing someone who returns to Paris after being absent for nine months.

I would have naturally wished that the news you give me about the sales of the book were better. Perhaps the success of the work in England will ultimately have an influence on your public. In France, we are going to issue a new edition; it is the third one in less than ten months, and each edition has been so substantial that the first three printings of the *Old Regime* amount to almost as many copies as the first six editions of the *Democracy*. What you tell me about the opinion of Mr. Bancroft touches me greatly. The interest expressed in the letter of your mother, Mrs. Sedgwick, has touched me even more. Do you know that in this learned Europe, which still prides itself on being the center of the movements of the human mind, and above all, in this France which once had a literary life, do you know that one could meet very few women who display the admirable curiosity and intellectual activity of your mother, Mrs. Sedgwick, as revealed by the fragment of the letter that you have sent to me? I would add that one could meet few women who were able to read a work such as that of Grote[36] and to pass such a true and accurate judgment on it. You tell me that you are proud of your mother, Mrs. Sedgwick, and you are certainly right to be so.

I read with great interest what you told me about your political affairs. How can you excuse yourself for the length of your letter? It seemed to me too short. You have enabled me to understand better than ever before how a very sizeable part of the population in the North voted for Mr. Buchanan. Please God that the latter should justify the hopes that you have placed in him! I know that he is a very distinguished man. But he has a very difficult task. I agree with you that the greatest domestic danger threatening the northern states today is less slavery than the corruption of democratic institutions, a corruption whose seeds it was already easy to perceive twenty-five years ago when I was in the United States, and which, it seems to me, I foresaw quite well, but which, if I am to believe what I am being told, has progressed more quickly than I feared. As for the policy allowing slavery to develop on a whole part of the earth where it had previously been unknown, I acknowledge like you, if you will, that for the sake of the specific and current interest of the Union, the only thing that one can do is to allow it to spread in this manner. But, for me as a foreigner, I confess that this sight makes me despair and horrifies me. I cannot change my views on this issue. I cannot accept that, given such a horrible calamity, the majority of a great people are not entitled to have an opinion and to act. I am unwilling to admit that any contract whatsoever could include among its terms the annihilation of the right and the duty that the present generation has to prevent the most horrible of all social evils from spreading over millions and millions of people belonging to future generations. And I thank God that I am not placed in the painful situation of being obliged either, as a citizen, to jeopardize such a great present good as the Union, or, as a human being, to allow a dreadful plague to spread over a large part of the inhabitable earth, and perhaps for as long as the world will last. I feel that I could write on this subject for two hours; but I am running out of paper and the fear of annoying you leads me to change the subject and take up a more pleasant one: your first voyage to Europe.[37] We will welcome you here with open arms. You know that already. Your daughters, the Misses Sedgwick, will be welcomed by my wife as old friends and we shall do our best to make their stay as pleasant as possible. We would very much hope that you should bring them to Tocqueville and not to Paris. People do not see each other here, regardless of their desire to meet. A few days in the countryside furthers mutual acquaintance more than two months in Paris. From July 15 onward, we shall be in Normandy and we shall not move from there until next spring. It is there that you should seek us out if you come this year. The journey is a little long, but the countryside is beautiful and full of those memories of old Europe which, I am sure, will be of interest to the Misses Sedgwick.

The death of my father is already placing in my hands – and will certainly soon place more – an amount of capital that I would be tempted to invest in America if, without risking the capital, I could gain from my money a little over 5%, a rate which one could not exceed in Europe now without endangering the capital. If you have any advice on this matter, at your earliest opportunity I would be very pleased if you shared it with me.

Two days ago, I received here a young American to whom you had given a letter of introduction in March of last year. He traveled through Italy before coming to Paris, so your letter traveled with him before reaching me. The person concerned is Mr. Alfred Pell. I have endeavored to introduce him to a distinguished lawyer from the Paris Bar who is a good friend of mine. Mr. Pell is a very pleasant young man; because he is not fluent in French yet, he will perhaps have a difficult time dealing with our lawyers, who in general speak only their own language.

Nothing would be easier than to present a book to the Academy of Moral [and Political] Sciences. It would be enough to send a copy to the permanent secretary. But it would be better to have it presented by a member who, in offering the book, could make a brief analysis of it. I do not need to tell you how delighted I would be to take upon myself the task of being that person. The only difficulty is to know if your book could arrive in Paris in time to find me still here.[38] I shall not be in Paris after June 15. At that time, I shall go to England. If your work could reach me around June 1, that would be perfect. I would immediately present it to the Academy, and would write an account without delay that would be included in our printed proceedings. If you cannot ensure that your book reaches me within the time indicated, I shall try to find a colleague to present and summarize it in my stead.[39] You will perhaps lose nothing by this change. But it would be a pleasure for me to act as your rapporteur. Hence, do not lose any time in having the book sent to me.

I add to my letter another letter for Mr. Bonner. Would you please forward it to him?

My apologies for the length of this letter, and above all, my apologies for my poor handwriting, which you will have great difficulty in reading. Please believe in my most sincere friendship.

A. de Tocqueville

P. S. I have not responded at all to that part of your letter in which you speak to me in such a moving way about your recent loss, because I know from experience that one should not re-open such wounds. But please believe, dear Mr. Sedgwick, that you could not find anyone more capable of understanding and empathizing with you than me. To that end, it is sufficient to return into myself and to consider what I would feel if I were to go through a similar ordeal.

138. Alexis de Tocqueville to Charles Sumner[40]

Friday, May 1, 1857

Dear Mr. Sumner,

Do you have a ticket for tomorrow or should I send you mine?[41] I need to know because the ticket that I have for you is in great demand. I hope you are doing well.

A. de Tocqueville

139. Edward Vernon Childe to Alexis de Tocqueville

Baltimore, MD, May 2, [18]57

My dear M. de Tocqueville,

I have delayed for a few days to answer your exceeding kind and most welcome letter of the 2nd of April – just a month ago! I wanted to see Edward before doing so, that he might add a line or two; but he tells me that he wrote to you from Cuba (he having arrived here yesterday), and now would merely say, in addition to the love he sends you, that he has terminated his two months' voyage much to his satisfaction. After visiting Cuba, he went through the great West, and I am inclined to think that he has had enough of American travelling. You will soon receive a letter from him.

Since you are so indulgent toward my poor notions of public affairs, and as I know how much you are, and have been always, interested (not without knowledge) in American concerns, I will, before closing this letter, give you some of my impressions of a general nature, which are the result of being in communication with some of the distinguished men of the South.

But I would first tell you somewhat of myself and of mine, assured, as I am, of the interest you feel for us. The advice contained in your last favor tallies so well with the facts – the hard facts and necessities of our case, that we shall probably follow it with exactitude. Edward is disgusted with Boston – with its climate, its moral and intellectual sameness, flatness and unprofitableness, – its professional peculiarities on the part of the men, and its woodeny, conventional and unpoetical bearing on the part of its women. As yet he knows nothing, practically, about this place. Whether he will return to Paris the next autumn or in the spring is a matter of uncertainty. Were it not for his unwillingness to quit his father and sister, he would stay here but a short time. I have told him to do as he shall see fit to do, nor shall I urge him to remain longer than the summer. It is hard luck to be separated from the few that one loves, but I am in some measure accustomed to suffering. Mary *must*, as you truly say, remain in this country, and I must, of course, hire or buy a house and furniture so as to give her a home. Unfortunately her *near* relatives, with someone of whom a girl of her tender years should reside, are so circumstanced that a home with them (though freely and heartily offered) is wholly impracticable. One uncle is a farmer in Virginia, with a host of boys in his house and no means of instruction at hand; a second is at a navy yard, liable to be sent to sea at any moment and sure to quit his post (in Philadelphia) next year; a third fighting the Indians in the far South-West; and poor Mrs. Marshall, at whose house we are staying, is wholly powerless in hand and foot. Then, as well as I can guess, there is little or no chance of my crossing the Atlantic for years to come. My present notion is that I shall fix my residence in Baltimore. The climate of *all* this country is, in my eyes, detestable, but since it is my duty to remain here (and better would it have been for us all, if years ago we had left Europe). I can no more complain of its vicissitudes with reason, than can the soldier, whose vocation keeps him in an atmosphere of gun-powder, find fault with the smell of sulphur and saltpetre.

I am very happy to know that your health is so well established – may you go on prospering and to prosper! *I* never am well, and yet my health seems in no way to fail. At times my spirits are shockingly bad, and, as poor Hamlet says, "I have bad dreams." What a blessing it would be to me if I had a little even of *your* mental capacity to employ one's self agreeably and profitably, without taking into account the "wide world's fame."

I have just returned from a visit to Virginia, and never was I more disappointed in a country on this side of the Atlantic. In city and in the country no signs or realities of hospitality are wanting; but the impression made upon one's mind is that the inhabitants of Vir[gini]a are many years behind those of Mass[achuse]tts. The roads are execrable and even unsafe, the bridges dangerous, and the ferries, where no impediment exists to the construction of bridges, so imperfect in material that the gentleman in whose carriage I crossed looked very nervous, and I, for my part, was all-prepared for a swim. Then, their hotels – the condition of which necessary [*sic*] in modern times is a certain index of civilization – are abominable. In the category of gentlemen one half, at least, would, if they once attempted to speak or act according to their kind, find themselves quite at sea in any well-regulated saloon either in Boston or Paris. They are self-confident, and, if other southerners partake of the like self-admiration, no fear of consequences will deter them from the rashest of all resolves – a separation from the free states. It appears, much to my surprise, that the party for disunion is by no means feeble in the slave-holding states. Their only point of difference among themselves is the matter of cooperation – that is, whether one state, South Carolina, for example, shall declare itself a secessionist, calling on other states to rally around her, or whether no move shall be made in the matter till some 5 or 6 states have agreed on withdrawing from the Union. There are some persons who, being much better informed than myself, believe in a dissolution of the Union. I do *not* believe in such a disaster. Nay, more, even if it were to happen, I am not so clear but that much good would be the result of the rupture for the free states. You will perceive, then, that with my views I am without fear in the question.

In the actual administration of this country we have, I am told, two or three most able and honest men. The President, Buchanan, from all that I hear of him, is a weak and not overfaithful person. He is pledged to the southern interests, they say, but I doubt if he dare to act his part in the southern sense. In spite of him, and of the man he has sent to govern Kansas, that territory will be, I think, a non-holding slave state. Mr. Cass, Buchanan's foreign secretary, is a twaddler and unfit for his place. Our foreign relations will, according to present appearances, be of a pacific nature. Buchanan and Cass are both old men, and age is seldom coupled with a pugnacious disposition.

The last accounts from Walker describe that gentleman as being in a most precarious predicament, but he has so often contrived to emerge from a flood of difficulties that it will cause no surprise to me to hear that he has again got his head above water. The hope, however, is now that he will be hung. He is surrounded by numerous enemies, through whose ranks he has tried in vain to break a passage, and his lieutenant, with reinforcements, has failed to fight his way to Walker's relief.

The more I see and learn of slavery, the greater is my disrespect for the "institution." Slave owners admit that it is not profitable in the true sense of the word, that is, that their profits are not such as they ought to be from the capital employed. Of men, women and children in slavery on a plantation not one half can earn a penny. The master must support them. And yet the traffic in slaves – the transportation of them from Africa to America – is carried on to-day to a frightful extent!

Since our arrival in this country, with the exception of 3 or 4 weeks, the weather has been ferociously disagreeable. We have been grieved at hearing of the failure of our friends the Greenes. As yet I have not received the volume you were so kind as to give me and to leave with them.

Adieu, my dear friend, and believe, I pray you, in the expression of all my esteem and affection.

E. V. Childe

Beinecke Rare Book and Manuscript Library, Yale University, Uncat MSS 324; also available as Bonnel copy in MS Vault Tocqueville, D II A, folder "Bonnel's copies of letters from Americans to Tocqueville."

140. Francis Lieber to Alexis de Tocqueville

New York, May 30, 1857

It is now almost a year I wrote to you last, my dear de Tocqueville, and many, many months since I received your letter; but you will not, I feel sure, ascribe my long silence to any abatement of the friendship I feel for you. On the contrary, you have occupied my mind very much. I have read and re-read your excellent work, and have now directed my youngest son, Norman, who is studying law at Cambridge, to read it with great care in conjunction with my *Civil Liberty*. I have delayed writing to you, because I did not exactly know what would become of me, and it is not pleasant to commune with distant friends when we are in a state of uncertainty. Then, I had it in contemplation to go to Europe, and to surprise you, after my departure from Columbia S.C., but I found it unadvisable to make the trip, and now have the pleasure of informing you that I have been elected professor of History and Political Science in Columbia College in this city. The chair is a newly created one. The institution has lately much increased the number of chairs, and a university course is to be added. The revenue of the institution is rapidly increasing, owing to its possessing a great deal [of] land, which is fast filling up with houses, and it is the plan of the trustees to enlarge the institution as the means increase, so as ultimately to form a real university. It was gratifying to me that I was unanimously elected by a Board consisting of some 25 members. The chair is considered the most important, and, if I add that my *Civil Liberty* and my *Pol[itical] Ethics* have been repeatedly cited in the courts of justice as authority in questions of constitutional difficulty, you will allow that my position is not a wholly subordinate one. Will you have the goodness of seeing that in the publications of the Institute I am called *Professeur de l'Histoire et des Sciences Politiques au Columbia College, à New York*? You would do me a favour by seeing the change made.

And now a word on your *Ancien Régime*. I do not know how the translation by Bonner, which is exceedingly well done, has sold. I dare say, not very well, simply because profound works never do, but every one in the United States who is a judge of political works of wisdom and profundity, is delighted with it and speaks of it as a most remarkable work. I was greatly delighted when I found that Mr. Samuel Tyler,[42] of Maryland, a lawyer of great eminence and member of the Law Reform Committee of that state, and a ripe philosopher, the friend of Senator William Hamilton – when I found that he had grouped Montesquieu, de Tocqueville, and Lieber as forming a distinct class of modern political philosophers and distinguished by their rising from the broad ground of history and human reality to the highest speculations, by their true wisdom and by real statesmanship, the only modern publicists resembling Aristotle.

Soon after I had perused your work, I took it to a dinner party, and read your last page (of the work, not of the appendix) to the assembled guests before we went to the dinner. Bonner has translated that page peculiarly well, and Mr. Petigru,[43] of Charleston, whom you may remember as the first lawyer in the South, exclaimed: "Good heavens, who is that? What book do you read from? Since Tacitus, there has not been written such a page." Almost the very words I had used to some friends a few days before. I think I shall deliver a course of lectures during next winter on the history of the 19th century down to the laying of the sub-Atlantic telegraph.[44] Give me any advice you think proper. I made an ode on this telegraph, which has gone through all the papers here.

Pray let me hear soon from you and be a good Christian not rewarding silence with silence. My best regards to Madame de Tocqueville.

Very sincerely my dear de Tocqueville,
                    Your faithful friend,
                    Francis Lieber

Remember me very friendly to de Beaumont.

Beinecke Rare Book and Manuscript Library, Yale University, Bonnel copy in MS Vault Tocqueville, D II A, folder "Bonnel's copies of letters from Americans to Tocqueville."

141. Alexis de Tocqueville to William H. Prescott

Paris, June 6, 1857

Sir,

Mr. Ticknor has kindly agreed to bring you the book that I published a year ago on *The Old Regime and the Revolution*. I have been wanting to send it to you for a long time, but have been unsure about what means to use to that end. Please accept this book as a token of the esteem that I have for you and as a way of thanking you for the pleasure that I experienced in reading your works.[45] I hope, Sir, that you will continue to instruct us and interest us with new works worthy of the previous ones.

Please accept the expression of my distinguished consideration.
                    A. de Tocqueville

142. George Ticknor to Alexis de Tocqueville

Hotel Bristol, June 10, 1857

My dear Sir,

I have received the three copies of your admirable work that you have done me the favor to send me. For my own I thank you very heartily. The two others I will send to their respective addressees, when I reach Boston, if not before.

But, I hope we shall see you again and soon. We are at home almost every evening after VII and to-morrow morning Circourt breakfasts with us at X, and we shall talk, I think, till XII. I wish you could come and help us.

> Y[ou]rs very faithfully,
> George Ticknor

143. Alexis de Tocqueville to Massachusetts Historical Society[46]

[June 1857]

Sir,

I have received the letter you wrote to me announcing that I had been unanimously elected an honorary member of the Massachusetts Historical Society.

I pray you to tell in my name to your colleagues that I accept with the deepest feeling of gratitude the title they have conferred to me.

I know that your society (which is already an ancient and celebrated institution) has produced excellent works and contains many very distinguished members and I consider as highly honorable for me to be nearly connected with it.

All the links which bind me with the American people are very dear in my estimation and I feel very proud and happy when I know that my name is not unknown in your grand and glorious country.

Believe me, Sir, your very humble servant.

> [Alexis de Tocqueville]

144. Alexis de Tocqueville to Theodore Sedgwick

Paris, June 13, 1857

Dear Sedgwick,

I am a little worried about what happened to a letter that I wrote to you about three months ago.[47] Not only have you not responded to it yet; but that letter contained another one addressed to the translator of my work, who has also not replied to me. The coincidence of these two facts makes me fear that the letter has not arrived, which, however, is improbable, since the postal service that delivers the letters to America works very well. At all events, if these few words cannot make up for the lost letter, I hope that they will at least succeed in shaking you out of your lethargy and encouraging you to give me news about you.

You also announced to me the publication of a work written by you that has not reached me yet. Nevertheless, I would very much wish that it should have reached me before my departure from Paris, so as to allow me to present it in your name to the Academy of Moral and Political Sciences, by adding a short commentary of my own, which would then be printed in the proceedings of the Academy. Here I am on the last day of my stay in this city. I am leaving today, and thus it is only at the end of winter, around the month of February, that I shall be able to have the pleasure of introducing you to my colleagues. Perhaps you will not want to wait until then. At all events, please send me your instructions. If the presentation of the book cannot be done by me, I shall make sure that you do not lose anything, which will not be very difficult.

At the present moment, I am not returning to my home but am going to England where I have many friends whom I have not seen for a long time and whom, moreover, I want to visit in order to make inquiries of documents concerning the French Revolution.[48] It is said that the British Museum owns the most complete collection of documents of this kind in the world.[49] This would appear surprising if we were not familiar with the habit of the English of using their great resources to obtain rare things, even those things on which they sometimes set a small value and in which they are hardly interested. Therefore, I am leaving for London and shall return to Tocqueville only at the end of July. I would very much wish that this year does not pass without seeing you and your family. But I have little hope of determining you to come here this year.

I apologize for the insignificance of this letter. But the frequent violation of the secrecy of correspondence makes it very difficult to send to a foreigner any interesting news about what is going on in France. I want to be sure that this letter reaches you. This is why I do not want in any way to touch upon politics here.

You are not, thank God, in the same situation, and I hope that, when writing to me, you will not forget to tell me a little about the public affairs in your country, in which, as you know, I take an interest which is no less great for being disinterested. Is the government of the new President capable of calming the almost revolutionary agitation that his election has caused? I would very much hope so. During the last electoral battles, passions seemed to have reached a high level of violence which would be the infallible sign of civil war in Europe and which, even in America, could end by leading to it in the near future, if they cannot be calmed. May God prevent such a terrible tragedy! When I think of the immense gifts that Providence has given you, of the almost superhuman prosperity that you enjoy, of the prodigious destinies that await you if you remain united; and when I see so many goods ready to be spoiled or lost by the evil passions of the people, I am tempted to cry with Molière:

"Man, I confess to you, is a wicked animal!"[50]

But it is even more just to say that he is a limited and imperfect animal who deserves pity more than anger. Nevertheless, I count on the practical common sense of the American people to give me a better opinion about our species.

Farewell, dear Sedgwick. My wife wishes kindly to be remembered to you, and I ask you to believe as always in my most sincere friendship.

A. de Tocqueville

145. Alexis de Tocqueville to Edward Everett

Paris, June 17, 1857

I avail myself of an opportunity that presents itself to send you the last volume that I have published (*The Old Regime and the Revolution*); I should have sent it to you much earlier, since this book is already a year old and has had three editions. I have been prevented from doing so by a very unfortunate event, the death of my father, which coincided with the publication of my book. As you can imagine, this event has profoundly affected me. I immediately left Paris and have only recently returned here. This is my excuse. I hope that you would be so kind as to accept it. At all events, please receive this book as a very small testimony of the great esteem that I have for your ability.

Please receive, Sir, the expression of my most distinguished consideration.

Alexis de Tocqueville
Member of the Institute

146. Alexis de Tocqueville to Edward Vernon Childe

July 7, 1857

Dear Mr. Childe,

I have been truly touched by your last letter.[51] What you tell me about yourself and your family saddens me greatly. I see that your country has become a painful and difficult dwelling place for you and that, although you have close relatives, you are, in fact, isolated there. I fear that the sadness of this situation and the rigors of a climate to which you are no longer accustomed might end up having a nefarious influence on your health, or at least, that they might increase your natural inclination to melancholy and might finish by getting the better, not of your courage (I know that you have enough of that), but of your physical and moral energies. I continue to believe that the best chance of happiness for Miss Mary is to remain in her country, to preserve the taste, spirit, and habits of it, and, finally, to choose her husband there. But that, it seems to me, could be done without condemning you to absolute immobility. Why do you not come with her soon on a short trip to Europe? I do not mean settling down here, nor do I mean a long stay, but a voyage of a few months as you Americans often do without having the impression of undertaking a great enterprise! I do not think that this distraction would be detrimental to Miss Childe, and as for yourself, I am sure that it will do you good. You will refresh your impressions. The sight of our continent will no doubt recall many painful memories, but on your way you will meet good friends whom, I believe, you will be very pleased to greet. I am happy to see that in this Paris which is so frivolous, where it is said that everything is so quickly forgotten, people remember the person who was so dear to you. What pleased me, without surprising me, was also to hear the two or three people who spent the most time with you, above all de Pins,[52] speak about you in particular with the tone of genuine affection and as if you had just left us. Undoubtedly, if you came to settle in Paris, in the long term your position would seem to you less agreeable than in the past; but, on the other hand, I do not doubt that a simple visit among us would be very enjoyable to you. I believe that you would notice especially that your absence has changed nothing among those whom you call your friends and whom you used to welcome in your house. You will find in them the same high-spiritedness, the same confidence, and the same friendship as in the past. This would be beneficial to a temperament like yours which, beneath its cold exterior, inspires sympathy and is in need of receiving sympathy. Like you, I believe that at the present moment your first duty is toward the young girl whose only guide and support you were made by Providence. But in her interest, you must try to preserve yourself, not just your life, but also that state of mind which allows one to be useful to oneself and to others. How would she ever be able to replace such an affectionate father as you, and one so devoted to your children, as I know you to be? This is a treasure for which you are entirely responsible to them and of which you should not risk depriving them. Having said that, dear Mr. Childe, I repeat, as I have already done in my previous letter, that I do not intend at all to give you any advice. One always proceeds tentatively when attempting to enter into the mind of another person, because there are always thousands of facts or feelings with which one is unfamiliar and which would modify what one would say to that person if one knew them. Hence, I offer you the previous considerations only as impressions that you alone can best judge. What I am certain of is that they come from a very sincere wish to be of service to you.

Please thank Mr. Edward, if he is with you, for a very friendly and very interesting letter that he wrote to me from Cuba.

I am writing to you as I am about to leave for England, where I shall spend a month before returning to Normandy. You can write to me at the Institute, care of M. Pingard, Chief Secretary. Your letter will be forwarded to me wherever I shall be at that moment. What you tell me about America seemed very interesting to me; and when you write, I shall always be extremely delighted if you give me news about that country and about what is going on there. For me, it is one of the greatest objects of curiosity in the world, and everything that a friend as thoughtful as you are could teach me about it is extremely valuable.

I would happily render to you the same service for Europe if that were of any interest to you. But letters are often read, especially when they are written to foreigners; and when they displease, they are disposed of. In order to make my correspondence more secure, I am obliged to cut out what might make it more interesting. But I can give you news about the acquaintances and friends whom I have recently seen. The Duchess de Rauzan,[53] whose voice, I think, you would be very pleased to hear, is doing a little better; Belvèze[54] and de Pins are doing well. Both are presently in Paris. The Circourts,[55] whom I place among your acquaintances rather than friends, are in the countryside.

Farewell, dear Mr. Childe. Please think of me; I often think of you and of everything that your name reminds me of. Do not forget to remember me to Mr. Edward and Miss Mary and please believe in my sincere affection.

A. de Tocqueville

147. Susan Sedgwick[56] to Alexis de Tocqueville

Massachusetts,
Northhampton, July 11, 1857

Sir,

I was entrusted by my father with the task of writing to you. It is a long time ago that my father received your letter containing another one for Mr. Bonner, but unfortunately, he has been too unwell to write to you ever since.[57] He has just received a second letter from you, and not wanting to keep silent any longer, he asks you to kindly accept these few lines on my part. Upon receiving your letter, he sent it to Mr. Bonner and has not received any news from him yet.

In the hope of recovering from a very serious neuralgia attack, my father has placed himself for the last few weeks in a water cure establishment; he is doing a little better now but we cannot delude ourselves that he will recover very quickly. He sends you his sincere thanks and hopes to write to you personally before long.

Please also accept, Sir, the expression of my profound gratitude for the kindness that Madame de Tocqueville and you have shown to my sister and I. It would be impossible for us to experience a greater pleasure than seeing Europe and particularly your beautiful France, and we would be extremely happy to benefit from your kind hospitality. Perhaps we will be so fortunate in another year.

Please, Sir, pay my respects and those of my sister to Madame de Tocqueville and accept the expression of my most distinguished consideration.

Susan Sedgwick

P. S. – My dear M. de Tocqueville, I have been quite ill and still am very weak; I shall write to you when I can. Many thanks for your kind letters. Theodore Sedgwick

Beinecke Rare Book and Manuscript Library, Yale University, Bonnel copy in MS Vault Tocqueville, D II A, folder "Bonnel's copies of letters from Americans to Tocqueville."

148. Alexis de Tocqueville to Jared Sparks

Paris, July 15, 1857

Dear Mr. Sparks,

I hope that you will forgive me for sending you my book a year after its publication and when it has already had three editions. You ought to have been one of the first Americans to whom I should have offered this book, for in America I scarcely have an older friend than you.[58] An unfortunate circumstance has prevented me from fulfilling my desire in this regard. At the very moment when my book appeared a year ago, I had the misfortune of losing my father toward whom I was deeply attached. This event so powerfully and profoundly affected me that I had to leave Paris immediately after it occurred, without taking any steps for distributing my work to my friends. When I returned here, a few months ago, the second edition of my *Old Regime [and the Revolution]* had sold out. I had to wait for the third edition and then for an opportunity to send you the volume that I had reserved for you. The best of all opportunities has just presented itself. Our mutual friend, Mr. Ticknor, is leaving Europe to return to New England. He is willing to bring you my work. Please receive it, dear Mr. Sparks, with goodwill and as testimony to all the sentiments of esteem and friendship that I have for you.

If you reply to me, the most reliable way of doing so is to address your letters to *the Institute, care of M. Pingard, Chief Secretary*. The latter will forward them to me wherever I shall be residing at that time. I would be very happy to learn how you are, what you are doing, what kind of work you are currently undertaking (I know that you cannot remain idle). Everything that you might tell me about your country will also be of great interest to me. The crisis into which it is thrown by the issue of slavery is the subject of my worries and I would very much wish that you could reassure me about the future of the Union to which perhaps is attached that of liberty in the world.[59]

Farewell, dear Mr. Sparks. Please believe in all my sentiments of esteem and friendship.

Alexis de Tocqueville

149. Edward Vernon Childe to Alexis de Tocqueville

White-Sulphur-Springs, Virginia
July 16, 1857

It is exactly one month, my dear Mon[sieur] de Tocqueville, since you wrote to me your last and most kindly affectionate letter, which contained exceeding good and reasonable advice, such as I needed. I have been again and again on the point of acknowledging, and thanking you for it; but so many business letters have kept me employed, and so much have I been upon the move, that, as usual, what ought to have been done has been left undone, and, as is not usual, my inclination has not been duly consulted. My agent, long-tried and faithful, Mr. Cotting, died about six weeks ago, and his son, a youth of 25 or 26 years, my new agent, has need of my constant counsel. Besides, ever since we parted, my health has been far from good – spirits somewhat under par, and appetite clean gone. Yet nothing of a serious nature has occurred except, some 3 or 4 weeks since, a violent attack of flying-gout in the breast tormented me during a few hours.

After visiting some relatives in this state, and passing a while in Baltimore with my brother-in-law (Edward and Mary being with me), my son and I accompanied his sister, her aunt Mrs. Col. Lee and her cousin – a girl of about Mary's age – to Berkeley Springs in Morgan county of this state, where we left them for the benefit of Mrs. Lee's health and of my daughter's well-being, and then we came to this place to drink the waters, which are supposed to be of great efficacy in a case like mine.

I have, however, very little faith in mineral waters for hereditary diseases – thus much concerning the health of one you take such a kind and flattering interest in. And I will repeat, what was in my last letter, how truly happy it makes me to learn that your own health is vastly improved. The wise DeWitt said well – that life, as compared with health, is a worthless thing. As for the American climate, disagreeable to the feelings, it is still more injurious to the health. I heard a Scotchman remark in Baltimore that, tho' now accustomed to it, he lost 25 or 30 pounds in the process of becoming acclimated.

All that you say respecting my dear little Mary is most true. It still appears to me a judicious step, the bringing of her to this country, where she has become attached to many relations, whom she never had seen, and with whom she is a very great favorite. Wherever she goes, it is a great source of happiness to me to see that she gains friends. For her sake I shall remain here – how long who can tell? – I have taken a furnished house for two years and two years are a term of time quite long enough for a man past 50 years to look before him. Were it not that duty and affection both point out the line to be pursued, I would embark with Edward for Europe, never to return here but at the call of necessity. The people – and by that word I mean all, with few exceptions, high, half way and low, rich, well to do and poor – the people, taken by and large, please me less and less, the more I see and know of them. This is, of course, to be imputed to a certain wryness in my vision or way of thought. Either I am fastidious by nature or perverted by a residence in foreign countries. To whatever cause the thing may be attributed, it is not less a reality, and in my case a sad reality, that the sober side of Americans resembles the gloom of an old-fashioned puritanical Sunday, while the opposite side is more like the hilarity of an automaton, or of a hireling, paid to giggle, than of a sentient being rejoicing from the heart. But whatever be the condition of things, and men, here I *must* remain. In the course of time Mary will be married, it is to be presumed. For here, as in Europe, a young lady who is reputed to be rich, or who is one of few heirs of a man enjoying that reputation, is no less exposed to the fortune hunter than in other countries. Fortunately the child has a deal of common sense, and is dearly attached to her father and brother.

How much I should like to see you and my other friends in Europe, I need not say. Do, whenever you see them, remember me to them – to de Pins, Mérimée, Belvèze, Cuvier, and to Madame de Rauzan,[60] whose kindness in our extremity, I shall never forget. To these and to the "good duke" I would be recalled in all warmth of heart. Edward within these few days has written to you, or I would add his words to mine. He will, however, I hope, be able before long to tell you in person how much we speak of you, and how highly we prize your counsel and friendship.

You will see in Paris about the month of September an old friend of yours – Mr. Sparks, whom I like much, among other reasons, for his unpretending demeanor and gentle nature. You will always delight me by giving good tidings of my friends in Paris – friends such as one rarely meets, and such as proved themselves true as the thrice-tried steel in the hour of our sore trouble and distress. I would like, too, always to hear of those, who, missing the current of friendship through some original slackness of feeling or looseness, perhaps of the heart's fiber, are content to float along on the dull unbroken tide of mere acquaintance. It will ever be a gratification to learn whatever may regard that "admirable work," M. de Circourt – that wonderful congregation of facts – hating none and hated by none – unloving as unloved. And his wife. Does she continue to display her wares, intellectual and moral, with the air of one who alone knows how to value them?

I regret much that the P.O.[61] should dare to come between me and the information on European politics that you could give me. I regret it, not merely because here, without newspapers from the other side of the water, and reading nothing but garbled accounts cut haphazard from lying, stupid or ignorant correspondents, we know nothing, but especially because it is from *you* that I should get such information. If, however, your occupation ever permits you to enlighten me, a letter to me, under cover to Messr. Monroe and Cie, 5 rue de la Paix, would reach [me] safely. By the word *here* in the last line of the last page I do not mean this poor corner of Virginia, but the whole of the South, which from all that I can see and learn is, at least 50 years behind New-England and "the non-holding slave states." Till I came to the South and met southerners, many of whom are assembled here, a spot where 1, 000 are lodged and not a dozen northerners, to "leaven the lump" – I had no conception of the intense dislike, amounting, I suspect, often to rabid hatred, with which the people of the North and East are regarded. Strong indeed must be the material interests which keep together a congregation of such communities for any great length of time. Fortunately these are as strong as material interests can well be. There must be a saving virtue in the people at large, or before now a wreck would have destroyed all.

At the present moment there is much to disquiet a looker on. There is, as I have said, dislike, on the past of the South towards the North, mingled with some contempt and no little envy – indifference on the side of the north – the Kansas difficulty, which is far from a settlement – the Mormon affair, which is nest of troubles, and added to these, we have a host of Central American affairs to arrange, with a president,[62] who is said to be the "meanest of white men," aided by a foreign secretary,[63] who is but one remove from an old woman. And yet all goes on well, and all will, I doubt not, continue to go on well enough to the end of the chapter.

The Press, we constantly hear, is of all-powerful influence in this country. If it be so, its conductors must be either weak or wicked; for an increasing disregard for law, and a stronger disposition to substitute might for right, cannot but be remarked in many portions of the land. Lynch-law, it must be admitted, has been at times a horrible necessity in territories far distant from the old states, where the only choice to men of order, who had wives and daughters and property to protect, was between such law (misnamed as it was) and utter lawlessness. But what can be said in extenuation when Lynch-law is carried out to the extremity of public execution in one of the oldest and most respectable of our communities – in the very state where now I am writing? Yet such has been the fact within two months! Yet such is, has been and, for aught I see, is like to be the fact in N. York City, in Phil[adelphi]a and in Baltimore. Men in these places go armed habitually, they engage in regular pitched battles, much in the same way as in the wars upon the borders of England and Scotland. Within the last week or 10 days New-York has been a scene of bloodshed. Instead of bringing the military to act at once, which would be in the long run an act of mercy, a few constables are sent to oppose armed ruffians – to be maimed and slaughtered. In Baltimore the same game has been enacted on a smaller scale. And such is the nature of the lower orders in the latter city (and in the others also, I presume), that gentlemen never go out of the home unprepared for an assault – at least some that I know. My brother-in-law, for example, Judge Marshall, carries a dagger, and his son a revolver. As another instance, while residing at their house the weather was so hot that Edward and I could not in dressing support our *robes de chambre* and were in our "shirt sleeves." Although in a 2nd storey and although between us and a neighbor (a retired baker) there were two yards, courts or gardens and a street, this ruffian chose to blackguard us in a high and insulting tone, and to threaten to shoot the "damned old grey head." By advice (for no assistance or protection could be had from the police) I never for a week left the house without a weapon of defense. This is a charming state of things for a quiet man to encounter! And all this should be overcome and suppressed by the public sentiment through the Press, if the Press were what it ought and pretends to be.

It is true that there are in this country a host of men with whom it is a pleasure and a profit to hold daily communion. There are here at this moment, among others, Judge Wayne[64] of the U. S. Supreme Court, and Mr. Gilpin, whom you knew in Phil[adelphi]a and in Paris, but such men are so scattered – there being no Paris for them to meet in – that, for a waif upon this social ocean, like myself, they might almost as well not be as be. In Baltimore, where, as said, I have fixed myself for Mary's sake, I know not a single individual of the kind I have described.

I have lately had occasion to change investment of property, and perhaps the result of my inquiries may interest you. I have directed my agent to buy Pennsylvania 5 percent stocks at 81 and 82 – the par value being 100, and perhaps I shall purchase Massachusetts and Boston city bonds, which are the surest in the land, and which will pay 5 and $\frac{1}{2}$ per cent. To the N.Y. State stocks, such as you have, I have no objection if they can be bought at a paying price, i.e., so as to yield 6 p[e]r c[en]t.

By enclosing to Monroe and Co. I hope you will be able to instruct me as to the *reality* of European affairs, about which I know nothing.

Do not, I pray you, allow my absence to dim your remembrance of me and of mine. And rest assured that I am always your most truly and affectionately,

E. V. Childe

Beinecke Rare Book and Manuscript Library, Yale University, Uncat MSS 324; also available as Bonnel copy in MS Vault Tocqueville, D II A, folder "Bonnel's copies of letters from Americans to Tocqueville."

150. Alexis de Tocqueville to Charles Sumner

[July 1857]

Several times every week, very good steamships leave the coast of England, from Weymouth (Southampton), Dorset, for Granville, touching at Jersey. The coast of Granville is itself worth visiting. Close to Granville, to its South, lies the *Mont St. Michel*, one of the most beautiful and most unusual examples of Gothic architecture, placed on a rock in the middle of the sea. Close to Granville, to the North, on the road to Cherbourg, lies *Coutances*, whose location and cathedral are famous.

From Granville to Cherbourg, there is, I believe, a coach, twice a day, that arrives in eight or ten hours at Cherbourg. If you prefer, you can stop five leagues from Cherbourg, in the town of Valognes, where you can easily find a cabriolet or a barouche to bring you to Tocqueville. Perhaps it would be preferable, however, to go to Cherbourg where you can find a better inn (*Hôtel de l'Europe*) and better coaches. The time necessary to go from Cherbourg to Tocqueville is shorter than from Valognes to Tocqueville.

The whole road from Granville to Cherbourg passes through the historical and heroic Normandy, the Normandy that gave a part of its soldiers to William the Conqueror; the Normandy where the Tancrèdes de Hauteville,[65] who conquered Sicily, were born along with their main companions.

The route from Dieppe or Le Havre or Calais:

From Le Havre to Cherbourg, there is a steamship twice a week that goes from one of these towns to the other in seven or eight hours.

If you want to travel over land, you have to reach *Caen* by the shortest route. From Caen, there are two coaches every day that take eight or nine hours to get to Cherbourg.

Nota. Ask for the residence of M. Alexis de Tocqueville, close to St. Pierre-Église, and not that of the Count de Tocqueville. The latter is my older brother, and since he owns an estate in the vicinity of Cherbourg, it is possible to make a mistake.

> M. Alexis de Tocqueville
> at Tocqueville, par St. Pierre-Église
> (Manche)

151. Charles Sumner to Alexis de Tocqueville

> Athenaeum Club,
> August 4, [18] 57

My dear M. de Tocqueville,

My present hope is to take the packet at Weymouth for Jersey on Saturday 8th August, and to come to you as soon as I can make the journey from Granville – stopping at Cherbourg.

I do not expect to trouble you more than two nights, when I shall run away to Switzerland.

Everybody here speaks with interest and admiration with regard to you, and Lord Lansdowne told me that he envied me the opportunity I was about to enjoy in visiting you.

Believe me, with much regard,

> Ever sincerely yours,
> Charles Sumner

Beinecke Rare Book and Manuscript Library, Yale University, Uncat MSS 324; also available as Bonnel copy in MS Vault Tocqueville, D II A, folder "Bonnel's copies of letters from Americans to Tocqueville."

152. Maria Weston Chapman to Alexis de Tocqueville

> Weymouth – near Boston, U. S.
> August 7, 1857

Dear Monsieur de Tocqueville,

A thousand thanks for your welcome volume which I have but just received. I had just been reading again your account of my country.

How true and just! I do hope we may be able to redeem it from the curse of slavery before we leave life – but it matters little. We shall leave as a heritage to our children, if not a free country, yet the noblest battle for the world's freedom that the sun has over looked upon. I say the freedom of the *world*, for it is the position for the United States as holding slaves, yet claiming the foremost place among free nations, that constitutes the strongest obstacle to the world's advance. Your testimony is registered against slavery. Renew it from time to time, I entreat you. Our statesmen and men of literature can only be reached by those whom they look up to, in other countries. Do you notice the absurd efforts some of them are making, to be thought the representative men of our nation, while they yet advocate slavery? It is only too true that at this hour they are so – but they feel that their hour is short. Politically, their course has been their death blow.[66] Every word against slavery, uttered by European celebrities, hastens the time when the atrocious system shall be abolished. Already the public opinion is slowly and surely seen to change. How many times lately have I been visited by the surviving friends of persons who spent their youth in reproaching mine for harsh language against slavery. Now, they come to beg me to find, if I can in our anti-slavery archives, some "recorded execration" which they may use as an ornament to their fathers' sepulchres: so short-sighted are the generations of men!

Pardon so long a note. I only meant to ask you for one more page for our annual volume, "The Liberty Bell." We shall never cease to be grateful for the one you have already written.[67]

Maria Weston Chapman

Beinecke Rare Book and Manuscript Library, Yale University, Uncat MSS 324; also available as Bonnel copy in MS Vault Tocqueville, D II A, folder "Bonnel's copies of letters from Americans to Tocqueville."

153. Alexis de Tocqueville to Edward Vernon Childe

Tocqueville, September 2, 1857

Dear Mr. Childe,

It has already been some time since I received your letter of July 16. I would have responded to it earlier if, upon my return here, I had not been beset by a host of small matters to which I had first to attend. During the first months of the summer, I made a trip to England which was of great interest. I had not visited that country for twenty years. I was welcomed there with tokens of interest and affection that deeply touched me. There was nothing people did not do to show me the respect that they had toward me and the approval given to my latest book. Your letter reached me upon returning from this trip. I was very pleased to find in it good news about your health. Your last letter had worried me a little and I was hoping to learn that your mind and body had returned to a more tranquil condition. You know that I have a genuine friendship for you and you should not doubt the sincere interest that I take and shall always take in anything concerning you.

Although I would have liked to have seen you, it is, however, with great satisfaction that I learned that your health allows you to remain in America for a few more years. I believe that this is essential to the future happiness of your beloved daughter Mary who, I hope, will be a great consolation in your old age, when the latter will finally arrive. What you, as well as Mr. Edward, tell me about the pleasant character and good sense of this young girl brought me great joy. I hope to see her again one day in the company of her venerable father and with a good husband who knows how to appreciate and love her. What you tell me about America is very interesting and matches only too well the news that has reached me from other sources. Nothing would be more agreeable to me than to know your impressions about everything that is going on in your country.

What is happening in ours can be summarized in a few words. The situation has changed very little since you left France. The government continues to have the appearance of a very strong power, lacking any *strong* supporters, and dominating as a consequence of the powerlessness, confusion, and apathy reigning among its adversaries, and not through the support and devotion of its friends; a power capable of doing everything today, but one that lacks any future in people's minds; a power that, in spite of its duration, is as separated as it has ever been from all the people who distinguish themselves through their position, talents, or intellect; a power that is as despised by its representatives as it has always been; a power that continues, however, to survive, without anyone knowing for sure how long it can last. You saw this spectacle with your own eyes. It has hardly changed since you left us, and it would be sufficient for you to consult your memory to imagine our present situation. The elections were, however, an important event.[68] In all of the towns, a fearless opposition showed its face, and this despite the actions of the administration and of oppressive laws. Even the villages voted with a muffled clamor against the ridiculous game that they were forced to play. You know about the elections in Paris. Throughout France, and perhaps even more so at the courts of foreign powers, they produced a powerful impression. They have revealed the clay from which the feet of the colossus are made and showed that the French Revolution has been suspended but is not yet finished. I do not believe that the government would dare risking a second electoral contest.

I do not need to call your attention to the extreme gravity, especially for Europe, of events in English India.[69] At the present moment, everybody here, as well as across the continent, is closely following this situation. It is likely that for some time to come, the English will find themselves paralyzed, as it were, in their foreign politics and, if so, this would open a new sphere of action for ambitions on the continent. For the first time in forty years, France would be ready to reconsider the treaties of 1815. England is disarmed and, moreover, it is on very bad terms with Russia; Austria and Russia hate each other; there are no coalitions to fear and France, I believe, would easily be able to form new alliances. If Louis-Napoléon had been successful in his projects fifteen years ago, it is certain that he would have taken advantage of such fortunate circumstances, had they occurred at that time. But, today, I am led to believe that he will limit himself to the role of a spectator; he is getting old and I believe that he prefers the entertainments, pleasures, and appearance of being the arbitrator of Europe – something that is easily granted to him – to the more substantial, but less easily secured, enjoyments of a conquering ambition. Hence, I believe that he will not take advantage of the new circumstances that emerge. But who knows what will be the outcome in India? We are watching only the first act of a drama which could abruptly end at any time, but which, if it persists, could change the course of events.

Farewell, dear Mr. Childe. From time to time please give me news about you. I imagine that Mr. Edward will leave you soon, if he has not already done so. He did not tell me when I could write to him c/o Mr. Baring. I shall send my letters there.

A thousand friendly and affectionate regards. Thank you very much for everything you tell me about economic matters in America. This subject has always been of great interest to me. Please continue to write to me at the Institute.

A. de Tocqueville

154. Alexis de Tocqueville to Edward Lee Childe

Tocqueville, September 12, 1857

Dear Mr. Edward,

Although in your letter you did not tell me the exact date of your arrival in Europe, I assume that it must take place soon. Hence, I am writing to you at the address in London that you indicated. Moreover, this address is known to me, for I know Mr. Thomas Baring personally, and I have had dealings with his firm.

Since, with a trust that touches me greatly, you are so kind as to share with me your plans and ask for my opinion, I shall tell you that I very much approve of the voyage that you are about to undertake. I do not see what you could do that would be better at this moment. Moreover, for some time, my feeling has been that, without separating yourself from America in a definitive manner, it would be good for you sometimes to distance yourself from it. Unfortunately, there is little natural harmony between the qualities of your country and your own qualities, and you have already arrived at an age when it is quite difficult to fight effectively against the habits of thinking and affection which have become, as it were, an integral part of your mind and heart. Such a course would make you very unhappy, without any guarantee of future success. Moreover, I do not think that it would be in the interest of your venerable father to have you around him, if he were to see you suffering from boredom and dissatisfied with your condition. This sight would do him more harm than good. In returning to him, after having spent some time in the old world, you would bring him a refreshed spirit, fortified by new impressions, and he will be very happy to see you again. Hence, I believe that you can abandon yourself to the pleasures that you expect from your voyage without any painful second thoughts. The letter that I received from your father a short time after having received your own contains good news about him and excellent news about your sister. Everything that he and you report to me about that young girl fills me with joy. I hope that she will be a great source of happiness for your father. Everything that she does gives evidence of an exceptional common sense, and after all, it is with this ingredient that one organizes one's life and that of others. There is nothing I want more than seeing your father happy. Nobody is more deserving of it than him.

You are going to undertake a remarkable voyage and I envy you for being able to embark upon it. After completing it, you should come and spend a few weeks in Paris. I realize that returning to this city would wring your heart. I myself cannot pass through the *rue de la Ville-l'Évêque* without feeling a very painful emotion.[70] I advise you, however, to show resolve in overcoming such a natural hesitation. After all, Paris is the place that contains the greatest number of people, things, and ideas that are in accord with your tastes and inclinations. There is no other city in Europe which could offer you so many resources, and, moreover, resources of which you can make such a good use. Hence, you should not abandon the idea of visiting a place which is your second, I would even say, your first homeland. Moreover, you will find in Paris, more so than anywhere else, friends and people who would be willing and pleased to see you again. Sooner or later, you will have to overcome the painful emotion evoked by Paris and your memories of it. It is better to gain this victory as soon as possible. I conclude, therefore, by saying that you would do well to make a short stay in Paris before returning to America. You know that I shall be extremely delighted to see you there; I shall probably be in the city from March 1 until June 15. From what I understand, people usually return from the East around that time. Goodbye for now, I hope; please believe in my profound and sincere affection.

A. de Tocqueville

155. N. W. Beckwith to Alexis de Tocqueville

Genève – Suisse
September 20, 1857

My dear M. de Tocqueville,

I have just arrived from England, and am indebted to you for increasing the pleasure of my return by your note of the 19[th] Aug[us]t which I have this moment read.

What a pity for me not to have met you in London!

Mr. Sumner called in my absence and I missed him also.

Your remarks on India and China[71] are very interesting, and very just.

'Tis true that the English seem to wonder at the discontent of their eastern subjects; by[72] why need they?

The laws, religion, civilization, of one race does [*sic*] not suit another race. Each must develop these things for itself in its own image, its own spirit, its own time, its own way and after its own fashion: there is little which one can borrow from another without alteration, and the best things are repulsive and become the worst, when forced against the will;

one people should never govern another people: what business have the English in India? That country was conquered little by little, harassed, worried, slaughtered into subjection; but those people and the memory of their sufferings have passed away; new generations have come up, and find themselves governed by a handful of foreigners, for the most part striplings, mere boys, pretentious and ignorant, who do not understand the native languages nor can make themselves understood without an interpreter; they do not respect the native religion nor customs, and they hold in supercilious disdain their princes and princesses, their men and their women.

It needs not "oppression and misrule"; the administration of law may be mild and just (which it is not!) but to the native millions the very presence of the intrusive stranger is oppression and insult of the most unbearable kind, and rebellion is as natural and certain, as that the memory of sufferings fades away, and human feelings and passions remain.

What matters it, from whence came the particular spark which set this material in flame? The discussions upon greased cartridges is a waste and a stupidity.[73] The cause is in the circumstances on one side and in the natural fire of the human breast on the other: the aversion of race to be governed by race is ineradicable (for a wise purpose no doubt). In the past we see, in some races closely allied to each other, fusion, and individuality lost, but in other cases where the difference was greater, as between the Anglican and Indian, American or Asiatic, no fusion takes place, and extermination of one or both is the result; but while they last, war lasts.

The grand difficulty of England is to supply fighting men; her dominion *à la Rome*, has become too extended for her breeding ground; she is rich by commerce and conquest, but has more money than men.

The time was ill chosen for the revolt – had it occurred during the Russian war, or had that war lasted; but the movement, like a disease in the human body, is spreading slowly through all the subjugated peoples, notwithstanding the pretensions of the Br[itish] press to the contrary.

But we shall see that the troubles will be "at an end" a great many times before they are finished.

The nature of the discontent, and the inadequate means of the English to crush it suddenly, indicate a long strain on their resources of men and money, for the forces must be permanently augmented.

But England is at peace in Europe and I see nothing for the future of India but slaughter, destruction of property, interruption of industry, famine, pestilence and rapid depopulation.

Can Christian civilization be introduced in India by the sword? The Br[itish] Govt has never read the New Testament; it takes its religion and its policy from the Old – conquest and revenge are the divine right of the strongest party; but J[ohn] Bull[74] bellows tremendously when for a moment strength inclines to the other side!

Mean time the war in China is suspended for want of men.[75]

Here again it is easy for England to deliver heavy blows upon that old gong which may have rung in the days of Abraham, and have been a tradition in the time of Moses – easy to shatter the power and weaken the authority of the govt, render life and property unsafe, disturb industry and destroy commerce – but can she reorganize, rebuild and restore? Her success in India is not very encouraging, anarchy once established in China, industry will be deranged and commerce annihilated and that vast population will perish by millions of starvation.

Even the local disturbance of industry and suspension of trade at Canton has reduced the people to great distress for food, and our commercial establishment there, though its ordinary business is entirely suspended at that port, is nevertheless fully employed in importing food from Siam and the sea islands, to feed the people of Canton.

The means of transport indeed are insufficient and, as the season of the monsoons approaches, the voyages will be lengthened and the deficiency still more felt. I have recently engaged in England, three large steamers (and conditionally three more) now on their way out with troops for India, to proceed thence to China where we are to employ them in the transport of food for the Cantonese. It is due to the English to say that they do not obstruct the importation of food into the Canton river, but I must add, that creeks and passages behind Macao, through the delta and numerous islands, are so many, so intricate and so well known to the Chinese, that any attempt to guard them by the Br[itish] force now present would be a total failure. We might indeed resume the export trade in teas and silks, but for the incomparable firmness of Yeh, who will not permit his people to trade while an armed enemy stands at his gate; no other man on either side in this affair, has yet shown so much (I will not say intelligence) but *ability* and *firmness* as Yeh.

You are doubtless aware of the fact and of the reasons, why the Br[itish] Govt has avowed the abandonment of its original designs of territorial conquest and permanent occupations, though they are not yet in general publicly known. You know also that England most needs from China, tea and the revenue from tea – that France for the first time can't well do without Chinese raw silk, and that the E[ast] I[ndia] Company must have a market for opium, or suffer a deficit in her treasury. These are pressing necessities, and depend upon keeping the ports open in China and if hard pushed China will close her ports to trade as she has done at Canton.

In this state of things, with the change of Govt plans, there is a growing feeling in England, *among those who know any thing about it,* and (they are not very numerous even in the government) that China had better be left alone.

True, the Chinese are "insolent" but they must always be nothing if not insolent; you may destroy but you can't change them, nor can they change themselves any more than the leopard his spots: killing a goose merely because she *is* a goose is a stupidity so long as she lays her eggs.

The India affair surged up at the right moment to confirm the already changing views of England, and she will now be glad to retire from China on any terms short of disgrace.

My chief fear is that that stiff and proud people will not yield such terms to England as will permit her to withdraw, but will compel her to fight for her "honor."

The delay of the troops is favorable; if a large force was present and public expectation was pressing, Lord Elgin[76] might be obliged to fight, but as it is he has time to try other means and he is strongly inclined to conciliate. I believe in point of fact, he thinks better of Governor Yeh, than he does of Governor Bowring.[77]

There is reason to hope he may succeed but I do not feel very confident of it.

I may mention, entre nous,[78] *which is not to be repeated,* that my Br[other]-in-law at the last dates had proposed a plan for opening an *underground* communication on his own account (but with the knowledge and desire of Lord Elgin) with the Emperor at Pekin, with a view to serve both parties in a friendly way and promote a reconciliation.

His emissary is a skillful and able Chinese of great experience, formerly governor of Canton, but now under a cloud, and whether he will succeed in reaching the ear of the govt I don't know; he thinks he can and that it will even restore him to favour. I think it just as likely he will lose his head; but he should know best; the grand difficulty is to pass over Governor Yeh, and convey correct information to the govt at Pekin, in a way that it will be accepted as reliable.

I learned something also from Prince Gortschakoff[79] at Kissingen some months since, which is interesting.

It just occurs to me that perhaps I am writing too freely. In these days of post office spies one does not know who is to read one's letters – and I might suggest a suspicion to other minds that that [sic] even you were taking an interest in matters about which you neither know nor wish to know anything whatsoever.

I have no right to do this, and will drop the subject, with the hope that a miserable war in China which can do no possible good, but produce great suffering, may be avoided.

I am totally at a loss to comprehend the position of France in China – an ally of England – but with every interest traditional and present, in the opposite scale. I can't help imagining that she has chosen her position as the best for modifying and controlling the action and policy of England in China and of diminishing the barbarities of naval-coast warfare, by preventing the destruction of defenseless towns and unarmed people, as she did in the Black Sea; that modification, with the concessions to neutrals, were [sic] the chief advance in humanity exhibited in the Russian war, and I believe are due wholly to the French Govt.

Your remarks upon the state of things in America, give me a feeling which inclines me both to laugh and to cry!

As to the exposure of property to destruction by violence, and the insecurity of life, notwithstanding the gravity with which you speak of it, I cannot see it in a serious light.

The greatest insecurity for life is in New York, and the greatest danger there, is that of being run over by an omnibus; of that I confess there is some probability, and a stranger not accustomed to the rush of things, might feel himself in a terrible condition of exposure.

But I have not heard of any wanton destruction of property, nor of life, of an alarming character.

There have been some street rows between the Irish and the Germans, and some bloody work for the moment.

But these were not movements involving any political principle nor had they any public character: nothing which would extend and unite larger bodies of men, and disturb the general repose, or endanger even the local tribunals, much less the government.

On the contrary they were but an aggregation of personal quarrels, growing chiefly out of individual piques and animosities of nationality and limited to small bodies of men and certain localities of the city. The very appearance of a few clerks and mechanics in showy uniforms, with swords and muskets, commanded by the great "General Sandford,"[80] himself a small red faced lawyer, put an end to the whole matter, or rather it was at an end before these worthy people got together, and the fierce belligerents themselves formed part of the crowd, who always come round anything like a show of soldiers in the parks.

'Tis true, the newspapers, some of them, said these disorderly proceedings were connected with the dispute and litigation between the mayor and the new police-Board about the *legality of a law*. But still it was the German street sweepers who wanted to stay in and the Irish who wanted to get in; a quarrel about who should sweep the streets, and nobody was more surprised and frightened than both the mayor and the new Board, at the dust their followers kicked up.

America receives great numbers of energetic, ignorant, and vicious people from the whole earth. Released from their habitual restraints and admitted to a large personal liberty, they often abuse it; they usually quarrel together, and draw in more or less of their neighbors who have been longer in the country or may have been born in it.

But I discover nothing in the character of these disgraceful riots, which threatens the general safety, or the govt, or the Union. They manifest no discontent with the govt, or laws, and considering all the circumstances, instead of discouragement from the occurrence of these events, I derive from their nature and infrequency, renewed confidence in the renovating influence of freedom on all men, confidence in the self respect it inspires, and confidence in the ability of man for self government. Thus, we arrive at opposite conclusions from the same premises.

But little as I think of the danger from this source, I look with serious alarm upon the danger to property and to society from another source.

It was formerly the custom for freebooters to roam in distant seas for plunder – it is now the fashion for organized bands to assemble in large cities, not to destroy property by violence, but to conspire against values of all kinds, sinking and depreciating the property of thousands, to enrich themselves, and this is done in such cunning ways that laws are not yet cunning enough to prevent it.

What is the difference in principle between one who sets fire to a house that he may steal the furniture carried into the street and one who attacks credit and character, that he may reduce values within his reach?

The incendiary on land, the pirate on the sea, and the "Bear" on change are men of equally bad character, and should be dealt with by society on equal terms of severity.

More insecurity is given to values and more property destroyed by the conspirations of these "Bears" than by violence, and all[81] casualties, not excepting the dangers of the seas.

Yet these modern pirates sit in high places, do arms to be seen of men, and their blood-offerings are not rejected; they are even respected as were those great sea-robbers, Cook, Drake, Cavendish, Daupier, etc., became successful and wealthy. The only palliation for the deeds of those men is the poor excuse of the lax morals of their age; they would not be tolerated now, and if there be any such thing as moral progress, the day must come when the deeds of the modern "pirate on change" will be held in horror.

Mean time the ruin and demoralization they produce is truly alarming. New-York is now in a shocking crisis brought about by the crimes of those men, and Paris itself seems on the brink of it; it requires some study and considerable credulity to accept the whole truth in regard to the deliberate wickedness of their doings, and the magnitude of the effects.

German riots and Irish quarrels for the privilege of sweeping the streets are mere trifles, in a moral point of view, compared with the influence of the Stock Exchange.

If this terrible nuisance were the offspring of democratic institutions or confined to America I should begin to doubt if it were not time the Republic was suppressed!

Looking at the venality which prevails at Washington, the rascality of Wall Street, the monetary frauds and political wickedness of England, the system which prevails in France for enriching the new Court, the savage war in Algeria, the homicides in India and the murders in China – the moral aspect of things is not cheering – and worst of all these are the peoples claiming to be most advanced in Christian civilization.

But the proverb says "it is always darkest just before day."

I have engaged teachers for my children and my passage, but shall not leave till the beginning of Nov[embe]r – as to personal safety in the East I feel no uneasiness what ever, and rather like the excitement of the changing state of things.

I thank you much for the expression of your friendly feelings and good wishes and can only say how warmly they are appreciated and reciprocated by us. And I shall expect the intimated letter from Madame de Tocqueville before we leave.

With best regards to Madame and yourself we remain,

Very truly yours,

NWB

Beinecke Rare Book and Manuscript Library, Yale University, Uncat MSS 324; also available as Bonnel copy in MS Vault Tocqueville, D II A, folder "Bonnel's copies of letters from Americans to Tocqueville."

156. Charles J. Ingersoll to Alexis de Tocqueville[82]

Foresthill, near Philad[elph]ia,
Sept[ember] [18]57

Sir,

During the twenty years that have passed since I had the honor of making your acquaintance at my home in this country,[83] and constantly inspired by the most noble literary and philosophical work written by any foreigner about our new and still-experimental American institutions but which are, I hope, best adapted to our position and development, I have not ceased to follow with the greatest interest, although being so far away from you, your subsequent career even up to the report recently made with so much patriotism to the deputies of your great country.[84]

Often my friend Mr. Rush and I talk about you. More often I read and study your incomparable writing which I see with pleasure, but without being surprised, has already reached its third edition. It is destined to take its rank along with the immortal *Spirit of the Laws* by Montesquieu.

My son, his wife, and their sons will soon leave us in order to spend the winter in Europe; I cannot let them leave without entrusting them, through this letter, with my most respectful regards for you in your eminent position, and I ask you to be so kind as to accept the sincere compliments of a far-away admirer and your obedient servant,

C. J. Ingersoll

Beinecke Rare Book and Manuscript Library, Yale University, Uncat MSS 324; also available as Bonnel copy in MS Vault Tocqueville, D II A, Paquet 12, pp. 66–67.

157. William H. Prescott[85] to Alexis de Tocqueville

Peppesell, Mass.
Sept[ember] 29, [18]57

My dear Sir,

My friend Mr. Ticknor placed in my hands a short time since your *Ancien Régime et la Révolution*, which you have done me the honor to send me.[86] I should have acknowledged your kindness at once; but I was then about to change my residence for the country, where I pass the autumn. I shall not attempt now to skim through the pages before I thank you for the present. Indeed it would not be easy to pass lightly over what you write. Reading your compositions is to meditate and to study. This I well know from the study which I have given to your great work on the institutions of my own country, which you have discussed in that profoundly philosophical spirit which leaves you without a rival.

I need not say how gratifying it is to me that you should have paid me the compliment of sending me a copy of your latest work. I may say, with the rest of the world, *Da, Jupiter, amos;*[87] and with years may you have health and leisure to complete the great task which you have undertaken.

Believe me, my dear Sir,

With sentiments of high regard,

Very truly yours,

Wm. H. Prescott

Beinecke Rare Book and Manuscript Library, Yale University, Uncat MSS 324; also available as Bonnel copy in MS Vault Tocqueville, D II A, folder "Bonnel's copies of letters from Americans to Tocqueville."

158. Alexis de Tocqueville to Edward Lee Childe

Tocqueville, par St. Pierre-Église
October 8, 1857

Dear Mr. Edward,

Thank you for your friendly and affectionate letter. I was touched by it as much as I am by anything coming from you. I was very pleased to learn that you are going to embark on a voyage to the East. I hope that you will find both health and pleasure in those far away countries. The novelty of things alone will suffice, I believe, to please a young and vivid imagination such as yours. Ever since I received your letter, I have been racking my brains to know to whom I could recommend you in the countries where you are going. No name comes to mind, which is not at all extraordinary, since my trips have all been toward the West and the South, and I have never seen the East but on the map. The only possibility would be to find French diplomats whom I know in the regions that you are going to visit. Unfortunately, I am so completely withdrawn from the world of affairs that I do not even know who these diplomats are today. I have written to one of my young friends,[88] who still has a position in the Ministry of Foreign Affairs, and I hope to obtain through him several letters that might be useful to you abroad. It is always good to be able to get in touch with diplomats; it is true that they often have only preconceived ideas about the region where they live, but through them one can become acquainted with the people who could give you more accurate information. I would hope that you will not make this journey only as a tourist, but that you will try to obtain an accurate picture of the people that you will visit and the condition of the countries that you will go through. You possess everything that is needed to retain from your travels more than a knowledge of monuments and the recollection of mountains and rivers. After all, there is nothing that is more genuinely interesting for man on this earth than man himself.

I am delighted by the good news that you give me about your venerable father and your sister. The portrait of the latter that you draw leads me to believe that she will be happy. The good sense necessary to conduct oneself and the art of making friends, there is no other secret for achieving happiness in this world. I hope to see you in Paris upon your return from the East. I think that I shall be in the city from April until mid-June. You can be sure that I shall greet you with all my heart. I believe that Paris in the spring will be more to your liking than it would have been during this autumn. You will find here people who will welcome you as a friend. Madame de Rauzan, who was very pleased to receive a letter from you, wrote to me to ask where she could reply to you. I am giving her your address.

I shall write to you again shortly. A thousand friendly regards and be well; be resolute and, above all, have a light and contented heart. Please do not forget to remember me to your father when writing to him. I was very fortunate not to have anything with Greene during the catastrophe.[89] What has become of him?

A. de Tocqueville

159. Alexis de Tocqueville to Francis Lieber

Tocqueville, par St. Pierre-Église (Manche)
October 9, 1857

My dear Lieber,

I was beginning to believe that you had forgotten me when I received your letter of last May 30. When saying I received it, I mean when I read it, which has occurred very recently. At the time when your letter arrived at my home, I was in England where I had gone for both pleasure and business. I wanted to see again friends from whom I had been separated for a long time, and it was also my intention to take advantage of their positions in government to obtain information from the Queen's archives that it would have been otherwise impossible for me to get were I not to have these friends in the government, but which I needed for the sequel to my book.[90] I have completely achieved my goal and my journey was as successful as it was pleasant.

We were extremely delighted by your letter informing us of your new position. It is very creditable in itself and you have achieved it in a manner befitting, namely, by a unanimous election. Please accept our most sincere congratulations. I hope that, regardless of the ever changing terrain (however firm below the surface) of American society, you have now reached a stable position. It is said that this is always difficult for a foreigner, especially when he does not belong to the English race. Regarding this great and singular country in which I take such a sincere and profound interest, when replying please tell me what you think of the present situation. I am talking not only of the state of the parties, but of what is more permanent than their squabbles, that is, the very foundation of mores and political customs. I hear many Europeans, even those with good intentions, or sometimes even American themselves, who, upon returning from the United States, say things that I find distressing. People affirm that the part of the population in the States that still has violent mores and uncouth habits increasingly sets the tone for the rest; that acts of personal violence, the cases of people taking justice into their hands, are becoming more and more common and to such an extent that many peaceful people carry arms with them in case they have to resort to legitimate self-defense.[91] People add that this situation is furthered by the increasingly imperfect state of the justice system which, by becoming more and more unstable and dependent on the multitude or the parties (because of the election of judges by universal suffrage and due to the short duration of their mandate), often fails to offer a sufficient guarantee to the individual such as to encourage him not to take up the task of defending himself. What is there of truth in all this? Please give me a candid response. I do not intend to make any use *whatsoever* of your answer, but only to enlighten myself on this topic and to reach a conclusion about an issue that stirs up my interest to the highest degree.

I am very flattered by your good opinion of my latest work and by what you tell me of its favorable reception among the competent judges whom you mention.[92] In France, I have already had three *large* editions in eleven months, and the third one will soon be sold out. At this present time, I am very absorbed in the labor which will allow me to complete my work.

Farewell, dear Lieber. Be well and think sometimes of those who have a sincere friendship for you.

A. de Tocqueville

P. S. Since I never know when I am here or in Paris, I take the liberty of asking you to continue to address your letters to the *Institute*, care of M. Pingard, Chief-Secretary of the Institute.

160. Alexis de Tocqueville to Edward Lee Childe

October 13, 1857

Dear Mr. Edward,

I am writing only a few words to tell you that, as I informed you, I have asked a friend of mine, a very pleasant young man who occupies a quite important position in the Ministry of Foreign Affairs, to write letters for you. He answered without delay that he would be very happy to fulfill my request. I have just written to him again in order to ask him to deposit the letters that he is preparing for you with M. Hottinguer. Please see to it that they are sent to you. I believe that they will be to your liking and perhaps of use in the far-away countries that you will visit and where the diplomats of the great powers of Europe are important persons. I can only tell you this much for the moment and end by wishing you from all my heart a safe voyage. Remain in good health and, above all, please do not be melancholic! A thousand friendly regards.

A. de Tocqueville

P. S. The name of my friend from the Ministry of Foreign Affairs is the Baron d'Avril. He has traveled in many of the countries that you will visit. He is a young and distinguished man whom you would be well advised to thank. His address in Paris is 18 Avenue Marbeuf. It would be good to meet him upon your return.

161. Alexis de Tocqueville to Susan Sedgwick

Tocqueville, par. St. Pierre-Église (Manche)
October 30, 1857

Dear Miss Sedgwick,

Please allow me to write to you to thank you for the care that you have taken to give me news about your father. In a short note that he added to your letter, he promised me that he would himself inform me of his recovery. His silence worries me somewhat. Therefore, I would again ask you to be so kind as to write a few words to inform me about how Mr. Sedgwick is doing and to let me know if the events that have destroyed so many fortunes in America and Europe have not also affected him. I hope that you will excuse these questions in light of the genuine interest that has prompted me to ask them.

Please accept, Miss, the expression of my respect.

A. de Tocqueville

162. Charles Sumner to Alexis de Tocqueville

Teddesley Park-Penkridge,
Nov[ember] 3, [18]57

My dear M. de Tocqueville,

Since I parted from you at Cherbourg I have seen much – Paris – Rheims – Strasbourg – Baden-Baden – the Rhine – Switzerland, its lakes and mountains, the Alps, which I passed by St. Gothard and then repassed by St. Bernard – Mt. Blanc – and afterwards Holland, from which I returned to London. Then taking a new start I visited for five days the Manchester Exhibition, and commenced a very rapid tour through Scotland, stopping at Dunrobin Castle,[93] the seat of the Duke of Sutherland, Haddo House,[94] the seat of Lord Aberdeen – Inverary Castle,[95] the seat of Duke of Argyll, and also several other places. The hospitality everywhere was complete and elegant, and everywhere we talked of you.

Returning to England, after various visits, including Castle Howard,[96] I have reached the kindest of homes with our friends Lord and Lady Hatherton.[97] To-day I start for Liverpool, stopping on the way with John Bright,[98] Gladstone[99], and the Marquess of Westminster[100] – for a single night each, and sailing for Boston on Saturday.

I suppose that you will be reading this missive while I am embarking. I hope you have not forgotten your promise to let me hear from you, if only a word, in America, where during the session of Congress, my address will be at *Washington* – afterwards at *Boston*.

The financial crisis in America seems the beginning of a crisis which is to disturb the whole financial world. I fear that France will suffer severely. Indeed, the present Govt by its course provokes bankruptcy.

Notwithstanding the bad look of things in America, I am sanguine that there will be a speedy revival there. The country was never so rich or abundant in resources. Your interests have suffered most – the railroad and manufacturing. In my neighborhood large manufacturers, who have been supposed to have great wealth, are prostrated and their luxurious houses are sold to pay their creditors. The merchants as a class have suffered much less.

Meanwhile Mr. Buchanan and his pro-slavery supporters are trying to introduce slavery into Kansas in order to make this beautiful territory a slave-holding state and to have two new slave-holding senators. For such baseness I have no tolerance. As I look at my country from a distance, I see more clearly than ever the importance of overthrowing the Slave Power which now predominates over the Republic, vulgarizing the whole Government.

You have been here – at Teddesley – and know how pleasant and hospitable it is. My hosts talk of you much. Their house has been full of company and all their guests have been happy. This English country life – even to the *cravate blanche*[101] – is *sui generis* and *unique*. It is *urbs in rure*.[102] To a stranger from any country it is a most interesting experience.

The Duchess of Sutherland and the Duchess of Argyll both inquired much about you, and spoke of the pleasure they had in seeing you and in your conversation. So also did Lord Aberdeen. Remember [me] kindly to Madame de Tocqueville and believe me

Ever sincerely yours,
Charles Sumner

Beinecke Rare Book and Manuscript Library, Yale University, Uncat MSS 324; also available as Bonnel copy in MS Vault Tocqueville, D II A, folder "Bonnel's copies of letters from Americans to Tocqueville."

163. Henry P. Tappan[103] to Alexis de Tocqueville

New York, Nov[ember] 14, 1857

My dear M. de Tocqueville,

Perhaps you will recollect that in the course of conversation at your house at Versailles I mentioned to you a translation of La Fontaine by a Yankee of Boston. I have availed myself of an opportunity to send you this work as a literary curiosity.

Knowing the interest you take in everything relating to my country I have taken the liberty to send you also a little tract of mine on *University Education*. This highest form of Education is a great merit with us. My little book will show you at least what we are aspiring after. We have many things for which to bless God and to be satisfied with in the United States; but, I feel sad when I think how far we are behind you in the means of the higher culture. When shall we have here the libraries, the University, and the Institute of France? This is the question I often ask myself, and I feel a strong impulse to make some effort towards this grand realization.

I regret that I could not have remained longer in Paris. I cannot express to you the delight your noble Institutions of learning and the Arts afforded me.

I hope at no distant time to visit France again to acquaint myself more fully with what I feel I have only looked at superficially.

Mrs. Tappan and my daughter unite with me in grateful remembrances of your kind attention to us.

Please present my most respectful regards to Madame de Tocqueville and believe me

> With high esteem,
> yours very sincerely,
> Henry P. Tappan

P. S. I send you this through the American Consul, Mr. Goodrich.

Beinecke Rare Book and Manuscript Library, Yale University, Uncat MSS 324; also available as Bonnel copy in MS Vault Tocqueville, D II A, Paquet 12, pp. 38–39.

164. Alexis de Tocqueville to Charles Sumner

> Tocqueville, par St. Pierre-Eglise (Manche)
> November 14, 1857

Dear Mr. Sumner,

I was starting to believe that you had forgotten us and that the splendors of Dunrobin Castle had completely overshadowed the small manor house of Tocqueville.[104] But I was slandering you. For, in the midst of your very busy and pleasantly occupied life, you have found time to think of us and you have written me a very friendly letter, for which I thank you.

Since you have already returned to America, I would very much like you to provide me with information that it is very important for me to have.

I am counting on the clarity of your mind and your sound judgment to provide it in such a way as to be useful to me. I have some funds invested in America. I shall name the enterprises in which they are placed in the order of importance of the funds.

1. The *Michigan Central Railway*. I have bonds issued by this company. Based on the information that has already been given to me by M. Baring, whose advice I followed in purchasing these bonds, this company, although in a difficult situation, should recover. This railroad is excellent; it has not ceased to increase its profits for the last few years, and bond owners cannot fear a serious loss. The bulk of my funds is invested there.
2. The *Chicago and Galena Railway*. I also have bonds of this company, but in a smaller quantity than in the Michigan Central.
3. The *Marietta and Cincinnati Railway*. I only have two bonds in this enterprise.
4. Finally, I own a very small number of shares in the *Lacrosse and Milwaukee Railroad*.

You will understand how important it is for me to be aware of anything that is happening with regard to these railroads, especially those of the Michigan and Galena. You would render me a truly *friendly service* by informing me, for as long as this terrible crisis lasts, of the fate of these enterprises and of any important details regarding them. I am asking you to render this service to me, and hope, dear M. Sumner, that you will not refuse me, given the critical circumstances in which we find ourselves at the present moment. In Europe, investments placed in a similar way to those that I own in the Michigan and Galena would be sheltered from any crisis; but the financial upheaval that troubles your country is so violent that it is impossible to say what might occur under such exceptional circumstances. This, of course, must remain between us. I speak about my affairs in this way for *you alone*.

I have not forgotten the promise that I made to keep you informed of events in Europe. But since you have just left our continent, there is nothing new as yet to bring to your attention. The financial crisis in America will affect all of us; I am convinced of that. And financial affairs will remain for some time the most important issues for any government.

I have been very pleased to see that the inhabitants of Kansas have made a choice in the direction of liberty![105] Please God that slavery is vanquished on that disputed soil! Please make sure to tell me in your reply (*which I ask you to please send to me as soon as possible*) how you have found the issue of slavery upon your return, an issue that interests you so much.

A thousand friendly regards to your brother.[106] Please do not forget to remember me to the Ticknor family, if you meet them in Boston. My wife wishes to be kindly remembered to you. Please believe in all my sentiments of esteem and friendship.

A. de Tocqueville

165. Theodore Sedgwick to Alexis de Tocqueville[107]

Owlistead, Dec[ember] 6, 1857

My dear M. de Tocqueville,

My daughter has just received your letter. I am writing to you from my small house on the Bay of New York, where Ampère came to see me. I have not yet recovered enough from my neuralgia attack to return to my study and the only thing I do is to vegetate. I have not been in any danger but I have suffered terribly, partly from sharp pains, but what was worse, from a complete lack of sleep; for three months I have almost not slept at all. For many nights, I did not close my eyes, and even without any pain, the suffering was intolerable. But finally, all that passed along with all the miseries of life and I am recovering steadily, albeit slowly. And once I am fully recovered, I shall say farewell to my profession which is killing me. I shall plant cabbages or stroll through Europe, but no more law for me.

We have had a small squall in the financial world, in part due to the great principle of action and reaction governing all beings, above all, those belonging to an organization as execrable as that of ours, and in part due to souls whose extravagance is boundless. The country that you saw almost in its cradle is indeed an odd one. The mixture of activity, intelligence, and presumption, energy, religion, complete indifference toward any dogma, cold blood, capacity for business, carelessness and absolute negligence, good faith, morality, fraud and shameless swindling, all this creates a painting that a master like you should contemplate. You have seen only a light sketch.

Are you still interested in the railways here? The *Michigan Central* has had serious difficulties but it has come back, at least for the moment. The *Galena Chicago* has suffered a lot, as everyone else has, from the decrease in the number of carriers, but I do not think that it is seriously affected by that. I know nothing about the *Haarlem*.

If you still have your [. . .][108] let me know what their value is, for I am not sure that I remember them, and I shall write you a report about them. All our railroads have been doing very *badly* and a great number have been administered very dishonestly for the last three or four years.[109] Please remember me to Madame de Tocqueville and Ampère, if he is not in Italy. I hope to see Europe next year. May that not remain a mere hope![110]

As the greatest pleasure of my life I promise myself that I will come to Europe with my two daughters. One is now seventeen years old;[111] the other will soon be nineteen.[112] I shall be happy to introduce them to Madame de Tocqueville. They would be extremely happy (what we call a *privilege*) if they were admitted into your social and private circle, and had a chance to see you and listen to you. It serves no point therefore to tell you that our firm intention is to come as soon as I am able to do so.

Perhaps one day I shall bother you with a request. I have almost finished the printing of a book on our *Statutory and Constitutional Law*,[113] and I shall perhaps ask you how to present a copy to your Academy.[114] I would not mind submitting it to the approval or rather the examination of some of your distinguished men who are law specialists in the most general and widest sense of the word. A great part of my work is devoted to our narrow and technical law, but a part also deals with more general and universal issues.

Farewell, my dear M. de Tocqueville. Please thank Madame de Tocqueville for her interest and sympathy, stay healthy, and retain for me a small place in your heart. I am your devoted,

Theodore Sedgwick

P. S. If you send something to Mr. Bonner, the translator, he would be very flattered. You could send your letter to me. I would very much like to know that this letter has reached you.

(In the margin)[115]: When will your second volume be published ? I shall send you my work shortly.

Please address your letters as in the past simply to New York.

I shall see Mr. Harper this week and will find out from him how they are doing with the sale of your book.

Mr. Bancroft and many other readers and thinkers have spoken to me about your book with the strongest and most sincere praise – but, as I have told you, it has appeared here at a very bad moment. And in general, we know far too little about your history and politics in order to appreciate them. When will the next volume be published?

166. Edward Everett to Alexis de Tocqueville[116]

Boston, U. S. of America
Dec[embe]r 8, 1857

My dear M. de Tocqueville,

It is only a few days ago that I received the copy of *The Old Regime and the Revolution* that you had the kindness to send to me through Mr. Ticknor. I had already known this remarkable work by reputation and very much wanted to have the opportunity to study it. During the few days since I have had the book, I have not been able to do more than browse through it quickly, which I have done, however, with the greatest interest, immensely enjoying the profound and sound philosophy, the equally novel and striking observations, and above all the courage, not to mention, all things considered, the boldness with which in certain places you express yourself on points regarding the current state of things in France. I greatly admire the independence which you show. I would almost say that in daring to speak on certain issues and boldly attempting comparisons with so much openness, you contradict your sad complaint that the French are satisfied with a regime which "takes away from them the freedom of thought and the freedom of writing." You can certainly be proud of the fact that this precious liberty has not been taken away from you.

How unfortunate that everywhere people abuse their privileges so much! In our country, where people fully enjoy freedoms so dearly obtained, so painfully acquired elsewhere, they push them so far beyond their legitimate exercise that the abuse threatens to become a more unbearable evil than their total absence.

I know well that I write to you in very poor French. I do it in order to transport myself better in imagination to your beautiful France which I so much desire to see again, and to renew the few friendships that time has spared for me there, and among which I cherish yours so much. Please, my dear M. de Tocqueville, afford me the pleasure of writing a few lines to me and accept the affection of your sincere friend.

Edward Everett

167. N. W. Beckwith to Alexis de Tocqueville

Geneva, Switzerland, Dec[embe]r 18 [1857 ?][117]

My dear M. de Tocqueville,

I am delighted by the warmth of your language in regard to slavery.[118] It was the custom of slave owners to admit their misfortunes, and ask with apparent candor, how they were to get rid of them? This seemed reasonable and made us considerate and patient, and tolerant.

But now that they have abandoned that position, and confess that they were never in earnest, we are losing patience with them; so are you, and I am glad to see it. It is high time; they are faithless, demoralized, and false, and like depraved men and women fallen from (apparent) virtue, they face you and put you to shame by boasting of their vices, justifying them, and calling them virtues; this is offensive and disgusting, and it is more: it is dangerous.

Seeing the manifest and increasing depravity and crimes of slavery and the disgrace and danger it brings to free institutions, I cannot imagine any one remaining indifferent and tolerant of it, who has any hope or any faith in human progress, or who believes in the retributive law of deliberate wickedness. Like yourself, I am not an abolitionist, in the correct sense which you give to that word. The abolitionists are few in numbers, and without much power of good or of evil: Garret Smith[119] is their head and front.[120] Mrs. Abigail Folsom[121] is the right wing and main body and the rest of their organs are incomplete. It is a wild, crazy, impracticable deformity, but of no great consequence; the worst thing it has done is to create a bad name, which is misapplied by slave owners to another class of persons, very numerous, very discreet, right-minded, well poised, deliberate, practiced and resolute, but with very different aims from those of the abolitionists; these are the only men whom the slave owners fear; they do not fear the abolitionists. I confess however that I never could see any danger in immediate emancipation, to be generous and just is not the way to make people hate you and try to kill you; a good-natured, laughing, thoughtless happy-go-lucky race, which bears and forbears and does not rise against its masters when afflicted with the greatest wrongs at their hands, is not likely to turn against them and cut their throats when, from being oppressors they become protectors and friends; all pretence of danger from this source is vile sham.

He must be a fool who believes it, or a coward conscience that fears it; but those who pretend to, are, in general, only knaves.

But as regards the negroes themselves, they, like the servile race led by Moses out of Egypt, are not fit for freedom; they require a sojourn of 40 years in the wilderness to give time for the old and unimprovable to die off, and for the rising generation to be bred up in habits of personal independence.

Nevertheless, if negroes are men I desire to see them treated like men; but if they are only property, mere chattels, why not kill' em and eat' em like other chattels? They would be better eating than a horse!

But I am content to turn over all these nice points to the metaphysics of slave holders, and to the *sovereign* states, where they reside! I claim no more right to meddle in the affair, than in the affairs of Naples or Greece or Turkey or Russia or Persia. But when we step out from the area of local sovereignties, and meet on common federal ground, as in the federal Congress, and federal councils of the Nation, (when there is a limited scope for constitutional action) and especially when we enter the territories, which are the common property of all; when every man in the Union is a co-proprietor, the owner of a joint and undivided interest, here on this ground it is the clear right and duty of every one to speak out and act out that which is within him.

This is the position of the *Free Soilers*,[122] of those who wish this new ground to remain free, who are opposed to the farther spread of slavery, and I am one of them! The slave holders hate us and fear us, and they call us "black republicans," "negro worshipers," "abolitionists" and other names derived from the nomenclature of plantations.

"Abolitionist" is particularly odious and false in its application, because it means a man of bad faith who disregards his obligation to his neighbour; one who acts on the principle of the slave holder in this, that like the slave owner, he would be a law to himself, and would enforce his will as law upon others, in their own sphere, in their own dominions, in their own homes and houses. *We* claim nothing of the sort; we denounce that principle, in the abolitionist and in the slave holder alike. It is the principle which holds the slave subject to the will of his master. We condemn it everywhere in every form and forever.

We allow precisely the same freedom and scope, to the will and the action of every man in his own sphere, and of every body of men in their own sphere, as we claim for ourselves. This leaves slavery and everything else, to those to whom it belongs, within their own dominions and there we are content to leave it, with the responsibility and the shame to them.

Well, with these views on which we intend to act in good faith, we leave the domain of local sovereignties and enter on the new and common ground: we admit the equal right of the slaveholders to come there, on the principle and in the spirit that we come, and (theoretically) as much entitled to carry out their views and plant slavery, as we are to carry out our views and prevent it; we thus stand face to face in presence of each other, opposed to each other, both being in the exercise of our respective[123] and equal rights, and we cannot agree; the case does not admit of compromise; the property cannot be divided; we have tried that, but it will not stay divided, because slavery is faithless; when it has filled up one half it "repeals the compromise" and breaks into the other half; this other half must now be slave or free; it cannot be both, one party or the other must yield, but neither will yield; now what are we to do? There are but two ways of getting out of this difficulty: the first and old fashioned way is to fight and sometimes it is not a bad way, but generally it is bad.

Freedom seldom gains by fighting; if often loses, if it wins it loses, because it introduces permanent bad feeling, military law, reaction, military despotism, and after liberty has won it finds itself lost.

The second way of relief, and the only one which we consider legitimate, is an appeal to the voice of the majority and we are willing to abide by this; this [is] the umpire of peace and of freedom, and we do not wish to know any other. Well, we agree, both parties, to this appeal, and when the ballot boxes are prepared and opened, in rushes faithless slavery, led by *Senators* Atchison[124] and Stringfellow[125] from the slave state of Missouri close by, with an armed mob of slave dealers, drive our people from the polls, fill the boxes with spurious ballots, commit riots, destroy property, kill a number of men, insult the women, and then proclaim that the ballot has decided in favour of slavery.

This is the old trick and habit of slavery; how many elections were carried in this manner, in the old Forum of Rome, by noble senators backed by armed slaves? Slavery never acted nor ever will act in any other way, and it is this which makes it fatal to liberty; it will never abide by law, but will ever resort to force, because it is of the nature of force.

But this is rather a narrow view of the subject. The real contest is political and the question political, and the place of action is Washington; shall the sovereign power continue in the hands of the majority, or shall it pass to the minority? Shall we give up government by the people and substitute the rule of an oligarchy of slaveholders?

This is the only question; the real contest is on this, and the question of the extension of slavery is subsidiary to it: no party is pushing for abolition and no party fears it; the pretence of danger to the "institution" is a humbug for political effect.

The slaveholders are struggling to extend slavery, and the Free Soilers are struggling against it, because on its success or defeat depends in a great degree the other question: who is to rule, the minority or the majority?

It is true, the slaveholders contend that limitation is abolition in disguise, that it will eventually destroy slavery; if it cannot spread it must die, (say we).[126]

It is not very clear why this effect should follow, seeing the vast room it still has to spread in; but admitting it to be true, it is no reason for not limiting it; we did not agree to sustain slavery by spreading it; we only agreed not to abolish it where it existed; but seeing its growing evils, and illegal and faithless efforts to gain power, and consequent danger to liberty, we have no choice left in self-preservation but to limit it, and we have the right to do so.

It is no objection to a right act that it may have remote and indirect consequences, good also,[127] although we might not have the right to aim directly at those remote results; the opposite rule would bar all reforms, would prohibit all right actions lest the force of their example should deter evil doers and thus thwart the wishes of those who are interested in perpetuating wrong. If the limiting of slavery should deprive it of political power, which is the direct object, and surrounding it by free labor, should render it valueless – (which is the indirect result) so that, having lost its power and its value, slaveholders would from interest and of their own action, gradually abandon it, that we consider a desirable end, by legitimate means and without any breach of faith.

The first step violates no agreement, no faith, but is requisite for self defense, and if the other effects follow, so much the better, say we; to this extent and in this way we are abolitionists and in no other way.

This is the nature and the shape of the contest; it was apparent to all sagacious men from the first, that the principle of popular sovereignty based on the rule of the majority, and the opposite principle of the rule of the minority which is the principle of slavery, that two such opposite principles could not co-exist in harmony, in the presence of each other, that each would aim at supremacy, and that they would probably come into conflict.

Short sighted men hoped to avoid this by limiting the sphere of action of the minority principle to the subject of slavery and to the area of the slave states. But the future contest of principles was rendered certain by giving to slavery political power; making 5 slaves count as 3 free men, that is, making a slave owner who has 500 slaves of as much weight as 300 individual freemen, was the most fatal mistake and the most vicious bargain in the whole American system; this blunder sends 23 false members to Congress from the slave states.

But the bargain was made and we don't ask to break it; we intend to keep the agreement and beat them besides.

Government was always carried on by parties, but they were formed upon political theories, commercial theories etc. etc., and slave owners were divided upon them as much as the men of the free states.

But the free states were money-making and busy and left politics to the idle South. The Plantation sovereigns naturally plotted for power, and having no other means of securing it, drew us into war, two wars, for territory to spread in.

At length the people of the free states began to comprehend what all this really meant, and their own danger, which they were very slow to believe.

But it was necessary that this conviction should become very strong, strong enough to break up all existing party ties, habits and organizations and override all commercial and other political, and internal questions, and for the free states, Whigs, democrats and all sorts, friends and enemies, to unite, or an entire majority of them, in one party against the slave states.

Much as they may hate slavery, no regard for the negroes would ever bring the free states to sink all other feelings and unite on this one; nothing but a clear connection[128] of danger, to themselves has power to do this — and this is the element now at work — this is the change now going on.

In the midst of this transition comes on the Presidential election.

The south is fully organized, compact, resolute and desperate. The North is yet in confusion and disorder — has thrown off its old leaders, but has not got well into drill under the new ones.

The south openly threatens *disunion* if defeated. Consider the power of that word *disunion*: a man must know America to appreciate it — it goes to the heart and chills the blood of every American, for they are proud of the Union and they love it; and as they are ready to make great sacrifices for it, they are slow and fearful of doing any thing which may endanger it.

Under these circumstances, the well organized South has been able to carry with it enough of the North, the timid, the fearful, and those accustomed to go with that party – united to the whole influence of the Govt, patronage and all, to turn to scale against freedom, and in favour of Buchanan.

But it was a small majority – my surprise is that it was no larger; the Dutchmen in Pennsylvania, the Railroad governed New Jersey and the south part of Indiana settled by people from the slave state of Kentucky, turned the scale against us; even the Irish vote would have saved us; but they went in a body, church and all for slavery.

One of these days that good hearted people will open their eyes to their true interests and then they will go with us.

But see how we swept all New England, New York, Ohio, Michigan, all but carried the election, at the first trial and under all disadvantages – so far from being disappointed or discouraged I am full of confidence for the future.

But it is not Mr. Buchanan nor Mr. Frémont, nor any one man, who can settle this question; whoever is in power, the contest is of the people, for the people, and can only be settled by the action of the whole people. Slavery is a great interest and a great power to overthrow, and there are great difficulties in the way and it requires time and patience.

The first successes are in favor of the ready and the desperate, but that will not last.

Some of the considerations which I rely on with so much confidence for final success are these.

1st The disunion cry, so potent, will lose its power, because it is an impossibility and a monstrous sham; the leaders it is true are in earnest but they cannot carry their own people with them; they see too clearly that disunion would lead to certain speedy and total abolition, preceded by servile insurrection. Slavery only exists by the good faith and forbearance of the north; let the free states once cast a controlling vote for free soil and show themselves ready to back that vote and enforce the federal authority. How can a handful of slave holders – with few men and little money and a servile race ready to rise, how can they defy the authority of the laws of the federal Govt.? Rest assured from that day, the word *disunion* will cease to be uttered; but it takes time for the whole people to see this and feel its truth and know it, and act on it, in the face of grave preparations and threats. But they will come to the knowledge of this fact, and will act on it.

2nd Free Labor is the thing in issue; the free laborers are the whole physical force, and the whole electoral majority, and control the ballot. They are beginning to see that the extension of slavery shuts them from the territories; that it degrades and disgraces their[129] all, which is their labor, that they are the most directly and largely and personally interested, no free laborer will work beside a slave, it takes time to get this into their dull brains, but it is making its way, with constant help, and these men will come right by and by; nothing can stop them.

3rd The excess of slavery.

It has thrown off all disguise and comes forth in frightful ugliness; it asserts itself to be right necessary and just – approved of God and needful to men; it claims to be the true basis of white freedom, and to be entitled to political power; it demands the patronage of the Govt, and the protection of the treasury; it is resolved on the re-opening of the African slave trade, for the benefit *of the Africans*, the re-enslaving of the Haitians, the conquest of Cuba to prevent emancipation, the conquest of Central America to spread in, the enslaving of poor white men to get rid of them, it requires to be spoken of with respect, and justifies the bludgeon in the Senate and force in every form out of doors, to make itself if not respected, at least feared – it affects religion, piety and morality, it denies all the settled maxims of experience, wisdom and justice and boldly denies and belies the most self evident truths; it manifests itself every day more factious, turbulent, imprudent, odious, revolting and dangerous; it is rushing backwards to barbarism, degradation and crime.

All this, and much more like it, is dressed up daily in the southern press, with sophistry, skill and fine language, but no concealment, openly and shamelessly.

It cannot stop in this career, it is the nature of it, and must go on.

I rejoice at it; it is a great power, this self exposure: no genius could exhibit it so revoltingly as it exhibits itself.

This was the thing wanting; while it was meek and humble and hypocritical, men would not believe it so bad; now it speaks in its own voice and its own sentiments, men hear it and see it and are amazed.

We have everything to hope from the excesses of slavery and it will not disappoint us; it is helping us as we could not help ourselves. These things alone are enough to assure us of the future: time and patience and constancy will win the battle for freedom, and without much fighting.

Now as to Mr. Buchanan – he is in the hands of his party; he is a man of ability and experience and of good intentions. But he is undecided and the Chief to follow and not to lead; the Ostend manifesto was not his; it was Jef[ferson] Davis's and Soulé's and Slidell's; Buchanan was drilled into it; he has the faculty of *assentation*, but from lack of enterprise and will he is not affirmatively dangerous – only negatively dangerous.

As to his foreign policy, civilization has not much to hope and not much to fear from him; whatever threatening appearances the slave holders may get up, I think they will end in smoke; the only danger in regard to Cuba, is that her stupid and timid government will in some of its panics commit acts which will drag us all into *retaliation*.

This is all that I am afraid of in that quarter. As to his internal policy, he will try to be President – he will coax and listen and take advice – and in trying to please all, will probably fail with all. As to any decided vigorous and manly policy – I think it impossible; but if he cuts from extremes and takes to a middle and moderate course, he will be well sustained and I think he is most likely to do this. His election will retard the settlement of the slavery contest, somewhat; but that is a matter not to be much hastened nor retarded by any man.

We shall yet have many violent and threatening scenes, if not worse than that; I think we may have serious local disturbances, and acts that will mortify and disgrace us. But as to the final result, let every one be of good cheer, and recollect that pretty story of Ariosto,[130] of the Fairy, whose fate it was to descend at intervals from the Celestial regions, assume the form of a loathsome Reptile and grovel upon the earth, an object of repulsion and disgust – shunned, abused, despised, pointed at and trod upon by the thoughtless; occasionally an individual had penetration enough to see through her disguise, and discover her divine nature, and to compassionate, befriend and protect her; the period of her humiliation past, she reassumed her celestial form, reascended to her native abode, and became the presiding genius of those who had befriended her in her hour of disgrace, and never failed to protect and bless them.

So with Liberty: she is often doomed to violence, humiliation and disgrace, that is her fate; but she never fails to warm the hearts and cheer the souls of those who know her and defend her, and love her for her own sake.

I owe you an apology for a letter that I am sure will be tedious to you, but recollect that you gave me an occasion to gossip and on a subject that I am so full of, I never know when to stop. You doubtless observe that the proposition to exempt property on the high seas from seizure is making progress. Russia has formally assented to it, Palmerston[131] has spoken publicly in its favour, and no power has yet objected to it.

We are in good health and good spirits and do not find the weather disagreeable but walk a great deal.

With a thousand good wishes for you and for Madame de Tocqueville from Mrs. Beckwith and myself, I remain sincerely yours,

N. W. Beckwith

N. B. I have a note from poor Sedgwick informing me of the death of his wife – a noble woman – which leaves him in great grief.[132]

Beinecke Rare Book and Manuscript Library, Yale University, Bonnel copy, MS Vault Tocqueville, D II a, folder "Bonnel's copies of letter for Americans to Tocqueville."

168. Alexis de Tocqueville to Theodore Sedgwick

Tocqueville, par St. Pierre-Eglise (Manche)
December 24, 1857

Dear Mr. Sedgwick,

I have just received your letter of the 6th, and I want to tell you immediately that it brings me great joy. You can flatter yourself that you frightened us greatly by your prolonged silence. The short note that you wrote to me a few months ago announced that, if your health were to allow it, you would write again shortly. Since we have not seen anything arriving from you, we were beginning, I confess, to form very dark thoughts about you. What made us entertain them was not hearing anything about the book which you had mentioned to me and which I had promised to present to the Institute. An author who no longer occupies himself with the fate of his works did not seem to me to be a healthy person. These fears were unfounded.[133] God be praised! You should not have allowed people who take a genuine interest in you to entertain them. I have known and still know many Americans for whom I have genuine regard; but you are the only one who seems to have in your nature something which is entirely *congenial*[134] to our European nature. Hence, from now on, do not commit the same sin again! But, above all, do get well and return to us. You know that Tocqueville is always open to you and your family, and that, whenever you can come here, you will always be received with open arms.

Many, many thanks for having given thought to our material interests. They have been very affected by your unfortunate financial problems, and if I ever manage to recover from the hands of your companies the greater part of the funds that I entrusted to them, I should be, as our peasants say, eternally grateful to God. Here, however, is my exact situation; I take the liberty of calling your kind attention to it:

1. I own, to a considerable amount, bonds of the *Central Michigan Railway*. It is by far the most important of all my American investments. I have two kinds of bonds: some will mature in 1860, the others in 1869.
2. The biggest of my investments after this is in bonds of the *Galena and Chicago Railway*.
3. In addition, we own two bonds of the *Cincinnati and Marietta Railway*.
4. And, finally, a very small number of shares in the *Lacrosse and Milwaukee Railway*.

If I could save what I had lent to the first two companies, I would easily reconcile myself with losing the remainder. But a considerable loss with regard to the first two investments, especially the first, would have a very detrimental impact on my assets.

This is the situation. Trusting in your friendship, I am asking you to gather all the information that might enlighten me on the *present* and *future* situation of the businesses in question; on the *payment of interest,* or *the fortunes of the capital assets,* and to bring it to my attention as soon as possible. You will understand that we are experiencing an anxiety that is very natural given the semi-ignorance in which we find ourselves.

Should you be absent from America, could you please indicate to us a *reliable* correspondent in New York whom we can contact in order to keep ourselves informed of what is going on there in the world of business? Moreover, it was at the recommendation of Mr. Baring in London and M. Hottinguer in Paris that I made the first two investments mentioned above.

Without being disquieting, the news that your letter contains about yourself, dear Mr. Sedgwick, shows, however, that you have been through cruel ordeals and that you have not fully recovered from them as yet. For the first time, I have learned from your letter that the arduous labor which your profession imposes on you must be given pride of place among the causes of your suffering. I am sorry that your clients who, it is said, have benefited much from your assistance, will see you abandoning a career in which you were so successful. But as for yourself, I am happy to see you making a decision that, I believe, is very wise. Forget then, I concur, the *dossiers,* but do not forget your friends.

I realize that you are not at all inclined to do this, given the interest with which you ask me for news about Ampère. He is doing very well, but he almost does not exist for us, since he is always absent.[135] Rome detains him to the point that I doubt that he will ever leave it, except for very short periods.

I continue to spend a lot of time working on the sequel to my book.[136] But there are great difficulties to overcome and I advance only very slowly.

Farewell, dear Mr. Sedgwick. Next time, please do not let so much time pass without writing to us. Be well, and believe in the affection that the inhabitants of the old cottage known as the Tocqueville chateau have for you.

A. de Tocqueville

P.S. The surest thing is always to write to me here. For the time being, I do not have a residence in Paris.

169. Alexis de Tocqueville to Edward Vernon Childe

Tocqueville, January 23, 1858

Dear Mr. Childe,

I have just received your last letter from Baltimore. I am surprised and frustrated to see that you have not received a letter that I wrote to you on November 8 last, and that I addressed, following the instructions that you had given me, to Messrs. Monroe & Co., 5 rue de la Paix. I do not understand why this letter has not been forwarded to you. I am distressed because this long silence might have led you to believe that I had forgotten you, which is the thing in the world that I am the least inclined to do. For my part, I was surprised not to have news from you, for in the letter that was withheld, I asked you for information that it was very important for me to obtain at the time. As I am certain of your friendship, I was worried about your health. I am very pleased to see that the second is no more compromised than the first. Dear Mr. Childe, may you be able to preserve for a very long time this first of all possessions, and continue to contribute to the happiness of the two good and lovely children that God has given to you, and of whom you should always think when dark thoughts enter your mind! I am extremely delighted to learn what you tell me about Miss Mary. Please tell her that I shall be truly happy when I am able to see her again by your side. How many painful memories are attached to the last meeting that I had with that young girl! These are memories that cause distress but also ones that bind people together. Mr. Edward wrote to me at very the moment he was embarking on his trip up the Nile. He seemed happy about his voyage, enchanted by this first sight of the East, and in better spirits than I have often seen him. I fear that, in vain, I have promised him letters for our diplomats in Asia Minor and Greece; the person to whom I addressed myself at the Ministry of Foreign Affairs (the Baron d'Avril) and who promised to help me, abruptly left on a mission, before receiving the letter in which, at his request, I had given him all the details that would have allowed him to write useful letters. I could not tell you how annoyed I am by this incident that seems irreparable; for, if I were now to ask someone else to write letters, I would not know how to make them reach Edward in due course. Mr. Edward must be on his way back and I very much hope to meet him in Paris toward the end of next Spring.

For the last six months since I returned here, I have been living a very secluded and productive life and, in short, one entirely suitable to my inclinations. I believe that the revolutions which violently brushed me aside from the path that I was following have put me back, despite myself, on the path that I should have always followed. I must acknowledge that in the midst of the affairs in which I was involved, and in the small part that I was able to take in government, I have never found anything resembling the inner peace and the harmony of faculties and desires that I often now enjoy. I say *often* and not *always*, for my mind has a certain restlessness of which I shall never be able to rid myself.[137] But if this illness is not entirely cured, at least it torments me infinitely less than it has done before. My health is also better than previously. My work does not advance quickly, but it goes forward at a regular pace. I do not plan on returning to Paris before the end of February and it will not be easy for me to give up my solitude . You will see, dear Mr. Childe, that I practice what I preach; I speak to you about myself because I know that you are genuinely interested in anything that happens to me. I have said enough to make you understand that I wish you to do the same and keep me informed of anything regarding you. I assure you that I shall always read with great interest everything that you write to me on this subject.

I have nothing to tell you about public affairs that you would not already know from newspapers. Abominable crimes, similar to the one that has just been committed against the Emperor, can nowhere revive the cause of liberty.[138] The cause is good, but those who pretend to represent it are often, one must admit, horrible rascals. It is sad to be placed, as we are now, between despotism and a band of murderers, and nowhere to find solid foundations upon which a liberal and non-demagogic party could be established.

You have not told me anything about your commercial crisis and the current state of business in America which, however, would have interested me greatly. I hope that the abolitionist cause will triumph in Kansas. I desire this with all my heart, in the interest of the whole of mankind. The Mormons could give you much trouble in the future.[139] Is it not strange to see thus emerging from the bosom of old civilized societies the institution which is most characteristic of nascent societies or nearly barbaric ones, polygamy?

Farewell, dear Mr. Childe. I address this letter to you in Baltimore, fearing that it might have the same fate as the previous one. Please reply to me at the Institute. I am very annoyed that my previous communication has been intercepted. Please allow me to offer you another copy of my book, and this time, I shall hand it to your son himself. I shall be very pleased to see again that *dear Edward*, as he was always called by his poor mother, taken away so cruelly from her family and friends, and who, for as long as I shall live, will retain such a great place in my memory.

A. de Tocqueville

170. Alexis de Tocqueville to N. W. Beckwith

Tocqueville, February 6, 1858

Dear Mr. Beckwith,

The aim of this letter is not to give you news from Europe. I am unaware of any such news that the newspapers could not tell you directly. I only want you to know that there are people at the antipodes, or almost, who still think of you and take a serious interest in your fortunes. My wife and I are very eager to learn how your long voyage went. Although the Americans are even more than the English a *moving race*,[140] and in spite of the fact that, for them, traveling three thousand leagues is a common thing, nonetheless, even for them going so far away with a large family is not a small matter. Please hurry therefore to give us news about you as well as news about Mrs. Beckwith and your children.

In addition to knowing how you are, we are most interested in learning how you have found the situation in China and your impressions of that peculiar country. This is the first time I can hear an original and perceptive mind pass judgment on what is going on there.

In Europe, at the present moment people are expecting to learn that the English and the French have attacked Canton.[141]

Nobody knows for sure why people fight; nonetheless, there is a lot of interest in the outcome of a battle that seems so unequal at first sight. I see that the Americans continue to keep themselves at a distance and I am quite inclined to believe that they are right to do so. But perhaps, given their nature as *barbarians*, they will end up by being drawn into the battle against their will. The English have on their hands two difficult tasks. As far as one can judge from a distance, the situation in India is fraught with more difficulties than initially thought. It is clear that order cannot be restored and maintained in that country except with the aid of a significant European army, and that the only thing which it is difficult for the English to find is soldiers.

If that nation had, as is the case with the peoples on the Continent, the possibility of limitless recruitment, I believe that the entire world would end by being the object of its covetousness. Fortunately, the limits of its armies impose necessary constraints on its ambition.

You will have learned from the newspapers about the attempt against the Emperor's life. This event is meant to make all friends of absolute governments rejoice; but it makes those who, like myself, continue to support *the good old cause*[142] of liberty despair. In the eyes of the masses it justifies all kinds of violence that is permitted against them. After such an incident, those in power can do anything. The only danger for them is to abuse their own power.

I am writing to you from the heart of our retreat at Tocqueville where we have been living so happily that it is only with sadness that we see the time approaching when we shall have to leave here in order to spend a few months in Paris. Please send me your reply there. Since I do not know as yet where I shall reside in Paris, I ask you to address your letter to M. de Tocqueville, care of M. Pingard, Chief Secretary of the Institute. We have been well throughout the winter and I have been working assiduously. To good effect? I cannot say; only the future will tell.

Here is a letter of too little interest to be sent so far, but, as I was saying at the beginning, I know nothing. I add that there is nothing, I believe, truly significant to learn at present about public affairs in Europe. All the great questions are either resolved or postponed. Do not therefore look in this letter for anything else than the token of our friendship for you, which is sincere and toward which, I believe, you are not indifferent. Our affectionate remembrances to Mrs. Beckwith.

[Alexis de Tocqueville]

171. Theodore Sedgwick to Alexis de Tocqueville[143]

Office of the District Attorney of the United States, for the Southern District of New York.

New York, Feb[ruary] 15, 1858

My very dear M. de Tocqueville,

I have just received your letter of [...].[144] I contacted my friend *Belmont*, your ex-chargé in The Hague and the representative of the Rothschilds in this country. I know him well and you can rely on the good faith and wisdom of his advice. He wrote a note which I am forwarding to you enclosed and I am confident that what he says is likely to allay your fears regarding the most significant part of your American investments.

Thank you very much for your kind invitation. Please retain for me a small place in your and Madame de Tocqueville's heart as well as in your chateau, for the brightest hope that I have for the future is to bring my daughters there with me in order for them to see the old Europe. And of course, in Europe I shall have no greater [...][145] than to show them a sample of the [...][146] French nobility as it exists under your roof. Perhaps that will happen this year, perhaps next year, but it is certain that if I live, I shall come.

I use my official letterhead in order to convince you in the clearest and most striking way that I have been made "District Attorney."[147] The position was offered to me in the most gracious manner by the President when I was too ill to work and I told him [...][148] yet he nominated me. I accepted it thinking that at least I had the duty to try and, fortunately, either because of the excitement coming from the new job or simply from the work of God, my health has greatly improved since I have been in the saddle. As you know, public positions count for little in our country, but any new experience is pleasant and my work is light and easy.

I am sending with the same steamer a package containing my work.[149] I have sent it care of Mr. Mason, the Minister of the United States in Paris, and if you are so kind as to send for it at the legation in Paris, you will receive the book at no cost. I very much appreciate your promise to bring it to the attention of the Institute and when you do so, please send me your note. A great part of the work is purely [...]^{150} technical. But the first, the fifth, and the tenth chapters address those general questions that any historian of a country governed by written laws or a constitution must study and consider [...].^{151} You, who understand our country so well, will easily notice the line that I have endeavored to follow and the task that I set for myself.

We are right in the middle of the *Kansas* question but I believe that we are coming closer to its end. But unfortunately it is only the end of *this part* of the eternal issue of slavery. Slavery still remains a cause of shame and misfortune for us. But any country as well as any individual has its weak side and taking everything into account, we are or should be very happy with our situation. Shall we have the wisdom to remain united? That is the great question on which our future depends. I believe that we shall have the good sense not to slaughter each other during my lifetime.

The country is gradually recovering from our financial troubles, but it will still be at least a year until affairs resume their regular course.

The arts are beginning to flourish greatly in our country. *Belmont* brought from Europe a very nice collection of works by modern artists that cost him more than 300,000 francs and opened it to the public. *Aspenwell*, another major businessman, is about to open a beautiful gallery of paintings which he has just bought in Europe; so we are following right in the footsteps of old Europe.

Farewell, my dear M. de Tocqueville. Please convey my respects to Madame de Tocqueville and believe that I am always your devoted,

Theodore Sedgwick

P. S. I hope to receive news from you soon.

Beinecke Rare Book and Manuscript Library, Yale Library, Bonnel copy, MS Vault Tocqueville, D II a, folder "Bonnel's copies of letters from Americans to Tocqueville."

172. Alexis de Tocqueville to Charles Sumner

Tocqueville, par St.-Pierre-Église (Manche)
March 28, 1858.

Dear Mr. Sumner,

I have been meaning to write to you for some time in order to thank you for the useful information that you have given us regarding our financial affairs. The fear of disturbing you has kept me from doing so. At this very moment, you must have more important things to do than to read letters from Europe that can teach you nothing. It is becoming more and more dangerous for the French to write about the state of public affairs. Do not expect me, then, to write about politics, unless it is about American politics. Besides, the latter also interests me greatly; but no matter how hard I read what the newspapers have to say about it, I hardly understand anything from them. Will Kansas be condemned to the horrors of slavery? Will it be able to escape this destiny? As a friend of America and of humanity, I am interested in the answer you could give to this question.[152]

In Europe, many people are starting to accuse you of engaging in the slave trade. I do not know if this accusation is well-founded. Not only slave trade on behalf of the countries in which slavery is still established, but also slave trade on your own account. From time to time, our newspapers report about shipments of blacks being unloaded in the southern states bordering the Gulf of Mexico. Is there any basis for this accusation?

But what is even more damaging to your reputation in the opinion of Europe, where, as you know, people are not concerned much with slavery, is the behavior that people have begun to attribute to a great number of those who are involved in public life in America, and who lead either the public affairs of the individual states or those of the Union. People are constantly telling us anecdotes, undoubtedly false or exaggerated, but all of which tend to make public opinion in Europe believe that in America the majority of public officials lack moderation, sometimes probity, above all education, and that they belong to a race of political adventurers, an energetic race, intelligent but violent, vulgar, and without principles. Note that I am far from saying that this is the case in reality. I speak only about the impression given to the public and the consequent harm done to America and its institutions. Since I take the most profound interest in your country, I often suffer when hearing how people in France, and even in England, speak about it. Without subscribing, as I said earlier, to the claims that are being made, I am led to believe that in your country the movement of an unlimited democracy often elevates to the government of society men who are more aptly made for obedience than leadership, and that, *in general*, those who govern are inferior to the governed. Am I mistaken?

I have remained here since I last saw you, being as ever both engaged in study and occupied with agriculture, as you well know. But the time when I am obliged to return to Paris has arrived. Since I do not know how long I shall remain there, I ask you to address your response to the *Institute, Paris, care of M. Pingard*. I expect to return here in a few months.

Please send us your news and be reassured that no one in Europe is more interested than us in receiving good news about you. Kindly remember us to your brother and believe in my sincere friendship.

A. de Tocqueville

173. Alexis de Tocqueville to Edward Lee Childe

Paris, April 10, 1858

Dear Mr. Edward,

For a very long time I have been reproaching myself for not having written to you. In fact, I should have carried out this plan a long time ago. Instead of requesting news directly from you, I have been asking for it from your father. What a strange detour to address oneself to an inhabitant of Baltimore in order to know how an Egyptian is doing![153] The truth is that I have been so vexed at not being able to send you the letters of recommendation that were *promised* to me, that the pleasure of writing to you would have been diminished. I attached great importance to sending those letters, which I thought would not only please you, but could also be useful in certain circumstances. I do not know if Mr. Childe has informed you about how, between the moment when the offer was made to me and the moment when it was supposed to be fulfilled, the friend from the Foreign Affairs who had taken this task upon himself was obliged to leave France suddenly. I thought that the letters had already been sent out when I learned that it was too late for them to reach you. This is what it means to be no longer *anything* in your own country! One cannot even render the simplest services to one's friends!

Upon my arrival here eight days ago, I went to M. Hottinguer in order to inquire about you. He had no news from you, other than the fact that you were on your way to Constantinople, where any correspondence for you had to be addressed. Hence, I shall send this letter to you there. If you receive it, something I am not certain of, please let me know how you are doing as soon as possible. Your letter from Egypt was very interesting and I do not doubt that the remainder of your voyage will add many lively impressions to those that the first encounter with Egypt gave you.[154] I hope that on your return you will stop in Paris where I expect to be. My intention is to stay here until the end of June. I am, in fact, obliged to remain here during this time in order to continue the research that I have started and whose outcome is of particular interest to me. If you stop in Paris, as I hope you will do, we will spend some time together. I would be truly delighted to see you; moreover, I believe that I will not be the only one to do so and that you will find again a number of friends who have not forgotten you and in whose hearts the memory of your mother is still very much alive. For my part, I repeat that I am one of them. Even assuming for a moment that I did not have the true friendship that I feel toward you, I would still be attached to you by such a precious memory.

I am not going to write more to you today, foreseeing that perhaps by the time this letter arrives in Constantinople you will have left the city. If you receive it, please write a few words without delay. Address your letter to the Institute, care of M. Pingard. Be reassured that I shall be very pleased to learn that you are doing well, and to know everything that might contribute to your happiness. The latest news that I received from your venerable father was very good, and his letters are always full of the tender affection that he has for his children.

Goodbye for now; from all my heart, yours,

A. de Tocqueville

174. Alexis de Tocqueville to Edward Lee Childe

Paris, April 30, 1858

Dear Mr. Edward,

An unforeseen circumstance has forced me to leave Paris and will undoubtedly deprive me of the pleasure of seeing you on your passage through the city. I regret this very much. You will find enclosed a copy of my latest book that I ask you to offer to your venerable father. I have already sent him one but it did not reach him.

A thousand sincere and friendly regards.

A. de Tocqueville

P. S. I hope that you received the letter that I wrote to you in Constantinople.

175. Charles Sumner to Alexis de Tocqueville

May 7, 1858

I was very happy, my dear Monsieur de Tocqueville, to hear from you; but I should have been happier still had you written me a few words about affairs in your own country. Everything there seems to portend great changes soon. The present unnatural system of compression cannot endure always.

Our politics here continue convulsed by the eternal slavery question; and this will not end until justice prevails. Mr. Buchanan has disappointed large numbers of his supporters by the extent to which he has gone in behalf of slavery. Many expected from him greater moderation; for myself I am not disappointed. He is essentially a politician rather than a statesman, and is governed by vulgar ideas. All his sympathies are given to the most ultra-school of pro-slavery. The usurpations and atrocities in order to plant slavery in Kansas have all received his sanction. Indeed, I doubt if history can record acts of meaner tyranny. He thinks that the Kansas question is now settled; but it is only postponed. Meanwhile Mr. Mason[155] writes from Paris that the opposition to slavery from France and England is dying away. This is curious, while Russia is just beginning her great act of emancipation. At present all our ministers in Europe are creatures of slavery, and think only how they can serve its purposes. Of course, they belong to an inferior class of public men.

I am grateful that your interest in my country does not abate, and that you so often say a kind word for us. Be assured that many of those things by which we are degraded are caused by slavery, even in states where slavery does not exist. This has demoralized our government, and introduced everywhere the vulgar principles of force, which, as you know, underlies slavery. Let a party prevail founded on hostility to slavery, and although abuses and excesses may not all cease, yet I cannot doubt that the very principle on which it is founded will diffuse a new civilization over the whole country. And now, my dear friend, if you hear the American Republic abused, pray charge its evil deeds to slavery, and say that there are good people here who are determined that this source of all our woes shall cease – at all events, that it shall no longer give its tone to our government and to our national character.

Why will not Spain follow the example of European powers – and now of Russia – and declare emancipation in her colonies? This would do more to settle the slavery question than any blow ever before struck. It would at once take Cuba from the field of Mr. Buchanan's lawless desires, and destroy the aliment of filibusters; besides it would be an act of noble justice, as well as of wise statesmanship.

I notice the publication of M. Guizot's *Memoirs*, and look forward to their perusal with great interest.[156] Remember me kindly to M. de Circourt and M. Ampère, and do commend me to Madame de Tocqueville.

Originally published in *Memoirs and Letters of Charles Sumner*, edited by Edward L. Pierce, vol. III, 1845–1860 (Boston: Roberts Brothers, 1894), pp. 561–62.

176. Alexis de Tocqueville to Theodore Sedgwick

Tocqueville, par St.-Pierre-Église (Manche)
May 28, 1858

Dear Mr. Sedgwick,

I am writing to you with great delay. I ask for your forgiveness. During these past months, my life has been full of unforeseen incidents that have not allowed me to pursue any project whatsoever.[157] I went to Paris last April, as I believe I told you I had planned to do. My intention was to spend four months there. But after a fortnight, events forced me to return here, where it is likely that I shall spend the entire summer. Upon my arrival in Paris, my first concern was to pay a visit to the American Minister in order to gain possession of the volume which I was expecting from you and which, in fact, I found there to my great satisfaction. I began to read it, and at the very moment when I was going to present it to the Academy, I was obliged to leave Paris. I wrote a report on your work[158] and, not wanting to wait for my return in order to draw the attention of the Academy to it, I decided to send my report to M. Mignet, asking him to be so kind as to bring it to the attention of my colleagues. I would have preferred to speak rather than write about it. But I did not want to wait, perhaps until the next winter, to present it to the Academy. My short report which, according to the custom, is quite brief, and whose only goal is to call the attention of the Academy to it, will be printed in our yearbook, and as soon as it appears, I will send it to you.

Now, please allow me to tell you my opinion of your work. I want to assure you, without flattery, that I found it to be excellent. It has a merit, to be sure, but it is one that can only strike an American jurist, namely, the scope and solidity of the science of laws and legal customs that you reveal. I cannot pass judgment on this, since these issues are largely beyond my understanding. But the general part of your subject was well within my reach and my mind focused itself so well on the latter that I remained deeply interested in it during the entire reading of your work. It seems to me that you have wonderfully highlighted what is peculiar to the position of the judiciary in America and have allowed us to understand the consequences that such a judicial system can have on the political system as a whole. Your book, which must be useful to American jurists, is also likely to attract the attention of all the people who study the science of government, and is, in my opinion, indispensable for studying it well. This is precisely the point that I have sought to highlight clearly in the short report of a few pages that I have sent to the Academy. I also thought it appropriate to offer to the Academy the copy that you were so kind as to send to me, so that the latter could be placed in its library where it can be consulted. When you come to Europe, I demand that you to bring me another copy. It is also my wish that you should place it yourself among my books in my study.

When will you be able to afford me that pleasure? I fear that it might not be very soon. Here you are, retained not only by your private concerns, but also by public duties which perhaps will not allow you to travel for a few years from now.[159] If you can escape, I hope you will come to Europe. You have promised to bring your children here. We do not release you from your promise.

In the meantime, however, please give us news about you and some news about your country, in which I have taken such a profound interest for such a long time. In my mind, the memories of America are united to the memories of my youth. This is enough to tell you that sometimes my heart turns toward that side of the Atlantic where you live.

I would have many things to tell you about our old world. But in order to do that, I would need the intervention of a friend who would agree to deliver the letter to you in person. For, using the mail to send letters that speak about our affairs to a foreigner means taking the risk that these letters never arrive at their destination. I have had this experience more than once.

Therefore, I end here. My wife sends you many friendly regards and I do the same. As soon as my report is published, I shall hasten to send it to you, as if that were worth doing. Could you please excuse all the deletions, the scribbling, and the ink blots that cover this letter? I am incapable of writing without making a large number of such silly mistakes. Please excuse me for them and wish that I should never make any greater ones. Again, a thousand friendly regards.

A. de Tocqueville

177. Alexis de Tocqueville to Edward Lee Childe

Tocqueville, par St. Pierre-Église (Manche)
July 6, 1858

Dear Mr. Edward,

An acquaintance of mine has informed me that you are in Paris. This makes me regret even more that I am not there. You should have received a second letter from me after the one to which you had replied from Constantinople. In this last letter, I explained to you what forced me to leave Paris in the month of May rather than remaining there until the end of June, as I was initially planning to do. I would very much like to know if your present sojourn in France is likely to make you abandon the trip that you had the intention of undertaking next winter. I would be very saddened by such a change of plans because it would deprive me of the pleasure of meeting you. Hence, I would very much like to know as soon as possible what I should expect in this regard. Please write a few words to me at Tocqueville to answer my questions.

Since I do not know if this letter will ever reach you, I shall add nothing to these words other than saying that it would be extremely painful for me if I were to give up the idea of greeting you a few months from now. I hope that you have good news from America. In all probability you will have received a book from M. Hottinguer that I had left there for you to pick up when passing by. If you return immediately to America, I hope that you will give it to your venerable father as a token of the *lasting* affection that I have for him as well as for his son.

A. de Tocqueville

178. Alexis de Tocqueville to Edward Lee Childe

Tocqueville, par St. Pierre-Église (Manche)
July 19, 1858

Dear Mr. Edward,

Your letter[160] was most welcome. I was a little surprised that you had been in Paris without letting me know. I see that you have yet some friendship for me, and I think that you are right, since I hold you in genuine affection.

I note that you have not received the letter in which I had informed you of the change in my plans. As for myself, I believe that I have received all your letters. All of them were full of very interesting details for which I thank you. In the letter that has not reached you, I expressed the opinion that if everything was going well in America, it would be useful for you to remain in France for at least a few months during the winter, so as *to renew the chain of time*, as Louis XVIII said in vain with regard to the Charter.[161] You would be able to utter these words with more justice. Your presence in Paris would place you again in the world in the midst of which you have previously lived and where the memory of your mother is still alive. I am beginning to lose hope of making you *less French*. That being said, you must preserve in France the position that you desire. I believe that you will be received everywhere with genuine kindness. A few days ago, I received a letter from the Duchess de Rauzan, from which I copy the following: "I am informed that Edward Childe has returned; he seems, it is said, to be happy with his voyage. I hope to see him when passing through Paris. I have remained extremely interested in him. He loved his mother in such an affectionate manner that this has always given me a good impression of him." She adds (since one remains a woman even if one is a Duchess and an old woman): "People say that he has not shaved his beard." In the same letter, Madame de Rauzan informs me that she should pass through Paris soon. I think that you would do well during your passage through the city to try to find out if she is there or if she is due to return soon.

My own intention is to pass through Paris during the month of October. So, if you return at harvest time, as you say, we shall finally be able to meet. For my part, I assure you that this would afford me great pleasure.

You asked me for serious books worth reading. A few have appeared since your departure that, without being outstanding, nevertheless deserve to be read. Do you know the book by the Prince de Broglie on the Church in the fourth century?[162] It is interesting, and a man who returns from the East would above all take an interest in the description of a Christianity whose composition is still three quarters Oriental. You would see millions of people fighting over the doctrine of the Trinity in a place where the only thing you can hear over the roof tops is the cry: "God is great and Mahomet is his prophet!" There is also the work by Villemain on M. de Chateaubriand that is very nicely written and awakens many still recent memories.[163] Have you read the memoirs of the Duke de Raguse?[164] Do you know those of M. Miot on the same period?[165] I believe that these authors are interesting even for a foreigner, but above all in the eyes of a foreigner who loves France and who often wishes to live there. If I were to search for more, I could find a few more books; but these are enough for the time being. A book has just appeared in England that has caused quite a stir there and has suddenly transformed an unknown man into a *lion*; it is the book of a certain Mr. Buckle, *The History of Civilisation*,[166] nothing less than that. Only the introduction has appeared thus far; but it has

800 pages. Such a weighty volume on such a serious subject is frightening at first sight. It seems that the garnish is good enough to make such an unappealing offering palatable. People say that the style is full of charm, and even women, I am assured, have been taken with the author during the last season. He seeks to prove that we are only simple machines and that, at all events, we have the advantage of resembling animals much more than intelligent people usually think. These beautiful discoveries seem to please the English immensely.

Farewell. Please speak kindly of me to your father and always count on my sincere affection.

A. de Tocqueville

179. Alexis de Tocqueville to N. W. Beckwith

Tocqueville, September 7, 1858

Dear Mr. Beckwith,

You have written the most interesting letters to us. The one addressed to me, dated the end of last June, has delighted me as much as it has educated me.[167] Although it was long, I found that it ended much too soon, and I could hardly console myself that you did not have time to speak even more about the strange country where you live.[168] If you knew how delighted I am to receive your letters, you would agree, from time to time, to take a few moments away from your onerous activities to write to us. It is a fortunate occurrence to see such a strange people judged by an observer endowed with such a penetrating and original mind. We earnestly ask that you please continue to write to us. At the very moment when I am writing to you, people in Europe have learned officially of the peace treaty that has just been signed between the Christian powers and the Son of Heaven.[169] The terms of the treaty seem propitious to me; and if they are faithfully executed, China will find itself more open with regard to Europe than it has ever been before. But will this treaty be implemented in actual fact? This is what I still doubt, and especially that it will be permanently implemented. I imagine that the clauses will be implemented at the outset; but I think that people will not be slow in attempting to avoid them by all sorts of pretexts. I would be very curious to know what you think of the likely effects of the events that have just occurred.

Nothing has surprised me more than what you tell me about the almost chivalrous probity of the Chinese in matters of trade. The facts that you cite are conclusive but, nonetheless, they are in disagreement with common opinion in Europe, according to which the Chinese are as cheating as they are intelligent. This is an additional proof that nothing is more subject to error than common opinion. To my mind, in reality a good single observer carries more weight than thousands of superficial or biased testimonies coming from people who repeat each other.

Another fairly common opinion, and on which I would be very curious to have your view, is that regarding the religious beliefs of the Chinese. All those who return from China, mainly the missionaries, assure us that China is the country of the world in which religion properly speaking exists the least among the enlightened classes and comes closest to being a pure philosophy. According to them, the religion of Buddha has passionate and convinced supporters only among the lowest class of the people, and even there it is in decline, as one can observe by looking at the great number of temples that are falling into ruin. Above the people, religious sentiment, or at least the sentiment attached to a positive religion, is almost unknown. The same persons add that, of all people, the Chinese have surrendered most to a practical Epicureanism, which leads them to look only for worldly pleasures and to live only with that goal in mind. This is possible, but such a state is rare and in general lasts only for a short time among human beings. I doubt that anyone has ever seen in the past a great mass of people who are moved only by the passion for material well-being.[170] From time to time, more elevated aspirations and yearnings of the soul toward an invisible world have never failed to manifest themselves. It would be as odd to imagine the opposite phenomenon as it would be sad to consider it. Hence I ask you this question. I could ask you a thousand others, for everything arouses my curiosity to the highest degree with regard to the country where you are living; so feel free to write to me about these issues as you think fit. Please be so kind as to write whenever your business affairs allow you to do so.

I would very much like to pay you back for your news about China with European news in such a way as to discharge my debt to you; but I have nothing to give you that would be of equal worth to what you have sent me. The newspapers can give you a knowledge of the facts better than I could do it. The only thing left for me is to communicate my own opinions to you. I believe that, at least for some time, peace is certain. The French government which, after the horrible attack committed in the month of

January,[171] appeared briefly to be struck by a sort of vertigo, seems to have recovered its composure. During the first moments of fear and anger, it seemed that the government wanted to adopt a politics of violence, with which the nation, in spite of being tired of political turmoil, would not have put up for long. Abroad, more and more threats were made, which led the English to believe that we were planning a major strike against them. At home, as well as abroad, these unfortunate measures created fears, uncertainties, and excitement in the minds of the people, which, combined with the last effects of the industrial crisis, ended by paralyzing the entire course of affairs; but, more recently, the French government has taken a better path. Benefiting from the unusual ability that consists in recognizing errors and from the ease with which all absolute powers repair the errors that they have committed, the government has managed to reassure the nation about internal violence and irrational adventures abroad. It has made prodigious efforts, partly successful, to bring the English government back into a close alliance. My very firm opinion is that the consequence of all this will be a fairly rapid resumption of relations. Without being outstanding, the harvest is sufficient and this allows the government to allocate to industry the capital that it would have been necessary to use in order to buy grain with gold. Hence I believe in an imminent return to public prosperity which, since the crisis in America, has been absent on the old as well as on the new continent. What will be the limits of this recovery? How long will it last? I believe that nobody can tell for sure, since it depends in part on what might happen in the mind of one man, who hardly speaks and communicates only through his actions. Until now, fortune has been leading him as if by the hand.

I do not know if anyone on earth has ever seen ten years of misfortune succeeded by such unheard-of prosperity. There have been almost no events in the last ten years that have not served him well and, as it were, have not led him to success. But, as one must recognize, knowing how to *follow* fortune is already no small merit; there are so many people who stubbornly persist in turning their backs to it!

Remember us fondly to Mrs. Beckwith. And if, for your part, you retain a little friendship for us, write to us from time to time, since your letters bring us great pleasure.

My wife thanks you warmly for what you have written to her.

[A. de Tocqueville]

180. Alexis de Tocqueville to John Young Mason[172]

Tocqueville, par St.-Pierre-Église (Manche)
September 21, 1858

Sir,

I hope that you will be so kind as to excuse the approach that I am making toward you by taking into consideration that the sentiment that has motivated me to do so is an extreme confidence in your knowledge and your character.

I am the owner of two *second issue* bonds of the American railway Marietta and Cincinnati. Messrs. Greene & Co., through whom I acquired these two bonds, have just sent me an offer from a Mr. Samuel Hallet, from which it seems that Mr. Hallet would take upon himself, at his own risk, to sell the railway. At least 75% of the price would be distributed to the owners of *second issue* bonds. Mr. Greene has cited your name in support of Mr. S. Hallet's offer. He asks me to accept his offer *as soon as possible*. The purpose of this letter is to ask you if you think that the person and scheme of Mr. Hallet offers sufficiently serious guarantees for me to accept the offer that has been made to me. You can be sure that I shall give considerable weight to your opinion and I take the liberty of asking you to give it to me as soon as possible, since I must respond to Mr. Greene.

Please accept, Sir, along with my excuses, the expression of my most distinguished consideration.

Alexis de Tocqueville
Member of the Institute

181. Alexis de Tocqueville to Edward Lee Childe

Monday, October 11, 1858

My dear Mr. Edward,

I have been here for six days and received your letter upon my arrival. But I arrived very ill, suffering from a bronchitis that has taken away my voice and has made me entirely unfit for company.[173] I would like, however, to shake your hand. Could you stop by to see me tomorrow at noon? I am living at the Hotel Bedford, 17 rue de l'Arcade. We shall exchange only a few words, but for my part they will certainly come from all my heart.

A thousand friendly regards,

A. de Tocqueville

182. Alexis de Tocqueville to Edward Lee Childe

Friday morning, October 15, 1858

Dear Mr. Edward,

Seeing that you have not come here, as I asked you to do in my last letter, I concluded that you were not in Paris. I stopped by at your lodgings yesterday and there, indeed, I learned that you had left the city and are expected to return tomorrow, Saturday. If you were to arrive on Saturday before noon and stopped by to see me at that hour, you would afford me great pleasure. But you will probably only arrive in the evening.

If you cannot come to see me on Saturday, please do not come for a few days after that, since I shall undergo some medical treatment that will make me unsuitable for company for a few days, and I would like to be able to enjoy your presence. Moreover, I shall write to you again. A thousand friendly and affectionate regards.

A. de Tocqueville

183. Alexis de Tocqueville to Edward Lee Childe

Tuesday morning, October 19, 1856

Dear Mr. Edward,

Today I have a little more strength in my voice than usual and want to profit from it in order to visit you between eleven and noon. I shall not retain you for a long time since I am forbidden to have long conversations. At least, I shall greet you with all my heart. I am arranging the *rendez-vous* at your lodgings and not at my own in order to be able to speak more freely. I stopped by yesterday, but you had already left. Until soon, therefore, *if the weather remains fine*.

A. de Tocqueville

184. Alexis de Tocqueville to Edward Lee Childe

Cannes, December 4, 1858

Dear Mr. Edward,

I reproach myself greatly for not having written to you sooner. For you are one of the very few persons in whose friendship I believe, and these persons should always take precedence in all correspondence. I have not written to you because, for some time, I have been unable to do so and, above all, I have lacked the desire to write. In order to arrive here, I have made the most difficult journey.[174] The sudden fall in temperature, the length of the journey and several incidents which it would take too much time to relate to you, all this has worsened my condition and, above all, has greatly exhausted me. It has taken me almost two weeks to recover from this initial exhaustion. But, since then, my health has not ceased to improve and I have regained my strength to the point that I am now beginning to feel like a different person and my doctor promises me a complete recovery. I am told that there are some newspapers claiming, on the contrary, that I am very ill. This is what we call, in the language of the street, a *hoax*.

Upon your return from England, you wrote me a short letter which proved to me that, despite the fact that you are a literary spirit, you know, when you want to, how to speak about business affairs in a clear and concise way (the two great qualities of the genre). I thank you for the information that you gave me. It confirmed what I already knew; for some time I have been wanting to change gradually the funds that I have in the railway bonds so as to place them in a more secure situation. But the question is how to act at such a distance and in such a way as to risk nothing and to choose the favorable moment? I return to what I have already told you, namely, that I see your father as the only person whom I can reliably consult on this matter; I shall also write to him in the next few days and shall send you my letter as you suggested. If you have the occasion to see M. Hottinguer (you should not go there for this alone), please ask him to give you the latest quotations from the New York Stock Exchange. With the arrival of each steamship he receives newspapers that list them. If he could give you one of these, I would be obliged if you could send it to me. I think of you very often, and often with sadness, since I do not know what advice to give you. The lack of a regular occupation is the cause of the malaise that torments you. This is certain. But how can one find a regular occupation suitable to a man who is independently wealthy and has no passionate taste for anything? The problem is insoluble. Only necessity, *dira necessitas*,[175] could force a disposition such as yours to obtain the invaluable good that is a profession. But thus far you have escaped from all obligations deriving from a profession. Be convinced, dear Edward, that being free from all ties is not a condition suitable to man in this world. It is contrary to his nature and, sooner or later, nature takes revenge. I have often regretted, for the sake of your happiness, that you were not born an artisan. I venture to tell you that by making a potter's wheel turn for eight hours you would arrive at the end of your day calmer and more content to be alive than you often seem to be. This is what led me to believe that, since you lack the ties and obligations provided by an industrial career or a *profession*, the only thing left to you to overcome this situation would be to accept the ties and obligations of marriage. I aspire to take away from you the unlimited liberty that you enjoy and which will lead you to *spleen*. But how does one get married? I confess that you put me in a difficult situation when asking me this question. But if you were to perceive its utility and desirability and if you were inclined to do it, that would already be a great step forward. From this first would follow all the others. I do not think that I criticize you too much when saying that the society in the midst of which you have lived has given you a great contempt for women and a certain taste for easy pleasures. This would be a bad frame of mind for marriage. I could say much more about the things that come to mind when I think of you. But I am beginning to become tired and leave the continuation of our dialogue for another time. If you have the occasion to see Miss Lagden,[176] please send her our friendly regards and give her news about me. Farewell, dear Edward. Please believe in my genuine affection for you.

A. de Tocqueville

185. Alexis de Tocqueville to Edward Lee Childe

Cannes, December 11, 1858

Dear Edward,

I hasten to send you by return mail the item that you have borrowed from M. Hottinguer. I delay for a while longer from responding to your letter of the 7th that has profoundly touched me.[177] I would have already written to your father if, in that same letter, you had not told me: "I have just received a letter from my father ... there is in his letter advice and information that I shall send to you soon." I thought that it might be useful to know what he had already said before writing to him.

A thousand friendly and affectionate regards,

A. de Tocqueville

186. Alexis de Tocqueville to Edward Lee Childe

Cannes, December 22, 1858

Dear Mr. Edward,

Please excuse me for not having responded to you sooner. When your last letter arrived, I was suffering a little more than both previously and since. Moreover, the current treatment to which I have subjected myself, although useful to the body, is crushing for the mind. It is absolute silence. I only see my wife and my brother and speak to them only when it is impossible to do otherwise. It is this sort of intellectual solitude to which I am confined that throws me into a listlessness of mind that makes every kind of correspondence difficult to me, even that with my best friends. Dear Edward, you certainly belong among the latter. I already held you in great affection, and this has increased even more in light of the interest that comes out from your letters. We understand each other very well.

I turn at once to the most important things, since I do not want to write a long letter. I read what your venerable father has to say about my affairs. I still need two or three days to decide myself how I should respond to him; hence you will not have any letter for him today.

And now let us talk about you. You say that you have some confidential things to tell me if you see me. Instead of that, do not delay for a single moment to share them with me in writing, for the advice of a true friend can always be useful. Moreover, when shall we be able to talk in person? I do not know. You would have to come here or else I would only be able to correspond with you in writing. One of my oldest friends, M. de Malartic,[178] is here at the moment. This is what we are reduced to. Therefore, write without delay, and for God's sake, speak without fear or embarrassment. I imagine that there is a woman at the heart of your secret. I was once young. I was familiar not only with the temptations of the flesh, but also with the passions of the heart. Hence, you can speak without fearing that you would find a man devoid of feelings.

As to what you want me to do with regard to your father, I am ready to demonstrate to him that you are made only for living in Europe. I have already tried to convince him of this several times and I assure you that I shall return forcefully to this subject. I am also very willing to insist that he make a return trip to Europe, instead of wishing to lure you back to America. But I could not promise to press him to settle here at the present moment. My conscience would be troubled by that, for I believe strongly that it is in the interest of your sister, who has again become an American, to remain an American and consequently to get married in America rather than here. All I can do for you therefore with regard to this last issue is not to raise it with your father.

I am doing as well as one can do given the state of my illness. I sleep well, have a good appetite, and walk a lot. But I continue to cough a little and would like so much to see the end of this illness which, if not cured soon, would end by becoming serious.

Farewell, very dear Edward. A thousand affectionate regards, to which I would like to add in closing my wishes for the new year, which is not an empty wish since it comes from the bottom of my heart.

A. de Tocqueville

187. Alexis de Tocqueville to Edward Lee Childe

Cannes, December 26, 1858

My dear Edward,

I have received your letter and I must immediately answer since it troubles me.[179] I am not happy with you. Your mind is obviously in a highly agitated state. Something extraordinary and particularly painful is going on in your life. Not far away, you have a reliable and trustworthy friend, with a rich experience in the great torments of life (for, believe me, my existence has not been a quiet one at all!), and yet you refuse to open yourself up to him after having revealed enough of your inner state to worry him deeply as a friend. This is unreasonable and unfair toward a man who has as much affection for you as I do. Let go, dear Mr. Edward, and open your heart to he who will know how to listen to you and perhaps help you with his advice! What do you fear? Do you not know that I am the most trustworthy confidant? As mute as silence! If you do not want to leave a written trace of what you would have to tell me, after having read it I shall send your letter back to you by return mail, and you will have the satisfaction of burning it. But do write, my friend, I ask you in earnest; I do not need to dwell on what I already know; it troubles and worries me.

In truth, what do you have in mind when begging me not to mention a single word about it to your father? Do you think that I am insane as well as being capable of betraying a secret? Do I not know your venerable father as if I had spent my entire life with him? My intention was to tell him only that I had found you to be very fragile and, all things considered, tired from your travels. From that, I would have developed an argument to prevent you from making the voyage to America, or at least to postpone it. But if even that is not to your liking, please tell me when you reply to me and I shall not touch upon the subject anymore. Nonetheless, I believe that the point is very much worth making and I see no disadvantage in doing it. Write, write, and for God's sake, remember that you do not have a better friend than me!

A. de Tocqueville

188. Jared Sparks to Alexis de Tocqueville

Cambridge, Massachusetts, Dec[ember] 28, 1858

My dear M. [de] Tocqueville,

On my return from Europe, I received from Mr. Ticknor the letter and the volume, which you sent to me by him from Paris. For these tokens of your friendship and kindness, I beg you will accept my best thanks. I have perused your work with very great satisfaction, not only as containing a rich fund of historical facts, but as presenting a clear and vivid picture of the internal state of France during the important period which it embraces. I have nowhere seen the causes and the gradual progress of the Revolution so completely developed. The work throughout bears evidence of great labor and research in collecting the materials of which it is formed, and it must ever be regarded as a most valuable acquisition to the historical literature of France. In my library it will stand by the side of the *Démocratie en Amérique* and together they will serve as a perpetual agreeable memorial of their author.

What can I say to you concerning the state of public affairs in this country? No man understands better than yourself the principles and practical operations of our political system. No essential change has taken place since you were in America. There is a constant conflict of parties, but so it will always be in a free government. The rapid extension of settlements at the west, and the addition of new states in that quarter, produce gradual changes in our internal affairs, yet no material inconveniences have been found to result from these acquisitions, although new states are now forming on the Pacific ocean, nearly four thousand miles from the Capitol at Washington.

Slavery is the absorbing topic, which occupies all minds. It is indeed most formidable, whether regarded as bearing on the present or future prospects of the country. Emancipation is the hope and ardent desire of every friend of humanity, but how or when this is to be effected, no one can venture to predict. And even if all the slaves were now emancipated, what could be done with these millions of people, differing in race, color, and condition from those around them constituting the mass of the nation? The tendency of the evil, as it now exists, is to produce a geographical division in the opinions and interests of different states. Such a division must always be unfavorable to the Union. As yet, however, there are no serious apprehensions of difficulty from this source. The future must be left to the guidance of a wise and beneficent Providence.

I shall ever be most happy to hear from you. With best wishes for your success in all your undertakings.

I am, my dear Mr. [de] Tocqueville, most truly your friend,

Jared Sparks

P. S. The enclosed recap, cut from one of our University Catalogues, will indicate to you some of the Societies of which I am member. [A partly illegible note follows, with all the societies of which Jared Sparks was a member].

Beinecke Rare Book and Manuscript Library, Yale University, Bonnel copy, D II a, folder "Bonnel's copies of letters from Americans to Tocqueville." This letter was partly published in Herbert Adams, *Jared Sparks and Alexis de Tocqueville*, 1898, pp. 46–47.

189. Robert Walsh to Alexis de Tocqueville

Paris, Jan[uar]y 11, 1859

Dear Sir,

Last month, the literary and philosophical world was much alarmed and distressed by a report in the journals, that you were grievously ill. Every one who knows you, and can appreciate your character and writings, rejoiced when the intelligence was given of your gradual recovery. No one of the number felt more satisfaction than my humble self. I have been, for many years, engaged at intervals, in preparing personal or private memoirs to be published after my death. My main purpose is to furnish correct public history. You must remember the case of the quintuple treaty for the repression of the slave trade.[180] As a member of the Chamber of Deputies, you bore a distinguished and influential part in the discussion. Of late years, it has been repeatedly proclaimed in the United States that the sentiments and votes of the Chamber and the final refusal of M. Guizot to adopt the treaty, were produced or determined by a small pamphlet from the pen of General Cass, minister plenipotentiary of the United States at the epoch 1841–42. I was in this capital at the time, Consul, and closely attentive to the proceedings in the Chambers in regard to the treaty. General Cass placed in my hands the proof sheets of his pamphlet which impugned the project of Four Powers. My recollection is that the pamphlet was not issued, or known to the Chamber of Deputies before the decisive vote; that the opposition of the Chamber was original, and its measures produced by the general repugnance to the stipulation of the Treaty, in particular the mutual visitation and search; and moreover that M. Guizot yielded only to the manifestations and resolves of the Deputies and the prevailing sentiments of the Chamber of Peers.[181]

Now, what you may remember, would operate conclusively with me in my record; perhaps you can refer me to some publication in which the circumstances are accurately related. I pray you to lend no attention whatever to this note, in case any effort of your memory or employment of your pen should be irksome, and have a tendency to interfere, in any degree with the progress of your convalescence.

The reestablishment of your health is a common solicitude. I share in this sympathy and have the honor to be,

> Dear Sir,
> with the utmost respect,
> your obedient servant,
> Robert Walsh
> N° 124, Rue de Faubourg, St. Honoré

Beinecke Rare Book and Manuscript Library, Yale University, Uncat MSS 324; also Bonnel copy in MS Vault Tocqueville, D II a, folder "Bonnel's copies of letters from Americans to Tocqueville."

190. Alexis de Tocqueville to Edward Lee Childe

Cannes, February 4, 1859

Dear Mr. Edward,

You ask me why I have not written to you lately. The reason is that until now, I have been incapable of writing, either to you or to anyone else.

The illness that struck me five weeks ago has been much more serious than I myself had initially thought.[182] I am now convalescing, but because of the extreme weakness which I continue to experience, I am still unable to write a long letter or even to put several ideas together. Apart from that, my doctor is satisfied. Be reassured that I am very concerned and worried about you and that the first use that I shall make of my strength will be to write to you at length. In the meantime, I can only shake your hand from all my heart.

A. de Tocqueville

191. Alexis de Tocqueville to Edward Lee Childe

Cannes, February 8, 1859

Dear Edward,

My recovery is becoming more and more pronounced and I have regained just enough strength to be able to respond, if not at length, at least effectively, I hope, to what you might have to tell me. But for the past five weeks since I was plunged into this abyss of death, I have not been able to follow you. I do not know if something new has occurred. Please write to me immediately about your situation. I shall try to answer without delay.

A thousand friendly and affectionate regards,

A. de Tocqueville

192. Alexis de Tocqueville to Edward Vernon Childe

Cannes (Var), February 19, 1859

Dear Mr. Childe,

So many months have passed since I wrote to you! Regardless of how long the silence has been, I am sure, however, that you have not attributed it to forgetfulness. For I do not need to tell you that you do not have a more reliable or better friend than me on this side of the Atlantic. Moreover, you were aware of what were the true and only reasons of this silence and how a bronchitis that no doctor has been able to diagnose, after having tormented me during the whole of last summer, has finally forced me to spend the winter in the south. This last measure could be very successful. My doctor promises to send me back home next summer fully recovered. May God hear him!

Your wonderful son, I know, has updated you about my financial affairs in America and you have promptly shown a deep and sincere desire to help me with your advice. In this gesture I recognized your old friendship and was profoundly touched by it. You could not imagine, dear Mr. Childe, the anxiety that these matters have caused me during the commercial and monetary crisis. I believe that they have had a very unfortunate influence on my health. I am no longer worried today but I remain very preoccupied by what I have to do. I count in great part on you, dear Mr. Childe, to help me overcome this difficult situation through your wise advice. You could not provide me with a more tangible proof of an affection upon which, moreover, you have taught me to rely.

In a separate note I have gathered together everything concerning my business affairs; I hope that you will be so kind as to respond to this part of my letter as soon as possible. How fortunate I am that you are in America at the present moment! I turn therefore without delay to a subject which will naturally interest you more than my business affairs, that of your son. I saw him when passing through Paris and found him very much changed to his advantage, *fully grown* as a result of his travels and, in all, a complete *gentleman*. I also know that he is very well regarded in the highest Parisian circles. From this point of view, you could only derive the greatest satisfaction. But, on the other hand, it also seemed to me that he has not been strengthened by his lengthy voyages. I found him very thin and looking tired. He was coughing a little during that time and the Duchess de Rauzan, with the almost motherly affection that she has for him, noticed it like me. I sensed that, given this condition of his health, Edward was a little fearful of undertaking immediately such a long sea voyage as the one to which he will have to subject himself in order to go to America, and where he will find himself subject to a climate that he has never regarded as good for him. I confess to you that I myself was also thinking the same. Nonetheless, he passionately desires to see you again; he speaks only about his father and he does so only with the most affectionate tone. All this has suggested to me a plan that seems beneficial to both your son and yourself. Instead of making the young man return to America, why do you not make a small voyage this year to Europe where your friends will be so happy to see you again? Miss Mary must have almost finished her education. Would she not be pleased again to see for a few months the Europe which she was not yet able to judge when she left it, and to revisit the places where she spent her childhood? I am sure that this young girl would be received with open arms by all the women who knew her mother and above all by the

Duchess de Rauzan, who has preserved such warm memories of her. You will understand that I am not speaking about *settling* in Europe – you know my ideas on this subject – but about a simple voyage similar to the many ones made by your compatriots. This trip would fill your son with joy and gratitude, would be interesting and instructive for your daughter, and would give to all the numerous friends that you left behind in France a very precious occasion to shake your hand once more. As for myself, apart from this reason which makes me wish that you would accept the plan I am proposing to you, in giving you this advice, I have been motivated by the fear that the return of your son to America *this year* might be very harmful to him. The reason that made me speak will lead you, I hope, to forgive me for having interfered in your affairs without being asked to give an opinion.

I shake your hand from all my heart.

A. de Tocqueville

Undated and Partially Dated Letters

193. George Sumner to Alexis de Tocqueville

418 rue St. Honoré – Friday, June 20[183]

Dear Sir,

Permit me to recall myself to your recollection in order to present you the respectful compliments of my brother (who had the honor to meet you occasionally in Paris in 1840) and also to trouble you with a request on his part. You have seen, perhaps, from time to time the reports of the "*Prison Discipline Society*" of Boston, which reports have for several years past breathed a spirit of bitter hostility towards the system of Philadelphia. This has been owing in a great degree to the personal feeling of the *Secretary* of the Society; a feeling which has been allowed for too long a time to go on unchecked.

My brother writes me, under date Boston 1st June.

"At the last annual meeting of our Prison Discipline Society, a few days since, when the Secretary had made his Report, abusing as is his custom, the Philadelphia System, I came forward and endeavored to answer some of his charges, moving then the reference of his Report to a select Committee. Of that committee I am a member, and I hope that we shall be able to make a thorough report on the two systems;[184] but for this we shall be much aided if you could obtain from Messieurs de Tocqueville and de Beaumont, copies of their different reports and speeches on the subject; and also if you could send any other documents that have lately appeared in Europe. Any thing from Messrs. Tocqueville or Beaumont has great weight, from the confidence which their learning and honorable character inspire."

Charles Sumner

I know how precious your moments are, but still I venture to hope that, when you are least occupied, you will think of this, and furnish me with such matter relative to the subject as you can conveniently lay your hands upon; above all I hope you will not forget the admirable discourses of last year at the Chamber of Deputies.

With sentiments of the highest respect, I have the honor to be, Sir,
your very obedient servant,
George Sumner

Beinecke Rare Book and Manuscript Library, Yale University, Tocqueville Vault, MSS 324.

194. N. W. Beckwith to Alexis de Tocqueville

[undated][185]

I do not rightly comprehend your remarks on America, my friend, till I received your last note: the subject is now clear.

You hear it said "that in America people, when offended, resort to violence and even to arms quicker than in other countries, that acts of individual violence are more frequent and less punished than in France or in England, that life is of less weight than in other civilized countries, that persons when aggrieved oftener take justice into their own hands, and consequently, habits of violence are becoming more and more a feature of the national character."

A comparison between America and Europe in this respect is extremely difficult; in the absence of ample statistics few persons are well enough informed of the state of society in both countries to give an opinion of any value.

People are apt to speak from momentary feeling, or isolated facts, or prejudice, or partiality or ignorance or, in fact, any thing but fullness of knowledge.

As to the relative value set upon life, I confess that I have no opinion, or rather no conviction: people will arrive at different conclusions depending on the *tests* which they adopt.

For example: in Geneva a few months since, a Frenchman and a Pole had a dispute, and one shot the other dead.

The dead man was placed beside a tree with a pistol in his hand and deliberately left in that condition (he was a gentleman) where several days afterwards he was found by a farmer.

This was followed by no public inquest, no movement of the authorities, no legal process, and there were not a thousand newspapers to occupy themselves with it for days.

A little inquiry was made; one of the parties volunteered a short statement – a mere paragraph in the journal, which was never verified, and there the matter dropped like a pebble into the lake, without commotion and with little comment.

One might infer from this that life was held cheap; even investigation and publicity, the only punishment which could be inflicted on the survivors who had probably fled, was not resorted to.

My inference however was that the apparent neglect was no evidence of indifference, but that the people were shocked, mortified and ashamed, and did not wish to hear a word said about it: they would have concealed it if they could, as a public disgrace.

Or, if we take as a test, the late doings in the Crimea, Algeria, India, China, we shall fail of any evidence that governments at least, set any high value on life.

If there be not fair tests, neither are the duels in America, and much less the accidents of steam or drowning, so often cited.

When a man is killed by accident or by design, or a dozen are blown up or smashed – if we take as a test the manifestations of affliction – the shows of grief, how shall we measure the relative quantity of these things?

Many persons would say the proper test is the pains taken to avoid accidents and to preserve life in the community.

Here they would find a difference between America and Europe.

In Europe, the govts take great care to prevent, and they use diligence to investigate and zeal to punish even inattention and carelessness.

In America, there is less of this and in regard to punishment for carelessness, I think they are too lenient.

But in Europe the govts do a hundred things for the people which in America the people are left to do for themselves: people in Europe are treated like ignorant children who require a great deal of minute caring for; in America they pretend that the people have intelligence enough to take more care of themselves, that they can do it better than it can be done for them and that it quickens and develops their intelligence to charge them with more self-care.

This is our system: we may carry it too far, or may be wrong, but we have the same end in view that you have; it is only a difference in the way of arriving at it, and nothing could be more illusive and erroneous than to infer from this difference of custom that life is held in higher esteem in Europe than in America.

It is a feature of the system of self-government: the care taken of the people in these matters should bear relation to their intelligence – relaxing as their intelligence rises – and whether we estimate this intelligence too high or you estimate it too low, *for the benefit of the people*, is a point on which doctors may differ: and it is a difference which prevails throughout – in the laws in regard to minors – and among parents in regard to family discipline etc. It extends from the head of the state to the fireside of families; and it is worthy of study on both sides, but should not lead to wrong conclusions on either side.

In regard to punishments for crimes and offenses there is also a wide difference: a great difference in the *Rule or Measure* of damages, and some difference in the degrees of punishment awarded for similar offenses. In these things there is a wide difference between the French and the English, which the American and English systems approximate very nearly.

I see the reports of trials daily in France, where *consequences* – consequential damages, are investigated, and dealt with on the footing of *direct effects* of the act complained of, both in civil and criminal matters, and this is carried to remote and doubtful effects.

In England and in America, this is not the Rule: remote effects – consequential damages, are not investigated, but are stricken out and the proceeding is limited to the direct effects of the act, or thing complained of.

Consequently many things go unpunished, which in France would be punished, and lighter penalties are inflicted, where all secondary effects are excluded from consideration.

To illustrate this, I take the following from a newspaper which is before me. In Paris an Englishman (probably in bed) sent his servant in the morning to get a newspaper of a woman who kept a dépôt.[186] The servant took with him a poodle, the newspaper woman also kept a poodle – and on entering the shop, the servant's poodle and woman's poodle flew at each other.

Madame had a heart, and could not see her poodle scratched by an Englishman's poodle, with indifference. She was excited and in her emotion stepped backward, fell over a chair and broke her thigh.

She sued the *master* of the servant, of the dog, and recovered 1,000 francs fine, and a pension of 500 francs per year for life, of the master, who by this time must have waked up [*sic*].

In England or America, this case would not come within the *purview* of the law, it would have been ruled out of court.

If one dog had damaged the other dog, that would have been a direct effect of the act of fighting and a thing to be paid for.

But the broken leg of the woman was the direct effect of her emotion, or of her carelessness, or of a misplaced chair, or of her own stupidity, or of her mistake in supposing there was a danger when there was none, or of any other thing, or even if you please, it was the indirect effect of the assault of the strange dog on her dog, or of the ill nature and ill manners of her own dog – but being *indirect* it is *uncertain*, and could not be remedied by English law or American law.

There is nothing which differs more than the extent to which consequential damages are traced among different peoples, and at different epochs among the same people – but whatever the variations and the differences, nothing is to be inferred from them as to the different values set upon life or upon personal rights.

The only question is, as to how far it is just and wise and safe to pursue the endless chain of cause and effect, in dealing with human actions. The practical conclusion of the Anglican race at this day is, that the direct and certain effects of men's actions is as much as it is wise to hold them responsible for, and even for these, milder penalties are more hopeful of reform, more likely to soften the passions and improve humanity than severe ones; and I think it must be admitted that this is the spirit in which the ancient dispensation was rebuked by the Christian founder of all modern improvement in the dealings of man with his fellow man, and in our necessary attempts to judge each other.

But peoples and races differ, and a system may be wisely and well adopted to one which would be unsuitable for another. Comparisons of systems therefore throw little light on the wisdom of them, for that depends on the people and circumstances to which each is applicable.

The idea that universal suffrage begets indifference of life, or that absolutism is tender of the lives of its people, will do for a monarch or for a slaveholder, but we democrats think the people are likely to set a higher value on themselves than any body will set upon them, and that in many cases they can take better care of themselves than can be taken of them; we even think that our people are better off because they are less cared for in many things, and more cared for in others, as in their means of education.

But it is a curious fact, the low value set upon life everywhere, even by its possessors; nothing is held so cheap as life; the moral sense is dull in regard to it; men expose their lives uselessly, sell them for a trifle, give them away or wantonly destroy them, to gratify the smallest want, the weakest passion, the most transient whim, of the moment.

Indeed this mysterious principle of life, which is everywhere supported by death, is one of the most puzzling subjects.

The grass, the leaves, every drop of water, the air, teem with life: every animal as well as man drinks it and feeds upon it – and most strange of all, be it an ox grazing in the field or a man meditating in his humblest mood, at every step, at every move, a thousand death-pangs are unconsciously inflicted: how often the eye falls by accident on the agonies of expiring life under foot.

This profusion of life – its unprotected condition – the utter careless-ness of it, as if it had no value – and I do not see any difference in regard to life in the higher or lower organisms – all are exposed and without pro-tection, against innumerable unseen dangers, which extinguish it: where a man destroys one tiger for safety or a tiger destroys one man for food, both destroy innumerable lives without design and uselessly: we seem to exist but upon the condition of extinguishing life, at every moment, every pulsation.

If the principle of organic life were of any consequence, why leave it in this condition?

But instinct is better than observation in this case: we can't comprehend the mystery, but we feel that life is of importance, we respect it, and feel rather disposed to sympathise with the Egyptians who consecrated (to protect) life, in its lowest forms, *seeing* it to be useful to man and *feeling* it to be the most direct manifestation of Deity.

But this is rather foreign to the subject: if there were a convenient test I think it would appear that human sensibilities are nearly equal, that the same high or low value is set upon human life everywhere among peoples of equal civilization, however different the modes and customs by which the feeling is expressed.

If the question of demoralization in America be taken in another form, if it be asked if it is progressive, if America as compared with herself is worse than she was – I think I am well enough informed to answer – and

I must confess that she is worse, much worse; that she degenerates in morals and manners, manifestly and clearly – I have not a doubt of it.

You have also heard it said that the principal causes are,

1st the predominant influence of "the people" in public affairs.

2nd the increase of adventurers from all parts,

and 3rd the ultra democratic constitution of the courts of justice, the judges being elected by universal suffrage, for short tenures of offices, dependant on party or popularity, whereby justice is rendered uncertain and people will not resort to the tribunals, but prefer to redress their own grievances in their own way.

I admit the degeneracy in its full length and breadth, but I reject the cause to which it is assigned.

As to the last, the courts and judges – the judges are not elected by universal suffrage in all the states; in 8 or 10, they are appointed by executive and legislative authority, their term is not short, but usually for 6, 8 or 10 years, which is a large share of a man's life after he is old enough to be a judge and not too old to be unfit for one; a judge should have vigor and industry and *lively sympathies* with humanity: cold justice would cut us all off: the increase of disorder is not confined to the states which elect by the people but is common to all; if there is a difference it is in favor of the states which elect: but this arises from other causes: some of the northern states which elect, are the best behaved in the Union and some of the middle and southern which appoint are the worst behaved. But in fact the elective judiciary is yet in its infancy; it is on its trial; it has not had time to tell on the public morals [sic] and you may rest assured that whoever expresses an opinion on this subject for or against the system, takes his opinion from preconceived notions, theories, and not from experience and the study of facts.

In regard to the 2nd cause, the increase of adventures, they do increase and swell the number of disorderly persons, but not to such an extent as to tell perceptibly on the national character.

And as to the 1st cause the share which "the people" have in affairs, it was the same from the beginning; they have always had the preponderance, they have received no important accessions of power, or influence, some small property qualifications which existed at first have been removed, but the increase of number at the polls from this source is not great, and such is the distribution of property that if those restrictions were restored they could exclude very few from the polls.

Had the increased power of the people from this source been all bad, very bad, it would not go for much, but it was not all bad: and the disorders are not most among non property holders; they do not prevail most in the class which would be excluded from power by any property qualification which ever existed in America, *or which now exists in England.*

These disorders occur most *among those who in Europe would not be called "the people" but a middle or better class.*

If these things be so, and I believe they are facts and fairly stated, it follows that the three causes stated will not account for, nor help much to account for, *progressive* demoralization.

Now, I beg you to look at the subject from another point of view.

Great changes have occurred since you were there: America was then a large area, the parts were remote, there was but little and slow intercourse between them – different ideas and habits prevailed in different localities, the parts scarcely knew each other.

Now, all is changed; brought together by steam and the telegraph and for 6 mo[nth]s of the year, the country is concentrated at Washington.

The Govt is there and has grown *big*; the Congress sits more than half the time; it has a large commerce to regulate, money to spend, with patronage and power.

A great throng of people is drawn round it: many thousands, who come and go, and go and come quickly from all parts of the country – keeping up a lively intercourse with the people. The prevailing spirit and habits of the Govt, and of Congress, are naturally imbibed by this throng and thus spread over the country.

The Congress at length breaks up and goes back to the people, each member with his congressional spirit and habits.

Near one half this body is bred in the slave states: trained in habits of self will, the quick hand, ready and violent action: no other system would enable one man to hold one hundred in direct and absolute control: the quick and fearless hand, is better for this than courts and judges and law books.

With this spirit and these habits the South meets the North in Congress and in the government; violence begets violence, attacks stirs up defense, and the northern soon becomes as fierce as the southern.

Every body knows that slavery has introduced the pistol and the knife into Congress; ancient senators brought their armed slaves to the Forum, and did not conceal them; togas were without pockets and pantaloons were not invented, but the modern senator stuffs his coat and trousers' pockets with arms and is not ashamed to use them himself, that which the Roman thought might be done by the hand of a slave, is done by the hand of the modern master.[187]

The spirit of violence born on the plantation is thus like poison introduced into the heart of the nation at Washington, and flows into the arteries
and out into all the veins, tainting the whole system.

When the hot season comes, the Govt, the Congress and the south come
north and reassemble at all the resorts, sea-sides, springs, great hotels
and places of relaxation.

It becomes fashionable and looks lucky and jaunty to carry a pistol
and a knife, cock the hat on one side, sport cigars and kid gloves – he's
not afraid, not he; he can help himself, he is independent of judges and
constables – they are for women and weak people – he can take care of
himself, he is a sovereign, and delights in a row. But of course he is on
the straight road to barbarism; marching to the rear, and will soon be in
the place of dishonor.

Slavery is the cause, I do not say the sole cause, but cause enough
obvious and certain, to produce the progressive demoralization you have
indicated.

Probably 7 cases out of 10, of the lawless violence which disgrace the
nation and disgust the world, do not occur among "the people" but among
the young or middle aged and pretentious persons, who call themselves
gentlemen, and think themselves best qualified to participate in affairs
and even to govern; it is they who despise the "people" and speak of
them with contempt, unless seeking for office, and then no adulation of
the people is too gross.

But the people is really and truly pretty well behaved, and though
you may meet with crooks who seeing these evils and not perceiving the
cause of them, ascribe them to universal suffrage, elective judges and the
influence of the people, be assured my friend they are totally mistaken.

It is not the people who are corrupting the manners and morals, it [is]
the leaders who corrupt the people.

I am satisfied, abundantly satisfied, that the evils we lament do not
spring from democratic institutions, nor from the largest liberty: on the
contrary, seeing how little of governing we have, and how much voluntary
restraint is necessary in the people to preserve a decent appearance
in general, and tolerable security, and that this exists in the presence
[of] the corrupting and enormous influence of slavery and in the midst
of a prosperity which is anomalous in its magnitude and in its general
diffusion among all classes – a thing in itself more trying to human virtue
than calamity – seeing these things renews my faith in the people, and
my confidence in free and elective institutions.

I rely on "the people" to do, what nothing else could do, which is to exterminate slavery.

Under any other system, with slavery deep rooted and wealthy as it is, it would rally round the central power, seize it and hold it, perpetuating power and itself.

But labor is the property of the people; they know its value and its power, and are determined that it shall not be dishonored but shall be free and respected.

This is a power which works slow, but it is this alone which holds slavery in check and will finally conquer it, and with the diminution and disappearance of the disturbing cause we may anticipate a diminution of its effects.

If we ever get back to a better condition of things, and the spirit of violence becomes quenched, we shall owe it alone to "the people," to their great influence and predominance in public affairs.

I for one am not discouraged, and I believe that those who study the case and are capable of tracing effects to their causes, will see nothing in the existing disorders to the discredit of free institutions, but will perceive that *universal suffrage* is the sole possible remedy.

(written en route at different places)

Ever yours,

N. W. B.

Beinecke Rare Book and Manuscript Library, Yale University, Uncat MSS 324; also available as Bonnel copy, MS Vault Tocqueville, D II a, folder "Bonnel's copies of letters from Americans to Tocqueville."

SECTION E

Letters between Tocqueville and His French and Other Correspondents

Introduction

The letters selected in this section cover the period 1847 to 1857 and were exchanged between Tocqueville and some of his closest friends such as Gustave de Beaumont, Louis de Kergorlay, Jean-Jacques Ampère, Arthur de Gobineau (author of the controversial *Essai sur l'inégalité des races humaines*), Nassau Senior (a well-known nineteenth-century British economist), and the Count and Countess de Circourt. Throughout the 1850s, Tocqueville attended the *salon* hosted by the Countess de Circourt and he exchanged a lengthy correspondence with the Count de Circourt, mostly concerning diplomatic affairs.

The selections from the letters included in this section touch upon many of the themes to be found in the correspondence between Tocqueville and his American friends and acquaintances after 1840. In his letters to Beaumont, for example, Tocqueville's worries about his investments in America loomed large and he also made references to the immigration of large numbers of Germans who arrived in American without any knowledge or familiarity with the traditions of liberty and self-government. The letters received from Adolphe de Circourt – for the most part written against the backdrop of the Crimean War that had brought England and France into conflict with Russia – confirmed Tocqueville's growing sense that, as the 1850s progressed, the United States was increasingly acting as an expansionist power, ready to intervene in the affairs of the old world and often in a reckless manner. These letters also echoed the news he was receiving about the potentially dangerous turn of domestic events in the United States as the country edged ever closer to the break-up of the Union.

The most interesting exchanges translated in this section are arguably those with Jean-Jacques Ampère and Arthur de Gobineau. From the outset, Tocqueville was deeply troubled by the racial theories of Gobineau and he went to great lengths to ensure that the latter fully understood the nature of his objections. Having just received Gobineau's *Essay on the Inequality of Human Races*, he wrote; "I have a great prejudice against what appears to me to be your main idea. I confess that this seems to me to belong to the family of materialist theories and to be one of the most dangerous of its kind, because it is the fatality of constitution applied not only to individuals but to those collections of individuals called *races* and which are still alive."[1] Tocqueville repeated these objections to many of his other correspondents and it is clear that, upon their first acquaintance, he had grave doubts about Gobineau's intellectual seriousness.[2] These fragments confirm Tocqueville's hostility to Gobineau's theses and also locate this hostility in the context of the United States. Gobineau's pursuit of personal recognition as a thinker is countered by Tocqueville's assertion that his ideas will only be taken up by the supporters of slavery and that, despite support from the pulpit, his theories must be seen as being inescapably in opposition to the core beliefs of Christianity.

J.-J. Ampère was not only an inveterate traveler but also someone who became one of Tocqueville's closest and most devoted friends. He visited the United States from September 1851 to May 1852, stopping in many of the places visited by Tocqueville and meeting some of the people whom Tocqueville had met on his own voyage in the early 1830s. For his part, Ampère did not hide the fact that his interest in the New World had been awoken by a reading of *Democracy in America*. "Every day, every hour spent in the United States," he wrote to Tocqueville, "was a commentary upon your work, a verification of your thoughts." Accordingly, it was to Tocqueville that Ampère's *Promenade en Amérique* was dedicated.[3]

The most intriguing of Ampère's encounters was with John C. Spencer, author of a preface to the first American edition of *Democracy in America* and a correspondent of Tocqueville. Ampère introduced his account of this discussion by noting that Americans were almost universally agreed that on one thing Tocqueville had been mistaken: the possibility of a tyranny of the majority was unfounded and greatly exaggerated.[4] On this view, the ever-changing nature of majority opinion ensured that no "lasting tyranny" could be established on the soil of the New World. Spencer himself attributed Tocqueville's error to the peculiar political circumstances during his stay: namely, the support of the majority for General Jackson's populist measures. Ampère, however, was not convinced by Spencer's argument. That the oppressed could themselves become one day the oppressors was no safeguard for liberty. Moreover, the new majority might simply continue to voice many of the opinions of the previous majority. This was especially true in the states of the South where freedom of expression on the subject of slavery did not exist. Tocqueville, Ampère consequently affirmed, had been right to diagnose the existence of a "radical infirmity" existing at the heart of American society: "the possible tyranny of number where numbers counted for everything."[5]

Not surprisingly, there was much in Ampère's account that echoed the ideas of Tocqueville. Like so many visitors before him, he saw the importance of religion in American life and recognized the place attributed to hard work in individual success. He was surprised by the relative sophistication and European character of American cultural life. But he saw two problems looming on the near horizon. The first was that of keeping the Union intact. Having witnessed the "hideous scene" of seeing slaves sold at market, he observed that nothing could justify slavery and that all the talk of "humane" masters changed none of this. Secondly, Ampère wondered what foreign adventures would be produced by the growing sense among Americans themselves of their own superiority. Here he was clearly thinking of American expansionist designs on Mexico and Cuba. But his broader concern was that territorial expansion would pose problems for the federal system of government and that it would change the character of America.

Tocqueville's response to Ampère also reveals his continuing fascination with life in America and an eagerness to learn of what had changed there since his visit. Elsewhere we see the re-appearance of themes addressed in *Democracy in America*, most notably the connection between politics and religion. We glimpse Tocqueville's enduring interest in the mores of Americans, especially young Americans. But these letters also reveal his devotion to his American friends, especially the Childes, and the depth of friendship evoked by memories of his own visit to North America. Finally, we again are witness to his increasing fears about the future of the Union. As Tocqueville neared his own end, America – the *puer robustus* – edged ever closer to the abyss of civil war.

195. Alexis de Tocqueville to Louis de Kergorlay[6]

Clairoix par Compiègne (Oise),
October 18, 1847

[. . .] I am delighted to hear you say that the politicians whom you meet generally share your view on the situation in Germany. Two days ago in Paris I saw an Englishmen of great distinction whose name is Senior.[7] He has just returned from Germany. I conversed with him and was delighted to learn that he appeared to have had the same impressions of Prussia as you. At least, this is what I was able to judge. For me this is a serious guarantee that you are on the right track. The difficulty will be to make this visible to the French reader and to paint him a clear picture of a state of society and of mind that is so different not only from what we imagine but, above all, from what our feelings about ourselves lead us to imagine. The great difficulty of the subject is not our ignorance but the natural prejudice arising from the contemplation of our country and the memories of our history. Unfortunately, on this matter I can give you no advice, except constantly to return upon yourself and to ask yourself what you were naturally led to think about Germany before studying it; to be aware of the path you took in moving from your instinctive to your reasoned opinions and to attempt to make your readers follow the same path. I am sure that this must be your goal. Only the author himself can be the judge of this question. Is it necessary to explain the differences and resemblances that the two countries may display or simply speak in such a way as to make them evident? I do not know. In my own work on America, I almost always followed the second method. Although I rarely spoke of France in that book, I did not write a page without thinking of her and without always having her, as it were, before my eyes. And above all, what I tried to highlight in the United States and to explain was less a complete picture of that foreign society than the contrasts and resemblances with our own. It was always, either through opposition or analogy with the one, that I endeavored to present a fair and, above all, interesting image of the other. I say this not to give you an example to follow, but as useful advice. In my opinion, the return that I constantly made to France, without making it known, was one of the main causes of the success of the book.

With regard to religious passions, you pose me a question[8] which, I believe, is insoluble; that is to say, not amenable to resolution through recourse to a general and absolute truth. I think it indisputable that political liberty has sometimes deadened and sometimes enlivened religious passions. This has depended upon many circumstances: on the nature of religions, on the age reached by either the religious passion or the political passion when they met each other; because for the passions, as for everything else in the world, there is a pattern of growth, virility, and decline. When religious passion was declining and political passion was initially rising, the second led us to forget the first one. These circumstances, and many others which I do not mention, can serve to explain the enormous differences presented in this respect by time and location. If, however, it was necessary, over and above these particular cases, to find what one may regard as the most common and general truth in this matter, I would be inclined to agree with the views of your Germans rather than with your own views. As a general thesis I believe that political liberty enlivens religious passions more than it extinguishes them. I believe, first of all, that there are far more family resemblances between political passions and religious passions than you suppose. On both sides, general, and in some degree immaterial, interests are kept in sight; on both sides, an ideal of human society is pursued, a certain perfecting of the human species, the picture of which raises our souls above the contemplation of minor, private interests and carries them away. For my part, I understand far more easily a man animated at one and the same time by religious passion and political passion than by political passion and the passion for well-being, for example. The first two can exist together and may be found in the same soul, but not the second two. There is another reason, no less general and no less important and perhaps a more conclusive one, which explains how the two passions go together and stimulate each other to their mutual benefit. It lies in the service that they are often called upon to render to each other. Free institutions are often the natural and, sometimes, indispensable instruments of religious passions. Almost all the efforts that the moderns have made towards liberty have been made because of the need to demonstrate or defend their religious beliefs. It was religious passion that drove the Puritans to America and led them to want to govern themselves there. The two revolutions in England were carried out so as to obtain liberty of conscience. It was this same need which led the Huguenot nobility of sixteenth-century France to incline toward republican opinions. In all these cases, it was religious passions that aroused political passions and political passions served the free development of other passions. If religious passions were never constrained in their expression, this effect would possibly not be produced. But they are almost always hampered. When they have obtained satisfaction in everything they desired, this effect may equally cease to be produced. Your theory may perhaps be applicable to a society that is religious without being troubled by controversies or religious passions. It is possible then that public affairs will gradually and almost exclusively absorb the attention of citizens. And yet I am still not certain of this, at least if the public political circumstances are not very lively. Most often it is the case that the agitation created and kept alive at the bottom of our souls by political liberty arouses and stirs up the religious ferment which might remain alive in the country. In my opinion, this is what is happening in America and about which you have spoken to me. In my view, in America the passing of time and the increase of well-being . . . have deprived the religious element of three-quarters of its original strength. Nevertheless, whatever remains of it is still very lively. Religious people come together, speak to each other, and act in common far more in the United States than anywhere else. I believe that the habits of political liberty and the impetus that liberty has given to everything do play an important role in the particular movement that one perceives at the heart of the religious element still existing in the country. I believe that, without being able to give back to it the all-powerful quality it once had, these circumstances preserve it and give to it all the strength that it might still have. We must be careful not to confuse political liberty with some of the effects it sometimes produces. Once it is well established and operates in a peaceful environment, it encourages people to pursue and develop a taste for well-being, to care and be passionate about making a fortune. And, as a consequence, these tastes, these needs, and these cares extinguish religious passions. But these are distant and secondary outcomes of political liberty which harm political passion as much as religious passion.

This is what I have to say on this particular point which, moreover, I am far from having examined with all the care that its importance requires. The only absolute truth that I see on this subject is that there is no absolute truth. It is best therefore, in my view, to concentrate upon the examination of particular circumstances. [. . .]

Farewell. I embrace you with all my heart.
Write to me soon.
[Alexis]

196. Alexis de Tocqueville to Jean-Jacques Ampère[9]

Paris, October 6, 1851

My dear friend,

We were very happy the other day to receive your first letter from America, posted from Boston and dated September 13.[10] We were beginning, not exactly to be worried about you, but to be surprised that we had not received news from you. You have had a successful voyage and are happy with what you have seen thus far: this is good. I shall be extremely curious and interested to speak with you on your return about the country that you are visiting in order to learn what you saw in the same way as I did and what you saw differently from me; to learn what has changed over the past twenty years, not only with regard to the superficial and material aspect of society, but concerning its very foundations. It is impossible that the temperament of the people has not changed in the midst of such rapid growth.

But it is not about America that you want me to speak at the moment. It is about France, your friends and your acquaintances. [. . .] Your *escapade* is still little known. All those who learn of it are thrown into the most profound astonishment, as if America was still three months from France and as if you were visiting the antipodes. Villemain asked me with concern *if you were grieving about something.* I have answered that I was only aware of your being troubled by the fact that you do not know America.[11] [. . .]

I would very much like to know in which direction you are going to trace your steps. The United States are so well-known to me and are still so present to my mind after twenty years that you would not be able to go anywhere where I could not easily follow you in my imagination.

Farewell, my dear friend. I embrace you with all my heart. My wife sends you a thousand affectionate wishes.

A. de Tocqueville

197. Jean-Jacques Ampère to Alexis de Tocqueville

New York, November 7, 1851

My dear friend,

I returned here a few days ago after a trip of a thousand miles that, from Quebec, took me to Illinois and Cincinnati. I was extremely interested by my voyage but rather tired by it, suffering at one and the same time from all my illnesses: of the throat and the stomach. I therefore have not hesitated to rest up this winter, all the more since several days of predicted cold weather have convinced me that this temperature does not suit me.

I have had several very sad moments here. I did not see Mr. Sedgwick again, whom I had believed to be in the country, and at this moment, I have just received news that caused me deep and profound grief: the death of the Viscountess de Noailles, toward whom I felt a sincere affection.[12]

Here I have had several interesting meetings and have made some interesting acquaintances. I went to Albany, carrying your letter to Mr. Spencer. He appreciated this gesture and showered me with signs of enthusiasm toward you. I had very fine weather on the Hudson and was satisfied with this trip, as I was with all the parts of my journey. I came here to find new ideas and notions: I have found more of them than I had anticipated. My curious mind, faced with a constellation of new facts, is enjoying them to the fullest.

I do not dare ask you to write to me, as I sense how much you must be absorbed by present events.

However, a few words would be very kind.

Farewell, my dear friend. I will head for the south via Philadelphia and Washington. As ever and as always, my affection.

J.-J. Ampère

198. Jean-Jacques Ampère to Alexis de Tocqueville

New York, November 12, 1851

My dear friend,

Hardly had I sent you my letter than yours arrived here. I am extremely grateful, as I know how gloomy and preoccupied you must be.

Since you wrote to me, an event has occurred which perhaps might change something of the deplorable certitude of which you have spoken to me.[13] But I am not really informed about the situation, being so far away and not reading the French newspapers; they are very hard to come by here. At the *reading-room*, a place very well provided with English journals and American newspapers, they receive only *La Presse* and only once a month.[14]

On the other hand, I speak with many distinguished, or at least well-informed, people. Each day I learn much. And I also would be extremely delighted to converse about all of this with you and to talk about what has changed. Nothing of substance, I think: the rule of the majority, the energy of individual efforts, the strength of associations to do what elsewhere is done by the government, all this remains in its essentials. Each object that I see, each daily incident, is a commentary upon and a demonstration of your book. The most important changes that have occurred since your visit result above all from the railroads which expand every day and which have already had such an influence upon the development of the East, the West and the northern part of the Union. A more profound change, and one which transforms the fundamental policies of the United States, is, in my opinion, a disposition to interfere in the affairs of Europe and this is beginning to prevail. The enthusiasm for M. Kossuth is important as a demonstration of this new tendency, so contrary to the old direction. On this subject there is much exaggeration in the newspapers which dream of an anti-absolutist crusade and speak of bombarding Saint-Petersburg. But there is also something real about it, and M. Sedgwick believes that this new principle in the politics of the country exists. It is a sequel to the attitude that began with the war with Mexico, but it grows every day and takes on a very unusual character.

I am inclined not to be of your opinion on the religious future of the United States. Thus far I do not see that propensity toward philosophy and Catholicism, but it is a question that I still need to study in detail.

Farewell, dear friend. Please express my warmest respects to Madame de Tocqueville.

J.-J. Ampère

199. Jean-Jacques Ampère to Alexis de Tocqueville

New Orleans, January 23, 1852

My dear friend,

I thank you affectionately for having written to me. After what has just happened, I was in great need of being reassured by yourself, since one of the newspapers announced your arrest.[15]

Now, I think of the moral suffering that you are enduring in seeing the ideas of true liberty so alien to France, the parties that divide her, and brutal force triumphing in December as in February.[16] Indeed, I believe that under the regime which is beginning there will be no place in what will call itself an assembly for a sincere friend of liberty; but for you there will be better things to do than to be there. I rejoice in advance at seeing you working and at working with you at Tocqueville. My impression is that if something can give a chance to constitutional monarchy in the future, it is what is happening now; because such a monarchy will appear as a return to a normal situation. Faced with a real danger to society, France can deliver herself up to a master who will defend her, but sooner or later comes weariness. However that may be, happy are those who, like you, in writing history, can await the hour to make history! Here the public does not understand and adheres to the view that the French are not ready for a better government. The politicians whom I have seen in Washington say that it is perhaps necessary for anarchist passions to be kept in check by a dictatorship. At such a time, I am not sorry to leave the United States. I believe that I have learnt something here. I have been to the North and the West and now I am in the South. Everywhere I have lived with the most distinguished people, talked extensively, examined and received a great deal of information. Only the temperature displeases me.

I hope to find warmth in Havana, and warm myself in the sun and rest. Perhaps I will also go to Jamaica, before returning for my courses in May. My sincere respects to Madame de Tocqueville. With fondest love.

J.-J. Ampère

200. Adolphe de Circourt[17] to Alexis de Tocqueville

La Celle Saint-Cloud, August 25, 1853

My dear Sir,

[...] Whereas among us peace is wanted almost unanimously, almost with passion, by statesmen of all persuasions, by the professions and all classes, in England the party of war gets stronger by the day in Parliament, in the Cabinet and even in the City. [...] Nevertheless, the violence that would be directed against Russia is, of necessity, compensated for by a disastrous complacency toward the United States. The latter are getting bolder at intervening in the most undisguised manner in the affairs of the old world. The dispatch of Mr. Soulé to Madrid is a scandal;[18] his official statements present a foreboding of his instructions; and I confess to being astonished at seeing the English Cabinet think so much about Moldavia when concerning itself so little with Cuba.

[...] I have finished with great pleasure my reading of the sketches of M. Ampère. He has not shaken me from my aversion to slavery and my conviction that this national scourge, raised to the level of a fundamental principle by self-interested sophists, will be the cause of the political degradation, perhaps even the future dissolution, of the southern States of the Union. But it is impossible to touch upon this question with greater judgment or wisdom than M. Ampère has done.

[...] This Mr. Soulé, about whom I have spoken to you, sees many people in Paris and the vicinity. He modestly announces his mission in Madrid as having as its goal the *purchase* by the United States of the island of Cuba. He is a demagogue, an enthusiastic supporter of slavery, and a man who affects to speak well, if ever there was one.

[...] I remain, with the highest and most affectionate consideration, your devoted,

Adolphe de Circourt

201. Alexis de Tocqueville to Gustave de Beaumont[19]

November 3, 1853

My dear friend,

I forewarned you in my letter that I do not reckon on sending back the books to Paris before the 10th. Thus you have in advance authorization to keep Haxthausen for the time necessary to read it carefully.[20] It merits this attention from everybody, but especially from you.[21] Although extremely boring, it is however very instructive and throws great light on the Slavs. There is certainly in the mores he describes something which characterizes this race and that you need to know about. Gobineau has just sent me a big book written by him intended to prove that all the events occurring in this world are explained by the difference of races, a theory more appropriate to a horse dealer than a statesman.[22] I do not believe anything of it at all. Nevertheless, I think that there is in each nation, whether it comes from race or rather the education of the centuries, something very tenacious, perhaps of a permanent character, which combines itself with all the episodes of a nation's destiny and which can be perceived through all its fortunes and at all epochs of its history. Above all, this is true of semi-civilized nations who have lived in isolation for a long time. Properly to identify the specific characteristics which distinguish their physiognomy from the mass of humankind is a necessary condition for speaking accurately about them. In addition, in Haxthausen is presented a very extraordinary picture that on its own compensates for the boredom of reading his work: that of a people still in the infancy of serfdom and communal property and nevertheless enjoying in part the institutions and, even in some respects, sharing the mentality of the democratic and civilized times in which we live. On one side, the glebe of the tenth century, on the other, the perpetual movement of place and state that characterizes the Americans. For the rest, what makes our author so boring is not only the faculty – with which he is blessed – of writing in a diffuse, prolix, and tiring manner, but also the natural and inevitable tedium that cannot fail to arise from looking at the lower levels of Russian society, where everything is perfectly uniform in terms of ideas, laws, habits, down to the most minute details of the exterior appearance of objects. It makes one think of an America without enlightenment and liberty. A democratic society to be frightened of.[23]

[...] I only have time to embrace you and to ask you to speak of us to Madame de Beaumont by recalling us warmly to her memory,

A. de Tocqueville

202. Adolphe de Circourt to Alexis de Tocqueville

La Celle-Saint-Cloud, November 9, 1853

My dear Sir,

[...] It is truly a pleasure for me to be able to tell you that my wife has received a detailed letter from the Countess Kuczkowka, sister-in-law of Florence Soltyk.[24] It would not be possible to make a better beginning to real life and the life of a family than this poor young girl has done in Galicia. She has been extremely well received by her mother-in-law and the other relatives of her husband. She lives in her beautiful chateau in Balice and seems to be developing a taste for the countryside; until now, she and her husband have been getting on well. Mr. Childe received this good news at the very moment that he disembarked from America, bringing Edward with him who, from all appearances, has decided to lead a life of leisure as a club man rather than a *lounger* on Broadway – what a sad alternative!

[...] Please give my respectful regards to Madame de Tocqueville and accept my sincere wishes for your health, your work, and happiness.

Very faithfully yours,
A.C.

203. Alexis de Tocqueville to Madame de Circourt

Saint-Cyr, November 26, 1853

Madame,

[...] Among all this bad news I was extremely delighted by the news conveyed by M. de Circourt about the excellent reception of Madame de Soltyk in Poland. I see that this young woman has every chance of happiness, if only she were willing to help herself a little. But will she want it? This is not impossible. The young Americans are such strange creatures! Capable of committing the most audacious and stupid things in order to gain a husband, and then of carrying out the wisest resolutions to the end. It is true that the latter, while completely preserving the faults of her country, might well have gained some of those of our own. This good news delighted me because of her parents to whom I wrote immediately to express my joy. They deserve to have a little pleasure after the cruel and undeserved trials of last winter. I have yet to forgive the world for the ridiculous severity of its judgments on this occasion and whenever I think about it I am disposed to have more friendship for Mr. and Mrs. Childe. [...]

Farewell, Madame. Here you have a rather uninteresting letter; but what else can you expect from a solitary man? [...] Please accept the expression of my sentiments of respectful friendship. Madame de Tocqueville wishes me to recall her particularly to you.

A. de Tocqueville

204. Alexis de Tocqueville to Gustave de Beaumont

Bonn, August 6, 1854

My dear friend,

We are worried about Antonin[25] and hope that you will let us know the results of the examination as soon as you know them yourself. [...] We are still in Bonn, where I would continue to find myself in excellent health, were it not for the fact that, a week ago, Marie went down with acute rheumatism in the joint of her wrist and the thumb of her right hand. She cannot make the slightest use of this hand without crying. [...] We have found here several families who informally receive us among them and whose manners please us well. Private life in Germany clearly has its attractive sides. But what poor citizens! When I see the long practice of absolute power, the softness of this power, the traditions of liberty so absent from mores, the centralization, the widespread passion for positions and dependency everywhere, I ask myself if they will ever be very different from what they are today. Moreover, one can sense that the feeling of *instability* about everything seems general.

The other day I had a very interesting conversation with a Prussian who had just returned from the United States, where he had been ambassador for ten years.[26] He astounded me by saying that last year German emigration to the United States reached the incredible figure of 140, 000 individuals, and that it continues at this level. Formerly, they came only from among the poor; but today they come from the comfortably off and even the rich. I asked him from which parts of the country these people generally came and what motives led them to emigrate. Very few come from Prussia. They number 10, 000 out of 140, 000 Germans. But the former are almost all well-educated and well-off people. The others come mainly from the small states at the centre of Germany and also in large numbers from Baden, from Württemberg and from Bavaria. According to the person with whom I spoke, all these Germans take their ideas with them to the United States and, to a certain extent, preserve them there. They retain their language. They do not mix with the natives of the country. In general, they stay together and, although, through imitation and especially in the second generation, they finish up adopting a part of American political habits, they still remain a distinct and foreign component. In brief, what he said confirmed what I had always thought, namely that the rapid introduction of foreigners into the United States and thus into the English race is the greatest danger faced by America and what makes the final success of democratic institutions still an unresolved issue. I forgot to say that my interlocutor attributed the departure of most of the families who today leave Germany for America to the insistent invitations sent by their parents and friends who had already emigrated. But what *German* cause led the latter to emigrate? This was what I could not get him explain clearly and is most important to know.

[. . .] My wife received a letter from your wife for which she was eager to express her thanks herself. But her infirmity, as you will understand, makes all writing impossible at this time. Please explain this to Madame de Beaumont and, as always, pass on our warmest friendship to her. Farewell, dear friend. I embrace you.

Alexis

205. Adolphe de Circourt to Alexis de Tocqueville

La Celle-Saint-Cloud, November 26, 1854

My dear Sir,

[. . .] The attitude of America causes [the English] grave concern.[27] It is here, the trades people say today, that lies the most serious and the most dangerous question. The treaty concluded with the Russian court brings forth a complete fusion of commercial interests between the two countries, at a minimum a defensive league in matters relating to commercial navigation.[28] Mr. Mason[29] and Mr. Buchanan say loudly that by spring their country could well be at war with England. Given such a danger, the army and the diplomats are making enormous efforts in the Crimea, in Vienna, and in Berlin; but fortune seems reluctant to help them. [. . .]

Please accept the expression of my high consideration and my entire devotion.

[A. de Circourt]

206. Adolphe de Circourt to Alexis de Tocqueville

La Celle-Saint-Cloud, November 1, 1855

My dear Sir,

[. . .] If America had a government now, I would regard a break with England as both near and certain. But for as long as Pierce[30] and his miserable government are running things, it is probable that matters will remain at the level of threats, moral antipathy, the exchange of insults, and mockery. It is nevertheless a real diversion in Russia's favor. England runs the risk of perishing if the bread and cotton of America were suddenly no longer available to it, if American privateers were to intercept its commerce with her colonies. And it is with this that it is openly threatened. Frankly, we can no longer have any sympathy for England. Our master[31] seems very decided not to allow himself, under any circumstances, to be drawn into following England into a break with America. In his fashion, he takes an *interest* in Spain, rather as the Moncades of the past concerned themselves with the Babets.[32] But at no price does he wish to guarantee the independence of Cuba. His treaty with Espartero,[33] it is said, is signed, a treaty with which England will have nothing to do with. For a subsidy of between 40–50 millions, Espartero will provide 25, 000 Spaniards, not however to be stationed in Crimea but to relieve from Rome and from the south of France an equal number of French troops that can be sent to the Orient. You will see that we are returning to the principles of 1804.[34] But Espartero wants France to forbid America from acquiring both Cuba and Haiti. Now, to break with America, which alone can preserve us from famine and from the revolutionary consequences of famine, cannot be done. The chorus leaders of the government party would shout it from the rooftops. [. . .]

Very faithfully yours,
A. de Circourt

207. Arthur de Gobineau[35] to Alexis de Tocqueville

Tehran, March 20, 1856

Sir,

[. . .] I follow with great interest the impression produced by my book in different places. In Germany where, in general, people are more concerned with the intrinsic truth than we are, it seems that they have been a little shocked but that they persevere. I there have made three precious friendships. In France, people ask whether I am a legitimist, a republican, a supporter of the imperial regime, for or against the L'Univers,[36] but they are not pleased to see that I do not prove that the French are the leading people of the world. [. . .] In America, the situation is stranger than anywhere else. Three distinguished persons, whom I do not know, have done me the honor of writing to me.[37] One of them has translated the entire systematic part of my work and asks for my advice on the second edition that he intends to publish, the first being almost sold out. I have not seen the first edition, but from what he has said to me, he has kept everything which establishes the permanence of the races and the effects of miscegenation, that is to say, the essential part of my system. He did not dare to present to the public the part explaining the consequences. He did not want to tell them that from the moment that two races are unequal, marriage with an inferior race would entail degeneration. At the same time, I have an inkling that he did not hide from them that the Anglo-Saxon family of the United States is superior to the Mexicans and that this proposition has been accepted without difficulty. What he assuredly did not translate was my chapter on the United States. Whatever may be the case, he tells me that even the abolitionist newspapers recognize the exactitude of my principles. Thus, this very practical nation, despite these alterations and incoherencies, has succeeded in turning a purely scientific theory into a hefty volume that the parties throw at each other. This does not trouble me, but what does disturb me is that you, Sir, who likes me, maintain a doubt about the morality of my conception. [...]

Farewell, Sir. We send you and Madame de Tocqueville all our tender and affectionate regards. Think of us and of the devoted respect that you know I have for you.

Count A. de Gobineau

208. Adolphe de Circourt to Alexis de Tocqueville

Paris, June 7, 1856

My dear Sir,

[...] What is happening in America is very serious.[38] England will have difficulty avoiding war in preserving its honor. America takes upon itself the vengeance of the Russians, and the injustice with which British interests are treated in the West is payment for the injustice with which English interests have treated the Oriental populations. Such is the march of Providence. It does nothing to prevent evil; it does everything to punish it. [...] I shall write to you from Germany and will follow your instructions most faithfully, if I have a chance again to visit that pleasant city, Bonn. Next Thursday, I shall be in Geneva. My ... [39]

Adolphe de Circourt

209. Adolphe de Circourt to Alexis de Tocqueville

Geneva, June 15, 1856

My dear Sir,

[...] I would ask you to thank Mrs. Childe on my behalf for her news from Paris and her husband for the information on America, which I owe to their kindness. The argument between Pierce and Palmerston seems to be reaching a very un-chivalrous conclusion. Moreover, the struggle, if it has been postponed this time, will only be delayed. It seems to me impossible that such opposed principles and such conflicting interests can be settled without a trial of force, and that the Isthmus of Panama should be auctioned without a fight.[40] [...]

My respectful regards to Madame de Tocqueville; once more, the sincere expression of my sympathy and good wishes.

A. C.

210. Alexis de Tocqueville to Madame de Circourt

Tocqueville, near Saint-Pierre-L'Eglise
(Manche)
July 5, 1856

Dear Madame,

[...] The very day that I left Paris I received the news of an event that, even in my great sadness,[41] deeply grieved me: the death of Mrs. Childe, whose illness I had only heard about two days before.[42] For many years, Mrs. Childe showed me a friendship that I was very happy to return. In according me greater confidence than she habitually displayed in her relations with the world, she enabled me to appreciate the many genuine qualities that she possessed. People were often unfair in the judgments they made of her and I will always hold her memory in the greatest esteem and affection. [...]

Farewell, Madame. Please believe in all my sentiments of sincere and respectful devotion.

A. de Tocqueville

211. Alexis de Tocqueville to Arthur de Gobineau

Tocqueville, near Saint-Pierre-L'Eglise
(Manche)
July 30, 1856

My dear friend,

[...] You know that I cannot reconcile myself to your system in any way and that my ideas are so *obstinate* in this regard that the very reasons with which you are trying to make them acceptable to me deepen my opposition, which only remains *latent* because of my affection for you. In your last but one letter, you compared yourself to a doctor who informs his patient that he is mortally ill and you say: what is immoral about that?

I reply that even though the act itself might not be immoral in itself, it can only produce immoral and pernicious consequences. [...] If the English and the Americans are interested in you, this will only be a reflection of the ephemeral views of parties. This is so with the Americans whom you mention and who have translated your book and are known to me as the devoted leaders of the anti-abolitionist party. They translated the part of your book which agrees with their prejudices, the part which tends to prove that the blacks belong to a separate and inferior race; but they said nothing of the part of your book which would lead one to think that the Anglo-Saxon race, like all the others, is declining. Therefore I think that a book of real merit such as yours will occupy a considerable place in the minds of thinkers everywhere but, with the exception perhaps of Germany, it is not destined to excite the mass of readers [...]

> With many friendly regards,
> A. de Tocqueville

212. Alexis de Tocqueville to Nassau Senior[43]

Tocqueville, September 4, 1856

My dear Senior,

[...] I must say that America is a *puer robustus*. Yet I cannot desire, as many persons do, its dismemberment. Such an event would inflict a great wound on the whole human race; for it would introduce war into a great continent from whence it has been banished for more than a century.

The breaking up of the American Union will be a solemn moment in the history of the world. I never met an American who did not feel this, and I believe that it will not be rashly undertaken. There will always be, before actual rupture, a last interval in which one or both parties will draw back. Has not this occurred twice?

> Alexis de Tocqueville

213. Adolphe de Circourt to Alexis de Tocqueville

La Celle, November 4, 1856

My dear Sir,

[...] Ticknor is very worried by the nature of public affairs in America. He thinks that during the administration of Buchanan, the breakup will be forestalled and the explosion suppressed, but that, with the electoral campaign of 1860, the dikes will be breached and a deluge of blood will cover the North as well as the South. [...]

My respectful regards to Madame de Tocqueville; my wife thanks you very much for your kind memento. Very faithfully yours.

[A.C.]

214. Alexis de Tocqueville to Arthur de Gobineau

Tocqueville, January 24, 1857

My dear friend,

[...] Plainly Christianity seeks to make all men brothers and equals. Your doctrine makes them cousins at best whose common father is in the heavens: here there are only victors and vanquished, masters and slaves by right of birth. And this is so true that your doctrines are approved, cited and commented upon by whom? By slave owners and by those who favor the perpetuation of slavery founded upon the fundamental difference of race. I know that at this very moment, there are in the south of the United States Christian priests and perhaps good priests (though they are the owners of slaves) who preach from their pulpit doctrines which are undoubtedly analogous to yours. But be assured that the majority of Christians, comprising those whose interests do not incline, without their knowledge, toward your ideas – be assured, I say, that in this world the majority of Christians cannot have the least sympathy for your doctrines. [...]

A thousand friendly and sincere regards. Please be reassured that I shall not forget about your academic interests.

A. de Tocqueville

215. Adolphe de Circourt to Alexis de Tocqueville

La Celle, October 14, 1857

My dear Sir,

[...] The financial disasters of the United States have not touched the personal fortune of Mr. Ticknor. But those of his wife's brother, a niece, and the husband of a niece have perished in this great shipwreck. But you know of the great stoicism with which Americans accept such catastrophes. Already three people are at work to re-establish their business affairs and it is to be hoped that they will achieve this when the squall has passed. M. Ticknor thinks that Buchanan will not favor the new attempts of the filibusters, will make no effort towards the acquisition of Cuba and will leave Kansas free to give itself a constitution that rejects slavery. *Utinam.*[44]

Adolphe de Circourt

216. Alexis de Tocqueville to Gustave de Beaumont

Tocqueville, November 16, 1857

My dear friend,

I am terribly late in replying. You must forgive me. Assuredly, my silence does not come from a lack of interest in the things that regard you. [...]

I do not need to tell you that all this time I have been greatly preoccupied and often very concerned about our business affairs in America. I do not know if my wife has explained to yours the grounds that we had for hoping that we would escape from this cataclysm without being completely drowned. According to the figures provided by an American friend,[45] whose opinion has in addition been corroborated by that of Mr. Baring (as you know, the head of the leading bank in England), it seems fairly certain that the principal railroad in which we have invested is one of the best in America;[46] that its revenues have not ceased to grow for many years, to the extent that if suddenly, they were to be reduced by half instead of still growing further, it would still have more than was necessary to pay the interest on its redeemable stock (debts which take precedence over all the others). Despite these figures and these assurances, I confess that I live in a state of great anxiety from which I fear that I will not quickly escape. Moreover, in France, too, we will have difficulty in avoiding a crisis that, though dissimilar, will be no less serious. The shortage of money has already had the effect of lowering prices. Everyone is frightened to buy. [...]

Farewell. Remember me very fondly to Madame de Beaumont and be reassured that we are deeply attached to both of you.

Alexis

217. Alexis de Tocqueville to Gustave de Beaumont

Tocqueville, December 6, 1857

My dear friend,

I have received your letter of the 3rd. I should have replied to you earlier. But on the one hand, I have, although not fruitfully, returned to work in earnest and, on the other hand, I wanted to put an end to this awful habit where we seem to write to each other the moment we are about to receive a letter, with the result that we never reply to each other. [. . .]

I have not replied to the pressing questions that your friendship led you to ask in your last but one letter about our business affairs in America; because I think that I explained everything in the letter which crossed with yours. The near totality of the considerable funds that we have in America is held in *bonds* with two railroads: 1. the *Central Michigan Railway*. 2. the *Galena-Chicago*. It is above all in the *Central Michigan* that we have invested. Everything that we have heard said about these railroads, both before we loaned them our money and since, makes us certain that the railroads in question, when the crisis arrived, were regarded as the best on the whole continent and were in a position of great prosperity. You will know that in America, as in Europe, the lenders have a mortgage on the railroad; that they must be paid before giving anything to the shareholders and that, in order for them not to receive interest on their money, it would be necessary, so to speak, for the railroad to yield no return. This is all I know. I see in *The Times* that the *Michigan Railway* is still listed on the Stock Exchange and that the *bonds* are at seventy-five. This leads me to believe that people think that it will survive the crisis which led it to suspend all payments in America. But until we arrive at a day of payment for the period of interest, we cannot know if they will continue or not to pay us. It seems to me that the capital runs no great danger, but a suspension of interest would already be a serious inconvenience in the present and a cause of worry for the future. In brief, although business is improving in America and although I am not as *upset* as I was at first, my anxiety is still considerable and painful. It is not so much the scale of the risk that worries me in this matter but the scale of what is at stake for me. Thus, it is with great impatience that I await direct news from America. Unfortunately, I have few regular correspondents. Sedgwick, who was the best, is dead or dying.[47] Others are absent from the country. I wrote to Sumner (the Senator),[48] who came to see me here this summer. He is a well-known barrister in New York. I do not doubt that he would know much and would be very eager to inform me about what is happening there; but, despite the steamship, it takes a long time to receive a response from the United States and I do not expect this for at least three weeks. This is all that I can tell you for now: the improving business situation, the good health of the railroad itself, the opinion of Baring, all should reassure us a little. But one is not easily reassured when a large part of one's fortune is at stake.

This whole crisis in America has put me in a mood little favorable to work and many times I would have abandoned the subject which preoccupies me were it not for the fact that I become so miserable when, after a certain amount of time, I have done nothing of seeming importance. [. . .]

Farewell. Many warm regards to your dear and lovely wife.

The tragedy of the poor Lamoricière family has affected us greatly.[49] What a persecution by destiny.

[Alexis]

PART II

SPEECHES, ARTICLES, AND
DIPLOMATIC PAPERS

General Introduction

The documents in Part II are drawn from a variety of sources – electoral and parliamentary speeches, academic discourses, private letters, diplomatic exchanges, and newspaper articles – that shed fresh light on the evolution of Tocqueville's views on America after 1840. As with his letters, they provide ample evidence that America never ceased to be an object of inquiry and interest for Tocqueville after the publication of Volume Two of *Democracy in America*. Indeed, their content complements the correspondence published in Part I of our book and in them we see clearly the influence of Tocqueville's exchanges with his American friends and acquaintances after 1840.

Two themes stand out in this regard. The first is Tocqueville's view that France and America made natural allies, especially when faced with the imperial ambitions of Great Britain. The second is Tocqueville's eagerness in the 1840s to cite America as an example of successful, constitutional government from which lessons could be drawn. These lessons included the benefits of federalism, bicameralism, judicial review, and respect for private property.

Nonetheless, America was largely absent from Tocqueville's last book, *The Old Regime and the Revolution* (1856). To understand the nature of feudal rights he turned his attention to Germany. To assess the mentality of the pre-revolutionary French peasantry he delved into the departmental archives at Tours and in Normandy. It was now England, the subject of several visits by Tocqueville,[1] that provided the counterexample of a free and successful polity and also revealed an open and progressive nobility.[2] If a few references to America appeared in Tocqueville's second masterpiece, it was not because of any light that the American Revolution might have shed upon its later French counterpart but, as we have already noted, as part of a common Anglo-American tradition that fascinated Tocqueville. The English and Americans, unlike the French, displayed respect "for the feelings of the majority of their fellow citizens,"[3] and their rulers observed the rule of law. In America, as in England, the traditions of municipal independence were recognized, with the result that individuals "uniting together do everything" and "the towns became almost like independent municipalities."[4]

Comparing the French propensity to centralization with the situation in America, Tocqueville remarked that in the United States "the government is no longer involved in anything." The comparison was extended to cover the decentralized British colonial regime in North America and the centralized regime of French Canada. Tocqueville believed that "it is in the colonies that one can best judge the form of the metropolitan government."[5] In French Canada, the regulatory and overseeing powers of the state were such as to extinguish all individual initiatives. "In Canada," Tocqueville concluded, "at least as long as Canada remained French, equality was joined with absolute government; in the United States it was combined with freedom."[6]

Finally, another important feature of the texts included in Part II of the present volume is worthy of comment. We have seen that in Tocqueville's correspondence from the 1850s the mood changed from one of relative optimism to a certain form of pessimism regarding America's future. What is striking is that this change is not evident in his published writings and speeches from this period. At no point did Tocqueville make known to a wider audience his increasing fears for the Union as the controversy over slavery gathered in intensity in the 1850s. Rather, he was content to share his views only with a few of his closest American friends and chose to remain publicly silent about the disquieting signs of an impending political crisis in America, especially beginning with 1852. We might want to speculate as to why Tocqueville never publicly disclosed his doubts and fears about the country to which he owed so much, but it is safe to assume that we shall never know his hidden reasons for doing it. Nonetheless, what we do know for sure is that in some of these scattered fragments collected here, most notably in the texts written in the 1840s, we see that for all his concerns about the prospects for liberty in America, Tocqueville still retained parts of the optimistic vision that he had absorbed and expressed in the 1830s.

America in the 1840s

General Introduction

In 1838, Tocqueville was elected a member of the *Academy of Moral and Political Sciences*; a year later, he was elected as a deputy to the Chamber of Deputies. In 1844, he became one of the proprietors of a newspaper published in Paris, *Le Commerce*. The two texts below reflect these different aspects of Tocqueville's political career. The first was written as a speech before the Chamber of Deputies, the second as a report to the *Academy of Moral and Political Sciences*. The importance Tocqueville attached to the latter is perhaps best judged by the fact that Tocqueville subsequently republished this text as an appendix to the twelfth French edition of *Democracy in America* (1848).

If Tocqueville's parliamentary career during the 1840s was something of a disappointment to him, on one subject at least he had an important impact. In 1844, he presented a report before parliament on prison reform. The context was one of a perceived increase in lawlessness and of growing fears of popular disorder. In presenting his report, Tocqueville drew extensively upon his earlier investigations in America and, in effect, restated the arguments both for and against the Philadelphia and Auburn systems, opting decisively for what he regarded as a meliorated and slightly relaxed version of the former. There is no need here to rehearse the detailed (and often heated) polemics that took place over this issue, but it was Tocqueville's view that the Philadelphia system of solitary confinement was the more effective and efficient of the two alternatives. He strongly denied that solitary confinement had the deleterious effects upon the minds and bodies of prisoners sometimes imagined by its critics, citing detailed statistics on the death rates and mental health of inmates. Under the

Philadelphia system, there was less evidence of re-offending and, as sentences could be shorter, it was less costly in the long run. The French system, by contrast, he believed to be both punitive and inefficient.[7]

Debate on this issue was not limited to the parliamentary arena. In February 1844, Tocqueville found his proposals for the adoption of the Philadelphia system under challenge from within the *Academy of Moral and Political Sciences*. Again, he denied the charge that solitary confinement was cruel, countering (with a harshness not unknown elsewhere in his writings) that criminals did not have "a divine right" to live in common and that the solitary confinement of inmates prevented the spread of immoral and criminal practices. At a minimum, Tocqueville suggested, we should hope that prison did not make criminals worse, and there was ample evidence from Philadelphia to prove this.[8]

In some respects, however, the most interesting dimension of this exchange related to the thorny issue of the legitimacy of comparison between two countries. Tocqueville's challenger, Charles Lucas, contended that France had little or nothing to learn from the American experience. Tocqueville, to his credit, accepted the legitimacy of the objection, leading him to make the following interesting remark: "With regard to political constitutions, I accept that placing two nations such as France and America in parallel is not without danger. It might not be expedient to transport an institution that works in one to the other. This I accept. But what is at issue here? It is a matter of the physical constitution of man and of his health."[9] The implication was clear. If, for Tocqueville, a criminal was much the same in France and America, the same rule did not apply to their citizens.

Tocqueville's involvement in the publication of *Le Commerce* sheds additional light on the evolution of his views of America in the 1840s. The published prospectus announced the paper's attachment to the defense of political liberty, equality before the law, and constitutional government.[10] It proved not to be a successful enterprise, and within a year Tocqueville ceased his involvement with it. Apart from his own articles, his one significant initiative was an undertaking to publish letters from correspondents abroad. As the newspaper's American correspondent, Tocqueville chose Francis Lieber.[11] Lieber published four short pieces, none of which will have reassured Tocqueville about America's future. Among other things, Lieber detailed mounting political corruption in Washington, D.C. and divisions within the

Protestant churches over the issue of slavery. He also wrote of the political tensions arising from American designs on Oregon, Mexico, and Texas, predicting that the repercussions of the annexation of the latter for the extension of slavery ran the risk of greatly weakening the bonds that tied the Union together.[12]

It is well known that Tocqueville was not a successful parliamentary orator and this might explain why he was not called to make his speech about Oregon in January 1846. Tocqueville himself blamed his fellow parliamentarian, Adolphe Thiers, for stealing his turn. Nonetheless, there can be no doubt as to the importance that Tocqueville attached to this proposed intervention. From the moment that Tocqueville entered the Chamber of Deputies, he became increasingly preoccupied with questions of empire and foreign affairs. In 1840, the Eastern Question, as it was then called, was dramatically brought back to life when, on July 15 of that year, Great Britain, Austria, Prussia, and Russia signed a treaty committing themselves to maintaining the integrity of the Ottoman Empire. Brushed to one side and humiliated, France voiced its outrage in a wave of chauvinism and Anglophobia, from which Tocqueville himself was far from immune. In his speeches to the Chamber of Deputies, he repeatedly proclaimed that France must not accept its fate with "resignation" and that it must seek to maintain its place amongst the "first rank" of nations.[13] Within that geo-political vision, America came to occupy the place of an all-important counterbalance to British imperial power. Upon the basis of shared international and commercial interests, America was France's natural ally. No similar confluence of interests existed between France and Britain.

This, for example, was how Tocqueville assessed the strategic and commercial importance of American expansion into the Caribbean, at that time largely controlled by the British. "The Mississippi River," he wrote in 1843, "empties into these waters. No one can doubt that the Mississippi soon will be called the greatest commercial waterway in the world. The Mississippi valley is, in a way, all of North America. The valley is a thousand leagues long and almost as wide; it is irrigated by fifty-seven navigable rivers, several of which themselves, like the river into which they flow, are a thousand leagues long. The soil of most of the valley is the richest in the New World. This is why this valley, which was deserted forty years ago, contains more than ten million men today. Every day, new hordes of immigrants arrive; every year they form new states."[14]

"Now," Tocqueville went on, "to connect most of the points in this immense valley to the rest of the world requires going toward the Mississippi; the river's mouth in the Gulf of Mexico is, so to speak, the only way out. Thus more and more of the wealth that is contained in the whole northern continent and exploited by the Anglo-American race with such prodigious success and such rare energy will come through the Mississippi. The sea that serves as the commercial road of the Antilles themselves, of Colombia, of Mexico, and perhaps China, and which is in addition the outlet for almost all the products of North America, this sea certainly must be considered one of the most important points of the globe." He predicted that "it will become more and more *the Mediterranean* of the New World," the center of important business and significant maritime influence. "It is there," Tocqueville concluded, "that domination of the ocean will be fought for and won."[15]

The second international issue that preoccupied Tocqueville was that of the French Empire, and Algeria in particular. Tocqueville's position on this issue is now well known.[16] He believed that a thriving Empire was necessary for the strength and greatness of France. Less well observed have been the parallels that Tocqueville was prepared to draw between Algeria and America. When faced with the remorseless activity and expansion of Algiers, he commented that it was "Cincinnati transported onto the soil of Africa."[17] He also saw quite clearly that France must not repeat the errors of America with regard to the indigenous population. In words that recalled those used to describe the treatment of the American Indians in the closing chapter of the first volume of *Democracy in America*, he wrote: "It is not just violent behavior that is to be feared. Civilized peoples often repress and dispirit barbarous peoples by their mere contact, without intending it: the same rules of administration and justice that seem to the European to be the guarantee of liberty and property, seem intolerable oppression to the barbarian. . . . the forms that we call tutelary, they call tyrannical, and they would rather withdraw than submit to them. This is how, without recourse to the sword, the Europeans in North America ended up pushing the Indians off their territory. We must take care that it is not the same for us."[18] After acknowledging the violence involved in the process of uprooting, he concluded: "Let us not begin the conquest of America over again. Let us not imitate the bloody examples that the opinion of the human race has stigmatized."[19]

Just as importantly, the American experience told Tocqueville that in its pursuit of Empire, France should not abandon the seas. "Look," Tocqueville declared, "at the other side of the ocean, at the growth of this great people, of the United States of America, which, without colonies, ... , through the resources of its territory, its vital spirit, and its genius already possesses half of the maritime strength of England and has a level of trade equivalent to two thirds of that of Great Britain: do you believe that it is at the moment when such an ever-growing maritime power enters the lists that it is the right time to abandon the seas?"[20]

The territorial expansion of the United States attained a new intensity in the 1840s. In part, this was inspired by fears of possible intrusion by France and Great Britain into the North American continent but also by the ideology of America's "manifest destiny." By the end of the decade, this had resulted in America's annexation of Texas, the settlement of the Oregon dispute, and the acquisition of California, New Mexico, and Utah. But, throughout the 1840s, friction and disagreement existed between the United States and the European powers. One zone of disagreement was Oregon, a vast swathe of undeveloped land on the Western Coast. In 1818, Great Britain and the United States had negotiated its joint occupation, but as America moved westward and pioneers set off across the Oregon Trail, this settlement no longer seemed acceptable. James K. Polk, an enthusiastic expansionist, won the presidential election of 1844 on a program calling for the 'reoccupation of Oregon' up to 54° 40'. In the event, Oregon was divided along the 49th parallel.

François Guizot, Prime Minister of France, set out France's policy toward the United States in two speeches on January 12 and 21, 1846. Tocqueville's projected speech was a response to this statement of France's new American policy and the implications it would have for French actions over Texas, California, and Oregon. In brief, Guizot's central premise was that if equilibrium were to be preserved within the international system, the expansion of American power had to be checked. In his view, France needed to cooperate with Britain in order to prevent America's onward march to the Pacific coast and beyond. If this were not done, within a generation or two, America would pose a threat to European interests and civilization.

With this argument, as the notes of his speech reveal, Tocqueville was in complete disagreement. Guizot's declaration of French neutrality in the dispute between Britain and the United States was contrary to the interests of both the United States and of France. Moreover, an alliance with the United States would reduce British domination of the open seas. This was an argument that Tocqueville was to repeat in his address to the citizens of Cherbourg in 1848.[21]

There was one further dimension in which America entered Tocqueville's thoughts as a parliamentarian. From the moment of his election, he had displayed a deep distaste toward what he saw as the corrupt and unprincipled parliamentary practices of his day, marked by selfishness, insincerity, gullibility, and stupidity. This sense only intensified as the years of the 1840s passed and France's political malaise deepened. "What we meet least in our day," Tocqueville wrote to his friend Ampère in August 1841, "are passions, true and solid passions, that bind up and lead life. We no longer know how to want, or love, or hate. Doubt and philanthropy make us incapable of all things, of great evil as well as great good, and we flutter heavily around a multitude of small objects, none of which either attracts us, or strongly repels us, or holds us."[22] In those circumstances, he could not but reflect upon how in America, where revolutionary fervor was extinguished, "public spirit" had remained "active and vibrant."[23]

Given the reputation of Switzerland as a country of bland normality, it might seem surprising that Tocqueville should devote not one but two texts to an analysis of its political institutions. The first and most important text was a long commentary on Cherbuliez's book, *De la Démocratie en Suisse*, which, although focused on political developments in Switzerland, contains important references to America and its political institutions. In particular, Tocqueville reminded his readers that "judicial power, which hardly exists in Switzerland, is the real moderator of American democracy" and reiterated that the principle of democracy has peacefully penetrated everywhere and dominates everything in the United States. The second text, not translated here, was an article that appeared in *Le Commerce* in 1845.[24] In fact, from the end of the eighteenth century until the 1840s, Switzerland was a country racked by political turmoil, revolution, and *coups d'état*. As Tocqueville wrote in *Le Commerce*, "upon the tranquility of Switzerland may depend the peace of Europe."[25] Switzerland also provided a vivid – and one at France's immediate borders – example of the painful transition from an aristocratic to a democratic society. Additionally, when contrasted with America's own happy experience, it illustrated how not to effect this transition and how not to institute a federal system of government. In Tocqueville's opinion, America was not only a "more tranquil and prosperous democratic society," but it proved the point that a federal constitution could provide strong, respected, and effective government.

The key points of reference here are Chapters 6 and 8 of Part One of Volume One of *Democracy in America*, and in particular the sub-section on "What distinguishes the Federal Constitution of the United States of America from all other Federal Constitutions." Citing Switzerland, the German Empire, and the Republic of the Netherlands as examples, Tocqueville there argued that "the federal government in these different peoples has almost always remained feeble and powerless, whereas the Union conducts affairs with vigor and ease."[26] This could be explained by the fact that in America the federal power acted "without an intermediary on the governed." Where this did not operate, "all unions have come to civil war, to enslavement or to inertia."

Ten years later, Tocqueville was able to confirm this analysis and restate his faith in the virtues of the American federal system. As he wrote (again in *Le Commerce*): "Let us compare the constitution of the United States to that of Switzerland: Congress has no more rights than the Diet, but why does Congress do what the Diet does not do? Because it has instruments which are properly its own. Because, in order to put its wishes into effect, it has no need, as is the case with the Diet, to borrow its means of action from any another power. Like the Diet, its sphere of action is limited by the sovereignty of the individual States; but within its sphere, it is at least supplied with everything it needs to act promptly and efficiently. When the American government decides to raise money it has its own tax collectors who tell every American citizen the share that he must pay. When it recruits its army, it has its own agents to muster the troops. When it sets up customs posts, it has its own customs officers. When, finally, the taxpayer refuses to pay, the soldier to march, and the customs officer to obey, it has its courts which represent only itself and which oblige the citizens to obey its laws."[27] In addition, he was able to confirm the central importance of an independently constituted judicial power as a break upon the tyranny of democratic government. In 1848, as in 1835, he remained convinced that judicial power is "the real moderator of American democracy." The "experience, skill and wisdom" of the American people showed that the principle of the sovereignty of the people need not have the disastrous consequences it had been allowed to engender in Switzerland. In brief, when contrasted with Switzerland, the American constitution showed that the problem lay

not in a federal constitution but in the particular form taken by the
Swiss institutions. There was, therefore, no need for the Swiss to abandon a federal constitution and substitute it with "a unitary republic."
Tocqueville sought to apply these important lessons after the Revolution of 1848.

I. Outline of a speech on the Oregon Affair[28]

The speech by M. Guizot has given the question of America a new aspect.
It is no longer a matter of the past, but of the future. Not the future of Texas,
but of Oregon. France has clearly expressed its view. She has announced
a great resolve to the world.

I shall not remain within the framework of these important questions
about the balance of power which have been dealt with so prudently. I
will limit myself to saying a word about these three nations that oppose
each other, while we are stationary, in this *modest* and *moderate* position
of which I take note without approving of it.

Which is the one which should cause us the least offence? America.
Which is the one which we seem to offend most? America. I recall this to
the conscience of each one of you.

But I wish to descend from generalities to the particular.

In general the question of Oregon is badly understood. What is happening there? Is it just a few square miles of wilderness about which two
great peoples quarrel? No, the question is of great importance. Of huge
importance for England, of huge importance for America, and of great
importance for us.

I do not speak of the balance of power on the seas. Let us leave this
aside. I speak of a matter of greater interest. Are we indifferent as to
whether there are American ports or English ports in the Pacific Ocean?
What was your ambition in the ridiculous expedition to Tahiti?[29]

The Pacific Ocean entirely in the hands of the English or those of the
half-civilized republics of Spanish America. . . .

This is the question. You wish to let it be decided entirely by other
people. You proclaim your neutrality. So be it, but we have a right to ask
if this neutrality of which you speak is sincere. In proclaiming it, what is
your true goal? What will be its limits?

You say that you will observe a position of neutrality between America
and England. But for the past two years you have violated this principle
to the detriment of the Americans.

It has been shown how your *actions* and your language are contrary to the interests of France. I wish to show the extent to which they are ineffectual and from this obvious ineffectiveness I will draw out the hidden goal of your conduct. . . .

You wished to prevent the United States from taking possession of Texas.[30] This was a failure. In support of these actions and contrary to all diplomatic practices, you produced theories about the necessity of stopping the territorial expansion of the United States. It was a failure . . .

I do not accuse you of having committed the error implied by your actions and your words. You knew America too well to fall into such stupid errors. If your intention was not that implied by your actions and words, what was it?

Here it is:

While the immeasurable Oregon affair continued, the two nations negotiated. Do you know what was one of the great strengths of America in these negotiations? A *doubt* about the disposition of France.

The English were fearful that we wanted to favor the Americans. The Americans were inclined to hope so. And why did they hope so? Their reason: our interests, *their interests*, old links of friendship.

You wanted to deprive them of this strength. And in order to do this, you first sought an occasion to display your bad faith, an occasion which could show you to the world as being united with the English against them, and when finally this occasion did not arise, you hastened to let them know that they could expect nothing from you.

This was the secret goal of all your conduct. . . .

But if to proclaim this neutrality in advance is so damaging to America, is it wise for us? Why tie our hands in advance? Why publicly withdraw from the affairs of the world when these affairs could perhaps become so important? In any case, how do you understand this position of neutrality? We need to know and the principal intention of this speech is to demand this. Is it the armed neutrality of the Northern powers in 1800?[31]

It is not we, the opposition, that needs to know, but France.

✻

The significance of actions and words.

Actions: official documents.

Three things follow from this:

1. That French policy not only joins forces with English policy, but is entirely identical to it.

Since independently of the things that are done in *concert*, of the documents that are communicated, general orders are given to our agents to understand one another.

And nonetheless, while it is admitted that we have an interest – a distant interest – in the question, it is accepted that the interest of the English is greatly superior to our own.

2. How far the documents indicate that we would have gone:

Nothing indicates that we would not have gone as far as *breaking off relations* or even war, if the United States had wanted to take possession of Texas.

If the treaty of annexation had been ratified by the Senate, France would have opposed this (dispatch of August 1, 1844) and have gone even further: the opposition of the Senate excused France and England from having to loudly denounce this treaty.[32]

Not only would these actions have engaged France on a path that would have ended in war with the United States but it would have led her to something that is no less absurd: guaranteeing the reciprocal existence of Texas and Mexico.[33] In short, it would have involved us in all the quarrels that might have arisen between these two States.

3. The documents and, even more so, the speeches of M. Guizot commit the future. This is the most serious outcome. It represents not only the completion of a bad process but a future threat.

It must never be forgotten that immediately behind the question of Texas appeared that of Oregon. And that all the reasons given by M. Guizot to justify intervention in the question of Texas apply equally to the question of Oregon.

It is not because of this or that *particular* and *momentary* reason that France intervened in the question of Texas. It is for a *general* and *permanent* reason. The interest that France has in preserving the *United States* within its boundaries and of creating an equilibrium in America are both doctrines that apply equally to the question of Oregon as to the question of Texas.

When one reflects upon the philosophical, historical, and non-diplomatic character that M. Guizot has given to this debate, however partial to abstract ideas as he might be, I cannot believe that he gave way to the inclination of his mind. He followed a fixed plan and this plan was:

1. To aid the English in their continuing negotiations with a threat from France.

2. To play a waiting game that would enable him still better to aid the English if a conflict had taken place.

All this amounted to a defensive alliance with England against America: this is the right word. A comparison of the language of Guizot with that of Lord John Russell.[34]

✠

The policy indicated by these actions and these words, does it conform to our interests?

This policy is *new*, the first step on a road not only *different* but *entirely contrary* to that followed by France for eighty years.

On this single point, Louis XVI, the Republic, Napoléon, who went so far as to give up the most beautiful colony with the single thought of creating something analogous to what you wanted to prevent, namely to extend the maritime strength of the United States, and the Revolution of July were all in agreement. Only the Restoration seemed not to speak the same language, even if it did not stray away from this policy.

The same language has always been used. And if I had difficulty in convincing the Minister of Foreign Affairs on this point, I would call to my aid the Minister of the Interior and would beg him to repeat to his colleague what he said in 1834. Here are his words: . . .[35]

But, says M. Guizot, the United States itself does not want this close alliance. Its fundamental policy is not to enter any contract of this kind.

This is true but a truth that can be contested.

America did not ally itself with us in 1793. It did not enter into conflict with us, but it was on the point of doing so. One can say that the majority of the American people wanted it. Washington made *use* of his immense popularity to prevent it.

But let us admit that no properly so-called alliance was to be hoped for.

It is not exactly through its alliance that *America* serves us. It is through its greatness, it is by sharing the seas, it is by re-establishing the maritime *equilibrium*.

It serves us without willing it, without seeking to be in agreement with us. A recent example: the question of boarding rights.[36]

I believe that around a *common, clearly-defined, and limited* interest we would easily arrive at a close alliance. . . .

Even the message of the president,[37] upon which we have relied to demonstrate the *egotistical* policy of the Americans, shows this: "France," he said, "which has been our ancient ally, this country has a common interest with us in maintaining the freedom of the seas."

II. Report on *Democracy in Switzerland*[38]

January 15, 1848

Gentlemen,

I feel that the importance of the subject addressed by the author[39] warrants a detailed examination of his book;[40] and, thinking that such an examination might prove of some use, I have undertaken it.

I intend to place myself completely outside the preoccupations of the moment, as is appropriate in this place, and to pass over in silence present events which do not concern us, so as to study not the behavior of political society in Switzerland but rather that society itself, the laws which shape it, and their origin, tendencies, and character. I hope that thus circumscribed, my sketch will still be worthy of interest. What is happening in Switzerland is no isolated phenomenon.[41] It is a particular instance of a general movement that is hastening the ruin of the entire ancient fabric of European institutions. The stage may be small but there is greatness in the play. Above all, it has a particular originality. Nowhere else is the democratic revolution which is shaking the world taking place in such complicated and strange circumstances. One people composed of several races, speaking several languages, professing different religious beliefs, with various dissident sects and two churches both equally established and privileged, such that all political questions quickly become religious questions and all religious questions end up as political questions. And finally two societies, one very old and one very young, married together despite the differences in their ages. Such is the picture offered by Switzerland.[42] To paint it well, in my opinion, the author should have placed himself at a higher vantage point. In his preface, M. Cherbuliez announces, and I take the claim to be very sincere, that he sought to observe the rule of impartiality, to the point that he feared that the completely impartial quality of his work might give a monotonous quality to his subject. This fear is certainly unjustified. The author does indeed want to be impartial, but he is unsuccessful. In his book, there is knowledge, perspicacity, real ability, and evident good faith that stand out even in his most passionate statements. But what one precisely does not see is impartiality. At one and the same time, there is plenty of intelligence but little freedom of thought.

Toward what forms of political society does the author incline? At first this seems hard to say. While to a certain extent he approves of the political conduct of the most fervent Catholics in Switzerland, he is so decidedly opposed to Catholicism that he is not far from wanting legislative measures to prevent the spread of Catholicism to places where it is not dominant. On the other hand, he is very much against the dissident Protestant sects. Opposed to the government of the people, he is likewise opposed to that of the nobility. In religion, a Protestant church controlled by the State; in politics, a State ruled by an aristocratic bourgeoisie: this would seem to be the author's ideal. It is Geneva before the last revolutions.[43]

But if one does not always easily discern what he likes, what he hates is perceived without difficulty. What he hates is democracy. The democratic revolution that he describes was an affront to his opinions, to his friendships, and perhaps also to his interests, and he speaks of it always as an enemy. He does not only attack democracy because of one or other of its outcomes, but for its very principles. He does not see the qualities that it possesses; he pursues the defects that it has. Of the ills that may arise from it, he does not distinguish between those that are fundamental and permanent and those that are accidental and passing, between what must be accepted as being inevitable and what one should seek to remedy. Perhaps the subject cannot be addressed in such a way by a man who has been as heavily involved in the conflicts of his country as M. Cherbuliez? We should regret this, for, as we continue this analysis, we will see that Swiss democracy has great need of someone to shed light on the imperfections of its laws. But to do that effectively, the first requirement was not to hate it.

M. Cherbuliez has called his book, *De la Démocratie en Suisse*. This might lead one to believe that, in the eyes of the author, Switzerland is a country which provides the material for a theoretical study of democracy and where one is afforded the opportunity to judge democratic institutions in themselves. In my view, this is the origin of almost all the errors in this book. Its correct title should have been: *De la Révolution démocratique en Suisse*.[44] Switzerland has, in fact, been for the past fifteen years a country in a state of revolution.[45] There democracy is less a stable form of government than a weapon used habitually to destroy, and sometimes to defend, the old society. One can well study there the specific phenomena which accompany a state of revolution in our democratic era, but one cannot take it as a description of democracy in a permanent and peaceful condition. Anyone who does not keep this point of departure constantly in mind will only understand with difficulty the picture presented to him by the institutions of Switzerland; and, for my part, I should find it impossibly difficult to explain how I judge what exists without saying how I understand what went before.

In general, people have a mistaken impression of Switzerland at the time when the French Revolution broke out. As the Swiss had for a long time been living in a republic, it was easily imagined that they came much closer than the other inhabitants of the continent of Europe to the institutions which embody and to the spirit which animates modern liberty. But the opposite is the case.[46]

Although Swiss independence was born out of an insurrection against aristocracy, most of the governments then founded soon borrowed from the aristocracy their habits and laws, and even some of their opinions and propensities. In their eyes, liberty was never seen as anything other than a privilege and the idea of a general and pre-existing right of all men to be free was something that remained as alien to their way of thinking as it did to that of the princes of Austria whom they had vanquished. It was not long therefore before all powers were brought into and kept in the hands of small aristocracies, which were either closed or self-recruiting. In the north, these aristocracies took on an industrial character, while in the south they had a military constitution. But, in both cases, they were equally restricted and exclusive. In most of the cantons three quarters of the population were excluded from any participation, whether direct or indirect, in the administration of the country. Moreover, each canton had subject populations.[47]

These little societies, which had been established in the midst of such great turmoil, soon became so stable that no further movement was felt within them. The aristocracy, finding itself neither pressed by the people nor guided by the king, kept the social body both immobile and clothed in the old garments of the Middle Ages.

The passage of time has long since allowed the new spirit to penetrate into the most monarchical societies of Europe, but Switzerland still remained closed to it.

The principle of the separation of powers was accepted by all writers, but in Switzerland it did not apply. Freedom of the press, which, in fact at least, existed in several absolute monarchies on the Continent existed neither in fact nor law in Switzerland. The right of political association was neither exercised nor recognized. Freedom of speech was restricted within very narrow limits. Equal taxation, toward which all enlightened governments were tending, was as unknown there as equality before the law. Industry faced a thousand impediments, and there was no legal guarantee of individual liberty. Freedom of religion, which was beginning to penetrate even the most orthodox states, had still made no appearance in Switzerland. Dissident sects were entirely prohibited in some cantons and obstructed in all. Differences in belief almost everywhere resulted in political disabilities.

Switzerland was still in this condition when the French Revolution entered its territory by force of arms.[48] For the moment, it overthrew the old institutions but it put nothing solid and stable in their place. Napoléon, who, a few years later saved the Swiss from anarchy by the Act of Mediation, gave them equality but not liberty.[49] The political laws that he imposed were so constituted as to paralyze political life. Power, exercised in the name of the people but placed very far out of its reach, was entirely located in the hands of the executive authorities.

When, a few years afterwards, the Act of Mediation fell along with its author, the Swiss did not gain liberty but only lost their equality.[50] Everywhere the old aristocracies again took up the reins of government, and again put in force the exclusive and outdated principles that had prevailed before the revolution. Matters then returned, as M. Cherbuliez rightly says, to the point where they were before 1798. The allied kings are wrongly accused of having imposed this restoration upon Switzerland by force. It was done in agreement with them but not by them. The truth is that the Swiss, along with the other peoples on the Continent, were carried away by the temporary but universal reaction which suddenly revived the old society throughout Europe. And since, in their case, the restoration was not brought about by the princes whose interests, after all, are distinct from those of the former privileged classes, but by the former privileged themselves, it was more complete, more blind and more obstinate than in the rest of Europe. It did not show itself to be tyrannical, but very exclusive. A legislative power entirely subordinated to the executive; the latter exclusively in the hands of an aristocracy of birth; the middle class excluded from the administration; the whole of the people barred from political life: such is the spectacle presented by almost every part of Switzerland up to 1830.

It was then that the new age of democracy opened for her!

The object of this short exposition is to enable us to understand two things.

First, that Switzerland is one of the countries of Europe where the revolution was the least profound and the following restoration was the most complete. So that, since the institutions foreign or hostile to the new spirit had either retained or regained much of their influence, the revolutionary impulse was bound to be more powerful there.

Second, that in the greater part of Switzerland up to our day the people have never taken the smallest role in government and so the judicial forms guaranteeing civil liberty, freedom of association, freedom of speech, freedom of the press, and freedom of religion have always been as much, I might almost say more, unknown to the great majority of the citizens of these republics than they could ever have been, at the same time, to the subjects of most monarchies.

This is something of which M. Cherbuliez often loses sight, but which we must constantly bear in mind in the careful examination which we are going to make of the institutions which Switzerland has given herself.

Everyone knows that in Switzerland sovereignty is divided into two parts: on one side, there is the federal power; on the other, the cantonal governments.

M. Cherbuliez begins by speaking of what occurs in the cantons, and he is right to do so, for it is there that resides the real government of society. I will follow him in this path and like him concern myself with the cantonal constitutions.

Today all the cantonal constitutions are democratic, but democracy does not display the same characteristics in all of them.

In the majority of the cantons, the people have handed over the exercise of their powers to assemblies which represent them, but in a few of them they have kept it for themselves. They come together as a body and govern. M. Cherbuliez calls the former *representative democracies* and the latter *pure democracies*.

I will ask the Academy's permission not to follow the author in the very interesting examination that he makes of pure democracies. I have several reasons for acting in this manner. Although the cantons which live under a pure democracy have played a great role in history, and may still have a considerable role in politics, they would provide grounds for an odd study rather than a useful one.

Pure democracy is something almost unique in the world and very exceptional even in Switzerland, for only one thirteenth of the population is governed in this way. Moreover, it is a passing phase. It is not well enough known that in the Swiss cantons where the people have most preserved the exercise of their power, there exists a representative body upon which rests some of the functions of government. Now, it is easy to see when studying the recent history of Switzerland that gradually those matters with which the people in Switzerland concern themselves are becoming less in number, whereas those dealt with by their representatives are every day becoming more numerous and more varied. In sum, the principle of pure democracy is losing ground that is being taken by the opposing principle. The former is imperceptibly becoming the exception and the latter the rule.

Moreover, the pure democracies of Switzerland belong to another age; they can teach us nothing about the present or about the future. Although, in order to describe them, we are obliged to make use of a term taken from modern science, they live only in the past. Each century has its dominating spirit which nothing can resist. If any principles foreign or contrary to it are introduced within its realm, it is not slow in penetrating them and, when it cannot do away with them, it appropriates or assimilates them. In the end the Middle Ages came to give an aristocratic form even to democratic freedom. In the midst of the most republican laws and even by the side of universal suffrage, it found a place for religious beliefs, opinions, sentiments, habits, associations, and families who, distanced from the people, retained the real power. The little Swiss cantons must be seen as being like the democratic governments of the Middle Ages, as the last revered relics of a world which no longer exists.

However, the representative democracies of Switzerland are the off-spring of the modern spirit. They are all founded upon the ruins of a former aristocratic society. All proceed from the single principle of the sovereignty of the people. All have applied this principle in an almost identical fashion to their laws.

As we shall see, these laws are very imperfect, and, without the evidence of history, they serve to show that in Switzerland democracy and even liberty are new forces lacking in experience.

First, we should note that, even in the representative democracies of Switzerland, the people have retained in their own hands the direct exercise of part of their power. In some cantons, when the most important laws have secured the approval of the legislature, they must still be submitted to the *veto* of the people. Thus, in these specific cases, representative democracy has degenerated into pure democracy.

In almost all cantons, the people must be consulted from time to time, usually at frequent intervals, about whether they wish to modify or maintain the constitution. This, at intervals, disturbs all the laws at one and the same time.

All the legislative powers which the people have not retained in their own hands have been conferred upon a single assembly which acts in their sight and in their name. In no canton is the legislature divided into two branches. Everywhere it is composed of one body. Not only are its activities not delayed by the need to come to an understanding with another assembly, but its desires do not even have to face the obstacle of prolonged deliberation. Discussions of general laws are subject to certain formalities that extend them, but the most important resolutions can be proposed, discussed, and approved on the spot in the form of decrees. These decrees turn secondary laws into something as important, as hasty, and as irresistible as the passions of the multitude.

Outside the legislature, there is nothing that can resist. The separation, and above all, the relative independence, of the legislative, administrative and judicial powers does not in fact exist.

In no canton are the representatives of executive power directly elected by the people. It is the legislature that chooses them. Consequently the executive power is endowed with no power which is properly its own. It is only the creation and can only but be the servile agent of another power. To this weakness are added several others. Nowhere is executive power exercised by a single person. It is confided to a small assembly, where its responsibility is divided and its decisions are put into effect. Several of the rights inherent to the executive power are moreover denied to it. It has either no veto or only an ineffectual one over the laws. It does not possess the prerogative of mercy; nor does it either appoint or dismiss its officers. One might even say that it has no officers of its own, for it is usually obliged to make use of public magistrates.

But, above all, the defects of the laws of Swiss democracy arise from the bad constitution and bad composition of judicial power. M. Cherbuliez remarks on this, but, in my view, not sufficiently. He does not seem properly to understand that in democracies it is judicial power that is principally intended to be both a barrier to, and a protector of, the people.

The concept of the independence of judicial power is a modern concept. The Middle Ages had no sense of it, or at least conceived of it in a very confused manner. One may say that in all the nations of Europe executive power and judicial power were initially combined. Even in France, where by exceptional good fortune the law quickly developed a vigorous individual existence, one can nevertheless say that the separation of the two powers remained very incomplete. It is true that it was not the administration that kept the system of justice in its hands, but the judiciary that took hold of part of the administration.

Switzerland, however, was of all the countries of Europe the one perhaps where the system of justice was most completely confounded with political power and where it became most completely one of its attributes. One may say that the idea that we have of the law as an impartial and independent power which interposes itself between all interests and between all powers in order to call them all back to a respect for the law is an idea that was always absent from the minds of the Swiss and that even today is very poorly understood.

The new constitutions have unquestionably given the courts more of a separate existence than they had among the former powers, but it is not an independent existence. The lower courts are elected by the people and subject to re-election. The highest court of each canton is chosen not by the executive power but by the legislative power, and nothing protects its members against the daily whims of the majority.

Not only do the people or the assembly which represents them choose the judges, but they impose no constraints upon their choice. As a rule, no special abilities are demanded. Moreover, as the judge simply enforces the law, he has no right to question whether the law conforms to the constitution. In truth, it is the majority itself which judges through the medium of its magistrates.

Moreover, even if the law had given to the judicial power in Switzerland both the independence and the rights necessary for it, the judges would still have difficulty in performing their function since the law is based upon tradition and opinion which need the support of judicial conceptions and mores.

It would be easy to accentuate the defects in the institutions that I have just described and to show that they tend to make the government of the people irregular in its behavior, precipitate in its decisions, and tyrannical in its actions. But this would take me too far from my subject. I will rather limit myself to comparing these laws to those of an older, more tranquil, and prosperous democratic society. M. Cherbuliez thinks that the imperfect institutions of the Swiss cantons are the only ones which democracy can put forward or permit. The comparison that I am about to make will prove the contrary and will show how, starting from the principle of the sovereignty of the people, it has been possible elsewhere, through more experience, skill and wisdom, to arrive at different outcomes. I will take as my example the State of New York, which of itself contains as many inhabitants as the whole of Switzerland.

In the State of New York, as in the Swiss cantons, the principle of government is the sovereignty of the people, put into practice through universal suffrage. But the people exercise their sovereignty for one day only, when they choose their delegates. In general, in no case do the people retain any part whatsoever of the legislative, executive, and judicial power. They choose those who will govern in their name and until the next election they step down.

Although the laws are changeable, their foundation is stable. Nobody has ever conceived in advance the idea of submitting the constitution, as is the case in Switzerland, to repeated and periodic revision whose occurrence or mere anticipation keeps the social body in suspense. When a new need is felt, the law-maker establishes that a modification of the constitution has become necessary, and the next legislature puts it into operation.

Even if the legislature cannot escape the force of public opinion any less than it does in Switzerland, it is organized in such a way as to resist its whims. No proposition can become law until it has been subject to consideration by two assemblies. These two branches of the legislature are elected in the same way and are composed of the same elements. Both originate equally in the people, but they do not represent it in exactly the same way. One is charged with reflecting the impressions of the moment; the other is concerned with habitual instincts and permanent inclinations.

In New York, the separation of powers exists not only in appearance, but also in reality.

The executive power is exercised not by a body but by a single individual with full responsibility, who uses his rights and prerogatives firmly and decisively. Elected by the people, he is not, as in Switzerland, a creature and an agent of the legislature. He acts as its equal, and like it, he represents the sovereign in the name of which both act, although in a different sphere. Both derive their authority from the same source. He possesses executive power not only in name, but exercises its natural and legitimate prerogatives. He is the head of the armed forces and appoints their principal officers. He selects several of the most important officials. He has the right to grant pardon. The *veto* by which he can oppose the wishes of the legislature, without being absolute, is nevertheless efficient. If the governor of the State of New York is undoubtedly less powerful than a European constitutional monarch, he is certainly more so than a little Swiss council.

But the most striking difference lies in the organization of judicial power.

The judge, although he emanates from the people and depends upon them, is a power to which the people themselves submit.

Judicial power derives this exceptional position from its origin, permanence, competence, and, above all, from public mores and opinion.

The members of the higher courts are not chosen, as in Switzerland, by the legislature, a collective power which is often impassioned, sometimes blind and always irresponsible, but by the Governor of the State. Once appointed, a judge is regarded as immovable. No trial falls outside his jurisdiction and no punishment can be imposed by anyone else. He not only interprets the law but may be said to judge it. When the legislature, because of the hasty actions of the parties, distances itself from the spirit and the letter of the constitution, the courts bring it back by refusing to apply its decisions. In this way, if the judge cannot oblige the people to maintain the constitution, he can at least oblige them to respect it as it exists. The judge does not direct the people, but he does constrain and limit them. Judicial power, which hardly exists in Switzerland, is the real moderator of American democracy.

Today, when one examines this constitution in its smallest details, one finds not the slightest trace of aristocracy. There is nothing which resembles a class or a privilege, the same rights everywhere, all powers deriving from and returning to the people, the same spirit animating all institutions, with no contradictory tendencies: the principle of democracy has penetrated everywhere and dominates everything. And yet these governments, so completely democratic in character, have a far greater stability, a much more peaceable character and much more regular ways than the democratic governments of Switzerland.

One may say that this derives in part from differences in law.

The laws of the State of New York, which I have just described, are arranged in such a way as to combat the natural defects of democracy. The Swiss institutions, which I have sketched, seem intended, on the contrary, to increase them. Here they restrain the people, there they push them forward. In America, the fear is that their power might be tyrannical, whereas in Switzerland the intention seems to be to make it irresistible.

I do not exaggerate the influence that legal mechanisms may have on the destiny of peoples. I know that the great events in this world are chiefly explained by deeper and more general causes; but one cannot deny that institutions have their own virtues and that they do contribute to the prosperity or the poverty of societies.

If, instead of almost totally rejecting all the laws of his country, M. Cherbuliez had revealed their defects and how their arrangement could

be improved without alteration of principle, he would have written a book
of more lasting value and of greater use to his contemporaries.

Having examined democracy in the cantons, the author next explores
the influence that it has over the Confederation itself.

Before following M. Cherbuliez in this regard, we must do something
that he fails to do, that is, make clear what the federal government is, how
it is organized in theory and in practice, and how it works.

It is legitimate first to ask if the law-makers of the Swiss Confederation
intended to establish a federal constitution or merely a league; in other
words, whether or not they intended to sacrifice a part of the sovereignty
of the cantons or to transfer any of it. If one considers that the cantons
gave up several of the rights that are inherent to sovereignty and that
they conceded them in a permanent manner to the federal government,
if one imagines that, with regard to these matters thus handed over to
the government, the majority was to make the law, then one cannot doubt
that the law-makers of the Swiss Confederation intended to create a truly
federal constitution and not a league. But one must admit that they set
about it the wrong way to succeed.

I have no hesitation in saying that, in my opinion, the Swiss Federal
Constitution is the most imperfect of all the constitutions of this kind
yet to be seen in the world. Reading it, one might believe oneself to
have returned to the height of the Middle Ages, and one cannot but be
surprised that this confused and incomplete work is the product of a
century as learned and experienced as our own.

It is often repeated, and not without good cause, that the pact unduly
limited the rights of the Confederation, that it left outside the sphere of the
government representing it some issues of an essentially national nature
and which have naturally come within the competence of the Diet; such
as, for example, the postal service, the regulation of weights and measures,
and coinage.... And the weakness of the federal power is attributed to
the small number of functions entrusted to it.

It is certainly true that the pact withheld from the constitution of the
government of the Confederation several of the rights which are naturally
and even necessarily part of government. But it is not here that resides the
principal cause of its weakness, for the rights granted by the pact would
have been enough if it could have used them, either to acquire quickly
all those that it lacked or, at any rate, to conquer them.

The Diet can muster troops, raise money, make war, conclude peace,
negotiate commercial treaties, and appoint ambassadors. The constitutions of the cantons and the basic principles of equality before the law are

placed under its protection. This would have allowed it, when the need arose, to interfere in all local affairs.

Public tolls and rights over roads are controlled by the Diet, thus giving it authority to direct and supervise great public works.

Finally, the Diet, according to Article 4 of the pact, *takes all measures necessary to the internal and external security of Switzerland*, thereby giving it license to do everything.

The strongest federal governments have not had greater prerogatives, and far from thinking that in Switzerland the competence of the central power is too restricted, I am led to think that its limits have not been defined with sufficient care.

How then is it that, with such fine privileges, the government of the Confederation has in general so little power? The reason is simple. It has not been given the means of doing what has been granted to it, the right to want something.

Never has a government been better destined for apathy and condemned to impotence by the imperfection of its organs.

It is of the essence of federal governments to act, not in the name of the people, but in the name of the States who make up the confederation. If it were otherwise, the constitution would cease immediately to be federal.

Among the other necessary and inevitable of consequences of this, it follows that federal governments are usually less bold in their decisions and slower in their movements than the others.

Most of the lawmakers of the confederations have endeavored, through the use of more or less ingenious devices, which I do not need to go into here, partly to correct this natural flaw of the federal system. The Swiss have made this flaw much more noticeable than elsewhere as a consequence of the particular forms which they have adopted. In their system, not only do the members of the Diet act only in the name of the various cantons they represent, but in general they cannot take any decision that has not been previously considered or approved by them. Hardly anything is left to their free choice. Everyone believes himself subject to a binding mandate, imposed beforehand. As a consequence, the Diet is a deliberating assembly where, to tell the truth, there is no interest in deliberation, where one speaks not before those who must make the decision but before those who only have the right to apply it. The Diet is a government which wants nothing by itself but which is limited to giving effect to what twenty-two other governments have separately decided upon. It is a government which, whatever the nature of events, can decide nothing, foresee nothing, or provide nothing. One cannot imagine any arrangement better suited to increase the natural inertia of a federal government and to turn this weakness into a form of senile debility.

There are still other causes which, independently of the flaws inherent in all federal constitutions, serve to explain the habitual impotence of the government of the Swiss Confederation.

Not only has the Confederation a weak government, but one might say that it does not have a government of its own. In this respect, its constitution is unique in the world. At its head the Confederation places leaders who do not represent it. The directorate which forms the executive power in Switzerland is chosen not by the Diet and even less by the Swiss people. It is a government based on chance that the government borrows every two years from Berne, Zurich or Lucerne. Elected by the inhabitants of a canton to manage the affairs of a canton, this power thus becomes in addition the head and the arm of the whole country. This may certainly pass for one of the great political curiosities presented by the history of human laws. The consequences of such a state of affairs are always deplorable and often surprising. Nothing could be stranger, for example, than what happened in 1839. That year the Diet was sitting in Zurich and the confederation had as its government the directory of the State of Zurich. There occurred a cantonal revolution in Zurich. A popular revolution overthrew the established authorities. The Diet found itself immediately without a president and the life of the federation remained suspended until it pleased the canton to give itself new laws and new leaders. By changing their local administration, the people of Zurich had unintentionally decapitated Switzerland.

Even if the Confederation had an executive power of its own, the government would still be powerless to make itself obeyed as it could not act directly and immediately on its citizens. This in itself is a greater cause of weakness than all the others put together, but in order for it to be properly understand, there is need to do more than just mention it.

A federal government may have a fairly limited sphere of action and yet be strong if, within this narrow sphere it may act of its own volition, without intermediaries, as is the case with ordinary governments in the unlimited sphere in which they move. If it has officials who have direct contact with each citizen, its own courts which oblige each citizen to obey its laws, it can easily compel obedience, because it always has only individual resistance to fear, and all difficulties it gives rise to are resolved in the courts.

On the other hand, a federal government may have a very extensive field of activity and yet still enjoy only a very weak and precarious authority if, instead of having direct contact with each citizen, it has to deal with the cantonal governments; for, if the latter resist, the federal power immediately finds itself faced less by a subject than by a rival who can only be brought to reason by war.

The power of a federal government therefore resides less in the extent of the rights conferred upon it than in the degree of opportunity it is allowed to exercise them for itself. It is always strong when it can give orders to its citizens; it is always weak when it is reduced to giving orders only to local governments.

The history of confederations provides examples of these two systems but, as far as I know, there is no confederation where the central power is as completely divested of all action on its citizens as is that of Switzerland. Here, as it were, there is not a single right that the federal government can exercise on its own account. There are no officials dependent on it alone and no courts which represent its sovereignty exclusively. One might say that it was a being to whom life had been given but who has been deprived of all organs.

Such is the federal Constitution as it has been established by the pact. Now let us briefly follow the author of the book we are analyzing in assessing what influence democracy has on it.

It cannot be denied that the democratic revolutions which have successively changed almost all the cantonal constitutions in the last fifteen years have had a great influence upon the federal government. But this influence has been felt in two very different ways. It is very necessary to take into account both aspects of this phenomenon.

The democratic revolutions that have taken place in the cantons have had the effect of producing more activity and power at a local level. The new governments created by these revolutions, drawing support from the people and pushed forward by them, have found themselves to be both much stronger and to have a more elevated idea of their strength than the governments which they overthrew. And as no similar renewal took place at the same time in the federal government, it followed naturally as a result that the latter became weaker in comparison with the former than had previously been the case. Cantonal pride, the feeling of local independence, impatience with all control in the internal affairs of each canton, and jealousy of any supreme, central authority, these are all feelings that have grown with the coming of democracy. And from this point of view, one can say that it has weakened the already frail government of the Confederation and has made its daily and habitual job harder and more difficult.

But from another perspective, this has given it an energy and, one might say, an existence that it had not had before.

The establishment of democratic institutions in Switzerland has introduced two entirely new things.

Up to now each canton has had its separate interests and a separate spirit. The coming of democracy has divided all the Swiss of whatever canton they belong into two parties, the one supporting democratic principles, the other opposed to them. It has created common interests and common passions which, in order to be satisfied, have felt the need of a general and common power extending at the same time over the entire country. Thus, the federal government for the first time possessed a great strength that it had previously lacked. It has been able to draw upon the support of a party, a dangerous force, but one that is indispensable in free countries where the government can hardly do anything without it.

At the same time that democracy was dividing the Swiss into two parties, it drew Switzerland into one of the great parties that are dividing up the world. It created the need for a foreign policy. If it gave it natural friends, it created inevitable enmity. So as to cultivate and keep the one and watch over and guard against the other, the country has felt the irresistible need for a government. Local public sentiment has been succeeded by national public sentiment.

These are the direct ways in which democracy has strengthened the federal government. The indirect influence that it has exercised and will exercise in the long run in particular is no less important.

The resistance and the difficulties met by a federal government are greater and more numerous to the extent that the populations that make up the confederation are more diverse in their institutions, feelings, customs and ideas. It is less the similarity of interests than the perfect correspondence of laws, opinions and social conditions that makes the job of government so easy in the American Union. By the same token, one can say that the unusual weakness of the former Swiss federal government was due principally to the extraordinary difference and the widespread contradiction between the spirit, views, and laws of the various populations over which it had to rule. To keep men so naturally remote and so dissimilar from one another under the same leadership pursuing the same policies was a very arduous task. A much better constituted government, and one provided with a wiser organization, might not have succeeded in this. The democratic revolution taking place in Switzerland has the effect of bringing about in each canton the dominance of certain institutions, certain maxims of government, and certain similar ideas. If the democratic revolution strengthens the independence of the cantons in relation to the central government, on the other hand, it facilitates the actions of this power. To a large extent, it does away with the causes of resistance, and, without making the cantonal governments more eager to obey the federal government, it makes obedience to its wishes infinitely easier to achieve.

In order to understand both the present and the future condition of the country we need to study very carefully the two contradictory effects that I have just described.

By paying attention to only one of these two tendencies one is induced to believe that the coming of democracy to the cantonal governments will lead immediately and easily to an extension of the legislative sphere of the federal government and to the concentration in its hands of the daily direction of local affairs: in brief, to a modification of the whole structure of the pact in a direction favorable to centralization. For my part, I am convinced that such a revolution will continue to meet resistance for a much longer time than one might imagine. Today's cantonal governments show no more taste than their predecessors for a revolution of this kind, and they will do everything they can to avoid it.

Nevertheless, I think that despite this resistance, the federal government is destined day by day to increase its power. Circumstances will help this more than laws. It will not perhaps very obviously extend its prerogatives, but it will use them differently and more often. In reality it will grow, even if it retains the same legal status; it will develop more through the interpretation of the pact than by changing it; and it will dominate Switzerland before it is in a position to govern it.

Equally, one can foresee that the very people who, until now, have been most opposed to its steady extension, will not be slow in wishing for it, either to escape from the intermittent pressure of such an ill-constituted power or to secure protection from the much nearer and heavier tyranny of the local governments.

What is certain is that henceforth, whatever may be the modifications made to the letter of the pact, the federal constitution of Switzerland has been profoundly and irrevocably changed. The Confederation has changed its nature. It has become something new in Europe. A policy of action has replaced a policy of inertia and neutrality. A purely municipal existence has become a national one, producing an existence which is more arduous, more troubled, more precarious, and greater.

America and the Revolution of 1848

Introduction

The protests that erupted in February 1848, leading to the hasty abdication of King Louis-Philippe and the birth of the Second Republic, found republicans in France not only weak but also divided, both ideologically and organizationally. It was to these individuals, however, that (quite unexpectedly) was to fall the task of steering France toward yet another constitution. Now, for the first time republicans saw the opportunity of establishing a Republic which would embody not just the political equality of the ballot box but also the social and economic demands they had campaigned for over the previous decades. These views were no better expressed than by the socialist Louis Blanc. Liberty, on his view, was seen not just as a "right" but as the "ability" to exercise our faculties to the full. If Blanc recognized the importance of those liberties which he himself listed as liberty of the press, of conscience, and of association, he believed that the socialist conception of liberty had to be pushed much further, so as to embrace a range of liberties which would abolish the servitude which arose from poverty and hunger. By liberty, then, was meant not just the narrow conception of the absence of restraint, but something which was tied to a different vision of society: the *social* Republic.

If Tocqueville, somewhat reluctantly, rallied to the Second Republic, he was equally determined that it should not be pushed in a radical direction and that the republicans should not be allowed to relive the revolutionary fantasies of the past. As we shall see in the next section, this call to moderation was most obvious in his contributions to the framing of the new constitution and in his opposition to the recognition of the "right to work." The two texts published below, both taken from 1848, serve to illustrate the continuing importance of America to Tocqueville at this critical juncture in French history.

Discussion of America and of the relevance of the American constitutional model was by no means confined to the parliamentary chamber and its constitutional commission.[1] The text of the American constitution was reprinted in several new editions and it was the subject of frequent commentary in the French press, not least by Tocqueville's old rival, Michel Chevalier.[2] It was also debated in numerous brochures and pamphlets of that time.[3] In 1848 Édouard Laboulaye,[4] the most vigorous and articulate member of the so-called "American school" in France, published his *Considérations sur la Constitution*,[5] presenting a systematic critique of those constitutional proposals which ignored the lessons to be learnt from America. A year later, his inaugural lecture at the *Collège de France* was entitled *De la Constitution Américaine et de l'Utilité de son étude*.[6] In response to those who disputed the relevance of the American model to a France which, by their own admission, loved equality more than it loved liberty and which continued to prize an indivisible sovereign will, the defenders of America replied that it was not a question of slavishly copying the American constitution. Rather, it was a question of recognizing the merits of a system that had brought internal peace, prosperity, and liberty. Tocqueville was among those who defended the latter view.

The two texts below have decidedly different origins. The first was an impromptu speech given in Cherbourg on March 19, 1848 as Tocqueville campaigned to secure re-election as parliamentary deputy for his local constituency of the Manche. Somewhere in the region of 1, 500–2, 000 people were present and it appears to have been one of the few occasions where Tocqueville enjoyed genuine success as a public speaker. As he was later to recall in his *Recollections*, "I very much wanted to speak, but I was not on the list, and besides I did not quite see how to begin. A reference by one of the orators. . . . to the memory of Colonel Briqueville gave me my chance. I asked to speak, and the meeting chose to hear me. When I found myself mounted on the rostrum, or rather on the professor's chair raised twenty feet above the audience, I felt a little confused. But I soon recovered my presence of mind and delivered a touching little obituary address."[7] Tocqueville's call to elicit American support in order to overcome British supremacy of the seas cannot but have appealed to the patriotic sentiments of his Cherbourg audience.

The second text appeared as a new introduction to the twelfth edition of *Democracy in America*. It is not clear if a re-issue had been planned before the revolutionary events of February 1848, but Tocqueville's new publisher, Pagnerre, brought out the first cheap edition running to 4,000 copies. It quickly sold out, with two more editions going to press that same year. According to Hugh Brogan, "this introduction repays study as Tocqueville's manifesto for the Second Republic, expressing principles which he maintained throughout its brief and stormy existence."[8]

In both texts, Tocqueville's message was crystal clear. The importance of the American experience was undiminished. Indeed, as France now found itself divested of monarchy, it had grown in importance. This did not mean that France should make "a servile copy" of American institutions, but it did mean, Tocqueville affirmed, that the "principles of order, balance of powers, true liberty, sincere and deep respect for law" were indispensable to all republics. Similarly, his impassioned speech before the citizens of Cherbourg pointed out that "in America, the Republic is not a dictatorship exercised in the name of liberty, it is liberty itself, genuine, true liberty for all citizens." Wherever these principles were not to be found, as Tocqueville clearly believed might be the case in France, the republic will cease to exist. It was this vision of a stable and moderate republic where liberty was guaranteed and secured by the rule of law that Tocqueville defended as a member of the Chamber of Deputies.

I. Popular Banquet at Cherbourg[9]

I was not expecting to speak and, despite the kind manner in which my name has been mentioned a few minutes ago, I would not have done so had I not been, as it were, pushed to this rostrum by the emotion brought upon me by the tribute just made to the memory of a man for whom I have the deepest esteem and the liveliest affection: I speak of the courageous Colonel Briqueville.[10] Yes, I was moved in hearing his name resound again among a people who were so dear to him. I was moved in hearing the acclamations he received. I was moved in seeing this public and solemn justice rendered to such a noble memory and I felt the need to join my feeble voice to the strong voice of the country. If only Briqueville had been here in my place! Would he not have been overjoyed by the spectacle presented by this assembly where society in its entirety is represented, he who never considered himself to be the deputy of one class but of all classes, and who held all the people in his heart? Let us always recall the name of Briqueville. As we cannot bring his person back to life, let us try to revive among us the great qualities that led us to admire him so much. Let us honor his memory by seeking to follow his example. There was never a spirit more generous, a heart more noble, a soul more fearless.

As I am at this rostrum, please allow me, before I descend, to propose a toast in my turn.

In everything that has just been said there are two words that have been constantly repeated and that I heard with distinct pleasure: these are the two words of UNION and of CONCORD. Never was our union and our concord more necessary to save the country. Therefore, let union be always on our lips and in our hearts. Why would it not be so? What have we to reproach one another for? During the course of this great revolution that has just taken place, no attempt was made to interfere with property, nor with the existence nor the liberty of persons. Union therefore is not only necessary, it must also be easy to achieve. The union between peoples is no less important; above all, the union between peoples who have similar institutions. I therefore propose this toast to you: TO THE CLOSE UNION OF REPUBLICS! And I add in particular: TO THE UNION OF THE TWO GREATEST REPUBLICS WHICH EXIST ON THE EARTH TODAY: THE FRENCH REPUBLIC AND THE REPUBLIC OF THE UNITED STATES OF AMERICA.

Many among us still take fright at the name of the Republic because they worry about the proud but sad memories of our own history instead of reflecting upon what has occurred and is occurring elsewhere in the world. Should they cast their eyes across the ocean and to the shores that surround it and confront the other side of the Atlantic, they will discover a great people, spread across a territory far larger than that of France, and which for sixty years has had democratic and republican institutions. For me, who has lived within this immense Republic and whose laws I have earlier tried to describe, I think ceaselessly of it so as to reassure myself about the future of our own institutions. No other country in the world can furnish us with such useful examples and suggest such legitimate hopes. In America, the Republic is not a dictatorship exercised in the name of liberty, it is liberty itself, genuine, true liberty for all citizens; it is the honest government of the country by the country, the uncontested dominion of the majority, the rule of law. Protected by the laws of America, property is secure, order firmly maintained, industry free, taxation light, the tyranny of one or several persons unknown, and it has been so for sixty years. For these sixty years, during which Europe has been torn apart by discord, wars and revolutions, republican and democratic America has not had even a riot. I was therefore right in saying to you that we must turn our eyes toward it in order to find great examples to follow and great hopes to entertain. But we must ask it for still more. In uniting ourselves with it we must demand the liberty of the seas.

The earth is free but the sea is still held in serfdom. One country reigns there, not only in domination, but in tyranny. A single nation has insolently appropriated to itself what was the common domain of all. The sea is still held in serfdom. And why is it not free? Because the two great powers which at one and the same time have the most obvious interest in breaking her chains and the most power to attain that end, but which have been separated more by a difference of institutions than by distance, have still not come to agree and unite with each other. What was not possible a month ago is possible today. Let the French Republic and the American Republic stretch their arms across the seas that separate them; let them shake hands and the sea will be free. There will not even be need for war to attain that end, and God forbid that I should call for war. The sight alone of their close union will render their common will all powerful.

Is there a single place in the world where it is more natural and more legitimate to express these views than here in Cherbourg? What is Cherbourg if not a living protest against the serfdom of the seas? What is the significance of these magnificent dockyards that I can almost see from the spot on which I speak? What are these jetties, these dock basins cut out from the rock, this new town composed of shipyards and arsenals, this magnificent island called forth by the voice of man from the heart of the waves to stop the sea and protect the shore? What is all this, if not the greatest and most energetic effort ever made by France to set free the Ocean?

It is therefore at Cherbourg that it is most appropriate to propose this toast: to the close union of the two Republics! And through it, the freedom of the seas.

II. Preface to the twelfth edition of *Democracy in America* (1848)[11]

However great and sudden the events which have just occurred in an instant under our very eyes, the author of this book has the right to say that he has not been surprised by them at all. This book was written fifteen years ago, with a mind constantly preoccupied by one single thought: the imminent, irreversible and universal advent of democracy in the world. If one rereads it, one will find on every page a solemn warning that reminds people that society is changing its form, humanity is changing its condition, and that a new destiny is upon us.

At the outset the following words were written:

> *"The gradual development of equality is a providential fact. It has all its main traits: it is universal, it is durable, every day it escapes human power, and all events, as well as all men, have contributed to its development. Would it be wise to believe that a social movement that comes from so far can be stopped by one generation? Can anyone believe that democracy, after having destroyed the feudal system and vanquished kings, will retreat before the bourgeois and the rich? Will it stop now that it has become so strong and its adversaries have become so weak?"*

The person, who, in the presence of a monarchy which had been strengthened rather than shaken by the July Revolution, wrote these lines made prophetic by events, can today, without fear, call the attention of the public to his work.

He must also be allowed to add that the present circumstances give to his book an immediate interest and a practical utility which it did not have when it appeared for the first time.

Royalty existed then. Today, it is destroyed. The institutions of America, which were only a subject of curiosity for monarchical France, must be a subject of study for republican France. It is not force alone that establishes a new government; good laws do that. After the combatant comes the legislator. The one has destroyed, the other is a founder. Each has his own work to do. Although it is no longer a question of whether we shall have a monarchy or a republic in France, we have yet to learn if we shall have an disorderly republic or a peaceful republic, a regular republic or an irregular one, a pacific republic or a warlike one, a liberal republic or an oppressive republic, a republic that threatens the sacred rights of property and the family or a republic that recognizes and consecrates them. This is a terrible question, the solution of which concerns not only France, but the entire civilized world. If we manage to save ourselves, we shall at the same time save all the peoples who surround us. If we lose our way, they will all be lost along with us. Depending on whether we have democratic liberty or democratic tyranny, the destiny of the world will be different, and one could say that today it depends upon us whether the republic will end by being established everywhere or will be abolished everywhere.

Now, this question that we have only recently posed, America had solved more than sixty years ago. For sixty years, the principle of the sovereignty of the people which we have introduced among us only yesterday, has there reigned unchallenged. It is there put into practice in the most direct, unlimited, and absolute manner. For sixty years, the people who have made it the source of all their laws have increased constantly in population, in territory, in wealth, and, note this well, it finds itself to have been, during that period, not only the most prosperous, but also the most stable of all the peoples of the earth. While all the nations of Europe were devastated by war or torn by civil discord, only the American people in the entire civilized world remained at peace. Almost the whole of Europe was turned upside down by revolutions; America did not have even a single riot; there the republic was not a disruptive force but the conserver of all rights; individual property has had more guarantees there than in any other country of the world, and anarchy has remained there as unknown as despotism.

Where else could we find greater hopes and more important lessons? Let us not look at America in order to copy in a servile manner the institutions that she has established for herself, but in order to understand better those institutions that suit us, less in order to find examples than to draw lessons, in order to borrow her principles rather than the details of her laws. The laws of the French Republic can and must be in many cases different from those that govern in the United States, but the principles on which the American constitutions rest, those principles of order, balance of powers, true liberty, sincere and deep respect for law, all these principles are indispensable to all republics and must be common to all of them. And it can be said beforehand that, where they are not to be found, the republic will soon cease to exist.

SECTION C

Tocqueville's Contributions to the Debates on the Constitution of the Second Republic

Introduction

The April 16, 1848 diary entry of Richard Rush, U. S. Minister to France, reads as follows: "M. de Tocqueville, the well-known author of the celebrated work on the political institutions of the United States, comes to see me. We get into conversation on some of the points of Republican Government. I mention what I had heard of M. Lamartine's objections to a double branch of the Legislative power under the new republic. We converse on this part of the subject. I say that the American experience is all in favor of two branches. For the illustration from history showing the dangers of a single branch and advantages of a double branch, I refer him to the learned and logical work of the elder Adams, formerly President of the United States, and one of the foremost patriots and sages of the American Revolution ... M. de Tocqueville seemed familiar with the historical facts and reasoning in favor of the double branch but wished to know what work of repute there was in our country which defended the single branch. I replied, none that I knew of and that not only did the Constitution of the United States establish a double branch in the two houses of Congress, but all the States, amounting to thirty, which composed the federal Union at present, had adopted the double branch; or, if exceptions existed, I was not aware of them. The only exception in our past history was in the constitution first formed by Pennsylvania after the breaking out of the Revolutionary War. I remembered no other. But the same state changed it afterwards for a Constitution with the double branch. Was there any work in Pennsylvania, he asked, embodying the argument for the single branch when her Constitution was formed? None that I was able to specify, I said."[1] At this

377

point, Rush recorded, the conversation came to an end, as Tocqueville hastened off to join his regiment in the National Guards.

Less than two weeks later, Rush again found himself in the presence of Tocqueville and, upon this occasion, also of George Bancroft, U. S. Minister in London.[2] "We had much conversation," Rush recorded, "on the new form of government in France; especially as regards the federative principle and centralization. M. de Tocqueville gave an account of the powers and jurisdiction of the Parliaments now existing in the departments. He sees great difficulty in constructing out of them anything like our State governments in France. She is too disposed to centralization from long habit, which had become a conviction. His views were perspicuously presented."[3] At the end of the following month, on May 31, the two men again exchanged their views. "M. de Tocqueville visits me," Rush remarked. "He is one of the committee of eighteen appointed by the National Assembly to prepare a draft of the New Constitution. We have much conversation on the subject. The work is advancing, and he thinks from present appearances that the committee will report in favor of a single Executive and a single Chamber." Tocqueville, he added, seemed a "little sanguine" about the prospects for France where "the idea of centralization is so deep-rooted."[4]

Rush and Tocqueville once more discussed the new constitution two days later, this time at a reception hosted by Madame de Tocqueville. On June 20, Rush's diary entry noted that the "anxiously expected Constitution" had been placed before the National Assembly. "A number of its clauses," Rush commented, "are similar to the Constitution of the United States. Other parts, and those elementary, are altogether different; as is to be expected when different races, acting under different moral and physical causes, found systems of government."[5] Three days later, on June 23, 1848, popular insurrection broke out in Paris. The June Days had begun. Rush's account of these events spoke of "the scenes of havoc and slaughter."

In brief, it seems that, from February 1848 onward, Rush was constantly visited by "French gentlemen calling for information about our constitution" and that among these gentlemen was Alexis de Tocqueville. The relevance of the American precedent was much in people's minds and Rush himself seems to have taken on the curious role of acting as an interpreter of the principles of the American constitution to the committee preparing the draft of the new constitution of the Second Republic. To his guests he patiently explained the system of checks and balances, the differences between Senate and House, and the principles of federalism. For Tocqueville himself, it must have been something like a refresher course, recalling the days, a decade earlier, when he had reflected on the position of the president of the United States and the federal powers.

Upon this occasion, however, Tocqueville was to be no idle academic commentator for, as an elected member of the Constituent Assembly in May 1848, he was chosen to sit on a committee of eighteen members delegated with the task of providing France with yet another new constitution.[6] Tocqueville's own account of its proceedings – written in Sorrento in March 1851 – is a litany of dashed hopes and expectations. "Taking the Committee as a whole," he wrote, "it was easy to see that nothing very remarkable was to be expected of it." Its members, he continued, "bore little resemblance to those men, so sure of their aim and so well acquainted with the best means to reach it, who drafted the American Constitution sixty years ago with Washington in the chair." Moreover, as Tocqueville also recounted, as their hurried discussions took place, "socialism was at our doors."[7]

Tocqueville's abiding obsession was so to construct the Second Republic as to prevent it, unlike its predecessor, from becoming a threat to both liberty and property. To that end, he focused his attention on three key points: bicameralism, the right to work (and the "social Republic"), and the mode of election of the president of the Second French Republic.[8] On each of these subjects, the example of America provided Tocqueville with crucial evidence on which he confidently drew in his public speeches and interventions translated in this section. Tocqueville reluctantly acknowledged that bicameralism was a lost cause in 1848. The prevailing view among French republicans was that the existence of two parliamentary chambers would destroy the unity of popular sovereignty. Nonetheless, this did not prevent Tocqueville from reminding his fellow parliamentarians that all of America's states possessed two chambers and that, where the experiment of one chamber had been tried (in Massachusetts and Pennsylvania), it had quickly been abandoned. As the example of America demonstrated, there was nothing aristocratic about a bicameral system; in practice, the latter could effectively serve to provide stable and moderate government.

In a speech drafted during this period, Tocqueville emphasized the centrality of bicameralism to political freedom and free government which he, interestingly, equated with moderate government: "This question embraces all the others. It is the question of moderate government which subsequently recurs again in many forms. It is not the theory of *balanced* but of *moderate* governments."[9] The same draft ended with the following prescient warning: "The question of two Chambers is a question of *liberty*. It is the future of free government. The single Chamber is dictatorship, prolonged dictatorship, the advent of a master."[10]

The debate over the right to work went to the heart of the aspirations associated with the Second French Republic. The Committee itself proposed a constitutional article stipulating that the Republic should "through fraternal assistance assure the livelihood of needy citizens, either by procuring them work within the limits of its resources, or, when there was no family, by giving aid to those not in a condition to work." Nonetheless, an amendment proposed that the Republic "recognizes the right of all citizens to education, work and assistance." It was Tocqueville's view that behind this amendment lay socialism. And behind all this lay the question of whether the 1848 Revolution was a socialist revolution. Tocqueville's position on this issue was clear: socialism stood for materialism, an attack upon the principles of individual property, and a deep distrust of liberty. America served his argument against socialism because it allowed him to counter the claim that socialism was the legitimate development of democracy. America was the most democratic country in the world but there, according to Tocqueville, one searched in vain for the least sign of socialism. And it was undoubtedly with the American example in mind that Tocqueville proclaimed from the tribune: "There is nothing there that obliges the State to replace individual foresight, thrift, and individual honesty. There is nothing there that authorizes the State to intervene in industry, to impose restrictions upon it, to tyrannize the individual in order better to govern him or, as is insolently maintained, to save him from himself."[11]

Tocqueville was also aware that there were other means, apart from bicameralism, of reducing the dangers posed by a unicameral legislature. The chosen device in 1848 was that of strengthening the executive.[12] At the committee stage, Tocqueville let it be known that, in his view, "the excessive influence of the President would be an immense danger." Nevertheless, he supported the view that ministers should be responsible to the president and that the latter should also possess the initiative for legislation. Without this clause, the outcome would be anarchy and a dangerous absence of power at the heart of the executive. Moreover, Tocqueville was displeased by the recommendation of the Constitutional Commission that proposed that the president of the Second Republic be elected by universal manhood suffrage. This recommendation, he believed, was fraught with significant dangers as subsequent developments clearly demonstrated. With the benefit of hindsight, Tocqueville deplored this mistake in his *Recollections* and regretted that the Commission did not choose the system of an indirect vote.[13]

On the basis of his earlier acquaintance with America, Tocqueville also argued that the president should not be eligible for re-election on the grounds that it would subject society to the corrupting influence of a president seeking to extend his term of office.[14] He made the further suggestion that France might adopt the two-level American electoral college model for choosing the president, a model that successfully averted "intrigues, conspiracy [and] violence."[15] This recommendation was rejected. He returned to this theme, and to the American example, again in 1851, when the question of the revision of the Constitution was raised.

For once Tocqueville's knowledge of America served him ill. His (and Gustave de Beaumont's) awareness that the re-election of the American president encouraged corruption and excessive patronage led them, as he recalls in his *Recollections*, to make a "big mistake" which had "untoward consequences." Given the vote, the people chose as their head of state an individual   Louis Napoléon Bonaparte – who was determined to remain in power, irrespective of what the Constitution stipulated. The days of the Second Republic were numbered and France was destined again to return to authoritarian rule.

I. Drafting of the Constitution, Meetings of May 25 and May 27, 1848[16]

Session of May 25 (1848) – 1 pm

President: M. Cormenin.[17] 17 members present.

M. Marrast:[18] I begin by stating as a fact that the system of two chambers is a system with no chance of winning.

It has no sufficient justification, logic condemns the theory that public opinion has struck down in advance. M. Barrot[19] himself recognizes this, when he says that the system of a single chamber appears more rational and more logical.

Indeed, why have two representations, two sovereignties for a single people? In reality this system of equilibrium sought by M. Barrot has never existed anywhere; there has only ever been one force which, under one name or another, has dominated the other forces in a country.

For example, in England it is said that there are three forces but, in truth, there is only one and this has absorbed the other two, an aristocracy which used to tell the Crown what it wanted and which gave only a semblance of power to the people.

In America, democracy is everything.

Moreover, I include the two chambers within the monarchical system, because the third power can settle the quarrels which arise between the two legislative chambers, but in a republic who can bring these differences to an end? In a situation of equilibrium between the three powers, it is unity that dominates, but two chambers in a republic form a detestable regime that I cannot understand.

It is certainly true that with a single chamber we are exposed to passions, to being carried away by our character, to pressure from outside and to current events, but the equilibrium necessary for its preservation can be looked for within the Chamber itself.

Through the Constitution one can establish several levels of discussion, as is done in England.

One can establish a Council of State which, in public sessions, would precede and prepare the discussions of the National Assembly.

All these precautions can give sufficient guarantees against the allurement of a single power; but in order to preserve national unity, it is indispensable to have a single chamber because there is only one people.

M. Vivien[20] asks if all the regulations in the world could provide guarantees against the initiative of members of the Assembly and against calls for urgent action.

M. Marrast replies that precautions against these eventualities could be written into the constitution itself.

M. de Tocqueville: I recognize that the cause that I am going to defend does not have the support of opinion, but I would be failing in my duty if I did not support what I believe to be best in the interest of the Republic and to which we shall return if we wish to establish a lasting republic.

It is not in any way necessary to dwell too much upon historical examples because we ought to seek to do something original and which arises from our own situation.

In the world there exists only one democratic republic, that of the United States; it has two chambers.

I shall not avail myself of the Constitution of the United States, a true work of art from which one could borrow much; but, aside from that, there are in North America thirty republics which are in a situation similar to our own; all have two chambers and there is not a single American who is of the opinion that one could proceed otherwise.

One should not say that the setting up of two chambers is an English tradition, because the Union began by having only one chamber and then returned to having two of them.

In Massachusetts, in Pennsylvania, a single chamber was first established; after thirteen years of testing and a thoughtful discussion, public reason accepted the necessity of two chambers; this example is striking.

I believe that the opinion in favor of a single chamber, so prevalent in France, derives from a misunderstanding.

It is imagined that the system of two chambers is an aristocratic institution because it gives expression to two different portions of the people. This is an error.

In no way do I want aristocracy. I recognize that our society is overwhelmingly democratic and that if one desired to introduce a single particle, one atom of aristocracy, into it, this would be an ingredient of ruin.

But it is necessary that, as in America, the two chambers should represent in the same way, by similar means, the same interests and the same groups of people.

It will be said that, if the second chamber does not represent some sort of aristocracy, it serves no purpose. This is a mistake, because its utility, although of a secondary nature, is not insignificant. That utility is primarily of three kinds:

1. Executive power ought to be strong, but in order to prevent it from abusing its power one can place alongside it a body, small in number, unobserved, chosen from among the second chamber, and charged with controlling certain important acts, such as a nomination to high public office, a treaty of alliance, etc.

This kind of advantage can be sought in a Council of State; but there are other advantages that can only be obtained with two chambers.

2. Executive power is in a perilous situation if you place it opposite a single chamber; there are ceaseless conflicts at the end of which the executive branch destroys the legislative power, or at least this power absorbs or swallows up the other power, in one way or another, after a very short struggle.

3. There are maladies that affect the best constituted bodies; the chronic disease which kills the power that makes the laws is legislative intemperance, it is the tyranny of a power that wants to legislate constantly.

Without doubt, two chambers will not prevent revolutions, but they will prevent the bad government which brings forth revolutions.

Wherever there is a single body, it laughs at the obstacles placed in its path. The body that represents all thoughts, all interests, and drives everything, that body crushes everything and is irresistible.

All the palliatives designed to stop it produce some beneficial effects, but only for a very short time.

In order to render this power less strong and less precipitate it is necessary to divide it into two chambers composed of the same elements; and, if you do not try to hold back the sovereignty of all the classes in the name of one class, you will have two bodies representing the same interests but which will not always have the same thoughts.

There will be between them a diversity of views, from which all will profit. There will be two examinations made by diverse minds.

There is also the further advantage that no faction will be able to establish itself within the assembly and make itself master of national sovereignty.

People speak of the two readings that will be required before the single chamber, but this remedy is sterile, because two readings made before the same men is something no more effective than an appeal lodged against a judgment made before the very men who made the judgment.

The leprosy of democracies is impetuosity, what one might call legislative thoughtlessness, and at the extremity of that thoughtlessness lays oppression.

I am convinced that the Republic will perish unless it adopts a system of two chambers.

M. Coquerel:[21] I believe that we are fated, as it were, to defer the question; the two chambers are an institution that both theory and reason seem to support; but we have against us the torrent of public opinion whetted by the February Revolution and toward which it would be wise to concede at the present time.

That which lacks counterbalances cannot preserve its equilibrium; a single assembly is sovereign and dominating because it is irresponsible; it is probable that we will come back to the system of two chambers; but today this is not possible. Thus it is necessary to combine the present necessity of a single chamber with the possibility of a return to two chambers.

The chapter on the revision of the Constitution ought to be written in such a way as to allow a return to the system of two chambers without revolution.

M. Martin:[22] It is not before the torrent that we must yield but before reason. In February, long before February, public opinion called for a single chamber. Every time that there have been two chambers, it has been a conciliation, a compromise, between aristocracy and democracy. If you establish two chambers, this institution will lead you to revolution. The French character demands unity and one can find within the chamber itself the necessary counterbalance to its action.

M. Vivien: The French character, impetuous and hasty, demands on the contrary a system of double examination; the Chamber of Deputies has very often been happy to acknowledge that it has too easily given way; I take fright before a single, irresponsible, chamber which laughs at the obstacles placed in its path and which will be able to exercise a terrible dictatorship.

It is said that the question is lost. I do not believe this. On the contrary, I believe that the system of a single chamber has for its supporters only the clubs and a few men said to be progressive; but if the elections had taken place with this question in mind, as was the case with the question of the peerage in 1831, I believe that French public opinion would not have favored the system of a single chamber. It is not necessary that one of the two chambers should be in a privileged position; the two chambers should be two chambers hewn from the same trunk, but there must be two of them; without this, there is a danger for the republic.

M. Martin: In the past, in France the utility of two chambers was real only with regard to minor questions; it was non-existent with regard to significant ones.

Those who, before the revolution of February, did not want the republic, today want two chambers, because this regime is not a republican regime. You cannot have two chambers without a factitious mechanism which will produce nothing of good for the country.

M. Considérant:[23] There are two sides to the logical arguments for one or the other system, because society is not in a logical state; but what must dictate the question is the present state of the French spirit.

The Senate, the Chamber of Peers, a second Chamber, whatever name one chooses to use, has never been greatly subject to consideration because it does not conform to the general way of thinking.

But to guard a single chamber from its excesses there would be need of a Council of State that could *revise* the laws.

M. Cormenin: No . . . . . *prepare* the laws.

M. Dufaure: Along with M. Martin, I accept that I could be under the sway of earlier parliamentary prejudices associated with constitutional monarchy, but still I want to say how the question appears to me.

As regards human laws, I acknowledge the sovereignty of the people. This sovereignty is exercised only through delegation. Logic does not tell me if it is better to entrust this delegation to two chambers rather than one.

Prudence alone can tell me if, for the republic to endure, it is better to establish two chambers or one.

What role will the executive power have in the introduction, discussion and approval of laws?

What is decided with respect to this will have an influence upon how I make up my mind, but in the meantime it is necessary to choose.

I see that, in the past, public opinion has only attached itself to a single chamber and has rendered the other nearly useless, to the extent that the latter has been more of a danger than an advantage. I do not believe that in the future two chambers will be of any greater service.

The example drawn from America is of importance; but I believe that between this people and our own there exist differences that considerably weaken the authority of this precedent.

Among us, public opinion, the true queen, must concentrate upon a single point, in the past upon royal power, later upon one man, Napoléon, then upon a single chamber. I fear that a second chamber will only weaken the first and will prevent it from resisting executive power, because I believe that this last power will have more authority than one imagines, since it will be the representative of all of France and will not be exposed to the problems and dangers that animated monarchies with their long reigns, their regencies, etc.

If the second chamber possesses no advantages with respect to the matters I have just indicated, it has no other merit than to restrain the enthusiasm, the unrestrained behavior, of the first chamber. Well! This advantage will not be obtained because the first chamber will always trifle with the second one.

I believe that the choice between one or two chambers is a matter of prudence and I would prefer to adopt a single chamber.

M. de Tocqueville reaffirmed the authority of the precedent to be found in America; without question, there are there many institutions that could not be transposed to France, but with regard to the two chambers the same arguments applied in both countries.

M. Dupin[24] that this question was at one and the same time the most difficult and the most fecund of all those that the Commission had to resolve, that it was influenced by the past and the present.

He then outlined the history of French constitutions in relation to this question.

The Constitution of 1791 only established one chamber; but the cause of its downfall did not lay there and it is certain moreover that, if it had established two chambers, one of these two chambers would, as Louis XVI tried, have placed a *veto* upon what the other wanted to do and never would the two chambers have destroyed all the old institutions whose abolition was necessary to institute the principles upon which the French Revolution rested.

In 1793 there was nothing but a tyranny, a hydra with a thousand heads.

In the Year III a return was made to the system of two chambers owing to memories of the past, because people saw that the first single chamber had devoured the executive power in 1792 and that the second was itself devoured.

It was not the system of two chambers that destroyed the Constitution of the Year III but the poor organization of executive power which was multiple; it was the disrepute with which it was regarded; the Convention had at least aroused hatred, the Directory had evoked only contempt. Moreover, the second chamber had not been able to defend the Constitution; it had protected the projects of Bonaparte.

The Empire had multiplied the wheels of government; it had divided in order to rule and had left a place only for the power of a single person.

When the Empire fell in 1814, there was only democracy in France, but people had wanted to remake an aristocracy from a few shreds of the former regime and from revolutionaries who imagined they could become feudal lords by adopting ridiculous titles.

The Chamber of 1815 challenged it in a servile manner in the Chamber of Peers.

The movement of 1830 possessed a populist element; its aim had been to rid France of a race that France had proscribed, and it was because of this that we wished for it and were very enthusiastic about it.

When the Revolution of 1848 arrived we supported it because the nation wanted it, because this revolution is legitimate in the same way as that of 1830; it is the work of the nation.

There exists this difference between the men of 1830 and the legitimists; the latter see their king even abroad, even outside the wishes of the nation, whereas we want only what the nation wishes for itself.

The French people are not as changeable as people say. They have always wanted the same thing. Since 1830 they have exhibited the same longing, they want free and popular institutions.

The power of 1830 lost because, instead of extending itself, it sought to concentrate itself among a small number of people who formed an arrangement of mutual assurance; everything that tended toward the enlargement of the electoral sphere was excluded.

Today we have a blank sheet. The king and the Chambers are overturned. There is a sovereign assembly in both law and fact and this has never been seen so clearly in any other epoch.

In order to decide upon the power that should come out of this revolution, we need not give way to the torrent; we need to find what is the most useful.

I believe that the system of one chamber is preferable; it is more logical, less exposed to disagreements and conflicts; the only thing to fear is the impulsiveness of a single power; we can take precautions against this inconvenience and can find support in public opinion.

But two chambers would also rival each other in obsequiousness toward the people, because all powers are flattered. It is best to prefer the simplest means and adopt a single chamber.

M. Pagès:[25] I admire the way that men, without knowing it, are the servants of events. Two chambers with a president, this is the likeness of royalty.

I want a single Chamber, because I want it to be strong and capable of resisting executive power.

This executive power has always mastered us either by subduing us or by misleading us.

The Committee of Public Safety devoured the Convention, as Napoléon devoured the councils of the nation. I fear that this evil may produce itself again.

America at times has had one chamber, at times two chambers, depending upon necessity. We too must march with the times and with the century. I do not know what we will do in ten years, but in the interim we can only think today of establishing a single chamber.

M. de Beaumont: I do not believe that the danger facing the republic derives from the excessive strength of the executive power. I think on the contrary that, if there is not a strong executive power, the republic will not last six months, and this power will not be strong if the Assembly dominates it too much.

But when, as I think, even the best reasons are on the side of the system of two chambers, the facts dominate: we can deliberate in the abstract. Well! I accept the facts when I cannot combat them. I yield before public opinion and I accept a single chamber. What is more, there are means to combat the dangers of impulsiveness presented by this system.

M. Barrot: We are here in order to express our thoughts and we must be open. With a single chamber, you will continue the revolution; with two chambers you balance the powers and you can arrive at stability.

After this discussion a vote was taken; 14 voted in favor of a single chamber; 3 for two chambers.

[...]

Session of May 27 (1848) – 1 pm.

President: *M. Cormenin*.

After having decided upon the powers of the legislative body, it is advisable to consider the precautions that can be taken to prevent that body from yielding to impulsiveness. In order to achieve this outcome, *M. Marrast* argues, it is necessary that, with regard to the form of its deliberations and the framing of laws, the assembly should be constrained by the Constitution.

At this point, *M. Cormenin* proposes, on the one hand, certain measures and the re-reading of proposed legislation and, on the other hand, the setting up of a Council of State.

He asks if it would not be advisable to give to this Council of State an element of control over the law after it has been passed.

M. Dupin rejects this idea and believes that the Council of State, which ought only to have a consultative voice, should not figure under the rubric of the legislative body.

M. de Beaumont thinks that, as in America, one could grant the executive power not a right of *veto*, but the faculty of suspending the promulgation and the execution of the law for a short delay so as to give the Chamber time for reflection.

M. de Tocqueville believes that, before attending to the executive power, it would be necessary to settle the regulations according to which it is appropriate:

1. to frame the laws
2. to pass them with an element of slowness and after the delay of discussion
3. then to delay promulgation by certain formalities.

M. Coquerel: I have more confidence in the means which will arise after the law has been voted than in those that will precede it.

M. Marrast: One could have three readings of the proposed law. After the first reading, which would be a kind of preliminary consideration by the Chamber, there would be a requisite referral to the Council of State, which would examine the project in its form and its drafting. Then the project put in order by the Council of State would come back to the Chamber, where it would be supported by a member of the Council of State.

Finally, if the majority secured by the law when voted upon the second time is small, the executive power could request a revision of the law by the Chamber.

Following the observation made by *M. Dufaure*,[26] the Commission accepted that all these questions will be more easily resolved when the nature of executive power had been determined.

And the Commission moved to this section.

But prior to this, the Commission decides that it will insert into the section on constitutional guarantees an article affirming that the first of these guarantees consists in the separation of powers.

Of executive power.

M. Cormenin says that there are three systems for the composition of this power.

1. The assembly itself exercising executive power through its delegates.
2. Three or five consuls or delegates.
3. A president or consul.

The Commission decides unanimously and without discussion that unity is necessary and indispensable and that executive power ought to be conferred upon a single person.

M. Dupin proposes thus to define the executive power.

Executive power is exercised by an elected functionary who carries the title of president of the Republic.

Everyone is agreed on the adoption of the title of president, but the drafting will be revised.

Then the question of determining the age of the president is addressed, some proposing forty years, others thirty-five, others thirty years.

The Commission decides by a majority of eight votes out of 14 that the president must be at least thirty years of age.

Then the Commission proceeds to determine the term of the executive power and if this power will have the same duration as the legislative power, if the president will be re-eligible.

M. Cormenin proposes that the executive power should be nominated for three years and should be re-eligible upon one occasion.

M. de Beaumont believes that re-election is a dangerous thing because the president will concern himself principally with taking measures designed to secure his re-election; it will be to that end that he will spend his time and that he will employ his immense power.

M. Woirhaye[27] supports re-election upon one occasion; he believes that it is essential not to deprive oneself of the services of a man loved by the nation and necessary to make the Constitution sufficiently elastic so as not to be easily broken by the impossibilities it imposes.

M. Dufaure: In America the legislative power and the executive power are normally nominated and renewed at the same time. This regulation seems to me to be very wise; it avoids the conflicts that can break out if the two powers do not have a simultaneous origin, if they owe their election to currents of opinion contrary to one another.

If the powers are nominated at the same time, they will be nominated by the same opinions and will be able to harmonize together; if one is young while the other is old, there will be an antagonism between them that will produce only disorder.

M. Marrast: I believe on the contrary that it would be a grave inconvenience to renew at fixed times, for example every three years, all the powers which govern society, on the grounds that the legislature could not continue for any longer.

Precisely because democracy is changeable by nature it is necessary to give a firm foundation to power, it is necessary to organize movement in such a way as to make it turn around a fixed pivot and it is to expose the republic to disruption to give it, as it were, a new skin at the end of three years.

M. de Tocqueville: The two difficulties, that of the re-election of the president and that of the equal or different duration of the legislative and executive powers, exacerbate one another; but I think that, to begin with, we cannot accept the principle of immediate re-election.

M. de Beaumont has already said, and he has very rightly said, that if the president is re-eligible, his major concern will be to think of his re-election; in order to be re-elected, he will govern in the interest of one party.

This disadvantage makes itself strongly felt in America and it grows without cease and appears more and more vexatious. But in France the harm would be yet greater.

392 C. Tocqueville's Contributions to the Debates on the Constitution

For in America, the president has little power; he nominates only a small number of post holders, but in France, where the executive power disposes of a very large number of posts and can create many protégés, the excessive influence of the president will be an immense danger.

It is true, on the other hand, that if the president is not re-eligible, one can cast an enormous discontent upon the mind of an eminent man who cannot extend his power and bring about the grand designs he contemplates; this would leave him with only the ambition of despair and inspire in him the thought of defying the Constitution.

This is a difficulty but I would rather see the Constitution exposed to an accidental and transitory danger than see society habitually subject to the corrupting influence of a president who employs the strength he possesses to prolong his power.[28]

I also believe that a legislature of four years is too long and, despite the disadvantages noted by M. Dufaure, I think that this legislature should last for only three years and that one ought to give four or five years to the executive power.

M. Vaulabelle:[29] asks if one could not give to the legislature and the executive power a duration of two years.

M. Dupin: believes that the president and the Assembly should be nominated for three years.

The Chamber will be the preponderant power; it will direct policy and business by giving them continuity through the re-election of a large number of men who made up the dissolved chamber.

M. Marrast: The one-year difference between the election of the president and that of the Chamber is a very small matter; the difference of currents of opinion of which M. Dufaure has spoken impresses me little; what worries me is a practical question, the necessity of imparting a spirit of continuity and tradition. If the powers are all renewed at the same time every three years, there will be three months lost during which the executive power and the legislative power, untested with one another, will embark on their education: that is the danger to be avoided above all.

Then a vote was taken on the question of re-election. It was decided by a majority of twelve votes to two that the president will not be re-eligible if this was not after a period of. . . .

Next the duration of executive power was determined: various members proposed three, four or five years.

By a majority of eight votes to six it was decided that the executive power would be nominated for four years.

Method of nomination.

M. Cormenin proposes that the president should be nominated by direct, universal suffrage, by a relative majority, and by not less than two million votes.

M. Marrast proposes a system of candidature according to which the National Assembly would propose five candidates from within itself and the nation would choose one of them. This system would avoid any possible surprises.

M. Coquerel believes that, with this system, the Assembly could select men of no merit in order to ensure the election of the fifth [candidate] whom it prefers.

M. Considérant says that this necessity for the people to limit its choice to certain men is an attack upon national sovereignty.

M. de Beaumont believes that an assembly may become enthusiastic either for or against a man and that it is important not to allow the Assembly to exercise such a great influence upon the choice of the executive power.

M. Dufaure says that he had voted for a single chamber thinking that the executive power would be strong because it would be the product of universal suffrage. If it were otherwise, this would upset the ideas that have developed on the authority of the various powers of the Republic.

He adds that, as there will be parties in the assembly, the latter would only choose candidates from the majority, whereas the nation might be disposed to prefer a man from the minority.

Following these observations, the commission decides that the president will be chosen by the entire nation, without formal presentation and by secret vote.

Next was examined what majority will be required, [and] if a minimum number of votes will be necessary.

It is accepted that one has to be satisfied with a relative majority. Several members propose a minimum of one million, others two million, another member believes that one could demand a minimum of votes proportionate to the number of electors.

The Commission decides that the choice of president will only be valid if he receives a minimum of two million votes.

M. Cormenin next reads a section devoted to the Council of State and the ministers and the extent of executive power; but all these questions are put back to the next session. It was agreed, following a proposal by M. Coquerel and M. de Tocqueville, *that the Constitution will be concluded by the indication of the organic laws intended to complete it and to put it into practice.*

II. Speech Made before the Constituent Assembly during the Discussion of the New Constitution on the Right to Work[30]

Session of September 12, 1848

If I am not mistaken you are not expecting me to respond to the last part of the speech that you have just heard. It contains the statement of a complete and complicated system to which I do not intend to oppose another system.

My aim now is simply to discuss the amendment in favor of which, or rather concerning which, the preceding speaker has just spoken.

What is this amendment? What is its bearing? What, as I see it, is its fatal tendency? This is what I have to examine.

First, a word on the work of the Commission.

The Commission, as the preceding speaker told you, had in reality two drafts but fundamentally it had and it continues to have only one thought. To begin with, it had a first formulation. The words which have been expressed at this tribune and elsewhere, and better than the words, the facts themselves have shown that this formulation was an incomplete and dangerous expression of its thought. It has rejected not the thought but the form.

This formulation is now taken up again. This is what we presently find ourselves confronting.

The two versions are placed before us. So be it. Let us compare them in the new light of the facts.

In its latest formulation, the Commission limits itself to imposing on society the duty to come to the aid, be it by work or by assistance strictly speaking, of all hardships to the extent of its resources. In saying this, the Commission undoubtedly wanted to impose on the state a more extensive and more sacred duty than that which has been imposed until now; but it did not want to create something absolutely new; it wanted to expand, consecrate, and regularize public charity; it did not want to generate anything other than public charity. The amendment, in contrast, does something different, and does much more. The amendment, with the meaning given to it in speeches and, above all, by recent actions, the amendment, which grants to each individual the general, absolute and irresistible right to work, this amendment leads necessarily to one of the following consequences. Either the state will undertake to provide work to all unemployed workers who come forward, thus being drawn little by little into the industrial process; or, as it is the industrial contractor that operates everywhere, the only one which cannot refuse to provide work and the one which usually imposes the least work, it is invincibly led to become the principal, and soon, as it were, the only industrial entrepreneur. Once this point has been reached, taxation is no longer the means of funding the machinery of government but the principal means of supporting industry. By thus accumulating in its hands all individual capital, the state finally becomes the sole owner of everything. Well, this is communism. [Disturbance]

On the other hand, if the state wishes to escape from the fatal logic which I have just described, if it wishes to provide work for all workers who come forward, not by itself or through its own resources but by seeing to it that they find it in private industry, it is led inevitably to the regulation of industry adopted, if I am not mistaken, in the system of the last honorable speaker. It is obliged to ensure that there is no unemployment; this leads it inevitably to distribute workers in such a way as they do not compete with one another, to regulate wages, sometimes in order to restrain production, sometimes to accelerate it, in short, to become the great and sole organizer of labor. [Movement]

Thus, although at first sight the texts of the Commission and that of the amendment seem to come together, these two texts lead to quite contrary results. There are two paths which, beginning at the same point, finish up by being separated by an immense gulf: one leads to an extension of public charity; at the end of the other, what do we see? – Socialism. [Expressions of agreement]

Let us not deceive ourselves. We gain nothing by postponing discussions whose principle involves the very foundations of society and which, sooner or later, come to the surface in one way or another, sometimes in words and sometimes in actions. Today what is at stake behind the amendment of the honorable M. Mathieu, perhaps unbeknownst to the author, but which I at least for my part see as clear as day, is socialism. [Prolonged disturbance – murmuring from the left].

Yes, gentlemen, sooner or later the question of socialism, which everybody fears and which nobody has dared to discuss until now, must come before this tribune. This Assembly must settle this question; we must relieve the country of the burden that it is made to bear by this idea of socialism. With regard to this amendment, and I confess that it is principally because of this that I have come to the tribune, the question of socialism must be resolved. It is necessary that we know, that the Assembly, that all of France knows, whether the February Revolution is or is not a socialist revolution. [Very good]

Behind the June barricades, did I not hear the cry, said and repeated again and again: *Long live the democratic and social Republic!* What is meant by these words? We need to know. Above all, the National Assembly must say.

The Assembly will understand that my intention is not to examine before you all the various systems comprised under the same word of socialism. I wish simply to try to identify, in as few words as possible, the distinctive characteristics found in all these systems so as to see if the thing which has this physiognomy and which bears these characteristics was the goal of the February Revolution.

If I am not mistaken, gentlemen, the first distinctive characteristic of all the systems which bear the name of socialism is an energetic, continuous, immoderate appeal to the material passions of men. [Signs of approbation]

Thus, there are those who have said that "it is a matter of rehabilitating the flesh." Others have said that "labor, even of the harshest kind, must not only be useful but agreeable." Still others have said that "men must be rewarded not according to their merits but according to their needs." And finally, the last of the socialists of whom I wish to speak has just told you that the goal of socialism and, according to him, the goal of the February Revolution was to secure *unlimited consumption* for everybody.

I am therefore right in saying, gentlemen, that the general and typical characteristic of all the schools of socialism is an energetic and continuous appeal to the material passions of man.

There is a second characteristic: an attack, sometimes direct, sometimes indirect, but always continuous, against the very principles of private property. Since the first socialist[31] who said fifty years ago that *property was the origin of all the evils of the world*, to the socialist whom we heard at this tribune and who, less charitably than the first, shifting from property to the property owner, told us that *property was theft*,[32] all socialists, all of them, I am bold enough to say, attack individual property either directly or indirectly. [It's true; it's true]. I do not pretend to say that everyone attacks it in the open and, if I may say, rather brutal manner adopted by one of our colleagues; but I say that all of them, by more or less circuitous means, if they do not destroy it, transform it, diminish it, constrain it, limit it, and make of it something else than the private property that we know and that we have known since the beginning of the world. [Very vigorous signs of agreement]

We come to the third and last characteristic, the one which above all exemplifies socialists of every color, of every school: the deep distrust of liberty, of human reason, a profound scorn for the individual in his own right, for the human condition. There is a continuous, diverse, incessant attempt to mutilate, to curtail, and to constrain human freedom in every possible way. There is the idea that the state must not only direct society but must be, as it were, the master of every man – how should I put it? – the idea that the state must be his master, his tutor, his teacher [Very good]; that from fear of letting him fall, the state must always be by his side, above him, around him, in order to guide him, protect him, sustain him, restrain him. In brief, as I have just said, it is the elimination of human freedom to a lesser or greater extent. [More signs of agreement] If, at this point, I had to find a definitive and general formula to express what socialism as a whole appears to me to be, I would say that it is a new form of servitude. [Vigorous approval]

You see, gentlemen, that I have not gone into the details of these systems. I have portrayed socialism according to its principal characteristics, but these are sufficient to identify it. Wherever you see them, rest assured that socialism is present, and wherever you see socialism, be assured that these characteristics will be found.

Well, gentlemen, what does all of this mean? Is this, as has been claimed on many occasions, the continuation, the legitimate complement, the perfecting of the French Revolution? Is it, as had been said many times, the complement and legitimate development of democracy? No, gentlemen, it is neither one nor the other. Recall the French Revolution, gentlemen. Return to the terrible and glorious origin of our modern history. Did the French Revolution, as a speaker claimed yesterday, achieve the great deeds that rendered it illustrious in the world by appealing to the material sentiments, to the material needs of man? Do you believe that it was by speaking of wages, of well-being, of limitless consumption, of the unlimited satisfaction of physical needs?

Citizen Mathieu (from the Drôme):[33] I said no such thing.

Citizen de Tocqueville: Do you believe that it was by speaking of such things that it was able to awaken, that it excited, that it organized, rushed to the frontiers, threw before the hazards of war, placed before death, a whole generation? No, gentlemen, no. It was by speaking of higher and finer things, by speaking of love of country, by speaking of virtue, of generosity, of disinterestedness, of glory, that these great things were done. Let us be certain, gentlemen, that there is only one secret to making men do great things, and this is by appealing to great feelings.[34] [Very good. Very good]

And property, gentlemen, property! Without doubt the French Revolution waged a cruel and energetic war against some property owners, but as for the principle of private property itself, it always respected and honored it. It gave property pride of place in its constitutions. No other people have treated it more magnificently. They have engraved it even on the title page of their laws.

The French Revolution did more. Not only did it consecrate individual property, it extended it, and thereby caused a greater number of citizens to share in it. [Several exclamations – That is what we ask!]

And today, gentlemen, it is thanks to this that we do not have to fear the fatal consequences of the doctrines which the socialists are spreading through the country and within these walls. It is because the French Revolution peopled this country of France with ten million property holders that we can allow your doctrines to appear before this tribune without danger. Undoubtedly they can upset society, but, thanks to the French Revolution, they will not prevail against it or destroy it. [Very good!]

And finally, gentlemen, as for liberty, one thing strikes me. The Old Regime, whose opinions, we must acknowledge, undeniably differed from those of the socialists on many points, was with regard to political ideas far less removed from it than one might believe. All things considered, it was closer to them than to us. Indeed, the Old Regime was of the opinion that wisdom resides in the state alone, that its subjects are weak and infirm beings whom one must always lead by the hand for fear that they might fall or hurt themselves; that it is good continually to constrict, to oppose, to constrain individual liberties; that it is necessary to regulate industry, to guarantee the quality of goods, to prevent free competition. On this point, the Old Regime thought precisely like the socialists of today. And who was it, I ask, that thought differently? The French Revolution.

Gentlemen, who was it that broke all those fetters which on all sides restricted the free movement of persons, of goods, of ideas? What was it that restored man to his individual greatness, to his true greatness, what? The French Revolution itself. [Approval and uproar] It is the French Revolution which abolished all these restrictions, which broke the chains that, under another name, you would like to re-establish. And this was not only true of the members of the Constituent Assembly, that immortal assembly which founded liberty not only in France but throughout the world.[35] It was not only the members of that illustrious Assembly that rejected the doctrines of the Old Regime. It was true of the eminent men of all the assemblies which followed it. It was true even of the representative of the bloody dictatorship of the Convention. The other day I was reading his words again. Here they are.

"Flee", said Robespierre, "the old obsession" – you see, it is not new [Smiles] – "flee the old obsession of wanting to govern too much; allow individuals and families the right to do freely anything that does not harm others; allow the communes the right to run their own affairs; in short, return to the liberty of the individual everything that has been illegitimately taken way, whatever does not necessarily belong to the public authority."[36] [Excitement]

Well, gentlemen, is it likely that this great movement of the French Revolution would lead only to this society painted for us with delight by the socialists, to a regulated, ordered, formalized society where the state is responsible for everything, where the individual is nothing, where society gathers and contains in itself all power and all life, where the goal assigned to man is well-being alone, a society without air and where light hardly penetrates? Was it for a society of bees or beavers, for a society of clever animals rather than of free and civilized men, that the French Revolution was made? Was it for this that so many famous men would die on the field of battle or upon the scaffold, that so much glorious blood flooded the earth? Was it for this that so many passions were aroused, that so much genius, so many virtues, were to appear in the world?

No, no! I swear by the men who succumbed to this great cause. No, it is not for this that they died. It was for something greater, more sacred, more worthy of them and of humanity. [Very good] If that was all there was to do, the revolution was useless, an improved old regime would have sufficed. [Prolonged reaction]

I was just saying that socialism has claimed to be the legitimate development of democracy. Unlike several of our colleagues, I will not try to search out the true etymology of this word democracy. I will not explore the garden of Greek roots in order to discover from where this word comes, as was done yesterday. [Laughter]. I will seek democracy where I have seen it, living, active, triumphant, in the only country on earth where it exists, where it has been able to establish something great and lasting here in the modern world, in America. [Whispers]

There you will see a nation in which all conditions are even more equal than they are among us, where the social state, mores, laws, are all democratic, where everything derives from and returns to the people, but where each individual enjoys a more complete independence and a greater freedom than at any other time or in any other country in the world, an essentially democratic country, I repeat, the only democracy that exists today in the world, the only truly democratic republics known to history. And in these republics you will search in vain for socialism. Not only have socialist theories not taken hold in the public mind, but they have played such a small part in the discussions and the affairs of this great nation that one has not even had the right to say that people feared them.

Today America is the country in the world where democracy is practiced to the greatest extent, and it is also the one where socialist doctrines, which you claim to be so in accord with democracy, have the least currency, the country in the universe where those who support its doctrines would have the least advantage in presenting themselves. For my part, I confess that I would see no great inconvenience were they to go to America, but in their own interest I do not advise them to do so. [Loud laughter]

A Representative: Their belongings are being sold at this very moment.[37]

Citizen de Tocqueville: No, gentlemen, democracy and socialism are not linked to each other. They are not only different but contradictory things. What if by chance, democracy were to consist of a government more interfering, more detailed, more restrictive than all others, the only difference being that it would be elected by the people and would act in the name of the people? In that case, what would you have done, if not have given to tyranny an aura of legitimacy that it did not previously possess and to have secured for it the strength and omnipotence that it lacked? Democracy extends the sphere of individual independence, socialism restricts it. Democracy gives the greatest possible value to every man, socialism turns every man into an agent, an instrument, a number. Democracy and socialism are linked by only one word, equality; but note the difference: democracy wants equality in liberty, and socialism wants equality through constraint and servitude. [Very good! Very good!]

Therefore, the February revolution should not be social. If it must not be, it is important to have the courage to say so. If this must not be the case, we must have the strength to proclaim it openly, as I am doing myself here. When one does not want the ends, one must not wish for the means. If one does not want the goal, one must not set out on the path that leads there. Today, it is being proposed that we take this path.

We must not follow the course of action long ago set out by Babeuf, the grandfather of all modern socialists. [Approving laughter] We must not fall into the trap that he himself pointed out, or rather which was pointed out in his name by his historian, his friend, his pupil, Buonarroti.[38] Listen to what Buonarroti said. It merits being listened to even fifty years later.

A Representative: There is no Babouvist here.

Citizen de Tocqueville: "The abolition of individual property and the establishment of the great national community was the final goal of his labors (of Babeuf). But he was very guarded about making it the object of a decree on the day after victory; he believed that it was necessary to act in such a way as to cause the entire people to prescribe individual property out of need and out of interest."

Here are the principal directives which he counted on using himself (it is his own eulogist who is speaking): "Establish by law a public order in which property owners, while provisionally retaining their property, would no longer obtain abundance, gratification or consideration; where, forced to spend the greater part of their income to cover the costs of cultivation and of taxation, crushed beneath the weight of progressive taxation, removed from public affairs, deprived of all influence, forming nothing more than a suspect class of foreigners within the State, they would be forced to emigrate while abandoning their possessions or be reduced themselves to ratifying the establishment of the universal community." [Laughter]

A Representative: There we are!

Citizen de Tocqueville: There, gentlemen, is the program of Babeuf. With all my heart I desire that it should not be the program of the February Republic. No, the February republic must be democratic, but it must not be socialist.

A Voice from the left: Yes! [No! No! Interruption]

Citizen de Tocqueville: And if it is not socialist, what therefore shall it be?

A representative on the left: Royalist!

Citizen de Tocqueville, turning towards this side: It might perhaps be so if we left it to you, [vigorous approval] but this will not happen.

If the February Revolution is not socialist, what therefore will it be? Is it, as many people say and think, a pure accident? Must it be no more than a simple change of men and of laws? I do not think so.

When, last January, I spoke in the Chamber of Deputies before the then majority, which grumbled on these benches, for other reasons admittedly but in the same way that they grumbled just now.... [Very good! Very good!]

[The speaker gestures to the left]

I said to it: Take care, the wind of revolution is rising: do you not feel it? Revolutions are coming: do you not see them? We are sitting on a volcano. I said that: *Le Moniteur* testifies to it. And why did I say it?.... [Interruptions on the left].

Was I feeble-minded enough to believe that revolutions were approaching because this or that man was in power, because this or that incident of political life excited the country for a moment? No, gentlemen, what made me believe that revolutions were approaching, what, in effect, produced the revolution, was this: I saw that, due to a profound departure from the most sacred principles spread across the world by the French Revolution, power, influence, honors, in short, life itself, had been confined within the very narrow limits of a single class. I saw that there was no country in the world which presented a single comparable example. Even in aristocratic England, the England that we then so often made the mistake of taking as an example and as a model, even in aristocratic England the people participated, if not completely and directly, at least widely and indirectly, in public affairs. If they did not vote themselves (and they did often vote), at least they made their voice heard. The people made known their will to those who governed and they listened to each other.[39]

Here, there was nothing of the kind. I repeat: all rights; all power; all influence; all honors, political life in its entirety, was confined within an extremely narrow class; and, beneath that, nothing!

This is what made me believe that revolution was at our gates. I saw that within this small privileged class, something was happening that always occurred in the long run in small, exclusive aristocracies: public life was being extinguished, corruption was spreading every day, intrigue was taking the place of public virtues, and everything was weakening and deteriorating.

So much for the top of society.

And what was happening at the bottom of society? Beneath what was then called the legal country, the people properly so-called, the people who were less badly treated than is said (since we must be just above all toward the fallen powers) but to whom little thought was given, the people, living, so to speak, outside the official world, were creating a life of their own. Psychologically and emotionally separating themselves ever more from those competent to lead them, they gave their mind and their heart to those who, naturally, were in contact with them, and many of the latter were ineffectual utopians, as we have just seen, or dangerous demagogues.

It is because I saw these two classes, one small, one large, separating themselves little by little from one another, the one filled with jealousy, defiance and anger, the other with thoughtlessness and sometimes egoism and insensitiveness, because I saw these two classes moving in isolation and in opposite directions, that I said and I had the right to say: the winds of revolution are rising and soon revolution is going to come. [Very good]

Was it to accomplish something like this that the February revolution occurred? No, gentlemen, I do not think so. As much as any of you, I think the contrary. I desire the contrary. I desire it not only in the interest of liberty but also in the interest of public security.

I confess that I myself did not work for the February revolution and I do not have the right to say so, but given that the Revolution has occurred, I want it to be a genuine revolution because I want it to be the last. I know that it is only genuine revolutions which endure. A revolution which produces nothing, which is sterile from birth, whose loins are barren, can serve only one purpose; that of giving birth to more revolutions to follow. [Approval]

Therefore, I want the February revolution to have a clear, precise, perceptible meaning that shines everywhere and that everyone can see.

And what is that meaning? I will express it succinctly: the February revolution must be the true continuation, the real and sincere fulfillment, of what the French revolution had looked for, it must be the implementation of what our fathers could only have thought about. [Strong approval]

Citizen Ledru-Rollin:[40] I request permission to speak.

Citizen de Tocqueville: That is what the February revolution must be, neither more nor less. The French Revolution had willed that there should be no classes in society. It never had the idea of dividing citizens, as you are doing, into proprietors and proletarians. You will not find any of these hate-filled and warlike words in any of the great documents of the French Revolution. Politically, the Revolution desired that there should be no classes: the Restoration, the July Monarchy wanted the opposite. We must want what our fathers wanted.

The Revolution wanted that public burdens should be equal, really equal for all citizens. It failed in that. Public burdens have remained unequal in certain areas. We must make certain that they are equal. On this point we must want what our fathers wanted and put into practice what they were unable to do. [Very good]

As I have already told you, the French Revolution did not have the ridiculous pretension of creating a social power which would itself directly produce each citizen's fortune, well-being and ease of life, which would substitute the highly questionable wisdom of governments for the practical and self-interested wisdom of the governed. It believed that it had sufficiently fulfilled its role in giving enlightenment and liberty to every citizen. [Very good!]

It had the strong, noble, and proud belief, which you seem to lack, that for an honest and courageous man it is sufficient to have these two things, enlightenment and liberty, and that he need ask for nothing more from those who governed him.

The Revolution wanted this. It lacked the time and the means to accomplish it. We must want it and do it.

Finally, the French Revolution had the desire, and it was this desire that made it not only sacred but holy in the eyes of the world, it had the desire to introduce charity into politics. It conceived a broader, more general and higher idea than previously held of the obligations of the state toward the poor, towards those citizens who suffered. It is this idea that we must take up again, not, I repeat, in order to substitute the foresight and wisdom of the state for the foresight and wisdom of the individual but by using the means at the state's disposal efficiently and really to aid all those who suffer, aid all those who, after having exhausted all their own resources, would be reduced to poverty if the state did not hold out its hand.

This is what the French Revolution wanted to do. This is what we ourselves must do.

Is there any socialism in this?

On the left; Yes! Yes! There is only that!

Citizen de Tocqueville: No! No! No, there is no socialism there. There is Christian charity applied to politics. There is nothing there.... [Interruption]

The President of the Assembly: You disagree. This is as clear as day. You do not have the same opinion. You will mount the tribune, but do not interrupt.

Citizen de Tocqueville: There is nothing there that gives the workers a right in respect of the state. There is nothing there that obliges the state to replace individual foresight, thrift, and individual honesty. There is nothing there that authorizes the state to intervene in industry, to impose restrictions upon it, to tyrannize the individual in order better to govern him or, as is insolently maintained, to save him from himself. Here is nothing else than Christianity applied to politics.

Yes, the February revolution must be Christian and democratic, but it must not be socialist. These words summarize my thoughts, and I end by pronouncing them. [Very good! Very good!]

III. Extracts from a Speech on the Election of the President[41]

Session of October 5, 1848

Citizen de Tocqueville. [...] The honorable previous speaker, if he will permit me for saying so, has painted you a somewhat imaginary picture of the power of the president as envisaged by the Constitutional project. Gentlemen, let us examine things more closely and you will see that even with popular election, this power is reduced to little and, were this origin to be denied it, it would be nothing.

As envisaged in the Constitutional project, in the legislative sphere the president can do nothing: he has neither the absolute veto of the constitutional monarch nor the suspensive veto of the president of the United States. The previous honorable speaker described him to you as the rival of the Assembly. In point of fact, he is only the simple executor of its laws, the simple agent of its will; nothing more, its arm, to make use of a comparison that has already been used.

In the sphere which is the president's own, the creative sphere, look at the extent to which he is under its influence and dominion! It has been said that the Council of State has as its end and would have as its effect that of limiting the power of the National Assembly, of acting, in some way, as a counterbalance. Gentlemen, this is an error: on the contrary, the Council of State would have as its principal effect that of allowing the legislative power to enter the executive sphere in a regular and deep way. It is through the Council of State, nominated by the Assembly and removable by it, that the National Assembly participates in the execution of laws, makes up its mind about the nomination of senior civil servants, and judges politicians about whom it has complaints.

But it is above all through the institution of the council of responsible ministers that the Assembly exercises a control over the daily actions of the executive power, something of which the previous honorable speaker appears to be unaware.

As envisaged by the Constitutional project, the council of ministers appears to me as an institution without precedent and consequently I ask permission briefly to draw the attention of the Assembly to it.

When it comes to constitutions, there are as a matter of fact two distinct systems: a first system in which the head of the executive power is not responsible; but as, in reality, he can do nothing without the support of his ministers and as these ministers are placed under the observation, in the heart and within the reach of the legislative Assembly, the influence of the latter over the government remains very substantial. This is the system of constitutional monarchies. There is a second system. Within this one, the head of the executive power is directly responsible; but, at the same time, to act he does not need the support of any of his ministers; his ministers are chosen by him from outside the Assembly.

It is this system that until now has been employed in all the republics which have not merged the powers together: it is to be found not only in the

Constitution of the United States but also in France with the Constitution of Year III.[42] As a matter of fact, the heads of executive power were responsible, but they were able to act freely. The Constitution of the United States presented the same characteristic.

Here, on the contrary, what have we done? Something new, something unheard of, if I may be so bold as to say so. At one and the same time we have declared the head of executive power to be responsible, unlike the king was, and we have placed besides him a council of ministers which is equally responsible, without which he can do nothing, and which can reduce him to impotence, in the same way as it would have been able to reduce a constitutional monarch to impotence; and in such a way that the National Assembly alone can place the president on trial if he fails in his duty. But as every day it can impose its will upon him in every detail by forcing upon him ministers without whom he cannot act, it submits him to its own authority and that of his ministers: it can even constrain him, guide him, restrict him, direct him better than if, after having nominated him, it had left him free to act alone.

That is the executive power as envisaged by the Constitutional project: impotence in the sphere of legislative power; total dependence in that which is properly his. We are here very far from what the honorable previous speaker, who saw a monster with two heads, told us.

No, Gentlemen, the Republic has only one head; it is the National Assembly; the head of the executive power is only one of its agents, and he will soon be its slave if you allow him to be elected by it.

[...]

IV. Report Presented by M. de Tocqueville in the name of the Commission charged with examining the proposals for the revision of the constitution[43]

Session of July 8, 1851

[...]

Nations which have a federal existence, even those which, without having divided up sovereignty, possess an aristocracy, or who possess provincial liberties that are deeply rooted in their customs, can exist for a good while with a weak government, and even tolerate for a short period the complete absence of a government. Each element of the people has its own life that allows society to remain upright for a time when general life is impeded or suspended. But are we one of these nations? Have we not centralized everything and thus created of all governments the one which is in truth the easiest to overthrow but which, at the same time, is the most difficult to do without for a single moment?

[...] One can imagine the anxiety and the terror that take hold of everyone at the thought one day of finding empty this vast space occupied by government among us. Is it not to be feared that, in this confusion and this anxiety, at the last moment the electors will feel themselves pushed, not out of enthusiasm for a name or a man but through fear of the unknown and a horror of anarchy, to maintain illegally, and by a kind of popular act, executive power in the hands of those who hold it?

Examine the system of presidential election established by the Constitution itself and one will see that it facilitates, as much as the law can do, this revolutionary and disastrous outcome. A great nation spread across a vast stretch of land, a nation where the sphere of executive power is almost without limit and where the single representative of this power is elected by all citizens, voting directly and separately, without having had any means to enlighten themselves, to inform themselves, and to agree among themselves, such a nation, I have no fear in saying, has never been seen on the earth. The only country in the world which presents something vaguely analogous is America. But look at the remarkable difference! In America, direct and universal suffrage is the norm; only one exception to this great principle has been introduced and this applies precisely to the election of the president. The president of the United States of America also emanates from universal suffrage but not directly. And nevertheless, gentlemen, the role of the executive power in the Union, compared to what it is and will always be in France, whatever one does, is a small role. Despite this, in this country where, one might say, the republic has existed since the beginning, under the monarchy, in its practices, ideas and manners, and where it only had to appear rather than being born, in this country one did not dare entrust the election of the representative of the executive power to the accident of a direct and universal vote. The power to be elected appeared too great and, above all, too distant from the elector for the choice of the latter to be well-informed and mature. The American nation only chooses delegates, who themselves choose the president. The latter undoubtedly represent the general spirit of the country, its inclinations, its tastes, often its passions and prejudices, but they are provided with less knowledge than the people might have. They can reach an exact idea of the general needs of the people, of its true dangers; they can know the candidates, compare their merits, weigh up, choose what each citizen, from the depth of his home, and often his ignorance, in the midst of his work and of the demands of his private life, is incapable of doing. Also, have we not seen that, for the past sixty years, the Americans have often denied the highest office of the republic to the best known, sometimes the most renowned, of its citizens and have chosen relatively obscure men, but who respond better to the political needs of the moment?

If on this question the dangers of direct and universal suffrage have roused the legislators of the United States, how the more so should they strike us, we who live in a country where most citizens have not yet acquired the habit of concerning themselves with political matters, where they consider them only by chance, and do not even know the name of the majority of those who lead them or believe themselves to lead them! A country where furthermore the people have already sufficiently acquired the passions awakened by democracy not to like placing one of their equals at the head of government, and have not yet acquired enough of the knowledge and experience required by democratic peoples to resolve these matters. Beyond perhaps the famous demagogues who call attention to and who commend self-interested and violent passions or princes whose birth enables them to be seen from afar and places them beyond compare, who is the only person whose name easily comes to mind and is fixed solidly in the memory of those millions of electors who cover the surface of France, if not that of the man through whom public power has been exercised for some years, who, in the eyes of each citizen, has personified this central administration, who here we see everywhere, who one senses in everything and who every day one discovers either above or beside oneself?

[. . .] France is again delivered up to the whims of the crowd and to the hazards of force. [. . .]

The Poussin Affair

Introduction

Alexis de Tocqueville became Minister of Foreign Affairs on June 2, 1849. He occupied this office for barely five months.[1] Two areas of foreign policy most preoccupied Tocqueville during this brief period: the so-called Roman affair, where France dispatched an expeditionary force with the dual aim of restoring the temporal power of the Pope and of imposing liberal institutions on central Italy; the repression of the Hungarian rising and the fate of its defeated supporters (which included Lajos Kossuth) seeking asylum in Turkey. However, events in the New World also attracted Tocqueville's attention in the form of the so-called Poussin Affair.

Guillaume-Tell Poussin was born in France around 1795. With the fall of Napoléon, he left for America and in 1817 became a topographical engineer in the United States Army. He subsequently became a naturalized American citizen but later returned to France. In 1841, he published *Considérations sur le Principe démocratique qui régit l'Union Américaine et d'autres états*.[2] In essence, this was a detailed commentary upon Tocqueville's *Democracy in America*, written by a man who, as he immediately told his readers, claimed to know more about America than his illustrious compatriot. In 1848 he played a decisive role in convincing Richard Rush, U. S. Minister to France, to recognize the new French Republic.[3] The following year, when Poussin was appointed French Minister in Washington, D.C., his appointment was warmly welcomed by the American administration as, in the words of President James K. Polk, "a new pledge of the friendly feelings of the French Republic."

However, as the documents below reveal, events quickly took an unhappy turn, with a series of minor incidents escalating into a diplomatic quarrel that also involved Tocqueville and threatened a serious rupture of relations between France and the United States. In brief, the first incident concerned a claim for damages raised by a French citizen named Port over the wrongful sale of bales of tobacco seized by the American army following the Mexican War. Poussin took up this claim with the newly appointed Secretary of State, John Middleton Clayton. Not satisfied with the reply he received from the latter, Poussin sent off another letter, in which he included the words: "the Government of the United States must be convinced, that it is more honorable to acquit fairly a debt contracted during war, under the pressure of necessity, than to avoid its payment in an endeavor to brand the character of an honest man." Outraged, Clayton summoned Poussin to Washington, D.C. and demanded that this offensive passage was withdrawn. This Poussin did.

No sooner was this matter resolved than a similar incident occurred, this time over the actions of Carpender, commander of the United States vessel *Iris*, to secure salvage for the rescue of a French ship, the *Eugènie*, which had run aground in the Gulf of Mexico. Although in practice, this issue was quickly resolved, Poussin wrote to Clayton asking that Carpender be censured and, when this was not done, sent a further letter in which he concluded that "I am induced to believe, that your Government subscribes to the strange doctrines professed by Commander Carpender of the war steamer *Iris*, and I have only too protest, in the name of my Government, against these doctrines."

At this point, the American administration decided to place the whole matter before the French government through the intermediary of its Minister in Paris, Richard Rush. As we already know, Rush was well known to Tocqueville, the two having spent much time together during 1848 in discussions of France's new constitution, and thus one might have expected a quick resolution to the issue. However, Tocqueville's reply failed to satisfy the administration in Washington, D.C., for in addition to observing that both Poussin and Clayton might be said to have used undiplomatic language, he added that the latter's note of April 21 was rather "an imperious summons than a diplomatic invitation." In response, President Taylor informed Poussin on September 24 that the United States government would have no further dealings with him. For his part, Clayton wrote directly to Tocqueville, informing him that he had not been invited "to construct an apology for that Minister, by indiscriminately censuring both parties to the correspondence." Neither side seemed prepared to yield, with the French government deciding that it would not receive the new American Minister to France, William Rives, until adequate explanations had been provided. These the Americans refused to supply. Clayton informed Tocqueville in a note of November 7, 1849 that "The President finds nothing in the conduct of this Government, which requires any expression of his intentions, views or wishes." At this point, the outbreak of war between France and America seemed not improbable. The Poussin Affair was widely reported in the French and American press. It is worth pointing out that American newspapers were not uncritical of the actions of their own government.

Here we should note that these exchanges preceded the completion of the transatlantic telegraph cable and that they were dependent upon steam ship, usually via Liverpool, a journey that could often last up to three weeks. The exchange of diplomatic correspondence was therefore subject to considerable delay. Thus, even after his dismissal from office, Tocqueville continued to receive updates on the situation in the United States from his emissary, Charles de Montholon. In these letters, we see the practices of quiet and informal diplomacy at work. We should also note that Poussin's letters to Tocqueville emphasize not just the political dynamics operating in Washington, D.C., casting American politics in an unfavorable light, but the growing American intervention in Central America, a subject which was to preoccupy Tocqueville in the 1850s.

The affair was brought to a speedy close. On November 8, 1849, Louis-Napoléon, President of France, having dismissed his government, received William Rives, assuring him of his consideration for the United States. The sixth paragraph of Zachary Taylor's Annual Message, December 4, 1849, indicated that "a slight interruption of diplomatic intercourse between this Government and France" had been terminated and that the U.S. Minister, Rives, had now been received in Paris. The following March, Bois-le-Comte was received as France's new Minister to the United States.

It serves no purpose to discuss who was right and who was wrong in this diplomatic squabble. Poussin undoubtedly used provocative and intemperate language. For his part, Clayton, directed by the inexperienced Zachary Taylor, seemed intent on provoking a fight with America's old ally. As for Tocqueville himself, for all his efforts to deal with the issue in an even-handed way, he seems to have displayed an element of naivety in his dealings with the American administration.

A face-saving diplomatic reshuffle might have been the wisest move. What cannot be denied, as the two letters he sent to Gustave de Beaumont reveal, is that Tocqueville was personally wounded and affronted by the Poussin Affair, feeling that it had seriously damaged his reputation. The irony of presiding over a breakdown of diplomatic relations with the United States cannot have been lost by him. Moreover, in his letter to Gustave de Beaumont on October 12, 1849, the man who had so warmly praised the character of the Americans in his published writings now felt able to describe these very same people as "animals."

The documents in this section not only shed fresh light on an important, yet little known, episode in the relations between the United States and France, but also allow us to understand what was probably Tocqueville's least happy engagement with America. They also permit us to re-evaluate the image of American democracy in France. The conventional picture of a peaceful and prosperous republic, embraced by Tocqueville himself in his own classic text, sits uneasily by the side of Charles de Montholon's reference, in his letter of November 11, 1849, to "the habits of hazardous enterprise and domination of the American people, its remarkable natural presumption, the illusions it always holds about its greatness and about the need that people have, beyond the seas, of its industrial and commercial wealth."

Our intention in this section has been to reconstruct the exchanges that took place over the Poussin Affair and thus, upon occasion, we have included a few relevant letters not written by or addressed to Tocqueville. Some of the documents in this section were translated from French; the others were originally written in English. Unless otherwise stated, the original documents are taken from the microfilms of the archives of the French Ministry of Foreign Affairs held at the Quai d'Orsay in Paris. They can be found under two headings: *Mémoires et documents: Etats-Unis*, Vol. 25 and *Correspondences Diplomatiques, Etats-Unis*, Vol. 104.[4]

I. Richard Rush to Alexis de Tocqueville

Paris, July 7, 1849

Sir,

I have the honor to enclose to your Excellency under instructions from the government of the United States copies of a correspondence, and documents connected with it, which has recently passed between the Secretary of State and M. Poussin, Minister of the French Republic at Washington.

It will be seen by these papers that in October last Commander Carpender of the United States Navy, while in command of the war steamer 'Iris,' saved from imminent peril if not certain destruction the French barque Eugénie, which had struck the Bank of Piso, near the anchorage of Anton-Lizardo on the coast of Mexico; that the commander of the 'Iris,' believing the service rendered laid a just claim for salvage in view of the case that has been sanctioned by the opinion of the Attorney General of the United States, made such a claim, though he afterwards delivered up the barque which at first he had detained, to the free control of her captain, thus waving the claim; that M. Poussin in a note to the Secretary of State of the 12th of May, written it would seem under instructions from the Minister of Foreign Affairs, founded that time on a report of the case from the acting council of the Republic at Vera Cruz, imputed arbitrary conduct to the Commander of the Iris, and invoked upon it the censure of the American government; and that the Secretary of State in receiving his note, lost no time in transmitting it to the Secretary of the Navy, which produced from that member of the Cabinet a full and circumstantial report on the transaction. The copy of his letter is marked A and the documents it transmitted, B, C, & D in the enclosed here sent to your Excellency.

All were enclosed to M. Poussin in a letter from the Secretary of State of the 25th of May, with the expression of a hope that they would remove any misapprehension which might have existed on the part of the French government relative to the conduct of the American Commander.

Explanations so official and full, given the moment attainable, and which then for the first time had been afforded from the American side, it might have been supposed would be transmitted by the Minister to his government, and its judgment awaited under the new lights thrown upon the transaction. He acted otherwise. On the day but one following, he repeated in a note to the Secretary of State his accusations of the American Commander and spoke to the American government of its duties, in terms to foreclose further discussion.

My instructions compel me to add that the attention of the American government was the more strongly attracted to the tone of this note, as the Minister had only a short time before (the month of April), in one written in support of a French claim, used language so objectionable that it was necessary he should withdraw it. The document showing it is marked E, and the words within brackets at the conclusion, are those that were withdrawn. The letter of the Secretary of State to the

Minister (marked F) points to the promptness with which the retraction was expected. In overlooking words incautiously used on that occasion the department of State was guided by a sincere desire to omit nothing which would tend to promote the friendly and harmonious relations of the two governments.

But in now submitting, by direction of the President, the whole of these papers to the consideration of the French government, your Excellency will not fail to perceive that the absence of due forbearance, in diction and tone, in diplomatic correspondence, must tend to embarrass rather than promote a friendly and frank discussion of questions that concern the honor and interests of the two Republics.

I eagerly seize this opportunity of tendering to your Excellency assurances of the distinguished consideration with which I have the honor to be
your most faithful and most
obedient humble servant,
Richard Rush

[From Guillaume-Tell Poussin]
Legation of France
Washington, April 1849[5]

To the Hon[ora]ble J. M. Clayton
Secretary of State

Sir,

I received on the 10[th] instant the letter which you did me the honor to address to me in answer to the one wherein I presented the principal reasons, which should, in my opinion, induce you to admit the claim of M. A[lexis] Port.

You endeavor to establish in that letter that M. Port knew at the moment when he became the purchaser of the tobacco, that it was the property of M. Domercq and not of the United States; then, proceeding upon this hypothesis you go on to say that M. Port, so far from being entitled to reimbursement of the sums lost by him in consequence of the annulment of the sale made by him to M. Abadie, did not even deserve to have restored to him the sums which he had paid into the hands of Quartermaster Webster, as the price of what he had bought from the United States.

Permit me, Mr. Secretary of State, to observe to you that in reasoning thus, you go rather singularly beyond the decision of the Court Martial held at Puebla on the 17th November 1847.[6]

This military court, which permitted Col. Childs[7] to carry out, without interruption, his string of calumnies incredible, was certainly by no means over favorable to M. Port; yet it refused to recognize in M. Port that bad faith which, in your opinion, might relieve the United States' government from the charge of returning to this Frenchman the sums paid by him into the American coffers and employed for the support of the army.

It is among the evidence given before the Court, which did not admit the charge of bad faith, that you seek for proofs of that bad faith. You cite with this object, the questions addressed by M. Port to M. Dumercq and the answers given by the latter. It would be easy, M. Secretary of State, for me by examining each word of this portion of the inquiries, to establish beyond question that, so far from it being against us, it serves effectively to overthrow the allegations of Col. Childs, but I shall limit myself to an account of the explanations given on the subject by M. Dumercq himself to the Legation of France, on the 12th of April 1849.

M. Dumercq then declared

1. That, while in Puebla, he gave no notice whatsoever, in a direct manner to M. Port, before the day of the sale of the 500 bales of tobacco.

2. That while at Puebla, he did not, except on the 19th of October, address to Col. Childs' Secretary his claims which, from reasons which we do not, and wish not to learn, remained without effect.

3. That the conversation between M. Port and the son of the Spanish Consul to which allusion was made in the Court at Puebla, may have related, not to the 500 bales of tobacco already bought by M. Port, but to the other lots of the same tobacco, which were afterwards to be sold at the same place.

These declarations, Sir, are in support of those of M. Port. I do not therefore hesitate to believe that, taking into consideration the different proofs which favor M. Port, and admitting on the other hand that a man should always be considered as acting in good faith until the contrary be proved, you will acknowledge the good faith of M. Port.

I have yet, Sir, to answer two objections which you have made to the reasoning contained in my letter of the 30th.

When I told you that *M. Port is not a tobacco dealer* I meant this in answer to the deposition of Col. Childs, where he uses these words "Witness is of the opinion that M. Port has rendered himself guilty of collusion with his Secretary, that they had a criminal understanding with each other to speculate in the tobacco to the injury of the first purchaser, Domercq; his reason for this first opinion is that so large a quantity of tobacco could not have been sold in Puebla without the fact being known to all tobacco dealers."

My reasoning was this: a man not habitually engaged in the tobacco trade, but who entered into it once, only when seduced by opportunity, may very fairly be supposed to be ignorant of the special operations of that business, which tobacco dealers alone are interested in learning; but, even if M. Port were a tobacco dealer, does it specifically follow, as Col. Childs concludes, that he must have engaged in a criminal understanding with M. Wingieski, and have rendered himself guilty of collusion? Really, Sir, if there is in all this an unqualified assertion, it is not mine, but that of Col. Childs, which you have not hesitated to endorse.

Finally, Mr. Secretary of State, I said in my note of 30th that M. Port quitted Puebla on the 10th of September, and did not return until 15th of October 1847. You answer that this assertion of mine is not supported by any evidence, and you therefore consider yourself justified in rejecting it entirely. I shall therefore annex to this letter some documents, the mere reading of which should convince you of the reality of the statement made by me; and you will also see, that the Legation of France, which could never consent to being the organ of a criminal accusation, does not venture, without proofs, to advance an assertion of a fact of the most innocent nature.

Allow me to hope, Mr. Secretary of State, that this letter may be the last of the correspondence, which has already been too long on an affair so clear. (The government of the United States must be convinced, that it is more honorable to acquit fairly a debt contracted during war, under the pressure of necessity, than to avoid its payment by endeavoring to brand the character of an honest man.)[8]

Accept, I pray you, Sir, the assurance of my high consideration.

Guillaume-Tell Poussin

Document F

Department of State
Washington, April 21, 1849

Sir,

On the afternoon of the 18th instant, a communication from you dated Washington, April 1849 (without showing the day on which it was written) was received at this office, relative to the claim of Mr. Port on the government of the United States, and having just had reason to address you a private note, I learn through the messenger who was to deliver it that you have been for the last two weeks absent from Washington and that the period of your return hither from New York was quite uncertain.

Under these circumstances, after the perusal of your note which was laid before me this morning, I lose not a moment in requesting you to repair to this city without unnecessary delay.

I have the honor to be,
Very respectfully, Sir,
Your obedient servant
John M. Clayton

✻ ✻ ✻

II. Richard Rush to John M. Clayton[9]

No. 98	Legation of the U. States
Hon[orable] J. M. Clayton	Paris, July 11, 1849
Sec[retary] of State	

Sir,

I paused a few days before acting upon the instructions of your No. 36 relating to M. Poussin, thinking it possible that the steamer succeeding the one which brought them, might bring me the full opinion of the Attorney General, the abstract of which, sent to you by Mr. Johnson at a moment when he was leaving Washington, came with your dispatch. The full opinion and precedents it probably embodies on the question of salvage are not indeed necessary to me under the turn the case took, and would have been desirable only for incidental reference. They may not be wanted for that.

Not receiving the opinion *in extenso*, I proceeded last week, after looking into some authorities on the point myself, to seek an interview with the Minister of Foreign Affairs,[10] and obtained one on the 6th inst. Considering the nature of the papers I was to communicate to him, I thought it best to smooth the way for his reception of them by a conversation beforehand; and this the good personal relations I have been so fortunate as to enjoy with M. de Tocqueville ever since being in France, enabled me the better to do. I explained the case verbally to him. Carrying your despatch with me, I also read such of your comments on M. Poussin's correspondence as I thought I might with advantage, and made other observations seeming appropriate to the interview. The Minister gave every attention to what I said. He remarked that the case was not entirely new to him tho' he had not examined it, but would be prepared to do so as soon as all the papers came under his view. He expressed the most cordial sentiments towards the U. States, in the sincerity of which I have the more reliance from my knowledge of his character; and I did not fail to say in return on this, as I do on all fit occasions, how precious to the U. States was the friendship of France.

On the day following, I drew up a note which yesterday morning I sent to him accompanied by copies of all the papers. A copy of my note is enclosed. In the evening I dined at the Ministry. It was a large entertainment given to the President of the Republic, to which the diplomatic corps, a portion of the home ministers, General Changarnier[11] and others were invited. After dinner I again sought an opportunity of conversing with M. de Tocqueville about the correspondence of M. Poussin. He had received my note and the papers and promised to examine them fully and carefully at the earliest moment in his power.

The Italian question is still making its pressure upon the time of the cabinet altho' Rome has surrendered to the French Army. I will barely add that whilst my conversations with him have been frank and free, under the just reserves, even towards M. Poussin, I have avoided even the least allusion to the course for the government to adopt on the occasion, leaving that, at this stage of the case more especially, to its own judgment entirely; although I could not forget that our history in analogous cases supplies precedents for the best course.

I have received Mr. Draper's exequatuor[12] from the Minister of Foreign Affairs under the application I made for it, and have the honor to remain etc.

Rich[ar]d Rush

✳ ✳ ✳

III. Guillaume-Tell Poussin to Alexis de Tocqueville

French Legation to the United States
New York,
July 16, 1849

Minister,

I received on the 13th instant the letter which you did me the honor of writing to me dated June 4 and identified by stamp no. 21, which informed me that the President of the Republic had recently conferred upon you the Foreign Affairs portfolio.

I am delighted, Minister, to be called upon with you to occupy myself with the questions and interests of our country in relation to the United States, of which, in so many ways, you are such a fine judge and well-informed authority. You can count on my loyal and enthusiastic support in everything that will be of a nature to interest the service of the government and upon the reliability and vigor of my efforts to find the most favorable solutions to all the tasks conferred upon me.

Be assured, Minister, of my highest consideration.

Guillaume-Tell Poussin

✵ ✵ ✵

IV. Alexis de Tocqueville to Richard Rush

Paris,
August 9, 1849

Sir,

I acknowledge receipt of the letter that you did me the honor of writing to me on the 7th of last month, the copies of the correspondence which took place between the Secretary of State for Foreign Affairs of the United States and the Minister of France in Washington concerning two demands that the latter was instructed to present to the Federal Government, one against the improper detention of the French vessel, the *Eugénie* by Commander Carpender off Vera Cruz, the other requesting compensation in favor of M. Port, a French trader, because of the invalidation of the sale of a certain quantity of tobacco belonging to him decided upon by the commanding officer of American forces at Pueblo.

These two affairs, having been until now discussed in Washington and having there to be resolved, I am not fully familiar with the details. Moreover, I am too sure of the honesty of the government of the Union to doubt that it will not recognize all lawful complaints, and for its part it should not think that the French government will allow itself to be led by the desire to protect its nationals or to support claims that are not well-founded in justice.

This sentiment of mutual confidence, which is of a nature to avoid disagreements and misunderstandings in matters relating to discussions of private interests and which can only further complicate these issues, is such that we have witnessed with astonishment as much as regret the course taken by the correspondence exchanged between our envoy and Mr. Clayton. Even before I had received the letter that you wrote me in order to bring this to my attention, M. Poussin had already forwarded copies to me. I was painfully struck to find in this correspondence a tone of sourness and a severity hardly appropriate to the friendly relations between two countries, but I feel obliged to say, without entering into pointless recriminations and without wishing to identify who was first at fault, that this observation applies not solely to the letters written by the Minister of France. M. Poussin, doubtlessly badly interpreting several statements that were addressed to him by the Secretary of State, believed he there saw a lack of respect toward which he expressed his sense of injury too strongly; but if a passage in his letter of.....[13] April offended Mr. Clayton, it seems to me that one is no longer entitled to act against him, when he has agreed to withdraw it and he has given sufficient evidence of his spirit of reconciliation by not responding to a phrase in the reply of the Minister of April 21, which, if read with undue susceptibility, might have appeared more as an imperious summons than as a diplomatic invitation.

Moreover, Sir, I do not need to say that I completely share the opinion that you expressed to me concerning the necessity of not putting aside in our negotiations the considerations and the manners of a benevolent courtesy. I have reminded M. Poussin never to forget this rule in the relations he has with the government of the United States, and I am confident that he will receive the same treatment by way of reciprocity.

❊ ❊ ❊

V. Guillaume-Tell Poussin to Alexis de Tocqueville

New York,
August 16, 1849

Minister,

I have the honor of indicating to you that I have received the despatches addressed to me up to no. 26 and to the date of July 6.

The President of the Unites States has just issued a proclamation that strongly indicates the honesty of his pacific intentions and how, with regard to himself at least, it is the intention to respect religiously the international agreements which bind the Union to friendly nations.

An armed expedition which had the intention of invading the island of Cuba has recently been discovered and has served as the pretext for this proclamation which I judge, Minister, to be of sufficient general interest to be translated in its entirety and transmitted to you.[14]

A Proclamation

There is reason to believe that an armed expedition is about to be fitted out in the United States with an intention to invade the island of Cuba or some of the provinces of Mexico. The best information which the Executive has been able to obtain points to the island of Cuba as the object of this expedition. It is the duty of this Government to observe the faith of the treaties and to prevent any aggression by our citizens upon the territories of friendly nations. I have therefore thought it necessary and proper to issue this my proclamation to warn all citizens of the United States who shall connect themselves with an enterprise so grossly in violation of our laws and our treaty obligations that they will thereby subject themselves to the heavy penalties denounced against them by the acts of Congress and will forfeit their claim to the protection of their country. No such persons must expect the interference of this Government in any form on their behalf, no matter to what extremities they may be reduced in consequence of their conduct. An enterprise to invade the territories of a friendly nation, set on foot and prosecuted within the limits of the United States, is in the highest degree criminal, as tending to endanger the peace and compromise the honor of this nation; and therefore I exhort all good citizens, as they regard our national reputation, as they respect their own laws and the laws of nations, as they value the blessings of peace and the welfare of their country, to discountenance and prevent by all lawful means any such enterprise; and I call upon every officer of this Government, civil or military, to use all efforts in his power to arrest for trial and punishment every such offender against the laws providing for the performance of our sacred obligations to friendly powers.

Given under my hand the 11th of August A.D. 1849, and the seventy-fourth of the independence of the United States.

Z. Taylor

By the President

J. M. Clayton

Secretary of State

Will this act of honesty, prudence and courage on the part of the President of the United States be sufficient to prevent the realization of a political fact destined in due time to be accomplished? I think not, Minister. It could perhaps have the effect of suspending its execution but not of changing the future.

In effect, the expedition against Cuba, based upon already existing interests in favor of annexation in the two countries and which attracts more supporters every day, was brought about intemperately by the Canadian insurrection,[15] to which it is connected and for which it serves as a counterbalance: because Cuba and Canada, it must be recognized, are two satellites of the United States irresistibly and inevitably drawn into the sphere of the Union and destined from that time onwards to submit simultaneously to its law. When the time comes, the Americans, while protesting their respect for international treaties, will march no less resolutely toward the realization of their ambition. While waiting they will proclaim their complete neutrality towards Cuba for as long as no other country intervenes in its affairs or that this island does not pass into the hands of another power apart from Spain, but when this situation changes it will act according to the demands of its own security and its interests.

Please accept, Minister, the assurance of my highest consideration.

Guillaume-Tell Poussin

❆ ❆ ❆

VI. John M. Clayton to Alexis de Tocqueville

Department of State
Washington
September 8, 1849

M. Alexis de Tocqueville
    Minister of Foreign Affairs
        of the French Republic

Sir,

I have received a despatch from Mr. Rush, the American Minister in Paris of the 13th of August, covering a note from you to him, dated the 9th of that month. Both have been submitted to the President, with the correspondence to which they relate. As Mr. Rush is returning home and Mr. Rives, who has been appointed to succeed him as Minister to France, has probably not yet arrived in Paris, I hasten to avail myself of the only means of communication, between the Governments we represent by addressing you directly on the subject of your note.

You acknowledge the receipt of the correspondence "which took place between the Secretary of State for Foreign Affairs of the United States and the Minister of France at Washington," from which, it must have been obvious to your mind, that his letter had repeatedly and gratuitously addressed communications to this Government highly offensive and discourteous both in manner and in substance.

That correspondence was submitted simply to enable your Government to decide upon the proper course to be taken in regards to its own Minister. You appear to have considered the occasion as one which called upon you to construct an apology for that Minister, by indiscriminately censuring both parties to the correspondence. You were not invited to decide as an arbiter upon the words in which the American Government conducted that correspondence, which was not only courteous and respectful in terms, but entirely unexceptionable in spirit, and you could not have failed to observe that this Department had not, in any instance, descended to recrimination, whether useless or otherwise, with M. Poussin.

Should the correspondence of any Minister of this Republic prove insulting to the friendly Government of France, that Government is too confident of our desires to maintain kind relations with it, to doubt that the President of the United States should feel it to be a high duty to examine the complaints, and to render a prompt and proper atonement for the inquiry. But the issue, presented in the correspondence of M. Poussin, cannot be evaded by any charge of recriminations. If that charge can be made, with any shadow of truth, let it be separately presented, and it will be promptly and most respectfully considered.

The President instructs me to say to your Excellency that, as from the whole tone of your communication to Mr. Rush, which has struck him with much surprise, it would seem that the disrespectful language of the French Minister at Washington has been received with indulgence, and held worthy of palliation by his distinguished Minister of Foreign Affairs of France, who has manifested no disposition to redress his wrong, he, as the Chief Magistrate of the United States, feels himself now at perfect liberty, and in fact constrained, with a view to preclude opportunities which might be again abused, to perform without any further delay, an unpleasant duty from which he had hoped his friendly appeal to the French Government, would have relieved him.

This Government is the guarantor of its own honor, and, as on all occasions, it seeks to avoid giving cause of offence, so, will it never submit to intentional disrespect. By the time this letter reaches your Excellency, M. Poussin will have been informed, that no further correspondence will be held with him by the Executive of the United States, and that, every proper facility will be afforded him, should he desire to return to France.

The President further instructs me to express to your Excellency the friendly sentiments of himself and of this Government, for the President, the Government, and the People of France. He does not doubt that these kind sentiments are reciprocated by them, and he anticipates, with lively satisfaction, the arrival of M. Poussin's successor, with whom it will be the duty of this Government to cultivate agreeable and friendly intercourse, in the terms and the spirit of mutual courtesy, which will be equally honorable to both the sister Republics.

In the mean time, prompt and respectful attention will be given to any communications touching the interests of our respective countries, which may be made through any other diplomatic agent whom the French Government may see fit to select.

I avail myself of this opportunity to offer to your Excellency the assurance of my most distinguished consideration.

John M. Clayton

✖ ✖ ✖

VII. Letter from Guillaume-Tell Poussin to Alexis de Tocqueville

Washington,
September 22, 1849

Addressed to: M. Alexis de Tocqueville, Minister of Foreign Affairs,

Minister,

A decision of the utmost importance taken by the government in Washington has resulted in the sudden and violent rupture of communications between the Legation of France to the United States and the Secretary of State. Given this decision, Minister, I feel constrained to explain to you the plan of action I have followed in my diplomatic relations with the present American administration; the decisions I have taken following my receipt of the strange note that has just reached me, the content of which it is for you to judge; and finally the inconsistencies that have preceded, accompanied and followed the dispatch of this note.

I have had two important items of business to conduct with Mr. Clayton, the present Secretary of State:

1. that concerning M. Port and the compensation claimed for losses occurred during the war with Mexico as a consequence of American military actions.

2. that concerning the French ship *Eugénie* for services rendered by the American warship Iris, whose commander, entertaining improper expectations of remuneration, illegally detained for over 48 hours our vessel in order to ensure the attainment of his demands.

These two issues, the soundness of which cannot be doubted by anyone, were specifically brought to my attention by the Minister of Foreign Affairs; they have not had a satisfactory outcome and I have, Minister, forwarded to you all correspondence relating to their subject. You yourself have observed a regrettable unpleasantness of expression in this correspondence; but one fact which moreover cannot have escaped your attention is that on this issue we have not ceased to be provoked by the government of the United States. We were obliged to respond with the same severity that had been deployed towards us. Thus, when the Secretary of State refused to acknowledge the demands of M. Port, accusing this Frenchman of fraud and bad faith, we could not but have objected to such an unjustified reproach; and when, called upon to disown the actions of a high-ranking officer of the American navy, the Minister of State, far from giving satisfaction to the legitimate complaints of the French government, disdained even to grant them a serious consideration, we had no choice about the response to make: that of protesting in clear terms against the doctrine of international law practiced by Commander Carpender and sanctioned by the approval of the American government.

It was in this manner that I wrote on May 30, 1849. Mr. Clayton replied on the 5th June indicating that he intended to submit the correspondence to my government. This was the decision that, for my part, I took and put into effect by a dispatch of June 12.

Since then what has occurred?

Almost three months have elapsed. During these three months I had cause to communicate with the government of the United States on different matters and these received response.

Then, finally, on the 14th of this month I received the letter of which I attach both a copy and a faithful translation.

Department of State
Washington, September 14, 1849

Sir,

The President has devolved upon me the duty of announcing to you that the Government of the United States will hold no further correspondence with you as the Minister of France and that the necessity which has impelled him to take this step at the present moment has been made known to your government. In communicating the President's determination in regard to yourself personally I avail myself of the occasion to add that due attention will be cheerfully given to any communication from the government of France affecting the interests of our respective Republics which may reach this Department through any other channels. Your own government will be able to explain to you the reasons which have influenced the American Executive in delaying the present communication until this period.

The President has instructed me further to say that every proper facility for quitting the United States will be promptly given at any moment when you may be pleased to sign that it is your desire to return to France.

I am, sir, very respectfully,
Your most obedient servant,
John M. Clayton

On the 20th of this month, the *Republic*, the official journal of Washington, published, at the prompting of the government itself, an article which, making appeal to public opinion and disdaining to clarify the situation by a complete publication of the letters, thought fit to let only a part of my correspondence see the light of day.

The American press almost unanimously opposed this practice and this very morning, Minister, the complete correspondence appeared, including your letter to Mr. Rush of August 9, 1849 and the letter addressed to you by Mr. Clayton dated September 8, 1849.

Thanks to these publications, Minister, and thanks to them alone I understand the grievances of the American government against me. In my official letters I believe strongly that I always remained within the limits of the instructions of my government as well as at the same within those of the utmost propriety and the most scrupulous decorum. You, Minister, will be the judge of this, but in awaiting your decision this is the code of conduct that I have resolved upon as best according with the demands of the position which I hold.

Deriving both my title and my rank from the French Republic, it is from its orders alone that I can be deprived of them; it is also to it alone that I must account for the use that I have made of them.

I know, Minister, that henceforth my remaining here as Minister of France is impossible, but I have thought that I owe to those who appointed me, and also to myself, not to give way before the outrageous conduct directed against me by the American Executive. Therefore, irrespective of my desire to quit immediately this nation which, as it were, reared me and where today, without any justification, I meet so much injustice, harshness and ill will, I will await my recall to France in New York and, having returned to private life, all that I ask of France are the words of justice and the esteem of my fellow citizens.

I have sent to the Consular officials of France in the United States the circular here attached.

If there is need for communication between the legation of France and the American government, this will be carried out by my secretary at the legation acting according to my orders and instructions.

Please accept, Minister, the expression of my deepest consideration,

Guillaume-Tell Poussin

Copy of the letter addressed to the Consular officials
The Legation of France
To the United States

Washington, September 21, 1849

Sir,

I have the honor of informing you that, as a consequence of the disagreement that has arisen between the government of the United States and the Minister of France I have removed the seat of my Legation to New York until such time as the government decides otherwise. It is therefore to this residence that you should address the demands of any French citizens that might require my assistance.

Please accept, etc, etc . . .

✳ ✳ ✳

VIII. Extracts from Two Letters Written by Tocqueville to Gustave de Beaumont[16]

Paris,
October 5, 1849

My dear friend,

[...]

I would speak to you at greater length and better about all this were I not at this moment very troubled and, above all, horribly frustrated by the news which comes to me from America. Major Poussin (whom we have just replaced with Bois-le-Comte) has been dismissed without any sufficient motive and this information was directly announced to me in an impertinent fashion. From this whole experience I have received some very disagreeable damage to my reputation.

[...]

Alexis de Tocqueville

Paris,
October 12, 1849

My dear friend,

[...]

P.S. I am tired and a little discouraged as I write to you. At the moment there are so many and too many big questions to be dealt with. I am weighed down by the burden. And then, my dear friend, what a misery it is to direct the foreign affairs of a people which, having the memory of immense strength and in reality only limited power, aspires to do everything and, at bottom, does not wish or perhaps cannot dare to do anything.[17] It would be better to plant cabbages.

I hope that the business with America will be resolved without too much difficulty, Poussin having been removed from office before we knew what had happened in the United States and Rives having not yet been received here. But what animals these Americans are! More and more I take what Talleyrand said about them to be profound.[18]

✳ ✳ ✳

IX. John M. Clayton to Alexis de Tocqueville

Department of State
Washington,
November 10, 1849

M. Alexis de Tocqueville
Minister of Foreign Affairs of France

Sir,

I have received your note of the 11th of October last, and in reply I am directed by the President to refer your Excellency to my note of the 14th of September which expressed fully and frankly his views, sentiments and intentions, and states the circumstances which presented the only grounds of the dissatisfaction of this Government with M. Poussin. I am further directed by the President, to say, that he deems it neither necessary nor proper to add anything on those topics.

By his order the correspondence of M. Poussin with this department had been, as an act of courtesy, laid before the French Government and you had been apprised by Mr. Rush's note of the 7th July last, that the terms used by M. Poussin in his communication of the 30th of May (a copy of which was transmitted to you) were such as to foreclose any further discussion with him. The President did expect, that, on your becoming aware of the fact that M. Poussin had addressed this Government in tone and language so discourteous and disrespectful, the French government would have promptly marked its sense of what was due on such an occasion to a friendly power by recalling him, or at least, by requiring him without delay, to withdraw his unbecoming expressions, disavow the intention of offence and offer suitable acknowledgements of the serious error into which he had fallen. Between the 7th of July, when Mr. Rush's note of that date, was addressed to you and the receipt of your reply of the 9th of August, information was communicated to me, in a circuitous manner, through a private citizen (which you are pleased to denominate semi-official information) that M. Poussin would be recalled, and the President was thus induced to expect that the proceeding of the French government, though tardy, would, at last, be such as to dispel the slight cloud, which the misconduct of an individual had interposed between two countries whose relations had been so amicable. Your *official* note of the 9th of August, received here on the 5th day of September, put an end to all such expectations. In that note, Your Excellency distinctly intimated the anticipated continuance of M. Poussin's functions as Minister near this Government by apprizing it (through Mr. Rush) that you would instruct him as to the mode in which he was, in future, to conduct his correspondence with it; and you referred to the very case of Commander Carpender (as one of the subjects, the description of which was to be concluded here) in regard to which you had been informed, by Mr. Rush, that the terms of M. Poussin's last communication were such as to preclude further discussion with him. That I have not misunderstood Your Excellency's note of the 9th of August manifestly appears by your own construction of it, in the note to which I am now responding, in which you say, "I ended the letter written to Mr. Rush in answer to your (my) note by the promise to invite the French Agent never, in his intercourse, to deviate from the observance and forms of amicable courtesy." Nor did Your Excellency propose, that any reparation should be made for the injurious proceeding of M. Poussin, who, for more than three months, had been with great forbearance, allowed to remain in his position, in the expectation, entertained by this government, of ultimate redress. While there was abundant opportunity, during that long interval, to recall or instruct him, he himself offered no acknowledgement of error.

The President therefore, did not hesitate, after considering your note of the 9th of August, to adopt the only course which remained for him to pursue consistently with the honor and dignity of the United States.

Under these circumstances, of all which you were fully apprized before you wrote your last note, the President finds nothing in the conduct of this government which requires any expression of his intentions, views or wishes beyond that contained in my note to Your Excellency of the 14th September last.

The Government of the United States, Sir, is studious to observe, on its own part, the high courtesy which is appropriate to international intercourse, and it expects from the functionaries of other Governments, not the active avoidance of all expressions which might be misconstrued, under the influence of an undue susceptibility, but a substantial compliance with the usages, in this regard, of civilized nations. It asserts the right to decline correspondence with any foreign Minister who may, in its judgment, evince intentional discourtesy and disrespect in his intercourse with it; and it maintains that the exercise of that right affords no just ground of complaint or question upon the part of any other Government.

Accept, Sir, the assurance of the high consideration with which I have the honor to be Your Excellency's very humble and obedient servant.

John M. Clayton

❊ ❊ ❊

X. John M. Clayton to William C. Rives[19]

Department of State
Washington, September 14, 1849

Sir,

You will find in the archives of the Legation at Paris copies of the correspondence between M. Poussin, late Minister of France at Washington, and this Department relating to the claim of A. Port; and, to the complaint of the French Government against Commander Carpender. You will, also, find, among those archives, the correspondence between Mr. Rush and M. de Tocqueville, the French Minister of Foreign Affairs. The President, having informed M. Poussin that no further communication would be held with him by this Government, and that every proper facility would be afforded him, in case he should desire to return to France, it may become important that you should understand the views of your own Government in regard to that correspondence, and especially in regard to the communication of M. de Tocqueville of the 9th of August last. I therefore transmit to you, herewith a copy of that letter, and of my reply to it of the 8th inst. together with a copy of my note to M. Poussin, of this date.

On the 7th day of February last, the Minister of France, residing near this Government, M. William Tell Poussin in a note to the Honorable James Buchanan, my predecessor in office, stated that he was charged by the French Government to prosecute a claim against the Government of the United States "brought by a Frenchman, established in Mexico, named A. Port, for indemnification for damages sustained by him, from the acts of certain agents of the Army of the United States." His application might be regarded as being in the nature of an appeal from the sentence of a Military Court of Inquiry at Puebla which had made a decision unfavorable to the claim he presented. It appearing that no answer to this note was returned by Mr. Buchanan, I lost no time after the claim was thus presented, in devoting myself to a full and fair investigation of it, and from deference to the high authority under whose sanction it was presented postponed important public business in order to gratify M. Poussin's urgent demand for a speedy decision. In less than three weeks after I took charge of this Department and within ten days after the subject had been brought to my notice, I had reviewed the evidence submitted to me by the French Government, and all the evidence I could obtain, and on the 28th day of March last, announced to M. Poussin, in respectful language my decision, which was, "that M. Port had no just cause to be dissatisfied with the award of the Military Court of Inquiry." Not satisfied with this decision, that Minister on the 13th March last, addressed to this Department another note, in which he reviewed the grounds on which he supposed the decision had been made, and animadverted with much severity upon the testimony of Colonel Childs, a distinguished officer of the American Army in Mexico, who had been examined, as a witness before the Court of Inquiry at Puebla, which had unanimously condemned the claim of M. Port as unjust, and whose decision had been regularly sanctioned and approved by Major General Winfield Scott, the Commander in Chief.[20] Having entertained the appeal from the sentence of the Military Court, at the request of M. Poussin, and definitely decided it, upon a full view of all the evidence he had presented I might, with perfect propriety, have declined any further correspondence with him, on that subject. But my high respect for the Government he represented, induced me to reply on the 10th of April last, assigning reasons for the decision I had made, and respectfully controverting some of the positions he had assumed. On the 18th of April, I received from M. Poussin another note, on the same subject, in which, without the shadow of provocation, the French Minister, whom I had uniformly treated with courtesy, and to whom not a line had been penned by me, which could by possibility be deemed by any reasonable mind as discourteous or unkind, indulged in a strain of invective and opprobrium palpably intended to be highly offensive to the Government of the United States.

This being the first instance, in which any Minister of a foreign country, had addressed me in my official character, in language insulting to the American Government, I immediately submitted the correspondence to the President, by whose instructions "I lost not a moment in requesting M. Poussin to repair to this city without unnecessary delay." His offensive note was dated at Washington, while he was absent in New York upwards of two hundred miles distant form this City. Bearing on its face an insult to this Government deliberately given in the very capital of the United States, which if not satisfactorily explained or retracted, would have required at the hands of this Government that all correspondence with him as a Minister, should terminate without delay, as a measure indispensable to the maintenance of friendly relations so happily subsisting between the two nations. His note had made it important to himself and to his Government, that he should lose no time in repairing to this place. My note to him of the 21st of April was written after the receipt of his communication, and requested him to repair to this City with the kind intention of permitting him to retract the offensive passages in his note, and especially the following: *"the Government of the United States must be convinced that it is more honorable to acquit fairly, a debt contracted during war, under the pressure of necessity, than to evade its payment by endeavoring to brand the character of an honest man."* The same note contained an attack upon Colonel Childs, who had been sworn as a witness at Puebla in effect charging him with perjury, in giving his testimony before the Military Court; and it contained also an attack upon the distinguished officers composing that Court, who were charged with permitting him (Col. Childs) "to carry out without interruption, his string of calumnies incredible." And, it closed with the innuendo that this Department had become the organ of a criminal accusation, without proofs, against M. Port, which was but thinly veiled by his assertion that the Legation of France would never have consented to become such an organ. The arrogance, too, displayed in this note in haughtily closing the correspondence on the subject (a correspondence which he afterwards verbally expressed his expectation that I would renew!) will hardly be regarded by any impartial judge, when taken in connection with the rest of his letter, in any other light than as a studied effort to insult those, against whom, neither he nor his Government had the slightest cause of complaint.

Such were the circumstances, under which my note to M. Poussin of the 21st of April was written. That note contains the only portion of the correspondence, on my part, which it was pretended contained anything exceptionable, and which the Minister of Foreign Affairs of France had characterized as "an imperious summons." I cannot better show the injustice of the only excuse which his ingenuity has been able to devise, to palliate or justify the insults of the French Minister, than by here inserting that note at length.

Department of State
Washington, April 21, 1849.

Sir,

On the afternoon of the 18th instant, a communication from you, dated Washington, April 1849, (without showing the day on which it was written) was received at this office, relative to the claim of M. Port on the Government of the United States; and having just had occasion to address you a private note, I learn through the messenger who was dispatched to deliver it, that you have been for the last two weeks absent from Washington, and that the period of your return hither, from New York was quite uncertain.

Under these circumstances, after a perusal of your note which was laid before me this morning, I lose not a moment in requesting you to repair to this city without unnecessary delay.

I have the honor to be, very respectfully, sir, your obedient servant,

John M. Clayton

[To] M. William Tell Poussin

M. de Tocqueville has not condescended to instruct me in what other part of my correspondence he found that tone of acerbity and harshness with which he says he has been "so painfully impressed." But the note of the 21st of April, now perused by you, and known to have been written for the indulgent purpose of allowing the French Minister to retract the most offensive passage in his note, and thus escape the consequences of his own indiscretion, His Excellency, has been pleased to characterize as one "which, estimated with a certain degree of susceptibility, might have seemed to be rather an imperious summons than a diplomatic invitation." It would have been gratifying to learn from his Excellency what that certain degree of susceptibility must in his judgment be, which could have translated such a request into an imperious summons. He says that M. Poussin, doubtless, misconstrued some of my expressions, for which he may have manifested his resentment with too much spirit. If by that peculiar susceptibility which construed my request as an imperious summons, he meant that M. Poussin misunderstood the plainest language, or was ignorant of its meaning, I can only say that such ignorance was no justification or excuse for a previous insult, even though the distinguished Minister of Foreign Affairs of France has appeared as its apologist.

In the interview between M. Poussin and myself, which followed my note of the 21st April, I informed him that his letter was highly offensive, and that it contained language which this Government could not admit; and that he was permitted, from a friendly feeling, (which he seems not to have appreciated) to withdraw his note for the purpose indicated. The note was accordingly withdrawn for the purpose of availing himself of the offer, and on the following day it was returned, the most offensive passage in it being retracted and expunged. Anxious to maintain our amicable relations with France, the President then permitted this matter to drop, and the correspondence, in regard to the claim of M. Port, was thus finally disposed of. It was the President's earnest hope that M. Poussin had received an admonition that would have served the happy purpose of preceding any further collisions.

But it was not long permitted to cherish that delusion. On the 12th day of May last, M. Poussin, in a diplomatic note, represented to this Department "that Mr. Carpender, the Commander of the American War Steamer Iris, after hastening to the assistance of the French Ship Eugenie, of Havre, which had struck on the bank of Piso, near the anchorage of Anton-Lizardo, advanced claims wholly inadmissible, on account of remuneration for his services; and, to secure their acquittal, detained the Eugenie for two or three days. In consequence of the energetic remonstrances of M. Lavallïe and the honorable intervention of the Consul of the United States at Vera Cruz, Commander Carpender desisted from his pretensions." M. Poussin proceeded to say that "the Minister of Foreign Affairs of France requested him to address to the Cabinet of Washington the most serious observations on the abuse of authority committed by this office, in illegally detaining the ship Eugenie." He then concluded his note with the following remark. "You will easily comprehend Mr. Secretary of State, how important it is that such occurrences should not be repeated, and that severe blame, at least, should be laid on those who thus considered themselves empowered to substitute arbitrary measures for justice, and I doubt not that you will, without delay, give satisfaction to the just complaint of the French Republic." This note unaccompanied as it was by any testimony to justify the charge against Commander Carpender, and to enable the Government of the United States to form a judgment as to what punishment should be inflicted on the officer, who had thus offended the French Republic, was promptly referred to the Navy Department for the purpose of ascertaining the facts, upon which his condemnation was demanded. On the 24th May, the Secretary of the Navy, in reply, transmitted to this Department all the evidence in his possession, and that consisted only of two letters from Commander Carpender himself, the one dated New Orleans, the 16th November 1848, the other New York, the 19th May 1849. Copies of these letters are in your possession. In the entire absence of testimony to contradict the statements of the Commander, and of the knowledge of the existence of any testimony that could contradict them, the President thought that the character of the officer, against which this Government has never known an imperfection, made it incumbent on him to submit the explanations given by commander Carpender to the

French Minister and to express at the same time the hope, "that they would remove any misapprehension which might exist, on the part of the French Government, relative to his conduct on the occasion in question." By referring to this note, which is also in your possession, you will find it entirely respectful towards the French Minister. Was it wrong in the absence of all testimony against the Commander, to decline punishing him on the demand of M. Poussin, before the French Government had an opportunity of hearing his defense? A brief review of the facts, he relates, which facts have never been contradicted, within our knowledge, shows that the Commander, seeing the French barque Eugenie and her crew in imminent peril, high up on the rocks of Anton-Lizardo, and being appealed to for succor, hastened to her assistance with seamen from the Iris; and that the Captain of the French barque gave up the charge of his vessel on the reef, in order that the American officer might take the command to save her. At a moment when no other aid could be procured and when a norther so formidable to seamen on that coast, was expected, the American Commander labored all night with his sailors, got the French barque off the rocks, and anchored her in safety alongside the Iris. Was it unreasonable, that the Commander should have expected compensation for his men, who had toiled so laboriously and successfully, to secure the bark and her crew from destruction? He did ask for that compensation, and it is certain, that by the laws of his country, he was entitled to it. Such the officer stated was the decision of our Minister in Mexico, Mr. Clifford, formerly Attorney General of the United States when appealed to on the subject – such, too, is the opinion of the present Attorney General of the United States. The President would regret that any claims of our naval officers for salvage of French vessels should ever jeopardize peaceful relations with France. But is the French Government prepared to say, that it is for the interests of France, that the officers and crews of our national ships should never receive compensation for the preservation of French property, on the high seas, no matter how much of peril or toil may be encountered in the effort? This question however becomes immaterial in the consideration of Commander Carpender's conduct, where we know that although he had asked and expected salvage, yet in his own words "thirty hours" having elapsed without receiving an answer, he had already resolved to let the Captain resume the charge of her, when he received a note from the consignee saying, that he could not act in the matter, as the vessel was not yet in port; and at the same moment, the captain of the "Eugenie" coming on board, he returned the vessel to him.

It was under these circumstances, that M. Poussin wrote the note of the 30th of May last which follows:

Legation of France
Washington, May 30, 1849

Sir,

I received on the 28th of May, the note which you did me the honor to address to me on the same day, in answer to mine, calling upon the Government of the United States, to disavow the conduct of Commander Carpender, of the American war steamer Iris, towards the French ship Eugenie, of Havre, which had run upon the bank of Piso, near the anchorage of Anton-Lizardo. The explanations, given by Commander Carpender, are not of a nature, Mr. Secretary of State, such as to dispel the discontent, which his proceedings have caused to my Government.

He considered, as he says, and he still considers, that the case was one of salvage, that the rights acquired by him as the saver of the vessel saved, empowered him to keep possession of her until his extravagant pretensions were fully satisfied; but his opinions have little interest in our eyes, when we have to condemn his conduct.

I called on the Cabinet of Washington, Mr. Secretary of State, in the name of the French Government, to address a severe reproof to that officer of the American Navy, in order that the error, which he has committed, on a point involving the dignity of your national marine, might not be repeated hereafter.

From your answer, Mr. Secretary of State, I am unfortunately induced to believe, that your Government subscribes to the strange doctrines professed by Commander Carpender, of the war steamer Iris, and I have only to protest, in the name of my Government, against these doctrines.

I have the honor to be, with distinguished consideration, your most obedient servant.

Guillaume-Tell Poussin

Hon[ora]ble J. M. Clayton,
Secretary of State

This Government had advanced no "doctrine" whatever, in regard to the case of Commander Carpender, and there is not a word in the correspondence on the part of the American Executive, indicating any opinion on the subject of salvage, or the right of Commander Carpender to compensation; but M. Poussin, as if zealous to make a point for us, against which he might enter a protest and utter a denunciation assumed that some "strange doctrines" had been adopted by the Executive, which were unworthy of the dignity of our national marine.

His note describes his previous letter of the 12th of May merely as one "calling upon the Government of the United States to disavow the conduct of Commander Carpender." But his note of the 12th of that month, instead of simply calling for such a disavowal, represented how important it was "that severe blame, at least, should be laid on those who thus considered themselves empowered to substitute arbitrary measures for justice." A severe censure upon Commander Carpender might have been accompanied by a disavowal of his conduct; but a disavowal of the principle of salvage or of his conduct in claiming it, would not necessarily have carried with it any severe censure. This Government did not understand, and does not now understand, M. Poussin's note of the 12th of May as demanding of it merely to disavow the law which allowed salvage to Commander Carpender and his crew. It was supposed, that the charge in that letter against the Commander was that he had abused his authority, in illegally detaining the French ship. Had the President supposed, that the object of the French Government, as expressed in that letter, was to obtain from him a disavowal of a law of the land, as it actually existed, his answer would have been promptly given, that no such disavowal could be made by him, as he can neither make nor unmake the law and it is his duty, to see it faithfully executed.

I did not undertake to instruct M. Poussin, as to the usages of nations but it is quite possible that that Minister was ignorant that the demand of salvage was conformable to the usage of other European maritime powers.

The next thing worthy of particular observation is, that the Minister declined or omitted to send home the defense of Commander Carpender, for the consideration of his own Government, so as first to obtain its views, under the new aspect thus presented, before writing his note, notwithstanding the President had expressed the hope, that it would remove the misunderstanding, which existed on the part of the French Government. M. Poussin instantly denounced the commander without considering the defense, which he regarded as a matter of *little interest in his eyes*, when he had occasion to condemn the conduct of an officer of the United States. This imperious refusal to suffer an American officer to be heard, in his own defense by the Government which accused him, accompanied by the contemptuous sneer, that it had little interest in their eyes, when they had determined to condemn him, although his own Government had asked that act of common justice to a meritorious and faithful officer, and had attached so much interest and importance to it as to express the hope, that when seen it would be satisfactory, was deeply felt by the President as rude and unjust. It was naturally supposed that the conduct of that officer who had saved a French ship and abandoned his claim to salvage would exempt him from censure at least even though it might fail to receive, what he would have highly prized, the approbation of the French Government, and it was felt to be due to Commander Carpender that the French Government should not, under any circumstances condemn him without a hearing. M. Poussin thought otherwise, and expected this Government to censure him although, as I have already stated, it was in possession of no evidence against him. After speaking of the officer's "extravagant pretensions" (by which we understand that he only claimed reasonable salvage) M. Poussin decides the whole question of law against him, and announces that he has committed an error on the point involving the dignity of the American national marine, which strange doctrine, he says, he is unfortunately induced to believe this Government subscribes to, and he therefore protests "against these doctrines." He also declares that this is done in the name of the French Government, thus presenting that Government to us, as having commissioned him to lecture the Executive of the United States on a point involving the dignity of the American national marine, and to condemn the conduct of the President in subscribing to a doctrine in accordance with the settled law of the land. Were an American Minister to protest against a law of France, and demand of the French President to disavow it as unworthy [of] the dignity of the Government, it is not to be doubted that the high sense of national honor felt by the President of France, and (may I not add?) by M. de Tocqueville himself, would promptly lead that Government to decline any further communication with him.

On the receipt of this extraordinary letter, the President decided to submit M. Poussin's correspondence to the French Government without assuming to prescribe the censure which that Government should adopt under such peculiar circumstances towards a friendly Power; and M. Poussin was duly advised of their determination. In coming to this decision, the President was actuated by a profound regard for existing friendly relations with a sister Republic, and a sincere desire that those relations should continue undisturbed by any cause; but, more especially, by the caprices of an individual whose special office, he had announced to us, on his presentation to this Government as a Minister, was to foster and cherish those relations by every means within his power. Accordingly, the whole correspondence was communicated to His

Excellency, the Minister of French Affairs of France, on the 7th of July by Mr. Rush.

M. de Tocqueville's letter to Mr. Rush, on the 9th of August, attempts in vain to excuse the correspondence of the French Minister, which he seems to admit had painfully impelled him, on finding in it, a tone of acerbity and harshness; but he adds, that, "without entering into useless recriminations, without seeking for the side whence the first injuries proceeded, it had appeared to me [him] that this observation was not alone applicable to the letters written by the Minister of France." The fact is, His Excellency was not able to discover, in that correspondence, that any injuries, first or last, had proceeded from this Government; and whether he sought for them or not, he has given no evidence that any such has been committed, no such evidence existed. Candor ought to have compelled His Excellency to have admitted that there was no foundation for his insinuation that there had been any "recriminations," emanating from this Government, whether useless or otherwise. He fully admits that he did not attempt to do justice to the subject, by the confession that he had considered it, "without seeking for the side whence the first injuries proceeded." It required but little seeking to ascertain that side. It could not have escaped his attention that this Government had been twice insulted, without any provocation, by the Minister of France, and that there had not been the slightest degree of recrimination indulged in by way of reply, on either of the two occasions. His intimation that M. Poussin doubtless misconstrued or misunderstood some expressions in the letter that had been addressed to him, without designating what those expressions were, is no excuse for intentional insult. His entire omission also to notice the indecorous language in the letter of 30th May, for which he does not pretend to point out the slightest pretext, or to make any apology, although his attention had been especially invited to that letter, is in perfect accordance with the spirit which, disdaining to seek for the side whence the first injuries proceeded, chose to condemn both parties without discrimination, as if in order to shield the real aggressor.

The President, therefore, finding it apparent from the whole tone of M. de Tocqueville's communication, which has struck him with profound surprise, that the French Government wholly refused to redress the wrong inflicted by the French Minister, felt himself compelled to adopt the course indicated in the letter from this Department, of the 8th September, to M. de Tocqueville.

France has no right to consider this decision offensive to her. Every Government is the sole judge on points affecting its own honor. The usage of nations justifies the course adopted. During the Presidency of Mr. Madison, when the language of a British Minister, Mr. Jackson, residing in this country, had proved offensive to this Government, that Minister was promptly informed, without even first submitting his correspondence to his own Government, that no further communication would be received from him, and the reason for the step was afterwards made known to his Government. Mr. Jackson himself, in defending the positions he had taken accompanied his observations with the remark that "*beyond this, it suffices that I do not deviate from the respect due to the Government to which I am accredited.*" How, then, was this matter regarded at the British Foreign Office, at the head of which, at that time, was Lord Wellesley? His Lordship, to whom the correspondence had been submitted, expressed the concern of his Majesty that the interruption of the intercourse had taken place, by the command of this Government, before it had been possible for his Majesty, by any interposition of his authority, to manifest his invariable disposition to maintain the relations of amity with the Untied States. He conveyed the most positive assurances, from Mr. Jackson, that it had not been his purpose to give offence to the United States Government, by any expression contained in his letters, or by any part of his conduct. He suggested, indeed, that a better, and more usual course, would have been to convey to his Government a formal complaint against the Minister, with a view to suitable redress. And, although, he said, His Majesty had not marked with any expression of displeasure the conduct of Mr. Jackson, who had not appeared to him, on the occasion, to have committed any intentional offence against the Government of the United States; yet as he was always disposed to pay the utmost attention to the wishes and sentiments of States in amity with him, he had directed the return of Mr. Jackson to England. And in further testimony of a sincere desire to cultivate an intercourse with the United States on the most friendly terms, his Lordship added that he was authorized to assure this Government that His Majesty was ready to receive, with sentiments of undiminished amity, and good will, any communication which the Government of the United States might deem beneficial to the mutual interests of both countries, through any channel which might appear advantageous to the Government of the United States.

> I am, Sir, respectfully,
> Your obedient servant,
> John M. Clayton

❈ ❈ ❈

XI. Letter from Guillaume-Tell Poussin to Alexis de Tocqueville

M. Alexis de Tocqueville, Minister of Foreign Affairs,
                                New York, October 9, 1849

Minister,

Without entering into the details of an affair with which you are quite familiar, I believe nonetheless that it is my duty to remind you of the position in which the administration found itself at the moment when it judged it useful to divert public attention; the situation in which it finds itself presently also merits your attention.

President Taylor was not elected because he was a Whig but despite the fact that he was a Whig. People wanted to reward his military achievements. The hero of Mexico was nominated as president but it was not expected that he would surround himself with a Whig administration.

Also the democratic press has been incessant in its attacks either to find fault with nominations or to demand transfers; the slightest pretext is sufficient for it; thus it demanded the recall of the consul to Paris on the grounds that he was not republican enough.

The fall of Hungary,[21] where a representative had been sent with full powers to recognize a future republic, the expedition to Cuba, opposed by the administration and viewed with favor by the Democratic Party, awoke the resentment of the democratic press which was of the opinion that nothing had been done for Hungary and nothing had been done for Cuba.

It was at this moment that the newspapers of Washington recalled that in the message from the President of the French Republic no mention was made of the United States or of the gratitude of the French Republic. Suddenly the newspapers announced that the accreditation of the French Minister had been withdrawn. This unexpected news was received with incredulity. The stock-brokers, the journalists hurried from all parts to make their inquiries. The value of stocks fell by two per cent.

The administration, sensing that this measure had not been well-received, sought to justify its actions and it was then that it published the disconnected and badly-translated passages from the diplomatic letters and notes. The passages cited, when removed from the letters, at first misled public opinion and the press, taken by surprise, did not spare the French Minister. The democratic press viewed with an element of pride the response of the president towards an apparent insult.

However, there remained an element of incredulity in some people's minds. They expected and demanded the publication of the correspondence, and when this publication took place they saw that in the quoted passages words had been removed and that others had been badly translated. The insult did not exist; *you had to look hard to find it. Recourse to justice would decide in favor of the French Minister.*

The independent press, the moderate press took the initiative. The [*Journal of*] *Commerce*, which weighed up all the consequences of a severing of relations, became alarmed, and far from having a sentiment of hostility toward France, the country displayed only displeasure at the abrupt and unwarranted manner in which the whole affair had been handled by the administration.

It should be noted that the administration has always avoided concerning itself seriously with the substance of French protests and that it was with a particular *intent* that it fastened upon the form of words that it wished to find offensive.

Since then the administration has taken great care to call to mind the most unbelievable rumors and has not missed an opportunity to attach great importance to an alleged phrase pronounced by the President of the French Republic when speaking to Mr. Rush.

The democratic press and the moderate press, having examined and discussed the published documents, have come around to accusing the administration of acting with undue haste.

The recriminations have started again. The elections of members of Congress will produce adversaries and the president will probably find himself with a chamber in which he will have no majority.

In Washington, people seem finally to accept that it would have been better to have acted without this undue haste. Even the president has expressed himself in such a way as to make it known that he regards this entire affair as capable of being easily *resolved*.

We await news from France with impatience. The manner in which France has received the communication of the methods of the administration will have a major influence upon the fate of this administration. If it has succeeded in its pretensions, it will be praised; if it has failed, the opposition will unleash itself against it and it will be obliged to withdraw.

A misunderstanding with France in this country is an *unnatural state*; but by enflaming the masses and exciting national vanity one can, I fear, lead the United States to forget what it owes to France, and unfortunately in the United States, as elsewhere, the cleverest are not the wisest.

I can add that in the conduct of the administration toward the French Minister there has been nothing of a personal nature and that without the unfortunate salience given to this affair by the newspapers, relations would without doubt be established on their previous footing.

A letter written by one of the close friends of General Taylor suggests that any complications with France would be regarded with displeasure; to which are added the grievances voiced by the opposition against the administration. At any rate, faced with an administration whose existence is so precarious, a little procrastination would perhaps have the advantage of clearing the ground and allowing us to negotiate with a new administration that would not believe itself obliged to feel insulted when it had indeed not been so.

Please accept, Minister, the expression of my deepest consideration,

Guillaume-Tell Poussin

✵ ✵ ✵

XII. Letter from Guillaume-Tell Poussin to Alexis de Tocqueville

M. Alexis de Tocqueville,
Minister of Foreign Affairs,

New York, October 17, 1849

Minister,

Nothing has yet been explained of the cause of the brutal and unparalleled act of the Washington government toward the Minister of France. People have tried to find the cause in the correspondence exchanged between Mr. Clayton and M. Poussin but without success; this correspondence, analyzed and discussed in every detail, has proved on the contrary that there was no plausible reason for irritation and certainly no grounds for a break off of diplomatic relations. The New York newspaper, [the *Journal of*] *Commerce*, that I send you herewith, contains an article on this subject in which its author, a genuine American, shows after a serious and impartial discussion that all the faults in this unhappy affair are on the side of the honorable Secretary of State. This article was republished throughout the American press and has contributed greatly toward making public opinion more favorable to the Minister of France.

Naturally the opposition has taken advantage of this subject and, adding it to the old grievances that it has already raised against the administration, turned it into an issue of controversy in the last elections and as a consequence obtained a large majority in the states of Ohio and Pennsylvania. There exists little doubt that in the state of New York the opposition or the Democratic Party will also obtain a very large majority in the elections of next November. Also the newspapers are beginning to announce as a necessity of the situation a change of government for the next meeting of Congress and the replacement of Mr. Clayton.

For the rest, public opinion has very much overcome its fear of war with France as a consequence of the rupture with its government and people see in this regrettable difficulty only a misunderstanding that could be easily resolved through diplomatic means.

I must, Minister, bring to your attention a new fact in American politics which, in the present circumstances, could become a serious matter.

During the course of this summer the United States sent a Minister to the Republic of Nicaragua, who was received in July.[22] This diplomat used the occasion of his reception to make a speech where he alluded to the celebrated doctrine of President James Monroe and announced that his government had the intention of reviving its principles in the relations it had with the new states of America with whom it was in contact.

He formally announced that the Unites States, in agreement with the Republics of America, would oppose all intervention by any European nation in the affairs of the American continent.

Several months later this same Minister concluded a treaty with the authorities of Nicaragua by which the United States secured for itself in perpetuity the possession of a route of communication by canal across the isthmus of Nicaragua, in the same way that, through a treaty with New Granada,[23] it has sought to secure a route of communication between the two oceans across the isthmus of Panama.

Already, Great Britain, in recognizing the creation and the independence of the new kingdom of Mosquito,[24] has obtained from the king, its vassal, a recent concession to the exclusive right of navigation on the San Juan river, which is part of the concession made to an American company[25] in conformity with a treaty concluded by the Minister of the United States. The English consul in Nicaragua has already exchanged a correspondence on this subject with the Secretary of State of Nicaragua in which he claims the prior rights of Great Britain to a part of this new concession. The English Consul in New York has likewise made it known officially to the American company that Great Britain had the rights of navigation on the San Juan river, which it could not give up according to

its agreement with the King of Mosquito. It now remains to be seen how
the United States resolves this new difficulty with the government of Great
Britain.

Please accept, Minister, the expression of my deepest consideration,

Guillaume-Tell Poussin

※　※　※

XIII. Guillaume-Tell Poussin to Alexis de Tocqueville

M. Alexis de Tocqueville,
Minister of Foreign Affairs,

New York,
October 23, 1849

Minister,

The discontent that the diplomatic actions of the present Secretary of
State have given rise to is now evident throughout the American press.

Raised initially by the press of the Democratic Party and that of the
opposition, it soon manifested itself amongst even the organs of the administration or the Whig party, amongst whom it has created disunion, and
already amongst the latter, which includes the [National] Intelligencer of
Washington, people openly discuss the necessity of placing at the head of
the government a man who knows how to direct foreign affairs with more
prudence.

The cause of the disagreement between the government in Washington and the Minister of France is now decided upon. A better-informed
public opinion has completely discharged the Minister of France of all
responsibility and has laid the blame upon the exaggerated sensitiveness
and groundless annoyance of the Secretary of State. Everyone deplores
an interruption of relations for which not the least trace can be found in
the analysis of the official documents exchanged between the Secretary
of State and the Minister of France; and if I might be allowed to express
in my support an openly repeated opinion, it is said that if one were to
put to the vote at this moment the question of the recall of the Minister of
France to his post in Washington, it is beyond doubt that it would receive
a majority of 10 votes to one.

In this situation, Minister, would it not be appropriate, as much in
our international interests as for the dignity of France, to display less

eagerness to renew our diplomatic relations with this country until the reaction is complete, which itself cannot be long in occurring?

In 1820 and 1821, difficulties arose between the United States and France as a result of aggressive measures taken by Congress against the maritime commerce of France; but as a consequence of the wise reaction of M. de Villèle, public opinion, which at first appeared to agree with Congress, was not slow in changing its mind and, in the space of less than a year, forced the government of the United States to take the first steps to smooth over the difficulties and to solicit the sending of an ambassador, M. de Neuville, who was received with the greatest eagerness.

Please accept, Minister, the expression of my deepest consideration,

Guillaume-Tell Poussin

✳ ✳ ✳

XIV. Letter from Charles de Montholon to Alexis de Tocqueville[26]

M. A. de Tocqueville,
Minister of Foreign Affairs,

Washington,
November 4, 1849

Minister,

After a long and perilous journey I arrived three days ago in Washington. As I expected, the newspapers on this side of the Atlantic had predicted and announced my journey for some time. The American newspapers, which ordinarily do not hesitate to offer their views, relying upon my previous good relations with Mr. Clayton and upon the numerous and influential friendships that I had established in the United States, and anticipating the confidence that you wished to place in me, designated me from *the beginning of October*, as being charged by the government of the Republic to present to the government in Washington words of conciliation. After so many gratuitous conjectures with regard to myself, my presence therefore caused no surprise. It was everywhere interpreted as an indication of a happy solution. The stock market was affected by this, and the day after my passage through New York, federal bonds began an upward movement openly attributed to my alleged mission. I signal this fact in order to show you the dispositions existing in this country with regard to the matter outstanding between the two governments.

Despite the persistence that people show in seeing me as a peacemaker, according to the expression that Mr. Clayton himself appears to have used, I have retained all the reserve that you have imposed upon me. Nevertheless, while strictly maintaining my private role, I have already been able to gather some useful information, from which in my opinion one can conclude that there exists here a sincere desire to renew good relations between France and the United States. Several important politicians have spoken to me in this way and the Under-Secretary of State for Foreign Affairs used a similar language.

As for Mr. Clayton, I have yet to make contact with him. He has been ill for several days and his door remains closed to all, without exception. However, being informed of my arrival, he immediately sent one of our mutual friends to express the pleasure he felt at my return, and above all in order to inquire about the reasons that had brought me back. I replied that family matters had brought me back to America, but that, without being in the least accredited to the government in Washington, I was authorized to submit to him a few observations of a completely friendly nature and which, I hoped, would be received in the same spirit of cordiality.

I had hoped to see Mr. Clayton this morning but he let it be known that he was too ill to receive me and that it was better to write to him if I had something to communicate to him. As the instructions of your Excellency exclude all appearance of official mission I concluded that, without new instructions, I ought not to open any official correspondence with Mr. Clayton whatsoever. I will therefore await the recovery of the Minister and further instructions, if you judge them appropriate, being resolved until that point to limit myself to verbal negotiations.

Nevertheless, Minister, if I did not know Mr. Clayton to be truly ill, I would perhaps be inclined to react angrily to this lack of eagerness to confer with me. On the other hand, the dignified and firm attitude that you have taken with regard to the government of Washington could well, I willingly presume, inspire in him the desire to exercise at the present moment an element of reciprocity. In addition, it must be noted that as a result of the contestations that happened recently between the majority of the foreign representatives in Washington and the Secretary of State, Mr. Clayton has enveloped himself in an unaccustomed, not to say exaggerated, reserve, and that M. Poussin, through his recent actions, has not contributed to placing us in the personal favor of the Minister. With regard to the first two points, these are simply conjectures that I submit to your enlightened appreciation, but with regard to the behavior of

M. Poussin after the severing of his relations with Mr. Clayton I only have incomplete information to pass on to you at the moment.

I must add, Minister, that Mr. Clayton, undoubtedly being under an illusion as to the significance of his last despatch, was far from expecting the decision taken by the government of the French Republic provisionally to refuse temporarily the accreditation of Mr. Rives. The administration of General Taylor was greatly surprised by this, and from reliable sources I learnt that in the State Department people speak with bitterness of the unfriendly [words][27] pronounced against the representative of the United States in Paris. Such a commentary on the sentiments of the French government is quite surprising given the fact that Mr. Rives had obtained from yourself, Minister, unambiguous signs of friendly intentions.

Be that as it may, the difficulties, if they arise, will come from here. Mr. Clayton is no longer the only one who has the power to decide on this matter. The government in Washington has taken the affair in hand and its great dilemma at the present moment is to decide whether it is best to recall Mr. Rives or maintain him in his post. On the one hand, a return to harmonious relations, on the other, a complete severing of relations: this is the alternative by dint of which it finally realizes the consequences of its false and thoughtless interpretation of events. It is especially with regard to this subject that I regret not being able to have spoken yet to Mr. Clayton. My explanations, I am convinced, would have partly dissolved the obstacles that others have sought to raise for us on this issue. Nevertheless, the American government, which is usually prone to comment, this time is taking great care to remain silent on the current position of Mr. Rives, which encourages us to suppose that it still desires a peaceful and regular solution.

You will see, Minister, that I have faithfully observed your instructions to the letter, and I have been careful not to stray away from them in any way. In the eyes of everyone, I have neither official status nor mission. Moreover, this constraint does not prevent me from acting. It is in this spirit, and as personal advice, that I saw it as my duty to recommend to M. V.,[28] Secretary of our Legation, to abstain from making any official approach towards the State Department until you will have indicated to him the attitude that he should take under the current circumstances.

In summary, Minister, without having a meeting with Mr. Clayton, I believe myself entitled to hope that things are moving in a favorable direction. The fame and the proper consideration that surround your memory in the United States are for me a powerful guarantee of this.

In addition, as I was mentioning to you at the beginning, politicians - members of Senate and representatives of the federal Congress – have expressed to me the necessity for the two peoples to renew as soon as possible the strongest relations upon an amicable footing, perceiving at the bottom of this only a purely individual disagreement, only a quarrel over forms, as it were, to be resolved between M. Poussin and Mr. Clayton; this seems to me to underplay the question; but good dispositions exist and it is very important to take note of them.

In general, the press displays a veritable zeal for conciliation. I do not imagine that Mr. Clayton will seek to show more resistance and susceptibility than everybody else. It would in addition be rather imprudent on his part not to want a prompt termination. Congress will reconvene on the 4th of December and the Secretary of State will need, in one chamber or the other, to wage a battle which will be all the more serious given the fact that the opposition, which is already very hostile toward him, which was already solid last year, will this year be even stronger, if one judges by the recent elections and by those which are forthcoming. Despite this spirit of exclusive nationality that is particular to the Americans, people agree in finding the decision taken with regard to M. Poussin to have been too hasty. I do not doubt that criticisms will be addressed to the government in Washington about this subject, which when added to other debates about questions about foreign affairs that are no less important, will perhaps bring about a government reshuffle. It is still only a vague rumor but it seems that it does not lack substance. I am therefore led to believe that Mr. Clayton will perceive the inconveniences in delaying for any longer such a desirable meeting.

I regret, Minister, to have nothing to bring to your attention of a more positive nature. In the next few days I will certainly meet Mr. Clayton and I shall have the honor of communicating to you the outcome of this meeting. For the moment, I am keeping my distance; I am waiting for the Minister, once he has recovered, which cannot be long in occurring, to take the initiative, not wanting through an insistence that is beyond my powers, to compromise again the dignity of the government of the Republic.

> I have the honor of being with respect,
> Minister,
> Your humble and
> very obedient servant,
> Charles de Montholon

✳ ✳ ✳

XV. Letter from Charles de Montholon to Alexis de Tocqueville

Washington,
November 11, 1849

Minister,

I had the honor of announcing to you, on the 4th November, my arrival in Washington and to share with you my first impressions of the state of opinion in this country with regard to the question which divides our two governments. At that moment I had not yet had a meeting with Mr. Clayton on account of the state of his health and it was only on the following day that he indicated to me that he was in better state and that he desired to speak with me.

I found Mr. Clayton entrenched within the distrustful reserve that my last despatch had reported to you. However, after having rendered an account of what had occurred with regard to the communications that he had compelled me to pass on to the President of the French Republic, after having testified, whilst maintaining the dignity of my government, to our good intentions, at both the Elysée and the Ministry of Foreign Affairs, both with regard to the Union and to Mr. Rives in particular, and after having presented things in their true factual light, it seemed to me that the Secretary of State was returning towards sentiments of conciliation. After a long meeting, I left him without being able to presume what action he would take but, to judge by his disquiet and embarrassment, was satisfied by the impression that I had produced.

In the evening there was a Cabinet meeting which continued long into the night; and I do not doubt that the request made to me the following day by Mr. Clayton was the consequence.

The Secretary of State began by thanking me warmly for my communications with him. This time he spoke frankly of the pleasure he would feel from a happy outcome; but at the same time, he questioned me again in order to know whether I had an official or even semi-official mission to enter into negotiations with the Government in Washington. I replied (I had said the same thing to him the previous day) that I had only the authority verbally to transmit and to receive explanations; that I had approached him unofficially in the reciprocal interest of the two countries; finally, that he ought to believe in my word today as much as at the moment when he bestowed his confidence upon me, when I left for Paris. Mr. Clayton then replied that that he was sure of my honesty and that he would be happier to work with me than with anyone else, toward the re-establishment of a good harmony. Then, he expressed clearly and several times that he would be happier if I had a less secretive mission, and he concluded, in consequence, by expressing his profound regret at not being able to continue our talks about the present question under discussion.

Obviously, since the previous day something occurred that I do not properly understand. I would have liked, Minister, to find the key to this change of direction in the disposition of Mr. Clayton. Information that I received this morning, emanating from a person in whom I have complete confidence, leads me to attribute it to the attitude taken by General Taylor. His blind obstinacy, his puerile susceptibility to be offended, his restricted political vision, perhaps even his personal opinions, these are the obstacles against which the best intentions and the good faith of the government of the Republic have had to struggle. In no way do I presume to predict the future: however, if I believe what I am told in confidence, General Taylor intends to adopt a haughty tone towards us in this matter and to put an end to the unsettled position of Mr. Rives, either accrediting him elsewhere or by recalling him in order to give him a post in the administration. It seems certain that in this meeting of the Cabinet held following my first meeting with Mr. Clayton the majority of the ministers supported the position of the President, and that the Secretary of State had to give way to the majority. Does this not explain the insistence of the latter during our second meeting to return to the issue of my true position with regard to him, and the extreme vexation that he showed towards my negative response?

What sense, Minister, can be made of the line of conduct that General Taylor would seem to wish to pursue? It would not be impossible to find the reason in the secret ambition he would have in creating a new popularity upon the ruins of the Whig party, which is under threat almost everywhere. Every day General Taylor sees the dissipation of the confidence that his program inspired at the time of his accession to power. He understands that the sympathy of the States of the Union does not accompany him as it did in the past. By making in this way an appeal to national pride, so easily awoken on this side of the Atlantic, would he not hope to attract to himself those distancing themselves from him, to win new adherents, and to bring into existence a party of which he would be the nominal head and driving force? To my eyes, it would not be improbable that the enthusiasm aroused by the renown that he acquired during the last war with Mexico would not encourage him to stir the spirits even more with these appearances of patriotic presumptuousness that earned him here the nickname of "Rough and Ready". If one also takes into account the habits of hazardous enterprise and domination of the American people, its remarkable natural presumption, the illusions it always holds about its greatness and about the need that people have, beyond the seas, of its industrial and commercial wealth, one will see many motives that might induce General Taylor to try his chances with a policy so lacking in reason. All this seems of a nature to give credence to the communications I have had. I pass them on to our Excellency more as words of warning than as an echo of the truth.

If however, Minister, the Executive really had such plans, it must not be forgotten that it can, after all, only express a proposition and that the right of decision belongs to the Federal Government alone. In three weeks the Federal Congress will reassemble. The information relating to the disagreement will be placed before it. Already the results of the elections for the new sessions are known for the most part. The administration of General Taylor will have only a small majority in the House of Representatives, whereas the opposition will carry the Senate. The documents will therefore be looked at very closely, and I am strongly inclined to believe that the wisdom of Congress will deal fairly with these exaggerations that lack any solid foundation. Moreover, the Whigs have no roots in the country and I doubt that they would be in a position to resist their adversaries for long in a situation where the French question becomes perhaps a matter of party, which will certainly and at once complicate the central question of tariffs.

Such in brief, Minister, is the present situation. Although very simple at the outset, things have been made worse by the ill-will of the President. But public opinion continues to express itself in a peaceful direction and will soon protest against the policy of the Executive. I dare not hope therefore that the question will take on a new bearing before 4th December. Today, unfortunately, Washington is mostly deserted. Those men who could help us are for most part absent. We must await their return. I am resigning myself to this with extreme impatience and, in the meantime, I will try to obtain some influential contacts. As soon as the Chambers are sitting again I will hasten to transmit to your Excellency a copy of the Presidential address, informing you of the effect that it will have produced upon public opinion and of the consequences it might have upon the deliberations of Congress.

The slowness with which the Chamber usually arrives at its final organization, the election of the Speaker, especially important this year as the numerical strength of the parties is about even, then the Christmas vacations, will without doubt delay discussion of the address. This delay, Minister, and the letter that, I know, Mr. Clayton addresses to you in this despatch will allow you at one and the same time to recognize the justice of the observations that I have submitted for your consideration and to take the measures that you judge to be of a nature to produce a solution that might still satisfy the dignity of the two governments. From now until that point I will continue strictly to display the prudent action that I have observed since my return to Washington.

I have the honor of being with respect,

> Minister,
> Your very humble and very
> obedient servant,
> Charles de Montholon

SECTION E

Final Thoughts on the American Constitution

Introduction

As readers of this volume will be aware by now, Theodore Sedgwick was one of Tocqueville's most faithful correspondents after 1840. Tocqueville first became acquainted with the Sedgwick family when he and Beaumont visited them in Stocksbridge, Massachusetts, in September 1831. His friendship with the young Theodore was sealed when the latter was appointed as an attaché to Edward Livingston, U. S. Minister to France, in 1833. After returning to New York in 1834, he established a successful legal practice and was later U. S. District Attorney of the southern district of New York.

Despite ill health and the exacting demands of his legal profession, Sedgwick was also a prolific author. In his day, he was best known for his *Treatise on the Measure of Damages; or An Inquiry into the Principles Which Govern the Amount of Compensation Recovered in Suits at Law*, a compilation of English and American statutory and case law first published in 1847. Sedgwick was also the author of *Thoughts on the Proposed Annexation of Texas to the United States*,[1] in which he opposed annexation of the former independent republic on the grounds that it would weaken the Union by extending slavery and by reducing the nation's faith in constitutional law. Also worth noting is another book by Sedgwick entitled *The American Citizen: His True Position, Character and Duties*, where, in Tocquevillian tones, he proclaimed that "the true greatness" of America lay "in the equal condition of its people, and in the exercise of those virtues which forever flow from that equal condition."[2]

It was toward the end of his life that Sedgwick published his second influential legal treatise. Starting from the premise that "the very essence of our system may be said to be government of the written law," he set out his subject in unambiguous terms. Its object was the study of constitutional and statute law. This, he argued, was governed

455

"by rules peculiar to themselves, and subject to the necessity, incident to the imperfection of language, of constant interpretation and instruction." His ambition, therefore, was "to declare the rules of interpretation by which they are, in cases of doubt, to be expanded, and to illustrate those rules by the light of adjudged cases." Sedgwick recognized that the power of interpretation had fallen to judges but, in part, his intention was to limit judicial discretion. As he commented, "unless their authority be very carefully exercised and confined within strict limits, the boundary between the legislature and the judiciary would be gradually effaced and the most valuable parts of the law-making power would fall into the hands of that branch of government which is not intended to have any share whatsoever in the enactment of laws."[3]

Tocqueville clearly felt a strong personal obligation to bring Sedgwick's book to the attention of a French audience. However, it also provided him with the opportunity of expounding upon a practice that had for long been dear to him and which remained largely unknown in France: the role of judges as a necessary counterbalance to the abuse of legislative power. He had addressed this issue in his chapter "On Judicial Power in the United States and its Action on Political Society" in the first volume of *Democracy in America*. There he had recognized that "confined within its limits, the power granted to American courts to pronounce on the unconstitutionality of laws still forms one of the most powerful barriers that has ever been raised against the tyranny of political assemblies."[4] Now, toward the end of his life and with undiminished lucidity, he returned to this important theme, again taking America as his model. It should be underlined that Tocqueville's approval of judicial intervention ran counter to one of the most powerful principles of the French political tradition: the sovereignty of the legislative assembly. As Hugh Brogan observed, "it was perhaps fitting that Tocqueville's last public word should be on the subject which first made his name."[5]

Report on a work by Mr. Th. Sedgwick

Entitled: A Treatise on the Rules which Govern the Interpretation and the Application of Statutory and Constitutional Law

(July 1858)

I have the honor of presenting to the Academy, on behalf of the author, a book which has as its title: *A treatise on the Rules which govern the interpretation and the application of statutory and constitutional Law,* a treatise on the interpretation and application of laws and the constitution. This book is the work of Mr. *Theodore Sedgwick,* one of the most distinguished barristers of the city of New York where, in addition and in the name of the federal government, he has held very high judicial office.

I take the liberty of drawing this book to the especial attention of the Academy; it is worthy of it on more than one account. As a treatise on jurisprudence, it has great merit. The author shows a deep knowledge of his subject. His insightful, vigorous, and serious mind displays an ability to reveal on every point the main argument and the conclusive evidence, and thus enlighten the reader without ever overburdening him. A style that is always clear and simple leads easily from the letter of word to the idea.

Therefore the treatise of Mr. Sedgwick cannot fail to facilitate the study of American law, but it is above all necessary to those who concern themselves with the general science of laws and with the relationship between justice and the government of societies. It is on this point that it is helpful to recall a few facts which will facilitate the explanation of what will follow.

In our modern societies, the proper functions of the judicial system consist in the application of the law when it is clear, and its interpretation when it is obscure. When the language of the laws gives rise to two meanings, the judge has the right to choose the one that appears to him to be the most credible; but when the words of the legislators produce no ambiguity, it remains for the judge only to follow respectfully their wishes.

It is in this way that things occur everywhere in Europe. But it is otherwise in America, and there, unless I am mistaken, the judicial power, without any contestation, exercises rights which are *recognized* nowhere else.

The American judge does not only apply the law, nor does he only interpret it. In certain cases, he has the right to judge it and, after having acknowledged that it is plain in meaning, to declare that it is without force.

This singular form of legislation had existed in the United States for more than sixty years. It is not founded upon a legal text but has been born out of practice. No constitution has formally conceded such a great power to the courts. They took it upon themselves and no one objected. Public opinion approved of what the judges were doing and the legislators themselves, although they were the representatives of the sovereignty of the people and the product of a free and universal vote, submitted to it without protest. Today no principle seems more accepted or frequently applied in America than this one.

Mr. Sedgwick shows very clearly the origin from which the American courts derive this unusual right that I have just outlined, and explains how they exercise it.

The Academy knows that each of the States that make up the American Union has its own constitution which, having been freely discussed and voted upon by the people of each State, is the undeniable product of the will of the latter.

In addition, the American Union has a unique constitution that the American people in their entirety established as they were finishing their revolution and at the very moment when we were beginning our own. Each of these constitutions constrains not only the ordinary citizens but all those who govern in the name of the people: the legislators as much as the magistrates.

It is by drawing upon this principle that the judges claimed the right to establish limits to the law itself.

The people, they said, are as much the master of the legislator as they are our own. The latter have spoken in their name, but they are not free to exempt themselves from the general rules that the people, acting in their own name, have laid down in the constitution. From this they do not hesitate to invalidate laws that appear to them to be unconstitutional.

Several examples will better serve to illustrate the workings of this remarkable system of jurisprudence. The constitution of the State of New York (I choose this randomly, because all the American constitutions have arrangements similar to those about which I am going to speak) declares that no delinquent can be denied a trial by jury or, in any circumstance, deprived of the guarantees afforded by ordinary criminal proceedings.

Let us imagine that the legislature of the State of New York passes a law which withdraws from a certain category of criminals the guarantee of trial by jury, or which wishes to subject them to extraordinary proceedings, or deliver them over to authorities other than the judicial authorities: those who would be affected by the application of such a law could appeal to the State court, and the latter would have not only the right but also the duty to welcome their appeal.

Another example: the Constitution of the United States decrees that it is not permissible for any individual state to pass retrospective laws in penal matters. Let us imagine that the same legislature of the State of New York considers changing after the event the conditions of certain condemned persons or of drawing from their earlier conviction consequences that the judges would not have foreseen and of subjecting them to punishments that did not exist when the crime or the misdemeanor was committed.

These unfortunate persons, struck down by these tyrannical measures, would be able to appeal to one of the courts of the Union and the latter would not fail to declare that the intended irregular law, being contrary to the Constitution of the United States, could not take effect.

The Academy will note that it is not the principle invoked by the American judges that is *new*, but the use that they make of it.

That the constitution of a country constrains the legislator *in law* is recognized in Europe as much as it is in the United States. But in Europe it is usually revolutions which, from time to time, remind the great powers of the state that they are in breach of the constitution or that they are not respecting its spirit; whereas in America it is the judge who, whenever the executive power or the legislature breaches the constitution, stops them by refusing to give judicial sanction to their wishes.

Even in England this counterbalance has never been used. The author asks himself why the English, who show themselves so nobly in love with their liberty that they cannot abide arbitrary actions even on the part of the powers that they love and respect the most, have never employed the means that have so often been successful for the Americans in protecting themselves against the violence of the legislator. He provides a clever explanation which is worth citing: in England, he says, for centuries every effort of the nation has been directed against the despotism of the prince. It is against him and not against parliament that all precautions have been taken. People feared the arbitrary power of the king so much that they did not think about protecting themselves from the tyranny of the legislative body. In America, where executive power is weak and where legislative power is always clothed in the full prestige of the sovereignty of the people, the law itself would often become oppressive if the courts did not have the right to strike out from it everything that went beyond the limits of the constitution.

Reason, strength, and depth are not lacking here but this does not appear to me to be sufficient to explain entirely what surprises the author. Unless I am mistaken, we need to add the following: the English do not have a constitution properly so-called. It is true that there it is acknowledged that certain general principles are placed beyond the reach of the legislator and that the law itself cannot be violated. But these principles are infrequently set out in a precise form and in a text to which one can have recourse so as to oppose the letter of the constitution to that of the law. Since the limits set by the constitution are badly understood, it is often as difficult for the judge to indicate them clearly to the legislator as it is for the latter to respect them. From this it follows that the English courts of justice, which through interpretation, frequently evaded the laws that appeared to it to be contrary to the general principles of fairness and equity, have never formally refused to apply a law.

The actual purpose of Mr. Sedgwick's book is to show how American judges have exercised and ought to exercise the tutelary and, at the same time, formidable power that their fellow citizens have granted them. His intention is to indicate to the magistrates of his country the rules that can guide them in the exercise of their power and where lie their limits in a sphere which seems to be entirely delivered over to their arbitrary actions. In order to arrive at this end, he examines in turn all the subjects which have already given rise to their judgments and which might give rise to them in the future. In his examination of specific questions, as in his exposition of the general principles of the subject, he shows a deep knowledge of precedents, a rare gift of interpretation, and, in my opinion, good sense. It is by delving with him into the details that one can come to have a clear and complete idea of this immense judicial power that, alone in America, dares from time to time to look at democracy straight in the face and to set it limits.

I have said enough to attain my purpose. My objective was to indicate the general utility offered by a book which appears to consider only certain specific aspects of a foreign system of legislation. The author did not aim to write a work of political science; he limited himself to producing an excellent book on law. It is the work of a jurist, but I will venture to recommend all writers on politics to read it.

Tocqueville's American Correspondents

George Bancroft (1800–1891) was a prominent American scholar and diplomat, author of a multi-volume *History of the United States* (10 volumes, 1834–74; revised into six volumes by the author in 1876 and 1883–1885). Bancroft was well trained in classics and enrolled at Harvard at the age of thirteen. In 1820, he went to Berlin where he had a chance to attend Hegel's and Schleiermacher's lectures. He served as Secretary of the Navy under the Polk administration (1845–1846) and was instrumental in the founding of the U.S. Naval Academy at Annapolis. A supporter of the Mexican War, Bancroft also played a key role in the acquisition of California. He subsequently served as U.S. Minister to London (1846–1849) and Berlin (1867–1874). Bancroft was a supporter of President Buchanan and wrote speeches for Stephen A. Douglas during his 1860s unsuccessful presidential bid. In 1885, he was elected President of the American Historical Association. Bancroft made several visits to Paris from 1847 to 1849 and there he met Tocqueville. For more information, see Mark Anthony de Wolfe Howe, *The Life and Letters of George Bancroft*, 2 vols (New York: Charles Scribner, 1908) and Lillian Handlin, *George Bancroft, The Intellectual as Democrat* (New York: Harper & Row, 1984).

N. W. Beckwith. We have surprisingly little information about Beckwith, in spite of the fact that his letters from the late 1850s are among the longest and most interesting ones received by Tocqueville during that period. A note from the Beinecke Rare Book and Manuscript Library at Yale University describes him as "an American diplomat in Geneva, one of Tocqueville's most prolific and astute correspondents." A short biographical note published in Tocqueville, *OC* VII, 147, n. 5, states that Beckwith was an American businessman working for Russell and Co. who was involved in trade with China. It is not clear if he had any relationship with Nelson M. Beckwith (1807–1889), who had an interesting correspondence with John Bigelow and was described as "an American living in Paris who advocated an improved railroad system in the United States" (Bigelow Papers, The New York Public Library, Mss. Col. 3101).

Maria Weston Chapman (1806–1885) was a leading abolitionist in America and prominent member of the Boston Female Antislavery Society. She was also the publisher of *The Liberty Bell* from 1839 to 1858. Chapman was elected to the executive committee of the American Anti-Slavery Society in 1839 and from 1839 until 1842, she served as editor of the anti-slavery journal, *Non-Resistant*.

Edward Lee Childe (1832–1879) was the son of Edward Vernon Childe and Mildred Childe (see the entry for E. V. Childe below). His correspondence with Tocqueville in the late 1850s is important because it reveals an extremely private face of Tocqueville with which his readers may be less familiar.

Edward Vernon Childe (1804–1861) was an American living in Paris, correspondent to New York newspapers such as the *Times* and *Courier and Enquirer*. A graduate of Harvard, he married Robert E. Lee's younger sister, Catharine Mildred Lee (1811–1856). Their Parisian *salon* was a meeting place for many Americans in Paris, as well as for French admirers of America like Tocqueville. After Mrs. Childe's untimely death in Paris, the entire family returned to the United States in the autumn of 1856 and eventually settled in Baltimore, Maryland. The young Edward Lee travelled widely before returning to Europe a few years later. For more information, see *Quelques correspondants de Mr. et Mrs. Childe et de Edward Lee Childe* (1912).

William Alexander Duer (1780–1858) was an important politician, lawyer, and college president who played a leading role in the 1821 revision of New York's Constitution of 1777. Duer endorsed the popular election of justices and property qualifications for voting. A strong supporter of the independence of the judiciary, Duer later became judge in the New York's Third Circuit (around Albany). In 1829, Duer became President of Columbia College in New York City. In 1833, he published *Outlines of the Constitutional Jurisprudence of the United States* in which he emphasized the importance of the power of federal courts and expressed concerns for the potential abuse of presidential power. A revised version of this book was published ten years later as *A Course of Lectures on the Constitutional Jurisprudence of the United States*. Duer opposed the right to secession from the Union.

Edward Everett (1794–1865) was a prominent Whig Party politician from Massachusetts. A graduate of Harvard College, Everett went to the University of Göttingen where he obtained a doctorate in classical literature.

Two years later, he took up a position at Harvard and became the editor of the influential *North American Review*. He also sought to implement some core elements of the Prussian education system. A supporter of the administration of John Quincy Adams, Everett was elected to the U.S. House of Representatives and U. S. Senate (in 1853), and also served as Governor of Massachusetts (1835–1839), and later as President of Harvard University (1846–1849). He also was the U. S. Envoy Extraordinary and Minister Plenipotentiary to England. In 1852, President Fillmore appointed Everett as U. S. Secretary of State. In 1860, Everett was an unsuccessful candidate for Vice President of the United States on the Constitutional Union ticket that represented the remnants of the Whig Party. He is remembered today mostly for his two-hour oration at the dedication of the national cemetery in Gettysburg on November 19, 1863. Everett first met Tocqueville in America in 1832. Everett's *Orations and Speeches on Various Occasions* came out in four volumes between 1853 and 1868. For more information, see Stuart J. Horn, *Edward Everett and American Nationalism* (Ph. D. diss., City University of New York, 1972).

Henry D. Gilpin (1801–1860) was a prominent American lawyer and statesman who served as attorney for the Eastern District of Pennsylvania (1831), government director of the Bank of the United States (1833), and solicitor of the U.S. Treasury (1837). President Van Buren appointed Gilpin Attorney General of the United States (1840–1841). From 1853 until 1858, Gilpin was President of the Pennsylvania Academy of Fine Arts and a Vice President and trustee of the Philadelphia Historical Society. Gilpin edited the papers of James Madison.

Samuel Griswold Goodrich (1793–1860) was the author of *The Story of Captain Riley and His Adventures in Africa* (Philadelphia: Henry F. Anners, 1841).

Charles Jared Ingersoll (1782–1862) was an attorney, author, and congressman who was educated at Princeton and was first elected to Congress in 1812. An independent spirit, Ingersoll voiced his skepticism toward northern abolitionists and was in favor of a mediated settlement. He retired from Congress in 1849. Ingersoll's two-volume memoirs, *Recollections*, were published in 1861. He also published a history of the War of 1812. For more information, see William A. Meigs, *The Life of Charles Jared Ingersoll* (Philadelphia: J. B. Lipincott, 1897).

Francis Kidder (1803–1879), born in Winhall, Vermont, was a member of the Vermont State House of Representatives and of the Vermont State Senate.

Francis Lieber (1798–1872) was a prominent nineteenth-century political scientist. Born in Berlin, Lieber studied at Jena, Halle, Dresden, and Berlin before emigrating to America in 1827. He became a naturalized citizen five years later. Lieber assisted Tocqueville and Beaumont in their gathering of information about America, and wrote on prison reform, being in favor of the Philadelphia system of solitary confinement. He was the founder of the *Encyclopedia Americana*, wrote the Civil War–era code of military conduct (that has become the basis for modern war crimes trials), taught at South Carolina College in Charleston (1835–1856), and later at Columbia College (later University) in New York. Author of many books, including *Manual of Political Ethics* (1838), *Essays on Property and Labour* (1841), and *On Civil Liberty and Self Government* (1853) Lieber became famous for his contribution to international law and to the development of political science in the United States. For a recent edition of his writings, see *The Miscellaneous Writings of Francis Lieber: Contributions to Political Science* (Lawbook Exchange, 2003). For more information on Lieber, see *The Life and Letters of Francis Lieber* by Thomas Sergeant Perry (Lawbook Exchange, 2006); *Francis Lieber and the Culture of the Mind*, eds. Charles Mack and Henri Lesesne (Charleston, SC: University of South Carolina Press, 2005); Charles Mack and Ilona Mack, *Like a Sponge Thrown into Water: Francis Lieber's European Travel Journal of 1844–1845* (Charleston, SC: University of South Carolina Press, 2005); Mele Curti, "Francis Lieber and Nationalism," *Huntington Library Quarterly* 4 (1941): 263–93; James Farr, "Francis Lieber and the Interpretation of American Political Science," *Journal of Politics* 53 (1990): 1027–49; Mancini, *Alexis de Tocqueville and the American Intellectuals*, 29–45.

W. W. Mann was an American journalist based in Paris. His political views brought him in close contact with the Whig circles of New York.

John Young Mason (1788–1859) was a prominent American politician and diplomat who, from 1831 to 1837, served in the U.S. House of Representatives and chaired the U.S. House Committee on Foreign Affairs from 1835 to 1836. A decade later, he served as Secretary of the Navy and then as Attorney General In 1853, he was appointed U.S. Minister Plenipotentiary to France. With James Buchanan and Pierre Soulé, U.S. ministers to Great Britain and Spain, he was instrumental in drawing up the Ostend Manifesto in October 1854.

Nathaniel Niles (1791–1869) was an American diplomat who served as Secretary of the American Legation in Paris (1830–1833) where he met Tocqueville.

Benjamin Perley Poore (1820–1887) was an American diplomat who published an account of political life under the July Monarchy entitled *The Rise and Fall of Louis-Philippe* (1848). After 1854, he became the Washington-based editorialist and correspondent of the *Boston Journal.*

William Hickling Prescott (1796–1859) was a prominent historian, born into a family prominent in Massachusetts. A graduate of Harvard, Prescott was a close friend of Sparks, Ticknor, Everett, and Bancroft, and became a leading figure in Whig circles. He was the author of the *History of the Reign of Ferdinand and Isabella*, 3 vols (1838) and the *History of the Reign of Philip the Second* (1855; 1859).

Richard Rush (1780–1859) was a prominent politician and lawyer, who was born in Philadelphia and was educated at Princeton. A member of the Republican Party, Rush was nominated General Attorney of Pennsylvania in 1811 and soon afterwards became Comptroller of the Treasury. A close associate of President Madison, Rush was appointed by the latter as Attorney General in 1814 and from 1817 to 1825, as U.S. Minister to Great Britain. His subsequent positions included Secretary of the Treasury (1825–1828), and U.S. Minister to France under the Polk administration (1847–1849). Rush first met Tocqueville in Paris in late 1847. In their correspondence, they addressed a number of topics of common interest such as the advantages of bicameralism and political representation. For more information, see J. H. Powell, *Richard Rush: Republican Diplomat, 1780–1859* (Philadelphia: University of Pennsylvania Press, 1942).

Theodore Sedgwick III (1811–1859) was a prominent lawyer and legal theorist, born to a distinguished New England family. A graduate of Columbia University, Sedgwick was admitted to the New York Bar in 1833. Late that year, he was appointed as an attaché to Edward Livingston, U. S. Minister to France. Sedgwick first met Tocqueville during his American voyage in 1831–1832 and later in Paris in 1833–1834. In the 1840s, Sedgwick distinguished himself as a conservative democrat who espoused a moderate position on slavery. An opponent of the popular election of judges, he argued for the need to maintain strict constitutional checks on popular sovereignty. He was the author of many articles and books, including *A Treatise on the Rules Which Govern the Interpretation and Application of Statutory and Constitutional Law* (1857). Sedgwick visited France again in 1850–1851 and had a rich correspondence with Tocqueville to the end of their lives.

Jared Sparks (1789–1866) was a prominent historian and clergyman, educated at the Philips Exeter Academy (New Hampshire) and at Harvard. An editor of the *North American Review*, Sparks edited George Washington's papers *The Life and Writings of George Washington*, 12 vols (1834–1837). He also wrote *A Life of Governeur Morris* (1832) and edited *The Works of Benjamin Franklin* (1833–1840) as well as *The Library of American Biography* (1833–1849). Appointed Professor of Ancient and Modern History at Harvard in 1838, he became President of Harvard in 1849. Tocqueville first met Sparks in 1828 in Paris and then during his visit to America in 1831–1832 and remained in touch until his death. For more information, see Herbert Baxter Adams, *The Life and Writings of Jared Sparks* (Boston & New York: Houghton, Mifflin & Co., 1893).

John Canfield Spencer (1788–1855) was a prominent lawyer and politician, who graduated from Williams College and Union College. He was appointed state district attorney for New York's five western counties in 1815. Later, Spencer, served in the U.S. House of Representatives (1817–1819) and in the New York Senate (1825–1828). He met Tocqueville in America in 1831. A major member of the Whig Party and a leading member in anti-Masonic circles, Spencer was appointed as head of the War Department by President Tyler in 1841 (he was also nominated to the U.S. Supreme Court in 1843, but his nomination was opposed in the Congress). Spencer met Tocqueville in 1831 and six years later he edited Reeve's translation of *Democracy in America*.

Charles Sumner (1811–1874) was a prominent politician and lawyer. A graduate of Harvard, Sumner had a close relationship with Joseph Story and was also an acquaintance of Emerson. He was a passionate social reformer, devoting his energies to important causes, such as prison discipline and education, slavery, war, and racial integration in Boston's public schools. After 1848, when the U. S. seized new territories from Mexico, Sumner joined other politicians to form the new Free Soil Party. Elected to the U. S. Senate in 1851, Charles Sumner showed himself to be an eloquent reformer in Congress and member of the Republican Party fighting against the Fugitive Slave Act and endorsing the attempts to form a new Republican Party whose mission was the prevent the spread of slavery into the Western territories. In 1856, following a famous exchange with Senator Stephen A. Douglas, Sumner was physically abused on the Senate floor by Senator Preston Brooks, a congressman from South Carolina, and was able to resume his post only three years later. Later, Sumner was a close associate of President Lincoln and served as Chair of the Committee on Foreign Relations. For a biography of Sumner, see *Memoir and Letters of Charles Sumner*, ed. Edward L. Pierce, four volumes (Boston, MA: Roberts Brothers, 1878–1894).

George Sumner (1817–1863), brother of Senator Charles Sumner, took an active interest in penitentiary reform in America.

Henry Philip Tappan (1805–1881) was a prominent nineteenth-century American philosopher and academic. In 1832, Tappan became Professor of Moral Philosophy at the University of the City of New York (later New York University), where he pursued research on the philosophy of education. In 1837, along with seven other faculty members, he was dismissed from his post after raising complaints about the managerial incompetence of his university. He then opened a private school for girls in New York City and continued to write works on the philosophy of education. He traveled to Europe in order to study the European university system. In 1851, Tappan published *University Education* and a year later, *A Step from the New World to the Old and Back Again: with Thoughts on the Good and Evil in Both*. In 1852, he became President of the University of Michigan, where he continued to pursue a program of university reform. On his life and work, see Charles M. Perry, *Henry Philip Tappan: Philosopher and University President* (Ann Arbor, MI: University of Michigan Press, 1933).

George Ticknor (1791–1871) is best remembered today as one of the founders of the Boston Public Library. A close friend of Everett and Sparks, in 1817 he became professor of French and Spanish languages and literatures and professor of belles-lettres at Harvard. Ticknor was the author of a widely acclaimed *History of Spanish Literature*, 3 volumes (1849). He frequently traveled to Europe and met Tocqueville in Paris in the 1850s. For more information, see *Life, Letters and Journals of George Ticknor*, 2 vols (1876), eds. George S. Hillard and Mrs. Anna (Eliot) Ticknor and Miss Anna Eliot Ticknor; David Tyack, *George Ticknor and the Boston Brahmins* (Cambridge, MA: Harvard University Press, 1967).

Isaiah Townsend was a politician from Albany, New York, and an acquaintance of John C. Spencer. He first met Tocqueville in 1831, and renewed their acquaintance nine years later in Paris.

Robert Walsh (1784–1859), American publicist and diplomat, founder (in 1811) of the Philadelphia-based *American Review of History and Politics*, the first American quarterly review. He was also the editor of the *National Gazette* (1821–1836), a paper devoted to politics, science, letters, and the fine arts which was well regarded in Europe. Walsh also contributed to the influential *National Intelligencer* and published two volumes of essays, *Didactics* (1836). From 1844 to 1851, he served as Consul General of the United States in Paris, where he remained until his death in 1859. Walsh was also the author of a famous *Letter on the Genius and Disposition of the French Government*. Tocqueville and Beaumont first met Walsh in Philadelphia on October 15, 1831. For more information, see Pierson, *Tocqueville in America*, 475–76.

Henry Wheaton (1785–1848) was the translator of the Napoleonic Code and prominent U.S. diplomat, author of important books, including *History of the Peoples of the North* (1831), *Elements of International Law* (1836), and *Enquiry into the Validity of the British Claim to a Right of Visitation and Search of American Vessels Suspected to be Engaged in the African Slave Trade* (1842). Wheaton was elected as foreign correspondent of the French Academy in April 1842.

APPENDIX 2

Chronology

1805

Alexis Charles-Henri Clérel de Tocqueville was born on July 29 to a distinguished aristocratic family with roots in Normandy. The family had two other sons: Hippolyte, born in 1797, and Édouard, born in 1800. Tocqueville's great grandfather was Chrétien-Guillaume de Lamoignon de Malesherbes, who became famous as a minister during the reign of Louis XVI and defender of the King during his trial. Tocqueville's family suffered during the Revolution and his parents, Hervé and Louise-Madeleine, were imprisoned during the Terror, narrowly escaping the guillotine.

1812

In Paris, Tocqueville begins his education under the tutelage of Abbé Lesueur who became an important person in his life.

1814

The Tocqueville family endorses the return of the Bourbons to the throne of France. Louis XVIII arrives in Paris on May 3.

1820

Enrolls in a high school in Metz where his father moved after being appointed prefect of the Moselle. Graduates in 1823.

1823–1826

Tocqueville studies law at the University of Paris.

1826

In December, Tocqueville travels to Italy and Sicily, accompanied by his brother Édouard.

1827

Tocqueville is appointed *juge auditeur* at the tribunal in Versailles, a position that he will hold until 1830. In November, his father is appointed member of the Chamber of Peers.

1828

Tocqueville meets Gustave de Beaumont, who will accompany him to America three years later. The same year, he also meets Mary Mottley, an English Protestant, whom he was later to marry.

1829

Tocqueville and Beaumont attend François Guizot's course of lectures on the history of civilization in France at the Sorbonne in Paris. In October, he visits Switzerland.

1830

On July 25, Charles X dissolves the Chamber of Deputies. Protests follow that will eventually lead to the fall of the Bourbon dynasty on August 2, when the king abdicates. A peaceful change of dynasty ensues, with King Louis-Philippe, former Duke d'Orléans, ascending to the throne on August 9. Hervé de Tocqueville refuses to pledge his oath to the new monarch. As a public official, Alexis de Tocqueville is required to take the oath of loyalty, which he does on August 16 without enthusiasm.

1831–1832

From May 1831 to February 1832, Tocqueville travels to America, accompanied by Beaumont. The official reason was to study the penitentiary system in the New World. The two Frenchmen land in Newport, Rhode Island, visit New England, Lower Canada, and Upper Michigan. Later they travel down the Ohio River and the Mississippi and arrive in New Orleans. On their way back north, they visit Alabama, Georgia, the Carolinas, and Virginia. After a sojourn in Washington, Tocqueville and Beaumont leave for France on February 20.

1833

Tocqueville and Beaumont publish *Du Système pénitentiaire aux États-Unis et de son application en France*. First visit to England (August 3–September 7). In September, he starts working on Volume One of *Democracy in America*.

1834

The writing of Volume One of *Democracy* continues. Tocqueville consults with two Americans in Paris, Theodore Sedgwick and Francis Lippitt. The volume is sent to the printers in the autumn.

1835

Volume One of *Democracy in America* is published in January by Gosselin; immediately upon its publication, it is widely acclaimed as a masterpiece. Tocqueville writes the first *Memoir on Pauperism* published by the Academic Society of Cherbourg (a second memoir was drafted, but never published). Beaumont publishes *Marie*. Tocqueville undertakes a second trip to England and Ireland (April 23–August 23), accompanied by Beaumont. In late October, Tocqueville marries Mary Mottley against the wishes of his family.

1836

Tocqueville's mother passes away in January. *L'État social et politique de la France avant et après 1789* is published in English in the *London and Westminster Review*. From July to September, he travels to Switzerland and Germany.

1837

In June and August, Tocqueville publishes *Deux Lettres sur l'Algérie* in *La Presse de Seine-et-Oise*. In November, he runs for election to the Chamber of Deputies and is narrowly defeated.

1838

In January, Tocqueville becomes a member of the *Academy of Moral and Political Sciences*.

1839

Tocqueville is elected parliamentary deputy for Valognes. In June, Beaumont, who is also elected deputy later that year, publishes *L'Irlande sociale, politique et religieuse*. In July, Tocqueville presents a report to the Chamber of Deputies on slavery in the French colonies.

1840

Volume Two of *Democracy in America* is published by Gosselin in April. In June, he submits a report on prison reform. In October, the Thiers cabinet is dissolved, being replaced by the Soult-Guizot cabinet; Tocqueville feels alienated from politics.

1841

In May–June, Tocqueville undertakes his first trip to Algeria. In December, he is elected to the French Academy, replacing Lacuée de Cessac.

1842

In April, Tocqueville gives his inaugural speech in the French Academy. He is reelected to the Chamber of Deputies in July and is elected to the *General Council* of the department of the Manche.

1843

Tocqueville expresses his growing dissatisfaction with the politics of the Soult-Guizot government. Publishes six letters in *Le Siècle* in which he examines the internal situation of France. Tocqueville is also worried by the maritime supremacy of England.

1844–1845

In June, along with a group of friends, Tocqueville purchases a newspaper, *Le Commerce*. He obtains the collaboration of Francis Lieber from America. Journalism turns out to be an unsatisfying experience for Tocqueville. His collaboration with *Le Commerce* ends less than a year later.

Annexation of Texas in December 1845. The future Know-Nothing Party spreads to other states as the *Native American Party* and became a national party in 1845. James K. Polk is elected president, intent on pursuing an expansionist policy calling for "the reoccupation of Oregon."

1846

Reelected to the Chamber of Deputies in August, Tocqueville undertakes a second journey to Algeria in October and explores the possibility of forming a new "Young Left" with Auguste Billault and Armand Dufaure.

The American-Mexican war begins (it will end two years later). President Polk sends a detachment of troops under General Zachary Taylor to the disputed territory.

1847

In May and June, Tocqueville submits two critical reports on Algeria to the Chamber of Deputies. He abstains from attending the banquets launched by the opposition parties and which challenged the unwillingness of the Soult-Guizot cabinet to lower the property qualifications for voting.

1848

On January 15, Tocqueville presents to the *Academy of Moral and Political Sciences* his report on Cherbuliez's *De la démocratie en Suisse*. Twelve days later, he gives a powerful speech in the Chamber in which he warns of the dangers of a forthcoming revolution. On February 23, the Guizot cabinet falls and the king abdicates a day later when the Second Republic is proclaimed. Tocqueville stands for office again in March–April and is elected with a substantial majority of the votes in his department of the Manche. During the electoral campaign, Tocqueville gives a speech in Cherbourg (March 19) in which he expresses his support for an alliance between France and America in order to countervail British maritime supremacy. On May 4, the new Constituent Assembly meets in Paris and Tocqueville is elected a member of the committee for the drafting of a new Constitution. A popular insurrection takes place from June 23 to June 26 after the provisional government shuts down the public workshops in Paris. Tocqueville is concerned about a possible civil war and supports the measures taken by General Cavaignac. Tocqueville plays a key role in the constitutional committee. He cites the American example, rejects the right to work, and endorses the election of the President of the French Republic by the people. Tocqueville supports Cavaignac, who loses to Louis-Napoléon Bonaparte in the presidential election of December 10.

By the Treaty of Guadalupe Hidalgo, signed on February 2, Mexico agrees to cede California and New Mexico to the United States and to recognize the Rio Grande boundary of Texas. Zachary Taylor elected U. S. president.

1849

In May, Tocqueville visits Germany and is elected representative of the Manche to the new Legislative Assembly. On June 2, he is appointed Minister of Foreign Affairs in the Barrot cabinet. The new minister faces a major crisis in Italy where French forces were sent to help restore the power of Pope Pius IX. Tocqueville appoints Francisque de Corcelle as the French envoy to the Pope, but the mission proves to be a failure. Tocqueville will also be involved in an unfortunate diplomatic incident with the United States triggered by the correspondence between the French Minister to the United States, Guillaume-Tell Poussin, and the U.S. Secretary of State, John M. Clayton. The Barrot cabinet is dissolved on October 31 and Tocqueville's ministerial career comes to an abrupt end.

1850

First signs of tuberculosis in March. He begins writing the *Recollections* in June; the book will be published posthumously. In December, Tocqueville arrives in Sorrento (Italy) where he will spend the winter. In an important letter to Louis de Kergorlay (December 15, 1850), Tocqueville expresses his desire to write a book on the French Revolution.

Millard Fillmore becomes President of the United States. The U.S. Congress passes the Compromise of 1850, which attempted to resolve the territorial and slavery controversies arising from the Mexican-American War. It contained the Fugitive Slave Act, requiring all U.S. citizens to assist in the return of runaway slaves regardless of the legality of slavery in the specific states. California is admitted into the Union.

1851

Tocqueville returns to Paris in April and submits his report on revising the Constitution in July. The report is rejected in the Chamber. Prevented from being re-elected, Louis-Napoléon stages a *coup d'état* on

December 2. Members of the Assembly are arrested, including Tocqueville who was released two days later.

1852

In April, Tocqueville gives an important speech to the *Academy of Moral and Political Sciences* in which he outlines his ideas on the relationship between politics and political science. On April 29, he resigns from his post as general counselor in his department of the Manche. Tocqueville begins writing *The Old Regime and the Revolution*. On December 2, the Second Empire is proclaimed.

Franklin Pierce is elected U. S. president.

1853

Tocqueville's health continues to be fragile. His doctors advise him to avoid the climate of Normandy and spend some time further south. Consequently, Tocqueville and his wife decide to rent a house near Tours, in the Loire Valley.

1854

Tocqueville and his wife travel to Germany during the summer. The writing of *The Old Regime and the Revolution* goes on.

The Kansas–Nebraska Act overturned the Missouri Compromise of 1820 and the Compromise of 1850 by reopening the question of slavery in the West. It created the territories of Kansas and Nebraska and opened new lands for settlement, and allowed the settlers to decide whether or not to have slavery. The Know-Nothing Party gains momentum by attracting former members of the Whig Party. The signing of the so-called *Ostend Manifesto*, a secret document written in October 1854 by U. S. diplomats at Ostend, Belgium, describing a plan to acquire Cuba from Spain.

1856

Tocqueville's father dies on June 9. Volume One of *The Old Regime and the Revolution* appears in June, published by Michel-Lévy Frères. Intense correspondence between Tocqueville and Madame de Swetchine.

In May, the anti-slavery Senator Charles Sumner is physically assaulted by Senator Preston Brooks on the Senate floor. 'Bleeding Kansas' erupts into violence. James Buchanan is elected U.S. president.

1857

Tocqueville travels to England (June 19–July 24). He begins writing the chapters meant to be included in Volume Two of *The Old Regime and the Revolution*. Frequent correspondence with his American friends, in particular with E. V. Childe, Theodore Sedgwick, and N. W. Beckwith.

In March, two days after the inauguration of Buchanan, Chief Justice Roger B. Taney delivered the Dred Scott decision, asserting that Congress had no constitutional power to deprive persons of their property rights in slaves in the territories. The U.S. economy is shaken by a financial crisis.

1858

Tocqueville's health deteriorates in April. His doctors advise him to move south. He settles at Cannes in early November.

The Lincoln-Douglas debates, in which Lincoln places slavery "in the course of its ultimate extinction."

1859

Tocqueville's health continues to deteriorate. His friend Gustave de Beaumont is summoned to Cannes, where Tocqueville is also surrounded by his brothers. He dies on April 16. He is buried in Normandy at Tocqueville.

1860

Abraham Lincoln is elected U.S. president. By the time of his inauguration, seven southern states have seceded from the Union.

1861

The Civil War commences.

Sources for the Texts

The majority of the letters included in Part I were published in Alexis de Tocqueville's *Œuvres Complètes, VII. Correspondance étrangère d'Alexis de Tocqueville. Amérique. Europe continentale*, eds. François Mélonio, Lisa Queffélec, and Anthony Pleasance (Paris: Gallimard, 1986). There are three new letters of Tocqueville (included in this section) which were not published in *OC*, VII. These letters were sent by Tocqueville to: Theodore Sedgwick (May 1853, Beinecke Rare Book and Manuscript Library, Yale University), Richard Rush (June or July 1849, Firestone Library, Princeton University), and Jared Sparks (December 11, 1852, Houghton Library, Harvard University). The latter was discovered by Robert T. Gannett whose own translation (slightly different from the one included here) was originally published in the *Harvard Library Bulletin*, New Series, 14: 3 (2003): 10.

The majority of the letters received by Tocqueville from his American correspondents from 1840 to 1859 have never appeared in print before. They were collected by the editors of the present volume from various libraries in the United States: the Beinecke Rare Book and Manuscript Library (Yale University); the Firestone Library (Princeton University, Rush Family Papers, C0079, IV. Papers, Documents, and Correspondence, 1846–1849, relating to the French Mission); the Houghton Library (Harvard University); the Huntington Library (San Marino, California); the University of South Carolina Library (Columbia, S.C.); the Massachusetts Historical Society Library (Boston). Some of the letters included in Part I are available only as "Bonnel copies" at the Beinecke Rare Book and Manuscript Library.

The letters included in Part I, Section E were collected from the following volumes of Tocqueville's *OC*:

Letter of Tocqueville to Louis de Kergorlay (October 18, 1847), *OC*, XIII: 2, 209–11.

Selections from the correspondence between Tocqueville and Jean-Jacques Ampère, (October 6, 1851; November 7, 1851; November 12, 1851; January 23, 1852), *OC*, XI, 200–9.

Selections from the correspondence between Tocqueville and Arthur de Gobineau (October 11, 1853; March 20, 1856; May 1, 1856; July 30, 1856; January 24, 1857), *OC*, IX, 199, 260–61, 262–63, 265–68, 277.

Selections from the correspondence between Tocqueville and Gustave de Beaumont, (November 3, 1853; August 6, 1854; November 16, 1857; December 6, 1857), *OC*, VIII: 3, 163–64.

Selections from the correspondence between Tocqueville and Alphonse de Circourt and Madame de Circourt (August 25, 1853; November 9, 1853; November 26, 1853; November 26, 1854; November 1, 1855; June 7, 1856; June 15, 1856; July 5, 1856; November 4, 1856; October 14, 1857), *OC*, XVIII, 99–101, 111–12, 115, 224–25, 278–79, 309, 311, 315–16, 349, 422.

The fragment from a letter of Tocqueville to Nassau Senior, September 4, 1856 was taken from *Correspondence and Conversations of Alexis de Tocqueville with Nassau William Senior*, ed. M. C. M. Simpson (London: Henry King: 1872), II, 271.

The texts of Tocqueville included in Part II, Section A were originally published as follows: "Projet de discours sur l'affaire de l'Orégon" *OC*, III: 2, 441–46; "Rapport sur *La Démocratie en Suisse*," *OC*, XVI, 203–20. The texts included in Part II, Sections B and C were originally published as follows: Tocqueville's speech at the popular banquet of Cherbourg, March 1848 (*OC*, III: 3, 43–46); Tocqueville's preface to the twelfth edition of *Democracy in America* 1848 (*OC*, I: 1, XLIII–XLIV); Tocqueville's interventions during the drafting of the Constitution, sessions of May 25, 1848 (*OC*, III: 3, 81–91) and May 27, 1848 (*OC*, III: 3, 97–101); Tocqueville's speech made before the Constituent Assembly during the discussion of the new constitution on the right to work, September 12, 1848 (*OC*, III: 3, 167–80); Tocqueville's intervention in defense of bicameralism before the Constituent Assembly (*OC*, III: 3, 199–201); Tocqueville's discourse on the election of the President of the French Republic, October 5, 1848 (*OC*, III: 3, 211–22). Tocqueville's contribution to the debates on the revision of the Constitution of the Second Republic was published as "Rapport fait par M. de Tocqueville au nom de la Commission chargée d'examiner les propositions sur la revision de la Constitution," July 8, 1851 (*OC*, III: 3, selected fragments from 433–53).

The original documents included in Part II, Section D ("The Poussin Affair") were collected from the microfilms in the archives of the Ministry of Foreign Affairs of the French Republic held at Quai d'Orsay in Paris. They can be found under two headings: *Mémoires et documents: Etats-Unis*, 25 and *Correspondances Diplomatiques, Etats-Unis*, 104.

Tocqueville's review of Sedgwick's *A Treatise on the Rules which Govern the Interpretation and the Application of Statutory and Constitutional Law* (Part II, Section E) was originally published as "Rapport sur un ouvrage de M. Th. Sedgwick" [1858], in Tocqueville, *OC*, XVI, 243–47.

Selected Bibliography

The bibliography below lists only Tocqueville's works mentioned in this book and the major works that are relevant to our volume.

Tocqueville's complete works (in eighteen volumes) have been published by Gallimard since 1951. Most volumes have more than one part. Volume XVII, yet to appear, will complete the publication of Tocqueville's extensive correspondence. Listed below are the volumes to which references are made in our book:

Œuvres Complètes, I: 1. De la démocratie en Amérique, ed. J.-P. Mayer, introduction by Harold Laski (Paris: Gallimard, 1951).

Œuvres Complètes, I: 2. De la démocratie en Amérique, ed. J.-P. Mayer, introduction by Harold Laski (Paris: Gallimard, 1961).

Œuvres Complètes, III: 2. Écrits et discours politiques, ed. André Jardin (Paris: Gallimard, 1985).

Œuvres Complètes, III: 3. Écrits et discours politiques, ed. André Jardin (Paris: Gallimard, 1990).

Œuvres Complètes, IV: 1. Écrits sur le système pénitentiaire en France et à l'étranger, ed. Michelle Perrot (Paris: Gallimard, 1984).

Œuvres Complètes, IV: 2. Ecrits sur le système pénitentiaire en France et a l'etranger, ed. Michelle Perrot (Paris: Gallimard, 1984).

Œuvres Complètes, VI: 2. Correspondance anglaise. Correspondance et conversations d'Alexis de Tocqueville et Nassau William Senior, eds. Hugh Brogan and A. P. Kerr (Paris: Gallimard, 1991).

Œuvres Complètes, VII. Correspondance étrangère d'Alexis de Tocqueville. Amérique. Europe continentale, eds. Françoise Mélonio, Lisa Queffélec, and Anthony Pleasance (Paris: Gallimard, 1986).

Œuvres Complètes, VIII: 1. Correspondance d'Alexis de Tocqueville et de Gustave de Beaumont, ed. André Jardin (Paris: Gallimard, 1967).

Œuvres Complètes, VIII: 3. Correspondance d'Alexis de Tocqueville et de Gustave de Beaumont, ed. André Jardin (Paris: Gallimard, 1967).

Œuvres Complètes, IX. Correspondance d'Alexis de Tocqueville et d'Arthur de Gobineau, ed. M. Degros (Paris: Gallimard, 1959).

Œuvres Complètes, XI. Correspondance d'Alexis de Tocqueville et de Pierre-Paul Royer-Collard. Correspondance d'Alexis de Tocqueville et de Jean-Jacques Ampère, ed. André Jardin (Paris: Gallimard, 1970).

Œuvres Complètes, XIII: 2. Correspondance d'Alexis de Tocqueville et de Louis de Kergorlay, ed. André Jardin and Jean-Alain Lesourd (Paris: Gallimard, 1977).

Œuvres Complètes, XV: 2. Correspondance d'Alexis de Tocqueville et de Francisque de Corcelle. Correspondance d'Alexis de Tocqueville et de Madame Swetchine, ed. Pierre Gibert (Paris: Gallimard, 1983).

Œuvres Complètes, XVI. Mélanges, ed. Françoise Mélonio (Paris: Gallimard, 1983),

Œuvres Complètes: XVIII. Correspondance d'Alexis de Tocqueville avec Adolphe de Circourt et avec Madame de Circourt, ed. A. P. Kerr (Paris: Gallimard, 1983).

The most comprehensive edition of *Democracy in America*, containing Tocqueville's extensive notes from the Beinecke Rare Book and Manuscript Library at Yale University, was edited and published by Eduardo Nolla at Éditions Vrin in 1990 (two volumes). Liberty Fund will publish soon a bilingual edition of this monumental edition, translated by James T. Schleifer and edited by Eduardo Nolla.

Three volumes of Tocqueville's works have been published in the prestigious Bibliothèque de la Pléiade as follows:

Œuvres, I, eds. André Jardin, Françoise Mélonio, and Lisa Queffélec (Paris: Gallimard, 1991). This volume includes Tocqueville's travel notes (Sicily, America, Switzerland, and Algeria), his notes on India, and a selection of representative political and academic writings and speeches.

Œuvres, II, eds. Jean-Claude Lamberti and James T. Schleifer (Paris: Gallimard, 1992). This volume contains the text of *Democracy in America* along with a representative selection from Tocqueville's notes.

Œuvres, III, ed. Françoise Mélonio (Paris: Gallimard, 2004). Contains the two volumes of *The Old Regime and the Revolution*.

Other editions of Tocqueville's works cited in the present book:

Tocqueville, Alexis de. 1959. *The 'European Revolution' & Correspondence with Gobineau*, eds. and trans. **John Lukacs**. New York: Doubleday Anchor.

Tocqueville, Alexis de. 1964. *On the Penitentiary System in the United States and Its Application in France*, ed. **Thorsten Sellin**. Carbondale, IL: Southern Illinois University Press.

Tocqueville, Alexis de. 1968. *Tocqueville and Beaumont on Social Reform*, ed. and trans. **Seymour Drescher**. New York: Harper & Row.

Tocqueville, Alexis de. 1971. *Recollections*, eds. J. P. Mayer & A. P. Kerr, trans. George Lawrence. New York: Doubleday.

Tocqueville, Alexis de. 1985. *Selected Letters on Politics and Society*, ed. **Roger Boesche**, trans. **James Toupin** & **Roger Boesche**. Berkeley, CA: University of California Press.

Tocqueville, Alexis de. 1997. *Memoir on Pauperism*, trans. *Seymour Drescher, with an introduction by Gertrude Himmelfarb*. Chicago, IL: Ivan R. Dee.

Tocqueville, Alexis de. 1997. *Recollections*, ed. **J.-P. Mayer**. New Brunswick, NJ: Transactions.

Tocqueville, Alexis de. 2000. *Democracy in America*, trans. **Delba Winthrop** and **Harvey C. Mansfield**. Chicago, IL: University of Chicago Press.

Tocqueville, Alexis de. 2001. *Writings on Empire and Slavery*, ed. and trans. by **Jennifer Pitts**. Baltimore, MD: The Johns Hopkins University Press.

Tocqueville, Alexis de. 2002. *The Tocqueville Reader*, eds. **Oliver Zunz** and **Alan S. Kahan**. Oxford: Blackwell.

Tocqueville, Alexis de. 2003. *Lettres choisies. Souvenirs*, eds. **Françoise Mélonio** and **Laurence Guellec**. Paris: Gallimard.

Tocqueville, Alexis de. 2006. *Kleine politische Schriften*, eds. **Harald Bluhm** & **Skadi Krause**. Berlin: Academie Verlag.

II. Other Primary Texts

Adams, Herbert B. 1893. *The Life and Writings of Jared Sparks*, **2** vols. Boston, MA and New York: Houghton Mifflin & Co.

Ampère, Jean-Jacques. 1855. *Promenade en Amérique*, **2** vols. Paris: Michel-Lévy.

Beaumont, Gustave de. 1958. *Marie or Slavery in the United States*. Stanford, CA: Stanford University Press.

Carrel, Armand. 1832. *Untitled article*. Le National, May 29.

Chateaubriand, François-René. 1969. *Travels in America*, trans. **Richard Switzer**. Lexington, KY: University of Kentucky Press.

Colombel, Hyacinthe. 1848. *Quelques réflexions concernant la Constitution qu'on élabore pour la France*. Nantes: Courier de Nantes.

Crèvecoeur, J. Hector St. John de. 1957. *Letters from an American Farmer*. New York: Dutton.

DeWolfe Howe. M. A. ed. 1908. *The Life and Letters of George Bancroft*, **2** vols. New York: Charles Scribner's Sons.

Everett, Edward. 1836. "De Tocqueville's *Democracy* in *America*," *The North American Review*, **43**: **92**: 178–206.

Everett, Edward. 1838. "De Beaumont and de Tocqueville on the Penitentiary System," *The North American Review*, **37**: **80**: 117–38.

Guizot, François. 1858–65. *Mémoires pour servir à l'histoire de mon temps* (Paris: Michel-Lévy Frères), **8** vols.

Hamelin, Fortunée. ed. 1912. *Quelques correspondants de Mr. et Mrs. Childe et de Edward Lee Childe (1844–1879)*. London: R. Clays & Sons.

Hawkins, Richmond Laurin. 1928. "Unpublished Letters of Alexis de Tocqueville." *The Romanic Review*, **XIX**: **3**: 195–217.

Hawkins, Richmond Laurin. 1929. "Unpublished Letters of Alexis de Tocqueville." *The Romanic Review*, **XX**: **1**: 351–57.

Hawkins, Richmond Laurin. 1933. *Newly Discovered French Letters*. Cambridge, MA: Harvard University Press.

Laboulaye, Édouard. 1849. *Considérations sur la Constitution*. Paris: Durand.

Laboulaye, Édouard. 1850. *De la Constitution Américaine et de l'Utilité de son étude*. Paris: Hennuyer.

Lieber, Francis. 2003. *The Miscellaneous Writings of Francis Lieber: Contributions to Political Science*. Lawbook Exchange, Reprint.

Jacquemont, Victor. 1885. *Correspondance inedite avec sa famille et ses amis, 1824–1832*, Vol. **I**. Paris: Calmann-Lévy.

Montulé, Édouard de. 1951. *Travels in America, 1816–1817*. Bloomington, IN: Indiana University Press.

Perry, Thomas Sergeant, ed. 1882. *The Life and Letters of Francis Lieber*. Boston, MA: Osgood & Co.

Poussin, Guillaume-Tell. 1841. *Considérations sur le Principe démocratique qui régit l'Union Américaine et d'autres états*. Paris: Gosselin.

Rendu, Abel. 1850. *Les deux Républiques*. Paris: Dondey-Dupré.

Rush, Richard. 1860. *Occasional Productions, Political, Diplomatic, and Miscellaneous, including, among others, A Glance at the Court and Government of Louis-Philippe and the French revolution of 1848, while the author resided as envoy extraordinary and minister plenipotentiary from the United States at Paris*. Philadelphia, PA: J.B. Lippincott.

Saint-Victor, Jacques Benjamin. 1835. *Lettres sur les États-Unis d'Amérique*. Paris & Lyon: Perisse Frères.

Sedgwick, Theodore. 1844. *Thoughts on the Proposed Annexation of Texas to the United States*. New York: Fanshaw.

Sedgwick, Theodore. 1847. *The American Citizen: His True Position, Character and Duties*. New York: Wiley and Putnam.

Sedgwick, Theodore. 1857. *A Treatise on the Rules which Govern the Interpretation and Application of Statutory and Constitutional Law*. New York: J.S. Voorhier.

Sergeant Perry, Thomas, ed. 1892. *The Life and Letters of Francis Lieber*. Boston, MA: Osgood & Co.

Simpson M. C. M., ed., 1872. *Correspondence and Conversations of Alexis de Tocqueville with Nassau William Senior*, II. London: Henry King.

Staël, Germaine de. 1818. *Considerations on the Principal Events of the French Revolution*, 3 vols. London: Bladwin, Cradock, and Joy (Newly revised translation: ed. **Aurelian Craiutu**. Indianapolis, IN: Liberty Fund, 2008).

Stendhal. 1975. *On Love*, trans. **Gilbert** and **Suzanne Sale**. London: Penguin.

Story, Joseph. 1851. *Life and Letters of Joseph Story*, ed. **William W. Story**, 2 vols. Boston, MA: Little & Brown.

Sumner, Charles. 1878–1894. *Memoir and Letters of Charles Sumner*, ed. **Edward L. Pierce**, 4 vols. Boston, MA: Roberts Brothers.

III. Works of General Information

Bemis, Samuel Flagg. 1958. *The American Secretaries of State and their Diplomacy: John Middleton Clayton*. New York: Pageant Book Company.

Craveri, Piero, ed. 1985. *Genesi di una constituzione: Libertà e socialismo nel dibattito constituzionale del 1848 in Francia*. Napoli: Guida.

Duguit L., **Monnier H.**, and **Bonnard R.**, eds. 1952. *Les Constitutions et les principales lois politiques de la France depuis 1789*. Paris: Librairie Générale de Droit et de Jurisprudence.

Garraty, John A., and **Carnes, Mark C.**, eds. 1999. *American National Biography*, Vol. 17. New York: Oxford University Press.

Jaume, Lucien, ed. 1995. *Les Constitutions de la France depuis 1789*. Paris: Flammarion.

Le Commerce [journal]. 1844–1845, Microfilm, Bibliothquè Nationale, Paris.

IV. Secondary Sources

Adams, Herbert B. 1898. *Jared Sparks and Alexis de Tocqueville*. Baltimore, MD: The John Hopkins University Press.

Antoine, Agnès. 2003. *L'impensé de la démocratie: Tocqueville, la citoyenneté, et la religion*. Paris: Fayard.

Bears, Sara B. 1986. "The Federalist Career of George Washington Parke Custis," *Northern Virginia Heritage* 8 (February): 15–20.

Blumenthal, Henry. 1959. *A Reappraisal of Franco-American Relations 1830–1871*. Chapel Hill, NC: University of North Carolina Press.

Boesche, Roger. 1987. *The Strange Liberalism of Alexis de Tocqueville*. Ithaca, NY: Cornell University Press.

Boesche, Roger. 2006. *Tocqueville's Road Map: Methodology, Liberalism, Revolution, and Despotism*. Lanham, MD: Lexington Books, Rowman & Littlefield.

Boudon, Raymond. 1982. *The Unintended Consequences of Human Action*. New York: St. Martin's Press.

Boudon, Raymond. 2006. "L'exigence de Tocqueville: la 'science politique nouvelle,'" *The Tocqueville Review/La Revue Tocqueville* **XXVII**: 2 (2006): 13–34.

Brogan, Hugh. 1991. "Alexis de Tocqueville and the Coming of the American Civil War," *American Studies: Essays in Honour of Marcus Cunliffe*, eds. **Brian Holden Reid** & **John White**. New York: St. Martin's Press, 83–104.

Brogan, Hugh. 2006. *Alexis de Tocqueville: A Life*. New Haven, CT: Yale University Press.

Broglie, Gabriel, de. 1979. *Histoire politique de la Revue des Deux Mondes de 1829 à 1979*. Paris: Perrin.

Brown, Bernard Edward. 1951. *American Conservatives: The Political Thought of Francis Lieber and John W. Burgess*. New York: Columbia University Press.

Brown Pryor, Elizabeth. 2007. *Reading the Man: A Portait of Robert E. Lee Through His Private Letters*. New York: Viking.

Callahan, John Morton. 1898. *The Neutrality of the American Lakes and Anglo-American Relations*. Baltimore, MD: Johns Hopkins University Press.

Ceaser, James W. 1997. *Reconstructing America: The Symbol of America in Modern Thought*. New Haven, CT: Yale University Press.

Ceasar, James W. 2003. "A Genealogy of anti-Americanism." *Public Interest*, 152: 3–18.

Clinton, David. 2003. *Tocqueville, Lieber, and Bagehot: Liberalism Confronts the World*. New York: Palgrave.

Craiutu, Aurelian & **Jeffrey C. Isaac**, eds. 2009. *America through European Eyes: British and French Reflections on the New World from the 18th Century to the Present*. University Park, PA: Pennsylvania State University Press.

Craiutu, Aurelian. 2009. *"What Kind of Social Scientist Was Tocqueville?,"* in *Conversations with Tocqueville*, eds. **Aurelian Craiutu** and **Sheldon Gellar**. Lanham, MD: Lexington Books, Rowman and Littlefield, 55–81.

Craiutu, Aurelian. 2005. "Tocqueville's Paradoxical Moderation," *The Review of Politics*, **67**: 4: 599–629.

Craiutu, Aurelian. 2003. *Liberalism under Siege: The Political Thought of the French Doctrinaires*. Lanham, MD: Lexington Books, Rowman and Littlefield.

Crouzet, Michel. 2008. *Stendhal et l'Amérique : L'Amérique et la modernité*. Paris: Editions de Fallois.

Curti, Mele. 1941. "Francis Lieber and Nationalism," *Huntington Library Quarterly* 4: 263–93.

Currie, David P. 2005. *Constitution in Crisis: Descent into the Maelstrom 1829–61*. Chicago, IL: University of Chicago Press.

Curtis, Eugene N. 1924. "American Opinion of the French Nineteenth-Century Revolutions," *American Historical Review*, **29**: 2: 249–70.

Daspre, André. 1972. "Stendhal et la démocratie américaine," *Europe*, **519–521** (July–September): 79–88.

Drescher, Seymour. 1964. "Tocqueville's Two *Démocraties*," *Journal of the History of Ideas*, **25** (April–June 1964): 201–16.

Drescher, Seymour. 1968. *Dilemmas of Democracy*. Pittsburgh, PA: University of Pittsburgh Press.

Drescher, Seymour. 1988. "More than America: Comparison and Synthesis in Democracy in America," *in Reconsidering Tocqueville's Democracy in America*, ed. **Abraham S. Eisenstadt**. New Brunswick, NJ: Rutgers University Press, 77–93.

Drescher, Seymour. 2006. "Tocqueville's Comparisons: Choices and Lessons," *The Tocqueville Review/La Revue Tocqueville*, **XXVII**: **2**: 479–516.

Eisenstadt, Abraham S. ed. 1988. *Reconsidering Tocqueville's Democracy in America*. New Brunswick, NJ: Rutgers University Press.

Echeveria, Durand. 1957. *Mirage in the West: A History of the French Image of American Society to 1815*. Princeton, NJ: Princeton University Press.

Farr, James. 1990. "Francis Lieber and the Interpretation of American Political Science," *Journal of Politics*, **52**: **4**: 1027–1049.

Foner, Eric. 1970. *Free Soil, Free Labor, Free Man: The Ideology of the Republican Party before the Civil War*. Oxford: Oxford University Press.

Gannett, Robert T. 2003. *Tocqueville Unveiled: The Historian and His Sources for the Old Regime and the Revolution*. Chicago, IL: University of Chicago Press.

Gargan, Edward. 1955. *Alexis de Tocqueville: The Critical Years 1848–1851*. Washington, D.C.: The Catholic University of America Press.

Gray, Walter D. 1994. *Interpreting American Democracy in France: The Career of Édouard Laboulaye*. Newark, DE: University of Delaware Press.

Hadari, Saguiv A. 1988. *Theory in Practice: Tocqueville's New Science of Politics*. Stanford, CA: Stanford University Press.

Howe, Daniel Walker. 1979. *The Political Culture of the American Whigs*. Chicago, IL: University of Chicago Press.

Howe, Walker Daniel. 2007. *What Hath God Wrought: The Transformation of America, 1815–1848*. Oxford: Oxford University Press.

Hurd, Douglas. 1967. *The Arrow Wars: An Anglo-Chinese Confusion, 1856–60*. New York: Macmillan.

Janara, Laura. 2002. *Democracy Growing Up: Authority, Autonomy, and Passion in Tocqueville's Democracy in America*. Albany, NY: SUNY Press.

Jannet, Claudio. 1876. *Les États-Unis contemporains ou les Moeurs, les institutions et les idées depuis la guerre de Secession*. Paris.

Jardin, André. 1988. *Tocqueville: A Biography*. New York: Farrar, Straus, Giroux.

Jaume, Lucien. 2008. *Tocqueville. Les sources aristocratiques de la liberté*. Paris: Fayard.

Jaume, Lucien. 1991. "Tocqueville et le problem du pouvoir exécutif en 1848," *Revue Française de Science Politique*, **41**: **6**: 739–55.

Jennings, Lawrence C. 1977. "France, Great Britain, and the Repression of the Slave Trade, 1841–1845," *French Historical Studies*, **10**: **1**: 101–25.

Jennings, Jeremy, 2009. "French Visions of America: From Tocqueville to the Civil War," *in America through European Eyes*, eds. **Aurelian Craiutu** and **Jeffrey C. Isaac** (University Park: Penn State University Press, 2009), 161–84.

Johnson, Douglas. 1963. *Guizot: Aspects of French History, 1787–1874*. London: Routledge and Kegan Paul.

Kann, Mark E. 2005. *Punishment, Prisons, and Patriarchy: Liberty and Power in the Early American Republic*. New Your: New York University Press.

Lahmer, Marc. 2001. *La Constitution Américaine dans le débat français, 1795–1848*. Paris: L'Harmattan.

Lamberti, Jean-Claude. 1983, *Tocqueville et les Deux Démocraties*. Paris: PUF.

Lamberti, Jean-Claude. 1984. "Tocqueville en 1848." *Commentaire* **25**: 141–51.

Lewis, Orlando F. 2005. *The Development of American Prisons and Prison Customs, 1776–1845*. Kessinger Publishing.

Luchaire, François. 1998. *Naissance d'une Constitution: 1848*. Paris: Fayard.

Mack, Charles and **Lesesne, Henri**, eds. 2005. *Francis Lieber and the Culture of the Mind*. Charleston, SC: University of South Carolina Press.

Mack, Charles and **Mack, Ilona**. 2005. *Like a Sponge Thrown into Water: Francis Lieber's European Travel Journal of 1844–1845*. Charleston, SC: University of South Carolina Press.

Mancini, Matthew. 2005. *Alexis de Tocqueville and American Intellectuals*. Lanham, MD: Rowman and Littlefield.

Mancini, Matthew. 1994. *Alexis de Tocqueville*. Woodbridge, CT: Twayne Publishers.

Marshall, James F. 1949. "Stendhal and America," *The French American Review*, (October–December): 240–67.

Masugi Ken, ed. 1991. *Interpreting Tocqueville's Democracy in America*. Lanham, MD: Rowman and Littlefield.

Mathy, Jean-Philippe. 1993. *L'Extrême-Occident: French Intellectuals and America*. Chicago, IL: University of Chicago Press.

Meigs, William A. 1897. *The Life of Charles Jared Ingersoll*. Philadelphia, PA: J. B. Lippincott.

Mélonio, Françoise. 1987. *"Tocqueville et les malheurs de la démocratie américaine" (1831–1859)*. *Commentaire*, **38**: 381–89.

Mélonio, Françoise. 1998. *Tocqueville and the French*. Charlottesville, VA: University Press of Virginia.

Meyers, Marvin. 1957. *The Jacksonian Persuasion: Politics and Belief*. New York: Vintage.

Mitchell, Harvey. 2002. *America after Tocqueville: Democracy Against Difference*. Cambridge: Cambridge University Press.

Nolla, Eduardo ed., 1992. *Liberty, Equality, Democracy*. New York: New York University Press.

Perry, Charles M. 1933. *Henry Philip Tappan: Philosopher and University President*. Ann Arbor, MI: University of Michigan Press.

Pessen, Edward. 1973. *Riches, Class, and Power Before the Civil War*. Lexington, MA: D. C. Heath.

Pessen, Edward. 1985. *Jacksonian America. Society, Personality, and Politics*. 2nd revised edition. Urbana, IL: University of Illinois Press.

Pierson, George Wilson. 1996. *Tocqueville and Beaumont in America*, 2nd edition. Baltimore, MD: The Johns Hopkins University Press.

Pitts, Jennifer. 2006. *A Turn to Empire: The Rise of Imperial Liberalism in Britain and France*. Princeton, NJ: Princeton University Press.

Portes, Jacques. 2000. *Fascination and Misgivings: The United States in French Opinion, 1870–1914*. Cambridge: Cambridge University Press.

Potter, David M. 1976. *The Impending Crisis, 1848–1861*. New York: Harper.

Rémond, René. 1962. *Les États-Unis devant l'opinion française, 1815–1852*, 2 vols. Paris: Armand Colin.

Roger, Philippe. 2002. *L'Ennemi américain*. Paris: Seuil (English trans. *The American Enemy*. Chicago: University of Chicago Press, 2005).

Rosanvallon, Pierre. 1994. *La monarchie impossible. Les Chartes de 1814 et de 1830*. Paris: Fayard.

Rudelle, Odile. 1988. *"La France et l'expérience constitutionnelle américaine: Un modèle présent, perdu, retrouvé"* in *Et la constitution créa l'Amérique*, ed. **Marie-France Toinet** (Nancy: Presses Universitaires de Nancy), 35–52.

Saint-Victor, Jacques Benjamin. 1835, *Lettres sur les États-Unis d'Amérique*. Paris & Lyon: Perisse Frères.

Schleifer, James T. 2000. *The Making of Democracy in America*, 2nd expanded edition. Indianapolis, IN: Liberty Fund.

Schlesinger, Arthur. Jr. 1945. *The Age of Jackson*. Boston, MA: Little, Brown & Co.

Sellers, Charles. 1994. *The Market Revolution: Jacksonian America, 1815–1846*. Oxford: Oxford University Press.

Smith, Rogers S. 1993. "Beyond Tocqueville, Myrdal, and Hartz: The Multiple Traditions in America." *American Political Science Review* 87 (3): 549–66.

Smith, Rogers M. 1997. *Civic Ideals*. New Haven, CT: Yale University Press.

Songy, Benedict Gaston. 1969. *Alexis de Tocqueville and Slavery: Judgments and Predictions*. Unpublished Ph. D. Diss. Saint-Louis University, St. Louis, MO.

Spandri, Francesco, 2006. "La vision de l'histoire chez Stendhal et Tocqueville," *Revue d'Histoire littéraire de la France*, 106:1: 47–66.

Stampp, Kenneth M. 1989. *America in 1857: A Nation on the Brink*. New York: Oxford University Press.

Troper, Michel. 2006. *Terminer la Révolution: La Constitution de 1795*. Paris: Fayard.

Tyack, David B. 1967. *George Ticknor and the Boston Brahmins*. Cambridge, MA: Harvard University Press.

Watkins, Sharon. 2003. *Alexis de Tocqueville and the Second Republic, 1848–1852: A Study in Political Practice and Principles*. Lanham, MD: University Press of America.

Welch, Cheryl. 2001. *De Tocqueville*. Oxford: Oxford University Press.

Welch, Cheryl. 2006, ed. *The Cambridge Companion to Tocqueville*. Cambridge: Cambridge University Press.

Welter, Rush. 1975. *The Mind of America: 1820–1860*. New York: Columbia University Press.

Wilentz, Sean. 1988. "Many Democracies: On Tocqueville and Jacksonian America," *in Reconsidering Tocqueville's Democracy in America*, ed. Abraham S. Eisenstadt. New Brunswick, NJ: Rutgers University Press, 207–28.

Wilentz, Sean. 2005. *The Rise of American Democracy: Jefferson to Lincoln*. New York: Norton.

Wills, Gary. 2004. "Did Tocqueville 'Get' America?" *New York Review of Books*, April 29, 52–56.

Wolin, Sheldon. 2001. *Tocqueville between Two Worlds: The Making of a Political and Theoretical Life*. Princeton, NJ: Princeton.

Zunz, Oliver. 2006. "Tocqueville and the Americans: Democracy in America as Read in Nineteenth-Century America" in *The Cambridge Companion to Tocqueville*, ed. Cheryl B. Welch, 359–96.

Notes

The Third *Democracy*: Tocqueville's Views of America after 1840

1. A shorter version of this text appeared in the *American Political Science Review*, 98: 3 (2004): 391–404, and was originally presented at the Annual Meeting of the American Political Science Association, Philadelphia, August 27–31, 2003. We would like to thank *APSR* and *Cambridge University Press* for the permission to reprint significant parts of our article. Also special thanks are due to Barbara Allen, Sheldon Gellar, Matthew Mancini, Vincent Ostrom, Jennifer Pitts, James Schleifer, and Lee Sigelman for their editorial comments and suggestions.

2. See Tocqueville's letter to E. V. Childe (December 12, 1856), Part I, section C, below.

3. See C. A. Sainte-Beuve, *Nouveaux Lundis*, Vol. X (Paris: Michel-Lévy Frères, 1874), 330.

4. *Democracy in America*, trans. Stephen D. Grant (Indianapolis, IN: Hackett, 2000); *Democracy in America*, trans. Delba Winthrop and Harvey C. Mansfield (Chicago, IL: University of Chicago Press, 2001); *Democracy in America*, trans. Gerald E. Bevan (London: Penguin, 2003); *Democracy in America*, trans. Arthur Goldhammer (New York: The Library of America, 2004). To this list one could also add the recent republication of Henry Reeve's old translation of *Democracy in America*, edited by Isaac Kramnick in the Norton Critical Edition series (New York: Norton, 2007).

5. Alexis de Tocqueville, *The Old Regime and the Revolution*, vol. I, trans. Alan S. Kahan (Chicago, IL: University of Chicago Press, 1998); and *The Old Regime and the Revolution*, vol. II, trans. Alan S. Kahan (Chicago, IL: University of Chicago Press, 2001). There is also another new English translation of Volume One of *The Old Regime and the Revolution* by Gerald Bevan (London: Penguin, 2008).

6. For an overview of recent work on Tocqueville see Cheryl Welch, "Introduction: Tocqueville in the Twenty-First Century," in *The Cambridge Companion to Tocqueville*, ed. Cheryl B. Welch (Cambridge, MA: Cambridge University Press, 2006), pp. 1–20. Also worth mentioning are the texts published in special issue of *The Tocqueville Review/La Revue Tocqueville*, XXVII: 2 (2006) and *The Review of Politics*, 67: 4 (Fall 2005) assembled to commemorate the bicentennial of Tocqueville's birth. Here is a list of some of the most important recent works on Tocqueville: Lucien Jaume, *Tocqueville. Les sources aristocratiques de la*

489

liberté (Paris: Fayard, 2008); Hugh Brogan, *Alexis de Tocqueville: A Life* (New Haven, CT: Yale University Press, 2007); Roger Boesche, *Tocqueville's Road Map: Methodology, Liberalism, Revolution, and Despotism* (Lanham, MD: Lexington Books, 2006); Barbara Allen, *Tocqueville, Covenant, and the Democratic Revolution* (Lanham, MD: Lexington Books, 2005); Matthew Mancini, *Alexis de Tocqueville and American Intellectuals: From His Time to Ours* (Lanham, MD: Rowman & Littlefield, 2005). Jean-Louis Benoît, *Tocqueville moraliste* (Paris: Honoré Champion, 2004); Laurence Guellec, *Tocqueville et les langages de la démocratie* (Paris, 2004); Serge Audier, *Tocqueville retrouvé. Genèse et enjeux du renouveau tocquevillien français* (Paris: EHESS/Vrin, 2004); M. R. R. Ossewaarde, *Tocqueville's Political and Moral Thought: New Liberalism* (London: Routledge, 2004); Agnès Antoine, *L'impensé de la démocratie: Tocqueville, la citoyenneté, et la religion* (Paris: Fayard, 2003); Michael Drolet, *Tocqueville, Democracy, and Social Reform* (Hampshire and New York: Palgrave, 2003); Robert T. Gannett, *Tocqueville Unveiled: The Historian and His Sources for the Old Regime and the Revolution* (Chicago, IL: University of Chicago Press, 2003); Sheldon Wolin, *Tocqueville Between Two Worlds: The Making of a Political and Theoretical Life* (Princeton, NJ: Princeton University Press, 2001); Cheryl Welch, *De Tocqueville* (Oxford: Oxford University Press, 2001); Eric Keslassy (*Le Libéralisme de Tocqueville à l'épreuve du paupérisme*, 2000). Also worth noting are the following collections: Alexis de Tocqueville, *Writings on Empire and Slavery*, ed. and trans. Jennifer Pitts (Baltimore, MD: The Johns Hopkins University Press, 2000); *The Tocqueville Reader*, eds. Oliver Zunz and Alan S. Kahan (Oxford: Blackwell, 2002); Alexis de Tocqueville, *Lettres choisies. Souvenirs*, eds. Françoise Mélonio and Laurence Guellec (Paris: Gallimard, 2003); Alexis de Tocqueville, *Textes économiques: Anthologie critique*, de Alexis de Tocqueville, eds. Jean-Louis Benoit and Eric Keslassy (Paris: Pocket, 2005). On the importance of Tocqueville's letters, see François Furet, "The Passions of Tocqueville," *The New York Review of Books* (June 27, 1985): 23–27; Françoise Mélonio, "Tocqueville entre la révolution et la démocratie," in Tocqueville, *Lettres choisies. Souvenirs*, 11–33; Roger Boesche, "Introduction," in Tocqueville, *Selected Letters on Politics and Society*, ed. Roger Boesche, trans. James Toupin and Roger Boesche (Berkeley, CA: University of California Press, 1985), 1–20.

7. Welch, *De Tocqueville*, 1.
8. Wolin, *Tocqueville between Two Worlds*, 564–65.
9. Ibid., 3.
10. Tocqueville scholars often disagree over whether *Democracy in America* forms one book or two different ones. Seymour Drescher ("Tocqueville's Two Démocraties," *Journal of the History of Ideas*, 25 [April–June 1964]: 201–16) and Jean-Claude Lamberti (*Tocqueville et les deux démocraties* [Paris: PUF, 1983]) insisted on the existence of a clear shift between the two halves of *De la démocratie en Amérique*. In particular, Drescher highlighted the profound differences between the two volumes that, in his opinion, constituted two separate studies rather than two parts of a single study. The opposite view can be found in James T. Schleifer (*The Making of Tocqueville's Democracy in America*, 2nd expanded edition. Indianapolis: Liberty Fund, 2000) and George Wilson Pierson (*Tocqueville in America*, 2nd edition. Baltimore: Johns Hopkins University Press, 1996). Also worth consulting are Drescher's "More Than America:

Comparison and Synthesis in Democracy in America," in *Reconsidering Toc-queville's Democracy in America*, ed. Abraham S. Eisenstadt (New Brunswick, NJ: Rutgers University Press, 1988), 77–93 and Schleifer's "How Many Democracies?" reprinted in *The Making of Tocqueville's Democracy in America*, 2nd expanded edition, 354–68; Schleifer's text was originally published in Eduardo Nolla ed., *Liberty, Equality, Democracy* (New York: New York University Press, 1992).

11. For example, Roger Boesche's excellent selection from Tocqueville's letters (*Selected Letters on Politics and Society*) contains only one letter from Tocqueville's correspondence with his American friends after 1840. Nonetheless, this superb edition represents a seminal instrument for any student of Tocqueville and we are happy to acknowledge our debt to it.

12. Tocqueville's letters were published in *Œuvres Complètes, VII: Correspondance étrangère d'Alexis de Tocqueville. Amérique. Europe continentale*, eds. Françoise Mélonio, Lisa Queffélec, and Anthony Pleasance (Paris: Gallimard, 1986); henceforth abbreviated as *OC*, VII. In general, the evolution of Tocqueville's views of America after 1840 has been overlooked by many exegeses of Tocqueville. Two such important collections that gloss over this topic are *Reconsidering Tocqueville's Democracy in America*, ed. Abraham S. Eisenstadt (New Brunswick, NJ: Rutgers University Press, 1988) and *Interpreting Tocqueville's Democracy in America*, ed. Ken Masugi (Lanham, MD: Rowman & Littlefield, 1991). In *De Tocqueville*, Cheryl Welch devotes a footnote to this topic while other recent interpretations of Tocqueville such as Harvey Mitchell, *America After Tocqueville: Democracy Against Difference* (Cambridge: Cambridge University Press, 2002) and Laura Janara, *Democracy Growing Up: Authority, Autonomy, and Passion in Tocqueville's Democracy in America* (Albany, NY: SUNY Press, 2002) have nothing to say about the evolution of Tocqueville's views of America after the publication of Volume Two of *Democracy in America*.

13. Our present volume draws inspiration from the work of historians who pointed out the importance of studying the evolution of Tocqueville's views of America after 1840. In particular, we would like to highlight the following important contributions: Françoise Mélonio, "Tocqueville et les malheurs de la démocratie américaine" (1831–1859). *Commentaire*, 38: (1987): 381–89; Hugh Brogan, "Alexis de Tocqueville and the Coming of the American Civil War," in *American Studies: Essays in Honour of Marcus Cunliffe*, eds. Brian Holden Reid & John White (New York: St. Martin's Press, 1991), 83–104; and Benedict Gaston Songy, *Alexis de Tocqueville and Slavery: Judgments and Predictions*, unpublished Ph.D. diss. (Saint-Louis University, St. Louis, MO, 1969, especially chapter III, "Correspondence with Americans," 125–84). Although Songy's work focuses mostly on Tocqueville's views on slavery, it makes a convincing case for studying Tocqueville's correspondence with his American friends in the 1850s. Matthew Mancini devoted a portion of his most recent book on Tocqueville and American intellectuals to exploring Tocqueville's views of American events in the 1850s (see *Alexis de Tocqueville and American Intellectuals*, 55–63). Among the issues touched upon by Mancini are the decline in mores, imperialism, slavery, and Tocqueville's reaction to the Kansas-Nebraska Act.

14. On this topic, see Philippe Roger, *L'Ennemi américain* (Paris: Seuil, 2002); English translation, *The American Enemy*, trans. Sharon Bowman (Chicago: University of Chicago Press, 2005); Jean-Philippe Mathy, *L'Extrême-Occident: French*

Intellectuals and America (Chicago, IL: University of Chicago Press, 1993). For a concise discussion of the history and significance of the symbol of America and the sources of anti-Americanism, see James Ceasar, "A Genealogy of anti-Americanism," *Public Interest* 152 (2003): 3–18; also Ceasar, *Reconstructing America: The Symbol of America in Modern Thought* (New Haven, CT: Yale University Press, 1997).

15. A methodological caveat is in order here. Interpreting Tocqueville's correspondence as a hypothetical third volume of *Democracy in America* is a speculative enterprise that must be undertaken with an element of caution. Such an endeavor is subject to the possible criticism that the views expressed in private letters are not those that would have been expressed in public, and thus no firm conclusions can be drawn about how Tocqueville might have changed his views on America after 1840. If, it might be argued, in published texts Tocqueville's fears for America were likely to be expressed obliquely, then in personal correspondence there is less reticence about expressing views more openly and, therefore, more harshly. Similarly, it can be contended that Tocqueville might have tailored his comments to suit the views of his individual correspondents. If these methodological reservations are accepted, it would be easy to conclude that the criticisms of America voiced by Tocqueville in his letters after 1840 were not substantially different in either substance or tone from the sense of foreboding that is clearly evident in some parts of Volume Two of *Democracy in America*.

16. From Boesche's introduction to Tocqueville, *Selected Letters*, 20.

17. Tocqueville, *OC*, VIII: 1, 93.

18. Tocqueville, *Selected Letters*, 143.

19. Tocqueville, *Recollections* (New York: Doubleday, 1971), 105; all emphases added.

20. Three names stand out in this regard: Crèvecoeur and La Fayette. The first was a Frenchman who emigrated to the United States and became a farmer in Orange Country, New York. He was the author of the *Letters from an American Farmer* (first published in London in 1782). Because of his support for the American republic, La Fayette gained the status of mythical hero in the United States and enjoyed a prominent political status in France. Necker also praised the virtues of the American Constitution in two of his most important works: *Du Pouvoir exécutif dans les grands états* (1782), Part II, Chapters 1–4 and *De la Révolution française* (1796), Part IV, Chapter 1. Yet Necker also pointed out the major cultural, geographical and sociological differences between France and America and concluded that, because of these differences, the American political system could not be exported to France.

21. See, for example, J. Hector St. John de Crèvecoeur, *Letters from an American Farmer* (New York: Dutton, 1957), 7–8. Durand Echeverria's classic book, *Mirage in the West: A History of the French Image of American Society to 1815* (Princeton, NJ: Princeton University Press, 1957) is an indispensable point of departure for anyone interested in this topic. On this topic, also see Jacques Portes, *Fascination and Misgivings: The United States in French Opinion, 1870–1914* (Cambridge: Cambridge University Press, 2000); *America through European Eyes: British and French Reflections on the New World from the 18th Century to the Present*, eds. Aurelian Craiutu and Jeffrey C. Isaac (University Park, PA: Pennsylvania State University Park, 2009).

22. See Réné Rémond, *Les États-Unis devant l'opinion française, 1815–1852* (Paris: Armand Colin, 1962), II, 340; 650–51. The French *Idéologues* (Destutt de Tracy, Daunou, Cabanis, Volney, and others) admired America and it was not a mere coincidence that Thomas Jefferson translated into English Destutt de Tracy's commentary on Montesquieu's *The Spirit of the Laws* (the book appeared first in English in 1811 and eight years later in French). In turn, Madame de Staël expressed her appreciation for the American political experiment, and equated the government of the United States with the government of reason. For more details, see Madame de Staël's *Considerations on the Principal Events of the French Revolution*, ed. Aurelian Craiutu (Indianapolis, IN: Liberty Fund, 2008), 707; Rémond, *Les États-Unis devant l'opinion française*, II, 552, 636–37.

23. Scheffer as quoted in Rémond *Les États-Unis devant l'opinion française*, II, 532.

24. For more details on references to the American model, see ibid., 657, n. 11.

25. Alexis Carrel, Untitled article. *Le National*, May 29, 1832.

26. For more details, see Rémond, *Les États-Unis devant l'opinion française*, II, 540–43.

27. Vinet as quoted in Rémond, *Les États-Unis devant l'opinion française*, II, 549, n. 32. Vinet's *Memoir in Favor of Liberty* was published in 1825.

28. "Arbitrary power is unknown here; everyone enjoys a liberty moderated by the need to use it," wrote Dumersan in 1822 (as quoted in Rémond, *Les États-Unis devant l'opinion française*, II, 544).

29. As quoted in Rémond, *Les États-Unis devant l'opinion française*, II, 545.

30. See, for example, the following statement of Dupont de Nemours dating from 1812: "Concerning education, the United States are more advanced than most other political societies" (as quoted in Rémond, *Les États-Unis devant l'opinion française*, II, 554, n. 59).

31. "America," wrote Gustave de Beaumont, "is the land of the free who cannot do without slaves. America is the cradle of equality, and no country in Europe contains so much servitude" (*Marie or Slavery in the United States* [Stanford: Stanford University Press, 1958], 57).

32. The fact is, however, that doubts about the virtues and qualities of America were voiced even before the moment of independence. As Philippe Roger has recently shown, the "pre-history" of French anti-Americanism is to be found in the Enlightenment.

33. Marchais and Dupont (in *Revue républicaine*, April 1834) as quoted in Rémond, *Les États-Unis devant l'opinion française*, II, 670, n. 17.

34. Cerise (in *L'Européen*, November 1835) as quoted in Rémond, *Les États-Unis devant l'opinion française*, II, 670, n. 18.

35. Guizot as quoted in Rémond, *Les États-Unis devant l'opinion française*, II, 664, n. 20.

36. Marchais and Dupont as quoted in ibid., 668.

37. Saulnier as quoted in Rémond, *Les États-Unis devant l'opinion française*, II, 737, n. 41.

38. The words are from a discourse of Lamartine from 1835 as quoted in Rémond, *Les États-Unis devant l'opinion française*, II, 741, n. 62.

39. Theodore Jouffroy as quoted in Rémond, *Les États-Unis devant l'opinion française*, II, 721.

40. Édouard de Montulé, *Travels in America, 1816–1817* (Bloomington, IN: Indiana University Press, 1951).

41. "The society of Charleston is the best I have met with in my travels, whether on this or on your side of the Atlantic. In respect to finish, and elegance of manners, it leaves nothing to be desired" (cited by Peter Campbell, "Achille Murat: A Precursor of de Tocqueville," *The Cambridge Journal*, VII: 5 [February 1954]: 302). For an English translation, see Murat, *A Moral and Political Sketch of the United States* (London: Effingham Wilson, 1833).

42. Murat as cited in Campbell, "Achille Murat: A Precursor of de Tocqueville," 303–4.

43. Murat, *A Moral and Political Sketch of the United States*, xxi.

44. Jacques Benjamin Saint-Victor, *Lettres sur les États-Unis d'Amérique* (Paris & Lyon: Perisse Frères, 1835), 26–27. Saint-Victor's second letter described in detail American mores. It is worth pointing out that Saint-Victor's letters, written in 1832–33 from America, were published in France in 1835, at the same time as Volume One of Tocqueville's *Democracy in America*.

45. La Mennais as quoted in Rémond, *Les États-Unis devant l'opinion française*, II, 763–64, n. 3.

46. Saint-Victor, *Lettres sur les États-Unis d'Amérique*, 30–31.

47. Chateaubriand, *Travels in America*, trans. Richard Switzer (Lexington, KY: University of Kentucky Press, 1969).

48. Victor Jacquemont *Correspondance inédite avec sa famille et ses amis, 1824–1832*, I (Paris: Calmann-Lévy, 1885), 153. For an analysis of Jacquemont's views of America, see Aurelian Craiutu, "A Precursor of Tocqueville: Victor Jacquemont's Reflections on America," in *America through European Eyes*, 117–41.

49. Stendhal, *On Love*, trans. Gilbert and Suzanne Sale (London: Penguin, 1975), 164. On Stendhal's political thought, see Richard Boyd, "*Politesse* and Public Opinion in Stendhal's *Red and Black*," *European Journal of Political Theory* 4 (2005): 367–92. The relationship between Stendhal and Tocqueville is discussed in Francesco Spandri, "La vision de l'histoire chez Stendhal et Tocqueville," *Revue d'Histoire littéraire de la France*, 106:1 (2006): 47–66; James F, Marshall, "Stendhal and America," The *French American Review* (October–December 1949): 240–67; André Daspre, "Stendhal et la démocratie américaine," *Europe*, 519–21 (July–September 1972): 79–88 ; René Girard, "Stendhal and Tocqueville," *American Society of the Legion of Honor Magazine* 31 (1960): 73–83; Françoise Mélonio, *Tocqueville and the French* (Charlottesville, VA: The University Press of Virginia, 1996), 35. See also Michel Crouzet, *Stendhal et l'Amérique* (Paris: Editions de Fallois: 2008).

50. Stendhal, *On Love*, 163.

51. Ibid., 163.

52. See Saulnier's critique in Rémond, *Les États-Unis devant l'opinion française*, II, 690–91.

53. For more details, see Rémond, *Les États-Unis devant l'opinion française*, II, 698–703, 711–12.

54. The following statement appeared in *Le bonhomme Richard* published in September 1832: "It is in vain that some try to offer as remedies to our problems these institutions which are shaky and rotten on the very next day following their birth" (as quoted in Rémond, *Les États-Unis devant l'opinion française*, II, 713).

55. For a comprehensive account of the diversity of responses to Tocqueville's work, see Mélonio *Tocqueville and the French*.

56. Tocqueville, *Democracy in America*, trans. Delba Winthrop and Harvey C. Mansfield (Chicago, IL: University of Chicago Press, 2000), 326. All subsequent references in this introduction are to this edition.

57. For a comprehensive analysis of this topic, see Mitchell, *America After Tocqueville*, 132–81.

58. Tocqueville, *Democracy in America*, 352–53.

59. Ibid., 379.

60. Ibid., 382.

61. Ibid., 502.

62. See, for example, Tocqueville's correspondence with Royer-Collard, published in *Œuvres Complètes, XI: Correspondance d'Alexis de Tocqueville et de Pierre-Paul Royer-Collard. Correspondance d'Alexis de Tocqueville et de Jean-Jacques Ampère*, ed. André Jardin (Paris: Gallimard, 1971).

63. Tocqueville, *Democracy in America*, 532.

64. It is worth pointing out that Tocqueville was also the author of a *Memoir on Pauperism* written in early 1835 after his visit to England. For an English translation, see Alexis de Tocqueville, *Memoir on Pauperism* (Chicago, IL: Ivan R. Dee, 1997), as well as *Tocqueville and Beaumont on Social Reform*, 1–27. In this essay, Tocqueville addressed the paradox of the then most opulent country, England, having the greatest number of paupers. A defender of private charity, he argued against public charity which, in his view, had a series of unfortunate unforeseen consequences. Nonetheless, Tocqueville did not detect the same problems in America.

65. There are two other texts written before 1840 in which Tocqueville addressed American issues: "Note sur les pouvoirs du président des États-Unis" [1835?], *OC*, XVI, 85–87; "À MM. les électeurs de l'arrondissement de Valognes [1837]," *OC*, III: 2, 41–46.

66. See Tocqueville, *OC*, XI, v. In his review of Volume Two of *Democracy in America*, published in *Revue des Deux Mondes*, Pellegrino Rossi boldly reversed Tocqueville's prediction. America, he wrote, is bound to follow Europe, rather than vice-versa: "Les États-Unis presentent à l'observateur des faits qui, generalisés, conduiraient à de fausses inductions. Pays neuf, sans antecedents, sans histoire, et placé dans des circonstances économiques toutes particulières, l'Amérique offre entre l'égalité civile et l'égalité de fait un rapprochement qui n'appartient qu'à elle, qui n'existe pas et n'existera jamais dans nos vieilles sociétés, et qui cessera d'exister en Amérique à mesure que ce pays vieillira, que la population en deviendra de plus en plus dense, lorsqu'il n'y aura plus de terres fertile vacantes, et qu'un nombre plus ou moins considérable d'Américains, gorgés enfin de richesses, deviendront des hommes de loisir et commenceront à prouver d'autres besoins que celui de gagner de l'argent. *C'est l'Amérique qui, à sa maniere, marche vers l'Europe; l'Europe ne peut se faire américaine*" (Pellegrino Rossi, review of *De la démocratie en Amérique*, Vol. II, in *Revue des deux mondes*, 4th series, 23 [juillet–septembre 1840]: 903–4; all emphases added). On Rossi's review of Tocqueville, see Jaume, *Tocqueville*, 116–17; Mélonio, *Tocqueville and the French*, 69–70.

67. For more information, Mancini, *Alexis de Tocqueville and American Intellectuals*, and Olivier Zunz, "Tocqueville and the Americans: *Democracy in America* as Read in Nineteenth-Century America," in *The Cambridge Companion to Tocqueville*, 337–58.

For a general account of intellectual life in America during the first half of the
nineteenth century, see Rush Welter, *The Mind of America: 1820–1860* (New
York: Columbia University Press, 1975), 253–328. Welter's book also contains
a bibliographic essay (395–441).

68. Edward Everett, review of Tocqueville's *Democracy in America*, Volume One, in
    The North American Review, XLIII: 92 (July 1836): 179.
69. Ibid., 179.
70. President Adams' letter deserves to be quoted in full: "Mr. Alexis de Tocqueville,
    author of the work entitled "De la Démocratie en Amérique" – Paris. Quincy
    12 June 1837. Sir, Recollecting with much pleasure, the satisfaction which I
    enjoyed in your friendly society at Boston and at Washington, during your visit
    with M. de Beaumont to the United States, and indebted as I have been to the
    gentleman and to you for a copy of your very valuable joint work upon the
    penitentiary system in the United States, I have yet to express to you and to ask
    of you the favour to convey to him my thanks for your kind remembrance and
    attention.

    I read with entertainment and instruction your report upon our penitentiary
    systems, still susceptible of much improvement, and furnished by the result
    of your enquiries and observations with useful hints for accomplishing that
    improvement. In the progress of your great Revolution, there was a time when
    the theory of the *perfectibility* of man, with other fascinating theories, expanded
    into romantic enthusiasm, from which it was recalled by crime and calamity to
    that rational theory, of which I profess myself to be a believer, and in which
    I flatter myself with the idea of being a humble co-operator and associate of
    yours. I mean the theory that the improvement in the condition of man on Earth
    is *progressive*; and that however, like the apparent motion of the Planets, it may
    be sometimes stationary and sometimes retrograde, its real march is *onward*, and
    that as the only inhabitant of this planet endowed with the faculty of combin-
    ing cause and effect, it must be the nature and destiny of man to improve his
    condition; that he has, however imperfectly, fulfilled that condition and purpose
    of his existence, and that he will continue in the same progress improving his
    moral, physical and social condition to the end of time. I call not this *perfectibility*;
    believing that perfection belongs to another state of existence.

    Your work upon Democracy in the United States has but recently fallen into
    my hands, first in an English translation, and since then, in the original, an edi-
    tion published at Brussels in 1835. You have remarked upon the transcendent
    influence of language upon the sympathies of opinion, in different nations, and
    the incident to which I now refer may serve as an illustration of the observation.
    Celebrated as your book has been from its first appearance, though I had often
    heard of it, the first form in which it met my eye was in the Library of the
    Congress of the United States, in the language familiar to my own country; and
    it is only within a few days that I have seen it in the language of its author.
    Even in its transformation, I saw that it was well deserving of being translated
    into all the languages of the civilized world, and I foresaw that it would be read
    in every language which has words practically significant of the wants of the
    human being, Liberty and Society; Property and Government.

    Of the French travelers in the United States, who preceded you, and have
    published the result of their observations here, I have successively read the

Chevalier de Chatellux, Saint Jean de Crèvecoeur, (two works, published at several years distance from each other) Brissot de Marville, the Duc de Liancourt, Volney, General Turreau, Talleyrand and Barbé de Marbois. Most of these writers have taken more or less notice of the manners and institutions of this country at the respective periods of their visits here. All of them have remarked what was on the surface of the soil and of social life. Some of them have surveyed the country with favourable, and some with adverse partiality; no one I think with so wide a compass or so deep a penetration as yours.

Before you came to this country, I take it for granted that you had seen the letter from Mr. Turgot to Doctor Price, which was the occasion of my father's Defense of the Constitutions of the United States, as they existed under the Articles of Confederation which preceded the Constitution of the United States. You had doubtless also read the four letters of the Abbé de Mably, addressed to my father containing observations upon the American Constitutions, but I imagine you had not and probably have not yet met with my father's Letter to the Abbé de Mably, which at once induced the Abbé to abandon the intention he had formed of writing a history of the American Revolution, and to write the four letters of observations on our Constitutions, which were published, I believe, in the last year of his life, and afterwards in the Collection of his works. I mention this Letter of my father to the Abbé de Mably, because I do not think there is a copy of it extant. A French translation of it was published in London, at the close of the first volume of Defense of the American Constitutions. An Abridged French Translation of the Defense of the Constitutions was published by De la Croix, in 1792, but the letter to the Abbé de Mably was not included in it. There is in that Letter an outline of the organization of the British Colonies on the Continent before the American Revolution, the minute acquaintance with which he believed to be indispensable for the historian of the Revolution. It is that same organization, which so impressively attracted your attention, and of which you have given so clear and interesting an account. The organization of the towns and counties, chiefly in New England, and in the Northwestern new States, settled in part by emigrants from New England. You are, I believe, the first foreign traveler that has noticed this element of our history.

There is in your book one passage relating to myself, containing an erroneous statement of facts; to which I invite your attention with the hope that in future editions of the work it may be corrected or omitted. It is at the 221st page of the 1st volume of the edition now before me, in the following words:

"M. Quincy Adams, à son entrée au pouvoir, congédia le plus grand nombre de ceux qu'avait nommés son prédécesseur."

The truth is that I never dismissed a single individual named by my predecessor. It was a principle of my administration to dismiss no person from office, but for misconduct, and there were in the course of four years that I presided only two persons dismissed from civil executive office, both of them for gross official misdemeanors.

My successor, it is true, did pursue a different principle. He dismissed many subordinate executive officers – not however so generally as the remainder of the paragraph in your book, which I have cited, supposes. He left in office many of those who had been appointed by his predecessors; and would probably have left many more, but for the influences by which he was surrounded.

The general principle in support of which you adduced the supposed facts that I had removed a majority of the removable officers, named by my Predecessor, and that my Successor removed all those named by me, the want of fixity essential to the elective system, may itself deserve your further profound consideration. This is the year of the Jubilee, the fiftieth year since the Constitution of the United States was presented to the acceptance of the American People. The twelfth presidential term of four years, since its adoption has just commenced. The eighth President of the United States, is now quietly in office. Five Presidents have been elected from the Southern and three from the Northern division of the Union. The political *Doctrines* of the several Presidents have been as different as the features of their faces –but the cardinal points of Policy regulating the movement of the nation in its orbit have been as fixed and steady as those of the Austrian or the Russian Monarchy. I name them, because they are the only governments of Europe, which have, for the last half century, had any fixity in their systems at all. And even of them, if the reigns of the Emperors Joseph II and Paul were taken into account, their stability would bear no comparison with that of the United States.

But I will not enter into a discussion, which would lead me far from the objects for which I have taken the liberty of addressing to you this letter. They were to thank you and M. de Beaumont for the copy of the report on our penitentiary systems, which you had the goodness to send to me; and to express to you the admiration with which I read your work upon our American Democracy, requesting of your kindness the revisal of one error of fact related to myself.

And with it permit me to ask your acceptance of three compositions of my own, delivered in honour of three Patriots of our Revolution, one of them a distinguished leader of yours, and published as they were respectively called to pay the debt of nature: Monroe, La Fayette, and Madison.

And the cordial and respectful salutations of John Quincy Adams" (Beinecke Library, Yale University, MS Vault Tocqueville).

71. *Life and Letters of Joseph Story*, edited by William W. Story (Boston, MA: Little & Brown, 1851), II, 329–30. The phrase *sic vos non vobis* is borrowed from Virgil and refers to persons by whose labors others have profited.

72. *Life, Letters, and Journals of George Ticknor* (Boston, MA: Osgood & Co., 1876), I, 480.

73. See the editors' introduction to Part II, section D, below. On Poussin's account of America, see Jeremy Jennings, "French Visions of America: From Tocqueville to the Civil War," in *America through European Eyes*, 161–84. As Jennings points out, Poussin did not share the profound worries about American democracy that concerned Tocqueville.

74. Herbert B. Adams, *Jared Sparks and Alexis de Tocqueville* (Baltimore, MD: The Johns Hopkins Press, 1898), 605–6.

75. Ibid., 606.

76. See the editors' introduction to Part I, sections A–D, below.

77. See Marvin Myers, *The Jacksonian Persuasion: Politics and Belief* (New York: Vintage, 1957), 279. In his classic account of Jacksonian democracy, Myers devotes an entire chapter to Tocqueville and suggests the following possible criticism of *Democracy in America*: "that, beginning with a general conception of democracy, and then allowing for the unique varieties of American experience,

Tocqueville does not attempt an integration of both elements. At most one finds a series of American themes, variously juxtaposed according to the subject of observation, all rather loosely related to a common point of departure in the framework theory" (277–78).

78. Sean Wilentz, "Many Democracies: On Tocqueville and Jacksonian America," in *Reconsidering Tocqueville's Democracy in America*, ed. Abraham S. Eisenstadt (New Brunswick, NJ: Rutgers University Press, 1988), 226. On the constitution of democracy in nineteenth-century America, see Welter, *The Mind of America*, 219–49. On Jacksonian America, some of the most important references are: Edward Pessen, *Jacksonian America. Society, Personality, and Politics*, 2nd revised edition (Urbana, IL: University of Illinois Press, 1985); Charles Sellers, *The Market Revolution: Jacksonian America, 1815–1846* (Oxford: Oxford University Press, 1994); Sean Wilentz, *The Rise of American Democracy: Jefferson to Lincoln* (New York: Norton, 2005), and Daniel Walker Howe, *What Hath God Wrought: The Transformation of America, 1815–1848* (Oxford: Oxford University Press, 2007). A detailed analysis of American politics in the late 1850s can be found in Kenneth M. Stampp, *America in 1857: A Nation on the Brink* (New York: Oxford University Press, 1989).

79. As quoted in Jean-Claude Lamberti, *Tocqueville et les deux démocraties* (Paris: PUF, 1983), 26.

80. For a recent and original analysis of the writing of *The Old Regime and the Revolution*, see Gannett, *Tocqueville Unveiled*.

81. Lieber was born in 1798 (not in 1800, as some sources claim). We would like to thank Matthew Mancini for calling our attention to this point.

82. See Appendix 1 for biographical details of each of Tocqueville's American correspondents. The group of the Boston intellectuals with whom Tocqueville was in contact is analyzed in David B. Tyack, *George Ticknor and the Boston Brahmins* (Cambridge, Mass.: Harvard University Press, 1967).

83. Songy, *Alexis de Tocqueville and Slavery*, 148.

84. For a recent excellent selection from Tocqueville's letters, see *Lettres choisies. Souvenirs* (2003).

85. In this regard, our work draws inspiration from the writings of other Tocqueville scholars. In particular, we would like to acknowledge Seymour Drescher's *Dilemmas of Democracy: Tocqueville and Modernization* (Pittsburgh: University of Pittsburgh Press, 1968) that closely examined the legislative careers of Tocqueville and Beaumont. For an excellent anthology of Tocqueville's texts on social issues, including the abolition of slavery, see *Tocqueville and Beaumont on Social Reform*, ed. and trans. Seymour Drescher (New York: Harper, 1968).

86. See Tocqueville's letter to E. V. Childe, December 12, 1856 in Part 1, section C, below.

87. See Tocqueville's letter to N. Niles (June 15, 1843), Part I, section A, below.

88. Tocqueville's writings on prison reform were published in *OC*, IV: 1 and *OC*: IV: 2. A selection from Tocqueville's writings on prison reform from the 1840s was published in *Tocqueville and Beaumont on Social Reform*, 70–98.

89. An American translation of this book (by Francis Lieber) was published in 1833. For a recent English edition, see Alexis Tocqueville and Gustave de Beaumont, *On the Penitentiary System in the United States and Its Application in France*, ed. Thorsten Sellin (Carbondale, IL: Southern Illinois University Press, 1964).

90. See Tocqueville's letter of March 29, 1836 to a member of the Society of Moral Sciences of Seine-et-Oise, in *OC*, IV: 1, 30.

91. For more information, see Thorsten Sellin, "Tocqueville and Beaumont on Prison Reform in France," in Tocqueville and Beaumont, *On the Penitentiary System in the United States and Its Application in France*, xxxiv–xxxviii. Also worth consulting is M. Perrot's introduction to Tocqueville, *OC*, IV: 1, 7–44.

92. *OC*, III: 2, 471.

93. See especially Tocqueville, *OC*, III: 3, 55–166. For a discussion of Tocqueville's role in these debates, see Jean-Claude Lamberti, "Tocqueville en 1848," *Commentaire* 25 (1984): 141–51; Sharon B. Watkins, *Alexis de Tocqueville and the Second Republic, 1848–1852* (Lanham, MD: University Press of America, 2003), 81–140, 189–322; Edward Gargan, *Alexis de Tocqueville: The Critical Years 1848–1851* (Washington, D. C: The Catholic University of America Press, 1955), 70–121.

94. See Tocqueville's preface to the 12th edition of *Democracy in America*, Part II, section B, below.

95. Tocqueville, *OC*, III: 3, 82; see Part II, section C, below.

96. Ibid., 82–83; see Part II, section C, below.

97. See Spencer's letter (June 10, 1848), Part I, section B, below.

98. See Everett's letter (March 12, 1849), Part I, section B, below.

99. From "Deux esquisses de discours," in *OC*, III: 3, 203. Also see Tocqueville's notes, *OC*, III: 3, 207–10.

100. See Part II, section C, below.

101. See Part II, section C below.

102. On Tocqueville in 1848, also see Lucien Jaume, "Tocqueville et le problème du pouvoir exécutif en 1848," *Revue Française de Science Politique*, 41: 6 (1991): 739–55 (especially 749–53); Odile Rudelle, "La France et l'expérience constitutionnelle américaine: Un modèle présent, perdu, retrouvé," in *Et la constitution créa l'Amérique*, ed. Marie-France Toinet (Nancy: Presses Universitaires de Nancy, 1988), 35–52; Brogan, *Tocqueville: A Life*, 454, 467–68, 509–14, 603; Watkins, *Alexis de Tocqueville and the Second Republic*, 43–256.

103. These events are discussed in Part II, section D, below.

104. *The Tocqueville Reader*, 272.

105. On Tocqueville's sense of moral isolation, also see his letter to Madame Swetchine from October 20, 1856 republished in Tocqueville, *Lettres choisies. Souvenirs*, 1218. On Tocqueville's restlessness, see Aurelian Craiutu, "Tocqueville's Paradoxical Moderation," *The Review of Politics*, 67: 4 (2005): 599–629.

106. See, for example, Tocqueville's letter of February 15, 1850 to Everett (as well as Everett's response), Part I, section B, below.

107. In an important letter to Edward Vernon Childe (April 2, 1857), Tocqueville wrote about the American people in the following terms: "As with all sovereigns, the people naturally loves courtesans and flatterers; but I have enough confidence in their practical sense to believe that in times of crises, they would place their confidence in better hands. At least I hope so, because I passionately desire to see the success of the great experience of *Self-Government* that is currently taking place. If it fails, political liberty on earth would be finished for ever" (Part I, section D, below).

108. This point applies to Tocqueville's letters rather than his published writings during this period. For more information on the differences between the two, see the editors' introduction to Part II, below.

109. For more information, see Daniel Walker Howe, *The Political Culture of the American Whigs* (Chicago, IL: University of Chicago Press, 1979).

110. See Tocqueville's letter to Theodore Sedgwick (December 4, 1852), Part I, section B, below.

111. See Sparks' letter of June 13, 1853, Part I, section C, below.

112. See, for example, Tocqueville's letter (August 6, 1854) to Beaumont in Tocqueville, *OC*, VIII: 3, 228–29. Also see Tocqueville's letter (October 14, 1856) to Theodore Sedgwick, Part I, section C, below.

113. See Tocqueville's letter to Theodore Sedgwick (August 14, 1854), Part I section C, below.

114. See Tocqueville's letter to Theodore Sedgwick (August 29, 1856), Part I, section C, below.

115. See Tocqueville's letter to Jared Sparks (December 11, 1852), Part I, section B, below.

116. Ibid.

117. See Tocqueville's letter to Theodore Sedgwick (September 19, 1855), Part I, section C, below.

118. This is the subtitle of Stampp's book *America in 1857: A Nation on the Brink*.

119. See Tocqueville's letter to Francis Lieber (October 9, 1857), Part I, section D, below.

120. See Tocqueville's letter to Theodore Sedgwick (October 14, 1856), Part I, section C, below.

121. It is worth pointing out that in a letter to Corcelle from July 29, 1857, in which Tocqueville spoke admiringly of England, he praised that country's "perfect accord between religious and political morality" (Tocqueville, *Lettres choisies. Souvenirs*, 1253). A similar reference to the seminal relationship between religion and liberty in England can be found in Tocqueville's letter to Kergorlay from August 4, 1857 (Tocqueville, *Lettres choisies. Souvenirs*, 1256; translated in *Selected Letters*, 355–57).

122. For an excellent analysis of Tocqueville's views of religion, see Antoine, *L'impensé de la démocratie*.

123. See Tocqueville's letter to Theodore Sedgwick (October 14, 1856), Part I, section B, below.

124. It is worth pointing out that Tocqueville had used this metaphor in *Democracy in America*, 229.

125. See Tocqueville's letter to Theodore Sedgwick (August 29, 1856), Part I, section C, below.

126. It is worth pointing out that J. S. Mill had much the same attitude about political developments in America in the 1850s; he did reverse his position a decade later when praising the virtue of the Union during the Civil War. Tocqueville did not live long enough to witness the Civil War, but some of his letters to Edward Vernon Childe clearly show that he foresaw its coming.

127. Cited in Stampp, *America in 1857*, 25.

128. Ibid., 25.

129. See Tocqueville's letter to Jared Sparks (October 13, 1840), Part I, section A, below.

130. This phrase is from Everett's letter of March 29, 1850; see Part I, section B, below. Songy also quoted from this letter in *Alexis de Tocqueville and Slavery*, 146. For an excellent anthology of Tocqueville's texts on social issues, including

slavery, see *Tocqueville and Beaumont on Social Reform*, 98–136. For an analysis
of Tocqueville's position on the abolition of slavery, see Drescher, *Dilemmas
of Democracy*, 151–95; Brogan, "Alexis de Tocqueville and the Coming of the
American Civil War."

131. See Tocqueville's article in *Liberty Bell* (April 1855), Part I, section C, below.
Tocqueville's staunch opposition to slavery was also acknowledged by Charles
Sumner, who wrote in a diary note from 1857 that Tocqueville was "full of
feelings against slavery" (quoted in Songy, *Alexis de Tocqueville and Slavery*,
157).

132. See Tocqueville's article in *Liberty Bell* (April 1855), Part I, section C, below.

133. Songy, *Alexis de Tocqueville and Slavery*, 153.

134. An analysis of Tocqueville's position on colonization, abolition, and emancipation goes beyond the scope of this introduction. In 1835, Tocqueville became
a member of the *French Society for the Abolition of Slavery* and later called for the
abolition of slavery in the French West Indies. Yet, unlike radical French abolitionists, he argued that the state ought to give the former slave masters some
form of indemnification. For more details on this issue, see Tocqueville, *Writings
on Empire and Slavery* and *Tocqueville and Beaumont on Social Reform*, 98–173.

135. See Tocqueville's letter to Theodore Sedgwick (January 10, 1857), Part I,
section D, below.

136. See Tocqueville's letter to Theodore Sedgwick (April 13, 1857), Part I, section
D, below.

137. See Tocqueville's letter to Jared Sparks (July 15, 1857), Part I, section D,
below.

138. Gary Wills, "Did Tocqueville 'Get' America?" *New York Review of Books*, April 29
(2004): 52–56.

139. Wills, "Did Tocqueville 'Get' America?" 53.

140. Rogers M. Smith, "Beyond Tocqueville, Myrdal, and Hartz: The Multiple Traditions in America," *American Political Science Review* 87: 3 (1993): 549. For a more
comprehensive treatment of this topic, see Rogers M. Smith, *Civic Ideals* (New
Haven: Yale University Press, 1997).

141. Smith, "Beyond Tocqueville, Myrdal, and Hartz," 549.

142. Ibid., 549.

143. Raymond Boudon, "L'exigence de Tocqueville: la 'science politique nouvelle,'"
in *The Tocqueville Review/La Revue Tocqueville* XXVII : 2 (2006): 20. The scientific
nature of Tocqueville's approach was also emphasized in Raymond Boudon, *The
Unintended Consequences of Human Action* (New York: St. Martin's Press, 1982) and
Saguiv A. Hadari, *Theory in Practice: Tocqueville's New Science of Politics* (Stanford,
CA: Stanford University Press, 1988). On Tocqueville's method, see Aurelian
Craiutu, "What Kind of Social Scientist Was Tocqueville?" in *Conversations
with Tocqueville: The Global Democratic Revolution in the 21st Century*, eds. Aurelian
Craiutu and Sheldon Gellar (Lanham, MD: Rowman and Littlefield, Lexington
Books, 2009), 55–81.

144. Tocqueville, *Democracy in America*, 13.

145. Ibid., 663.

146. See Tocqueville, *OC*, XI, 67. The letter is also quoted in James T. Schleifer, *The
Making of Democracy in America*, 2nd revised edition (Indianapolis: Liberty Fund,
2000), 212.

147. In his notes, Tocqueville wrote: "Use Democracy to moderate Democracy. It is the only path to salvation that is open to us. To discern the feelings, the ideas, the laws which, without being hostile to the principle of Democracy, can nonetheless correct its troublesome tendencies" (quoted in Schleifer, *The Making of Democracy in America*, 234).

148. Tocqueville as quoted in Schleifer, *The Making of Democracy in America*, 232–33.

149. Ibid., 200, 233.

150. Undated letter of Beckwith, Part I, section D, below.

151. See Tocqueville's letter to Francis Lieber (September 1, 1856), Part I, section C, below.

152. It is interesting to note that in spite of his disillusionment about French politics in the late 1850s, Tocqueville refused to believe that despotism was the normal and definitive state of French society; see, for example, Tocqueville, *Lettres choisies. Souvenirs*, 1266. The dismal state of affairs in French politics under Napoléon III did not affect Tocqueville's strong belief in political liberty. For more evidence regarding his passion for liberty and his views on French society, see Tocqueville's letter to Beaumont from February 27, 1858 (Tocqueville, *Lettres choisies. Souvenirs*, 1292–96). An English translation can be found in Tocqueville, *Selected Letters*, 365–70.

153. See Tocqueville's letter to Francis Lieber (August 4, 1852), Part I, section B, below.

154. Tocqueville similarly came to express some doubts about the one other country that had attracted French liberals of his generation: England. Writing at the time of the Crimean war, he commented on the extent to which England suffered from the weakness and incapacity of its government. Yet in some of his letters to Corcelle, Beaumont, and Kergorlay written in 1857, Tocqueville expressed greater appreciation for England, its political culture, and tradition of self-government. For more details, see Tocqueville *Lettres choisies. Souvenirs*, 1255, 1260.

155. Seymour Drescher, "Tocqueville's Comparisons: Choices and Lessons," in *The Tocqueville Review/La Revue Tocqueville*, XXVI: 2 (2006): 508.

156. For references to America in Tocqueville's last book, see *The Old Regime and the Revolution*, I, 129 (reference to New England townships), 206 (religion in America), 280–81 (comparison between the U.S. and Canada), 300 (respect for majority in America), 145 (role of cities in America), 285–86 (the rule of law in America); also see *The Old Regime and the Revolution*, II, 86, 113. On this topic, see François Furet and Françoise Mélonio, Introduction to *The Old Regime and the Revolution*, I, 1–79; Drescher, "Tocqueville's Comparisons: Choices and Lessons," 479–516.

157. Sardou as quoted in Roger, *L'Ennemi américain*, 88. For another interesting critique of Tocqueville, see Claudio Jannet, *Les États-Unis contemporains ou les Moeurs, les institutions et les idées depuis la guerre de Secession* (Paris: 1876). Jannet criticized Tocqueville for having offered a distorted and idealized image of America. Jannet's book is mentioned in Jaume, *Tocqueville*, 84.

158. See Tocqueville's letter to Charles Sumner (March 28, 1858), Part I, section D, below.

PART I. LETTERS

A. Letters: 1840–1847

1. Tocqueville, *OC*, VII, 82–248. For more information, see Appendix 3.

2. These documents are: a letter from Tocqueville addressed to Harvard University and Jared Sparks (December 11, 1852), a letter of Tocqueville to Theodore Sedgwick (May 1853), and a letter from Tocqueville to Richard Rush (June 1849).

3. One of Tocqueville's letters to Sedgwick (August 14, 1854) was translated in Tocqueville, *Selected Letters on Politics and Society*, 310–11.

4. It is likely that some letters received by Tocqueville from his American correspondents have been lost.

5. Biographical information about Tocqueville's American correspondents can be found in Appendix 1.

6. See Tocqueville's letter to Madame de Swetchine (September 10, 1856), in Tocqueville, *Lettres choisies. Souvenirs*, 1210.

7. Brogan, *Alexis de Tocqueville: A Life*, 608.

8. For a short selection, see the correspondence included in Part I, section F, below.

9. See Tocqueville's letter to E. V. Childe (December 12, 1856), Part I, section C, below.

10. See Francis Lieber's letter to Tocqueville (September 25, 1846), Part I, section A, below.

11. See Tocqueville's letter to Francis Lieber (December 14, 1844), Part I, section A, below.

12. For more information, see Jardin, *Tocqueville: A Biography*, 358–59; also see the editors' introduction and Tocqueville's speech given at a popular banquet in Cherbourg (Part II, section A, below).

13. On this issue, see Seymour Drescher, *Dilemmas of Democracy*, 124–50.

14. See John C. Spencer's letter to Tocqueville (June 10, 1848), below.

15. See Jared Sparks's letter to Tocqueville (June 13, 1853), Part I, section C, below.

16. See Theodore Sedgwick's letter to Tocqueville (December 1, 1853), Part I, section C, below.

17. See Jared Sparks's letter to Tocqueville (June 13, 1853), Part I, section C, below.

18. Songy, *Alexis de Tocqueville and Slavery*, 159.

19. Drescher, *Dilemmas of Democracy*, 189.

20. See Tocqueville's letter (April 2, 1857), Part I, section D, below.

21. Songy, *Alexis de Tocqueville and Slavery*, 172.

22. See Theodore Sedgwick's letter to Tocqueville (September 19, 1856), Part I, section C, below.

23. See Edward Everett's letter to Tocqueville (December 8, 1857), Part I, section D, below.

24. See Charles Sumner's letter to Tocqueville (May 5, 1858), Part I, section D, below.

25. The ratification of the controversial Lecompton constitution marked an important turning point in the debates over the extension of slavery into the Western

territories. Initially, the Kansas voters ratified it on December 21, 1857. According to election officials, there were 6,000 votes for the constitution with slavery, and fewer than 600 for the constitution without slavery. On January 4, 1858, another referendum was organized and the entire constitution was rejected this time. The final decision was made on August 2, 1858, when the constitution was rejected again. For more information, see Stampp, *America in 1857: A Nation on the Brink*, 266–321; David Zarefsky, *Lincoln, Douglas, and Slavery in the Crucible of Public Debate* (Chicago: University of Chicago Press, 1990), 11–17.

26. Stampp, *America in 1857*, 322.

27. See N. Beckwith's undated letter, Part I, section D, below. Songy also commented on the importance of Beckwith's letters to Tocqueville in *Alexis de Tocqueville and Slavery*, 164–68.

28. See N. Beckwith's letter to Tocqueville (February 20, 1857), Part I, section D, below.

29. See N. Beckwith's undated letter to Tocqueville, Part I, section D, below. In spite of his agreement with the general agenda pursued by the American abolitionists, Tocqueville did not share all of their views. In particular, perhaps under the influence of Jared Sparks, he did not believe that it was possible to abolish slavery quickly in the South. For more information on this topic, see Songy, *Alexis de Tocqueville and Slavery*, 167–68; 187–245. In a path-breaking study published in 1968, Seymour Drescher highlighted the importance of the debates on the abolition of slavery for Tocqueville and interpreted the latter's views against the background of the moderate French liberal tradition represented by Victor de Broglie, Charles de Rémusat, Odilon Barrot, and Beaumont. For more details, see Drescher, *Dilemmas of Democracy*, 151–95.

30. See Tocqueville's letter to Theodore Sedgwick (December 4, 1852), Part I, section B, below.

31. See Tocqueville's letter to Theodore Sedgwick (August 14, 1854), Part I, section C, below.

32. See Tocqueville's letter to Francis Lieber (September 1, 1856), Part I, section C, below.

33. See Tocqueville's letter to Jared Sparks (July 15, 1857), Part I, section D, below.

34. See Tocqueville's "Rapport fait au nom de la Commission chargée d'éxaminer la proposition de M. de Tracy, relative aux esclaves des colonies" (July 1839) in *OC*, III: 1, 41–78. An English version of Tocqueville's report of July 23, 1839 was translated by Jared Sparks's wife as *Report Made to the Chamber of Deputies on the Abolition of Slavery in the French Colonies by Alexis de Tocqueville* (Boston, 1840). For a revised version of the 1840 original English translation, see *Tocqueville and Beaumont on Social Reform*, ed. and trans. Seymour Drescher (New York: Harper, 1968), 98–136. For an analysis of Tocqueville's position on the abolition of slavery, see Drescher, *Dilemmas of Democracy*, 151–95. Victor de Tracy (1781–1864), the son of Destutt de Tracy, was a prominent member of the Chamber of Deputies. Elected for the first time in 1822, he served until 1851.

35. The translation was done by Sparks's wife. For more information, see the previous note above.

36. Sparks spent two months in Paris (December 1840-January 1841), collecting original documents on the American War of Independence.

37. For more information about the reception of Tocqueville's work in nineteenth-century America, see Matthew Mancini, *Alexis de Tocqueville and American Intellectuals*, 1–98; and Oliver Zunz, "Tocqueville and the Americans: *Democracy in America* as Read in Nineteenth-Century America," in *The Cambridge Companion to Tocqueville*, 359–96. Zunz's article also has a useful bibliography of selected nineteenth-century reviews of Tocqueville's work. The classic work examining the reception of Tocqueville in France is Françoise Mélonio, *Tocqueville and the French* (Charlottesville, VA: University Press of Virginia, 1998).

38. Reference to the treaty signed between Great Britain, Russia, Prussia and Austria guaranteeing the integrity of the Ottoman Empire. Because France was excluded from the treaty, the French public opinion was outraged and called for war with England.

39. The title of the book is not mentioned by Goodrich. In 1841, Samuel Griswold Goodrich (1793–1860) published *The Story of Captain Riley and His Adventures in Africa* (Philadelphia: Henry F. Anners, 1841), which is likely to be the book sent to Tocqueville.

40. The letter from A. W. Paull informs Tocqueville of his election to the Whig Society at Princeton. The folder "Tocqueville and Beaumont: Honors in the United States" (MS Vault Tocqueville, D II a, Beinecke Rare Book and Manuscript Library), contains information about the following honors bestowed on Tocqueville: member of the Historical Society of Pennsylvania (February 6, 1832); member of the American Philosophical Society (January 21, 1832); honorary member of the Massachusetts Historical Society (May 14, 1857); member of the Whig Society, Princeton (September 30, 1841). More information about the honors received by Tocqueville in the United States can be found in MS Vault Tocqueville, Beinecke Rare Book and Manuscript Library, Yale University, E IV 2.

41. The Whig-Cliosophic Society of Princeton (1765, 1769) is the oldest college literary and debating club in the United States, whose role has been to promote literary and debating activities. Its founders were Hugh Henry Breckenridge, Justice of the Pennsylvania Supreme Court; Philip Freneau, a Revolutionary War Poet; William Bradford, Attorney General of the United States, and James Madison, the future President of the United States.

42. "Its" in the Bonnel copy.

43. Meaning unclear.

44. William Bradford (1755–1795) was a lawyer and judge from Philadelphia who served as the second United States Attorney General in 1794–95.

45. Henry Lee, Governor of Virginia, became famous for his involvement in the repression of the so-called Whiskey Rebellion (1791–94), the first act of rebellion against the U. S. government after the adoption of the Constitution. He was the father of Robert E. Lee (1756–1818).

46. Henry Brockholst Livingston (1757–1823) was a close supporter of Jefferson who served on the New York Supreme Court and the U.S. Supreme Court. Edward Livingston (1764–1836) was an eminent lawyer, member of the U.S. House of Representatives, and mayor of New York.

47. James Ashton Bayard (1767–1815) was a well-known lawyer and politician from Wilmington, Delaware. A graduate of the Princeton class of 1784, he represented the state of Delaware in the U.S. House of Representatives and the Senate.

48. Robert G. Harper ran as an independent candidate for Presidency in 1820.

49. David Hosack played a key role in creating a medical school at Rutgers University in the 1820s.

50. Thomas Johnson was appointed to the Supreme Court of the United States by President Washington and served as Associate Justice from 1792 to 1793.

51. John Sergeant (1779–1852) was a Pennsylvania lawyer and politician who graduated from Princeton in 1795.

52. John Forsyth served in the U. S. Senate and later as U. S. Minister to Spain.

53. On Richard Rush, see the biographical note in Appendix 1.

54. Hugh L. White (1773–1840) was a prominent nineteenth-century American politician who represented the state of Tennessee in the U. S. Senate from 1825 until his resignation in 1840. He was the Whig Party's candidate for Presidency in the 1836 elections.

55. John C. Calhoun (1782–1850) was a leading Southern politician who served as the seventh Vice-President of the United States (1825–1832). In 1832, he resigned from that position to run for the U. S. Senate. Calhoun represented the state of South Carolina in the Senate where he led the pro-slavery faction in the 1830s and 1840s. He also was a prominent political philosopher best known as a spokesman for local liberties and state rights.

56. Lewis Cass (1782–1866) was a prominent military officer and politician who served as governor, ambassador, and U.S. Senator. Cass was the nominee of the Democratic Party for President of the United States in 1848.

57. John Tyler (1790–1862), the tenth President of the United States (1841–1845), was the first Vice President to be elevated to the office of President by the death of his predecessor, President Harrison.

58. Daniel Webster (1782–1852), a graduate of Dartmouth College, was one of the most famous nineteenth-century American politicians who provided an alternative to Andrew Jackson and was one of the dominant figures of the Whig party during the 1840s. Webster endorsed the Compromise of 1850 engineered by Henry Clay, standing almost alone among northern Congressional Whigs. Embittered by his own failure to secure the presidential nomination of his own party in 1852, Webster refused to support the Whig ticket that year and died shortly thereafter on October 24, 1852. On Webster, see George Ticknor, *Remarks on the Life and Writings of Daniel Webster of Massachussetts* (1831).

59. Townsend began corresponding with Tocqueville before 1840. At the Beinecke Rare Book and Manuscript Library (Yale University), there is also an original letter (written in French) sent by Townsend to Tocqueville on September 12, 1838 (Uncat MSS 324).

60. For more information, see Tocqueville, *OC*, VII, 85, n. 4. MacLeod was a Canadian citizen involved in the murder of an American citizen in December 1837, during the controversies involving the border disputes between Canada and the United States. The Americans prosecuted MacLeod for his act. For

more information, see John Morton Callahan, *The Neutrality of the American Lakes and Anglo-American Relations* (Baltimore, MD: Johns Hopkins University Press, 1898), 91–135 and David P. Currie, *Constitution in Crisis: Descent into the Maelstrom 1829–61* (Chicago, IL: University of Chicago Press, 2005), 51–68. From 1837 onwards, tensions between the United States and England mounted over disputes concerning the United States' northern frontier.

61. It turned out that MacLeod had nothing to do with the murder and was subsequently acquitted.

62. Tocqueville married a middle-class Englishwoman, Mary Mottley, in 1835, against the wishes of his own family.

63. Tocqueville left for Algeria in May 1841 but, unfortunately, his trip was cut short by a bout of illness. Tocqueville was strongly interested in the colonization of Algeria and participated in the parliamentary debates on this issue (he gave an important speech on this topic in the Chamber of Deputies on June 9, 1846). Tocqueville returned to Algeria in the Fall of 1846, and then again in 1847; he submitted an official report on Algeria on February 27, 1847 (see *OC*, III: 1, 308–408) A cursory reading of these documents shows that Tocqueville was preoccupied with securing the greatness of France and strengthening its political influence in Europe at that time. He believed that the means of the colonization should be the implantation of an agricultural population through the creation of villages in which the distribution of landed property was unequal. A critic of bureaucratic centralization, Tocqueville denounced the mistakes made by the centralized administration of the civil and military authority in Algeria and insisted that the citizens of the colony should enjoy the same rights and be protected by the same laws as those of the mother country. Tocqueville's writings on Algeria were translated into English as *Writings on Empire and Slavery*. For more detail, see *OC*, V: 2, 189–218; Jardin, *Tocqueville: A Biography*, 316–42; Brogan, *Alexis de Tocqueville: A Life*, 397–402; and Pitts, "Introduction" to Alexis de Tocqueville, *Writings on Empire and Slavery*, xi–xxix.

64. For a biographical note on John Canfield Spencer (1788–1855), see Appendix 1. Spencer was responsible for the publication of the first American edition of *Democracy in America*; for more details, see Pierson, *Tocqueville in America*, 216–24.

65. Isaiah Townsend met Tocqueville in Paris at the recommendation of Spencer.

66. See Townsend's letter of November 2, 1841, Part I, section A, above, in which he informed Tocqueville of Spencer's appointment as head of the War Department.

67. A defensive alliance formed in 1686 by Holy Roman Emperor Leopold I with various German states, (including Bavaria and the Palatinate) as well as with Sweden and Spain. It was an acknowledgment of a community of German feeling against French expansion.

68. In the early 1840s, the U. S. and France regarded with increasing concern the growth of the maritime power of England. Tocqueville's position on this issue was later outlined in his speech at Cherbourg of March 23, 1848 (see Part II, section B, below). Also see Jardin, *Tocqueville: A Biography*, 354–59.

69. Passed in 1841, the bill introduced new tariffs on a number of merchandises, including wines, and triggered a strong reaction in France.

70. Lieber's book, *Essays on Property and Labour*, was originally published in 1841. Another edition was published by Harper & Bros. in 1862. Lieber defended

freedom from government action and emphasized the need to avoid placing property under the control of the majority. He argued that "the principle of freedom is to leave as much as possible to spontaneous action, and to confirm by law what has thus already grown up out of the free action of the people" (quoted in Bernard E. Brown, *American Conservatives: The Political Thought of Francis Lieber and John W. Burgess* [New York: Columbia University Press, 1951], 67). Yet Lieber was not a classical liberal in the strict sense of the word and the form of liberalism he endorsed, while recognizing the sacrosanct nature of private property, allowed a substantial scope for state action on behalf of its citizens.

71. The revised statutes of New York (1835–36) rejected the Philadelphia system and endorsed the Auburn system based on solitude during the night and common labor during the day.

72. For a biographical note on Francis Lieber (1798–1872), see Appendix 1. For a general presentation of his political philosophy, see Brown, *American Conservatives: The Political Thought of Francis Lieber and John W. Burgess*, 13–100.

73. Founded in 1829 by François Buloz, the *Revue des Deux Mondes* is arguably the oldest European journal still in print. In the nineteenth century, it was a bimonthly literary and political journal that published many prominent contributors such as Chateaubriand, Hugo, Rémusat, Heine, and Michelet. For a history of the publication, see Gabriel de Broglie, *Histoire politique de la Revue des deux mondes de 1829 à 1979* (Paris: Perrin, 1979).

74. For a biographical note on Henry Wheaton (1785–1848), see Appendix 1.

75. Lieber's candidature was never formally presented to the Institute in spite of the reassurances given by Tocqueville.

76. Tocqueville was elected member of the French Academy on December 23, 1841 to fill in the vacancy opened by the death of Jean-Gérard Lacuée de Cessac.

77. These speeches were published in Tocqueville, *OC*, XVI, 249–69.

78. See *OC*, IV: 2, pp. 117–76, 338. Tocqueville's first report was presented in 1840 on behalf of a committee that also included, among others, Gustave de Beaumont, Prosper Duvergier de Hauranne, and Hippolyte Carnot. An excellent interpretation of Tocqueville's and Beaumont's positions on prison reform in France can be found in Drescher, *Dilemmas of Democracy*, 124–150. Drescher duly notes the importance of this issue for Tocqueville in light of his views on centralization and state power: "It is significant it was social reform in general and prison reform in particular which first brought Tocqueville and Beaumont to an awareness of the insidious nature of the modern tendency toward centralization. It is equally significant that they readily agreed to centralized administration to accomplish reforms in this area" (145).

79. For a biographical note on Nathaniel Niles (1791–1869), see Appendix 1.

80. This letter sent by Niles was lost. We can surmise that the document mentioned by Tocqueville referred to the reform of the penitentiary system in America.

81. The discussion on this law triggered intense debates in the Chamber of Deputies in April–May 1844. For Tocqueville's report, see *OC*, IV: 2, 117–82. An English translation can be found in *Tocqueville and Beaumont on Social Reform*, ed. Drescher, 70–89. As Drescher pointed out, the opposition in both the press and the Chamber to importing the Philadelphia system to France was both vigorous and effective.

82. This letter has been lost.

83. Reference to Léon Faucher's three-part essay *Études sur l'Angleterre* (White-Chapel, Saint-Giles, Liverpool) published in the October-December 1843 issue of the *Revue des Deux Mondes*. In this long article, Faucher drew attention to the social problems in London and Liverpool and pointed out the huge differences in living conditions between the affluent residents of London's West End and those of White Chapel and Saint-Giles. Léon Faucher was a prominent French intellectual and politician during the July Monarchy. A frequent contributor to the *Revue des Deux Mondes*, he also wrote a review of Volume One of Tocqueville's *Democracy in America* in *Le Courrier français*, (December 1834), a few weeks before the actual publication of the book (see Jardin, *Tocqueville: A Biography*, 225). During the last years of the July Monarchy, Faucher served as Minister of the Interior.

84. The exhibition of French industry opened on May 1, 1844 and closed two months later.

85. For a biographical note on Robert Walsh (1784–1859), see Appendix 1

86. The report was drafted by Bignon and was presented on June 6, 1844.

87. Tocqueville was critical toward the report on secondary education drafted by the committee chaired by Thiers (June–July 1844).

88. For more information on Tocqueville's involvement in the publication of *Le Commerce*, see Roger Boesche, *Tocqueville's Road Map*, 189–209, and Jardin, *Tocqueville: A Biography*, 386–96.

89. Lieber's letter has been lost.

90. François Mignet (1796–1884), eminent historian and member of the French Academy (elected in 1836). He was the author of many influential books, including *Histoire de la Révolution française* (1824), *De la féodalité, des institutions de Saint Louis et de l'influence de la législation de ce prince* (1822), *Essai sur la formation territoriale et politique de la France depuis la fin du XIe siècle jusqu'à la fin du XVe* (1836). Mignet's letter to Tocqueville has been lost.

91. The English correspondent was Charles Buller (1806–1848), a friend of Henry Reeve, Tocqueville's translator.

92. Tocqueville obtained such contributions from Greece and Switzerland but was unable to find a German contributor to *Le Commerce*. For more information on *Le Commerce*, see Jardin, *Tocqueville: A Biography*, 388–96; Roger Boesche, *Tocqueville's Road Map* (Lanham, MD: Rowman and Littlefield, Lexington Books, 2006), 189–209.

93. After overcoming his initial hesitations, Lieber accepted to serve as the American correspondent for *Le Commerce*. He sent four articles that were published in the newspaper.

94. Frederick William IV of Prussia (1795–1861) reigned as King of Prussia from 1840 to 1861.

95. The word was added by Lieber above the line.

96. Reference to Lieber's letter of November 7, 1844, sent from Hamburg.

97. "As a friend" (in French, in the original)

98. *Negretia* was an old name for the region of Nigeria. In this case, it presumably was used by Lieber as a pejorative expression for the South where he lived at that time.

99. Also known as the Philadelphia system.

100. Friedrich Wilhelm Heinrich Alexander von Humboldt (1769–1859), was a prominent Prussian naturalist and explorer, famous for his geographic and

botanical explorations in South America (1799–1804) and Russia (1829). His brother was the equally well-known former Prussian minister, philosopher, and linguist Wilhelm von Humboldt. Between 1830 and 1848, Alexander von Humboldt was frequently employed in diplomatic missions to the court of Louis-Philippe, with whom he always maintained the most cordial personal relations. Upon the accession of the Crown Prince Frederick William IV in June 1840, von Humboldt's favor at court increased. The King enjoyed Humboldt's company and often confided in him.

101. "Between us, so to speak" (in French, in the original)
102. The Auburn system evolved an alternative to the Philadelphia system of solitary confinement.
103. Ludwig Gustav von Thile was Prime Minister of Prussia from 1841 to 1848.
104. Also known as the Philadelphia system.
105. In French, in the original.
106. The reference is to Charles Dickens's *American Notes* that described his five-month visit to America in 1842. Dickens visited the East Coast and the Great Lakes region of both the United States and Canada by steamship, rail, and coach. He was very interested in American prisons and mental institutions and became a vocal critic of slavery in the United States. For a recent edition, see Charles Dickens, *American Notes* (New York: The Modern Library, 1996). *Les Mystères de Paris*, a novel by Eugène Sue (1804–1857), was originally published in *Journal des Débats* in 1842–43.
107. "General prison inspectors" (in French, in the original).
108. Lieber's note (in French), in margin: "This too remains *entre nous*."
109. "Two distinguished penologists" (in French, in the original).
110. In French, in the original.
111. A corner of Lieber's original letter is torn and missing.
112. Marie de Tocqueville wrote this letter in English. The English version was published in *OC*, VII, 97–99, followed by Tocqueville's note in French.
113. According to Françoise Mélonio, the person to whom Marie de Tocqueville referred was most likely Alexandre-François-August Vivien (1799–1854), a distinguished lawyer and member of the *Conseil d'Etat* and the Chamber of Deputies.
114. King Louis-Philippe unsuccessfully sought to obtain an allowance of 500,000 francs for his second son, the Duke of Nemours. This unpopular proposal had to be withdrawn in 1843, after being contested in the Chamber of Deputies.
115. The *Juif errant* was published in *Le Constitutionnel* from June 25, 1844 to July 12, 1845.
116. Louis-Adolphe Thiers (1797–1877) was a prominent French politician and historian, author of an influential ten-volume *History of the French Revolution*. A rival of Guizot, he was one of the leading politicians during the July Monarchy (1830–1848), when he served twice as Prime Minister and Minister of Foreign Affairs. From 1871 to 1873 he served as Head of State and provisional President of the French Republic.
117. Tocqueville's note (written in French) is placed after his wife's letter to Lieber.
118. Tocqueville refers to the election of James Knox Polk (1795–1849) as the eleventh President of the United States.
119. This letter has been lost.

120. Charles-Arnold Scheffer (1796–1853) was the brother of the well-known painter Ary Scheffer, and former personal assistant to General La Fayette.

121. Marie de Tocqueville wrote this letter in English. The English version was published in *OC*, VII, 102–105.

122. The facts did not seem to support Marie de Tocqueville's account. *Le Commerce* did not increase its readership and was unknown abroad. For more information, see Jardin, *Tocqueville: A Biography*, 388–96.

123. As Françoise Mélonio pointed out (*OC*, VII, 103, n. 4), in November-December 1845, *Le Commerce* published a few unsigned articles on education that defended a pluralist view of educational reform and attacked the monopoly on education that both the state and the Catholic Church were seeking at that time. Some of these articles were written by Tocqueville.

124. Abel-François Villemain (1790–1870), eminent historian and Minister of Education in the Guizot-Soult cabinet formed on November 29, 1840.

125. It is unclear if this prospective correspondent was Mittelmaier. No correspondence from Heidelberg was ever published in *Le Commerce*.

126. Thiers and his friends criticized Tocqueville's prison report. One of the harshest critiques was made by Léon de Malleville in the parliamentary session of May 10, 1844.

127. "Apathetic" (in French, in the original text).

128. Marie de Tocqueville's note was originally written in English. The English version was published in *OC*, VII, 106.

129. *Le Commerce* lost many subscribers in 1845 and had serious financial difficulties that ultimately led to a change of ownership. The new owner was the financier Dutacq, who paid 100,000 francs for *Le Commerce*. His original intention was to include articles written for *Le Commerce* in the daily *Le Soleil*, but his plan failed. For more information, see Tocqueville, *Selected Letters on Politics and Society*, 168–76; Boesche, *Tocqueville's Road Map*, 189–209; Jardin, *Tocqueville: A Biography*, 395; Brogan, *Alexis de Tocqueville: A Life*, 379–80.

130. August Belmont (1816–1890) was a prominent New York banker.

131. The 1844–45 parliamentary session that ended on July 21, 1845 was dominated by intense and controversial political debates on important issues such as education reform and the funding of local schools. Tocqueville participated in these debates. For more information, see Jardin, *Tocqueville: A Biography*, 362–69.

132. Tocqueville intended to speak on this topic before the Chamber of Deputies. The annexation of the Republic of Texas by the United States occurred in 1845. For more information, see the editors' introduction to Part II, section A, below; Walker Howe, *What Hath God Wrought*, 671–708.

133. For a biographical note on Benjamin Perley Poore (1820–1887), see Appendix 1.

134. The letter was originally written in French by Townsend.

135. The comparison of Tocqueville with Montesquieu had previously been made by both Pierre-Paul Royer-Collard and John Stuart Mill in the mid 1830s.

136. The New York State has had five constitutions over time (1777, 1821, 1846, 1894, 1938). The Constitutional Convention of 1846 met in Albany and dealt with a number of important questions such as petitions for women suffrage and the demands of the tenant farmers' movement that played a key role in New York State politics in the 1840s.

137. Lieber's letter has been lost.
138. The elections were held on August 1, 1846. Tocqueville faced competition from Le Marois whom he easily defeated (by 410 votes to 70).
139. Lieber had sent Tocqueville a brochure on Laura Dewey Bridgman (1829–1889), a blind, deaf, and mute person who learned how to write and communicate by signs. As such, Bridgman was the first deaf-blind American child to gain a significant education in the English language. The person who helped her was Samuel Gridley Howe from the Perkins Institute in Boston. Howe's report became very popular in both the United States and Europe. Dickens referred to Bridgman in his *American Notes* (1842).
140. The Left lost over 30 seats in the August 1846 elections.
141. The government of Lord Russell came to power in July 1846. Lord Palmerston became Secretary of Foreign Affairs, replacing Lord Aberdeen who had had diplomatic relations with France and with Guizot in particular. Because of Guizot's direct intervention in Spanish affairs, the government in London expressed its dissatisfaction at the attempt of France to gain influence over Spain.
142. On Guizot in the late 1840s, see Douglas Johnson, *Guizot: Aspects of French History, 1787–1874* (London: Routledge and Kegan Paul, 1963), 263–319; and Gabriel de Broglie, *Guizot* (Paris: Perrin, 2002), 311–64. Laurent Theis's recently published *François Guizot* (Paris: Fayard, 2008) offers a new intellectual and intimate portrait of the great French statesman.
143. A similar description of the reign of Louis-Philippe can be found in the first two chapters of Tocqueville's *Recollections*.
144. Lieber's response can be found in his letter from September 25, 1846 in which he cautioned against drawing too close a comparison between the colonization of Algeria and that of America.
145. Marie de Tocqueville's note was originally written in English. The English version published in *OC*, VII, 112–13.
146. George Grote (1794–1871) was a prominent nineteenth-century English classical historian who belonged to the group of the so-called "philosophical radicals" and was influenced by Jeremy Bentham and James Mill. Grote became famous for his *History of Greece*, the first two volumes of which appeared in 1846. Ten further volumes appeared between 1847 and 1856. He later also authored a three-volume work on Plato, *Plato and the Other Companions of Socrates* (1865). He traveled frequently to France after 1830, and was a member of the House of Commons (1832–1841).
147. The date of the letter is uncertain. Walsh's response has not been found.
148. Although Tocqueville addressed the issue of the verification of powers in a speech given in the Chamber of Deputies on August 22, 1846, he made no references to America.
149. The *National Intelligencer* was published in Washington D.C. by William Winston Seaton and Joseph Gales, who served as its editors for more than fifty years. Originally founded in 1800 to endorse Jefferson (it later supported Madison and Monroe), the journal became a daily newspaper in 1813 and was until its disappearance in 1867 a leading source of information on American politics.
150. The meaning of this phrase is unclear in Lieber's original letter; possibly a grammatical error on Lieber's part.

151. Reference to Queen Christina of Sweden (1626–1689) who planned the execution of Monaldeschi, who had betrayed her plans to become the Queen of Naples in the autumn of 1657. He was stabbed by two of Christina's own domestics in an apartment adjoining that in which she herself was at that time at Fontainebleau.

152. Lieber's letter ends abruptly here.

153. For a biographical note on Charles Sumner (1811–1874), see Appendix 1. Sumner had this letter of Tocqueville published in several American newspapers, as part of his campaign to convince public opinion of the virtues of the Philadelphia system of solitary confinement. Because Tocqueville's name commanded a lot of respect in America, Sumner was hoping that his endorsement would sway his countrymen's views.

154. The *Boston Prison Discipline Society* was founded in 1825 and was dissolved in 1854. It published an *Annual Report on Prisons in America* (29 issues were published). The Secretary of the Society, Louis Dwight, was hostile to the system of solitary confinement practiced in Philadelphia. The alternative system at that time was the so-called Auburn system, a penal method in which persons worked during the day and were kept in solitary confinement at night, with enforced silence at all times. The silent system evolved during the 1820s at Auburn Prison in Auburn, New York, as an alternative to and modification of the Philadelphia system, which it gradually replaced in the United States. In May 1845, Charles Sumner challenged Dwight's views and asked for a revision of the report. The controversy continued in 1846 and the 1847 *Annual Report* moderated its criticism of the Philadelphia system, but in the end Sumner's opinions in the favor of the latter (published in *Boston Daily Advertiser* in July) did not prevail over Dwight's views. For more information, see Mark E. Kann, *Punishment, Prisons, and Patriarchy: Liberty and Power in the Early American Republic* (New York: New York University Press, 2005); Orlando F. Lewis, *The Development of American Prisons and Prison Customs, 1776–1845* (Kessinger Publishing, 2005).

155. Tocqueville and Beaumont had become members of the Boston Prison Discipline Society during their visit to the United States (May 1831-February 1832).

156. Nonetheless, in Prussia and Italy a few critics rejected the system of solitary confinement practiced in Philadelphia. Tocqueville's writings on penitentiary reform were published in *OC*, IV (2 volumes).

157. The Chamber of Deputies followed Tocqueville's report when voting on this issue in its session of May 8, 1844. The project of the law was subsequently submitted to the Chamber of Peers on January 25, 1847.

158. *Le Siècle.*

B. Letters: 1848–1852

1. Rush's letters from this period – all formal in style – were written in his capacity as U. S. Minister in Paris.

2. For more details on Tocqueville's involvement in the activities of this Committee, see the editors' introduction to Part II, Section C, below; also Jardin, *Tocqueville: A Biography*, 417–20; Brogan, *Tocqueville: A Life*, 451–75; Watkins, *Alexis de Tocqueville and the Second Republic*, 189–256; Gargan, *Alexis de Tocqueville: The Critical Years, 1848–1851*, 70–121.

3. In the margin, there is a short note by Tocqueville as follows: "*C'est notre ferme croyance qu'après Dieu, la cause à laquelle nous devons le maintien de nos institutions libres – c'est la division du pouvoir législatif*" ["It is our firm belief that, after God, the cause to which we owe the maintenance of our free institutions is the division of the legislative power"].

4. This point was made by Tocqueville in his contributions to the debates on the constitution of the Second Republic (see Part II, section C, below). Also see *Genesi di una costituzione: Libertà e socialismo nel dibattito costituzionale del 1848 in Francia*, ed. Piero Craveri (Napoli: Guida, 1985).

5. On *juste milieu* liberalism during the Bourbon Restoration (1814–1830) and the July Monarchy (1830–1848), see Lucien Jaume, *L'Individu effacé ou le paradoxe du libéralisme français* (Paris: Fayard, 1997); Aurelian Craiutu, *Liberalism under Siege: The Political Thought of the French Doctrinaires* (Lanham, MD: Lexington Books, Rowman and Littlefield, 2003), 19–85; 185–96; Pierre Rosanvallon, *Le Moment Guizot* (Paris: Gallimard, 1985).

6. For a biographical note on William Alexander Duer (1780–1858), see Appendix 1.

7. Theodore Lyman (1722–1849) was the author of *The diplomacy of the United States. Being an account of the foreign relations of the country, from the first treaty with France, in 1778, to the treaty of Ghent, in 1814, with Great Britain*, published by Wells and Lilly in 1826 in Boston. Lyman also authored *A short account of the Hartford Convention, taken from official documents, and addressed to the fair minded and the well disposed. To which is added an attested copy of the secret journal of that body* (Boston: Everett, 1823), written as a defense of Harrison Gray Otis's participation in the Hartford convention. In 1823, Otis was the unsuccessful Federalist candidate for the governorship of Massachusetts.

8. William Duer (1805–1879), a graduate of Columbia College, was a prominent American lawyer and statesman from New York City, who represented New York in the United States House of Representatives for two terms (1847–1851). President Fillmore appointed him as U. S. Consul to Valparaiso, Chile, in March 1851.

9. James Kent (1763–1847) was a prominent American jurist and legal scholar who taught law at Columbia College (1793–98). Tocqueville was familiar with Kent's most important book, *Commentaries on American Law* (four volumes, 1826–1830).

10. We only have the English translation of Tocqueville's letter (published in *OC*, VII, 119–20); the original French text has been lost.

11. According to Françoise Mélonio (in *OC*, VII, 119, n. 2), the name is uncertain. The printed copy of the letter has "Sognet," but no deputy with such a name could be identified. The person to whom Tocqueville refers might be Lignier.

12. On August 3, 1848, Alexandre Quentin-Bauchart presented the report of the inquiry commission of the National Assembly on the events of May 15 (when the Constituent Assembly was invaded by the crowd) and June 23 (when Paris succumbed once again to mob violence and the authority was delegated to General Cavaignac). For more details on the events of May–June 1848, see the second part of Tocqueville's *Recollections* and his letter of June 24, 1848 to Paul Clamorgan (Tocqueville, *Selected Letters*, 212–14). The context of the June

days is also discussed in Brogan, *Tocqueville: A Life*, 430–64; Watkins, *Alexis de Tocqueville and the Second Republic* , 141–88; Gargan, *Alexis de Tocqueville: The Critical Years, 1848–1851*, 55–69.

13. The President was General Louis-Eugène Cavaignac (1802–1857), who played a major role in the suppression of the popular revolt in June 1848 when the National Assembly gave him dictatorial powers and declared a state of emergency. As President of the Council of Ministers and *de facto* head of state, he continued to exercise power until the election of a regular President and harbored hopes of being elected to that position. Yet, the outcome of the elections of 1849 was a crushing defeat for Cavaignac, who lost to Louis-Napoléon, the future Emperor Napoléon III. Tocqueville voted for Cavaignac in 1849, but was ultimately disappointed by his actions.

14. The *Conseil d'État* was regarded as an institution capable of moderating popular impulses, along with bicameralism. In its session of March 3, 1849, the Assembly voted to make the *Conseil d'État* an intermediary body between government and Parliament and entrusted it with the responsibility of supervising the administration. The members of the *Conseil d'État* were supposed to be nominated by the legislative power.

15. Louis-Antoine Macarel was the author of *Cours de droit administratif professé à la Faculté de Droit de Paris* (1842–1845). Sébastien-Joseph Boulatignier (1805–1895) edited Joseph-Marie de Gérando's *Instituts de droit administratif français* (1842–1846). Louis de Cormenin (1778–1868) was a jurist and member of the Chamber of Deputies under the July Monarchy and the Constituent Assembly of the Second Republic. In his *Recollections*, Tocqueville criticized Cormenin's role in the drafting of the new constitution.

16. For a biographical note on Edward Everett (1794–1865), see Appendix 1. Tocqueville (and Beaumont) met Everett for the first time in Boston in 1831. For more details, see Pierson, *Tocqueville in America*, 393, 397. Everett belonged to the group of the "Boston Brahmins," along with George Ticknor, and William H. Prescott. The general context is analyzed in David B. Tyack, *George Ticknor and the Boston Brahmins* (Cambridge, MA: Harvard University Press, 1967).

17. Augustin-Henri Delattre (1801–1867), nineteenth-century French painter.

18. The issue of bicameralism was of paramount importance for Tocqueville in 1848. Some of his American friends, such as E. Everett, J. C. Spencer, R. Walsh, W. W. Duer, and G. Bancroft, praised the virtues of bicameralism as a fundamental political principle of American democracy. On the contrary, in France the existence of two parliamentary chambers was not seen as a pillar of liberty, and public opinion supported unicameralism. Even some of Tocqueville's closest associates and friends such as Dupin, Dufaure, and Beaumont voted against bicameralism, much to Tocqueville's chagrin. For more information, see J. C. Lamberti, "Tocqueville en 1848," *Commentaire*, 25 (1984): 141–51; Watkins, *Alexis de Tocqueville and the Second Republic*, 189–255. The importance of the years 1848–1851 for Tocqueville was highlighted by Gargan, *Alexis de Tocqueville: The Critical Years 1848–1851*, 55–121. Also see Tocqueville's own testimony in his *Recollections* (*OC*, XII, 184–86) as well as Tocqueville's parliamentary speeches (Part II, Section C, below).

19. Robert M. Walsh served as the American Consul in Paris in the 1840s.

20. "If the current constitution is not going to be modified soon, the republic will not last" (in French, in the original text). This is Tocqueville's statement in his letter to Everett from March 6, 1849.

21. Everett took a strong interest in these issues. In a previous letter to Robert Walsh from April 30, 1848 (Beinecke Rare Book and Manuscript Library, Yale University, Uncat MSS 324, Everett folder), he wrote: "Dear Sir, I have your obliging notes of the 22nd Jan. and 4th of February unacknowledged. I am greatly indebted to you for your continued attention in forwarding the *comptes rendus* both of the Physical and Moral Sciences. You may well suppose that all eyes are turned with intense anxiety on Europe generally and France in particular. I infer from numerous suggestions in the correspondence which finds its way into the journals here (a portion of it proceeding, if I mistake not, from your pen) that the French are studying our system with attention. I am glad that there are members of the provisional government, who will in their acquaintance with you possess the means of precise and accurate information. I hope you will enforce upon them the all-importance of two chambers. No matter how defective the theory (and with us, except as a historical necessity growing out of the pre-existing rights of the States as politically equal, the theoretical grounds for two chambers are very imperfect), the practical operation is most salutary. It is not at all necessary that the two houses should differ as to eligibility, or qualifications of candidates. In most of our states they do not differ in these respects. The mode of constituting the supreme executive is the point of greatest difficulty. For us I think we have hit about right. Improvements might be fancied; but it is doubtful if they would prove to be uncompensated with evils. A uniform district system would perhaps be better, if we were starting anew. This can be had without difficulty in France. The machinery of Presidential Electors has in practice proved of no value, in the way of making the elections less subject to popular influences; but I do not know that it does any harm. I think a term of five years – the President not to be re-eligible – would perhaps be an improvement. You see I take for granted that no monarchy will ever be restored – I mean by the deliberate act of any constituent assembly to be called for some time in France – and that some sort of an elective executive will be agreed upon. I own I look with extreme anxiety as to the result, for the movement appears to me to have its origin, not in struggles wise or unwise for a larger measure of political liberty; but to realize certain theories of social equality, which appear to me inconsistent with our present civilization. Pray excuse the freedom, with which I discuss subjects so much closer to your observation, and believe me with great respect ever sincerely yours, Edward Everett."

22. "At the end" (in French, in the original text).

23. In 1845, the United States annexed Texas, which had been an independent republic for ten years. The annexation angered the Mexican political elites and triggered a war between the two countries that began with a Mexican attack on American troops along the southern border of Texas on April 25, 1846. The war ended with the American occupation of Mexico City on September 14, 1847. The Peace Treaty, signed on February 2, 1848 at Guadalupe Hidalgo, recognized the annexation of Texas, California, and New Mexico (including all the present-day states of the Southwest) to the United States. For more information, see Walker Howe, *What Hath God Wrought*, 744–91.

24. Zachary Taylor (1784–1850) was the twelfth President of the United States (1849–1850). A native of Virginia, he became a prominent military officer who distinguished himself in the Mexican War. Taylor owned a plantation in Mississippi and had a home in Louisiana, but was not an advocate of slavery. He was nominated by the Whigs to run against the Democratic candidate, Lewis Cass, in the presidential elections of 1848. Taylor won the Presidency in a close election but his actions quickly disappointed his supporters in the South. He died in July 1850, while in office.

25. Edward Everett served as President of Harvard University from 1846 to 1849.

26. In French, in the original text.

27. For a biographical note on George Bancroft (1800–1891), see Appendix 1. Also see Tyack, *George Ticknor and the Boston Brahmins*, 43–64, 85–90, 102–108.

28. Tocqueville had just been appointed Minister of Foreign Affairs of the Second French Republic. For more information, see Watkins, *Alexis de Tocqueville and the Second Republic*, 323–84 and Gargan, *Alexis de Tocqueville: The Critical Years 1848–1851*, 121–79.

29. For a biographical note on Richard Rush (1780–1859), see Appendix 1. Rush first met Tocqueville in late 1847 in Paris.

30. We could not locate two other presumptive letters of Richard Rush to Tocqueville from June 5 and 27, 1849, mentioned by the editors of volume VII of Tocqueville's *OC*. The two letters are not listed on the catalogue of the Firestone Library (Princeton University), where Rush's correspondence and papers are preserved.

31. Partially dated. Most likely, this letter was written in August 1849. At the end of the letter, Tocqueville wrote: "Monday 1 [p.m.]"

32. On the tense relations between France and the U.S. during the Poussin affair of 1849, see Part II, section D, below.

33. The U. S. Secretary of State Clayton wrote to Tocqueville to express his discontent caused by the actions of the French Minister to Washington, Guillaume-Tell Poussin, and to inform him that he refused to communicate with the latter. In turn, Tocqueville delayed the reception of William C. Rives as U.S. Minister in Paris. For more information, see the documents translated in Part II, section D, below.

34. Tocqueville refers here to the Poussin Affair. For more details, see Part II, section D, below.

35. A reference to the American press coverage of the Poussin Affair.

36. "*La Presse* of 8 and 10 September" (note of W. W. Mann).

37. Moreover (in French, in the original text).

38. This letter, originally written in French, is only partially dated. It is likely that it was written in December 1849. George Sumner was the brother of Senator Charles Sumner; also see Appendix 1.

39. Jean-Gérard Lacuée de Cessac (1752–1841), prominent military officer and French politician, and member of the French Academy. On December 23, 1841, Tocqueville was elected member of the French Academy filling in the position vacated by Cessac's death.

40. Viscount Gérard de Cessac (1812–1885) was sent to St. Louis by his mother-in-law, the Countess de Montesquiou, to try to help her sons, Raymond and

Gonsalve de Montesquiou, who were accused of having killed Theronk Barnum. Upon the recommendation of Edward Everett, Gérard de Cessac chose a very able lawyer, Edward Bates (a prominent official under the Lincoln administration), who managed to convince the jury to acquit Raymond and to prove that his brother Gonsalve was mentally ill. Also see Everett's letter (January 8, 1850), Part I, section B, below.

41. Reference to the diplomatic tensions between France and the United States in the summer of 1849 as a result of the acrimonious exchanges between the French Minister to the U.S., Guillaume-Tell Poussin, and the U. S. Secretary of State John M. Clayton. For more information, see the diplomatic exchanges translated in Part II, section D, below.

42. Tocqueville's five-month tenure as Minister of Foreign Affairs ended on November 23, 1849.

43. "Means" (in French, in the original text).

44. "Credit" (in French, in the original text).

45. André-Ernest Olivier Sain de Bois-le-Comte became the Chief of Staff of Alphonse de Lamartine in 1848. He was appointed French Minister in Turin (1848–1849) and Washington (1849–1851), as a replacement for Guillaume-Tell Poussin, For more information, see *OC*, VII, 132, n. 63. Also see Tocqueville, *OC* (Pléiade) III, 260.

46. On the Poussin affair, see Part II, section D, below.

47. In this original letter, Everett used an incorrect spelling for Bois-le-Comte's name. We silently corrected it (see previous note above).

48. A reference to the intense controversies that led to the Compromise of 1850, when Henry Clay designed a series of resolutions intended to resolve divisions over the admission of California to statehood, the boundary of the state of Texas, the abolition of slavery in the District of Columbia, and the constitutional right to recover slaves. Although, Clay's compromise was ultimately unsuccessful, it provided the basis for a temporary settlement that endured for almost a decade. See Currie, *Constitution in Crisis*, 157–94; Wilentz, *The Rise of American Democracy*, 637–71. On Henry Clay, see Walker Howe, *The Political Culture of the American Whigs*, 123–49.

49. Nassau Senior's article on Lamartine was published in the *Edinburgh Review*.

50. Prominent lawyer from Albany, NY.

51. Sedgwick was frequently in ill health. During this trip, he met Tocqueville on two occasions: at the home of Tocqueville's friend, Rivet, and in Sorrento, Italy.

52. It is unclear what Bancroft refers to in this paragraph. The two letters from Tocqueville to Bancroft from this period (December 12, 1849 and February 15, 1850, Part I, section B, above) that have been preserved contain no reference to Louis-Napoléon.

53. For a biographical note of Henry Philip Tappan (1805–1881), see Appendix 1.

54. Reference to Henry Jarvis Raymond (1820–1869), Speaker of the Legislative Assembly of the State of New York. Mann and Raymond wanted to attend the debates of July 14 and 19, 1851 on the revision of the French constitution. For more information, see Mann's two letters of June 28 and July 12, 1851.

55. In the Bonnel copy, "have."

56. Unclear meaning in the Bonnel copy.

57. W. W. Mann was an American journalist who was based in Paris. His political views brought him in close contact with the Whig circles of New York. For more information, see *OC*, VII, 134–35.

58. See Tocqueville's letter (July 2, 1851), Part I, section B, above.

59. "Chief-Usher" of the Assembly of Deputies (in French, in the original text).

60. There is a repetition ("have have") is in Mann's original letter that was silently corrected.

61. Jean-Jacques Ampère (1800–1864) was the son of the famous physicist André-Marie Ampère (1775–1836) and a close friend of Tocqueville. Their correspondence was published in volume XI of Tocquevillle's *Œuvres Complètes* (Paris: Gallimard, 1970). Ampère's account of his eight-month American voyage was published as *Promenade en Amérique*, 2 vols. (1855). Chapters of the book were first published in the *Revue des Deux Mondes*. For more information on Ampère's view of America, see Jennings, "French Visions of America: From Tocqueville to the Civil War," in *America through European Eyes: British and French Reflections on the New World from the Eighteenth Century to the Present*, eds. Aurelian Craiutu and Jeffrey C. Isaac (University Park, PA: Pennsylvania State University Press, 2009), 161–84.

62. Everett's two-volume *Orations and Speeches* were published in 1850. For more information, see Everett's letter (March 15, 1852), Part I, section B, below.

63. A reference to the probability that Louis-Napoléon would seek to maintain his hold on executive power. The constitution of the Second Republic stipulated that the President was not eligible to stand for a second term of office.

64. After the Mexican War, the proponents of the annexation of Cuba found strong support from many American groups. This policy was endorsed not only by those who had previously supported the annexation of Texas and California, but also by those who had set their eyes on Cuba's rich natural resources and fertile territory. Most notably, it was Southern political leaders, interested in getting access to new slave regions, who were interested in the annexation of Cuba. In 1848, the U. S. made an offer of one hundred million dollars for Cuba, which was bluntly rejected by the Spanish government. Three years later, General Narciso Lopez attempted a flawed military expedition that worried many European leaders. On April 23, 1852, the English and French ministers to the U. S. asked the American government to join them in a tripartite guarantee of Cuba to Spain, an offer declined by President Fillmore later that year. In 1854, President Pierce asked the U. S. Ministers to Spain, England, and France (James Buchanan, John Young Mason, and Pierre Soulé) to adopt measures for concert of action in aid of the negotiations in Madrid. The three ministers assembled at Ostend on October 8, 1854 and later adjourned to Aix-la-Chapelle, where they completed the so-called *Ostend Manifesto*, which was published in the European and American press at that time (it was reproduced in *House Executive Documents*, 33 Cong, 2 Sess., X, 127–36). The "Ostend Manifesto" proclaimed the right of the United States to seize Cuba if Spain refused to sell it and expressed confidence that the United States ought, if possible, to purchase Cuba with as little delay as possible. The document also claimed that the purchase of Cuba would be in the national interest of the United States. For more information, see Wilentz, *The Rise of American Democracy*, 697–99.

65. Everett's spelling is again incorrect; the correct spelling is Bois-le-Comte.

66. "Intimately linked" (in French, in the original text).
67. The fragment from Vattemare's letter (written in French) is inserted into the English text. Here is original text: "J'avais à cœur de confirmer les espérances qu'il m'a été si agréable de vous donner, du côté de l'Académie des Sciences Morales et Politiques, par ma lettre du 19 octobre 1851. J'ai vu pour cela M. Guizot et M. Alexis de Tocqueville, tous les deux donnent les dispositions les plus favorables. Le premier, qui se souvient avec plaisir d'avoir été votre collègue à Londres, appuiera votre candidature de tout son pouvoir. Il me l'a déclaré avec un empressement qui marque sa considération pour votre caractère autant que pour votre talent. Le second m'a chargé de vous demander la liste exacte et complète des ouvrages que vous avez publiés, afin de déterminer la section de l'Académie à laquelle vous appartiendrez. Je dis *appartiendrez*; car le succès n'est pas douteux. La plus prochaine vacance, j'en ai la conviction, vous ouvrira les portes de notre Institut. Laissez-moi vous recommander, Monsieur, de m'envoyer sans retard, la liste qu'attend M. de Tocqueville."
68. "At the [Ministry of] Foreign Affairs" (in French, in the original text).
69. "Of good faith" (in French, in the original text).
70. "Occasional pieces" (in French, in the original text).
71. The *North American Review* was founded in 1815 in Boston and is the oldest literary review in the U. S. It was published continuously until 1940; a new series was founded in 1964. The list of its editors and contributors included such prominent names as John Adams, George Bancroft, Edward Everett, Jared Sparks, George Ticknor, and Daniel Webster. For more information, see Walker Howe, *What Hath God Wrought*, 627–29; Welter, *The Mind of America, 1820–1860*, 283–94. The connection between the *North American Review* and Tocqueville's American friends from Boston is examined in Tyack, *George Ticknor and the Boston Brahmins*, 108, 122.
72. Edward Everett, "De Beaumont and de Tocqueville on the Penitentiary System," *The North American Review*, 37: 80 (July 1833): 117–38; and "De Tocqueville's *Democracy in America*," *The North American Review*, 43: 92 (July 1836): 178–206.
73. Harvard University.
74. "Long and exacting" (in French, in the original text).
75. "At the ballot" (in French, in the original text).
76. Alexandre Vattemare (1796–1864) was a well-known French ventriloquist and traveler who created the first system for the international exchange of publications. His initiatives inspired such later exchanges as those of the Smithsonian Institution or the Brussels Convention. He visited the United States twice (1839–1841 and 1847–1849). One of his most impressive achievements was the creation of the American Library in Paris, which by 1860 contained some 14,000 volumes, for the most part official publications of the federal government, states or cities of the early United States. Vattemare was also instrumental in the creation of the Boston Public Library.
77. "Of good faith" (in French, in the original text).
78. Lajos Kossuth (1802–1894) was briefly President of Hungary in 1849 after the Hungarian Declaration of Independence. After the Russian invasion, Kossuth was forced to flee the country. He traveled to the United States where he was warmly received as a champion of freedom. As Minister of Foreign Affairs,

Tocqueville was involved in discussions about how Kossuth and his colleagues might avoid imprisonment in Russia.

79. "Exploit" (in French, in the original text).

80. Sedgwick's letter was originally written in French.

81. Reference to George Bancroft's multi-volume *History of the United States* (10 volumes, 1834–74; revised into 6 volumes by the author in 1876 and 1883–85). Bancroft's *History* enjoyed great reputation a century and a half ago, when it was seen as a landmark in American historiography. As Daniel Walker Howe pointed out (*What Hath God Wrought*, 704), "Bancroft's history portrayed his country fulfilling a providential destiny as an example of human liberty." Anti-British and intensely patriotic (the motto of the first volume, adapted from Berkeley, was "Westward the star of empire takes its way"), the *History* also showed Bancroft's strong commitment to democratic principles and institutions.

82. Sedgwick's journals (held at the Massachusetts Historical Society, Ms N-851) record that he visited Tocqueville on both these occasions. Of the first, he records that Tocqueville "received me very cordially" and "spoke very frankly of French politics." He was similarly well received in France.

83. In a letter to his mother, dated December 7, 1851, Sedgwick wrote: "We have had Ampère 4 or 5 times to pass the night. I like him very much. He seems to enjoy his life here. He spends it pretty much in the Society Library & undoubtedly intends to make a book on us. He is an estimable and highly educated man" (Massachusetts Historical Society, Ms N-851).

84. The Bonnel copy is unclear and contains a transcription error ("J'ai vu savez").

85. Bancroft's tenure as U. S. Minister in London ended after the election of Zachary Taylor as President. Bancroft returned from London to New York and resumed his public role after 1854, when he became influential in the Democratic Party.

86. "But who knows it?" (in Italian, in the original text).

87. This letter has been lost.

88. "At the waters of Hamburg, close to Franfurt-on-Mein" (in French, in the original text).

89. This letter has been lost.

90. The Constitution of the Second Republic forbade two consecutive terms for the President of the French Republic. In June 1851, 233 deputies signed a petition calling for the revision of the constitution. On June 25, Tocqueville was elected *rapporteur* of the committee that was supposed to propose amendments to the Constitution. He presented his report on July 8, 1851 (see *OC*, III: 3, 433–53) and debates on the amendments followed. The final vote was 446 in favor and 278 against, short of the majority of three-quarters needed to pass the proposed amendments (for more information, see Gargan, *Alexis de Tocqueville: The Critical Years 1848–1851*, 196–226). A new government was formed in late October 1851, almost a month before the *coup d'état* of December 2, and the Assembly resumed its deliberations on November 4. Louis-Napoléon was planning a coup followed by a new constitution to be approved by universal suffrage. To this effect, he wanted the Assembly to repeal the law of May 31, 1850 that limited universal suffrage. The text of the law can be found in *Les Constitutions et les principales lois politiques de la France depuis 1789*, eds. L. Duguit, H. Monnier, R. Bonnard (Paris: Librairie Générale de Droit et de Jurisprudence, 1952), 242–45. The Assembly rejected the abrogation of the Law passed on May 31, 1851; some deputies

even went so far as to propose a bill authorizing the Assembly to summon the army. Tocqueville and Beaumont were among the protesting deputies who were prevented from meeting at the Bourbon Palace and decided to meet at the town hall of the 10th arrondissement in Paris to vote for the deposition of Louis-Napoléon. They were arrested there on the morning of December 2, 1851. Tocqueville was transported to Vincennes and released on the evening of December 3; Beaumont was freed a day later. See Tocqueville's own account of these events, originally published in *The Times* of London, in Tocqueville, *Selected Letters on Politics and Society*, 266–78.

91. For more information about the genesis of *The Old Regime and the Revolution*, see Tocqueville's letter to Louis de Kergorlay (December 15, 1850) in Tocqueville, *Selected Letters on Politics and Society*, 252–58; and Gannett, *Tocqueville Unveiled*, 15–38.

92. Reference to Napoléon III's *coup d'état* of December 2, 1851.

93. The text of the Constitution approved by the people on December 20–21, 1851 and promulgated by Louis-Napoléon Bonaparte on January 14, 1852 can be found in *Les Constitutions et les principales lois politiques de la France depuis 1789*, 245–54. According to Article III of the Constitution, the President was elected for ten years and was responsible directly to the people. He enjoyed extensive rights including the right to appeal directly to the people and to nullify the laws passed by the Assembly. The Senate consisted of 80 members appointed for life by the President; the other chamber – *Corps législatif* – was elected by universal vote every six years by a uni-nominal system. The local mayors and the presidents of general councils were appointed by the government. The constitutional text was complemented by the *Décret organique pour l'élection des députés au Corps législatif* (February 2, 1852), containing more details about voting procedures and eligibility requirements.

94. This important letter is available only as Bonnel copy; unfortunately, the copy has many missing words and is difficult to read.

95. Léon de Malleville (1803–1879), prominent French lawyer and politician, who served as Minister of the Interior for a very short period (December 20–29, 1849) and was later elected senator under the Third Republic (1875–1879).

96. The first entire paragraph of this letter was written by George Sumner in French. Here is the original text: "Je vous écris pour vous rappeler votre promesse de me répondre. Dites-moi je vous en prie où en est la France? Etes-vous au beau milieu de l'Empire, restez-vous République? Ou bien auriez-vous une restauration de la Monarchie Constitutionnelle? Cette dernière me semble à moi la moins favorable de toutes les solutions. Grâce à vos Léon de Mallevilles, à vos Thiers, et *tutti quanti* vous avez perdu la Constitution de 48, et je craindrai fort que la nation ne soit pas reconnaissante envers le parti qui, plus que tout autre, a amené la situation actuelle. Mais vous me direz vous-même ce qu'il en est de tout cela."

97. Illegible word (Bonnel's note).

98. Illegible word (Bonnel's note).

99. Illegible word (Bonnel's note).

100. Illegible word (Bonnel's note).

101. Illegible word (Bonnel's note).

102. Bonnel has this word crossed out.

Notes to Pages 135–138

103. Illegible word (Bonnel's note).
104. "Long live the Republic!" (in French, in the original text).
105. Winfield Scott (1786–1866) was a U.S. Army general, diplomat, and presidential candidate of the Whig Party in the 1852 presidential elections. After he won his party's nomination against the incumbent President, Millard Fillmore, Scott lost to Franklin Pierce, the candidate of the Democratic Party.
106. Illegible word (Bonnel's note).
107. Illegible word (Bonnel's note).
108. Illegible word (Bonnel's note).
109. Illegible word (Bonnel's note).
110. This prediction proved to be incorrect. The candidate of the Free Soil Party, John P. Hale of New Hampshire, polled only 155,000 votes. Pierce won 254 electoral votes while Scott won 27.
111. Senator Charles Sumner.
112. Two illegible words (Bonnel's note).
113. Illegible word (Bonnel's note).
114. Illegible word (Bonnel's note).
115. Illegible word (Bonnel's note). Probably "letter."
116. "My second country" (in French, in the original text).
117. Illegible word (Bonnel's note).
118. Illegible word (Bonnel's note).
119. "Let me know what to respond to them" (in French in the original text).
120. "Throw it into the mail without being franked and it will reach me in 15 days. Farewell! I shall be happy to receive news from you" (in French, in the original text).
121. N. W. Beckwith was an American businessman (working for Russell and Co.) involved in commerce with China. See Appendix 1.
122. The reason was the censorship imposed by Napoléon III's regime.
123. Alexis Piron (1689–1773) was a distinguished poet elected to the French Academy in 1753. Louis XV refused to ratify his election because of a satirical poem Piron had composed a few years before.
124. Henry St. John, Viscount Bolingbroke (1678–1751), was a prominent English statesman and political writer, head of the Tory opposition to Robert Walpole's Whig government. For an analysis of Bolingbroke's political thought, see Isaac Kramnick, *Bolingbroke and His Circle* (Cambridge: Harvard University Press, 1968).
125. Loiret takes its source in a floral garden of 35 hectares located south of Orleans. Bolingbroke lived happily there in the 1720s, cultivating his garden and studying history. On this topic, see Kenneth Woodbridge, "Bolingbroke's Chateau of La Source," *Garden History*, 4: 3 (Fall 1976): 50–64.
126. Tocqueville's parliamentary career ended abruptly on December 2, 1851, when he was arrested following his protest against the *coup d'état* of Louis-Napoléon. For more information, see Tocqueville's own account originally published anonymously in *The Times* of London, December 11, 1851, reprinted in Tocqueville, *Selected Letters on Politics and Society*, 266–78. See also Jardin, *Tocqueville: A Biography*, 459–61; Brogan, *Tocqueville: A Life*, 502–24; Gargan, *Alexis de Tocqueville: The Critical Years, 1848–1851*, 227–50; Watkins, *Alexis de Tocqueville and the Second Republic*, 537–70.

127. Charles de Rémusat (1797–1875) was a scion of a distinguished family. A gifted writer and politician who became close to the French Doctrinaires (Guizot, Royer-Collard, Barante), Rémusat emerged as one of the most brilliant representatives of the young generation that came of age around 1820. He published numerous articles in *Le Globe* from 1824 to 1830 and was elected member of the French Academy in 1846. Rémusat was the author of many important books, including *L'Angleterre au XVIIIe siècle* (1856), *Passé et Présent* (1847), *Politique libérale* (1860), *Histoire de la philosophie en Angleterre* (1875). His five-volume *Mémoires de ma vie* are essential reading for any scholar of nineteenth-century French political thought.

128. Jules-Armand Dufaure (1798–1881), prominent lawyer and French politician, member of the Chamber of Deputies. In 1846, Dufaure allied himself with Tocqueville, Corcelle, Rivet, and Billault to create the so-called "Young Left." During the Second Republic, he sat on the Committee that drafted the Constitution and was briefly Minister of Interior under Cavaignac. In 1851, he voted against the revision of the Constitution. During the Second Empire he returned to his profession as lawyer. In 1863, Dufaure was elected member of the French Academy. Under the Third Republic, he became Minister of Justice and President of the Council (of Ministers) in 1876, a position he held until late 1877.

129. "Here are quite a few questions" (in French, in the original text).

130. Henriette Gertrud Walpurgis Sontag (1806–1854), one of the best German sopranos of her time. She made her debut in 1821 in Paris and moved to Vienna later. In 1852 she toured America. Marietta Alboni (1823–1894), Italian contralto, achieved success at *La Scala* in the early 1840s. She also performed in the United States in 1852.

131. For more information on Webster, see Walker Howe, *The Political Culture of the American Whigs*, 212–25.

132. After the death of President Zachary Taylor in 1850, William Rufus King became the thirteenth Vice-President of the United States in the administration of Millard Fillmore. King had previously served in the Senate and had been appointed by President Tyler as U. S. Minister to France between 1844 and 1846. His main mission was to convince France not to interfere with the U. S. intention to annex Texas. He died in April 1853.

133. Greene was Tocqueville's banker in Paris.

134. Tocqueville received a *honoris causa* diploma from Harvard in 1852.

135. For Spark's response, see his letter to Tocqueville (June 13, 1853), Part I, section C, below.

136. Reference to Lord Mahon's criticism of Sparks's edition of Washington's letters. In volume VI of his *History of England* published in 1851, Mahon claimed that Sparks deliberately left out a number of important documents. The latter responded in *A Reply to the Strictures of Lord Mahon and Others on the Mode of Editing the Writings of Washington* (1852).

137. *Vie, correspondance et écrits de Washington, publiés d'après l'édition américaine, et précédés d'une introduction sur l'influence et le caractère de Washington dans la révolution des États-Unis de l'Amérique* (Paris, 1839–1840).

138. This letter was not included in *OC*, VII. It was first published, along with an English translation, by Robert T. Gannett in the *Harvard Library Bulletin*, New

Series, 14: 3 (Fall 2003): 10. The current translation is by the editors of this volume. We would like to thank Dr. Gannett for having brought this letter to our attention and to the Houghton Library for permission to publish it.

139. Harvard University.
140. The first signs of Tocqueville's tuberculosis had appeared in 1850.

C. Letters: 1853–1856

1. The letter was written in French by Sedgwick.
2. Sedgwick was appointed President of the Board of Directors of this project. In the memoir assembled by Sedgwick's mother after his death, she commented: "With his imagination excited by all he had recently seen in Europe and animated by the idea of stimulating the genius of his country, the scheme commended itself to his taste and patriotism." Sedgwick believed the building to be "one of the most beautiful sites of the world" (Massachusetts Historical Society Library, Ms. N. 851).
3. This letter was *not* included in *OC*, VII. Its presumed date (May 8, 1853) is uncertain. The original as well as the English translation can be found at the Beinecke Rare Book and Manuscript Library, Yale University. The current translation is by the editors of this volume.
4. On March 31, 1853, Louis de Corn killed Eugène Melville, who had accused him of having had an affair with his wife. He was found guilty and was condemned to two years and ten months in prison.
5. Tocqueville was then renting a property owned by Rivet.
6. See Tocqueville's letter (December 11, 1852) to Harvard University, Part I, section B, above.
7. See the previous note about Kossuth, above as well as the reference to Kossuth in Everett's letter (May 11,1852), Part I, section B, above.
8. On Everett and the political thought of the American Whigs, see Walker Howe, *The Political Culture of the American Whigs*, 70–72, 100–103; Wilentz, *The Rise of American Democracy*, 490. The "politics of Whiggery" is analyzed in Welter, *The Mind of America, 1820–1860*, 190–218.
9. On Francis Kidder (1803–1879), see Appendix 1.
10. *The History of New Ipswich from its first grant in 1736 to the present time* (Boston: 1852).
11. Reference to the economic crises of 1837 and 1841.
12. In June 1853, Tocqueville rented a house in the village of Saint-Cyr-sur-Loire in the valley of the Choisille River, 3 km. from Tours; he stayed there until May 1854. During this time, he received visits from his friends Beaumont, Ampère, Corcelle, and Rivet and conducted daily archival research for *The Old Regime and the Revolution*. In spite of his fragile health, Tocqueville's work schedule was very strict, as he pointed out in a letter (February 1854) to Mrs. Grote: "I rise at half-past five, and work seriously till half-past nine; then dress for dejeuner at ten. I commonly walk half an hour afterward, then set to on some other study – usually of late in the German language – till two p.m., when I go out again and walk for two hours, if weather allows. In the evenings, I read to amuse myself, often reading aloud to Madame de Tocqueville, and go to bed at ten p.m. regularly every night" (quoted in Gannett, *Tocqueville Unveiled*, 81). For

more information about Tocqueville's work at Tours, see Gannett, *Tocqueville Unveiled*, 79–98.

13. Bonnel's note (in the margin): "At the beginning of this letter there is a seven-line annotation written across the page and completely illegible. It seems to be the handwriting of M. Alexis de Tocqueville. The annotation ends with these words : 'to attack Christianity.'"

14. Sedgwick's letter was originally written in French.

15. Illegible word (Bonnel's note).

16. Illegible word (Bonnel's note).

17. According to Bonnel, there are almost two illegible lines that have been crossed out.

18. In his letter of December 1, 1853, Sedgwick expressed his belief that Tocqueville's financial investments in America were sound and predicted that no serious economic crisis would occur in the short-term.

19. Sedgwick asked for some information about the religious wars in France from 1550 to 1600 and wanted some advice on the best ways of obtaining access to French archives.

20. M. de Chabrier and Pierre Cintrat.

21. For a biographical note on Edward Vernon Childe (1804–1861), see Appendix 1. Additional information can be found in *Quelques correspondants de Mr. et Mrs. Childe et de Edward Lee Childe* (Boston, 1912).

22. The older daughter of the Childes, Florence, had run away with an older Polish man, Prince Soltyk. Tocqueville gave Edward V. Childe a letter of introduction to an old friend, Auguste de la Rive. The latter convinced Soltyk to marry the girl and the couple later settled in Galicia. The affair triggered some less than kind comments in Paris.

23. Mary Custis Childe (1841–1867), the youngest daughter of the Childes.

24. Edward Lee Childe (born in 1832), son of the Mildred and Edward Vernon Childe, finally settled in France. For more information, see Appendix 1.

25. Solon Robinson's *Hot Corn* was a sentimental novel published in 1854. The novel was placed in an urban working-class setting, but it remained within Victorian tradition.

26. This is Bonnel's transcription; the correct word might be "Puritanism."

27. This is Bonnel's transcription; the correct word might be "terms."

28. The Kansas–Nebraska Act was passed in 1854. Stephen Douglas proposed that the Kansas and Nebraska territories be divided into two sections and that the Missouri Compromise be repealed, with settlers in each territory freely choosing whether or not to accept slavery. The effects of the Kansas-Nebraska Act were far reaching and had a decisive influence on party politics. Among other things, it contributed to the collapse of the Whig Party and to the emergence of the anti-immigrant and anti-Catholic Know-Nothing Party. At the same time, the Republican Party, which favored keeping slavery out of the new territories, gained strength in northwestern states. The Kansas-Nebraska Act also triggered violent episodes in Kansas leading to clashes between pro- and anti-slavery forces that rushed in to Kansas territory. For more information, see Wilentz, *The Rise of American Democracy*, 671–79, 698–700.

29. The so-called "Missouri Compromise" was an agreement passed in 1820 between the pro-slavery and anti-slavery groups in the United States Congress. It allowed

Missouri to be admitted into the Union as a slave state but prohibited slavery in the former Louisiana Territory north of the parallel 36°30' north. For more information, see Wilentz, *The Rise of American Democracy*, 241–52; Walker Howe, *What Hath God Wrought*, 147–60.

30. Illegible word (Bonnel's note).
31. "Time" according to Bonnel's copy. Most likely a transcription error on Bonnel's part.
32. George Washington Parke Custis (1781–1857) was the adopted son of George Washington. In 1802, he began the construction of Arlington House in Virginia which he wanted to serve as a memorial to his adoptive father. Two years later, he married Mary Lee Fitzhugh and their only surviving daughter, Mary Anna Randolph Custis, married Robert E. Lee in June 1831. Custis was a prominent orator and playwright. Two of his plays, *The Indian Prophecy; or Visions of Glory* (1827) and *Pocahontas or, The Settlers of Virginia* (1830), were published during his life. He also authored *Recollections and Private Memoirs of Washington*, posthumously published by his daughter. For more information, see Sara B. Bears, "The Federalist Career of George Washington Parke Custis," *Northern Virginia Heritage* 8 (Feb. 1986): 15–20; Elizabeth Brown Pryor, *Reading the Man: A Portait of Robert E. Lee Through His Private Letters* (New York: Viking, 2007), esp. 45–53, 126–30, 250–75, 311–14.
33. For a biographical note on Henry D. Gilpin (1801–1860), see Appendix 1.
34. These two letters were lost; we have a letter written by Sedgwick in French, dated December 1, 1853. It is safe to assume that in the lost letters, Sedgwick offered financial advice to Tocqueville with regard to his investments in America.
35. Tocqueville spent some time in Bonn and later in Wildbad (June–September 1854).
36. The Crimean War (1854–1856) between Russia and the coalition consisting of England, France, Turkey, and Sardinia. Most of the battles, including the long siege of Sevastopol (September 25, 1854–September 8, 1855) were conducted in Crimea and the region of Black Sea, but other military conflicts also occurred in western Turkey and the Baltic Sea. The Treaty of Paris in 1856 marked the end of the war and was a blow to Russia's imperial power.
37. Tocqueville was arguably familiar with Madame de Staël's book, *De l'Allemagne* (*On Germany*, 1813), which had made a similar point about the political habits of the Germans.
38. On the Crimean War, see previous note 36 above.
39. Sedgwick's letter was originally written in French. A fragment from this letter in French has previously been published in Tocqueville, *OC*, VII, 158, fn. 2.
40. Illegible word (Bonnel's note).
41. Illegible word (Bonnel's note). Most likely, "expression."
42. Illegible word (Bonnel's note). Most likely, "consideration."
43. This letter was previously translated in Tocqueville, *Selected Letters on Politics and Society*, 310–11. The present translation is ours.
44. Detail reported by Tocqueville to Beaumont in a letter from August 6, 1854. For more information, see Tocqueville, *OC*, VIII: 3, 228–29. There was a major influx of German immigrants to the U. S. between 1852 and 1854.
45. Bonnel crossed out "that."

46. Lieber's letter seems to draw here a parallel between political and constitutional controversies in Kansas and the home rule provision for the Capetown colony in South Africa. According to a note published in *New York Daily Times* on July 22, 1853, "At a meeting at Grahamstown the new Constitution was denounced as the greatest curse which had ever befallen the Colony; that under it the most barbarous of the natives could not only vote, but also become a candidate himself; and that so far as the franchise is concerned, they might as well have been born with black faces. The Cape Monitor in the excess of indignation against the terms of the peace says that in case of further trouble between the Colonists and the Aboriginal chiefs, England will not foot the bill for troops to subjugate, and asks what is to prevent the Assembly from invoking the aid of the French, Dutch, or even Americans." This might be the original affair mentioned by Lieber in his July 1854 letter. We would like to thank Russell L. Hanson for information on this point.

47. Unclear meaning and possibly missing words in the Bonnel copy.

48. Illegible word (Bonnel's note). Most likely, the word is "party."

49. The "Know-Nothing Party" was a nativist American political party that emerged as a popular reaction to the growing number of Irish Catholic immigrants to America in the 1840s and 1850s. It was a short-lived movement, that grew out of a dissatisfaction with the Democrats, who were seen as allies of Irish politicians. The Know-Nothing Party manifested itself mainly from 1854 to 1856 and its membership included mostly middle-class and Protestant citizens. Most of them were later absorbed by the Republican Party in the North. The origin of the "Know-Nothing" term was in the semi-secret nature of the organization of the party. When a member was asked about its activities, he was supposed to reply "I know nothing." The Know-Nothing Party filled the vacuum left by the disappearance of the Whig Party; nonetheless, its demise was equally fast. For more information, see Wilentz, *The Rise of American Democracy*, 681–85, 693–95. On the relations between the emerging Republican Party and the Know-Nothing movement, see Foner, *Free Soil, Free Labor, Free Man*, 226–60.

50. Illegible word (Bonnel's note). The word might be "confidential."

51. The reference is to the Crimean War; see previous note 36 above.

52. In September 1851, Jean-Jacques Ampère, member of the *French Academy*, set out for the United States and returned to France in May 1852. He visited many places that Tocqueville had previously seen as well as a few new cities like Chicago. See Part I, section E, below for extracts from the letters of Tocqueville and Ampère relating to this visit to the U. S. In a letter to Ampère from October 6, 1851, Tocqueville remarked: "I am longing to know in which direction you are going to direct your steps. The United States are so well-known to me and still so present to my mind after twenty years that you will not be able to be anywhere where I cannot follow you in my thoughts" (*OC*, XI, 202–203). By the same token, Tocqueville was intrigued to learn what had changed since his visit in 1831–32, mainly with regard to the effect of the rapid economic growth and unprecedented prosperity on the character of the American people. On Ampère's views of America, see Jennings, "French Visions of America: From Tocqueville to the Civil War," in *America through European Eyes*, eds. Craiutu and Isaac, 161–184.

53. A reference to the political events in Kansas.

54. Sedgwick's letter was originally written in French.
55. Theodore Sedgwick to Harper Brothers

New York n°44 Wall St,
February 11, 1856

Gentlemen,

M. de Tocqueville the author of the "Democracy in America" writes me from France that he is about to publish a work on the French Revolution and desires to make an arrangement for its reappearance translated in this country. He tells me he shall begin to publish the first volume about the 1st of March at Paris but that the times of publishing the other volume is uncertain. And he only wishes now to make a bargain for the first. He does not say whether a translation of the work is to appear in England or not. He says that he will send on the sheets here exclusively to any persons who will assume the translation and publication of the work so as far as possible to prevent competition. He does not state the size of the volume. Be good enough to let me know if you will undertake to have this volume translated here and will also undertake the publications and on what terms. Would you think it best to stereotype it? Be good enough to name the best terms you can. I suppose you will concur with me that M. de Tocqueville's familiar reputation in this country will insure for any work he may write a very considerable sale. If there is any difficulty in finding a translator here adequate for such a work, will you suggest any other mode of arriving at the result? Oblige me by an early answer.

Very Resp[ectfull]y Yours
Illegible signature [Theodore Sedgwick]

Harper Brothers to Theodore Sedgwick

Franklin Square, New-York July 12th 1856

Dear Sir,

In reply to your favour of last evening we beg to say,

1st, We shall be happy to publish M. de Tocqueville's proposed "History of the French Revolution", and to pay to him, or his legal representatives, in the usual way, ten per cent on the Trade Price, on each copy sold of said work.

2nd We will undertake to have the translation made, which, we presume, will cost from one hundred to one hundred and fifty dollars per volume. The cost of the translation, however, we should expect to deduct from the first amount due to M. de T. under this proposition.

Soon after our Mr. J. H. left you yesterday morning, he met with Dr. James, whom you probably know as fully capable of making the translation. He expressed a willingness to undertake it, using his utmost care, for the price to be decided within the limits above named, after he sees the work.

Respectfully your ob[edient]t servants,
Harper and Brothers

(Beinecke Rare Book and Manuscript Library, Yale University, Uncat MSS 324, and Bonnel copy, MS Vault Tocqueville, D II a, Paquet 12, pp. 85–86).

56. Illegible word (Bonnel's note). Possibly, "judging."

57. Missing word (Bonnel's note).

58. Sedgwick's opinions had an important influence on Tocqueville's views. In his letters to his American friends from the 1850s, Tocqueville reiterated some of the points raised by Sedgwick. For example, the Frenchman expressed his deep concern about the deterioration of the American political scene as illustrated by violent campaigns, lawlessness, and violence in the Western territories.

59. The letter was originally written in French.

60. Sedgwick's letter was originally written in French.

61. Sedgwick's letter was originally written in French.

62. "A good part of it" (in Latin, in the original text).

63. This is the only text that Tocqueville published in *The Liberty Bell* in 1856; it was reprinted in *The Liberator*, Boston, April 11, 1856. The original French text (written in 1855) has been lost. Tocqueville wrote this text at the invitation of Maria Weston Chapman (1806–1885), a leading abolitionist. For a biographical note on Chapman, see Appendix 1. Chapmans's letter to Tocqueville is published in Part I, section D, below.

64. *The Old Regime and the Revolution* appeared a month later, on June 19, 1856. It was published by Michel-Lévy Frères.

65. Tocqueville's book contained in total thirty proof sheets.

66. Reference to the peace following the Crimean War (1854–1856). France emerged stronger from the war and benefited from the alliance with England. The defeat of Russia and the alliance with England gave France increased authority in Europe and eventually emboldened her to declare war against Austria in the summer of 1859, after Napoléon III made a secret deal with Cavour, the Prime Minister of Piedmont.

67. Emperor Napoléon III.

68. Alphonse de Lamartine (1790–1869), French poet, historian, and statesman. His many books include the *History of the Girondists* (1847) which brought him a wide popularity. After the Revolution of February 1848, Lamartine became an influential member of the provisional government and occupied for some time the position of Minister of Foreign Affairs. He was also a presidential candidate in 1849. Louis-Napoléon's *coup d'etat* of December 2, 1851 put an end to Lamartine's political career. He returned to literature and history for the remainder of his life (he published several historical works such as the *History of the Revolution of 1848*, *The History of the Restoration*, *The History of Turkey*, *The History of Russia*).

69. "Trustee" or "authorized representative" (in French, in the original text).

70. The *Post Scriptum* was originally written in French.

71. Joseph-Dominique-Aldebert Pineton, Viscount de Chambrun (1821–1891), author of *Nos historiens, Guizot, Tocqueville, Thiers* (Paris, 1889).

72. Sedgwick's letter was originally written in French.

73. Illegible word (Bonnel's note). It is likely that Bonnel's transcription contains a few errors here.

74. Allusion to the tense relations between England and the United States following Washington's recognition of William Walker's government in Nicaragua (1856) and the revocation of Crampton, the English ambassador to the U. S., who had protested against the decision taken in Washington, DC.

75. The peace following the Crimean War.
76. *Lettres de marque* were issued by governments to an agent, allowing the latter to seize and destroy the personal effects of an enemy or the property of a hostile government. In theory, this practice ceased with the signing of the Treaty of Paris in 1856. The U. S. was not a signatory to the Treaty of Paris and announced that it would not abide by it.
77. Hervé de Tocqueville (1772–1856) died on June 9, 1856. In his partly published *Mémoires*, he recounted his acts and movements during the French Revolution. He joined Louis XVI's Constitutional Guard and was lucky enough to escape the guillotine (he was scheduled to be beheaded shortly after 9 Thermidor). It was the fall of Robespierre that ultimately saved his life.
78. Napoléon-Eugène-Louis-Jean-Joseph (1856–1879), son of Napoléon III.
79. Mrs. Childe died in June. Tocqueville wrote a moving portrait of Mrs. Childe that was published in *OC*, VII, 249–51.
80. In English, in the original text.
81. The first print sold out by the end of August 1856.
82. Reviews of the book appeared in *Le Constitutionnel*, *Le Siècle*, and *Le Journal des Débats* (June–July 1856).
83. This letter has been lost.
84. The Childes returned to the United States in the Fall of 1856 and eventually settled in Baltimore. Edward Vernon Childe later returned to Europe.
85. Sedgwick's letter was originally written in French.
86. Given the date of this letter, it must be read in conjunction with Tocqueville's letter to Sedgwick of July 1856. It is likely that the metaphorical "baptism" mentioned by Sedgwick refers to the publication of Tocqueville's book in America, with a planned foreword that was supposed to be written by Sedgwick himself.
87. In English, in the original text
88. "Man is a robust child," a phrase used by Hobbes in the preface to his book, *De Cive*.
89. Lieber taught at South Carolina College in Columbia S.C. before moving to Columbia University in New York. In reality, Lieber's letters to Tocqueville from South Carolina contain sarcastic and critical observations about life in the South.
90. Sedgwick's letter was originally written in French.
91. See Tocqueville's letter (August 29, 1856), Part I, section C, above.
92. The Sedgwick family home was in Stockbridge, Mass. Sedgwick's letters to his mother further testify to the immense grief caused by his wife's illness and subsequent death.
93. In English, in the original text.
94. "*Inter arena silicit*" (in the Bonnel copy); most likely a transcription error on Bonnel's part. "Inter arenas" means "among the sands," or generally "in sand (desert)," which would give some idea of "flint-stone among the sands," an image of futility (for "inter arenas silices)." Another possibility would be "inter arenas sulcat" ("he is plowing among the sands"), another image of futility. We would like to thank Owen Crawer for his expert advice on this issue.
95. This letter has been lost.
96. M. Dosseur, who was in charge of Tocqueville's private affairs.

97. This package, that has been lost or destroyed, might have contained the correspondence between Tocqueville and Mrs. Childe. No letter between the two has been retrieved.
98. Sedgwick also made this point in his letter of September 19, 1856.
99. Prosper de Mérimée (1803–1870), prominent French writer, member of the French Academy (elected in 1842), best known for his novella *Carmen* that became the basis of the opera Carmen. Mérimée had been a regular visitor to the salon of the Childes in Paris.
100. There were two different translations of the book published in England and the United States.

D. Letters: 1857–1859

1. This letter has been lost.
2. Greene & Co. was Tocqueville's banker.
3. Reference to the death of Sedgwick's wife, after a long illness.
4. Reference to the election of President Buchanan as the fifteenth President of the United States (1857–1861). A native of Pennsylvania, Buchanan served as diplomat, Senator in Congress, and as Secretary of State in the Polk administration before winning the White House in 1856 in an election against John C. Frémont and Millard Fillmore. Plagued by strong controversies around the issue of slavery, Buchanan's administration was unable to prevent the country from sliding toward civil war.
5. *The Old Regime and the Revolution*.
6. Sedgwick's letter was originally written in French.
7. Franklin Pierce, the fourteenth President of the United States (1853–1857).
8. On Douglas's role in securing the repeal, see David M. Potter, *The Impending Crisis, 1848–1861* (New York: Harper, 1976), 156–77.
9. At the Convention held in Cincinnati, the southern delegations first backed Pierce and then Douglas, largely because of their role in passing the Kansas-Nebraska Act. On the seventeenth ballot, James Buchanan was chosen, in part because he was thought to be sympathetic to southern views.
10. James Buchanan was American Minister to Great Britain at the time.
11. President Buchanan was a native of Pennsylvania.
12. The Bonnel copy incorrectly ends the letter at this point and places the remainder of the text in the letter written by Sedgwick to Tocqueville on December 6, 1857.
13. President Buchanan.
14. Prior to being elected president, Frémont had been a famous explorer of the American West.
15. The letter abruptly ends here.
16. The Buchanan administration.
17. Deseret was originally proposed as a name for the state of Utah. The Latter Day Saints-organized territory petitioned for statehood as the state of Deseret in 1849–1850, but the petition was rejected by the U. S. Congress. Deseret (honey bee) is a term originally derived from the Book of Mormon.
18. In 1856, the incumbent President, Franklin Pierce, was defeated in his effort to gain the nomination of the Democratic Party; the delegates voted for James Buchanan.

19. The editor John W. Forney (1817–1881) was an early supporter of James Buchanan, but upon his election as president, the latter failed to deliver on expected patronage and was unable to secure a political position for Forney. Forney subsequently shifted his political allegiance; he served as Secretary of State between 1861 and 1868.

20. Simon Cameron was elected to the Senate in 1857.

21. "Superfluous" (in French, in the original text).

22. "Scholars" (in French, in the original text).

23. "Colleague" (in French, in the original text).

24. Count Agenor de Gasparin (1810–1871) was one of the first investigators of table turning and telekinetic movements. His most famous book, *Des Tables tournantes, du surnaturel en general, et des esprits*, was published in 1854.

25. Probably a pun on Childe's part.

26. The real meaning of Childe's remark about Washington is unclear.

27. Most likely, the Duchess de Rauzan.

28. Edward Lee and Mary Childe.

29. Jean-Charles Rivet (1800–1872), prominent French politician and friend of Tocqueville, member of the Chamber of Deputies (1839–1846), the National Assembly (1848–1849), and the *Conseil d'État* (until December 1851).

30. Childe's letter was originally written in French.

31. Spanish ceder from which cigar boxes were made.

32. Missing words (Bonnel's note).

33. M. Dosseur.

34. It is worth pointing out that Tocqueville himself had married an English woman, Mary Mottley.

35. In English, in the original text.

36. Grote's *History of Greece*; see previous note about Grote above.

37. This was Sedgwick's first trip to Europe after his wife's death.

38. The title of Sedgwick's book was *A Treatise on the Rules which Govern the Interpretation and Application of Statutory and Constitutional Law* (New York, 1857). For Tocqueville's review of Sedgwick's book, see Part II, Section E, below.

39. The colleague finally chosen by Tocqueville for this task was François Mignet.

40. For a biographical note on Charles Sumner (1811–1874), see Appendix 1.

41. Presumably, an entry ticket to attend the meetings of the Institute of France.

42. Writer of a biography of Roger B. Taney, Chief Justice of the U. S. author of the famous Dred-Scott decision.

43. James Louis Petigru (1789–1863), lawyer, Unionist, and politician, born in South Carolina. He graduated from South Carolina College and became a prominent lawyer in Charleston, representing the disadvantaged, imprisoned paupers, free blacks, and abused women. For more details, see *American National Biography*, eds. John A. Garraty and Mark C. Carnes, Vol. 17 (New York: Oxford University Press, 1999), 399–401.

44. Begun in the 1840s, the project to lay an underwater Atlantic cable was not finally completed until the end of the 1860s, although the first successful telegraph line linking Ireland with Newfoundland operated briefly in 1858. For many, the completion of a transatlantic cable was the greatest technological achievement of the age.

45. For more information on Prescott's works, see Appendix 1.

46. Letter originally written in English; the English version was published in *OC*, VII, 199–200. Tocqueville was elected honorary member of the Massachusetts Historical Society on May 14, 1857.
47. Reference to Tocqueville's letter of April 13, 1857.
48. Tocqueville left for England on June 19 and returned on July 24, 1857.
49. For more detail on Tocqueville's stay in England, see Brogan, *Tocqueville: A Life*, 599–607. In London, Tocqueville was able only to study some diplomatic exchanges from 1789 to 1793.
50. Molière's *Tartuffe*, V, 6.
51. The content of the package is unknown. It might have contained some of the letters that Tocqueville had sent to Mrs. Childe.
52. Paul-Henri-Emmanuel Odon de Pins (1808–1882) was a close friend of the Childes in Paris.
53. Claire de Durfort de Duras, Duchess de Rauzan (1797–1863), was a close friend of the Childes in Paris.
54. Louis-Marie Gustave Dupuy de Belvèze (1809–1886).
55. Adolphe de Circourt and Anastasie de Klustine. Tocqueville's correspondence with the Circourts was published in *OC*, XVIII.
56. Susan Ridley Sedgwick (1838–1872) was the daughter of Theodore Sedgwick. This letter and the *Post-Scriptum* were originally written in French.
57. Theodore Sedgwick had fallen ill with pleurisy.
58. As Françoise Mélonio pointed out (in *OC*, VII, 206. fn. 2), Tocqueville did not originally include any American names on the initial list of the persons that were supposed to receive *The Old Regime and the Revolution*.
59. In March 1857, the Supreme Court had delivered judgment in the case of *Dred Scott v. Sandford*, deciding that a slave from Missouri was not allowed to sue in a federal court as a citizen. If the South was elated by this decision, it caused great anger in the North and was taken to indicate that President Buchanan and the Supreme Court had conspired to extend slavery throughout the entire country.
60. The Duchess de Rauzan held a famous Parisian *salon* where she received many friends of Tocqueville. She was a close friend of the Childes. For more information, see Jardin, *Tocqueville: A Biography*, 378.
61. Post Office.
62. President James Buchanan. The following sentence was added above the line here: "to do or direct all"; it is unclear if the addition was made by Childe or someone else.
63. Lewis Cass served as U. S. Secretary of State from March 6, 1857 to December 14, 1860.
64. James M. Wayne (1790–1867), U. S. Supreme Court Justice (1835–1867).
65. The three sons of Tancrède de Hauteville conquered much of the southern Italian peninsula, including Sicily, toward the end of the eleventh century, making them among the strongest of Christian monarchs.
66. This sentence was added by Chapman in the margin.
67. Tocqueville never sent another text to *Liberty Bell*. His letter was subsequently republished, along with those of other French writers, in *Letters on American Slavery* (Boston: American Anti – Slavery Society: 1860), 8.
68. The legislative elections were held in June 1857. In spite of the victory of the governing coalition, the opposition managed to make its voice heard, especially in the capital.

69. Revolts by the indigenous Indian population against the English broke out in May 1857; they were occasionally accompanied by massacres.
70. The former address of the Childes in Paris.
71. On Tocqueville's views on India, see Alexis de Tocqueville, *Œuvres*, I (Pléiade), 959–1080. Most of Tocqueville's notes comment on the English administration of India, but a few observations deal with religion and local politics in India as well.
72. Perhaps an error on Beckwith's part; the correct word might be "but."
73. Reference to an event in 1856 concerning greased cartridges for the Enfield rifles used by the Indian Army. This aroused religious passions among Muslim and Hindus because the offending grease used on the cartridges was either of pig or cow fat. The touching of the grease was seen as offensive by Muslims and Hindus alike. The following year, the Indian mutiny broke out.
74. A national personification of Great Britain, John Bull is usually described as endowed with common sense and loyal patriotism. He is portrayed as a solid man, wearing a Union Jack waist coat and he is often accompanied by a bulldog.
75. See Douglas Hurd, *The Arrow Wars: An Anglo-Chinese Confusion, 1856–60* (New York: Macmillan: 1967).
76. James Bruce, 8th Earl of Elgin, 1811–1863, British statesman, appointed governor-general of Canada in 1846, sent as special envoy to China in 1856, after the seizure of the "Arrow" by the Governor Yeh plunged England into a second war with China, known as the "Arrow War" of 1856. Canton was occupied by British and French troops and an ultimatum sent to the Governor Yeh on December 12, 1856. Soon afterwards, Elgin sent Yeh as prisoner to India. Nonetheless, Britain's difficulties with China did not end with this incident.
77. Sir John Bowring (1792–1872), English linguist, political economist and writer. In 1849, he was appointed British consul at Canton, and superintendent of trade in China (until 1853). A year later, he was appointed governor of Hong-Kong.
78. Between us (in French, in the original text).
79. Prince Gortschakoff (1789–1866) was an eminent Russian general who fought in Finland in 1809, in the Turkish War in 1810, in the French War 1812–1814, and the Crimean War.
80. General Sandford played a key role in the containment of the New York riots in June 1857. The events were triggered by a decision of the State Legislature to adopt a new charter for the city of New York, many of the provisions of which interfered with the existing rights of officers and were in conflict with the charter already in force.
81. Probably a mistake on Beckwith's part (instead of "more").
82. Ingersoll's letter was originally written in French. On Charles Jared Ingersoll (1782–1862), see Appendix 1.
83. Tocqueville first met Ingersoll on October 14, 1831 in Philadelphia. See George Wilson Pierson, *Tocqueville in America*, 480–82.
84. Given that Tocqueville had ceased to be a member of parliament a few years earlier, it is difficult to know to which report Ingersoll referred in this letter.
85. For a short biographical note on William H. Prescott (1796–1859), see Appendix 1.
86. In 1839, Prescott had sent his book, *History of Ferdinand and Isabella* to Tocqueville. We have a letter from August 31, 1839 to this effect. "Sir, I take the

liberty to request your acceptance of a work written by me, the *History of Ferdinand and Isabella*. I offer it as a most inadequate, but sincere, tribute of admiration for those writings, in which you have so philosophically expounded the principles of our Constitution to Europeans, and so well pointed out to Americans themselves the dangers and abuses, to which their institutions may be exposed by negligence or misconduct. The work which I have the honor to send to you, was published last year, simultaneously in England and my own country. But I have thought the American edition might prove more welcome to you, especially as it is as well executed as the English.

    With sentiments of sincere respect, I have the honor to be, Sir, Your obed[ien]t serv[an]t, Wm. H. Prescott. The parcel is delivered to my correspondents Messrs. B. G. Wainwright and Co., Rue Faub[our]g Poissonière, n° 50, and I shall be obliged by your taking the trouble to advise me, through them, if it reaches you safely" (Beinecke Rare Book and Manuscript Library, Yale University).

87. In Latin, in the original text. This is Prescott's actual transcription which contains an obvious transcription error. Most likely, he played upon a line from Juvenal's tenth satire ("The Vanity of Human Wishes") quoting a wish for long life: "da spatium uitae, multos da, Iuppiter, annos." Special thanks to Owen Cramer for his clarification on this point.

88. Louis-Marie Adolphe, Baron d'Avril (1822–1904).

89. Greene encountered serious financial problems in 1857.

90. Volume Two of *The Old Regime and the Revolution*.

91. The deterioration of mores is an important leitmotif in Tocqueville's correspondence with his American friends from 1855 onward. It must be placed in the larger context of the controversies triggered, among other things, by the Kansas-Nebraska Act and the Supreme Court decision in the Dred Scott affair.

92. In his letter of May 30, 1857, Lieber referred to the favorable opinion expressed by Samuel Tyler and James Louis Petigru, who compared Tocqueville's work to that of Aristotle, Tacitus, and Montesquieu.

93. Dunrobin Castle, the seat of the Earls and Dukes of Sutherland, on the east coast of northern Scotland. The Duke of Sutherland was a friend of Charles Sumner.

94. Built in 1732, Haddo House in Aberdeenshire (Scotland) was designed by William Adam and had been home to the Gordons of Methlick and to Earls and Marquesses of Aberdeen since it was built in 1732. In the nineteenth century, Haddo was home to Britain's Prime Minister, Lord Aberdeen.

95. The castle was built in 1744 by the third Duke of Argyll.

96. Castle Howard, in Yorkshire, is the home of the Howard family, originally built from 1699–1712 for the 3rd Earl of Carlisle.

97. In the Tocqueville archives at Beinecke, DIII f, there is a fragment from Lord Hatherton's journal from 1857 referring to both Tocqueville's and Sumner's visits to England. The entry of July 1 mentions Sumner; the entries of July 11–13, 1857 refer to Tocqueville's visit to Teddesley. On November 27, 1857 Tocqueville wrote to Lord Hatherton, remarking: "I received not long ago, my lord, a letter from our friend Sumner, dated from Teddesley. He tells me how kindly you talked of me". Tocqueville added: "Taddesley dwells in my memory as one of the pleasantest episodes in my English tour" (Tocqueville, *Selected Letters on Politics and Society*, 350).

98. John Bright (1811–1889), British Liberal statesman. A gifted orator elected to the House of Commons in 1843, he worked closely with Richard Cobden in the formation of Anti-Corn Law League and emerged as one of the fiercest critics of British foreign policy, especially during the Crimean War.

99. William Gladstone (1809–1898), one of the most prominent nineteenth-century British politicians. Educated at Eton and Oxford, he was first elected to Parliament in 1832 as a Tory. After Robert Peel's death in 1850, he emerged as a leader of the Peelites and was appointed in 1852 Chancellor of the Exchequer. It was during this time that he left the Tory Party and formed a new Liberal Party. Gladstone served as Prime Minister for a total of almost fifteen years (1868–1874, 1880–1885, 1886, and 1892–1894) and promoted a number of key political reforms.

100. Richard Grosvenor, second Marquess of Westminster (1795–1869). His main country seat was Eaton Hall in the county of Cheshire, close to Gladstone's own estate.

101. "White tie" (in French, in the original text).

102. "A city in the country" (in Latin, in the original text).

103. For a biographical note on Henry Philip Tappan (1805–1881), see Appendix 1.

104. In the autumn of 1857, Charles Sumner spent a few days at Dunrobin Castle, the seat of his friend, the Duke of Sutherland.

105. In October 1857, the Free Soil Party gained the majority in the legislature of Kansas.

106. George Sumner.

107. Sedgwick's letter was originally written in French.

108. In the Bonnel copy, "Lumières *sinistres*," most likely a transcription error on Bonnel's part. The sentence refers to Tocqueville's American investments.

109. The next two sentences in the Bonnel copy seem out of context here.

110. At this point of the text, the Bonnel copy incorrectly inserts here a part of the letter written by Sedgwick to Tocqueville on February 5, 1857.

111. Sarah Price Ashburner Sedgwick (1839–1879).

112. Susan Ridley Sedgwick (1838–1872).

113. *A Treatise on the Rules which Govern the Interpretation and Application of Statutory and Constitutional Law* (New York: J. S. Voorhier, 1857).

114. Tocqueville subsequently presented the book to the *Academy of Moral and Political Sciences*. It was to be Tocqueville's last public statement.

115. Bonnel's note.

116. Letter originally written in French.

117. The year is not indicated on Beckwith's letter; it was written either in 1857 or 1858.

118. Only two of Tocqueville's letters to Beckwith have been retrieved.

119. Garret Smith was a wealthy upstate New Yorker, ardent abolitionist and social reformer.

120. This is Bonnel's own transcription. The correct phrase might be "heart and soul."

121. Abigail Folsom (c. 1792–1867) dedicated herself to Christian reform and protested vociferously in Boston against the injustices of the fugitive slave laws. For her promulgation of antislavery doctrine, Folsom landed briefly in jail, and was eventually transferred to the Worcester Insane Asylum.

122. For more information on the Free Soil Party, see Foner, *Free Soil, Free Labor, Free Men*, 81–87, 124–31; Wilentz, *The Rise of American Democracy*, pp. 617–45, 658–73.

123. In the Bonnel copy, the word is "respection"; most likely, a transcription error.

124. David Rice Atchison (1807–1886), lawyer and U. S. Senator from Platte City, Missouri, elected President *pro tempore* of the Senate, on March 5, 1849. In the controversy over slavery, he increasingly allied himself with John C. Calhoun and other southern senators. He played a key role in securing the repeal of the Missouri Compromise as part of the Kansas–Nebraska Act of 1854. Atchison worked to secure the new Kansas territory for slavery and he organized groups of western Missourians, known as "border ruffians," to cross into the territory and influence elections at the ballot box, claiming that the Kansas–Nebraska Act made no provision for a residence requirement in voting. This resulted in the election of a pro-slavery legislature and a pro-slavery delegate to Congress. This was denounced by Free State leaders and led to open warfare on the Kansas plains.

125. Benjamin Stringfellow, noted newspaper editor in Kansas, who was a chief political ally of Atchison.

126. In the Bonnel copy, the sentence ends with "se ve." Most likely, a transcription error.

127. Meaning unclear (as per Bonnel copy).

128. This is the word in the Bonnel copy; probably a transcription error. The correct word might be "conception."

129. This is the word in the Bonnel copy; probably a transcription error. The correct word might be "them."

130. Reference to Ariosto's *Orlando Furioso* (1516).

131. Henry John Temple Palmerston, third Viscount Palmerston (1784–1865), was a prominent nineteenth-century British statesman who served as Secretary of War, Foreign Secretary, and Prime Minister (1855–1857).

132. Sedgwick's wife died on October 21, 1856.

133. Sedgwick's health was often very fragile. On this occasion, he had been diagnosed as suffering from pleurisy.

134. In English, in the original text.

135. In 1857, Ampère spent a lot of time in Rome. Tocqueville did not see Ampère during the last few years of his life. Ampère arrived in Cannes on April 17, 1859, two days after Tocqueville's death.

136. Volume Two of *The Old Regime and the Revolution* remained unfinished at the time of Tocqueville's death in 1859. An English translation was published by University of Chicago Press in 2001.

137. On this issue, see Craiutu, "Tocqueville's Paradoxical Moderation," 599–629.

138. Reference to Orsini's unsuccessful attempt on Napoléon III's life on January 14, 1858.

139. The relations between the federal government and the Mormons reached a critical point in May 1857 when federal troops were sent to Salt Lake City.

140. In English, in the original text.

141. The relations between France, England, and China deteriorated in 1856, after the murder of a French missionary and the arrest of the personnel of an English vessel.

142. In English, in the original text. For Tocqueville's passionate commitment to political liberty, see *The Old Regime and the Revolution*, vol. I, Book 2, Chapter 11 and Book 3, Chapter 4.

143. Sedgwick's letter was originally written in French.

144. Missing word (Bonnel's note).

145. Missing word (Bonnel's note). The missing word might be "pleasure."

146. Illegible word (Bonnel's note).

147. Sedgwick's appointment was not without opposition or controversy. In a letter to his sister, dated December 24, 1857, Sedgwick wrote: "The matter of the District Attorneyship remains undecided & I care little how long it is to continue. I have done nothing to get it. I am not sure that I am equal to it, & I shall be about as well-pleased one way or the other" (Massachusetts Historical Society, Ms. N. 851).

148. Missing word (Bonnel's note).

149. *Treatise on the Rules which Govern the Interpretation and Application of Statutory and Constitutional Law* (1857); for Tocqueville's review of Sedgwick's work, see Part II, section E, below.

150. Illegible word (Bonnel's note).

151. Illegible word (Bonnel's note).

152. The issue of Kansas joining the Union as a free state or as a slave state continued to trigger vigorous controversies during 1857–1858. The Lecompton constitution, drawn up in 1857, established slavery, but when this was put to the people of Kansas they voted by a large margin to reject it. When Kansas entered the Union in 1861 it was with a constitution that forbade slavery.

153. Edward Lee Childe was traveling at that time in Egypt.

154. This letter has been lost.

155. John Young Mason. For more information, see Appendix 1

156. The first volume of Guizot's memoirs, *Mémoires pour servir à l'histoire de mon temps* (Paris: Michel-Lévy Frères), was published in 1858. An English translation appeared the same year as *Memoirs to Illustrate the History of my Time*, vol. I, trans. J. W. Cole (London: R. Bentley, 1858).

157. Tocqueville's health deteriorated in 1858 and early 1859 and he had to undergo a series of painful treatments for tuberculosis that ultimately proved ineffective. The doctors that treated Tocqueville proved to be incompetent and did not convey to him the gravity of his illness on time. For more details, see Brogan, *Tocqueville: A Life*, 585–639.

158. For a translation of Tocqueville's report, see Part II, section E, below.

159. As Sedgwick pointed out in his letter of February 15, 1858, he had been appointed District Attorney of the United States, for the southern District of New York.

160. This letter has not been retrieved.

161. These words can be found in the opening lines of the Charter of 1814, the constitutional text granted by Louis XVIII, upon his return to the throne of France. The Charter marked the transition from the First Empire to the constitutional monarchy of the Bourbon Restoration (1814–1830). For more information, see Pierre Rosanvallon, *La monarchie impossible. Les Chartes de 1814 et de 1830* (Paris: Fayard, 1994).

162. Albert de Broglie, *L'Eglise et l'Empire romain au IVe siècle* (Paris, 1856).

163. Abel-François Villemain, *La tribune moderne, M. de Chateaubriand, sa vie, ses écrits, son influence littéraire et politique sur son temps* (Paris, 1858).
164. Marshal de Marmont, Duke de Raguse (1774–1852), *Mémoires*, 9 vols. (Paris, 1857).
165. Miot de Mélito, *Mémoires*, 3 vols. (Paris, 1858).
166. Henry Thomas Buckle (1821–1862) was the author of the unfinished *History of Civilization in England* of which only the first two volumes appeared. Buckle began by stating the general principles of his method and the general laws which govern the course of human progress. His plan was to illustrate these principles and laws by examining the histories of certain nations characterized by prominent and peculiar features, such as Germany, the United States, Spain, and Scotland.
167. It is unclear to which letter Tocqueville refers. For an undated letter of Beckwith, see below.
168. Beckwith was residing in China at that moment.
169. Reference to the Treaty of Tianjin signed in June 1858 between France, Russia, the United States, Britain and China bringing the Second Opium War to a close.
170. This point had been a recurrent theme in Tocqueville's *Recollections*, in which he took to task the July Monarchy for having encouraged excessively the materialism of the French people.
171. Reference to the criminal attempt at Napoléon III's life by Orsini on January 14, 1858. The relations with England deteriorated after the French discovered that the bomb used by Orsini had been made in England.
172. On John Young Mason (1788–1859), see Appendix 1.
173. For more information about Tocqueville's declining health, see Brogan, *Alexis de Tocqueville: A Life*, 613–39; Jardin, *Alexis de Tocqueville: A Biography*, 521–28.
174. For more detail, see Brogan, *Alexis de Tocqueville: A Life*, 619–20.
175. "The terrible necessity" (in Latin, in the original text).
176. Miss Lagden was a friend of Madame de Tocqueville and a close friend of Mérimée.
177. This letter has been lost.
178. Louis-Charles de Malartic de Fondat (1802–1885) was a childhood friend of Tocqueville's.
179. This letter has been lost.
180. For more details, see Lawrence C. Jennings, "France, Great Britain, and the Repression of the Slave Trade, 1841–1845," *French Historical Studies*, 10: 1 (1977): 101–25. Besides France and England, the other three countries that signed the treaty for the suppression of the African slave trade in December 1841 were Russia, Prussia, and Austria.
181. Walsh's account misses a few important details. While it is true that Guizot had refused the proposal made by Lord Palmerston in the summer of 1841 (in the context of the deterioration of the relations between France and England over the Eastern question), he sought to facilitate a rapprochement between the two countries by agreeing to the proposal of Lord Aberdeen, who served as foreign secretary in the subsequent Peel cabinet.
182. Tocqueville's health took a turn for the worse in January. Mérimée reported to a friend that Tocqueville "sees absolutely no one; neither does his wife. .... Of

the two doctors who are treating him, one thinks he is lost, the other has some hope" (quoted by Jardin, *Alexis de Tocqueville: A Biography*, 227).

183. The letter does not have a full date. Most likely, it was written in 1849.

184. The Auburn and Philadelphia penitentiary systems. For more information, see the editors' interpretative essay, "The Third Democracy," above.

185. The letter was written either in 1857 or 1858.

186. "Store" (in French, in the original text).

187. Reference to the famous episode in which Senator Charles Sumner was physically attacked in Congress by Senator Preston Brooks in 1856.

E. Letters between Tocqueville and his French and Other Correspondents

1. Letter of October 11, 1853, in Tocqueville, *OC*, IX, 199.

2. See, for example, the letter of August 23, 1847 to Louis de Kergorlay where he wrote that Gobineau had a "superficial mind" (*OC*, IX, 202–4).

3. J.-J. Ampère's *Promenade en Amérique*, 2 vols. (Paris: Michel Lévy, 1856).

4. The same point was made a few decades later by Lord Bryce.

5. See Ampère, *Promenade en Amérique*, I, 337–41.

6. Extract from Tocqueville, *OC*, XIII: 2, 209–11. Another translation of this letter to Kergorlay was previously published in Tocqueville, *Selected Letters on Politics and Society*, 189–95.

7. Nassau William Senior (1790–1864) was a professor of political economy at Oxford and one of the most famous economists of his time. He was a close friend and correspondent of Tocqueville. Their letters were published in *OC*, VI: 2.

8. In his letter of October 10, 1847 (published in Tocqueville, *OC*, XIII: 2, 205–7), Kergorlay reflected on the relationship between political liberty and religious passions. He invited Tocqueville to share with him his views on this topic: "What did you see in America? Are the passions of the sects there increasing or are they waning? If political liberty were ever to disappear, in your view, would these passions become weaker or stronger?" (*OC*, XIII: 2, 206).

9. Extracts from Tocqueville, *OC*, XI, 200–9.

10. This letter has not been found.

11. Abel-François Villemain (1790–1870) was a celebrated essayist and historian, elected to the *Académie française* in 1821. He also served as a parliamentary deputy under the July Monarchy.

12. Clothilde, Vicountess de Noailles (1791–1851) had cared for Ampère when he had been sick in 1841. They developed a deep attachment to one another.

13. It is not clear which event Ampère is here referring to, although it might be a reference to the possibility of Louis-Napoléon securing re-election to the Presidency.

14. At this time, *La Presse* supported Louis-Napoléon.

15. Reference to Louis-Napoléon's *coup d'état* of December 2, 1851, when Tocqueville, along with other opposition parliamentary deputies, was briefly imprisoned.

16. A reference to the revolutionary events of February 1848.

17. The extracts from Tocqueville's correspondence with the Circourts included in this section are taken from *OC*, XVIII, 99–101, 111–12, 115, 224–25, 278–79, 309, 311, 315–16, 349, 422.

18. Pierre Soulé (1801–1870), Senator from Louisiana, became American Ambassador to Madrid in April 1853. His appointment was a clear indication of America's intention to acquire the island of Cuba.

19. The extracts from the Tocqueville-Beaumont correspondence included in this section are taken from OC, VIII: 3, 163–64, 228–30, 271–73, 511–15, 520–24.

20. August von Haxthausen, *Etudes sur la situation intérieure et la vie nationale et les institutions rurales de la Russie*, 2 vols. (Hanover: 1847).

21. Beaumont was studying Russia for an article that appeared in the *Revue des Deux Mondes*, March 15, 1854.

22. Arthur de Gobineau, *Essai sur l'inégalité des races humaines* (Paris: Firmin Didot, 1853). Gobineau was also the author of another important book, *La Renaissance* (1877).

23. Tocqueville expressed the same views on Gobineau and Haxthausen in a letter to Adolphe de Circourt, dated December 7, 1853: OC, XVIII, 119–20. The horse trader comparison used by Tocqueville to describe the quality of Gobineau's thought is repeated in this letter and in another letter to Francisque de Corcelle, dated June 10, 1854 (*OC*, XV: 2, 105).

24. Née Florence Childe, the oldest daughter of the Childe family. Although only fifteen years old, Florence had run away to Geneva with the Prince Soltyk, a member of a distinguished Polish family and considerably older than her.

25. Born in 1838, Antonin was the son of Gustave de Beaumont.

26. It is not clear who this person might have been.

27. The British government had difficulty recruiting soldiers and sailors to fight in the Crimean War. Accordingly, it sought to recruit from America, a process which led the American government to break off diplomatic relations with Great Britain in 1856.

28. The issue here was Russian expansion along its Pacific coast and its control of the navigation routes.

29. John Young Mason (1799–1859) was elected to Congress in 1831. In 1853, he was appointed as U. S. Minister Plenipotentiary to Paris. For more information, see Appendix 1.

30. Franklin Pierce (1804–1857), the fourteenth President of the United States, elected in 1852.

31. Reference to Napoléon III.

32. The meaning of this comparison is unclear.

33. Baldomero Espartero (1792–1879) became head of the Spanish government in 1854, after a long military and political career.

34. Reference to a treaty between France and Spain through which Spain received a subsidy should it declare war on England.

35. The extracts from the Tocqueville-Gobineau correspondence included in this section are taken from Tocqueville, *OC*, IX, 260–61, 262–63, 265–68, 277; the translations belong to the editors of the present volume. Some of these letters have previously been translated in *The 'European Revolution' & Correspondence with Gobineau*, eds. and trans. John Lukacs (New York: Doubleday Anchor, 1959) and Tocqueville, *Selected Letters on Politics and Society* (trans. James Toupin and Roger Boesche).

36. A famous right-wing Catholic newspaper.

37. The three men concerned were: George Glidden (1809–1857), United States Consul at Alexandria; Josiah Nott (1804-1873), author of *Types of Mankind*

(1850) and later of *Indigenous Races of the Earth* (1857); and Henry Hotz, who translated Gobineau's *Essai*. While Gobineau was pleased to see his book translated in America, as he indicated in a letter to Tocqueville dated May 1, 1856, he was annoyed that it was not being taken seriously in France.

38. Under the Bulwer-Clayton Treaty of 1850 the United States and Great Britain agreed not to occupy any part of Central America. In 1856 a group of American adventurers under William Walker occupied Nicaragua. To the annoyance of the British government President Pierce immediately recognized Walker's government.

39. The end of the letter is missing.

40. In the event war did not take place between the two countries. In 1860 an agreement was reached which saw Great Britain giving up its protectorate on the Mosquito coast (present-day Nicaragua and Honduras). This issue had surfaced at the time of the Poussin Affair (see Part II, Section D, below).

41. Tocqueville's own father had just died.

42. Mrs. Childe had died after an unsuccessful surgical operation. Madame de Circourt had written of her death to Tocqueville in her letter of July 2, 1856. Letters written by Tocqueville to other correspondents, for example, Francisque de Corcelle, confirm the deep sense of loss he experienced on that occasion.

43. This extract is taken from *Correspondence and Conversations of Alexis de Tocqueville with Nassau William Senior*, ed. M. C. M. Simpson (London: Henry King: 1872), II, 271.

44. Circourt uses the Latin "Utinam" for *Please God [that he may be right]*. Ticknor was proved to be largely incorrect in his analysis. Buchanan tried to acquire Cuba and supported slavery in Kansas.

45. It is not clear who this American friend might have been.

46. The *Central Michigan Railroad*.

47. Theodore Sedgwick actually died two years later in 1859.

48. Charles Sumner (1811–1874). For more information, see Appendix 1.

49. Tocqueville's friend, General de Lamoricière, had just lost his only son.

PART II. SPEECHES, ARTICLES, AND DIPLOMATIC PAPERS

A. America in the 1840s

1. Despite frequent pleadings from his friends, it should be remembered that Tocqueville never returned to America after 1832.

2. See Gannett, *Tocqueville Unveiled*, 39–56.

3. Tocqueville, *The Old Regime and the Revolution*, I, 300.

4. Ibid., 281.

5. Ibid., 280.

6. Ibid., 281.

7. Tocqueville, *OC*, IV: 2, 117–83.

8. Ibid., pp. 183–214.

9. Ibid., 208.

10. On Tocqueville and *Le Commerce*, see Boesche, *Tocqueville's Road Map*, 189–209.

11. For the letters between Tocqueville and Lieber on this subject, see Part I, sections A–D, above.

12. See *Le Commerce*, April 19, May 18, and June 30, 1845.

13. See Tocqueville, *OC*, III: 2, 290–91.
14. Tocqueville, "The Emancipation of the Slaves," in *Writings on Slavery and Empire*, 205.
15. Ibid., 205.
16. See Jennifer Pitts, *A Turn to Empire: The Rise of Imperial Liberalism in Britain and France* (Princeton, NJ: Princeton University Press, 2006), 204–39.
17. Tocqueville, "Notes on the Voyage to Algeria" (1841), in *Writings on Slavery and Empire*, 36.
18. Tocqueville, "First Report on Algeria" (1847), in *Writings on Slavery and Empire*, 144.
19. Ibid., 146.
20. See *OC*, III: 2, 429–30.
21. Tocquevillle's speech, can be found in Part II, section B, below.
22. Tocqueville, *Selected Letters on Politics and Society*, 153.
23. Tocqueville, "Vers la creation d'un parti de la 'Jeune Gauche,'" *OC*, III: 2, 720.
24. This untitled article was reprinted in *OC*, III: 2, 468–71.
25. Ibid., 468.
26. Tocqueville, *Democracy in America*, 147.
27. *OC*, III: 2, 469–70.
28. Drafted in 1846. See *OC*, III: 2, 441–46. These notes relate to a speech that Tocqueville had intended to make in parliament in January 1846.
29. Despite Guizot's efforts to forge an alliance with Great Britain, the two countries clashed in 1843 when the French Admiral, Dupetit-Thouars, annexed Tahiti, imprisoning the British consul, Pritchard, in the process. Upon learning of this, the French government immediately repudiated these actions, declaring that Tahiti would revert to its status as a Franco-British protectorate. Tocqueville wrote four articles on Tahiti; they were published in *OC*, III: 2, 403–20.
30. In line with her policy to prevent American expansion into Central and Latin America, France favored the independence of the Lone Star Republic, to the point of contemplating the invasion of Texas in 1845.
31. The Northern League, set up by Czar Paul 1st, comprised Russia, Sweden, Denmark and Prussia. Without being a formal ally of France, it was hostile to England.
32. Because of fears that the annexation of Texas was being sought to protect slavery in the South, in 1844 Senate rejected the annexation treaty with Texas by 35 votes to 16.
33. The chronic financial and political situation of Mexico placed it in no position to defend itself against an expansionist United States, and it therefore depended upon European military intervention on its behalf. In the event, when the Mexican War broke out, the French adopted a position of strict neutrality.
34. John Russell, 1st Earl Russell (1792–1878), British Whig politician and Prime Minister. Russell had spoken on Anglo-American relations twice in January 1846, once in Glasgow and once in parliament. The point of Tocqueville's comparison is not clear.
35. A reference to Charles-Marie Tanneguy Duchâtel (1803–1867), prominent politician of the July Monarchy and close associate of Guizot. In his speech, Duchâtel had affirmed that it was in France's interest to have the closest possible alliance with the United States.

36. In relationship to the slave trade, treaties of 1831 and 1833 between England and France had allowed ships belonging to each power to board any vessel carrying the flag of the other in order to verify that they were not carrying slaves as cargo. The dominance of the British fleet meant that more French vessels were subject to search. After considerable controversy, Guizot was forced to negotiate a new treaty that abolished boarding rights.

37. James K. Polk, the eleventh President of the United States (1845–1849).

38. *OC*, XVI, 202–20. This report was first presented to the Academy of Moral and Political Sciences on January 15, 1848 and was published by the Academy in its proceedings later that year (Vol. 13, 97–119). Tocqueville subsequently republished it as an appendix to the 12th edition of *Démocratie en Amérique* (1848). Another English language version of this text was published in Alexis de Tocqueville, *Democracy in America*, trans. George Lawrence, ed. J-P. Mayer (New York: Harper & Row, 1966), 736–49. The present translation is by the editors of this volume. Tocqueville's skepticism toward the republican nature of the Swiss government can be traced back to the 1830s when he visited Switzerland. In a letter sent to Corcelle from Berne on July 27, 1836, Tocqueville wrote: "I thus already, in my capacity as an American, have conceived a very superb disdain for the federal constitution of Switzerland, which I unceremoniously call a league and not a federation" (Tocqueville, *Selected Letters on Politics and Society*, 108).

39. The author was Antoine-Élysée Cherbuliez (1797–1869), a barrister and professor of political economy from Geneva, best-known for his writings against socialism.

40. The title of the book was *De la Démocratie en Suisse*, published in two volumes in 1843.

41. Since the creation of the Helvetic Republic in 1798, there had been a general movement in Switzerland putting an end to the rule of a small number of privileged cities and families over the majority.

42. The period known as the Regeneration after 1830 saw mounting tension between liberals and Catholics. The conservative Catholic governments of some cantons in central Switzerland established a secret alliance, the *Sonderbund*, intended to act against the liberal governments of the other cantons, leading to a short civil war in 1847.

43. Geneva joined the Swiss Federation in 1813. In 1846, a revolution overthrew the conservative regime associated with the Restoration and established the constitution that is still in force today.

44. "On the democratic revolution in Switzerland."

45. Tocqueville's assessment was an accurate one. The new Federal Constitution of 1848 effectively put an end to an eighteen-year period of bitter conflict and political turmoil.

46. Prior to 1798, Switzerland consisted of a loose confederacy of thirteen cities and valley communities where, for the most part, a few families controlled state affairs.

47. The broad majority of the Swiss population, especially the peasantry, had no political rights.

48. French troops invaded Switzerland in 1798, annexing Geneva.

49. In October 1802, French troops again invaded Switzerland and brought civil war to an end. A new constitution was elaborated under Napoléon's "mediation,"

giving most power back to the nineteen cantons that made up the new Swiss Federation. After Napoléon's defeat in 1815, this regime came to an end.

50. This was the period of the so-called Restoration, when Switzerland returned to its former federal structure.

B. America and the Revolution of 1848

1. For more information on the influence of the American political model in France in 1848, see Marc Lahmer, *La Constitution Américaine dans le débat français, 1795–1848* (Paris: L'Harmattan, 2001); Watkins, *Alexis de Tocqueville and the Second Republic, 1848–1852*; and Gargan, *Alexis de Tocqueville: The Critical Years, 1848–1851.*

2. See, for example, Clarigny, "Des Institutions républicaines en France et aux États-Unis," *Le Constitutionnel,* June 10, 24 and July, 5, 1848 and J. A. Dréollé, "Lettres sur la Constitution américaine," *L'Opinion publique,* November 28, December 10, and 19, 1848. The latter specifically cited Tocqueville's "excellent work," but went on to contrast the political immaturity of the French with the maturity of the Americans. In America, Dréollé argued, the people were "proud of their government." Above all, see Michel Chevalier, "Étude sur la Constitution des États-Unis," *Le Journal des Débats Politiques et Littéraires,* May 25, June 6, 15, 22, July 4, 11, and 21, 1848. Chevalier used his study of the American constitution to present a far from flattering picture of France and its constitution makers.

3. See, for example, Hyacinthe Colombel, *Quelques réflexions concernant la Constitution qu'on élabore pour la France* (Nantes: Courier de Nantes, 1848); J. Magne, *Esquisse d'une Constitution. Ce que la France républicaine pourrait, avec avantage, emprunter aux institutions des États-Unis* (Paris: Revue Britannique, 1848); and Abel Rendu, *Les deux Républiques* (Paris: Dondey-Dupré, 1850).

4. See Walter D. Gray, *Interpreting American Democracy in France: The Career of Édouard Laboulaye* (Newark, DE: University of Delaware Press, 1994).

5. Édouard Laboulaye, *Considérations sur la Constitution* (Paris: Durand, 1849).

6. Édouard Laboulaye, *De la Constitution Américaine et de l'utilité de son étude* (Paris: Hennuyer, 1850).

7. Alexis de Tocqueville, *Recollections* (New York: Anchor Books, 1971), 116–17.

8. Brogan, *Alexis de Tocqueville: A Life,* 431.

9. *OC,* III: 3, 43–46.

10. Armand-François-Bon-Claude, Comte de Briqueville (1785–1844) was a cavalry officer in the Napoleonic army and later parliamentary deputy for the Manche.

11. *OC,* I: 1, xliii–xliv. Another English translation of this text was previously published in *Democracy in America,* trans. G. Lawrence (New York: Harper & Row, 1966), xiii–xiv.

C. Tocqueville's Contributions to the Debates on the Constitution of the Second Republic

1. Richard Rush, *Occasional Publications, Political, Diplomatic and Miscellaneous,* 384.

2. During his time in London, Bancroft made regular trips to Paris, visiting the French capital seven times between 1847 and 1849. The papers of George Bancroft, held at the Massachusetts Historical Society N-1795, record in great

detail his impressions of France at this time. See also *The Life and Letters of George Bancroft*, ed. M. A. De Wolfe Howe (New York: Charles Scribner, 1908).

3. Rush, *Occasional Publications, Political, Diplomatic and Miscellaneous*, 391.

4. Ibid., 421.

5. Ibid., 440.

6. For transcripts of the discussions of this committee, see Piero Craveri, *Genesi di una Constituzione* (Naples: Guida editori, 1985). More generally, see Watkins, *Alexis de Tocqueville and the Second Republic*, especially 43–140, 189–322, 481–536. The text of the Constitution, plus commentary, can be found in *Les Constitutions de la France depuis 1789*, ed. Lucien Jaume (Paris: Flammarion, 1995), 253–78. For a detailed commentary, see François Luchaire, *Naissance d'une Constitution: 1848* (Paris: Fayard, 1998).

7. Tocqueville, *Souvenirs* (Paris: Gallimard, 1999), 223–45.

8. In addition to the four texts translated in this section, it is also worth calling the reader's attention to the three sketches for parliamentary speeches included in *OC*, III: 3, 199–206. Each of them indicates not only Tocqueville's determination to cite the American example but also the fact that he was aware of the dangers of misusing it: "The example of the Americans. Do not misuse this. But nevertheless, make known what is most striking" (*OC*, III: 3, 206).

9. *OC*, III: 3, 205

10. *OC*, III: 3, 206.

11. See Tocqueville's speech (September 12, 1848) below.

12. On this issue see Lucien Jaume, "Tocqueville et le problème du pouvoir exécutif en 1848," *Revue Française de Science Politique* 41: 6 (1991): 739–55.

13. For more information, see Watkins, *Alexis de Tocqueville and the Second Republic*, 225–37.

14. See "On the Reelection of the President", in *Democracy in America*, 128–30. Tocqueville's argument here was that, as he was re-eligible, the president of the United States would be only a docile instrument in the hands of the majority.

15. *OC*, III: 3, 147.

16. *OC*, III: 3, 81–89, 97–101.

17. Louis-Marie de Lahaye de Cormenin (1788–1868), distinguished pamphleteer and parliamentarian who was first elected in 1828. Elected as Vice-President of the Constituent Assembly in 1848, he was chosen as President of the Constitutional Commission.

18. Armand Marrast (1801–1852), former editor of *Le National*, a republican who was nevertheless hostile to socialism.

19. Odilon Barrot (1791–1873) was a leading politician under the July Monarchy, who served as Prime Minister from December 1848 to October 1849.

20. Auguste Vivien de Goubert (1799–1854), lawyer and parliamentarian, served as deputy for Saint-Quentin from 1833–48 and then as *rapporteur* to the Constitutional Commission; briefly minister under Cavaignac, he resigned his seat on December 2, 1851.

21. Athanase Coquerel (1795–1868), Protestant pastor, publicist and noted orator; he enjoyed a brief parliament career under the Constituent and Legislative Assemblies of the Second Republic.

22. Édouard Martin (1801–1858), barrister and parliamentarian under the July Monarchy and elected member of the Constituent Assembly; a committed republican.

23. Victor Considérant (1808–1883), principal disciple of Charles Fourier and editor of *La Démocratie pacifique*, elected to the Constituent Assembly; he was forced into exile after the abortive uprising of June 13, 1849.

24. André-Marie Dupin (1783–1865), a consummate politician whose political career spanned from the Restoration to the Second Empire. Tocqueville said of him that "at heart he was selfish and cowardly."

25. Jean-Pierre Pagès (1784–1866), barrister and parliamentary deputy of liberal persuasion.

26. Jules-Armand-Stanislas Dufaure (1798–1881), deputy from 1834 onward, later minister under both the July Monarchy and the Second Republic (when he served as Minister of the Interior). Member of the French Academy.

27. Charles-François Woirhaye (1798–1878), barrister and supporter of Cavaignac under the Second Republic, he rallied to the Second Empire.

28. Tocqueville proved to be wrong in this regard and later regretted his mistake.

29. Achille Tenaille de Vaulabelle (1799–1879), prominent historian and journalist elected to the Constituent Assembly; in 1848; he served briefly as Minister of Public Instruction under Cavaignac. Vaulabelle was the author, among others, of *Histoire des deux Restaurations* (1844, 6 vols.)

30. *OC*, III: 3, 167–80. Another translation of this text (by Seymour Drescher) was previously published in *Tocqueville and Beaumont on Social Reform*, 179–92. The text printed here is a new translation of Tocqueville's speech. An analysis of this important text can be found in Watkins, *Alexis de Tocqueville and the Second Republic*, 207–21.

31. The author in question was François-Noël ("Gracchus") Babeuf (1760–1797), prominent political journalist and one of the first social revolutionaries in Europe, who became a revered figure on the left.

32. Reference to Pierre-Joseph Proudhon (1809–1865), prominent French socialist thinker, author of such important books such *Qu'est-ce que la propriété?* (1840) *De la création de l'ordre dans l'humanité* (1843), and *Système des contradictions économiques, ou philosophie de la misère*, (2 vols., 1846).

33. Antoine-Philippe Mathieu (1808–1865), elected deputy in 1848 and editor of *La Solidarité républicaine*.

34. Compare this with what Tocqueville had to say about the same issue in *The Old Regime and the Revolution*: "I have never met with a revolution where one could see at the start, in so many men, a more sincere patriotism, more disinterest, more true greatness.... This is 1789, a time of inexperience doubtless, but of generosity, of enthusiasm, of virility, and of greatness, a time of immortal memory" (*The Old Regime and the Revolution*, I, 208; 244).

35. It would be interesting to compare and contrast Tocqueville's rather favorable view of the Constituent Assembly with Burke's strong critique of the Assembly in his *Reflections on the Revolution in France* (1790). The hidden dialogue between Tocqueville and Burke is examined in Gannett, *Tocqueville Unveiled*, Chapter 4.

36. The fragment is taken from Robespierre's speech on the Constitution (May 10, 1793).

37. Reference to the communist colony founded by Cabet and his disciples in Texas in 1847.

38. Filippo Michele Buonarroti (1761–1837), disciple of "Gracchus" Babeuf and narrator of the latter's failed Conspiracy of the Equals. Babouvism has been

seen as one of the earliest examples of socialist ideology and conspiratorial practice.

39. Allusion to the successful Reform Bill of 1831–32 that extended the franchise in England. During the 1820s, the pressure for reform slowly mounted. The preservation of a corrupt and inadequate electoral system was regarded as out of step with the new spirit of the time, because it failed to represent properly the new industrial and commercial interests of the country. For more information, see Michael Brock, *The Great Reform Act* (London: Hutchinson University Library, 1973).

40. Alexandre-August Ledru-Rollin (1807–74), journalist under the July Monarchy, he was briefly Minister of the Interior under the Second Republic and then candidate for the Presidency (when he received only 370,000 votes). After the protests of June 13, 1849, he went into exile in England.

41. *OC*, III: 3, 212–14. Also see Watkins, *Alexis de Tocqueville and the Second Republic*, 225–37. As Watkins pointed out, Tocqueville's constitutional proposals on this topic (as well as on the right to work) followed the model of balanced government meant to avoid the danger of a "legislative dictatorship," a phrase used by Tocqueville in a draft for a speech (*OC*, III: 3, 206). In Tocqueville's view, the Second Republic was supposed to be conservative socially and had to rely on a system of checks and balances, much like its American counterpart. Initially, Tocqueville hoped that General Cavaignac, a man whose integrity he valued, would win the Presidency in 1848. But soon it became clear for Tocqueville that the candidacy of Cavaignac was doomed to failure and subsequent events proved him right.

42. On this issue, see Michel Troper, *Terminer la Révolution: La Constitution de 1795* (Paris: Fayard, 2006).

43. *OC*, III: 3, 439–42. Also see Watkins, *Alexis de Tocqueville and the Second Republic*, 481–536.

D. The Poussin Affair

1. Tocqueville's own account of his time as Minister of Foreign Affairs of the Second Republic can be found in his *Recollections* (New York: Doubleday, 1971), 285–327. He indicates that the head of government, Odilon Barrot, offered him the post "in despair." "If any one asks me," he wrote, "what profit I derived from such an anxious, thwarted and short period in office, without time to finish anything I had begun, my answer is that I gained one benefit, perhaps the greatest this world can give, namely confidence in myself" (287).

2. Poussin's book, *Considérations sur le Principe démocratique qui régit l'Union Américaine et d'autres états*, was published by Gosselin in Paris in 1841. It is worth noting that Gosselin had also published Tocqueville's *Democracy in America* a few years earlier.

3. Rush, *Occasional Productions, Political, Diplomatic, and Miscellaneous*, 299–520.

4. For more information, see the letters from Rush to Buchanan held in the National Archives and Records Administration (NARA) and listed under M34, reel 34, RG 59; Samuel Flagg Bemis, *The American Secretaries of State and their Diplomacy: John Middleton Clayton* (New York: Pageant Book Company, 1958); Henry Blumenthal, *A Reappraisal of Franco-American Relations 1830–1871* (Chapel Hill, NC: University of North Carolina Press, 1959).

5. The day is not specified.

6. A military court settled the dispute by handing the tobacco back to Domercq.

7. It was Colonel Childs of the United States Army who had offered the bales of tobacco for sale at public auction.

8. This was the section of Poussin's letter to be found most offensive. On the left hand margin of the letter is written the word 'Withdrawn.'

9. Princeton University, Firestone Library, Rush Family Papers (C0079), IV. Papers, Documents, and Correspondence (1846–1849) relating to the French Mission, 334–36.

10. Alexis de Tocqueville.

11. Nicolas Changarnier (1793–1877), French General and politician, commanded the National Guard in Paris after the June Days of 1848.

12. An *exequatuor* (also spelled as *exequatur*) is a patent which a head of state issues to a foreign consul which guarantees the consul's rights and privileges of the office and ensures recognition in the state to which the consul is appointed to exercise such powers.

13. Blank space in the text.

14. In 1849, Narciso Lopez, a former Cuban provincial governor, attempted to raise an army in order to invade Cuba and free it from Spanish control. Based in New Orleans, he was backed by prominent Southerners who supported American expansion into Latin America, and Cuba in particular. After President Taylor issued his proclamation forbidding Americans to participate in the venture, the planned expedition collapsed. Taylor's policy was to uphold U.S. neutrality.

15. Presumably a reference to the Canadian rebellion of 1837–1838, when a group of patriots crossed the American border into Canada in an attempt to drive the British out of Lower (Quebec) and Upper Canada (Ontario).

16. Beaumont was then acting as French Minister to Vienna, a key diplomatic post given the events in Rome and the place held by the Habsburg Empire in Italy. These short extracts are taken from Tocqueville, *OC,* VIII: 2, 181, 201–2.

17. These sentiments are echoed almost word for word in Tocqueville's *Recollections*, 298.

18. It is not clear which remarks by Talleyrand Tocqueville is referring to. However, in his account of his enforced exile to the United States, Talleyrand painted a picture of an uncultured yet religious people living on the edge of civilization (see Roger, *L'Ennemi américain*, 68–73).

19. Document from the Virginia Historical Society Library, MSS1P9267d761; reprinted here by permission. Special thanks to John M. Clure for bringing this document to our attention.

20. General Winfield Scott, along with Zachary Taylor, was one of the two victorious American Generals in the Mexican War. In February 1847, he landed troops at Vera Cruz and reached Mexico City by September of that year. He stood as Presidential candidate in the elections of 1852 and was defeated by Franklin Pierce.

21. In September 1849, troops loyal to the Habsburg monarchy had crushed the popular uprising in Hungary.

22. In the wake of the Mexican War, the British government was fearful that the United States would seize what was considered the best route across the isthmus in Nicaragua. Accordingly, in the name of the Mosquito Indians, the British established a protectorate in the region, extending to the mouth of the San

Juan River. In response, the American chargé to Guatemala, Elijah Hise, made a treaty with Nicaragua on June 21, 1849 which secured for the United States the exclusive right to build a canal by the Nicaraguan route. Poussin is presumably referring to Hise's replacement, E. George Squier, who was instructed to oppose British pretensions in Nicaragua and to make commercial treaties with the Central American states. Matters became increasingly complicated and Clayton was forced to admit that it would be unwise to impose the Monroe doctrine upon the region. The issue was finally resolved through the signing of the so-called Clayton-Bulwer treaty of 1850, through which the United States and Great Britain pledged to respect the neutrality of the region and to forego exclusive control over any future Ship-Canal.

23. The Republic of the New Granada was a republic formed primarily of Columbia and Panama, with smaller portions of Costa Rica, Venezuela, and Nicaragua. It was founded in 1830 and was dissolved in 1858.

24. The Mosquito coast was a narrow strip of territory fronting the Caribbean Ocean in present-day Nicaragua. It takes its name from the Miskito Indians.

25. The Atlantic and Pacific Ship-Canal Company of New York.

26. Although Tocqueville stood down as Minister of Foreign Affairs on October 31, 1849, the next two letters were addressed to him in his official capacity as Minister; they are held in the Quai d'Orsay archives. Their author was Charles de Montholon, French consul-general at Richmond, who was sent by Tocqueville in the autumn of 1849 as an unofficial emissary to Washington. Poussin was replaced as Minister by André-Ernest-Olivier Sain Bois-le-Comte, who served in this position until February 1851.

27. This is our conjecture. The word is not legible in the original text.

28. The name is not legible in the original text.

E. Final Thoughts on the American Constitution

1. Theodore Sedgwick, *Thoughts on the Proposed Annexation of Texas to the United States* (New York: Fanshaw, 1844).

2. Theodore Sedgwick, *The American Citizen: His True Position, Character and Duties* (New York: Wiley and Putnam, 1847).

3. Theodore Sedgwick, *A Treatise on the Rules which Govern the Interpretation and the Application of Statutory and Constitutional Law* (New York: J. S. Voorhier, 1857), 21–23.

4. Tocqueville, *Democracy in America*, 98.

5. Brogan, *Alexis de Tocqueville: A Life*, 613.

Index

Note: A few terms such as America, constitution, democracy, freedom, government, history, institutions, law, and society frequently appear in the text and have been indexed only in connection with the main themes of the book. Most sources cited in the endnotes have not been indexed.

TOCQUEVILLE ON AMERICA AFTER 1840

Alexis de Tocqueville's *Democracy in America* has been recognized as an indispensable starting point for understanding American politics. From the publication of the second volume in 1840 until his death in 1859, Tocqueville continued to monitor political developments in America and committed many of his thoughts to paper in letters to his friends in America. He also made frequent references to America in many articles and speeches. Did Tocqueville change his views on America outlined in the two volumes of *Democracy in America* published in 1835 and 1840? If so, which of his views changed and why? The texts translated in *Tocqueville on America after 1840: Letters and Other Writings* answer these questions and offer English-speaking readers the possibility of familiarizing themselves with this unduly neglected part of Tocqueville's work. The book points out a clear shift in emphasis especially after 1852 and documents Tocqueville's growing disenchantment with America, triggered by such issues as political corruption, slavery, expansionism, and the encroachment of the economic sphere upon the political.

Aurelian Craiutu is Associate Professor in the Department of Political Science at Indiana University, Bloomington. He received his Ph.D. in political theory from Princeton University in 1999 and was the 2000 winner of the American Political Science Association's Leo Strauss Award for the best dissertation in the field of political philosophy. Craiutu's *Liberalism under Siege: The Political Thought of the French Doctrinaires* won a 2004 CHOICE Outstanding Academic Title Award; a revised and enlarged version of the book was published in French as *Le Centre introuvable* (2006). Professor Craiutu has also edited several volumes, including *Guizot's History of the Origins of Representative Government in Europe*, Madame de Staël's *Considerations on the Principal Events of the French Revolution, Conversations with Tocqueville: The Global Democratic Revolution in the Twenty-First Century* (with Sheldon Gellar), and *America through European Eyes* (with Jeffrey C. Isaac).

Jeremy Jennings is Professor of Political Theory at Queen Mary, University of London, having previously held posts at the universities of Swansea and Birmingham (UK). He received his D.Phil. from the University of Oxford. In 2007, he was made a Chevalier in the Ordre des Palmes Académiques for services rendered to French culture. Professor Jennings has published extensively on the history of political thought in France, the role of intellectuals in politics, and the history of socialism. In 2002, he published a new edition of Georges Sorel's *Reflections on Violence* and, in 2005, co-edited a volume entitled *Republicanism in Theory and Practice*. He has recently published articles in the *American Political Science Review, Review of Politics, Journal of Political Ideologies*, and *Journal of the History of Ideas*.